Household Demand for Consumer Goods in Developing Countries

This book analyses the household demand for consumer goods using a diverse database, consisting of 45 developed and developing countries.

Household consumption patterns have undergone dramatic changes due to rapid economic growth, increasing household income and changing demographics. Using the most recent data available and the latest econometric techniques, the authors model demand for 12 different commodities such as food, alcohol and tobacco, housing, health, transport, health communication, and recreation and provide insightful comparisons of consumption patterns in developed and developing countries.

The analysis presented in this book highlights valuable policy insights for planning government budgetary allocations and implementing policies towards an enhanced standard of living for people. The book also provides some important guidance for researchers interested in the theory and empirical application of the analysis of consumer demand.

Eliyathamby A Selvanathan is the Director of the Economics Policy Analysis Program (EPAP) and Professor of Econometrics in the Economics and Business Statistics Discipline at Griffith University, Queensland, Australia.

Saroja Selvanathan is a Professor of Econometrics in the Economics and Business Statistics Discipline at Griffith University, Queensland, Australia.

Maneka Jayasinghe is the Head of the Business discipline and Senior Lecturer in Economics at the Asia Pacific College of Business and Law at Charles Darwin University, Darwin, Australia.

Routledge Studies in Development Economics

167 Industrialization and Economic Diversification
Post-Crisis Development Agenda in Asia and Africa
Banji Oyelaran-Oyeyinka and Kaushalesh Lal

168 Digitalization and Economic Development
Edited by Mohamed Sami Ben Ali

169 The Political Economy of Universal Healthcare in Africa
Evidence from Ghana
Philip C. Aka, Hassan Wahab, and Yvette M. Alex-Assensoh

170 State Building and Social Policies in Developing Countries
The Political Economy of Development
Rashed Al Mahmud Titumir

171 Taxation in the Digital Economy
New Models in Asia and the Pacific
Edited by Nella Hendriyetty, Chris Evans, Chul Ju Kim and Farhad Taghizadeh-Hesary

172 Human Capital and Gender Inequality in Middle-Income Countries
Schooling, Learning and Socioemotional Skills in the Labour Market
Elizabeth M. King and Dileni Gunewardena

173 Digital Financial Inclusion and Regulation
Ogochukwu Monye

174 Household Demand for Consumer Goods in Developing Countries
A Comparative Perspective with Developed Countries
Eliyathamby A Selvanathan, Saroja Selvanathan and Maneka Jayasinghe

For more information about this series, please visit: www.routledge.com/Routledge-Studies-in-Development-Economics/book-series/SE0266

Household Demand for Consumer Goods in Developing Countries

A Comparative Perspective with Developed Countries

Eliyathamby A Selvanathan, Saroja Selvanathan and Maneka Jayasinghe

Routledge
Taylor & Francis Group
LONDON AND NEW YORK

First published 2023
by Routledge
4 Park Square, Milton Park, Abingdon, Oxon OX14 4RN

and by Routledge
605 Third Avenue, New York, NY 10158

Routledge is an imprint of the Taylor & Francis Group, an informa business

British Library Cataloguing-in-Publication Data
A catalogue record for this book is available from the British Library

Library of Congress Cataloging-in-Publication Data
Names: Selvanathan, Eliyathamby A., author. | Selvanathan, Saroja, author. | Jayasinghe, Maneka, author.
Title: Household demand for consumer goods in developing countries : a comparative perspective with developed countries / Eliyathamby A. Selvanathan, Saroja Selvanathan and Maneka Jayasinghe.
Description: 1 Edition. | New York, NY : Routledge, 2023. | Series: Routledge studies in development economics | Includes bibliographical references and index.
Identifiers: LCCN 2022021997 (print) | LCCN 2022021998 (ebook) | ISBN 9780367190613 (hardback) | ISBN 9781032368788 (paperback) | ISBN 9780429200120 (ebook)
Subjects: LCSH: Consumers—Developing countries. | Consumption (Economics)—Developing countries.
Classification: LCC HC59.72.C6 S46 2023 (print) | LCC HC59.72.C6 (ebook) | DDC 339.4/7091724—dc23/eng/20220725
LC record available at https://lccn.loc.gov/2022021997
LC ebook record available at https://lccn.loc.gov/2022021998

ISBN: 978-0-367-19061-3 (hbk)
ISBN: 978-1-032-36878-8 (pbk)
ISBN: 978-0-429-20012-0 (ebk)

DOI: 10.4324/9780429200120

Typeset in Times New Roman
by codeMantra

To our parents
who have made enormous sacrifices to give us the most precious gift of education,

the late Mr Velupillai Eliyathamby
the late Mrs Pooranam Eliyathamby
the late Murugesapillai Pathmanathan
Mrs Parameswary Pathmanathan
the late Mr Hemathilake Jayasinghe
Mrs Prema Kauthanthri

Contents

Figures

Tables

The inverse of the matrix on the far left of equation (2.53) is

$$\begin{bmatrix} U & p \\ p' & 0 \end{bmatrix}^{-1} = \frac{1}{p'U^{-1}p} \begin{bmatrix} (p'U^{-1}p)U^{-1} - U^{-1}p(U^{-1}p)' & U^{-1}p \\ (U^{-1}p)' & -1 \end{bmatrix}.$$

Using this inverse, the solution of equation (2.53) is

$$\begin{bmatrix} \frac{\partial q}{\partial M} & \frac{\partial q}{\partial p'} \\ -\frac{\partial \lambda}{\partial M} & -\frac{\partial \lambda}{\partial p'} \end{bmatrix} = \frac{1}{p'U^{-1}p} \begin{bmatrix} (p'U^{-1}p)U^{-1} - U^{-1}p(U^{-1}p)' & U^{-1}p \\ (U^{-1}p)' & -1 \end{bmatrix} \begin{bmatrix} 0 & \lambda I \\ 1 & -q' \end{bmatrix}.$$

Carrying out the matrix multiplication block by block, we obtain

$$\frac{\partial q}{\partial M} = \frac{1}{p'U^{-1}p} U^{-1}p, \tag{2.54}$$

$$\frac{\partial q}{\partial p'} = \lambda U^{-1} - \frac{\lambda}{p'U^{-1}p} U^{-1}p(U^{-1}p)' - \frac{1}{p'U^{-1}p} U^{-1}pq', \tag{2.55}$$

$$\frac{\partial \lambda}{\partial M} = \frac{1}{p'U^{-1}p}, \tag{2.56}$$

and

$$\frac{\partial \lambda}{\partial p'} = -\frac{\lambda}{p'U^{-1}p} U^{-1}p - \frac{1}{p'U^{-1}p} q'. \tag{2.57}$$

To simplify these expressions, we use equation (2.56) to substitute $\partial\lambda/\partial M$ for the reciprocal of $p'U-1p$ in equations (2.54), (2.55) and (2.57). Equation (2.54) then becomes

$$\frac{\partial q}{\partial M} = \frac{\partial \lambda}{\partial M} U^{-1}p. \tag{2.58}$$

Next, we replace $U-1p$ in equations (2.55) and (2.57) with $\partial q/\partial M$ divided by $\partial\lambda/\partial M$, which follows from equation (2.58). This yields

$$\frac{\partial q}{\partial p'} = \lambda U^{-1} - \frac{\lambda}{\partial\lambda/\partial M} \frac{\partial q}{\partial M} \frac{\partial q'}{\partial M} - \frac{\partial q}{\partial M} q' \tag{2.59}$$

and

$$\frac{\partial \lambda}{\partial p'} = -\lambda \frac{\partial q'}{\partial M} - \frac{\partial \lambda}{\partial M} q'. \tag{2.60}$$

Table 6.4 Total alcohol consumption per capita (litres of pure alcohol, 15+ years of age)

	Country	*All persons*					*Male*					*Female*				
	(1)	2000 *(2)*	2005 *(3)*	2010 *(4)*	2015 *(5)*	2018 *(6)*	2000 *(7)*	2005 *(8)*	2010 *(9)*	2015 *(10)*	2018 *(11)*	2000 *(12)*	2005 *(13)*	2010 *(14)*	2015 *(15)*	2018 *(16)*
Developed countries																
1	Australia	11.7	12.1	12.4	10.8	10.5	17.9	18.3	18.7	16.4	16.0	5.7	6.0	6.1	5.3	5.2
2	Austria	13.1	12.8	12.2	12.1	12.0	20.4	19.9	19.0	18.7	18.5	6.4	6.2	5.9	5.8	5.8
3	Belgium	12.5	13.1	11.4	11.8	11.1	19.4	20.3	17.7	18.3	17.2	6.0	6.3	5.4	5.6	5.3
4	Canada	–	–	10.1	8.9	8.9	–	–	15.8	13.9	14.0	–	–	4.6	4.0	4.1
5	Denmark	12.7	12.3	11.0	10.4	10.3	19.5	18.9	16.9	16.0	15.8	6.1	5.9	5.2	4.9	4.9
6	Finland	11.7	13.1	12.6	11.2	10.8	18.3	20.4	19.5	17.4	16.8	5.5	6.3	6.0	5.3	5.1
7	France	14.1	13.1	12.4	12.6	12.3	21.8	20.3	19.3	19.7	19.2	6.8	6.3	5.9	6.0	5.8
8	Germany	14.2	13.3	12.6	13.1	12.9	22.0	20.6	19.6	20.1	19.9	6.8	6.4	6.0	6.3	6.2
9	Hong Kong	–	–	–	–	–	–	–	–	–	–	–	–	–	–	–
10	Iceland	7.0	7.7	7.5	8.7	9.1	10.8	11.8	11.4	13.3	13.9	3.3	3.7	3.5	4.2	4.3
11	Ireland	15.1	14.2	12.1	12.5	12.9	22.7	21.3	18.3	19.0	19.6	7.7	7.2	6.0	6.1	6.4
12	Israel	3.1	2.7	3.1	3.9	4.2	4.9	4.3	4.9	6.1	6.6	1.4	1.2	1.4	1.8	1.9
13	Italy	10.4	9.4	7.3	7.6	7.8	16.3	14.9	11.7	12.1	12.5	4.9	4.4	3.3	3.4	3.5
14	Japan	8.2	8.0	7.2	7.9	8.0	12.6	12.3	11.1	12.2	12.3	4.0	3.9	3.5	3.8	3.9
15	Luxembourg	14.3	13.6	13.0	13.2	12.9	21.8	20.7	19.7	19.8	19.5	7.2	6.8	6.4	6.5	6.4
16	Netherlands	11.1	10.7	10.2	9.6	9.6	17.1	16.5	15.7	14.8	14.8	5.3	5.1	4.8	4.5	4.5
17	New Zealand	10.4	10.9	11.3	10.4	10.6	16.2	16.9	17.5	16.1	16.4	5.0	5.3	5.5	5.1	5.2
18	Norway	8.0	8.9	8.9	7.5	7.4	12.2	13.6	13.6	11.4	11.2	3.9	4.3	4.4	3.6	3.6
19	Singapore	2.5	1.8	2.2	2.1	2.0	3.7	2.7	3.3	3.1	3.1	1.3	0.9	1.1	1.1	1.0
20	Slovenia	12.6	12.3	11.5	12.7	11.9	19.6	19.1	17.8	19.7	18.4	6.0	5.9	5.5	6.0	5.6
21	South Korea	12.3	10.6	10.0	10.0	9.7	18.6	16.0	15.1	15.2	14.7	6.2	5.2	4.9	5.0	4.8
22	Spain	12.4	12.8	10.0	11.3	12.7	19.3	19.9	15.7	17.9	20.1	5.9	6.1	4.6	5.1	5.8
23	Sweden	8.5	8.6	9.5	9.1	8.9	13.3	13.4	14.7	14.0	13.7	3.9	4.0	4.4	4.3	4.2
24	Switzerland	12.5	11.6	11.4	11.6	11.5	19.3	18.0	17.6	17.7	17.7	6.1	5.7	5.6	5.6	5.6
25	Taiwan	–	–	–	–	–	–	–	–	–	–	–	–	–	–	–
26	UK	13.7	13.9	12.1	11.2	11.5	21.4	21.5	18.7	17.4	17.8	6.6	6.8	5.7	5.3	5.4
27	USA	9.2	9.5	9.4	9.8	9.9	14.3	14.7	14.5	15.2	15.3	4.3	4.5	4.4	4.6	4.6
Mean (*Developed*)		10.9	10.7	10.1	10.0	10.0	16.8	16.5	15.5	15.4	15.4	5.3	5.2	4.8	4.8	4.8

Authors

Professor Eliyathamby A Selvanathan is the Director of the Economics Policy Analysis Program (EPAP) and Professor of Econometrics at Griffith University, Queensland, Australia. He has also taught previously at the University of Jaffna (Sri Lanka), Murdoch University (Australia) and The University of Western Australia. He was educated at the University of Jaffna, Murdoch University and The University of Western Australia. He is one of the authors of the best-selling textbook *Business Statistics* published by Cengage. His research interests include applied econometrics, tourism economics, consumer demand models and stochastic index numbers. He has published eight research monographs and well over 100 articles in leading journals such as *Review of Economic Studies*, *Journal of Econometrics*, *Journal of Business and Economic Statistics*, *Review of Economics and Statistics*, *Energy Economics*, *Journal of Travel Research* and *Tourism Economics*.

Professor Saroja Selvanathan is a Professor of Econometrics at Griffith University, Queensland, Australia, and the Co-Editor-in-Chief of the *Journal of the Asia Pacific Economy*. She has also taught previously at the University of Jaffna (Sri Lanka), Murdoch University (Australia) and The University of Western Australia. She was educated at the University of Jaffna, Murdoch University and The University of Western Australia. Her research interests include consumer demand, time-series analysis, tourism economics and applied econometrics. She has published five research monographs and over 75 journal articles. Her publications have appeared in internationally refereed journals such as *Review of Economics and Statistics*, *Energy Economics*, *Resource Economics*, *Economic Modelling*, *Journal of Travel Research*, *Tourism Analysis* and *Tourism Economics*. She is a co-author of the Australian best-selling textbook, *Business Statistics*, published by Cengage.

Dr Maneka Jayasinghe is the Head of the Business discipline and Senior Lecturer in Economics at the Asia Pacific College of Business and Law at Charles Darwin University, Darwin, Australia. She has also taught previously at Griffith University (Australia). She was educated at Griffith

University (Australia), National University of Singapore and University of Colombo (Sri Lanka). She is an Applied Economist, and her research interests include poverty and well-being, consumer demand analysis, energy economics and tourism analysis. She has published one research monograph and numerous articles in leading international refereed journals such as *Energy Economics*, *Journal of Travel Research*, *Applied Economics*, *Economic Record*, *Social Indicators Research*, *International Journal of Tourism Research* and a number of book chapters with leading publishers.

Associate Professor Ripon Kumar Mondal is the Head of the Department of Agricultural Economics at Sher-e-Bangla Agricultural University, Dhaka, Bangladesh. He has also worked as an Economist for the Food and Agriculture Organization (FAO) of the United Nations (UN). He pursued his education at Griffith University (Australia), Kobe University of Japan, and Bangladesh Agricultural University (Bangladesh). His research interests include agricultural economics, applied economics, food security, agriculture transformation, and economic development focusing on developing countries. He has published research articles in some leading international refereed journals such as *Applied Economics and Economic Analysis and Policy.*

Technical Notes

This book contains nine chapters. To aid the reader, each chapter has been written in such a way that it is more or less self-contained.

Each chapter contains several sections, subsections and a list of references. The sections in each chapter are numbered at two levels: the first level refers to the chapter number and the second level to the section in each chapter. For example, Section 2.3 refers to the third section in Chapter 2.

Equations are indicated by two numbers: the first refers to the chapter and the second to the order of the occurrence of equations within that chapter. For example, 'Equation (2.3)' refers to the third equation in Chapter 2.

Tables and figures are indicated by two numbers: the first refers to the chapter and the second to the order of the occurrence of tables or figures within that chapter. For example, 'Table 3.2' refers to the second table in Chapter 3 and 'Figure 3.1' refers to the first figure in Chapter 3.

Abbreviations

ABS	Australian Bureau of Statistics
ACT	Australian Capital Territory
AIDS	Almost Ideal Demand System
BBS	Bangladesh Bureau of Statistics
CBS	Central Bureau of Statistics (Demand Systems)
CGWM	Conditional Generalised Working's Model
DCS	Department of Census and Statistics (Sri Lanka)
EPEA	Expenditure Per Equivalent Adult
GDP	Gross Domestic Product
HES	Household Expenditure Survey
HIES	Household Income and Expenditure Survey
HRE	Health, Recreation and Education (group)
IHDS-II	Indian Human Development Survey II
LES	Linear Expenditure System
NSW	New South Wales
NT	Northern Territory
OECD	Organisation for Economic Co-operation and Development
PCE	Per capita Expenditure
PI	Preference Independence
RC	Relative Consumption
RP	Relative Prices
TCH	Transport, Communication and Housing (group)
UK	United Kingdom
USA	United States of America
US$	United States Dollar
WA	Western Australia
W-R	Workings-Rotterdam

Acknowledgements

We wish to express our sincere gratitude to our mentor Professor Ken Clements of The University of Western Australia for his encouragement and guidance to undertake our research. We also acknowledge the comments and suggestions of the anonymous reviewers and the editor of the book at Routledge. We wish to thank Ms Tanya Parker for her excellent research and editorial assistance.

We gratefully acknowledge the research grants received from the Griffith Asia Institute and Griffith Business School at Griffith University and the Asia Pacific College of Business and Law at Charles Darwin University to complete this book. Our special thanks are also extended to the Australian Bureau of Statistics, Bangladesh Bureau of Statistics, Department of Census and Statistics, Sri Lanka, and Indian Human Development Survey team for giving us permission and access to the cross-sectional microdata.

Last, but not least, our heartfelt appreciation is extended to our family and friends for their encouragement, support and understanding.

1 Introduction

E A Selvanathan, S Selvanathan and M Jayasinghe

1.1 Introduction

Over the past two decades, consumption patterns across countries have changed for various reasons, including increases in consumers' real income; rising consumers' demand for goods and services; and technical and structural changes in the world economy. Improved trade relationships between countries, reduction in the level of trade protection applied to goods-imports and improved travel mobility between countries have resulted in substantial changes in the relative prices of consumer goods and services. Removal of trade barriers between countries and increased open competition within countries have provided households and businesses across the world with access to low-cost imported and in-country goods in various categories such as food, clothing and durables. This has resulted in an increasing re-allocation of consumer income within each country to different goods and services such as health care, education, transport, recreation and financial services.

In light of this changing global market, it is essential to measure the effect of income and price changes on the demand for consumer goods. An in-depth analysis of household demand for consumer goods is extremely important in the perspective of many stakeholders. First, policy makers are very keen to identify household consumption patterns as these provide important signals for planning government budgetary allocations and implementing policies towards sustainable improvement of living standards for their citizens. For such planning, having up-to-date income and price elasticity estimates for consumer goods in each country is important as they are the key inputs for a number of policy applications such as changes to public finance policies and estimation of economy-wide models that are used in designing consumer welfare policies and individual government revenues. Second, a clear understanding of household consumption behaviour is vital for manufacturing industries, import and export businesses and investors to understand consumer preferences, to identify emerging market opportunities and to invest in research and development. The analysis presented in this book also provides some important guidance for researchers who are

DOI: 10.4324/9780429200120-1

interested in the theory and empirical application of the analysis of consumer demand.

To elaborate further, although Engel's (1857) Law suggests that as a country or consumer becomes more affluent, food budget share declines, food expenditure still constitutes a significant proportion of the household budget in most developing countries. Therefore, an in-depth analysis of demand for food and related goods provides valuable information for businesses engaged in various food industries. There have been some notable changes in the consumption of addictive goods such as tobacco and alcohol. A detailed analysis of household demand for alcohol, tobacco and non-alcoholic beverages is particularly important for governments and policy makers due to two reasons. First, taxes on alcohol and tobacco comprise a significant proportion of government revenue. Second, consumption of alcohol and tobacco contributes to various health problems. For these reasons, household alcohol and tobacco consumption patterns are of greater interest to industries such as health care and insurance. Furthermore, alcohol, tobacco and non-alcoholic beverage industries, including export- and import-oriented agencies, are also expected to be interested in the consumption patterns of these commodities. Similarly, with increasing household income levels, improved access to and affordability of transport services and the expanding availability of a wide variety of communication services, households appear to devote a significant proportion of their household spending on these services. A detailed analysis of the consumption patterns of these commodities provides important insights for the businesses providing these services to match their investment decisions with the changing patterns of consumption behaviours. Of further interest is that over the past several decades, there have been significant changes in demographic patterns in countries across the world. These changing demographic patterns within households have a significant impact on household consumption expenditure on health (Reinhardt 2003). For example, the increased proportion of elderly may link with a higher proportion of expenditure on health. On the other hand, declining school-age children within the household may lead to a reduction in education expenditure. Therefore, it is important to investigate the consumer demand for health and education expenditure as these findings provide important signals for policy makers to direct resources and formulate policies on government expenditure on health and education.

This book provides an in-depth analysis of household demand for food and non-food commodities using a diverse database, consisting of 45 developed and developing countries. In doing so, in the first part of the consumer demand analysis we focus on 12 commodities, namely, food, alcohol and tobacco, clothing, housing, durables, health, transport, communication, recreation, education, restaurants and miscellaneous. In the second part, we consider within-group analysis (or conditional analysis within a group) for three groups of goods: the first food group consisting of food, alcoholic beverages and restaurant meals; the second group consisting of transport, communication and housing (TCH); and the third group consisting of health, recreation and education (HRE). In particular, we estimate income, own-price and cross-price elasticities for different commodity groups and commodities within specific groups. For the analysis, we employ the well-known system-wide approach (Clements et al., 2006, 2020a, 2020b; Theil, 1975/76). We also present the demand for consumer goods using cross-sectional household data for selected countries in the Asia Pacific region using the conditional generalised Working's model (CGWM) approach developed by Selvanathan et al. (2021).

1.2 Measurement of Consumer Demand

The theory and measurement of consumer demand both have a long history dating back to the last century. Significant contributions started with the 19th-century pioneer works of Cournot (1838), Gossen (1854), Engel (1857), Menger (1871), Edgeworth (1881), Marshall (1898), Fisher (1892) and Walras (1896), followed by the works of Slutsky (1915), Jevons (1931), Frisch (1932), Hicks and Allen (1934), Working (1943), Houthakker (1957), Wold (1953), Stone (1954) and Samuelson (1965) in the 20th century. The earlier consumption studies mostly considered each commodity in isolation by considering single equations and later the modern system-wide approach for consumption economics introduced by Theil (1975/76) emphasised the equation system rather than single equations under which cross-commodity restrictions such as demand homogeneity and Slutsky symmetry can be imposed and tested.

The system-wide approach has attracted a lot of attention in the last half century and has been used in many time-series and cross-sectional international consumption comparison studies, which has resulted in several research monographs, including Barnett (1981), Chen (2001), Deaton and Muellbauer (1980), Lluch et al. (1977), Selvanathan and Clements (1995), Selvanathan and Selvanathan (1994, 2003, 2005), Selvanathan (1993), Theil and Clements (1987), Theil et al. (1989) and Theil and Suhm (1981). The use of the system-wide approach has gained popularity in the literature for three reasons. (1) When consumers have a fixed budget constraint, any increase in expenditure on one commodity requires a reduction in expenditure on at least one other commodity. Such adjustments to household budget allocation can only be analysed when the demand equations for all commodities are considered simultaneously, as facilitated in the system-wide approach. (2) Theories in consumption economics are based on certain constraints imposed to enhance the accuracy of the estimations, such as that demand equations are homogeneous of degree zero in income and prices, termed *demand homogeneity*. A system-wide approach facilitates specification of such demand theory constraints. (3) Only a system-wide approach will enable the testing of cross-equation restrictions such as *Slutsky symmetry*. Slutsky symmetry implies that if the consumer's real income is held constant, the quantity change in the consumption of a good – arising from a one-dollar increase in the price of a different good – will be exactly the same as the change in the consumption of the first good brought about by a one-dollar increase in the price of the latter good.

A review of the existing literature on the topic identifies that there are several highly influential cross-country studies such as Chen (2001); Clements et al. (2006, 2020a, 2020b); Clements and Theil (1996); Houthakker (1957, 1965); Kravis et al. (1982); Leser (1941, 1963); Lluch and Powell (1975); Lluch et al. (1977); Selvanathan (1993); Selvanathan and Selvanathan (2003, 2005) and Summers and Heston (1984). Laitinen et al. (1983) proposed an extension to the Working's (1943) model which allows the marginal share to be a linear function of the corresponding budget share. Selvanathan et al. (2021) derived the conditional (within a group of goods) version of Laitinen's generalised Working's model, which is an important and useful generalisation of the popular Working's model with respect to the conditional case. We have adopted the CGWM for the analysis of cross-sectional data.

1.3 A Preview of the Book

As stated above, this book focuses on international consumption comparisons of food, alcohol and tobacco, clothing, housing, durables, health, transport, communication, recreation, education, restaurants and miscellaneous across a number of developed and developing countries. A comparison of consumption patterns between the developed and developing countries is also presented throughout the book.

Chapter 2 presents an overview of consumer demand theory. This chapter starts with introducing the basics of consumption economics such as budget shares, marginal shares and income and price elasticities. We then introduce data summary tools for consumption data such as Divisia price and quantity indices and Divisia price and quantity variances, Divisia price-quantity covariances and correlations. In the next step, we discuss the well-known non-utility-based demand models such as double-log demand equations, Working's model, Box-Cox Engel curves and the generalised Working's Model. We then derive the utility-based demand models and their theoretical properties such as demand homogeneity and Slutsky symmetry and preference independence utility structure based on the modern system-wide approach. This is followed by derivation of the conditional demand systems under block independence preferences. Finally, we consider the parameterisation of the demand system to be used in estimation in the forthcoming chapters.

Chapter 3 describes the time-series consumption and price data for 45 countries and summarises data using the tools presented in Chapter 2. This chapter has only a preliminary status. We then analyse the demand for food using Working's model and derive the income and price elasticities for the 12 commodities using the double-log demand equations. We then test the famous Frisch's conjecture which states that the income elasticity of marginal utility of income decreases in absolute value as the consumer becomes more affluent. We also investigate the support for the preference independence hypothesis.

In Chapter 4, we formally apply the system-wide approach to estimate the three differential demand systems and obtain the income and price elasticities for the commodity groups in 45 countries. We also test the demand theory hypothesis such as demand homogeneity, Slutsky symmetry and preference independence utility structure.

Chapter 5 uses cross-sectional data in the form of household expenditure surveys for four selected countries, Australia, Bangladesh, India and Sri Lanka, where we have access to such data. This chapter also considers various characteristics of the consumers and presents a comparison of the consumption patterns of these four countries.

Consumer demand for food is an important consideration for policy makers and agribusiness market participants to plan and implement social, welfare and food security-related policies and business policies. Chapter 6 presents a comprehensive conditional analysis of the demand for the 'food group' consisting of food, alcoholic beverages and restaurant meals for 45 countries. A comprehensive analysis of cross-sectional household data of the food group for Australia, India and Sri Lanka is also presented in this chapter. In doing so, the chapter discusses the impact of food prices and income on demand for the food group as well as sub-groups within food.

In recent years, with rapidly changing income and travel and communication behaviours, analysis of demand for transport and communication and housing has become an important area of policy interest. These three commodities are found to be very closely interlinked, in the form of close substitutes or complementary goods. In Chapter 7, we analyse the conditional demand for the commodity group consisting of the TCH group, for 45 countries using time-series data and for Australia, Bangladesh, India, and Sri Lanka, using cross-sectional household survey data. In particular, the chapter discusses the own-price, income and cross-price elasticities of these three commodities that provide enhanced insights into welfare and pricing policies regarding these commodities.

Changing demographic composition in countries with noticeable population aging and an increasing level of international and local travel facilitated by rapidly growing income and transport facilities means that the health, education and recreation sectors have become important considerations in household budget allocations. Chapter 8 presents a comprehensive analysis of consumer demand for the HRE group. The chapter carries out a time-series analysis for 45 developed and developing countries and a cross-sectional analysis of the consumer behaviour in Australia, Bangladesh,

India and Sri Lanka. This analysis provides insights on the differences in the way in which consumers in developed and developing countries respond to price and income changes with respect to these goods and provides important policy insights for optimal allocation of resources to ensure the well-being of people.

Throughout Chapters 6–8, the data analytic techniques and the conditional demand model estimation methods provided in Chapter 2 are fully utilised to present a summary of the price-consumption data, to model the demand for individual commodities as well as groups of commodities and to obtain conditional income elasticities for each commodity within the group. Finally, Chapter 9 gives summary of the results, policy implications and conclusion.

References

Barnett, W.A. 1981. *Consumer demand and labor supply: goods, monetary assets and time*. Amsterdam: North Holland Publishing Company.

Chen, D.L. 2001. *World consumption economics*. Singapore, London: World Scientific.

Clements, K.W., Y. Lan, and H. Liu. 2020a. Understanding alcohol consumption across countries. *Applied Economics* 52(40): 4421-4439.

Clements, K.W., J. Si, E.A. Selvanathan, and S. Selvanathan. 2020b. Demand elasticities for 9 goods in 37 countries. *Applied Economics* 52(24): 2636–2655.

Clements, K.W. and H. Theil. 1996. Chapter 7: A cross-country analysis of consumption patterns, in H. Theil (ed.), *Studies in global econometrics*. New York: Springer, pp. 95–108.

Clements, K.W., Y. Wu, and J. Zhang. 2006. Comparing international consumption patterns. *Empirical Economics* 31: 1–30.

Cournot, A.A. 1838. *Recherches sur les principes mathématiques de la théorie des richesses*.

Deaton, A., and J. Muellbauer. 1980. *Economics and consumer behavior*. London: Cambridge University Press.

Edgeworth, F.Y. 1881. *Mathematical psychics: An essay on the application of mathematics to the moral sciences* (No. 10). New York: A.M. Kelley.

Engel, E. 1857. Die lebenskosten belgischer arbeiter-familien fruher und jetzt. *International Statistical Institute Bulletin* 9: 1–74.

Fisher, I. 1892. Mathematical investigations in the theory of value and prices. New York: Augustus M. Kelly Publishers.

Frisch, R. 1932. Capital production and consumer-taking: A rejoinder. *Journal of Political Economy* 40(2): 253–255.

Gossen, H.H. 1854. Entwickelung der Gesetze des menschlichen Verkehrs, und der daraus fließenden Regeln für menschliches Handeln. Friedrich Vieweg und Sohn.

Hicks, J. R., and R.G. Allen. 1934. A reconsideration of the theory of value. Part I. *Economica* 1(1): 52–76.

Houthakker, H.S. 1957. An international comparison of household expenditure patterns, commemorating the centenary of Engel's Law. *Econometrica* 25(4): 532–551.

Houthakker, H.S. 1965. New evidence on demand elasticities. *Econometrica* 33(2): 277–288.

Jevons, H.S. 1931. The second industrial revolution. *The Economic Journal* 41(161): 1–18.

Kravis, L.B., A.W. Heston, and R. Summers. 1982. *World product and income: International comparisons of real gross product.* Baltimore, MD: The Johns Hopkins University Press.

Laltinen, K., H. Theil, and T. Raparla. 1983. A generalized working's model. *Economics Letters* 13: 97–100.

Leser, C.E. 1963. Forms of Engel functions. *Econometrica* 31(4): 694–703.

Leser, C.E. 1941. Family budget data and price-elasticities of demand. *The Review of Economic Studies* 9(1): 40–57.

Lluch, C., and A. Powell. 1975. International comparisons of expenditure patterns. *European Economic Review* 6(3): 275–303.

Lluch, C., A.A. Powell, R.A. Williams, and R.R. Betancourt. 1977. *Patterns in household demand and saving.* Oxford: Oxford University Press.

Marshall, A. 1898. Distribution and exchange. *The Economic Journal* 8(29): 37–59.

Menger, C. 1871. *Grunds? tze Der Volkswirthschaftslehre.* Рипол Классик.

Reinhardt, E.U. 2003. Does the aging of the population really drive the demand for health care? *Health Affairs* 22(6): 27–39.

Samuelson, P.A. 1965. A Theory of induced innovation along Kennedy-Weisäcker lines. *The Review of Economics and Statistics* 47(4):343–356.

Selvanathan, E.A., and K. Clements. 1995. *Recent Developments in applied demand analysis: alcohol, advertising and global consumption.* Berlin: Springer-Verlag.

Selvanathan, E.A., and S. Selvanathan. 1994. *Regional consumption patterns: A system-wide approach.* Vermont: Ashgate Publishing Company.

Selvanathan, E.A., and S. Selvanathan. 2003. *International consumption comparisons: OECD versus LDC.* Singapore, Hackensack, NJ: World Scientific.

Selvanathan, S. 1993. *A system-wide analysis of international consumption patterns.* Boston, MA: Kluwer Academic Publishers.

Selvanathan, S. and E.A. Selvanathan. 2005. *The demand for alcohol, tobacco and marijuana: International evidence.* Vermont: Ashgate Publishing Company.

Selvanathan, S., S. Selvanathan, and M. Jayasinghe. 2021. A new approach to analyse conditional demand: An application to Australian energy consumption. *Energy Economics* 93: 1–8.

Slutsky, E. 1915. Sulla teoria del bilancio del consumatore. *Giornale degli economisti e rivista di statistica*, 1–26.

Stone, R. (1954). Linear expenditure systems and demand analysis: An application to the pattern of British demand. *The Economic Journal* 64(255): 511–527.

Summers, R., and A. Heston. 1984. Improved international comparisons of real product and its composition: 1950–1980. *Review of Income and Wealth* 30(2): 207–219.

Theil, H. 1975/76. *Theory and measurement of consumer demand.* Amsterdam: North-Holland Publishing Company.

Theil, H., and K.W. Clements. 1987. *Applied demand analysis: Results from system-wide approaches.* Cambridge, MA: Ballinger Publishing Company.

Theil, H., C.F. Chung, and J.L. Seale. 1989. *International evidence on consumption patterns* (Vol. 1). London: Jai Press Inc.

Theil, H., and F.E. Suhm. 1981. *International consumption comparisons: A system-wide approach*. Amsterdam.

Walras, L. 1896. Éléments d›économie politique pure, ou, Théorie de la richesse sociale. Paris: F. Rouge.

Wold, H. 1953. Some artificial experiments in factor analysis. *Nordic Psychology Monographs* 3: 43–64.

Working, H. 1943. Statistical laws of family expenditure. *Journal of the American Statistical Association* 38(221): 43–56.

2 An Overview of Consumer Demand

E A Selvanathan, S Selvanathan and M Jayasinghe

2.1 Introduction

This chapter presents an overview of consumer demand analysis. It also includes different approaches to deriving demand equations such as the utility/non-utility-based approach and single-equation/system-wide approach. We start with the basics of consumption theory and then derive demand systems to be used in the later chapters to analyse the demand for various consumer goods. We also present a detailed discussion on the importance of undertaking an in-depth analysis of consumer demand patterns.

Basic demand analysis postulates that the quantity demanded of a good by a consumer will be determined by his/her purchasing capacity (that is his/her income), the price of that particular good and the prices of other goods that are competing with the good under consideration (substitutes), and the price of other goods that are complementing it (complements). The functional form that relates the quantity demanded of a good to consumer's income and prices of all goods is called a *demand function*. This means that a demand function for a single commodity explains how the changes in consumers' income and prices of all goods affect the quantity demanded for that good. There are two approaches to deriving demand functions. The first approach, used in early applied demand research, demand functions was usually directly specified without any reference to the utility function. Under this direct approach, demand for a good is specified as a simple function of income and prices. The second and most popular approach is to derive demand functions by postulating that the consumer behaves as if he/she chooses the consumption basket to maximise a utility function subject to a budget constraint.

The chapter is structured as follows: Section 2.2 introduces the basics of consumption economics. Summary measures of prices and consumption in the form of Divisia indices are introduced in Section 2.3. Section 2.4 presents some of the non-utility-based popular demand models, while Sections 2.5–2.9 present the utility-based demand models and their variants.

DOI: 10.4324/9780429200120-2

2.2 Basics of Consumption Economics

The objective of consumption economics is to analyse the demand for consumer goods and services in terms of income and prices. Let there be n goods available for purchase at prices $p_1, p_2, \ldots, p_n$. Suppose at a particular point in time a consumer buys $q_1, q_2, \ldots, q_n$ quantities of those n goods so that the total amount the consumer spends M ("income" for short) is given by

$$M = \sum_{i=1}^{n} p_i q_i = \boldsymbol{p}'\boldsymbol{q}, \tag{2.1}$$

where $\boldsymbol{p} = (p_1, p_2, \ldots, p_n)'$ and $\boldsymbol{q} = (q_1, q_2, \ldots, q_n)'$ are $n \times 1$ price and quantity vectors, respectively.

2.2.1 *Budget Shares and Marginal Shares*

The proportion of income spent on commodity i is given by

$$w_i = \frac{p_i q_i}{M}, \quad i = 1,2,\ldots,n, \tag{2.2}$$

and is called the *budget share* of commodity i. Summing both sides of equation (2.2) over $i = 1, 2, \ldots, n$ and using equation (2.1), we find that these budget shares sum to one. That is,

$$\sum_{i=1}^{n} w_i = 1. \tag{2.3}$$

The *marginal share*, θ_i, of commodity i is given by

$$\theta_i = \frac{\partial(p_i q_i)}{\partial M}, \quad i = 1,2,\ldots,n. \tag{2.4}$$

This marginal share answers the question: if income increases by \$1, how much of that extra income will be spent on commodity i? Differentiating equation (2.1) with respect to M implies that, like budget shares, we can easily show that the marginal shares also sum to one. That is,

$$\sum_{i=1}^{n} \theta_i = \frac{\partial\left(\sum_{i} p_i q_i\right)}{\partial M} = 1. \tag{2.5}$$

2.2.2 Income and Price Elasticities

The *income elasticity* of commodity *i*, η_i, the ratio of proportionate change in consumption of commodity *i* to proportionate change in total income, is given by

$$\eta_i = \frac{\partial q_i / q_i}{\partial M / M} = \frac{\partial(\log q_i)}{\partial(\log M)}, \quad i = 1,2,\ldots,n. \tag{2.6}$$

The income elasticity answers the question: if income rises by 1 percent with prices held constant, what is the percentage change in the consumption of *i*? Commodities with income elasticity positive and less than 1 are called *necessities*, while those with income elasticity greater than 1 are called *luxuries*. If the income elasticity is negative, then that commodity is said to be an *inferior good* as its consumption falls with increasing income. We can also easily see that the income elasticity of *i* is the ratio of marginal share to budget share of *i*. That is,

$$\eta_i = \frac{\partial q_i / q_i}{\partial M / M} = \frac{\partial(p_i q_i)/\partial M}{p_i q_i / M} = \frac{\theta_i}{w_i}, \quad i = 1,2,\ldots,n. \tag{2.7}$$

From equations (2.7) and (2.5), we can easily show that the weighted sum of income elasticities with the corresponding budget shares as weights is equal to 1. That is,

$$\sum_{i=1}^{n} w_i \eta_i = \sum_{i=1}^{n} \theta_i = 1. \tag{2.8}$$

Equation (2.8) is also called *Engel aggregation*.

The differential of equation (2.2) gives

$$d(\log w_i) = d(\log q_i) + d(\log p_i) - d(\log M)$$

With constant prices, using equation (2.6), the above equation can be simplified to

$$d(\log w_i) = (\eta_i - 1)\, d(\log M). \tag{2.9}$$

Equation (2.9) states that the income elasticity of the budget share of commodity *i* is ($\eta_i - 1$). For necessities ($\eta_i < 1$), this means that an increase in income will reduce the budget share of *i*; and conversely for luxuries ($\eta_i > 1$), an increase in income will increase the budget share of *i*. For example, when the consumer becomes more affluent, then the amount he spends on food, a necessity, will rise less rapidly than income, causing the food budget share to fall. This inverse relationship between the food budget share and income is known as the *Engel's Law*, after Engel (1857).

The *uncompensated price elasticity* of commodity i with respect to the price of commodity j, η_{ij}, the ratio of proportionate change in consumption of commodity i to proportionate change in the price of commodity j, is given by

$$\eta_{ij} = \frac{\partial q_i / q_i}{\partial p_j / p_j} = \frac{\partial(\log q_i)}{\partial(\log p_j)}, \quad i, j = 1, 2, \ldots, n. \tag{2.10}$$

The price elasticity η_{ij} answers the question that, if the price of commodity j increases by 1 percent, with income and other prices held constant, what is the percentage change in the consumption of i? If $i = j$, η_{ij} is known as the *own-price elasticity* of commodity i and if $i \neq j$, η_{ij} is known as the *cross-price elasticity of commodity i with respect to commodity j*. If $i = j$, according to the law of demand, we would expect η_{ii} to be negative (ruling out Giffen[1] goods). If an increase in the price of commodity j increases (decreases) the demand for i, that is $\eta_{ij} > 0$ (<0), then i and j are called *gross substitutes* (*gross complements*).

2.3 Divisia Indices

The Divisia index numbers are simple tools available to summarise consumption (price and quantity) data. These indices can be treated as central measures and dispersion of the distribution of prices and quantities, with budget shares playing the role of weights.

We denote the logarithmic change in a variable x as $dx/x = d(\log x)$. In this notation, we have n price log-changes $d(\log p_1)$, $d(\log p_2)$, …, $d(\log p_n)$ and n quantity log-changes $d(\log q_1)$, $d(\log q_2)$, …, $d(\log q_n)$. To summarise the overall movement in the n price and quantity log-changes, we use the Divisia price and Divisia volume index, respectively, defined as

$$d(\log P) = \sum_{i=1}^{n} w_i d(\log p_i) \tag{2.11}$$

and

$$d(\log Q) = \sum_{i=1}^{n} w_i d(\log q_i). \tag{2.12}$$

In other words, the Divisia price index (2.11) is a weighted average of the n logarithmic price changes, $d(\log p_1)$, …, $d(\log p_n)$, with the weights being the corresponding budget shares. Similarly, we can interpret the Divisia quantity (volume) index given by equation (2.12). To see the link between the

Divisia volume and Divisia price index, we first consider the differential of equation (2.1):

$$\sum_{i=1}^{n} p_i dq_i + \sum_{i=1}^{n} q_i dp_i = dM.$$

Dividing both sides of the above equation by M, using the identity $dx/x = d(\log x)$ and using equations (2.11) and (2.12), we obtain

$$d(\log Q) + d(\log P) = d(\log M). \tag{2.13}$$

Equation (2.13) decomposes the change in income into a volume and price index.

The Divisia price index $d(\log P)$ is defined in equation (2.11) as a budget-share-weighted-average of the n logarithmic price changes $d(\log p_1)$, ..., $d(\log p_n)$. This can be viewed as a weighted first-order moment of the price changes. The corresponding second-order moment is the Divisia price variance

$$\Pi = \sum_{i=1}^{n} w_i \left[d(\log p_i) - d(\log P) \right]^2. \tag{2.14}$$

This price variance Π vanishes when all prices change proportionately and increases when prices change more disproportionately. In other words, Π is a measure of the changes in relative prices. Similarly, the Divisia quantity variance

$$K = \sum_{i=1}^{n} w_i [d(\log q_i) - d(\log Q)]^2 \tag{2.15}$$

is a measure of the changes in relative quantities. To measure the co-movement of prices and quantities, we can use the Divisia price-quantity covariance

$$\Gamma = \sum_{i=1}^{n} w_i \left[d(\log p_i) - d(\log P) \right] \left[d(\log q_i) - d(\log Q) \right] \tag{2.16}$$

and the corresponding price-quantity correlation is

$$\rho = \frac{\Gamma}{\sqrt{K\Pi}}. \tag{2.17}$$

This correlation measures the co-movement of prices and quantities. As those commodities having above-average price increases would tend to experience below-average increases in consumption and vice versa, ρ will usually be negative. However, as ρ includes a real-income component, in certain cases it may be positive (see Theil 1975/76, Chapter 11).

2.4 Non-Utility-Based Demand Models

In this section, we describe the most commonly used direct non-utility-based demand models.

The older traditional direct demand models, which go back to Cassel (1932) and Workings (1943), specify the demand for a particular good as a function of the consumer's income and its own price as well as the prices of other goods in the consumer's basket. Below, we consider four such well-known demand specifications, namely, the *double-log demand model, Working's (1943) model*, the *Box-Cox Engel function* and an extended Working's model known as the *generalised Working's model* proposed by Laitinen et al. (1983) and Selvanathan et al. (2021).

2.4.1 Double-Log Demand Model

Here, we analyse a widely used member of this family, the double-log demand model, which takes the form

$$\log q_i = \alpha_i + \eta_i \log M + \sum_{j=1}^{n} \eta_{ij} \log p_j, \quad i = 1,2,\ldots,n, \tag{2.18}$$

where q_i is the quantity consumed of good i (i = 1, ..., n); p_j is the price of good j; M is income; and α_i, η_i, and η_{ij} are constant coefficients. In equation (2.18), the coefficient of income is

$$\eta_i = \frac{\partial(\log q_i)}{\partial(\log M)}, \quad i = 1,2,\ldots,n.$$

is the *income elasticity* of demand for good i defined in equation (2.6).

Similarly, the coefficient

$$\eta_{ij} = \frac{\partial(\log q_i)}{\partial(\log p_j)}, \quad i, j = 1,2,\ldots,n.$$

is the *cross-price elasticity* – the elasticity of demand for i with respect to the price of j defined in equation (2.10). As equation (2.18) holds constant money income M, the η_{ij}'s include both the income and substitution effects of the price changes. This is expressed by saying that the η_{ij}'s are the *uncompensated price elasticities.* This η_{ij} is also called the *Cournot price elasticity.*

2.4.2 Working's Model

Another example of directly specified demand equations is the Working's (1943) model, which expresses the budget shares as linear functions of the logarithm of income:

$$w_i = \alpha_i + \beta_i \log M, \quad i = 1,2,\ldots,n. \tag{2.19}$$

As the budget shares sum to unity, it follows from equation (2.19) that the constant coefficients α_i and β_i satisfy $\Sigma_{i=1}^{n} \alpha_i = 1$ and $\Sigma_{i=1}^{n} \beta_i = 0$. When M = 1, the above equation reduces to wi = α_i. Therefore, a_i can be interpreted as the budget share of the ith household whose income equals 1. Taking the differentials of both sides of equation (2.19), we can write $dw_i = \beta_i$ $d(\log M)$; thus, we can interpret β_i as 100 times the change in w_i resulting from a 1 percent increase in income M. It is to be noted that equation (2.19) does not contain prices. Consequently, it can be applied to household surveys, where prices are approximately constant. However, the model needs to be extended by adding a substitution term in situations where prices are not constant, as in a time-series application.

Using equation (2.2) to replace w_i in equation (2.19) and multiplying both sides by M, we get

$$p_i q_i = \alpha_i M + \beta_i M \log M,$$

and then differentiating with respect to M gives

$$\theta_i = \frac{\partial(p_i q_i)}{\partial M} = \alpha_i + \beta_i(1 + \log M).$$

Substituting from equation (2.19), we get

$$\theta_i = w_i + \beta_i, \quad i = 1,2,\ldots,n. \tag{2.20}$$

Thus, under Working's model, the marginal share and the budget share for commodity i differ by the constant coefficient β_i. Furthermore, as the budget share w_i is not a constant over time, neither is the marginal share θ_i defined in equation (2.20). Dividing both sides of equation (2.20) by w_i, we obtain the income elasticity of commodity i under Working's model (2.19) as

$$\eta_i = 1 + \frac{\beta_i}{w_i}, \quad i = 1,2,\ldots,n. \tag{2.21}$$

This shows that a commodity is a necessity if β_i is negative and it is a luxury if β_i is positive.

As the budget share of a luxury increases with income, prices remaining constant, it follows from equation (2.21) that increasing income causes the income elasticity η_i of such a good to fall towards 1. The income elasticity of a necessity also declines with increasing income under equation (2.21). Thus, as the consumer becomes more affluent, all goods become less luxurious under Working's model, which is plausible.

2.4.3 Box-Cox Engel Function

Taking the Engel (1857) curve specified by Working's (1943) model given by equation (2.19) as the starting point, the Box and Cox (1964) Engel function for commodity *i* can be written as

$$w_i = \alpha_i + \beta_i M^{(\lambda)} \quad i = 1, 2, \ldots, n, \tag{2.22}$$

where w_i is the budget share on commodity *i* (i = 1, 2, …, *n*) consumed and $M^{(\lambda)}$ is the Box-Cox transformed household expenditure, defined as

$$M^{(\lambda)} = \begin{cases} \dfrac{M^{\lambda} - 1}{\lambda} & \text{if} \quad \lambda \neq 0 \\ \log M & \text{if} \quad \lambda = 0 \end{cases} \tag{2.23}$$

where λ is the Box-Cox transformation parameter.

Equation (2.22) provides a non-linear specification for the system of Engel curves. For the adding-up restriction to be satisfied, the model parameters of equation (2.22) are expected to satisfy the following conditions:

$$\sum_{i=1}^{n} \alpha_i = 1 \text{ and } \sum_{i=1}^{n} \beta_i = 0. \tag{2.24}$$

Estimation of the non-linear system of equation (2.22) for i = 1, 2, …, *n*, subject to equation (2.24), will provide an estimate for the parameter, λ. As discussed in Beneito (2003), when λ = 0, equation (2.22) becomes the Working's (1943) model given by equation (2.19) above; when λ = 1, equation (2.22) becomes the linear specification $w_i = \alpha_i + \beta_i M$. The Box-Cox method assigns an initial value for λ and continues searching for an optimal value for λ using equation (2.23).

Equation (2.22) represents the basic Engel curve specification, which displays the relationship between the budget share of a given commodity against expenditure. Studies have also shown that household socio-demographic factors significantly affect household consumption patterns (Bosch-Domènech 1991; Jayasinghe 2019).

We derive the income elasticity of commodity *i* from model (2.22) as

$$\eta_i = \frac{\partial(\log q_i)}{\partial(\log M)} = \frac{\partial q_i / q_i}{\partial M / M} = \frac{\partial p_i q_i / p_i q_i}{\partial M / M} = \frac{\partial(p_i q_i)}{\partial M} \frac{1}{p_i q_i / M}.$$

Noting the fact that $w_i = p_i q_i / M$, we can write this as

$$\eta_i = \frac{\partial(p_i q_i)}{\partial M} \frac{1}{w_i}. \tag{2.25}$$

We multiply both sides of equation (2.22) by M to give

$$p_i q_i = \alpha_i \cdot M + \beta_i M \cdot M^{(\lambda)}. \tag{2.26}$$

Differentiating equation (2.26) with respect to M and using equation (2.22), we obtain,

$$\frac{\partial p_i q_i}{\partial M} = \alpha_i + \beta_i M^{(\lambda)} + \beta_i M \frac{\partial\left(M^{(\lambda)}\right)}{\partial(M)} = w_i + \beta_i M \frac{\partial\left(M^{(\lambda)}\right)}{\partial(M)}. \tag{2.27}$$

Substituting equation (2.27) into equation (2.25), we get

$$\eta_i = 1 + \frac{\beta_i}{w_i} M \frac{\partial\left(M^{(\lambda)}\right)}{\partial(M)}. \tag{2.28}$$

Under Box-Cox transformation (2.23), we have

$$\frac{\partial\left(M^{(\lambda)}\right)}{\partial(M)} = \begin{cases} M^{\lambda-1} & \text{when } \lambda \neq 0 \\ \dfrac{1}{M} & \text{when } \lambda = 0. \end{cases}$$

Therefore, equation (2.28) becomes

$$\eta_i = \begin{cases} 1 + \dfrac{\beta_i}{w_i} M^{\lambda} & \text{when } \lambda \neq 0 \\ 1 + \dfrac{\beta_i}{w_i} & \text{when } \lambda = 0. \end{cases} \tag{2.29}$$

The income elasticity given by equation (2.29) when $\lambda = 0$ is the same as that given by equation (2.21) under Working's model (2.19).

2.4.4 Generalised Working's Model

Another variation of (2.22) was proposed by Laitinen et al. (1983)[2] as a generalisation of the Working's (1943) model in the form

$$w_i = \alpha_i M^{\lambda} + \beta_i \frac{\left(M^{\lambda} - 1\right)}{\lambda}, \quad i = 1,2,\ldots,n, \tag{2.30}$$

where α_i and β_i are constants satisfying

$$\sum_{i=1}^{n} \alpha_i = 1 \text{ and } \sum_{i=1}^{n} \beta_i = -\lambda.$$

Using L'Hospital's rule, when $\lambda \rightarrow 0$ we have $(M\lambda - 1)/\lambda \rightarrow \log M$. Therefore, it can be easily seen that when $\lambda \rightarrow 0$, the *generalised Working's model* given by equation (2.30) reduces to Working's model presented in equation (2.19). That is, Working's model is a special case of the generalised Working's model when $\lambda \rightarrow 0$.

By replacing w_i in equation (2.30) with $p_i q_i / M$ and multiplying both sides by M, we can easily show that the marginal share θ_i of good i is

$$\theta_i = \frac{\partial(p_i q_i)}{\partial M} = (1+\lambda)w_i + \beta_i, \quad i = 1,2,\ldots,n. \tag{2.31}$$

In equation (2.20) under Working's model (2.19), the marginal share θ_i is a linear function of the corresponding budget share w_i. As can be seen from equation (2.31) under the generalised Working's model (2.30), a similar linear relationship exists between θ_i and w_i. The implied income elasticity under the generalised Working's model is given by

$$\eta_i = \frac{\theta_i}{w_i} = (1+\lambda) + \frac{\beta_i}{w_i}, \quad i = 1,2,\ldots,n. \tag{2.32}$$

When $\lambda \rightarrow 0$, marginal share (2.31) and income elasticity (2.32) under the generalised Working's model reduce to the marginal share and income elasticity under Working's model given by equations (2.20) and (2.21), respectively.

2.5 Utility-Based Consumer Demand Models

The utility-based demand functions are obtained from the utility maximising theory. That is, when consumers purchase a number of goods simultaneously, they maximise their overall total utility subject to the amount of income they can allocate for this purpose, also known as their budget constraint.

2.5.1 Utility Maximisation of Consumer Demand

To derive the general form of consumer demand equations, we postulate that the consumer has a stable preference which can be described by means of a utility function of the form

$$u = u(q_1, q_2, \ldots q_n) = u(\boldsymbol{q}) \tag{2.33}$$

where $\boldsymbol{q} = (q_1, q_2, \ldots, q_n)'$ is a $n \times 1$ vector of quantities. We assume that the marginal utility of consumption is positive. That is,

$$\frac{\partial u}{\partial \boldsymbol{q}} > 0 \text{ or } \frac{\partial u}{\partial q_i} > 0, \quad i = 1, 2, \ldots, n. \tag{2.34}$$

Another assumption made on u is that it has a continuous second-order derivative and there is generalised diminishing marginal utility so that the Hessian matrix of u is negative definite. That is,

$$\boldsymbol{U} = \left[\frac{\partial^2 u}{\partial q_i \partial q_j}\right] = \left[\frac{\partial^2 u}{\partial \boldsymbol{q} \partial \boldsymbol{q}'}\right] \tag{2.35}$$

is a symmetric negative definite matrix of order $n \times n$, which is a sufficient condition that guarantees a budget constrained utility maximum.

We derive the demand equations by solving the consumer maximisation problem by maximising the consumer's utility subject to his/her budget constraint. That is,

$$\text{Maximise } u = u(q_1, q_2, \ldots q_n) = u(\boldsymbol{q}) \tag{2.36}$$

subject to $\boldsymbol{p}'\boldsymbol{q} = M$.

To find a solution to this maximisation problem, we write the Lagrangian function in matrix form,

$$u^*(\boldsymbol{q}, \lambda) = u(\boldsymbol{q}) - \lambda(\boldsymbol{p}'\boldsymbol{q} - M)$$

or, in scalar form,

$$u^*(q_1, \ldots q_n, \lambda) = u(q_1, \ldots q_n) - \lambda\left[\sum_{i=1}^{n} p_i q_i - M\right], \tag{2.37}$$

where λ is the *Lagrangian multiplier.*

Using the first-order conditions for the objective function (2.37), we obtain

$$\frac{\partial u}{\partial \boldsymbol{q}} = \lambda \boldsymbol{p} \text{ or } \frac{\partial u}{\partial q_i} = \lambda p_i, \quad i = 1, 2, \ldots, n, \tag{2.38}$$

and

$$\boldsymbol{p}'\boldsymbol{q} = M \text{ or } \sum_{i=1}^{n} p_i q_i = M. \tag{2.39}$$

The second-order condition for the maximisation problem in equation (2.37) is given by equation (2.35).

There are $(n + 1)$ first-order conditions, n in (2.38) and one in (2.39), which can be, in principle, solved for the $(n + 1)$ unknowns $q_1, q_2, \ldots, q_n$ and λ. As these solutions for quantities will depend on income and prices, we can write the solutions in the following general functional form:

$$\boldsymbol{q} = \boldsymbol{q}(M, \boldsymbol{p}) \text{ or } q_i = q_i(M, p_1, p_2, \ldots, p_n), \quad i = 1, 2, \ldots, n. \tag{2.40}$$

Equation (2.40) is a system of demand equations consisting of n demand equations, one for each good.

Since marginal utility given by equation (2.34) is positive and prices are positive, from equation (2.38), we conclude that λ is also positive. By rearranging condition (2.38), we can write

$$\frac{\partial u}{\partial(p_i q_i)} = \lambda, \quad i = 1, \ldots, n. \tag{2.41}$$

This means that when expenditure on any good or income increases by one dollar, the utility increases by the same λ units. Consequently, λ is known as the *marginal utility of income*.

2.5.2 Demand Theory Constraints

The demand equation (2.40) should satisfy several constraints which come directly from the utility maximisation problem (2.36). The consumer's maximisation problem implies two testable constraints on the demand equations.

2.5.2.1 Demand Homogeneity

The first constraint on the demand equations is demand homogeneity, which states that if income and prices all increase proportionally, then the quantity demanded of each good will remain unchanged. In other words, the consumer does not suffer from money illusion. For example, suppose that all prices and money income double, then demand homogeneity assures us that this change would have no effect on consumption [or, equivalently, the demand function (2.40) is homogenous of degree zero], that is,

$$q_i(\alpha M, \alpha p_1, \ldots, \alpha p_n) = \alpha q_i(M, p_1, \ldots, p_n) = q_i(M, p_1, \ldots, p_n).$$

If we apply Euler's theorem to demand equation (2.40), we obtain

$$M \frac{\partial q_i}{\partial M} + \sum_{j=1}^{n} p_j \frac{\partial q_i}{\partial p_j} = 0, \quad i = 1, 2, \ldots, n. \tag{2.42}$$

Dividing both sides of equation (2.42) by q_i yields

$$\frac{\partial q_i/q_i}{\partial M/M}+\sum_{j=1}^{n}\frac{\partial q_i/q_i}{\partial p_j/p_j}=0, \quad i=1,2,\ldots,n.$$

Thus, demand homogeneity can be expressed in elasticity form as

$$\eta_i+\sum_{j=1}^{n}\eta_{ij}=0, \quad i=1,2,\ldots,n. \tag{2.43}$$

The Slutsky equation decomposes the total substitution effect of a price change in commodity j on the demand for i as

$$\frac{\partial q_i}{\partial p_j}=\frac{\partial q_i^*}{\partial p_j}-q_j\frac{\partial q_i}{\partial M}, \quad i=1,2,\ldots,n, \tag{2.44}$$

where the superscript * denotes that utility remains constant, that is,

$$\frac{\partial q_i^*}{\partial p_j}=\left.\frac{\partial q_i}{\partial p_j}\right|_{du=0}.$$

As holding utility constant is equivalent to keeping real income unchanged, $\partial q_i^*/\partial p_j$ in equation (2.44) is known as the *substitution effect of a change in the price of commodity j on the demand for i.* The remaining term on the right of equation (2.44), $-q_j(\partial q_i/\partial M)$, is the effect on the demand for i on account of the fall in real income; real income falls as a result of the increase in price of j as nominal income M is held constant. This term is known as the *income effect of a change in the price of j on the demand for i.*

Equation (2.44) can be expressed in elasticity form as

$$\eta_{ij}=\eta_{ij}^*-w_j\eta_i, \quad i,j=1,2,\ldots,n, \tag{2.45}$$

where

$$\eta_{ij}^*=\frac{\partial(\log q_i^*)}{\partial(\log p_j)}$$

is called the *compensated price elasticity of i with respect to the price of j.* If $\eta_{ij}^*>0$ (<0), then the pair of goods i and j are called *net substitutes* (*net complements*). If we sum both sides of equation (2.45) over $j = 1, \ldots, n$, and then use equation (2.43) and the sum of budget shares is equal to 1, we obtain

$$\sum_{j=1}^{n}\eta_{ij}^*=0, \quad i=1,2,\ldots,n. \tag{2.46}$$

2.5.2.2 Slutsky Symmetry

The second constraint is the *Slutsky symmetry*. This states that, when real income is held constant, the effect of an increase in the price of commodity j on the demand for i is equal to the effect of a price increase of i on the demand for j. In other words, as the commodity subscripts can be interchanged, the substitution effects are symmetric in i and j:

$$\frac{\partial q_i^*}{\partial p_j} = \frac{\partial q_j^*}{\partial p_i}, \quad i, j = 1, 2, \ldots, n. \tag{2.47}$$

In elasticity form, this constraint becomes

$$w_i \eta_{ij}^* = w_j \eta_{ji}^*, \quad i, j = 1, 2, \ldots, n. \tag{2.48}$$

Summing both sides of equation (2.48) over $i = 1, 2, \ldots, n$, and using equation (2.46) yields

$$\sum_{i=1}^{n} w_i \eta_{ij}^* = 0, \quad j = 1, 2, \ldots, n. \tag{2.49}$$

From equation (2.45), we have $\eta_{ij}^* = \eta_{ij} + w_j \eta_i$, which we substitute in equation (2.49) to give

$$\sum_{i=1}^{n} w_i \eta_{ij} + w_j = 0, \quad j = 1, 2, \ldots, n, \tag{2.50}$$

where we have also used equation (2.8). Equations (2.49) and (2.50) are known as *Cournot aggregation*.

2.6 Comparative Statics and Demand Equations

In this section, we apply the method of comparative statics to obtain information about demand equation (2.40) in the form of partial derivatives. This involves the use of the first-order conditions (2.38) and (2.39) to ask: how do the values of the endogenous variables $q_1, \ldots, q_n$ and λ respond to changes in the exogenous variables $M, p_1, \ldots, p_n$?

We first differentiate the budget constraint (2.39) with respect to p_j and M to yield

$$\sum_{i=1}^{n} p_i \frac{\partial q_i}{\partial p_j} = -q_j, \quad j = 1, 2, \ldots, n,$$

and

$$\sum_{i=1}^{n} p_i \frac{\partial q_i}{\partial M} = 1.$$

These can be expressed in matrix form as

$$\boldsymbol{p}'\frac{\partial \boldsymbol{q}}{\partial \boldsymbol{p}'} = -\boldsymbol{q}' \text{ and } \boldsymbol{p}'\frac{\partial \boldsymbol{q}}{\partial M} = 1, \tag{2.51}$$

where $\partial \boldsymbol{q}/\partial \boldsymbol{p}' = [\partial q_j/\partial p_i]$ is the $n \times n$ matrix of price derivatives of the demand functions; and $\partial \boldsymbol{q}/\partial M = [\partial q_j/\partial M]$ is the vector of n income slopes of the demand functions.

Second, we differentiate the proportionality conditions (2.38) with respect to p_j and M to give

$$\sum_{k=1}^{n} \frac{\partial^2 u}{\partial q_i \partial q_k}\frac{\partial q_k}{\partial p_j} = \lambda \delta_{ij} + p_i \frac{\partial \lambda}{\partial p_j}, \quad i, j = 1, 2, \ldots, n,$$

and

$$\sum_{k=1}^{n} \frac{\partial^2 u}{\partial q_i \partial q_k}\frac{\partial q_k}{\partial M} = p_i \frac{\partial \lambda}{\partial M}, \quad i = 1, 2, \ldots, n,$$

where δ_{ij} is the Kronecker delta (= 1 if $i = j$, 0 otherwise). We write these in matrix form as

$$\boldsymbol{U}\frac{\partial \boldsymbol{q}}{\partial \boldsymbol{p}'} = \lambda \boldsymbol{I} + \boldsymbol{p}\frac{\partial \lambda}{\partial \boldsymbol{p}'} \text{ and } \boldsymbol{U}\frac{\partial \boldsymbol{q}}{\partial M} = \frac{\partial \lambda}{\partial M}\boldsymbol{p}, \tag{2.52}$$

where $\boldsymbol{U}$ is the Hessian matrix (2.35); $\boldsymbol{I}$ is the $n \times n$ identity matrix; and $\partial \lambda/\partial \boldsymbol{p}' = [\partial \lambda/\partial p_j]$.

Third, we combine equations (2.51) and (2.52) to give

$$\begin{bmatrix} \boldsymbol{U} & \boldsymbol{p} \\ \boldsymbol{p}' & 0 \end{bmatrix} \begin{bmatrix} \dfrac{\partial \boldsymbol{q}}{\partial M} & \dfrac{\partial \boldsymbol{q}}{\partial p'} \\ -\dfrac{\partial \lambda}{\partial M} & -\dfrac{\partial \lambda}{\partial \boldsymbol{p}'} \end{bmatrix} = \begin{bmatrix} 0 & \lambda \boldsymbol{I} \\ 1 & -\boldsymbol{q}' \end{bmatrix} \tag{2.53}$$

Equation (2.53) is known as *Barten's fundamental matrix equation* in consumption theory, after Barten (1964). The matrix immediately to the left of the equal sign contains the derivatives of all the endogenous variables with respect to all exogenous variables. Our next objective is to solve equation (2.53) for this matrix.

The inverse of the matrix on the far left of equation (2.53) is

$$\begin{bmatrix} \boldsymbol{U} & \boldsymbol{p} \\ \boldsymbol{p}' & 0 \end{bmatrix}^{-1} = \frac{1}{\boldsymbol{p}'\boldsymbol{U}^{-1}\boldsymbol{p}} \begin{bmatrix} \left(\boldsymbol{p}'\boldsymbol{U}^{-1}\boldsymbol{p}\right)\boldsymbol{U}^{-1} - \boldsymbol{U}^{-1}\boldsymbol{p}\left(\boldsymbol{U}^{-1}\boldsymbol{p}\right)' & \boldsymbol{U}^{-1}\boldsymbol{p} \\ \left(\boldsymbol{U}^{-1}\boldsymbol{p}\right)' & -1 \end{bmatrix}.$$

Using this inverse, the solution of equation (2.53) is

$$\begin{bmatrix} \frac{\partial \boldsymbol{q}}{\partial M} & \frac{\partial \boldsymbol{q}}{\partial \boldsymbol{p}'} \\ -\frac{\partial \lambda}{\partial M} & -\frac{\partial \lambda}{\partial \boldsymbol{p}'} \end{bmatrix} = \frac{1}{\boldsymbol{p}'\boldsymbol{U}^{-1}\boldsymbol{p}} \begin{bmatrix} \left(\boldsymbol{p}'\boldsymbol{U}^{-1}\boldsymbol{p}\right)\boldsymbol{U}^{-1} - \boldsymbol{U}^{-1}\boldsymbol{p}\left(\boldsymbol{U}^{-1}\boldsymbol{p}\right)' & \boldsymbol{U}^{-1}\boldsymbol{p} \\ \left(\boldsymbol{U}^{-1}\boldsymbol{p}\right)' & -1 \end{bmatrix} \begin{bmatrix} 0 & \lambda\boldsymbol{I} \\ 1 & -\boldsymbol{q}' \end{bmatrix}.$$

Carrying out the matrix multiplication block by block, we obtain

$$\frac{\partial \boldsymbol{q}}{\partial M} = \frac{1}{\boldsymbol{p}'\boldsymbol{U}^{-1}\boldsymbol{p}}\boldsymbol{U}^{-1}\boldsymbol{p}, \tag{2.54}$$

$$\frac{\partial \boldsymbol{q}}{\partial \boldsymbol{p}'} = \lambda\boldsymbol{U}^{-1} - \frac{\lambda}{\boldsymbol{p}'\boldsymbol{U}^{-1}\boldsymbol{p}}\boldsymbol{U}^{-1}\boldsymbol{p}\left(\boldsymbol{U}^{-1}\boldsymbol{p}\right)' - \frac{1}{\boldsymbol{p}'\boldsymbol{U}^{-1}\boldsymbol{p}}\boldsymbol{U}^{-1}\boldsymbol{p}\boldsymbol{q}', \tag{2.55}$$

$$\frac{\partial \lambda}{\partial M} = \frac{1}{\boldsymbol{p}'\boldsymbol{U}^{-1}\boldsymbol{p}}, \tag{2.56}$$

and

$$\frac{\partial \lambda}{\partial \boldsymbol{p}'} = -\frac{\lambda}{\boldsymbol{p}'\boldsymbol{U}^{-1}\boldsymbol{p}}\boldsymbol{U}^{-1}\boldsymbol{p} - \frac{1}{\boldsymbol{p}'\boldsymbol{U}^{-1}\boldsymbol{p}}\boldsymbol{q}'. \tag{2.57}$$

To simplify these expressions, we use equation (2.56) to substitute $\partial\lambda/\partial M$ for the reciprocal of $\boldsymbol{p}'\boldsymbol{U}{-}1\boldsymbol{p}$ in equations (2.54), (2.55) and (2.57). Equation (2.54) then becomes

$$\frac{\partial \mathbf{q}}{\partial M} = \frac{\partial \lambda}{\partial M}\mathbf{U}^{-1}\mathbf{p}. \tag{2.58}$$

Next, we replace $\boldsymbol{U}{-}1\boldsymbol{p}$ in equations (2.55) and (2.57) with $\partial\boldsymbol{q}/\partial\mathrm{M}$ divided by $\partial\lambda/\partial M$, which follows from equation (2.58). This yields

$$\frac{\partial \boldsymbol{q}}{\partial \boldsymbol{p}'} = \lambda\boldsymbol{U}^{-1} - \frac{\lambda}{\partial\lambda/\partial M}\frac{\partial \boldsymbol{q}}{\partial M}\frac{\partial \boldsymbol{q}'}{\partial M} - \frac{\partial \boldsymbol{q}}{\partial M}\boldsymbol{q}' \tag{2.59}$$

and

$$\frac{\partial \lambda}{\partial \boldsymbol{p}'} = -\lambda\frac{\partial \boldsymbol{q}'}{\partial M} - \frac{\partial \lambda}{\partial M}\boldsymbol{q}'. \tag{2.60}$$

Equations (2.58) and (2.59) give the income and price derivatives of the demand functions. We write equation (2.59) in scalar form as

$$\frac{\partial q_i}{\partial p_j} = \lambda u^{ij} - \frac{\lambda}{\partial \lambda / \partial M} \frac{\partial q_i}{\partial M} \frac{\partial q_j}{\partial M} - \frac{\partial q_i}{\partial M} q_j, \quad i, j = 1, 2, \ldots, n, \tag{2.61}$$

where u^{ij} is the (i, j)th element of U^{-1}. This shows that the effect of a change in p_j on q_i, with income and the other prices constant, is made up of three terms. The third term on the right of equation (2.61), $-q_j(\partial q_i/\partial M)$, is the *income effect* of the price change. The remaining two terms, thus, represent the *total substitution effect*, the response of q_i to a change in p_j with real income (and the other prices) held constant. This total substitution effect comprises the *specific substitution effect*, λu^{ij}, and the general substitution effect,

$$-\frac{\lambda}{\partial \lambda / \partial M} \frac{\partial q_i}{\partial M} \frac{\partial q_j}{\partial M},$$

using the terminology from Houthakker (1960). The latter effect is concerned with the competition of all goods for an extra dollar of the consumer's income, while the former deals with the interaction of goods *i* and *j* in the utility function.

For future reference, we write equation (2.58) in scalar terms as

$$\frac{\partial q_i}{\partial M} = \frac{\partial \lambda}{\partial M} \sum_{j=1}^{n} u^{ij} p_j, \quad i = 1, \ldots, n. \tag{2.62}$$

2.7 Differential Approach to Deriving Demand Models

In this section, we use the solution to the fundamental matrix equation presented in the previous section to derive a general system of differential demand equations.

The total differential of equation (2.40) is

$$dq_i = \frac{\partial q_i}{\partial M} dM + \sum_{j=1}^{n} \frac{\partial q_i}{\partial p_j} dp_j, \quad i = 1, 2, \ldots, n.$$

We transform this to logarithmic-differential form by multiplying both sides by p_i/M and using $w_i = p_i q_i/M$,

$$w_i d(\log q_i) = \theta_i d(\log M) + \sum_{j=1}^{n} \frac{p_i p_j}{M} \frac{\partial q_i}{\partial p_j} d(\log p_j) \quad i = 1, 2, \ldots, n. \tag{2.63}$$

We use equations (2.2), (2.4) and (2.61) to express the second term on the right of equation (2.63) as

$$\sum_{j=1}^{n} \frac{p_i p_j}{M} \frac{\partial q_i}{\partial p_j} d(\log p_j) = \sum_{j=1}^{n} \frac{p_i p_j}{M} \left[\lambda u^{ij} - \frac{\lambda}{\partial \lambda / \partial M} \frac{\partial q_i}{\partial M} \frac{\partial q_j}{\partial M} - \frac{\partial q_i}{\partial M} q_j \right] d(\log p_j)$$
$$= \sum_{j=1}^{n} \left[\frac{\lambda p_i p_j u^{ij}}{M} - \frac{\lambda / M}{\partial \lambda / \partial M} \theta_i \theta_j - w_j \theta_i \right] d(\log p_j).$$

Substituting this in equation (2.63) and rearranging gives

$$w_i d(\log q_i) = \theta_i \left[d(\log M) - \sum_{j=1}^{n} w_j d(\log p_j) \right] + \sum_{j=1}^{n} \left[\frac{\lambda p_i p_j u^{ij}}{M} - \frac{\lambda / M}{\partial \lambda / \partial M} \theta_i \theta_j \right]. \tag{2.64}$$

In view of equation (2.13), the term in the first square bracket on the right-hand side of equation (2.64) is the Divisia volume index $d(\log Q)$, which enables us to write

$$\theta_i \left[d(\log M) - \sum_{j=1}^{n} w_j d(\log p_j) \right] = \theta_i \, d(\log Q). \tag{2.65}$$

To simplify the price substitution term of equation (2.64), we define

$$\phi = \frac{\lambda / M}{\partial \lambda / \partial M} = \left[\frac{\partial(\log \lambda)}{\partial(\log M)} \right]^{-1} < 0 \tag{2.66}$$

as the reciprocal of the *income elasticity of the marginal utility of income*. For brevity, we shall refer to ϕ as the income flexibility. We also define

$$v_{ij} = \frac{\lambda}{M} p_i p_j u^{ij}, \quad i, j = 1, 2, \ldots, n. \tag{2.67}$$

We will show below that these coefficients satisfy

$$\sum_{j=1}^{n} v_{ij} = \phi \theta_i, \quad i = 1, 2, \ldots, n. \tag{2.68}$$

To show that ϕ is negative, as stated in equation (2.66), we use equations (2.67) and (2.68) to write

$$\sum_{j=1}^{n} \frac{\lambda}{M} p_i p_j u^{ij} = \phi \theta_i, \quad i = 1, 2, \ldots, n.$$

Summing both sides of the above equation over $i = 1, \ldots, n$ and using $\Sigma_{i=1}^{n} \theta_i = 1$, yields

$$\phi = \frac{\lambda}{M} \sum_{i=1}^{n} \sum_{j=1}^{n} p_i p_j u^{ij}. \tag{2.69}$$

The right-hand side is proportional to a quadratic form with matrix $\boldsymbol{U}^{-1}$ and vector $\boldsymbol{p}$. In view of equation (2.35), this matrix is negative definite, so that the quadratic form is negative. As the factor of proportionality λ/M on the right of equation (2.69) is positive, we conclude that $\phi < 0$.

To verify constraint (2.68), we multiply both sides of equation (2.58) by p_i, which yields

$$\theta_i = \frac{\partial \lambda}{\partial M} \sum_{j=1}^{n} p_i p_j u^{ij}, \quad i = 1, 2, \ldots, n.$$

We then use equation (2.67) and re-arrange the equation to obtain equation (2.68).

Using equations (2.67) and (2.68), the substitution term of equation (2.64) can then be expressed as

$$\begin{aligned} \sum_{j=1}^{n} \left[\frac{\lambda p_i p_j u^{ij}}{M} - \frac{\lambda / M}{\partial \lambda / \partial M} \theta_i \theta_j \right] d(\log p_j) &= \sum_{j=1}^{n} v_{ij} d(\log p_j) - \phi \theta_i d(\log P') \\ &= \sum_{j=1}^{n} v_{ij} \left[d(\log p_j) - d(\log P') \right] \end{aligned} \tag{2.70}$$

where

$$d(\log P') = \sum_{i=1}^{n} \theta_i d(\log p_i) \tag{2.71}$$

and is known as the *Frisch (1932) price index*. This index is different from the Divisia price index (2.11), which uses budget shares as weights rather than marginal shares.

2.7.1 Relative Price Version of the Demand Model

Using equations (2.65) and (2.71) in equation (2.64), the demand equation for good i becomes

$$w_i d(\log q_i) = \theta_i \; d(\log Q) + \sum_{j=1}^{n} v_{ij} \mathrm{d}\left[\log \frac{p_j}{P'} \right], \quad i = 1, 2, \ldots, n, \tag{2.72}$$

where $d[\log(p_j/P')]$ is interpreted as $d(\log p_j) - d(\log P')$.

The first term on the right of equation (2.72) gives the effect of real income on the demand for good i. This term is a multiple θ_i of the Divisia volume index $d(\log Q)$. As this volume index equals $d(\log M) - d(\log P)$, where $d(\log P)$ is the Divisia price index, it follows that the Divisia price index transforms the change in money income into the change in real income. Further, as the Divisia price index is budget-share-weighted, it follows that this index measures the income effect of the n price changes on the demand for the ith good.

The second term on the right of equation (2.72), $\Sigma_{j=1}^{n} v_{ij} d[\log(p_j/P')]$, deals with the effects of relative prices. The Frisch price index acts as a deflator of each price change, so that we refer to $d[\log(p_j/P')]$ as the change in the *Frisch-deflated price of j*. From equation (2.70), it can also be seen that the substitution term can be written as the difference between $\Sigma_{j=1}^{n} v_{ij} d(\log p_j)$, which is the specific substitution effect of the n prices on the demand for good i, and $\phi d(\log P')$, which is the general substitution effect. Accordingly, the general substitution effect acts as the deflator of the specific effect by transforming absolute prices into Frisch-deflated prices.

In the substitution term of equation (2.72), v_{ij} is the coefficient of the jth relative price, which shall be called the (i, j)th price coefficient. These price coefficients satisfy $\Sigma_{i=1}^{n} \Sigma_{j=1}^{n} v_{ij} = \phi$, which follows from equation (2.68) and the fact that $\Sigma_{i=1}^{n} \theta_i = 1$. If $v_{ij} > 0$, then an increase in the Frisch-deflated price of j causes consumption of i to increase. Consequently, we follow Houthakker (1960) and define goods i and j as specific substitutes (complements) if $v_{ij} > 0$ (< 0).

To further interpret the coefficient v_{ij}, we use equation (2.67) to define the $n \times n$ matrix

$$\left[v_{ij}\right] = \frac{\lambda}{M} \boldsymbol{P}' \boldsymbol{U}^{-1} \boldsymbol{P}, \tag{2.73}$$

where $\boldsymbol{P}$ is the diagonal matrix with $p1, \ldots, p_n$ on the diagonal and $\boldsymbol{U}^{-1}$ is the inverse of the Hessian of the utility function. On the right of equation (2.73), λ, $M > 0$; $\boldsymbol{P}$ is a symmetric positive definite matrix, and $\boldsymbol{U}^{-1}$ is a symmetric negative definite matrix. Therefore,

$$\left[v_{ij}\right] \text{is a symmetric negative definite } n \times n \text{ matrix} \tag{2.74}$$

Inverting both sides of equation (2.73), we obtain

$$v^{ij} = \frac{M}{\lambda} \frac{\partial^2 u}{\partial(p_i q_i) \partial(p_j q_j)}, \quad i, j = 1, 2, \ldots, n, \tag{2.75}$$

where v^{ij} is the (i, j)th element of $[v_{ij}]-1$. Since $\partial u/\partial(p_i q_i)$ is the marginal utility of a dollar spent on good i, $\partial^2 u/\partial(p_i q_i)\partial(p_j q_j)$ on the right of equation (2.75) is interpreted as the change in this marginal utility of good i when spending on good j increases by one dollar. Accordingly, equation (2.75) shows that $[v_{ij}]$ is inversely proportional to the Hessian matrix of the utility function in expenditure terms.

In contrast to the other approaches to generating demand equations, the differential approach requires no algebraic specification of the utility function. Consequently, the coefficients of the demand equation (2.72) need not be constants; they may be functions of income and prices. The decision about how to parameterise differential demand equations comes as the final step, which will be illustrated in Section 2.11.

2.7.2 Absolute Price Version of the Demand Model

The substitution term of equation (2.72) is formulated in terms of deflated prices. We use equation (2.71) to express the substitution term in absolute (or undeflated) prices as

$$\sum_{j=1}^{n} v_{ij} d\left[\log \frac{p_j}{P'}\right] = \sum_{j=1}^{n} \pi_{ij} d\left(\log p_j\right), \tag{2.76}$$

where

$$\pi_{ij} = v_{ij} - \phi\theta_i\theta_j, \quad i = 1, 2, \dots, n, \tag{2.77}$$

is the (i, j)th *Slutsky coefficient* (Slutsky, 1915). This coefficient gives the total substitution effect on the demand for good i of a change in the jth price. It can be easily verified that

$$\left[\pi_{ij}\right] \text{is a symmetric negative semi-definite } n \times n \text{ matrix with rank } n-l. \tag{2.78}$$

Substituting equation (2.76) into equation (2.72) yields the demand equation for good i in terms of absolute prices,

$$w_i d\left(\log q_i\right) = \theta_i \; d(\log Q) + \sum_{j=1}^{n} \pi_{ij} \mathrm{d}\left(\log p_j\right), \quad i = 1, 2, \dots, n. \tag{2.79}$$

In view of equation (2.77), the Slutsky coefficients are symmetric in i and j,

$$\pi_{ij} = \pi_{ji}, \quad i, j = 1, 2, \dots, n, \tag{2.80}$$

which is known as *Slutsky symmetry*. These coefficients also satisfy

$$\sum_{j=1}^{n} \pi_{ij} = 0, \quad i = 1,2,\ldots,n, \tag{2.81}$$

which follows from equations (2.68) and (2.77). Constraint (2.81) reflects the homogeneity property of the demand functions that a proportionate change in all prices has no effect on the demand for any good under the condition that real income is constant. Accordingly, equation (2.81) is known as *demand homogeneity*. As stated in equation (2.78), the Slutsky matrix $[\pi_{ij}]$ is *symmetric negative semidefinite with rank* $n-1$; the cause of the singularity is equation (2.81).

Dividing both sides of equation (2.79) by w_i, we find that the income and compensated price elasticities are

$$\eta_i = \frac{\theta_i}{w_i}, \quad \eta_{ij} = \frac{\pi_{ij}}{w_i}, \qquad i,j = 1,2,\ldots,n. \tag{2.82}$$

These elasticities satisfy demand homogeneity and Slutsky symmetry.

2.8 Demand Equations under Preference Independence

When the consumer's tastes can be described by means of a utility function which is the sum of n sub-utility functions, one for each good, the utility function equation (2.33) takes the form

$$u(q_1,\ldots,q_n) = \sum_{i=1}^{n} u_i(q_i), \tag{2.83}$$

and the marginal utility of good i is independent of the consumption of j, $i \neq j$. Accordingly, equation (2.83) is known as a utility function of the form of *preference independence*. If the commodities are fairly broad groups, such as food, housing, clothing and so on, then equation (2.83) could be a reasonable working hypothesis as it conveys the idea that total utility is obtained from the utility derived from food, utility from housing, utility from clothing and so on. These broad commodity groups can be interpreted as representing the *basic wants* of the consumer, which could be expected to exhibit little interaction in the utility function.

The two versions of the demand model discussed above, the absolute price version and the relative price version, both have their own attractions. The absolute price version (2.79) and the constraints (2.80) and (2.81) are linear in the parameters, which makes estimation and testing straightforward.

The number of unknown coefficients in a general system of demand equations such as (2.72) and (2.79) is of the order of n^2, where n is the number of commodities. This many number of coefficients can only be estimated precisely with data when n is very small; even for moderate-sized systems (n in the vicinity of 6), it is impossible to estimate such a large number of coefficients unless we have a large number of observations. For larger models (when n is large), it is necessary to use the relative price version of the model (2.72), which is non-linear in the parameters, with suitable constraints on the v_{ij}s. These constraints take the form of postulating that certain goods do not interact in the utility function. One such form is the preference independence, discussed above, when no goods interact with any other. The hypothesis of preference independence comes to the rescue, as it serves to simplify the form of the demand equations by greatly reducing the number of unknown coefficients to be estimated. Accordingly, there are two distinct justifications of preference independence: (i) the economic justification, in terms of preference independence being plausible when applied to broad aggregates; and (ii) the statistical justification when n is not small. The first justification is a testable hypothesis and there are various ways to test it. For a simulations-based test of preference independence, see Selvanathan (1987).

2.8.1 Preference Independent Version of the Demand System

We now analyse the implications of preference independence of the utility function for the demand equation (2.72). Under equation (2.83), the Hessian matrix U and its inverse are both diagonal. As $u^{ij} = 0$ for $i \neq j$, it follows from equations (2.67) and (2.68) that, under preference independence,

$$v_{ij} = 0 \text{ for } i \neq j \text{ and } v_{ii} = \phi\theta_i, \quad i, j = 1, 2, \ldots, n. \tag{2.84}$$

Therefore, the demand equation (2.72) takes the simpler form

$$w_i d(\log q_i) = \theta_i d(\log Q) + \phi\theta_i d\left[\log \frac{p_i}{P'}\right], \quad i = 1, 2, \ldots, n. \tag{2.85}$$

Therefore, preference independence implies that only the own deflated price appears in each demand equation, rather than all n such prices. In other words, preference independence implies that no pair of goods (i, j) can be either a specific substitute or a specific complement. In addition, for $[v_{ij}]$ to be a negative definite matrix with diagonal elements $\phi\theta 1$, …, $\phi\theta_n$ and off-diagonal elements zero, each marginal share θ_i must be positive. Consequently, the hypothesis of preference independence rules out inferior goods. The number of unconstrained coefficients in equation (2.85) for i = 1, …, n is n, which is made up of $n - 1$ unconstrained θ_i's (one is constrained by $\sum_{i=1}^{n} \theta_i = 1$) and ϕ.

2.8.2 An Example of a Preference Independent Demand System: Linear Expenditure System

One of the most popular and well-known demand models used by many studies in the 1950s–1970s is the Linear Expenditure System (LES), which is based on a specified preference independence type utility function. The LES can be derived by directly specifying the utility function as

$$U(\boldsymbol{q}) = u(q_1, q_2, \ldots, q_n) = \sum_{i=1}^{n} u_i(q_i) = \sum_{i=1}^{n} \beta_i \log(q_i - \gamma_i), \tag{2.86}$$

where $u_i(q_i) = \beta i \log(q_i - \gamma_i)$, $\beta_i > 0$, $\gamma_i < q_i$ and $\Sigma_{i=1}^{n} \beta_i = 1$. The utility function (2.86) is the well-known Stone-Geary utility function. This utility function has also been previously considered by Klein and Rubin (1948). Obviously, the utility function in the form of equation (2.86) is a utility function under preference independence.

If we apply the first-order condition (2.38) to the utility function (2.86), we obtain,

$$p_i q_i = p_i \gamma_i + \beta_i \left[M - \sum_{j=1}^{n} p_j \gamma_j \right], \quad i = 1, \ldots, n. \tag{2.87}$$

This is the algebraic form of the demand equation (2.40) associated with the Stone-Geary utility function (2.86).

As expenditure on good i is a linear function of the n prices and income, equation (2.87) is known as the LES. If the γ_i coefficients are all positive, then equation (2.87) has the following interpretation. The consumer first purchases γ_i units of good i at a cost of $p_i \gamma_i$; this can be termed *subsistence consumption* of that commodity. The total cost of subsistence is $\Sigma_{j=1}^{n} p_j \gamma_j$, which leaves $M - \Sigma_{j=1}^{n} p_j \gamma_j$ as supernumerary income. A fixed fraction β_i of supernumerary income is then spent on good i. The LES was first applied to data by Stone (1954); for other applications, see Deaton (1975) and Lluch and Powell (1975).

It follows from equation (2.87) that the marginal share $\theta_i = \partial(p_i q_i)/\partial M$ implied by the LES is equal to the constant coefficient β_i. Consequently, the income elasticity of i takes the form

$$\eta_i = \frac{\beta_i}{w_i}, \quad i = 1, \ldots, n. \tag{2.88}$$

A rise in income with prices held constant causes the budget shares of necessities to fall and those of luxuries to rise. It then follows from equation (2.88) that increasing affluence causes the income elasticities of necessities to rise, while those of luxuries fall; the elasticities of both types of goods become closer to unity. Take the case of food, a necessity. The linear expenditure system implies that as the consumer becomes richer, the income elasticity, η_i, for food increases, causing food to become less of a necessity or more of a luxury. This behaviour of the elasticity is implausible, as food should be less of a luxury for a richer consumer.

Recall that the coefficient β_i in the utility function (2.86) must be positive. As this coefficient is interpreted as the marginal share in equation (2.87), it follows that the LES does not admit inferior goods.

The uncompensated price elasticities under LES are given by

$$\eta_{ij} = \frac{(\gamma_i - q_i)}{q_i}\delta_{ij} - \beta_i \frac{\gamma_j p_j}{p_i q_i}, \quad i, j = 1, 2, \ldots, n. \tag{2.89}$$

2.9 Demand Equations under Block Independence

In the previous section, we analysed the case when preferences can be represented by a utility function that is additive in the n goods.

Under preference independence, only the own Frisch-deflated price appears in each demand equation, so that no pair of goods is either a specific substitute or complement. Furthermore, preference independence implies that each θ_i is positive, which rules out inferior goods. These implications of the preference independence assumption are rather drastic. A weaker version of preference independence is *block independence*, whereby the additive specification (2.83) is applied to groups of goods rather than to individual goods. Let the n goods be divided into $G < n$ groups, written $S_1, \ldots, S_G$ such that each good belongs to only one group. Further, let the consumer's preferences be such that the utility function is the sum of G group utility functions, each involving the quantities of only one group,

$$u(q_1, \ldots q_n) = \sum_{g=1}^{G} u_g(\boldsymbol{q}_g), \tag{2.90}$$

where $\boldsymbol{q}$g is the vector of the $q$is that fall under S_g. Under equation (2.90), the marginal utility of a good depends only on the consumption of goods belonging to the same group. When the goods are numbered appropriately, the Hessian of the utility function and its inverse become block-diagonal. Accordingly, specification (2.90) is known as *block-independent preferences*.

In view of equation (2.67), block independence implies that $[\nu_{ij}]$ is block-diagonal. Therefore, if i belongs to S_g, equations (2.72) and (2.68) can now be written as

$$w_i d(\log q_i) = \theta_i d(\log Q) + \sum_{j \in S_g} \nu_{ij} d\left[\log \frac{p_j}{P'}\right], \quad i \in S_g, \tag{2.91}$$

and

$$\sum_{j \in S_g} \nu_{ij} = \phi\theta_i, \quad i \in S_g. \tag{2.92}$$

Thus, block independence implies that the only deflated prices that appear in the ith demand equation are those of goods belonging to the same group as the commodity in question. As $v_{ij} = 0$ for i and j in different groups, under block independence no good is a specific substitute or complement of any good that belongs to a different group.

We write the group budget share and the group marginal share as

$$W_g = \sum_{i \in S_g} w_i \quad \text{and} \quad \Theta_g = \sum_{i \in S_g} \theta_i .$$

Hence, the conditional budget share and conditional marginal share can be written as

$$w_i' = \frac{w_i}{W_g} \quad \text{and} \quad \theta_i' = \frac{\theta_i}{\Theta_g}, \quad i \in S_g, \tag{2.93}$$

for the budget and marginal shares of group S_g. The marginal share Θ_g tells us the increase in expenditure on S_g as a result of a one-dollar increase in income. Summing both sides of equation (2.92) over $i \in S_g$ shows that

$$\sum_{i \in S_g} \sum_{j \in S_g} v_{ij} = \phi \Theta_g < 0, \tag{2.94}$$

where the inequality sign is based on the negative definiteness of the matrix $[v_{ij}]$. Accordingly, block independence means that no group as a whole can be inferior; members of the group can be inferior, however.

We define the group Divisia volume, Divisia price and Frisch price indexes as

$$d\left(\log Q_g\right) = \sum_{i \in S_g} w_i' d\left(\log q_i\right), \qquad d\left(\log P_g\right) = \sum_{i \in S_g} w_i' d\left(\log p_i\right) \tag{2.95}$$

and

$$d\left(\log P_g'\right) = \sum_{i \in S_g} \theta_i' d\left(\log p_i\right). \tag{2.96}$$

These three indexes aggregate consistently since a budget-share-weighted average of $d(\log Q_1)$, …, $d(\log Q_G)$ equals the Divisia volume index of all the n goods $d(\log Q)$; a budget-share-weighted average of $d(\log P_1)$, …, $d(\log P_G)$ equals the Divisia price index of all the n goods $d(\log P)$; and a marginal-share-weighted average of $d(\log P_1')$, …, $d(\log P_G')$ equals the overall Frisch price index $d(\log P')$. That is,

$$d(\log Q) = \sum_{g=1}^{G} W_g d\left(\log Q_g\right); \quad d(\log P) = \sum_{g=1}^{G} W_g d(\log P_g);$$

and

$$d(\log P') = \sum_{g=1}^{G} \Theta_g d\left(\log P_g'\right).$$

We obtain the demand equation for the group S_g as a whole under block independence by simply summing both sides of the demand equation for good i under block independence, equation (2.91), over $i \in S_g$. In view of equations (2.93) and (2.95), this yields

$$W_g\, d\left(\log Q_g\right) = \Theta_g\, d(\log Q) + \sum_{i\in S_g} \sum_{j\in S_g} v_{ij} d\left[\log \frac{p_j}{P'}\right], \quad g = 1,\ldots,G. \qquad (2.97)$$

Our objective is to simplify the price substitution term of this equation. As v_{ij} is symmetric in i and j [see equation (2.74)], equation (2.92) can be expressed as

$$\sum_{i\in S_g} v_{ij} = \phi\theta_j, \quad j \in S_g,$$

so that

$$\sum_{i\in S_g} \sum_{j\in S_g} v_{ij} d\left[\log \frac{p_j}{P'}\right] = \phi \sum_{j\in S_g} \theta_j d\left[\log \frac{p_j}{P'}\right] = \phi\Theta_g d\left[\log \frac{P_g'}{P'}\right],$$

where the second step is based on equations (2.93) and (2.96). Accordingly, equation (2.97) can be expressed as

$$W_g\, d\left(\log Q_g\right) = \theta_g\, d(\log Q) + \phi\theta_g d\left[\log \frac{P_g'}{P'}\right], \quad g = 1,\ldots,G. \qquad (2.98)$$

This is the *composite demand equation* for Sg as a group.

Equation (2.98) shows that under block independence, the demand for a group of goods as a whole depends on real income and the relative price of the group $d[\log(P_g'/P')]$. This relative price is the *Frisch-deflated Frisch price index* of the group. It is to be noted that the relative prices of goods outside the group in question play no role in equation (2.98). By dividing both sides of this equation by W_g, we find that

$$\eta_g = \frac{\theta_g}{W_g} \text{ and } \eta_{gg} = \frac{\phi\theta_g}{W_g}, \quad g = 1,\ldots,G, \qquad (2.99)$$

are the income elasticity of demand and the own-price elasticity, respectively, for the group. This latter elasticity is the elasticity of the Divisia volume index of the group with respect to the Frisch-deflated Frisch price index of the group.

It is instructive to compare equation (2.98) with equation (2.85), the demand equation for an individual good under preference independence. This comparison reveals that both equations have the same general form: $w_i d(\log q_i)$ on the left side of equation (2.85) becomes $W_g d(\log Q_g)$ in equation (2.98), and $\theta_i d(\log Q)$ and $\phi\theta_i d[\log (p_i/P')]$ on the right side of equation (2.85) are replaced with $\Theta_g d(\log Q)$ and $\phi\Theta_g d[\log (P_g'/P')]$ in equation (2.98). Therefore, in going from equation (2.85) to equation (2.98), each variable is replaced by the corresponding group concept, making the latter equation an uppercase version of the former. The reason for this is that the demand equation for the group (2.98) is based on block independence, while equation (2.85) holds under preference independence, and the utility function under block independence (2.90) exhibits preference independence with respect to groups of goods, rather than the individual commodities. Another way of expressing this is to note that if S_g consists of only one good, let it be the *i*th, then equation (2.98) for this group coincides with equation (2.85).

2.10 Conditional Demand Equations

As there are G groups of goods, there are G composite demand equations, each of the form (2.98). These equations give the allocation of income to each of the G groups. This allocation depends only on income and the G relative prices of the groups. Given the demand for a group, the next question is how expenditure on the group is allocated to the commodities within the group. This question is answered by the *conditional demand equations*. In this section, we analyse the form of the conditional demand equations under the assumption of block independence. To obtain the conditional demand equations, we first rearrange equation (2.98):

$$d(\log Q) = \frac{W_g}{\Theta_g} d\left(\log Q_g\right) - \phi d\left[\log \frac{P_g'}{P'}\right]. \tag{2.100}$$

It follows from equation (2.74) that the price coefficients are symmetric in *i* and *j* for commodities belonging to the same group.

$$v_{ij} = v_{ji}, \quad i, j \in S_g. \tag{2.101}$$

The v_{ij}s within S_g are also constrained by equation (2.92), which we repeat here:

$$\sum_{j \in S_g} v_{ij} = \phi\theta_i, \quad i \in S_g. \tag{2.102}$$

To derive the conditional demand equation, we first substitute the right side of equation (2.100) for $d(\log Q)$ in the unconditional equation (2.91), which yields

$$
\begin{aligned}
w_i d(\log q_i) &= \theta_i \left[\frac{W_g}{\Theta_g} d(\log Q_g) - \phi d\left[\log \frac{P_g'}{P'} \right] \right] + \sum_{j \in S_g} v_{ij} d\left[\log \frac{p_j}{P'} \right] \\
&= \theta_i' W_g\, d(\log Q_g) - \phi\theta_i \left[d(\log P_g') - d(\log P') \right] + \\
&= \sum_{j \in S_g} v_{ij} \left[d(\log p_j) - d(\log P') \right], \quad i \in S_g.
\end{aligned} \tag{2.103}
$$

In view of equation (2.102), the second term on the right in equation (2.103) can be expressed as

$$
-\phi\theta_i \left[d(\log P_g') - d(\log P') \right] = \sum_{j \in S_g} v_{ij} \left[d(\log P_g') - d(\log P') \right]. \tag{2.104}
$$

Therefore, using equation (2.104), equation (2.103) can be simplified as

$$
w_i d(\log q_i) = \theta_i' W_g\, d(\log Q_g) + \sum_{j \in S_g} v_{ij} d\left| \log \frac{p_j}{P_g'} \right|, \quad i \in S_g, \tag{2.105}
$$

where

$$
\theta_i' = \frac{\theta_i}{\Theta_g} \tag{2.106}
$$

is the *conditional marginal share* of good i within the group S_g, with $\Sigma_{i \in Sg}\, \theta_i' = 1$. This conditional share answers the question: If income increases by a certain amount, resulting in a certain additional amount spent on the group S_g, what is the proportion of this additional amount that is allocated to commodity i?

Equation (2.105) is the demand equation for $i \in S_g$, given the demand for the group as a whole $W_g d(\log Q_g)$. It is known as the *conditional demand equation* for $i \in S_g$. This equation shows that the allocation of expenditure to goods within the gth group depends on the total consumption of the group, as measured by $Wgd(\log Qg)$, and the relative prices of goods within the group. The deflator for these relative prices is the Frisch price index of the group $d(\log P_g')$, defined in equation (2.96). Consumption of other groups and the prices of goods outside S_g do not appear in equation (2.105). Consequently, the within-group allocation of expenditure depends only on variables pertaining to the group in question.

The conditional demand equation (2.105) is to be contrasted with equation (2.91), which can be described as the corresponding *unconditional demand equation*. The variables on the left of these two equations are the same, but the real income term in equation (2.91), $\theta_i d(\log Q)$ is replaced by $\theta_i' W_g d(\log Q_g)$ in equation (2.105). Also, the price substitution terms are identical, except that the Frisch price index of all goods acts as the deflator in equation (2.91), while the corresponding group concept $d(\log P_g')$ plays this role in equation (2.105).

Block-independent preferences imply that the consumer's problem can be solved in two steps. The first decision involves the allocation of income to the G groups, as described by the G group demand equation (2.98). Each of these demand equations contains real income and the relative price of the group in question but not the prices of the individual goods. Then in the second decision, for each of the groups, expenditure is allocated to the goods within the group. The conditional demand equation (2.105) describes this allocation and it contains the total consumption of the group, as determined by the previous decision, and relative prices within the group. Accordingly, there is a decision hierarchy under block independence.

The conditional demand equation (2.105) was obtained under block independence. These results also hold, however, under the weaker condition of blockwise dependence; see, for example, Theil (1975/76).

Equation (2.105) is based on relative prices. To obtain the conditional demand equations in absolute prices, we define the (i, j)th *conditional Slutsky coefficients* as

$$\pi_{ij}^g = \nu_{ij} - \phi\Theta_g \theta_i'\theta_j', \quad i,j \in S_g. \tag{2.107}$$

This coefficient measures the effect of a change in the price of good j on the consumption of i ($i, j \in S_g$) under the condition that other prices and total consumption of the group remain constant. The conditional Slutsky coefficients satisfy demand homogeneity,

$$\sum_{j \in S_g} \pi_{ij}^g = 0, \quad i \in S_g, \tag{2.108}$$

which follows from equations (2.102) and (2.107) and Slutsky symmetry,

$$\pi_{ij}^g = \pi_{ji}^g, \quad i,j \in S_g, \tag{2.109}$$

which follows from equations (2.101) and (2.107).

The absolute price version of the conditional demand equation can be written as

$$w_i d(\log q_i) = \theta_i' W_g d(\log Q_g) + \sum_{j \in S_g} \pi_{ij}^g d(\log p_j), \quad i \in S_g. \tag{2.110}$$

2.11 The Rotterdam Model

The coefficients of the unconditional demand equations, (2.72), (2.79) and (2.85), and the conditional demand equations, (2.98), (2.105) and (2.110), are functions of income and prices. In general, these coefficients need not be constants. The Rotterdam model, derived below, parameterises these coefficients.

Equations (2.72), (2.79), (2.85), (2.98), (2.105) and (2.110) are formulated in terms of infinitesimal changes. The corresponding unconditional and conditional versions of the Rotterdam demand model, developed by Barten (1964) and Theil (1965), are the finitechange versions of these equations. We write, $Dx_t = \log x_t - \log x_{t-1}$ for the finite logchange from period $t-1$ to t for any positive variable x. The variable $d(\log q_i)$ on the left of equation (2.105) becomes Dq_{it} and $d\left[\log\left(p_j/P'\right)\right]$ becomes $\left(Dp_{jt} - DP_t'\right)$, where $DP_t' = \sum_{i=1}^{n} \theta_i Dp_{it}$ is the finite-change version of the Frisch price index. Similarly, $d(\log Q)$ becomes DQ_t, $d(\log Q_g)$ becomes DQ_{gt} and $d\left[\log\left(P_g'/P'\right)\right]$ becomes $\left(DP_{gt}' - DP_t'\right)$. As the budget share w_i on the left of equation (2.105) does not involve a change, we could use either $w_{i,\,t-1}$ or $w_{i,\,t}$ or a combination thereof which treats t and $t-1$ symmetrically. The natural choice is to use the arithmetic average, $\bar{w}_{it} = ½(w_{i,\,t-1} + w_{i,\,t})$. The finitechange version of equation (2.105) is then

$$\bar{w}_{it} Dq_{it} = \theta_i DQ_t + \sum_{j=1}^{n} v_{ij}\left(Dp_{jt} - DP_t'\right), \quad i = 1,2,\ldots,n, \tag{2.111}$$

where $DQ_t = \sum_{i=1}^{n} \bar{w}_{it} Dq_{it}$ is a finitechange version of the Divisia volume index. When the coefficients of equation (2.111), θ_i and v_{ij}, are treated as constants, it is known as the ith *demand equation of the relative price version of the Rotterdam model.*

The finitechange version of the absolute price version (2.110) is

$$\bar{w}_{it}\, Dq_{it} = \theta_i\, DQ_t + \sum_{j=1}^{n} \pi_{ij} Dp_{jt}, \quad i = 1,2,\ldots,n. \tag{2.112}$$

When the coefficients θ_i and π_{ij} are specified as constants, equation (2.112) is known as the ith *demand equation of the absolute price version of the Rotterdam model.* It follows from the relationship, $\pi_{ij} = v_{ij} - \phi\theta_i\theta_j$, that the constancy of the coefficients θ_i, v_{ij} and ϕ in the relative price version of the Rotterdam model implies that the Slutsky coefficients π_{ij} are also constant in the absolute price version.

Under preference independence, we have from equation (2.84) that

$$v_{ij} = 0 \text{ for } i \neq j \text{ and } v_{ii} = \phi\theta_i \quad i, j = 1,2,\ldots,n.$$

The finite-change version of the Rotterdam model under preference independence for commodity i, equation (2.111), becomes

$$\bar{w}_{it} Dq_{it} = \theta_i DQ_t + \phi\theta_i \left(Dp_{it} - DP_t' \right), \quad i = 1,2,\ldots,n, \tag{2.113}$$

where the coefficients ϕ and θ_i are specified as constants.

The finite-change version of the Rotterdam group demand equation (2.98) for group g becomes

$$\bar{W}_{gt} DQ_{gt} = \theta_g DQ_{gt} + \phi\theta_g \left(DP_{gt}' - DP_t' \right), \quad g = 1,2,\ldots,G, \tag{2.114}$$

where the coefficients ϕ and θ_g are specified as constants.

The finitechange version of equation (2.105), the conditional Rotterdam model in relative prices is then

$$\bar{w}_{it} Dq_{it} = \theta_i' \bar{W}_{gt} DQ_{gt} + \sum_{j \in S_g} v_{ij} \left(Dp_{jt} - DP_{gt}' \right), \quad i \in S_g, \tag{2.115}$$

where the coefficients θ_i and v_{ij} are specified as constants. The finitechange version of the absolute price version (2.110) is

$$\bar{w}_{it} Dq_{it} = \theta_i' \bar{W}_{gt} DQ_{gt} + \sum_{j \in S_g} \pi_{ij}^g Dp_{jt}, \quad i \in S_g, \tag{2.116}$$

where the coefficients θ_i' and π_{ij}^g are specified as constants.

2.12 Other Popular Demand Systems

In this section, we introduce three other well-known demand systems, namely the Workings-Rotterdam (W-R) model, the Translog Demand System (TRANSLOG) and the Almost Ideal Demand System (AIDS).

2.12.1 Workings-Rotterdam (W-R) Demand System

The W-R demand system is Working's model re-parameterisation of the Rotterdam model. Under Working's (1943) model, we have marginal share given by equation (2.20) which we repeat here,

$$\theta_i = w_i + \beta_i, \quad i = 1,2,\ldots,n. \tag{2.117}$$

Under equation (2.117), the Rotterdam model in relative prices (2.111), in absolute prices (2.118) and under preference independence (2.119) can be written as follows.

2.12.1.1 W-R Demand System in Relative Prices

$$\bar{w}_{it} \left(Dq_{it} - DQ_t \right) = \beta_i DQ_t + \sum_{j=1}^{n} v_{ij} \left(Dp_{jt} - DP_t' \right), \quad i = 1,2,\ldots,n, \tag{2.118}$$

The demand system (2.118) is also known as the *CBS demand system in relative prices.*

2.12.1.2 W-R Demand System in Absolute Prices

$$\bar{w}_{it}\left(Dq_{it}-DQ_t\right)=\beta_i\, DQ_t+\sum_{j=1}^{n}\pi_{ij}Dp_{jt} \tag{2.119}$$

The demand system (2.119) is also known as the *CBS demand system in absolute prices.*
W-R demand system under PI:

$$\bar{w}_{it}\left(Dq_{it}-DQ_t\right)=\beta_i DQ_t+\phi\left(\beta_i+\bar{w}_{it}\right)\left(Dp_{it}-DP_t'\right) \tag{2.120}$$

where $DP_t'=\sum_{j=1}^{n}\left(\beta_j+\bar{w}_{jt}\right)Dp_{jt}$. The demand system (2.120) is also known as the *CBS/PI demand system.*

2.12.2 Translog Demand System

Another way of deriving the demand equations is by specifying the form of the indirect utility function. By substituting the demand equation (2.40) into the utility function $u = u(\mathbf{q})$, we can write the utility function as a function of income and prices,

$$u=u[\mathbf{q}(M,\mathbf{p})]=u_I(M,\mathbf{p}). \tag{2.121}$$

The function u_I is called the *indirect utility function* and it gives the maximum utility attainable corresponding to given values of income and prices.

Roy's (1942) theorem,

$$q_i=\frac{\partial u_I/\partial p_i}{\partial u_I/\partial M},\quad i=1,\dots,n, \tag{2.122}$$

gives a way of generating a system of demand equations from a specified form of the indirect utility function. Christensen et al. (1975) applied Roy's theorem to the following *translog indirect utility function,*

$$u_I(M,\mathbf{p})=\sum_{i=1}^{n}\beta_i\log\frac{p_i}{M}+\frac{1}{2}\sum_{i=1}^{n}\sum_{j=1}^{n}\beta_{ij}\log\frac{p_i}{M}\log\frac{p_j}{M}, \tag{2.123}$$

where coefficients β_i and β_{ij} are all constants. Application of equation (2.122) to equation (2.123) yields the following demand equations:

$$w_i = \frac{\beta_i + \sum_{j=1}^{n} \beta_{ij} \log \frac{p_j}{M}}{\sum_{k=1}^{n} \beta_k + \sum_{k=1}^{n} \sum_{j=1}^{n} \beta_{kj} \log \frac{p_j}{M}}, \quad i = 1, \ldots, n. \tag{2.124}$$

This demand system (2.124) is called the *translog demand system*.

2.12.3 Almost Ideal Demand System (AIDS)

The consumer's *cost function* is dual to the (direct) utility function in that it gives the minimum expenditure needed to attain a specified level of utility, given the prices. The cost function is also referred to as the expenditure function. By specifying the form of the cost function and then applying the Shephard's lemma

$$\frac{\partial C}{\partial p_i} = q_i, \quad i = 1, 2, \ldots, n, \tag{2.125}$$

we can derive the corresponding demand function. Deaton and Muellbauer (1980a, 1980b) specified the cost function as

$$C(u, \boldsymbol{p}) = e^{a(\boldsymbol{p}) + ub(\boldsymbol{p})}, \tag{2.126}$$

where

$$a(\boldsymbol{p}) = \sum_{i=1}^{n} \alpha_i \log p_i + \tfrac{1}{2} \sum_{i=1}^{n} \sum_{j=1}^{n} \gamma_{ij} \log p_i \log p_j$$

and

$$b(\boldsymbol{p}) = \beta_0 \prod_{i=1}^{n} p_i^{\beta_i},$$

with α_i, β_i and γ_I all being constants. Applying equation (2.125) to equation (2.126), the resulting demand system can be written in the form

$$w_i = \alpha_i + \beta_i \log \frac{M}{P} + \sum_{j=1}^{n} \gamma_{ij} \log p_j, \quad i = 1, 2, \ldots, n, \tag{2.127}$$

where

$$\log P = a(\boldsymbol{P}) = \sum_{i=1}^{n} \alpha_i \log p_i + \frac{1}{2} \sum_{i=1}^{n} \sum_{j=1}^{n} \gamma_{ij} \log p_i \log p_j. \tag{2.128}$$

Deaton and Muellbauer (1980a, 1980b) refer to (2.127) as the *Almost Ideal Demand System* or AIDS for short.

The income and uncompensated price elasticities implied by AIDS are

$$\eta_i = 1 + \frac{\beta_i}{w_i}, \quad i = 1, 2, \ldots, n, \tag{2.129}$$

and

$$\eta_{ij} = -\delta_{ij} + \frac{1}{w_i}\left[\gamma_{ij} - \beta_i \left\{ w_j - \beta_j \log\left(\frac{M}{P}\right)\right\}\right], \quad i = 1, 2, \ldots, n. \tag{2.130}$$

The estimation of equation (2.127) is more complicated when we use log P defined by equation (2.128). A simpler variant form of equation (2.128) is known as Stone's index,

$$\log P = \sum_k w_k \log p_k. \tag{2.131}$$

With equation (2.128) replaced by equation (2.131), the budget share equation (2.127) is linear in the parameters to be estimated, namely α_i, β_i and the γ_{ij}s and it becomes

$$w_i = \alpha_i + \beta_i \log \frac{M}{P} + \sum_{j=1}^{n} \gamma_{ij} \log p_j, \quad i = 1, 2, \ldots, n, \tag{2.132}$$

which is known as *Linear Approximation of AIDS* (LA-AIDS).

2.12.3.1 Group Generalised Working's Model

Clements et al. (1985) showed the group version of Working's (1943) model (2.19) as

$$W_g = A_g^* + B_g^* M^{\lambda}, \quad i \in S_g, \tag{2.133}$$

and

$$\theta_g = W_g + B_g, \tag{2.134}$$

where $A_g^* = -B_g/\lambda$. Income elasticity for group S_g is given by

$$\eta_g = \frac{\theta_g}{W_g} = 1 + \frac{B_g}{W_g}. \tag{2.135}$$

2.12.3.2 Conditional Generalised Working's Model (CGWM)

Selvanathan et al. (2021) derived the conditional version of Laitinen et al.'s (1983) generalised version of Working's (1943) model (2.30) as

$$w_i' = a_i' + b_i' M_g^{\lambda} \tag{2.136}$$

where $\sum_{i \in S_g} a_i' = 1$ and $\sum_{i \in S_g} b_i' = 0$.

Conditional marginal share θ_i' of CGWM is given by

$$\theta_i' = (1+\lambda)w_i' + \beta_i', \tag{2.137}$$

where $\beta_i' = -\lambda a_i'$. The conditional marginal share θ_i' answers the question: if the expenditure on group S_g increases by one dollar, how is this one dollar increase allocated to goods within that group' and the conditional income elasticity of CGWM is given by

$$\eta_i' = \frac{\theta_i'}{w_i'} = (1+\lambda) + \frac{\beta_i'}{w_i'}.$$

That is,

$$\eta_i' = (1+\lambda) - \lambda\frac{a_i'}{w_i'}. \tag{2.138}$$

Notes

1 Demand for a Giffen good rises when its price rises and falls when price falls. This situation in economic terms is known as 'upward sloping demand curve', which is in contrast to the traditional *Law of Demand* – the demand curve slopes down.

2 For some further properties of the generalised Working's model and an application, see Van Hoa (1983) and Van Hoa et al. (1983).

References

Barten, A.P. 1964. Consumer demand functions under conditions of almost additive preferences. *Econometrica* 32: 1–38.

Beneito, P. 2003. A complete system of Engel curves in the Spanish economy. *Applied Economics* 35(7), 803–816.

Bosch-Domènech, A. 1991. Economies of scale, location, age, and sex discrimination in household demand. *European Economic Review* 35(8), 1589–1595.

Box, G.E., and D.R. Cox. 1964. An analysis of transformations. *Journal of the Royal Statistical Society: Series B (Methodological)* 26(2): 211–243.

Cassel, G. 1932. *The theory of social economy.* Revised Edition. Translated from the 5th German Edition by S.L. Burrow. New York: Harcourt.

Christensen, L.R., D.W. Jorgenson, and L.J. Lau. 1975. Transcendental logarithmic utility functions. *American Economic Review* 65: 367–383.

Clements, K.W., P.S. Goldschmidt, and H. Theil 1985. A conditional version of Working's model. *Economic Letters* 18: 97–99.

Deaton, A. 1975. The analysis of consumer demand in the United Kingdom, 1900–1970. *Econometrica* 42: 341–61.

Deaton, A.S. and J. Muellbauer. 1980a. *Economics and consumer behavior.* Cambridge: Cambridge University Press.

Deaton, A.S., and J. Muellbauer. 1980b. An almost ideal demand system. *American Economic Review* 70: 321–326.

Engel, E. 1857. *Die productions- und consumptionsverhaltnisse des Königreichs Saichsen*, in Zeitschrift des Statischen Bureaus des Königlich Sachsischen Ministerium des Inneren.

Houthakker, H.S. 1960. Additive preferences. *Econometrica* 28: 244–257.

Jayasinghe, M. 2019. Dynamic trends in household poverty and inequality in Sri Lanka: do gender and ethnicity matter? *Journal of the Asia Pacific Economy* 24(2): 208–223.

Klein, L.R., and H. Rubin. 1948. A constant-utility index of the cost of living. *The Review of Economic Studies* 15: 84–87.

Laitinen, K., H. Theil, and T. Raparla. 1983. A generalization of Working's model. *Economics Letters* 13(1): 97–100.

Lluch, C., and A. Powell. 1975. International comparisons of expenditure patterns. *European Economic Review* 6(3): 275–303.

Roy, R. 1942. *De l'utilite.* Paris: Hermann et Cie.

Selvanathan, S. 1987. A Monte Carlo test of preference independence. *Economics Letters* 25(3): 259–261.

Selvanathan, S., E.A. Selvanathan, and Jayasinghe, M. 2021. A new approach to analyse conditional demand: An application to Australian energy consumption. *Energy Economics* 93. https://doi.org/10.1016/j.eneco.2020.105037.

Slutsky, E. 1915. Sulla teoria del bilancio del consumatore. *Giornale degli Economisti e Rivista di Statistica, Serie terza* 51(1): 1–26.

Stone, R. 1954. Linear expenditure systems and demand analysis: An application to the pattern of British demand. *Economic Journal* 64: 511–527.

Theil, H. 1965. The information approach to demand analysis. *Econometrica* 33: 67–87.

Theil, H. 1975/76. *Theory and measurement of consumer demand.* Amsterdam: North-Holland Publishing Company.

Van Hoa 1983. The integrability of generalised Working models. *Economics Letters* 13: 101–104.

Van Hoa, T., D.S. Ironmonger, and I. Manning. 1983. Energy consumption in Australia: evidence from a generalized working model. *Economics Letters* 12(3–4): 383–389.

Working, H. 1943. Statistical laws of family expenditure. *Journal of the American Statistical Association* 38: 43–56.

3 A Preliminary Analysis of Consumption Patterns

Developed vs Developing Countries

S Selvanathan, M Jayasinghe and E A Selvanathan

3.1 Introduction

This chapter provides a preliminary data analysis of the consumption patterns of 45 developed and developing countries using time-series data. The analysis is presented at two levels, namely (1) all countries combined and (2) grouping the 45 countries into two groups: developed (or high-income) countries and developing (or middle- to low-income) countries. Per capita GDP (income) was used as the approach to classify countries as either developed or developing countries with income above US\$25,000 classified as developed and below \$US25,000 as developing countries. Based on this classification, 27 countries fall in the developed category and the remaining 18 in the developing category. In this chapter, while presenting a preliminary analysis of the data, we also identify a number of empirical regularities of consumption patterns at the individual country level as well as at the group level.

Section 3.2 provides the details of the data source and characteristics of the data. Section 3.3 presents a summary of the data using various graphical and numerical data analytic techniques in the form of growth rates and Divisa indices. Section 3.4 considers the relationship between relative prices and relative consumption to construct a sampling distribution for an important parameter in consumption economics, *income flexibility*. The following section investigates whether this large consumption database supports the well-known *Engel's law*. Section 3.6 estimates the basic double-log demand system to obtain some preliminary estimates of income and price elasticities. The following section, Section 3.7, investigates whether the consumption data of the 45 countries give support for the famous Frisch's (1959) conjecture using the estimates of income flexibilities obtained in the previous section. Section 3.8 of this chapter uses the income and price elasticity estimates from Section 3.6 to investigate whether the consumption data of the 45 countries supports one of the simplifying assumptions for estimating demand systems used in empirical economics concerned with the structure of the consumer utility function, namely, *preference independence*. Section 3.9 presents the concluding comments.

DOI: 10.4324/9780429200120-3

3.2 Data Source

The annual consumption expenditures (in current and constant prices) and the population for the 45 Asia Pacific and the OECD countries (selected on the basis of data availability) are compiled from the *National Accounts of OECD Countries* (OECD: Paris, various issues) and various individual country *Government Statistical Department* websites and publications. In this chapter, we classify the consumer basket into 12 commodity groups as shown in Table 3.1. To overcome different formats of the publicly available data for some countries, for example, the country's statistical agency publishes information about commodities in less than 12 commodity groups or the small sample size (time periods) for the 12 commodity groups is small, we aggregate some of the commodities into a single group when we perform the final estimation in Chapter 4.

Table 3.2 provides details about the database. Column (1) of the table lists the 45 countries (in alphabetical order) and column (2) gives their local currencies. Column (3) gives the sample period of the available data for each country and column (4) gives the number of observations available for each country. Column (5) gives the number of commodity groups for each country. Columns (6) and (7) give the per capita GDP of each country in 2018 (in constant 2010 US$ and indexed US = 100, respectively). The last column presents the food and alcohol expenditure as a percentage of total expenditure (income) for each country. A comparison of column (7) with column (8) reveals that, in general, the higher a country's per capita GDP, the lower the budget share on food.

3.3 Data Summary

Let there be n commodities and let p_{ict} be the price and q_{ict} be the per capita quantity consumed of commodity i in country c in period t. We define price and quantity log-changes, for country c, as

$$Dp_{ict} = \log p_{ict} - \log p_{ict-1} \tag{3.1}$$

Table 3.1 Classification of commodities

	Commodity	*Description*
1	Food	Food and non-alcoholic beverages
2	Alcohol	Alcohol beverages and narcotics
3	Clothing	Clothing and footwear
4	Housing	Housing and utilities
5	Durables	Furniture, furnishings and household equipment and operation
6	Health	Medical care and health expenses
7	Transport	Transport expenses
8	Communication	Communications expenses
9	Recreation	Recreation, entertainment and cultural activities
10	Education	Educational activities
11	Restaurants	Restaurants and hotels
12	Miscellaneous	Miscellaneous goods and services

Table 3.2 Country characteristics, 45 countries

	Country	*Currency*	*Sample period*	*Number of observations*	*Number of commodities*	*Per capita GDP in 2018 (constant 2010 US$)*		*Mean budget share – food and alcohol*
						International $'s	*US=100*	
	(1)	*(2)*	*(3)*	*(4)*	*(5)*	*(6)*	*(7)*	*(8)*
1	Australia	Dollars (Aus)	1985–2014	30	12	56,842	104	14.60
2	Austria	European euro	1995–2015	21	12	50,020	92	13.75
3	Belgium	European euro	1995–2014	20	12	47,166	86	17.16
4	Canada	Dollars (Can)	1981–2015	35	12	51,392	94	14.65
5	Colombia	Colombian peso	2000–2014	15	12	7,692	14	22.25
6	Czech Republic	Czech koruna	1995–2015	21	12	23,359	43	24.30
7	Denmark	Danish krone	1995–2015	21	12	63,873	117	15.98
8	Estonia	European euro	1995–2015	21	12	19,954	37	28.85
9	Finland	European euro	1975–2015	41	12	48,749	89	22.00
10	France	European euro	1959–2015	57	12	43,664	80	20.68
11	Germany	European euro	1995–2014	20	12	47,478	87	14.35
12	Greece	European euro	1995–2015	21	12	23,558	43	20.73
13	Hong Kong	Hong Kong dollar	1972–2016	46	8	38,782	71	18.40
14	Hungary	Hungarian forint	1995–2015	21	12	16,648	31	25.67
15	Iceland	Icelandic krona	1995–2014	20	12	52,103	95	19.32
16	India	Indian rupee	1971–2015	46	8	2,101	4	50.60
17	Ireland	European euro	1996–2014	19	12	76,881	141	17.18
18	Israel	Israeli new shekel	1995–2014	20	12	34,746	64	18.14
19	Italy	European euro	1995–2014	20	12	35,432	65	19.29
20	Japan	Japanese yen	1970–2015	46	8	48,920	90	19.81
21	Latvia	European euro	1995–2014	20	12	16,269	30	32.94
22	Lithuania	European euro	1995–2014	20	12	17,709	32	35.42

23	Luxembourg	European euro	1995–2015	21	12	110,742	203	18.67
24	Malaysia	Malaysian ringgit	2000–2016	17	8	12,120	22	23.77
25	Mexico	Mexican peso	2003–2014	12	12	10,404	19	24.96
26	Netherlands	European euro	1995–2014	20	12	55,023	101	14.32
27	New Zealand	New Zealand dollar	1987–2014	28	12	37,997	70	19.53
28	Norway	Norwegian krone	1970–2014	45	12	92,078	169	21.43
29	Philippines	Philippine peso	1999–2016	18	8	3,022	6	43.19
30	Poland	Polish zloty	1995–2015	21	12	16,659	31	29.18
31	Portugal	European euro	1995–2015	21	12	23,995	44	20.29
32	Singapore	Singapore dollar	1964–2016	53	8	58,248	107	16.02
33	Slovakia	European euro	1995–2015	21	12	20,599	38	26.16
34	Slovenia	European euro	1995–2015	21	12	26,768	49	21.15
35	South Africa	South African rand	1975–2014	40	10	7,434	14	28.61
36	South Korea	South Korean won	1970–2015	46	12	26,762	49	26.95
37	Spain	European euro	1995–2014	20	12	32,950	60	18.07
38	Sri Lanka	Sri Lankan rupee	1975–2016	42	8	3,936	7	53.56
39	Sweden	Swedish krona	1993–2015	23	12	57,921	106	16.64
40	Switzerland	Swiss franc	1995–2013	19	12	79,214	145	13.47
41	Taiwan	New Taiwan dollar	1962–2016	55	8	28,432	52	24.05
42	Thailand	Thai baht	1967–2015	49	8	6,362	12	33.58
43	Turkey	Turkish lira	1998–2014	17	10	15,069	28	26.89
44	UK	Pound sterling	1996–2015	20	12	43,325	79	12.94
45	USA	US dollar	1975–2020	46	12	54,579	100	11.75

Note: In countries with ten commodities, alcohol is included in food, and communication is included in transport. In countries with eight commodities, communication is included in transport education is included in recreation.

and

$$Dq_{ict} = \log q_{ict} - \log q_{ict-1}, \tag{3.2}$$

respectively. When these price and quantity log-changes are multiplied by 100, they can be interpreted as percentage growth rates in price and quantity, respectively, from year $t-1$ to t. Here and elsewhere, log refers to the natural logarithm.

To summarise these price and quantity log-changes for each commodity i, for each country we calculate the averages over sample periods of each country defined as below:

$$D\bar{p}_{ic} = \frac{1}{T}\sum_{t=1}^{T} Dp_{ict}, \quad i = 1,\ldots,n, c = 1,\ldots,45; \tag{3.3}$$

$$D\bar{q}_{ic} = \frac{1}{T}\sum_{t=1}^{T} Dq_{ict}, \quad i = 1,\ldots,n, c = 1,\ldots,45. \tag{3.4}$$

Tables 3.3 and 3.4 present the mean price and quantity log-changes calculated as in equations (3.1)–(3.4) for each of the 45 countries considered in this study. The last three rows of the tables give the mean price and quantity log-changes averaged over all the countries, their standard deviation and coefficient of variation.

As can be seen from Table 3.3, the average growth in the price of food across the 45 countries varies between −4.2 percent (Portugal) and 16.5 percent (Turkey) with an average of 3.7 percent per annum. For all countries, the average annual growth in the price of alcohol is 4.5 percent, clothing 2.1 percent, housing 4.8 percent, durables 2.7 percent, health 4.1 percent, transport 3.8 percent, communication −0.3 percent, recreation 2.7 percent, education 4.9 percent and restaurants 4.2 percent.

Among the developed countries, the average growth in the price of food varies between −1.8 percent (Ireland) and 8 percent (South Korea) with an average of 2.7 percent per annum. The developed countries' average annual growth in the price of alcohol is 3.9 percent, clothing 1.1 percent, housing 3.4 percent, durables 1.8 percent, health 3 percent, transport 2.7 percent, communication −1.3 percent, recreation 1.5 percent, education 3.8 percent and restaurants 3.3 percent. Among the developing countries, the average growth in the price of food across countries varies between −4.2 percent (Portugal) and 16.5 percent (Turkey) with an average of 5.1 percent per annum. Average annual growth in the price of alcohol is 5.6 percent, clothing 3.6 percent, housing 7 percent, durables 4 percent, health 5.7 percent, transport 5.5 percent, communication 1.8 percent, recreation 4.6 percent, education 7 percent and restaurants 5.8 percent.

A comparison between the developed and developing groups reveals that for almost all goods (except communication), on average, prices in developing countries have grown at a rate more than twice that of developed countries. Another difference worth noting is that while in most developed countries, communication has become cheaper (negative price growth), consumers in developing countries continue to experience increasing prices for communication (positive price growth). A comparison of the CV values indicates that there is large variation in prices for clothing, communication, recreation and education.

As can be seen from Table 3.4, the average growth in per capita consumption of food varies between −0.3 percent (Belgium and Germany) per annum and 7.4 percent per annum (Portugal) with an average of 1.4 percent per annum across the 45 countries. The average annual growth in consumption of alcohol is 0.05 percent, clothing 2.7 percent, housing 2.1 percent, durables 2.9 percent, health 3.3 percent, transport 3.1 percent, communication 7.6 percent, recreation 3.7 percent, education 2.4 percent and restaurants 1.8 percent. Communication has had the highest growth in consumption among the commodity groups for all countries. This may be explained by the rapid advances in communication technologies around the world over the past two decades. In developing countries, the average growth in per capita consumption of food, clothing, durables, transport and restaurants is about twice that of developed countries. While the average growth in per capita consumption of alcohol is negative in most of the developed countries, it is positive in the majority of the developing countries.

Let M_t be the total expenditure (income for short) on the n commodities during period t. Therefore, the total expenditure $M_t = \sum_{i=1}^{n} p_{it}q_{it}$. The proportion of total expenditure devoted to commodity i, called the budget share of i, is

$$w_{it} = \frac{p_{it}q_{it}}{M_t}, \quad t = 1,2,\ldots,T, \tag{3.5}$$

where T is the sample size. Table 3.5 presents the budget shares at sample means for each commodity calculated as,

$$\bar{w}_i = \frac{1}{T}\sum_{t=1}^{T} w_{it}, \quad i = 1,\ldots,n, \tag{3.6}$$

for the 45 countries. For each commodity, the last three rows of the bottom part of the table present the mean budget share of each commodity group averaged over the 45 countries, $\bar{\bar{w}}_i = (1/45)\sum_{c=1}^{45} \bar{w}_i$, the corresponding standard deviation and coefficient of variation (CV). We also present mean budget shares, the corresponding standard deviations and CV for the developed countries and developing countries separately.

As can be seen from the food column of Table 3.5, among the 45 countries, on average, the British consumers allocate only about one-twelfth (8.6 percent per annum) of their income on food while the Sri Lankan consumers allocate more than half (53.6 percent per annum) of their income on food, which is more than six times that of the UK. On average, consumers in the 45 countries allocate about one-fifth of their income on food. The averages for

Table 3.3 Growth in prices, 12 commodities, 45 countries (Mean log-change x100)

	Country (1)	*Food* (2)	*Alcohol* (3)	*Clothing* (4)	*Housing* (5)	*Durables* (6)	*Health* (7)	*Transport* (8)	*Communication* (9)	*Recreation* (10)	*Education* (11)	*Restaurants* (12)	*Miscellaneous* (13)
Developed countries													
1	Australia	3.22	6.06	1.09	4.12	1.35	3.66	2.10	0.18	1.50	6.32	3.57	3.15
2	Austria	1.96	2.30	0.53	2.94	1.14	2.39	1.95	−3.00	0.21	4.45	2.45	1.07
3	Belgium	2.09	3.21	0.66	2.32	1.41	1.83	2.32	−0.86	0.84	1.86	2.74	0.95
4	Canada	2.51	4.72	1.05	2.80	1.57	3.07	2.62	1.58	1.52	5.24	3.36	2.48
5	Denmark	1.69	2.18	0.35	2.98	1.25	1.10	1.64	−3.27	0.44	3.03	2.45	1.38
6	Finland	3.26	4.66	2.81	4.61	3.13	4.87	4.18	0.36	3.10	5.05	5.13	4.04
7	France	3.80	4.87	3.61	5.25	3.23	3.06	4.29	0.36	2.72	5.53	5.63	4.51
8	Germany	1.49	2.59	0.52	1.86	0.80	1.33	2.06	−3.02	−0.23	1.53	1.68	0.50
9	Hong Kong	5.33	–	4.62	5.23	1.01	6.31	4.22	–	6.22	–	–	5.44
10	Iceland	3.97	5.37	1.04	6.32	3.82	4.49	5.34	2.60	3.38	4.93	4.63	2.31
11	Ireland	−1.80	0.44	−6.60	−3.48	−2.09	4.16	−3.87	−8.80	−4.09	−11.76	−3.14	−8.21
12	Israel	3.55	6.72	−1.51	3.86	1.27	3.12	3.88	−0.71	0.94	3.46	5.17	2.55
13	Italy	2.23	1.12	1.52	3.65	1.87	2.57	2.84	−3.06	0.69	2.78	2.66	1.92
14	Japan	2.54	–	2.85	2.56	0.20	2.10	2.43	–	1.86	–	–	2.61
15	Luxembourg	2.13	3.90	0.98	2.50	1.80	0.90	2.26	−4.53	1.41	3.22	2.81	0.76
16	Netherlands	1.73	3.99	0.65	3.20	1.49	2.24	2.65	−0.84	0.99	3.35	2.86	1.26
17	New Zealand	2.35	4.58	0.44	3.64	0.67	2.73	1.12	−4.01	0.36	7.72	2.37	2.19
18	Norway	4.29	6.28	1.93	5.05	3.59	5.29	5.20	0.22	3.29	5.72	5.75	5.70
19	Singapore	2.72	–	1.23	3.47	2.41	3.37	2.41	–	1.28	–	–	2.01
20	Slovenia	4.38	5.96	2.03	4.90	3.20	3.78	4.11	2.36	3.42	5.15	4.74	3.68
21	South Korea	7.96	7.40	7.08	9.82	6.65	6.58	7.82	4.21	6.32	10.49	8.52	6.63
22	Spain	2.55	3.06	1.52	3.42	2.09	2.03	3.07	−1.32	1.07	3.86	3.29	1.44
23	Sweden	1.30	2.27	1.01	2.21	0.51	3.01	1.72	−2.06	−0.80	3.34	2.43	1.75
24	Switzerland	−1.19	1.37	−0.37	−0.93	−0.89	−3.37	−1.59	−7.88	−1.70	−2.61	−0.15	−2.43
25	Taiwan	4.05	–	1.87	3.29	3.25	3.43	2.12	–	4.55	–	–	3.66
26	UK	2.19	3.06	−3.46	2.65	0.85	2.47	2.60	−0.45	−1.44	7.20	3.42	1.65

27	USA	3.69	4.38	1.10	4.30	1.88	5.10	3.43	1.33	1.19	6.55	4.24	3.82
	Mean	2.74	3.93	1.06	3.43	1.76	3.02	2.70	−1.33	1.45	3.76	3.33	2.10
	Std Dev	1.86	1.88	2.43	2.31	1.65	1.94	2.14	3.14	2.27	4.23	2.24	2.77
	CV	67.71	47.76	230.19	67.34	94.02	64.18	79.17	−235.64	156.91	112.64	67.30	131.61
Developing countries													
28	Colombia	5.22	6.59	3.26	4.46	2.96	5.00	5.72	2.56	1.82	5.40	5.39	3.55
29	Czech Republic	2.03	3.82	−0.62	5.53	0.50	3.36	1.00	1.67	1.57	4.02	4.26	2.33
30	Estonia	4.58	7.01	4.74	7.48	2.11	5.80	5.66	1.65	5.17	6.57	5.50	3.66
31	Greece	2.15	6.28	2.28	2.70	1.39	3.31	2.48	−0.31	2.63	2.83	2.71	2.06
32	Hungary	6.52	9.51	4.97	7.90	4.01	9.65	5.84	5.24	5.07	7.09	8.49	6.23
33	India	7.10	–	5.98	9.59	5.76	6.39	6.64	–	5.95	–	–	4.71
34	Latvia	4.21	6.14	2.76	8.95	2.55	5.96	5.56	2.28	3.67	6.80	5.35	4.73
35	Lithuania	2.94	3.63	0.12	6.86	1.79	3.65	4.63	1.31	1.37	4.90	3.34	4.64
36	Malaysia	3.25	–	−1.05	1.69	1.34	2.25	1.56	–	1.74	–	–	2.01
37	Mexico	5.61	4.39	5.65	3.89	4.07	4.36	5.23	−0.45	3.98	5.61	4.10	2.49
38	Philippines	4.00	–	3.32	4.51	2.05	5.22	4.56	–	5.13	–	–	3.87
39	Poland	4.12	5.51	−0.01	6.48	3.95	5.81	4.46	0.47	6.57	5.57	0.66	4.02
40	Portugal	−4.21	5.03	−1.82	5.90	2.17	1.71	2.84	0.23	1.89	2.60	3.02	2.66
41	Slovakia	2.93	3.20	1.87	6.08	0.22	1.78	1.54	4.55	2.12	7.35	3.01	4.19
42	South Africa	10.34	–	5.97	9.60	7.99	10.47	10.13	–	7.88	13.49	10.66	7.38
43	Sri Lanka	9.65	–	7.66	8.24	10.96	11.63	8.51	–	7.41	–	–	9.82
44	Thailand	4.78	–	4.68	4.83	3.96	3.25	4.93	–	3.89	–	–	5.21
45	Turkey	16.53	–	15.71	20.47	13.89	13.00	17.69	–	15.58	18.72	18.50	13.56
	Mean	5.10	5.56	3.64	6.95	3.98	5.70	5.50	1.75	4.64	7.00	5.77	4.84
	Std Dev	4.24	1.83	4.08	4.05	3.63	3.38	3.85	1.85	3.43	4.44	4.61	2.94
	CV	83.24	32.99	112.08	58.31	91.27	59.34	69.93	105.95	74.06	63.44	79.97	60.72
All countries													
	Mean	3.68	4.46	2.09	4.84	2.65	4.09	3.82	−0.34	2.72	4.93	4.21	3.20
	Std Dev	3.22	1.99	3.40	3.54	2.82	2.90	3.21	3.12	3.18	4.53	3.44	3.12
	CV	87.46	44.66	162.70	73.23	106.37	70.81	84.16	−929.36	116.72	91.91	81.80	97.40

Table 3.4 Growth in per capita quantity consumed, 12 commodities, 45 countries (Mean log-change x100)

	Country (1)	*Food* (2)	*Alcohol* (3)	*Clothing* (4)	*Housing* (5)	*Durables* (6)	*Health* (7)	*Transport* (8)	*Communication* (9)	*Recreation* (10)	*Education* (11)	*Restaurants* (12)	*Miscellaneous* (13)
	Developed countries												
1	Australia	0.82	−1.63	1.48	1.62	1.61	2.83	1.86	6.43	3.39	1.50	1.14	2.55
2	Austria	0.04	0.01	1.02	0.63	0.82	0.79	0.39	5.18	2.46	−0.73	0.89	1.59
3	Belgium	−0.31	−0.04	0.28	0.62	0.93	1.75	0.31	5.51	1.41	0.49	0.41	1.29
4	Canada	0.38	−1.58	1.37	1.67	1.62	2.72	1.66	3.81	2.75	1.49	0.33	2.52
5	Denmark	0.16	−1.40	1.73	0.23	0.71	2.44	0.29	6.81	2.37	0.08	0.74	1.34
6	Finland	1.01	0.11	2.08	2.19	1.84	2.67	1.15	7.67	2.95	2.62	0.64	2.70
7	France	1.32	0.17	0.71	2.60	2.08	4.20	2.43	8.58	3.87	1.53	0.67	2.66
8	Germany	−0.26	−1.57	0.01	0.61	0.31	2.98	0.10	6.81	2.55	2.77	0.42	1.79
9	Hong Kong	1.71	–	3.53	3.92	7.47	3.64	4.73	–	2.91	–	–	5.05
10	Iceland	1.56	0.80	1.74	1.24	2.38	2.33	2.09	7.83	2.07	1.59	3.48	4.43
11	Ireland	3.51	1.98	7.08	9.80	3.04	2.90	8.48	14.53	6.82	16.04	7.29	12.12
12	Israel	1.08	−0.19	2.54	1.41	1.65	1.61	2.39	5.82	1.96	2.06	−0.02	1.21
13	Italy	−0.66	1.19	−0.28	0.33	−0.77	−0.08	−0.65	6.25	1.47	−0.09	0.97	0.18
14	Japan	0.32	–	−0.54	2.84	2.71	3.64	2.97	–	3.36	–	–	1.85
15	Luxembourg	0.21	−1.12	1.23	0.78	−0.47	2.37	0.52	7.13	−0.05	4.30	−0.90	2.83
16	Netherlands	0.75	−1.02	1.47	0.73	0.01	−0.10	0.05	6.18	1.60	−0.34	0.19	0.70
17	New Zealand	1.40	−1.43	1.86	0.81	1.77	0.86	1.78	9.07	2.99	2.37	1.03	1.90
18	Norway	0.97	−0.31	3.27	1.79	2.75	2.76	1.94	7.66	4.42	1.46	2.34	2.39
19	Singapore	0.68	–	1.93	3.53	2.11	4.27	4.02	–	4.88	–	–	3.89
20	Slovenia	0.78	−0.51	2.86	1.19	1.75	4.69	1.50	6.30	2.25	2.91	1.20	3.30
21	South Korea	1.64	2.62	3.65	3.67	5.18	6.90	5.70	13.22	7.77	3.09	3.11	7.36
22	Spain	−0.64	−1.12	−0.31	2.51	−0.59	2.81	0.43	6.72	1.28	0.03	−0.68	1.70
23	Sweden	1.30	−0.53	2.08	0.20	3.76	2.20	1.73	7.46	4.29	2.58	2.52	2.48
24	Switzerland	1.99	−1.86	0.38	2.55	1.34	6.33	3.10	10.72	1.92	6.13	0.84	3.74
25	Taiwan	2.72	–	5.76	5.04	6.50	5.05	9.01	6.11	4.81	–	–	4.88
26	UK	0.51	−0.79	7.26	0.54	2.07	2.16	1.48	4.43	4.97	−2.14	0.11	2.08

27	USA	0.09	−0.12	2.56	1.38	2.47	2.45	1.58	4.92	4.83	0.07	1.40	2.42
	Mean	0.85	−0.36	2.10	2.02	2.04	2.86	2.26	7.30	3.20	2.17	1.22	3.00
	Std Dev	0.97	1.16	2.02	2.00	1.95	1.66	2.37	2.53	1.74	3.51	1.70	2.37
	CV	113.37	−320.98	96.17	99.37	95.40	58.17	104.87	34.61	54.46	162.21	139.24	78.95
Developing countries													
28	Colombia	1.15	−1.07	2.77	1.76	2.63	1.10	4.30	6.39	5.86	0.53	3.00	3.88
29	Czech Republic	2.32	0.20	3.33	0.69	4.02	2.89	3.61	5.47	2.33	0.88	1.04	3.03
30	Estonia	3.53	3.78	4.46	3.07	6.08	5.45	4.86	10.88	6.38	−0.05	5.66	7.92
31	Greece	1.09	−1.76	−1.88	1.21	0.43	−0.02	0.43	9.43	0.94	0.75	0.92	0.74
32	Hungary	0.74	0.16	2.12	1.11	2.50	1.20	2.84	6.89	2.49	0.96	1.75	1.94
33	India	1.27	–	5.12	1.83	5.24	4.48	6.39	–	4.03	–	–	7.50
34	Latvia	2.98	2.15	9.01	2.39	9.95	5.07	4.86	12.33	9.73	13.67	6.34	5.19
35	Lithuania	3.51	4.05	9.89	0.96	10.46	8.71	7.96	13.68	12.66	6.93	5.39	8.76
36	Malaysia	3.15	–	7.25	3.21	4.94	6.36	6.51	–	8.37	–	–	5.38
37	Mexico	1.01	1.97	0.72	0.72	0.93	−0.55	1.85	7.07	3.42	−0.59	−0.48	3.96
38	Philippines	2.86	–	0.17	2.21	2.15	4.08	4.25	–	2.79	–	–	3.57
39	Poland	1.25	0.95	6.62	2.85	4.99	5.62	5.48	8.24	1.42	3.36	7.01	6.63
40	Portugal	7.37	−2.08	4.68	−0.28	0.00	2.33	−0.14	3.96	−0.06	1.82	0.98	1.31
41	Slovakia	1.86	1.77	1.97	2.55	7.60	5.23	4.98	4.95	6.56	4.90	2.81	5.36
42	South Africa	0.01	–	3.08	2.28	0.78	2.38	1.46	–	2.07	−0.13	−0.05	4.22
43	Sri Lanka	1.97	–	4.17	7.55	2.74	2.18	8.13	–	5.23	–	–	3.48
44	Thailand	2.34	–	3.27	3.72	4.76	6.03	4.81	–	3.56	–	–	7.66
45	Turkey	1.34	–	−2.90	1.63	3.52	6.93	3.46	–	0.67	4.49	0.61	5.40
	Mean	2.21	0.92	3.55	2.19	4.10	3.86	4.22	8.12	4.36	2.89	2.69	4.77
	Std Dev	1.64	2.06	3.38	1.69	3.03	2.55	2.33	3.13	3.40	3.96	2.58	2.31
	CV	74.12	224.22	95.26	76.87	74.00	66.15	55.08	38.56	77.95	137.25	95.81	48.33
All countries													
	Mean	1.40	0.05	2.68	2.09	2.86	3.26	3.05	7.56	3.66	2.43	1.75	3.71
	Std Dev	1.43	1.60	2.71	1.86	2.61	2.10	2.52	2.71	2.57	3.64	2.15	2.48
	CV	102.29	3058.32	101.08	89.36	91.28	64.35	82.79	35.87	70.07	150.11	122.52	66.83

all countries reveal that the remaining income is spent on alcohol (5 percent), clothing (5.7 percent), housing (19.5 percent), durables (5.7 percent), health (4.1 percent), transport (13.2 percent), communication (2.7 percent), recreation (9.2 percent), education (1.4 percent), restaurants (7.4 percent) and miscellaneous (10.7 percent). There are some noticeable differences in the allocation of income on food between developed and developing countries. On average, while the developing group allocates more than one fourth of their income on food, the developed group allocates only one-seventh of their income on food (26.9 percent vs 14 percent). The other major difference in income allocation between developed and developing countries is in alcohol (4.5 percent vs 6.1 percent), housing (21.2 percent vs 16.9 percent), health (4.5 percent vs 3.5 percent), recreation (10.1 percent vs 7.7 percent) and restaurants (7.7 percent vs 6.8 percent). The CVs presented in the table reveal that there is more variation in the budget shares between developed and developing countries for food, housing, durables, health, transport, recreation, education and restaurants.

To measure the overall growth in consumption and prices, we use the Divisia volume and price indices introduced in Chapter 2. Below, we present the finite-change version of the Divisia indices. The Divisia volume index, DQ_t, for period t is the weighted sum of individual quantity log-changes with weights being the corresponding budget shares, defined as

$$DQ_t = \sum_{i=1}^{n} \bar{w}_{it} Dq_{it}, \quad t = 1,2,\ldots,T, \tag{3.7}$$

where $\bar{w}_{it} = ½(w_{it} + w_{it}–1)$ is the arithmetic average of the budget shares of commodity i in periods t and $t-1$. The Divisia volume index averaged over the whole sample period for each country is calculated as

$$D\bar{Q} = \frac{1}{T}\sum_{t=1}^{T} DQ_t. \tag{3.8}$$

The Divisia price index, DP_t, for the period t is the weighted sum of individual price log-changes with the corresponding budget shares being the weights, and is given by

$$DP_t = \sum_{i=1}^{n} \bar{w}_{it} Dp_{it}, \quad t = 1,2,\ldots,T. \tag{3.9}$$

The Divisia price index averaged over the whole sample period for each country is calculated as,

$$D\bar{P} = \frac{1}{T}\sum_{t=1}^{T} DP_t. \tag{3.10}$$

The Divisia quantity index (DQ_t) and the Divisia price index (DP_t) are first-order moments. The second-order moments, the Divisia quantity and price variances, are defined as

$$K_t = \sum_{i=1}^{n} \bar{w}_{it} \left[Dq_{it} - DQ_t \right]^2, \quad t = 1, 2, \ldots, T, \tag{3.11}$$

and

$$\Pi_t = \sum_{i=1}^{n} \bar{w}_{it} \left[Dp_{it} - DP_t \right]^2, \quad t = 1, 2, \ldots, T. \tag{3.12}$$

These two variances measure the degree to which the quantities and prices of the individual commodities change disproportionately. When all quantities and prices change proportionately, these two variances will vanish.

To measure the co-movement of prices and quantities, the Divisia price-quantity correlation is defined as

$$\rho_t = \frac{\Gamma_t}{\sqrt{K_t \Pi_t}}, \quad t = 1, 2, \ldots, T, \tag{3.13}$$

where $\Gamma_t = \Sigma_{i=1}^{n} \bar{w}_{it} \left(Dp_{it} - DP_t \right) \left(Dq_{it} - DQ_t \right)$ is the Divisia price-quantity covariance between prices and quantities. Since relative prices and relative consumptions are expected to move in the opposite direction, we would expect Divisia price-quantity correlation to be negative. The corresponding sample period averages for each country are calculated as

$$\bar{K} = \frac{1}{T} \sum_{t=1}^{T} K_t, \quad \bar{\Pi} = \frac{1}{T} \sum_{t=1}^{T} \Pi_t \quad \text{and} \quad \bar{\rho} = \frac{1}{T} \sum_{t=1}^{T} \rho_t. \tag{3.14}$$

Furthermore, if we regress the relative consumption $(Dq_{it} - DQ_t)$ against relative prices $(Dp_{it} - DP_t)$, then under the assumption of *unitary income elasticity*, we can show that the weighted least squares estimate of the slope of the regression equation is the measure of income flexibility (for example, see Selvanathan and Selvanathan 2003) given by

$$\hat{\phi}_t = \frac{\Gamma_t}{\Pi_t} = \rho_t \sqrt{\frac{K_t}{\Pi_t}}. \tag{3.15}$$

Tables 3.6–3.8 present the Divisia volume index, Divisia price index and Divisia price-quantity correlations for every country and for the whole sample period calculated using equations (3.7), (3.9) and (3.13), respectively. The last row of each table presents the corresponding sample mean values averaged over the respective time periods, given by equations (3.8), (3.10) and (3.14), respectively.

Table 3.9 presents the collection of the mean values in the last row of Tables 3.6–3.8. As can be seen from column (2), the overall growth in consumption in the 45 countries varies between 0.3 percent (Italy) and 7.5 percent (Ireland) with an overall average of 2.5 percent per annum across all countries. The average consumption growth across the developing countries (3.1 percent) is slightly higher than that of the developed countries (2.1 percent).

Table 3.5 Budget shares (means x100)

	Country	*Food*	*Alcohol*	*Clothing*	*Housing*	*Durables*	*Health*	*Transport*	*Communication*	*Recreation*	*Education*	*Restaurants*	*Miscellaneous*
	(1)	*(2)*	*(3)*	*(4)*	*(5)*	*(6)*	*(7)*	*(8)*	*(9)*	*(10)*	*(11)*	*(12)*	*(13)*
Developed countries													
1	Australia	10.76	3.84	4.29	20.68	5.65	5.12	11.99	2.16	10.82	3.18	7.00	14.50
2	Austria	10.29	3.46	6.47	20.61	6.88	3.66	12.94	2.32	10.45	0.74	11.69	10.49
3	Belgium	13.24	3.92	5.08	23.70	6.11	5.58	11.70	2.37	9.19	0.41	5.60	13.11
4	Canada	10.56	4.09	5.35	23.64	6.09	3.36	14.46	2.14	8.97	1.11	7.31	12.92
5	Denmark	11.71	4.27	4.49	27.22	5.32	2.71	12.35	2.01	11.22	0.76	5.50	12.43
6	Finland	16.08	5.92	5.13	22.43	5.30	3.38	13.25	1.96	10.87	0.35	6.64	8.68
7	France	16.49	4.19	7.36	20.30	6.62	3.01	13.35	1.91	8.72	0.65	6.06	11.33
8	Germany	10.81	3.54	5.49	24.08	7.09	4.36	14.31	2.64	9.57	0.68	5.03	12.39
9	Hong Kong	18.40	–	16.30	17.96	8.17	3.76	7.80	–	8.23	–	–	19.38
10	Iceland	14.38	4.94	5.15	19.80	6.55	2.99	15.03	2.15	11.4	1.24	8.19	8.19
11	Ireland	10.50	6.68	5.19	19.91	6.04	3.48	12.18	2.70	6.99	2.34	13.9	10.11
12	Israel	15.72	2.42	3.52	22.96	6.91	3.15	13.95	3.85	7.00	2.70	6.10	11.73
13	Italy	15.07	4.22	7.04	20.61	7.16	3.27	12.96	2.69	7.06	0.98	8.87	10.08
14	Japan	19.81	–	5.43	21.12	5.29	11.18	10.89	–	11.71	–	–	14.58
15	Luxembourg	9.49	9.18	5.24	21.53	6.61	1.95	16.67	1.65	7.18	0.67	7.33	12.5
16	Netherlands	11.13	3.19	5.44	20.22	6.31	3.95	13.37	3.50	11.39	0.70	7.20	13.62
17	New Zealand	14.18	5.35	4.55	25.38	6.11	2.20	14.04	2.81	10.03	0.88	5.80	8.68
18	Norway	16.66	4.77	6.76	21.24	6.69	2.34	14.83	2.16	10.49	0.46	5.12	8.49
19	Singapore	16.02	–	6.12	12.84	7.57	4.30	14.33	–	23.18	–	–	15.64
20	Slovenia	15.83	5.32	5.64	18.83	5.75	3.35	15.65	2.84	9.75	1.07	6.70	9.29
21	South Korea	22.84	4.11	7.74	14.50	3.95	3.69	10.26	2.40	6.34	5.33	8.40	10.45
22	Spain	13.82	4.25	5.48	18.34	5.19	3.41	11.59	2.46	8.13	1.55	16.37	9.40
23	Sweden	12.62	4.02	4.75	27.98	4.68	2.99	13.25	3.09	11.21	0.25	5.15	10.04
24	Switzerland	9.39	4.08	3.61	24.03	4.27	12.69	9.34	2.25	9.72	0.51	7.53	12.58
25	Taiwan	24.05	–	5.82	18.88	4.39	3.64	13.65	–	15.13	–	–	14.44

26	UK	8.62	4.32	5.28	25.48	5.11	1.52	13.35	1.95	10.43	1.30	9.45	13.19
27	USA	9.23	2.52	5.24	18.78	5.53	15.44	11.72	2.11	8.59	1.75	6.55	12.53
	Mean	13.99	4.16	5.85	21.22	5.98	4.46	12.93	2.44	10.14	1.29	7.72	11.88
	SD	4.06	1.12	2.32	3.44	1.03	3.29	1.92	0.52	3.23	1.16	2.84	2.58
	CV	29.05	31.73	39.58	16.21	17.30	73.63	14.87	21.51	31.88	90.32	36.82	21.70
Developing countries													
28	Colombia	18.85	3.10	6.72	16.71	4.53	3.25	10.64	4.21	4.91	4.97	11.17	10.64
29	Czech Republic	16.10	8.20	4.18	24.26	5.64	2.03	9.73	2.75	10.2	0.56	8.04	8.31
30	Estonia	20.88	7.[illegible]7	6.69	19.52	4.72	2.81	11.64	3.01	8.00	0.90	6.56	7.30
31	Greece	16.26	4.17	5.04	18.99	4.43	4.49	14.24	3.38	4.57	2.05	13.74	8.33
32	Hungary	18.51	7.[illegible]6	3.56	19.22	5.54	3.93	13.85	3.65	7.92	1.54	6.44	8.68
33	India	50.60	–	10.23	10.45	4.34	2.83	12.53	–	3.50	–	–	5.53
34	Latvia	24.08	8.36	5.00	20.05	3.05	3.92	11.58	2.75	8.21	1.72	5.51	5.28
35	Lithuania	27.78	7.54	6.37	16.46	5.34	4.10	13.73	2.35	6.27	0.59	2.93	6.43
36	Malaysia	23.77	–	2.80	17.03	5.48	2.34	19.67	–	15.60	–	–	13.31
37	Mexico	22.29	2.57	2.98	21.56	5.74	4.40	18.10	3.53	4.21	1.55	4.48	8.49
38	Philippines	43.19	–	1.70	12.29	4.87	2.38	13.72	–	5.72	–	–	16.13
39	Poland	21.41	7.77	5.01	20.70	4.52	3.90	10.68	2.73	7.90	1.14	2.97	11.25
40	Portugal	16.88	3.11	6.39	14.88	6.16	4.68	14.55	2.82	7.35	1.15	10.72	11.00
41	Slovakia	20.50	5.56	4.89	23.52	5.48	2.97	7.92	3.30	8.74	1.15	6.63	9.24
42	South Africa	28.61	–	6.30	12.95	9.34	5.78	15.64	–	5.52	2.08	2.77	11.02
43	Sri Lanka	53.56	–	7.15	8.00	4.78	1.70	17.20	–	3.55	–	–	4.06
44	Thailand	33.58	–	6.06	9.25	4.51	3.62	12.75	–	22.28	–	–	7.95
45	Turkey	26.89	–	7.22	17.43	7.75	3.48	18.00	–	4.47	1.08	6.22	7.47
	Mean	26.87	6.[illegible]1	5.46	16.85	5.35	3.48	13.68	3.13	7.72	1.58	6.78	8.91
	SD	11.37	2.[illegible]6	2.00	4.74	1.39	1.04	3.15	0.53	4.66	1.13	3.39	2.97
	CV	42.31	36.[illegible]4	36.65	28.11	25.99	30.02	23.07	17.05	60.34	71.63	49.93	33.29
All countries													
	Mean	19.14	4.[illegible]9	5.69	19.47	5.72	4.07	13.23	2.66	9.17	1.39	7.38	10.69
	Std Dev	10.02	1.[illegible]7	2.18	4.51	1.21	2.65	2.48	0.62	4.00	1.14	3.04	3.08
	CV	52.36	37.–2	38.29	23.17	21.22	65.20	18.77	23.10	43.61	82.14	41.13	28.81

Table 3.6a Divisia volume indices (x100), 27 developed countries

Year	*Australia*	*Austria*	*Belgium*	*Canada*	*Denmark*	*Finland*	*France*	*Germany*	*Hong Kong*	*Iceland*	*Ireland*	*Israel*	*Italy*
(1)	*(2)*	*(3)*	*(4)*	*(5)*	*(6)*	*(7)*	*(8)*	*(9)*	*(10)*	*(11)*	*(12)*	*(13)*	*(14)*
1960	–	–	–	–	–	–	3.70	–	–	–	–	–	–
1961	–	–	–	–	–	–	4.34	–	–	–	–	–	–
1962	–	–	–	–	–	–	5.88	–	–	–	–	–	–
1963	–	–	–	–	–	–	5.94	–	–	–	–	–	–
1964	–	–	–	–	–	–	4.05	–	–	–	–	–	–
1965	–	–	–	–	–	–	2.73	–	–	–	–	–	–
1966	–	–	–	–	–	–	3.82	–	–	–	–	–	–
1967	–	–	–	–	–	–	4.08	–	–	–	–	–	–
1968	–	–	–	–	–	–	3.46	–	–	–	–	–	–
1969	–	–	–	–	–	–	5.79	–	–	–	–	–	–
1970	–	–	–	–	–	–	3.86	–	–	–	–	–	–
1971	–	–	–	–	–	–	4.70	–	–	–	–	–	–
1972	–	–	–	–	–	–	4.08	–	5.68	–	–	–	–
1973	–	–	–	–	–	–	4.39	–	5.65	–	–	–	–
1974	–	–	–	–	–	–	1.93	–	–6.14	–	–	–	–
1975	–	–	–	–	–	–	1.27	–	0.82	–	–	–	–
1976	–	–	–	–	–	1.16	4.67	–	7.54	–	–	–	–
1977	–	–	–	–	–	−0.97	2.29	–	11.81	–	–	–	–
1978	–	–	–	–	–	2.39	3.90	–	13.46	–	–	–	–
1979	–	–	–	–	–	5.47	2.90	–	2.38	–	–	–	–
1980	–	–	–	–	–	2.10	0.87	–	5.37	–	–	–	–
1981	–	–	–	–	–	0.73	1.40	–	4.95	–	–	–	–
1982	–	–	–	−3.67	–	3.98	2.88	–	3.04	–	–	–	–
1983	–	–	–	1.21	–	2.21	0.72	–	4.44	–	–	–	–
1984	–	–	–	3.12	–	2.67	0.33	–	4.01	–	–	–	–
1985	–	–	–	3.76	–	3.30	1.34	–	2.90	–	–	–	–
1986	1.10	–	–	2.58	–	3.30	2.76	–	6.65	–	–	–	–
1987	2.07	–	–	2.19	–	4.23	2.52	–	9.94	–	–	–	–
1988	4.74	–	–	2.41	–	5.10	2.72	–	7.77	–	–	–	–
1989	3.12	–	–	1.45	–	4.01	2.98	–	2.65	–	–	–	–
1990	2.98	–	–	–0.76	–	−1.13	2.02	–	4.54	–	–	–	–
1991	3.49	–	–	−2.82	–	–3.42	0.25	–	5.91	–	–	–	–
1992	5.98	–	–	0.42	–	–4.42	0.68	–	8.03	–	–	–	–
1993	2.84	–	–	1.18	–	–1.91	–0.48	–	5.28	–	–	–	–
1994	1.96	–	–	2.68	–	2.40	1.15	–	3.08	–	–	–	–
1995	4.28	–	–	1.35	–	3.66	1.03	–	–0.59	–	–	–	–
1996	2.95	2.06	1.91	1.74	1.95	3.44	1.36	1.17	–0.43	4.09	–	2.37	0.75
1997	3.78	0.03	1.71	3.53	2.33	3.49	0.53	0.69	2.23	7.34	14.23	1.07	3.32
1998	5.02	2.83	2.64	2.48	1.73	4.11	3.60	1.25	−8.82	8.62	18.91	2.57	3.09
1999	5.99	2.46	1.40	2.79	−0.29	2.99	3.27	2.34	0.54	6.19	18.55	3.26	2.32
2000	5.37	2.77	2.60	2.97	0.33	1.76	3.24	2.06	4.59	2.35	24.33	5.01	2.43
2001	3.41	0.79	0.50	1.45	0.07	2.43	1.78	1.86	0.83	−1.86	11.31	−0.48	0.02
2002	3.62	0.33	−0.19	2.91	1.15	2.13	1.29	−0.82	0.26	−1.53	8.91	−0.92	−0.80
2003	3.76	1.00	−0.21	1.17	0.79	3.61	0.75	−0.14	−0.35	4.41	7.64	−1.59	−0.09
2004	4.94	1.81	0.78	2.08	4.52	3.07	1.61	0.88	6.67	5.12	7.24	3.38	0.51
2005	4.52	1.75	0.51	2.21	3.56	2.87	1.62	0.86	4.07	6.25	12.81	1.91	0.58
2006	5.30	1.54	0.83	2.60	2.46	3.73	1.65	1.96	5.38	1.17	13.27	2.49	1.06
2007	5.24	0.93	1.02	2.91	1.04	2.83	1.86	0.09	8.41	4.64	12.44	5.43	0.65
2008	21.68	1.05	0.80	1.44	−0.46	1.67	−0.26	0.71	2.04	−5.60	−2.11	−0.66	−1.56
2009	3.05	−0.48	−0.66	−1.01	−4.68	−4.26	−0.68	0.44	0.67	−4.96	−19.57	−1.52	−2.07
2010	7.53	0.78	1.84	1.95	0.52	2.90	0.99	0.68	7.45	−2.91	−3.14	2.74	1.06
2011	4.08	1.06	−0.20	0.93	−0.10	2.77	0.00	1.29	8.89	2.31	1.31	1.31	−0.04
2012	4.16	0.09	−0.39	0.71	−0.22	−0.12	−0.45	0.69	3.72	2.21	−0.90	0.73	−3.94
2013	5.98	−0.32	−0.08	1.47	−0.01	−1.12	−0.06	0.36	5.96	1.60	2.81	1.71	−2.72
2014	4.21	−0.72	−0.54	1.78	0.46	−0.33	−0.11	0.79	1.58	3.71	6.50	1.90	0.38
2015	–	0.01	–	1.30	2.07	0.45	1.01	–	1.78	–	–	–	–
2016	–	–	–	–	–	–	–	–	−0.99	–	–	–	–
2017	–	–	–	–	–	–	–	–	–	–	–	–	–
2018	–	–	–	–	–	–	–	–	–	–	–	–	–
2019	–	–	–	–	–	–	–	–	–	–	–	–	–
2020	–	–	–	–	–	–	–	–	–	–	–	–	–
Mean	4.73	0.99	0.75	1.54	0.86	1.83	2.21	0.90	3.86	2.27	7.47	1.62	0.26

Japan (15)	*Luxembourg* (16)	*Netherlands* (17)	*New Zealand* (18)	*Norway* (19)	*Singapore* (20)	*Slovenia* (21)	*South Korea* (22)	*Spain* (23)	*Sweden* (24)	*Switzerland* (25)	*Taiwan* (26)	*UK* (27)	*USA* (28)
–	–	–	–	–	–	–	–	–	–	–	–	–	–
–	–	–	–	–	–	–	–	–	–	–	–	–	–
–	–	–	–	–	–	–	–	–	–	–	–	–	–
–	–	–	–	–	–	–	–	–	–	–	3.95	–	–
–	–	–	–	–	−4.44	–	–	–	–	–	10.90	–	–
–	–	–	–	–	3.31	–	–	–	–	–	7.05	–	–
–	–	–	–	–	5.59	–	–	–	–	–	3.80	–	–
–	–	–	–	–	5.16	–	–	–	–	–	8.20	–	–
–	–	–	–	–	6.77	–	–	–	–	–	7.36	–	–
–	–	–	–	–	7.54	–	–	–	–	–	5.80	–	–
–	–	–	–	–	10.80	–	–	–	–	–	5.92	–	–
4.86	–	–	–	4.51	7.06	–	6.49	–	–	–	7.18	–	–
7.08	–	–	–	1.63	7.73	–	3.97	–	–	–	8.86	–	–
7.61	–	–	–	2.72	7.84	–	8.08	–	–	–	10.35	–	–
−1.58	–	–	–	2.09	5.95	–	4.11	–	–	–	3.26	–	–
2.62	–	–	–	4.44	1.08	–	3.37	–	–	–	4.59	–	–
2.44	–	–	–	5.25	3.68	–	6.65	–	–	–	5.57	–	2.89
2.95	–	–	–	5.51	5.41	–	3.78	–	–	–	5.72	–	5.11
4.03	–	–	–	−2.58	7.29	–	6.23	–	–	–	7.58	–	4.23
5.28	–	–	–	3.87	8.73	–	6.22	–	–	–	8.62	–	−1.54
0.74	–	–	–	1.82	7.25	–	−1.60	–	–	–	4.02	–	1.49
0.61	–	–	–	−0.35	3.96	–	3.20	–	–	–	1.97	–	4.56
3.59	–	–	–	−0.26	0.36	–	5.32	–	–	–	3.38	–	3.23
2.44	–	–	–	1.28	5.25	–	7.22	–	–	–	4.76	–	3.36
1.95	–	–	–	2.87	1.51	–	5.58	–	–	–	6.56	–	1.43
2.60	–	–	–	8.96	−2.34	–	5.12	–	–	–	3.76	–	−1.29
2.71	–	–	–	4.31	4.22	–	7.98	–	–	–	5.93	–	0.42
3.52	–	–	–	−1.65	8.28	–	7.46	–	–	–	10.19	–	0.01
4.27	–	–	2.14	−2.39	8.69	–	7.11	–	–	–	12.09	–	4.24
4.20	–	–	−0.09	−1.29	5.25	–	8.07	–	–	–	11.57	–	3.89
4.13	–	–	−0.86	0.70	4.97	–	7.95	–	–	–	7.36	–	4.02
2.17	–	–	−4.03	2.36	0.51	–	7.28	–	–	–	6.01	–	3.26
1.67	–	–	−1.28	1.62	3.46	–	5.92	–	–	–	8.09	–	2.13
0.80	–	–	2.06	1.95	6.76	–	5.84	–	–	–	6.52	–	3.07
1.71	–	–	4.56	2.99	1.18	–	7.67	–	1.45	–	6.50	–	1.83
2.00	–	–	2.68	3.04	−0.35	–	9.14	–	1.05	–	2.92	–	0.81
1.73	0.16	4.12	3.53	5.67	0.57	4.07	6.23	4.25	1.09	2.68	5.67	3.52	−0.85
0.91	3.78	3.08	1.56	2.29	0.57	3.59	3.56	2.06	2.60	3.79	6.20	3.60	2.46
−0.51	2.07	4.43	1.75	2.06	−7.34	1.75	−11.63	1.57	3.28	4.21	4.26	3.12	2.29
1.43	4.81	4.63	2.26	3.03	7.27	5.29	9.71	1.02	4.18	4.08	4.27	3.94	2.58
1.76	4.64	2.43	0.30	3.43	10.22	1.30	7.18	5.46	3.89	4.50	3.66	4.25	1.87
2.21	0.35	1.48	1.38	1.62	−0.59	2.53	4.72	3.41	1.61	4.20	0.26	2.73	2.22
1.42	3.71	0.28	3.46	2.22	1.36	2.25	6.96	7.54	2.43	−0.51	2.45	3.06	2.58
1.17	0.63	−0.89	4.41	2.16	0.80	3.02	−1.33	2.25	1.44	0.93	2.50	3.35	3.69
0.91	0.09	0.24	3.31	4.24	5.32	3.33	−0.86	2.20	2.22	3.56	4.52	2.70	4.06
1.46	−0.72	0.31	3.09	2.97	1.62	3.17	3.00	3.07	2.67	3.26	2.83	2.50	3.66
1.33	−0.32	−1.05	1.99	3.76	0.85	0.72	3.28	2.44	2.73	3.10	1.23	1.11	1.24
0.88	0.43	1.35	2.41	4.45	1.41	5.43	4.00	3.51	3.10	4.87	1.92	1.91	1.39
−0.23	−0.82	0.16	−1.98	0.18	−3.47	2.10	1.75	4.89	−0.66	3.63	−2.45	−1.39	2.08
0.31	−1.82	−2.82	0.44	−1.24	−5.04	−0.36	0.19	11.35	−0.32	0.54	−0.44	−3.74	2.94
1.85	−0.93	0.01	1.63	2.25	7.04	1.18	3.17	5.86	2.31	2.55	3.25	0.06	2.70
−0.11	0.50	0.02	2.21	0.52	2.78	−0.15	2.72	5.40	0.86	0.42	3.04	−1.19	1.81
1.88	−0.33	−1.52	1.68	1.70	0.06	−1.96	0.62	3.48	−0.16	3.14	1.55	1.14	1.40
2.75	−1.18	−1.38	2.23	0.76	0.84	−3.99	0.75	3.32	0.82	2.71	1.95	1.22	−1.50
−0.33	0.28	−0.25	1.74	0.30	0.81	1.59	1.40	3.39	1.79	–	2.84	1.30	−2.64
0.09	−1.68	–	–	–	2.24	0.80	1.10	–	2.34	–	2.65	1.47	1.18
–	–	–	–	–	0.51	–	–	–	–	–	3.22	–	1.55
–	–	–	–	–	–	–	–	–	–	–	–	–	0.50
–	–	–	–	–	–	–	–	–	–	–	–	–	0.83
–	–	–	–	–	–	–	–	–	–	–	–	–	2.22
–	–	–	–	–	–	–	–	–	–	–	–	–	2.48
2.12	0.68	0.77	1.58	2.18	3.33	1.78	4.33	4.02	1.85	2.87	5.03	1.73	2.00

Table 3.6b Divisia volume indices (x100), 18 developing countries (cont.)

Year	*Colombia*	*Czech Republic*	*Estonia*	*Greece*	*Hungary*	*India*	*Latvia*	*Lithuania*	*Malaysia*	*Mexico*	*Philippines*	*Poland*	*Portugal*	*Slovakia*	*South Africa*	*Sri Lanka*	*Thailand*	*Turkey*
(1)	*(2)*	*(3)*	*(4)*	*(5)*	*(6)*	*(7)*	*(8)*	*(9)*	*(10)*	*(11)*	*(12)*	*(13)*	*(14)*	*(15)*	*(16)*	*(17)*	*(18)*	*(19)*
1960	–	–	–	–	–	–	–	–	–	–	–	–	–	–	–	–	–	–
1961	–	–	–	–	–	–	–	–	–	–	–	–	–	–	–	–	–	–
1962	–	–	–	–	–	–	–	–	–	–	–	–	–	–	–	–	–	–
1963	–	–	–	–	–	–	–	–	–	–	–	–	–	–	–	–	–	–
1964	–	–	–	–	–	–	–	–	–	–	–	–	–	–	–	–	–	–
1965	–	–	–	–	–	–	–	–	–	–	–	–	–	–	–	–	–	–
1966	–	–	–	–	–	–	–	–	–	–	–	–	–	–	–	–	–	–
1967	–	–	–	–	–	–	–	–	–	–	–	–	–	–	–	–	–	–
1968	–	–	–	–	–	–	–	–	–	–	–	–	–	–	–	–	3.33	–
1969	–	–	–	–	–	–	–	–	–	–	–	–	–	–	–	–	3.08	–
1970	–	–	–	–	–	–	–	–	–	–	–	–	–	–	–	–	5.44	–
1971	–	–	–	–	–	0.63	–	–	–	–	–	–	–	–	–	–	3.29	–
1972	–	–	–	–	–	−4.41	–	–	–	–	–	–	–	–	–	–	3.95	–
1973	–	–	–	–	–	0.31	–	–	–	–	–	–	–	–	–	–	5.41	–
1974	–	–	–	–	–	−1.50	–	–	–	–	–	–	–	–	–	–	3.86	–
1975	–	–	–	–	–	5.10	–	–	–	–	–	–	–	–	–	–	3.11	–
1976	–	–	–	–	–	−2.31	–	–	–	–	–	–	–	–	−0.20	2.08	−4.41	–
1977	–	–	–	–	–	7.67	–	–	–	–	–	–	–	–	−2.51	9.57	5.92	–
1978	–	–	–	–	–	2.48	–	–	–	–	–	–	–	–	−0.96	0.26	4.54	–
1979	–	–	–	–	–	−1.95	–	–	–	–	–	–	–	–	1.05	8.29	4.15	–
1980	–	–	–	–	–	2.83	–	–	–	–	–	–	–	–	9.28	5.04	3.50	–
1981	–	–	–	–	–	2.17	–	–	–	–	–	–	–	–	5.09	2.04	0.73	–
1982	–	–	–	–	–	0.69	–	–	–	–	–	–	–	–	0.42	2.35	0.50	–
1983	–	–	–	–	–	4.87	–	–	–	–	–	–	–	–	0.23	−1.08	4.95	–
1984	–	–	–	–	–	1.53	–	–	–	–	–	–	–	–	2.89	−3.64	2.19	–
1985	–	–	–	–	–	1.47	–	–	–	–	–	–	–	–	−6.92	3.66	−0.61	–

1986	–	–	–	–	–	2.72	–	–	–	–	–	–	–	–	−1.19	−0.57	1.13	–
1987	–	–	–	–	–	1.54	–	–	–	–	–	–	–	–	1.33	2.72	6.73	–
1988	–	–	–	–	–	3.83	–	–	–	–	–	–	–	–	4.45	3.55	8.02	–
1989	–	–	–	–	–	2.21	–	–	–	–	–	–	–	–	0.59	−0.62	8.09	–
1990	–	–	–	–	–	1.75	–	–	–	–	–	–	–	–	2.17	−12.84	9.58	–
1991	–	–	–	–	–	−0.15	–	–	–	–	–	–	–	–	−1.92	−0.28	3.59	–
1992	–	–	–	–	–	1.97	–	–	–	–	–	–	–	–	−3.43	6.91	8.13	–
1993	–	–	–	–	–	2.63	–	–	–	–	–	–	–	–	−0.54	6.92	7.20	–
1994	–	–	–	–	–	2.39	–	–	–	–	–	–	–	–	1.60	6.43	5.51	–
1995	–	–	–	–	–	3.88	–	–	–	–	–	–	–	–	3.59	2.04	8.13	–
1996	–	7.68	16.67	1.86	−0.03	6.37	3.09	8.91	–	–	–	7.31	7.73	10.46	2.46	2.17	4.60	–
1997	–	2.85	10.55	5.12	3.17	7.76	6.72	8.06	–	–	–	6.32	5.88	8.51	1.52	7.94	−2.09	–
1998	–	−0.13	4.57	3.97	4.13	−0.05	2.07	7.33	–	–	–	4.26	6.78	6.20	0.66	8.58	−9.91	–
1999	–	2.51	−0.67	1.75	5.83	3.86	3.68	4.45	–	–	1.77	5.11	5.45	1.14	0.36	1.74	2.48	−3.15
2000	–	1.69	6.86	2.55	3.55	2.19	3.61	5.46	–	–	2.91	2.63	4.01	2.57	2.61	7.67	5.69	6.47
2001	0.20	2.88	5.90	2.88	4.18	3.68	6.36	6.35	3.29	–	1.89	1.69	1.58	6.80	1.90	3.57	4.95	−7.23
2002	0.27	1.69	8.06	5.87	3.70	1.10	7.94	6.85	2.03	–	2.86	3.75	1.24	4.27	2.40	8.82	5.50	3.32
2003	1.54	4.74	7.87	3.53	6.78	5.33	8.45	11.03	1.47	–	3.31	1.43	−0.48	1.52	1.40	4.65	5.87	7.08
2004	2.36	3.21	8.96	3.50	0.97	3.90	10.77	10.33	10.78	4.32	3.82	4.00	2.54	4.57	4.82	1.75	6.47	7.74
2005	2.59	4.12	9.10	3.03	3.05	6.74	9.42	11.95	8.19	2.95	2.50	1.54	1.10	5.10	4.61	3.76	3.52	5.38
2006	5.01	3.88	10.31	2.36	2.75	7.06	19.41	9.29	5.92	3.96	2.28	4.18	1.53	5.74	6.99	7.83	3.48	3.36
2007	5.42	3.02	7.05	3.38	−0.45	6.64	10.89	10.60	10.25	1.47	2.96	6.44	2.58	7.09	5.18	4.97	1.77	3.10
2008	2.13	1.07	−4.95	3.02	−0.40	4.86	−6.31	4.61	6.34	0.34	2.03	5.99	1.08	5.54	−0.08	6.49	2.41	−1.01
2009	−0.35	−0.61	−14.76	−2.85	−5.77	5.39	−16.16	−16.34	−1.00	−8.09	0.72	3.44	−2.52	−0.99	−3.88	−4.23	−2.52	−2.90
2010	3.50	0.38	−1.57	−7.17	−2.81	6.22	4.58	−0.52	4.20	3.94	1.66	2.19	2.74	0.41	2.63	8.47	5.58	3.90
2011	4.74	−0.02	3.55	−9.32	0.95	7.81	4.09	6.62	4.11	3.09	3.71	3.53	−3.03	−0.84	3.58	14.47	3.72	5.09
2012	3.30	−1.36	4.64	−7.38	−2.02	3.05	4.43	4.92	4.77	3.40	4.80	0.81	−4.91	−0.76	2.20	7.89	7.15	−1.53
2013	2.47	0.25	4.07	−0.76	0.63	5.61	6.76	4.81	5.77	0.76	3.89	0.48	−0.33	−0.95	1.75	2.67	2.94	3.11
2014	3.22	1.30	3.53	1.72	3.49	4.43	3.80	4.86	9.57	0.80	3.80	2.70	3.36	1.08	0.31	4.79	−0.16	0.44
2015	–	2.90	3.58	0.74	3.90	6.93	–	–	2.86	–	4.55	3.17	3.31	2.32	–	10.09	4.48	–
2016	–	–	–	–	–	–	–	–	3.98	–	5.22	–	–	–	–	−0.26	–	–
Mean	2.60	2.10	4.67	0.89	1.78	3.14	4.93	5.77	5.16	1.54	3.04	3.55	1.98	3.49	1.45	3.82	3.65	2.07

Table 3.7a Divisia price indices (x100), 27 developed countries

Year (1)	*Australia* (2)	*Austria* (3)	*Belgium* (4)	*Canada* (5)	*Denmark* (6)	*Finland* (7)	*France* (8)	*Germany* (9)	*Hong Kong* (10)	*Iceland* (11)	*Ireland* (12)	*Israel* (13)	*Italy* (14)
1960	–	–	–	–	–	–	3.17	–	–	–	–	–	–
1961	–	–	–	–	–	–	2.95	–	–	–	–	–	–
1962	–	–	–	–	–	–	4.20	–	–	–	–	–	–
1963	–	–	–	–	–	–	4.73	–	–	–	–	–	–
1964	–	–	–	–	–	–	3.25	–	–	–	–	–	–
1965	–	–	–	–	–	–	2.61	–	–	–	–	–	–
1966	–	–	–	–	–	–	2.97	–	–	–	–	–	–
1967	–	–	–	–	–	–	3.09	–	–	–	–	–	–
1968	–	–	–	–	–	–	4.91	–	–	–	–	–	–
1969	–	–	–	–	–	–	6.85	–	–	–	–	–	–
1970	–	–	–	–	–	–	4.89	–	–	–	–	–	–
1971	–	–	–	–	–	–	5.49	–	–	–	–	–	–
1972	–	–	–	–	–	–	5.72	–	6.86	–	–	–	–
1973	–	–	–	–	–	–	7.02	–	17.49	–	–	–	–
1974	–	–	–	–	–	–	13.45	–	14.57	–	–	–	–
1975	–	–	–	–	–	–	11.04	–	1.75	–	–	–	–
1976	–	–	–	–	–	12.05	9.20	–	5.16	–	–	–	–
1977	–	–	–	–	–	10.81	8.93	–	4.74	–	–	–	–
1978	–	–	–	–	–	7.67	8.35	–	5.94	–	–	–	–
1979	–	–	–	–	–	7.16	10.38	–	12.38	–	–	–	–
1980	–	–	–	–	–	10.40	12.29	–	13.23	–	–	–	–
1981	–	–	–	–	–	10.91	12.81	–	11.40	–	–	–	–
1982	–	–	–	9.55	–	8.51	11.16	–	9.60	–	–	–	–
1983	–	–	–	6.74	–	7.55	9.13	–	9.56	–	–	–	–
1984	–	–	–	4.31	–	6.54	7.61	–	8.75	–	–	–	–
1985	–	–	–	3.79	–	5.06	6.02	–	3.10	–	–	–	–
1986	8.19	–	–	4.20	–	3.65	2.67	–	5.33	–	–	–	–
1987	6.86	–	–	3.86	–	3.04	2.96	–	5.90	–	–	–	–
1988	6.49	–	–	4.00	–	4.36	2.66	–	7.15	–	–	–	–
1989	6.48	–	–	4.40	–	5.78	3.76	–	7.92	–	–	–	–
1990	5.28	–	–	4.18	–	5.50	2.84	–	7.98	–	–	–	–
1991	2.68	–	–	4.96	–	4.47	2.70	–	9.06	–	–	–	–
1992	1.83	–	–	1.48	–	3.13	2.53	–	7.23	–	–	–	–
1993	1.80	–	–	1.71	–	3.40	1.50	–	6.36	–	–	–	–
1994	2.04	–	–	0.87	–	0.63	0.93	–	7.84	–	–	–	–
1995	2.80	–	–	1.41	–	0.52	0.93	–	7.89	–	–	–	–
1996	1.44	1.45	0.58	1.69	1.58	0.88	1.54	0.90	5.73	2.41	–	7.55	4.12
1997	1.56	1.39	1.49	1.64	1.69	1.91	0.78	1.10	4.76	−0.44	−6.36	6.96	2.17
1998	0.82	0.23	1.20	1.05	1.44	1.74	0.22	0.42	0.88	1.15	−8.18	5.68	1.93
1999	1.85	0.07	0.60	1.72	1.81	1.46	−0.48	0.32	−5.38	2.99	−8.55	5.87	1.89
2000	4.43	2.11	3.14	2.25	2.58	3.05	2.28	0.79	−3.49	5.47	−10.52	1.94	3.24
2001	2.51	2.39	2.01	1.89	2.29	2.70	1.92	1.65	−1.05	6.71	−4.53	0.62	2.62
2002	2.90	1.14	1.34	1.97	1.82	1.71	1.06	1.32	−3.54	4.93	−3.00	4.86	2.91
2003	1.60	1.58	1.55	1.79	1.28	1.02	1.66	1.95	−2.83	1.13	−2.88	0.50	2.96
2004	1.68	1.84	2.37	1.52	1.05	0.27	2.09	1.24	−0.46	3.33	−3.82	0.05	2.43
2005	2.99	2.47	2.66	1.83	1.62	0.93	1.80	1.46	1.94	4.05	−6.71	1.65	2.06
2006	3.42	2.01	3.10	1.45	2.23	1.19	2.10	1.08	1.44	6.78	−6.59	2.47	2.56
2007	3.10	2.31	2.91	1.58	1.68	1.87	2.10	1.70	4.06	4.80	−6.04	1.47	2.30
2008	2.89	2.05	3.13	1.41	2.97	3.22	2.77	1.71	2.51	10.57	0.59	5.51	3.13
2009	2.51	0.39	−0.50	0.07	1.20	1.99	−1.49	−0.47	−1.14	9.23	5.08	1.92	−0.34
2010	2.04	1.67	1.72	1.80	2.35	1.27	1.19	1.82	1.95	2.83	−0.44	3.22	1.36
2011	2.53	3.24	2.98	2.19	2.39	3.14	1.81	1.99	4.46	3.42	−0.28	2.99	2.89
2012	2.67	2.45	1.96	1.34	2.37	2.87	1.43	1.51	3.64	5.51	0.37	1.57	2.68
2013	2.38	2.16	1.10	1.26	0.77	2.47	0.68	1.21	2.42	3.49	−0.79	1.98	1.20
2014	1.61	2.04	0.52	1.68	0.80	1.59	0.12	0.90	2.55	3.11	−2.16	0.50	0.26
2015	–	1.36	–	0.89	0.52	0.38	−0.20	–	1.28	–	–	–	–
2016	–	–	–	–	–	–	–	–	1.54	–	–	–	–
2017	–	–	–	–	–	–	–	–	–	–	–	–	–
2018	–	–	–	–	–	–	–	–	–	–	–	–	–
2019	–	–	–	–	–	–	–	–	–	–	–	–	–
2020	–	–	–	–	–	–	–	–	–	–	–	–	–
Mean	3.08	1.72	1.78	2.54	1.72	3.92	4.09	1.19	4.85	4.29	−3.60	3.04	2.23

Japan (15)	*Luxembourg* (16)	*Netherlands* (17)	*New Zealand* (18)	*Norway* (19)	*Singapore* (20)	*Slovenia* (21)	*South Korea* (22)	*Spain* (23)	*Sweden* (24)	*Switzerland* (25)	*Taiwan* (26)	*UK* (27)	*USA* (28)
–	–	–	–	–	–	–	–	–	–	–	–	–	–
–	–	–	–	–	–	–	–	–	–	–	–	–	–
–	–	–	–	–	–	–	–	–	–	–	–	–	–
–	–	–	–	–	–	–	–	–	–	–	0.63	–	–
–	–	–	–	–	1.06	–	–	–	–	–	0.91	–	–
–	–	–	–	–	0.39	–	–	–	–	–	0.75	–	–
–	–	–	–	–	1.88	–	–	–	–	–	0.25	–	–
–	–	–	–	–	2.11	–	–	–	–	–	3.81	–	–
–	–	–	–	–	1.13	–	–	–	–	–	5.69	–	–
–	–	–	–	–	0.02	–	–	–	–	–	3.57	–	–
–	–	–	–	–	1.20	–	–	–	–	–	4.05	–	–
5.60	–	–	–	6.05	3.66	–	13.76	–	–	–	1.97	–	–
4.91	–	–	–	6.69	2.70	–	12.65	–	–	–	4.00	–	–
9.11	–	–	–	7.14	13.74	–	11.40	–	–	–	10.99	–	–
19.34	–	–	–	9.18	11.83	–	28.79	–	–	–	30.38	–	–
10.91	–	–	–	10.55	2.28	–	23.60	–	–	–	5.25	–	–
8.74	–	–	–	8.20	0.93	–	16.46	–	–	–	1.95	–	4.09
7.09	–	–	–	8.32	1.94	–	14.48	–	–	–	8.49	–	3.33
4.63	–	–	–	7.55	3.11	–	19.79	–	–	–	7.13	–	5.17
3.46	–	–	–	5.10	3.47	–	17.54	–	–	–	10.06	–	9.73
6.72	–	–	–	9.23	5.84	–	24.85	–	–	–	19.59	–	7.97
4.23	–	–	–	12.69	4.38	–	17.33	–	–	–	13.91	–	5.38
2.51	–	–	–	11.15	0.55	–	5.04	–	–	–	2.92	–	6.29
3.00	–	–	–	8.21	−0.37	–	3.14	–	–	–	1.60	–	6.79
2.54	–	–	–	5.73	1.86	–	3.76	–	–	–	0.92	–	8.46
2.24	–	–	–	5.45	0.24	–	3.65	–	–	–	0.69	–	10.21
0.86	–	–	–	6.86	0.09	–	1.56	–	–	–	0.69	–	8.68
0.56	–	–	–	8.01	2.38	–	3.64	–	–	–	1.59	–	5.69
0.55	–	–	5.39	5.79	3.74	–	5.61	–	–	–	0.99	–	4.51
1.87	–	–	5.90	4.82	4.35	–	6.06	–	–	–	3.56	–	3.96
2.35	–	–	4.78	4.47	4.55	–	8.85	–	–	–	3.31	–	3.67
2.50	–	–	2.05	3.52	2.20	–	10.6	–	–	–	4.06	–	2.14
1.90	–	–	1.41	2.31	1.90	–	7.71	–	–	–	3.42	–	3.29
1.32	–	–	0.37	2.54	3.99	–	6.40	–	–	–	3.19	–	3.89
0.78	–	–	1.34	0.89	5.54	–	9.27	–	2.50	–	3.58	–	4.46
0.13	–	–	2.19	2.34	1.29	–	6.14	–	2.81	–	3.15	–	4.49
0.35	1.52	1.64	1.78	1.12	0.93	10.51	6.58	2.88	1.05	−1.15	3.05	3.13	3.46
1.21	1.31	2.08	1.26	2.47	2.23	8.05	5.94	2.71	1.26	−1.68	1.37	2.45	2.83
−0.76	1.24	2.40	1.63	2.36	−2.08	6.60	5.68	1.66	0.30	−2.17	1.47	1.55	2.64
−0.20	2.48	2.03	0.55	2.07	−2.36	6.19	2.83	2.16	1.32	−2.01	1.02	0.68	2.08
−0.66	4.51	3.05	2.35	2.91	−0.96	7.34	4.55	4.06	0.92	−1.71	1.04	0.60	2.08
−1.04	0.82	3.39	2.06	2.24	−0.81	7.33	4.23	3.50	1.71	−2.02	−0.25	0.22	2.12
−1.45	1.65	3.26	1.81	1.60	−1.41	7.46	3.29	2.87	1.43	−0.23	0.25	0.40	1.69
−1.20	1.98	2.01	0.46	2.59	−0.31	5.35	3.31	3.18	1.74	−0.40	−0.39	0.87	0.70
−0.25	3.08	1.61	1.67	0.92	0.54	2.90	3.20	3.57	0.74	−1.81	1.29	1.57	1.42
−0.23	3.84	1.61	2.00	1.19	0.01	2.24	2.47	3.31	0.98	−1.48	1.16	1.73	2.46
0.29	2.79	2.76	2.78	1.68	1.84	2.37	1.59	3.61	1.14	−1.39	0.79	2.55	1.84
−0.39	2.51	2.51	1.77	1.22	4.81	4.02	1.85	3.31	1.44	−2.29	1.29	1.98	1.32
1.29	3.13	2.36	3.93	3.34	5.82	5.37	3.92	3.56	3.06	−1.41	2.82	3.31	2.04
−2.13	−0.14	−0.91	1.93	2.34	1.01	0.97	2.18	−0.84	1.83	−1.14	−1.15	0.41	2.49
−0.75	2.14	0.97	1.86	2.37	3.79	1.46	2.78	1.91	1.87	−1.64	0.79	2.05	2.81
0.21	3.62	1.95	2.50	0.99	4.86	1.79	3.64	2.43	1.85	−0.79	0.91	3.66	2.68
0.77	2.50	1.40	0.67	1.15	3.71	1.44	2.13	2.37	0.53	−2.73	1.19	2.08	2.47
−0.64	1.34	2.13	0.75	1.84	1.36	0.94	1.11	0.97	0.69	−2.23	0.31	2.20	3.04
2.08	0.62	1.23	0.79	1.90	1.24	0.12	1.21	0.18	0.83	–	0.67	1.95	0.07
−0.22	−0.72	–	–	–	0.49	−0.43	0.94	–	0.76	–	−0.71	0.64	1.71
–	–	–	–	–	−0.44	–	–	–	–	–	0.85		2.48
–	–	–	–	–	–	–	–	–	–	–	–	–	1.95
–	–	–	–	–	–	–	–	–	–	–	–	–	1.31
–	–	–	–	–	–	–	–	–	–	–	–	–	1.43
–	–	–	–	–	–	–	–	–	–	–	–	–	0.28
2.31	2.01	2.03	2.07	4.52	2.23	4.10	7.68	2.49	1.40	−1.57	3.42	1.70	3.59

Table 3.7b Divisia price indices (x100), 18 developing countries (cont.)

Year	*Colombia*	*Czech Republic*	*Estonia*	*Greece*	*Hungary*	*India*	*Latvia*	*Lithuania*	*Malaysia*	*Mexico*	*Philippines*	*Poland*	*Portugal*	*Slovakia*	*South Africa*	*Sri Lanka*	*Thailand*	*Turkey*
(1)	*(2)*	*(3)*	*(4)*	*(5)*	*(6)*	*(7)*	*(8)*	*(9)*	*(10)*	*(11)*	*(12)*	*(13)*	*(14)*	*(15)*	*(16)*	*(17)*	*(18)*	*(19)*
1960	–	–	–	–	–	–	–	–	–	–	–	–	–	–	–	–	–	–
1961	–	–	–	–	–	–	–	–	–	–	–	–	–	–	–	–	–	–
1962	–	–	–	–	–	–	–	–	–	–	–	–	–	–	–	–	–	–
1963	–	–	–	–	–	–	–	–	–	–	–	–	–	–	–	–	–	–
1964	–	–	–	–	–	–	–	–	–	–	–	–	–	–	–	–	–	–
1965	–	–	–	–	–	–	–	–	–	–	–	–	–	–	–	–	–	–
1966	–	–	–	–	–	–	–	–	–	–	–	–	–	–	–	–	–	–
1967	–	–	–	–	–	–	–	–	–	–	–	–	–	–	–	–	–	–
1968	–	–	–	–	–	–	–	–	–	–	–	–	–	–	–	–	–	–
1969	–	–	–	–	–	–	–	–	–	–	–	–	–	–	–	–	1.38	–
1970	–	–	–	–	–	–	–	–	–	–	–	–	–	–	–	–	−0.26	–
1971	–	–	–	–	–	4.41	–	–	–	–	–	–	–	–	–	–	1.45	–
1972	–	–	–	–	–	11.15	–	–	–	–	–	–	–	–	–	–	4.18	–
1973	–	–	–	–	–	17.41	–	–	–	–	–	–	–	–	–	–	13.54	–
1974	–	–	–	–	–	18.41	–	–	–	–	–	–	–	–	–	–	19.44	–
1975	–	–	–	–	–	−5.45	–	–	–	–	–	–	–	–	–	–	5.27	–
1976	–	–	–	–	–	2.71	–	–	–	–	–	–	–	–	9.98	3.31	1.10	–
1977	–	–	–	–	–	4.77	–	–	–	–	–	–	–	–	10.31	4.80	5.92	–
1978	–	–	–	–	–	12.92	–	–	–	–	–	–	–	–	9.49	13.54	8.09	–
1979	–	–	–	–	–	7.77	–	–	–	–	–	–	–	–	11.41	13.17	10.12	–
1980	–	–	–	–	–	14.49	–	–	–	–	–	–	–	–	11.39	21.24	16.36	–
1981	–	–	–	–	–	9.12	–	–	–	–	–	–	–	–	13.92	12.07	10.95	–
1982	–	–	–	–	–	6.54	–	–	–	–	–	–	–	–	13.15	13.73	5.87	–
1983	–	–	–	–	–	8.85	–	–	–	–	–	–	–	–	12.57	17.45	3.65	–
1984	–	–	–	–	–	5.99	–	–	–	–	–	–	–	–	9.72	17.35	0.88	–
1985	–	–	–	–	–	5.50	–	–	–	–	–	–	–	–	17.13	2.85	3.27	–

1986	–	–	–	–	–	6.85	–	–	–	–	–	–	–	–	16.45	8.21	3.63	–
1987	–	–	–	–	–	7.64	–	–	–	–	–	–	–	–	14.47	3.50	2.85	–
1988	–	–	–	–	–	8.52	–	–	–	–	–	–	–	–	12.99	11.62	4.38	–
1989	–	–	–	–	–	7.02	–	–	–	–	–	–	–	–	14.33	11.57	5.64	–
1990	–	–	–	–	–	9.79	–	–	–	–	–	–	–	–	14.66	33.48	5.85	–
1991	–	–	–	–	–	12.75	–	–	–	–	–	–	–	–	13.85	15.8	5.65	–
1992	–	–	–	–	–	5.86	–	–	–	–	–	–	–	–	13.59	3.79	2.53	–
1993	–	–	–	–	–	7.59	–	–	–	–	–	–	–	–	9.67	5.88	2.84	–
1994	–	–	–	–	–	10.89	–	–	–	–	–	–	–	–	9.53	7.68	5.26	–
1995	–	–	–	–	–	9.74	–	–	–	–	–	–	–	–	7.86	8.27	4.35	–
1996	–	7.76	21.82	7.53	20.41	6.79	12.92	16.19	–	–	–	18.22	−2.28	0.87	7.23	10.73	5.15	–
1997	–	8.52	10.16	4.55	16.44	−2.02	7.40	6.60	–	–	–	13.94	0.37	1.69	8.28	2.10	4.97	–
1998	–	8.37	7.23	4.77	12.46	11.81	4.73	5.23	–	–	–	10.05	0.56	3.97	6.18	6.01	7.56	–
1999	–	2.40	4.03	2.83	8.71	5.98	3.10	0.18	–	–	5.86	6.30	1.58	8.65	7.07	7.74	0.62	42.77
2000	–	3.51	3.25	3.12	10.87	2.49	2.81	−0.98	–	–	4.05	9.43	3.03	7.43	7.99	7.19	0.77	42.93
2001	7.84	3.67	6.30	3.72	9.64	2.21	2.34	1.22	1.25	–	6.20	3.56	2.85	5.44	6.27	10.22	2.24	42.39
2002	5.54	1.61	3.75	2.52	6.36	1.55	5.51	−0.23	1.72	–	3.06	2.91	2.95	3.02	7.83	1.98	0.97	31.78
2003	5.96	−0.06	2.23	2.57	4.16	4.02	5.19	−1.50	0.97	–	3.26	0.56	3.12	6.50	5.26	5.28	1.95	20.21
2004	5.88	3.25	4.16	3.26	5.87	2.55	6.30	0.38	1.27	5.53	6.27	4.63	2.00	7.02	6.64	8.93	3.05	11.21
2005	4.45	1.17	4.46	2.87	3.80	8.57	9.54	2.46	2.60	4.59	6.65	2.14	3.57	2.96	4.57	9.12	4.27	8.00
2006	4.51	1.90	6.18	3.16	3.19	5.87	9.85	4.42	2.61	3.31	5.33	1.49	3.23	4.93	2.95	8.18	4.48	9.48
2007	4.49	2.99	7.76	3.60	7.07	4.58	11.42	6.69	1.63	4.89	3.30	2.21	3.07	2.57	6.57	13.24	2.73	6.43
2008	5.71	4.90	8.09	4.21	5.62	6.29	12.25	10.09	4.14	6.30	8.87	4.00	2.55	4.54	7.96	18.04	5.53	9.94
2009	3.70	0.69	−0.44	1.07	3.76	6.42	−3.14	3.51	1.19	4.93	2.00	2.53	−2.11	0.32	7.45	3.65	0.55	4.25
2010	2.62	0.62	3.36	3.57	3.89	8.20	−2.57	1.07	1.64	4.34	3.94	2.48	1.81	1.11	4.47	5.18	3.80	8.35
2011	4.51	1.49	5.44	2.12	3.60	1.61	6.01	4.48	2.77	3.30	4.83	4.82	1.62	3.96	5.48	6.48	3.98	9.72
2012	2.63	2.15	4.01	0.32	5.98	9.93	3.31	3.23	1.58	3.83	2.97	3.26	1.87	3.50	6.09	7.51	2.52	7.52
2013	2.10	0.87	2.92	−1.88	1.72	7.25	0.21	1.69	1.69	2.84	2.14	0.35	0.82	1.39	5.36	6.04	2.10	6.35
2014	3.07	0.73	0.83	−2.47	0.84	3.87	0.64	0.69	2.62	4.12	2.52	−0.13	0.41	−0.07	5.69	3.20	1.62	6.66
2015	–	0.09	0.19	−1.32	−0.28	−1.26	–	–	1.82	–	0.82	−1.38	0.86	−0.12	–	0.64	−0.64	–
2016	–	–	–	–	–	–	–	–	2.35	–	1.29	–	–	–	–	3.68	–	–
Mean	4.50	2.83	5.29	2.51	6.71	6.84	5.15	3.44	1.99	4.36	4.08	4.57	1.59	3.48	9.38	9.13	4.45	16.75

Table 3.8a Divisia quantity correlations (x100), 27 developed countries

Year	*Australia*	*Austria*	*Belgium*	*Canada*	*Denmark*	*Finland*	*France*	*Germany*	*Hong Kong*	*Iceland*	*Ireland*	*Israel*	*Italy*
(1)	*(2)*	*(3)*	*(4)*	*(5)*	*(6)*	*(7)*	*(8)*	*(9)*	*(10)*	*(11)*	*(12)*	*(13)*	*(14)*
1960	–	–	–	–	–	–	0.15	–	–	–	–	–	–
1961	–	–	–	–	–	–	−0.19	–	–	–	–	–	–
1962	–	–	–	–	–	–	−0.61	–	–	–	–	–	–
1963	–	–	–	–	–	–	−0.42	–	–	–	–	–	–
1964	–	–	–	–	–	–	−0.41	–	–	–	–	–	–
1965	–	–	–	–	–	–	0.31	–	–	–	–	–	–
1966	–	–	–	–	–	–	−0.01	–	–	–	–	–	–
1967	–	–	–	–	–	–	0.42	–	–	–	–	–	–
1968	–	–	–	–	–	–	0.07	–	–	–	–	–	–
1969	–	–	–	–	–	–	0.41	–	–	–	–	–	–
1970	–	–	–	–	–	–	0.32	–	–	–	–	–	–
1971	–	–	–	–	–	–	0.23	–	–	–	–	–	–
1972	–	–	–	–	–	–	−0.73	–	0.38	–	–	–	–
1973	–	–	–	–	–	–	−0.26	–	−0.65	–	–	–	–
1974	–	–	–	–	–	–	−0.21	–	−0.77	–	–	–	–
1975	–	–	–	–	–		−0.35	–	0.61	–	–	–	–
1976	–	–	–	–	–	−0.64	−0.04	–	0.01	–	–	–	–
1977	–	–	–	–	–	−0.70	−0.24	–	−0.78	–	–	–	–
1978	–	–	–	–	–	−0.74	−0.20	–	−0.80	–	–	–	–
1979	–	–	–	–	–	0.33	−0.33	–	−0.52	–	–	–	–
1980	–	–	–	–	–	−0.64	−0.39	–	0.11	–	–	–	–
1981	–	–	–	–	–	−0.21	−0.77	–	0.02	–	–	–	–
1982	–	–	–	−0.24	–	−0.60	−0.51	–	0.21	–	–	–	–
1983	–	–	–	−0.45	–	−0.22	−0.15	–	−0.61	–	–	–	–
1984	–	–	–	−0.73	–	−0.35	−0.18	–	−0.38	–	–	–	–
1985	–	–	–	−0.37	–	−0.75	−0.33	–	0.57	–	–	–	–
1986	−0.24	–	–	−0.50	–	0.49	−0.35	–	0.63	–	–	–	–
1987	−0.20	–	–	−0.62	–	0.37	−0.37	–	0.09	–	–	–	–
1988	−0.52	–	–	−0.43	–	−0.12	−0.49	–	−0.67	–	–	–	–
1989	−0.13	–	–	−0.50	–	0.52	−0.33	–	0.03	–	–	–	–
1990	−0.16	–	–	−0.50	–	0.11	−0.61	–	0.08	–	–	–	–
1991	−0.29	–	–	−0.46	–	0.04	−0.05	–	−0.80	–	–	–	–
1992	−0.60	–	–	−0.40	–	0.05	−0.04	–	−0.62	–	–	–	–
1993	−0.20	–	–	0.50	–	−0.17	−0.30	–	0.21	–	–	–	–
1994	−0.34	–	–	−0.39	–	−0.50	−0.18	–	−0.42	–	–	–	–
1995	−0.70	–	–	−0.61	–	−0.17	−0.54	–	−0.07	–	–	–	–
1996	−0.68	−0.15	−0.25	0.48	−0.29	0.15	−0.28	0.03	0.50	0.47		−0.18	−0.69
1997	−0.47	−0.76	−0.14	0.00	−0.84	−0.51	−0.57	−0.22	−0.46	−0.70	−0.98	0.02	−0.36
1998	−0.74	−0.80	−0.32	−0.05	−0.28	−0.62	−0.82	−0.74	0.42	−0.79	−0.86	−0.04	−0.11
1999	−0.68	−0.88	−0.17	−0.16	−0.70	−0.45	−0.63	−0.77	0.35	−0.62	−0.92	−0.73	−0.66
2000	−0.46	−0.71	0.21	−0.52	−0.31	−0.67	−0.60	−0.90	0.09	−0.43	−0.96	0.20	−0.67
2001	−0.22	−0.37	−0.54	−0.37	−0.04	−0.15	−0.76	−0.76	0.24	−0.22	−0.92	−0.28	−0.59
2002	−0.64	−0.70	−0.18	−0.49	−0.66	−0.43	−0.52	−0.25	−0.24	−0.09	−0.91	−0.26	−0.53
2003	−0.85	−0.43	0.55	−0.50	−0.48	−0.64	−0.71	−0.39	−0.72	0.25	−0.94	−0.40	−0.27
2004	−0.68	−0.40	−0.67	−0.62	0.10	−0.54	−0.82	−0.53	0.67	0.05	−0.94	0.09	−0.52
2005	−0.41	−0.56	−0.43	−0.39	−0.32	−0.10	−0.62	−0.71	0.58	−0.69	−0.93	−0.28	−0.41
2006	−0.69	−0.65	0.04	−0.72	−0.34	−0.72	−0.65	−0.63	−0.32	−0.63	−0.96	−0.46	−0.74
2007	−0.47	−0.45	−0.44	−0.66	−0.83	−0.69	−0.54	−0.76	0.56	−0.28	−0.83	−0.67	−0.76
2008	0.30	−0.71	0.06	−0.29	−0.46	−0.86	−0.37	−0.54	0.55	−0.60	−0.84	0.25	−0.64
2009	0.16	−0.54	0.13	0.19	0.45	0.26	−0.35	−0.81	−0.20	−0.85	−0.81	0.37	0.07
2010	−0.63	−0.42	−0.45	−0.12	−0.13	−0.15	−0.81	−0.51	−0.09	−0.17	−0.90	−0.06	−0.74
2011	−0.40	−0.52	−0.52	−0.30	−0.48	−0.46	−0.58	−0.18	−0.24	−0.18	−0.91	−0.74	−0.74
2012	−0.02	−0.41	−0.05	0.17	−0.85	−0.44	−0.67	−0.82	−0.78	0.28	−0.26	0.06	−0.20
2013	−0.75	0.32	−0.57	0.29	−0.19	−0.14	−0.78	−0.68	−0.87	−0.07	−0.98	−0.52	0.24
2014	−0.47	0.02	−0.32	−0.51	−0.57	−0.22	−0.86	−0.08	0.35	−0.34	−0.98	−0.47	−0.10
2015	–	−0.13	–	−0.59	−0.71	0.04	−0.39	–	−0.06	–	–	–	–
2016	–	–	–	–	–	–	–	–	0.88	–	–	–	–
2017	–	–	–	–	–	–	–	–	–	–	–	–	–
2018	–	–	–	–	–	–	–	–	–	–	–	–	–
2019	–	–	–	–	–	–	–	–	–	–	–	–	–
2020	–	–	–	–	–	–	–	–	–	–	–	–	–
Mean	−0.42	−0.46	−0.21	−0.32	−0.40	−0.28	−0.36	−0.54	−0.07	−0.30	−0.88	−0.22	−0.44

Japan (15)	*Luxembourg* (16)	*Netherlands* (17)	*New Zealand* (18)	*Norway* (19)	*Singapore* (20)	*Slovenia* (21)	*South Korea* (22)	*Spain* (23)	*Sweden* (24)	*Switzerland* (25)	*Taiwan* (26)	*UK* (27)	*USA* (28)
–	–	–	–	–	–	–	–	–	–	–	–	–	–
–	–	–	–	–	–	–	–	–	–	–	–	–	–
–	–	–	–	–	–	–	–	–	–	–	–	–	–
–	–	–	–	–	–	–	–	–	–	–	0.57	–	–
–	–	–	–	–	−0.41	–	–	–	–	–	−0.55	–	–
–	–	–	–	–	−0.31	–	–	–	–	–	−0.30	–	–
–	–	–	–	–	−0.69	–	–	–	–	–	−0.53	–	–
–	–	–	–	–	−0.48	–	–	–	–	–	−0.22	–	–
–	–	–	–	–	−0.72	–	–	–	–	–	−0.50	–	–
–	–	–	–	–	0.31	–	–	–	–	–	0.13	–	–
–	–	–	–	–	0.03	–	–	–	–	–	−0.59	–	–
0.07	–	–	–	−0.14	−0.21	–	−0.92	–	–	–	−0.45	–	–
−0.42	–	–	–	−0.39	0.65	–	0.06	–	–	–	−0.60	–	–
−0.52	–	–	–	−0.45	−0.57	–	−0.22	–	–	–	−0.63	–	–
−0.79	–	–	–	−0.33	−0.72	–	−0.42	–	–	–	−0.76	–	–
0.10	–	–	–	−0.77	−0.15	–	−0.52	–	–	–	−0.51	–	
−0.76	–	–	–	−0.27	−0.31	–	−0.29	–	–	–	0.45	–	0.29
−0.01	–	–	–	−0.35	−0.51	–	−0.42	–	–	–	0.14	–	−0.80
−0.19	–	–	–	−0.42	0.42	–	−0.57	–	–	–	−0.06	–	−0.96
0.03	–	–	–	−0.06	−0.34	–	−0.35	–	–	–	0.49	–	−0.75
−0.67	–	–	–	−0.59	−0.56	–	0.07	–	–	–	−0.08	–	−0.47
−0.19	–	–	–	−0.82	−0.72	–	−0.48	–	–	–	−0.49	–	−0.06
−0.44	–	–	–	−0.46	−0.77	–	−0.14	–	–	–	−0.42	–	−0.40
−0.32	–	–	–	−0.22	−0.82	–	0.07	–	–	–	0.55	–	−0.72
−0.66	–	–	–	−0.69	−0.05	–	−0.33	–	–	–	0.28	–	−0.83
−0.72	–	–	–	−0.09	−0.30	–	−0.48	–	–	–	−0.23	–	−0.77
−0.18	–	–	–	−0.24	0.27	–	−0.12	–	–	–	−0.44	–	−0.15
0.09	–	–	–	−0.38	0.21	–	−0.08	–	–	–	0.61	–	−0.22
−0.53	–	–	−0.56	−0.18	0.40	–	−0.19	–	–	–	−0.83	–	−0.32
−0.19	–	–	−0.86	−0.05	0.30	–	−0.26	–	–	–	−0.39	–	−0.80
−0.50	–	–	0.26	0.82	−0.42	–	−0.11	–	–	–	−0.24	–	−0.11
−0.61	–	–	−0.50	−0.77	0.19	–	−0.41	–	–	–	−0.01	–	−0.62
0.06	–	–	−0.65	−0.41	0.28	–	0.28	–	–	–	−0.43	–	−0.38
0.46	–	–	−0.29	−0.62	0.35	–	−0.12	–	–	–	0.18	–	−0.26
0.46	–	–	−0.53	−0.16	0.34	–	−0.75	–	−0.78	–	−0.23	–	−0.71
−0.39	–	–	−0.39	−0.63	0.71	–	−0.47	–	−0.06	–	0.23	–	0.32
−0.11	−0.68	0.34	−0.67	−0.67	0.23	0.03	−0.09	−0.16	−0.17	−0.98	0.10	−0.64	0.01
−0.28	−0.42	−0.71	0.00	−0.59	−0.58	−0.58	−0.14	−0.04	−0.80	−0.98	0.00	−0.24	−0.29
0.20	−0.03	−0.80	−0.83	−0.71	−0.49	−0.59	−0.32	−0.08	−0.48	−0.95	−0.51	−0.76	−0.50
−0.34	0.37	−0.81	−0.49	−0.90	0.06	0.07	−0.22	0.19	−0.01	−0.88	−0.02	−0.90	−0.55
−0.21	0.28	−0.65	−0.82	−0.68	−0.36	−0.57	−0.75	−0.45	−0.45	−0.95	0.61	−0.85	−0.61
−0.53	−0.42	−0.11	−0.41	−0.33	−0.26	−0.61	−0.33	−0.40	−0.13	−0.95	0.31	−0.83	−0.69
−0.23	0.19	−0.24	−0.62	−0.82	−0.09	0.09	−0.48	−0.52	−0.60	−0.86	−0.66	−0.79	−0.66
−0.66	−0.76	0.15	−0.76	−0.64	−0.22	−0.52	−0.12	−0.22	−0.62	−0.98	−0.22	−0.84	−0.76
−0.34	0.44	−0.52	−0.45	−0.56	−0.12	0.12	−0.45	−0.22	−0.42	−0.95	−0.25	−0.51	−0.82
−0.12	−0.28	−0.30	−0.67	−0.64	0.08	−0.13	−0.52	−0.33	−0.31	−0.94	−0.21	−0.73	−0.78
−0.09	−0.34	−0.24	−0.68	−0.63	−0.91	−0.05	−0.36	−0.13	−0.44	−0.86	−0.27	−0.86	0.18
−0.63	−0.08	−0.61	−0.63	−0.20	−0.76	−0.48	−0.47	−0.45	−0.79	−0.88	−0.68	−0.77	−0.26
−0.38	−0.66	−0.20	−0.54	−0.46	−0.32	−0.56	−0.37	−0.35	−0.54	−0.94	−0.55	−0.82	−0.78
0.37	−0.24	0.08	0.67	−0.51	0.54	−0.19	−0.72	0.29	−0.10	−0.74	−0.63	−0.25	−0.86
−0.67	−0.17	−0.39	−0.52	−0.32	0.11	−0.50	−0.13	−0.60	−0.14	−0.89	−0.56	−0.60	−0.90
−0.65	−0.06	−0.35	−0.76	−0.37	−0.64	−0.38	−0.24	−0.63	−0.48	−0.85	−0.38	−0.48	−0.84
−0.63	−0.67	−0.12	−0.69	−0.15	−0.32	−0.07	−0.51	0.13	−0.44	−0.93	−0.30	−0.57	−0.71
−0.63	−0.19	0.26	−0.61	0.22	−0.36	−0.43	0.10	0.01	−0.17	−0.94	−0.70	−0.80	−0.46
−0.39	−0.64	−0.48	−0.62	−0.26	−0.77	−0.42	−0.55	−0.01	−0.75	–	−0.86	−0.21	0.50
0.48	−0.14	–	–	–	−0.27	−0.62	−0.71	–	−0.53	–	−0.23	−0.58	−0.71
–	–	–	–	–	−0.60	–	–	–	–	–	−0.22	–	−0.65
–	–	–	–	–	–	–	–	–	–	–	–	–	−0.79
–	–	–	–	–	–	–	–	–	–	–	–	–	−0.82
–	–	–	–	–	–	–	–	–	–	–	–	–	−0.76
–	–	–	–	–	–	–	–	–	–	–	–	–	−0.37
−0.28	−0.23	−0.30	−0.50	−0.41	−0.20	−0.32	−0.32	−0.21	−0.42	−0.91	−0.22	−0.65	−0.50

Table 3.8b Divisia quantity correlations (x100), 18 developing countries (cont.)

Year	*Colombia*	*Czech Republic*	*Estonia*	*Greece*	*Hungary*	*India*	*Latvia*	*Lithuania*	*Malaysia*	*Mexico*	*Philippines*	*Poland*	*Portugal*	*Slovakia*	*South Africa*	*Sri Lanka*	*Thailand*	*Turkey*
(1)	*(2)*	*(3)*	*(4)*	*(5)*	*(6)*	*(7)*	*(8)*	*(9)*	*(10)*	*(11)*	*(12)*	*(13)*	*(14)*	*(15)*	*(16)*	*(17)*	*(18)*	*(19)*
1960	–	–	–	–	–	–	–	–	–	–	–	–	–	–	–	–	–	–
1961	–	–	–	–	–	–	–	–	–	–	–	–	–	–	–	–	–	–
1962	–	–	–	–	–	–	–	–	–	–	–	–	–	–	–	–	–	–
1963	–	–	–	–	–	–	–	–	–	–	–	–	–	–	–	–	–	–
1964	–	–	–	–	–	–	–	–	–	–	–	–	–	–	–	–	–	–
1965	–	–	–	–	–	–	–	–	–	–	–	–	–	–	–	–	–	–
1966	–	–	–	–	–	–	–	–	–	–	–	–	–	–	–	–	–	–
1967	–	–	–	–	–	–	–	–	–	–	–	–	–	–	–	–	–	–
1968	–	–	–	–	–	–	–	–	–	–	–	–	–	–	–	–	−0.07	–
1969	–	–	–	–	–	–	–	–	–	–	–	–	–	–	–	–	−0.17	–
1970	–	–	–	–	–	–	–	–	–	–	–	–	–	–	–	–	0.44	–
1971	–	–	–	–	–	0.76	–	–	–	–	–	–	–	–	–	–	0.44	–
1972	–	–	–	–	–	−0.96	–	–	–	–	–	–	–	–	–	–	−0.41	–
1973	–	–	–	–	–	−0.02	–	–	–	–	–	–	–	–	–	–	−0.33	–
1974	–	–	–	–	–	−0.17	–	–	–	–	–	–	–	–	–	–	−0.30	–
1975	–	–	–	–	–	−0.64	–	–	–	–	–	–	–	–	–	–	−0.02	–
1976	–	–	–	–	–	0.22	–	–	–	–	–	–	–	–	−0.76	−0.85	0.81	–
1977	–	–	–	–	–	−0.22	–	–	–	–	–	–	–	–	−0.45	−0.55	−0.29	–
1978	–	–	–	–	–	−0.12	–	–	–	–	–	–	–	–	−0.76	−0.72	−0.42	–
1979	–	–	–	–	–	−0.66	–	–	–	–	–	–	–	–	−0.62	−0.36	−0.60	–
1980	–	–	–	–	–	−0.70	–	–	–	–	–	–	–	–	−0.67	−0.11	0.32	–
1981	–	–	–	–	–	0.15	–	–	–	–	–	–	–	–	−0.70	−0.35	−0.73	–
1982	–	–	–	–	–	−0.26	–	–	–	–	–	–	–	–	−0.60	−0.63	0.24	–
1983	–	–	–	–	–	−0.02	–	–	–	–	–	–	–	–	0.86	−0.48	−0.48	–
1984	–	–	–	–	–	−0.35	–	–	–	–	–	–	–	–	−0.19	−0.52	0.43	–
1985	–	–	–	–	–	0.59	–	–	–	–	–	–	–	–	−0.83	0.50	−0.28	–

1986	–	–	–	–	–	−0.48	–	–	–	–	–	–	–	–	−0.48	0.09	−0.67	–
1987	–	–	–	–	–	−0.02	–	–	–	–	–	–	–	–	−0.89	−0.42	−0.69	–
1988	–	–	–	–	–	−0.34	–	–	–	–	–	–	–	–	−0.61	−0.77	−0.39	–
1989	–	–	–	–	–	−0.31	–	–	–	–	–	–	–	–	−0.45	−0.44	−0.44	–
1990	–	–	–	–	–	0.66	–	–	–	–	–	–	–	–	−0.72	−0.99	−0.03	–
1991	–	–	–	–	–	0.26	–	–	–	–	–	–	–	–	−0.69	−0.90	−0.39	–
1992	–	–	–	–	–	−0.18	–	–	–	–	–	–	–	–	−0.86	−0.88	−0.32	–
1993	–	–	–	–	–	0.09	–	–	–	–	–	–	–	–	−0.17	−0.87	0.25	–
1994	–	–	–	–	–	−0.78	–	–	–	–	–	–	–	–	−0.41	−0.03	−0.56	–
1995	–	–	–	–	–	0.40	–	–	–	–	–	–	–	–	−0.39	0.44	−0.75	–
1996	–	−0.86	0.02	0.01	−0.07	−0.08	−0.22	−0.34	–	–	–	−0.92	−0.99	−0.52	−0.38	−0.40	−0.46	–
1997	–	−0.36	−0.75	0.05	−0.39	−0.91	0.00	−0.07	–	–	–	−0.75	−0.97	−0.61	0.19	−0.69	−0.10	–
1998	–	−0.11	−0.36	−0.34	−0.50	0.58	0.50	0.17	–	–	–	−0.52	−0.95	−0.52	−0.89	−0.47	−0.18	–
1999	–	−0.91	−0.24	−0.39	−0.01	−0.09	0.10	−0.49	–	–	−0.13	−0.58	−0.69	0.16	0.19	−0.90	−0.58	0.21
2000	–	−0.41	−0.60	−0.52	−0.42	0.26	−0.04	−0.06	–	–	0.42	0.45	−0.74	−0.64	−0.08	−0.51	0.26	−0.37
2001	−0.22	−0.44	−0.73	0.11	−0.78	0.12	−0.27	0.16	0.31	–	0.54	−0.23	−0.71	−0.47	−0.33	−0.90	0.80	−0.84
2002	−0.34	−0.18	−0.86	−0.45	−0.59	0.77	−0.81	−0.12	0.14	–	−0.86	0.74	−0.67	−0.43	−0.65	−0.66	0.30	−0.59
2003	−0.22	−0.34	−0.58	0.02	−0.53	−0.61	−0.29	−0.86	0.33	–	−0.44	−0.34	−0.54	0.25	−0.44	−0.15	0.37	−0.82
2004	−0.11	−0.38	−0.58	0.12	−0.70	−0.47	−0.58	−0.62	−0.66	−0.45	0.15	−0.60	−0.78	0.02	−0.74	−0.18	−0.14	−0.78
2005	−0.21	−0.45	−0.81	0.13	−0.08	0.06	−0.32	−0.19	−0.50	−0.59	0.29	−0.25	−0.83	−0.78	−0.61	−0.70	−0.11	−0.38
2006	−0.86	−0.33	−0.63	−0.57	−0.62	−0.85	−0.68	−0.50	−0.76	−0.64	−0.71	−0.43	−0.68	−0.70	−0.85	−0.30	−0.71	−0.39
2007	−0.68	−0.40	−0.51	−0.56	−0.75	−0.24	−0.50	−0.84	−0.59	−0.34	−0.18	−0.58	−0.16	−0.64	−0.48	−0.57	−0.57	−0.48
2008	−0.35	−0.60	−0.24	−0.32	−0.46	−0.15	−0.36	−0.31	−0.78	−0.42	0.38	−0.66	−0.61	−0.87	−0.71	−0.80	−0.23	−0.06
2009	0.25	0.19	0.24	−0.34	0.33	−0.78	−0.73	−0.46	−0.08	−0.56	0.10	0.20	0.16	−0.72	0.18	−0.17	0.05	0.14
2010	−0.21	0.21	−0.33	−0.63	−0.82	−0.80	−0.11	−0.32	−0.72	0.00	−0.27	−0.92	−0.03	−0.21	0.04	−0.38	−0.57	−0.31
2011	−0.28	−0.05	0.01	−0.19	0.24	−0.85	−0.49	−0.57	−0.72	−0.02	−0.10	−0.25	−0.73	−0.16	−0.11	−0.28	−0.57	0.72
2012	−0.47	−0.02	−0.34	−0.46	−0.41	−0.91	−0.33	−0.65	−0.80	−0.85	−0.23	−0.56	0.11	−0.37	−0.07	0.85	−0.28	−0.74
2013	−0.12	−0.80	−0.54	−0.12	−0.38	0.24	−0.33	−0.84	−0.46	−0.39	−0.47	−0.72	−0.12	−0.39	−0.29	−0.43	−0.52	0.63
2014	−0.55	−0.27	−0.32	−0.15	0.00	−0.72	−0.06	−0.60	−0.17	−0.77	−0.36	−0.50	−0.37	−0.25	−0.47	−0.69	0.80	0.54
2015	–	−0.63	0.05	−0.60	0.46	0.22	–	–	−0.75	–	0.06	−0.48	−0.60	−0.72	–	−0.77	0.24	–
2016	–	–	–	–	–	–	–	–	−0.05	–	−0.01	–	–	–	–	−0.58	–	–
Mean	−0.31	−0.36	−0.41	−0.26	−0.32	−0.18	−0.29	−0.40	−0.39	−0.46	−0.10	−0.40	−0.55	−0.43	−0.43	−0.45	−0.16	−0.22

Table 3.9 Mean Divisia price and quantity indices and variances, price-quantity correlation and income flexibility, 45 countries

Country (1)	Divisia quantity index $D\bar{Q}$ (2)	Divisia price index $D\bar{P}$ (3)	Divisia quantity variance $\bar{K}$ (4)	Divisia price variance $\bar{\Pi}$ (5)	Divisia price-quantity correlation $\bar{\rho}$ (6)	Income flexibility (eq. 3.15) ϕ (7)	Income flexibility (eq. 3.19) ϕ (8)
Developed countries							
1 Australia	1.86	3.08	6.31	4.73	−0.42	−0.49	−0.51 (0.05)
2 Austria	0.99	1.72	5.18	4.27	−0.46	−0.51	−0.77 (0.06)
3 Belgium	0.75	1.78	5.65	5.20	−0.21	−0.22	−0.38 (0.08)
4 Canada	1.54	2.54	4.91	3.34	−0.32	−0.39	−0.43 (0.05)
5 Denmark	0.86	1.72	9.58	3.05	−0.40	−0.71	−0.85 (0.10)
6 Finland	1.83	3.92	11.69	6.46	−0.28	−0.38	−0.49 (0.07)
7 France	2.21	4.09	6.03	4.24	−0.36	−0.43	−0.70 (0.05)
8 Germany	0.90	1.19	7.15	3.82	−0.54	−0.74	−0.96 (0.07)
9 Hong Kong	3.86	4.85	31.43	10.21	−0.06	−0.11	−0.47 (0.09)
10 Iceland	2.27	4.29	43.69	20.52	−0.30	−0.44	−0.82 (0.10)
11 Ireland	7.48	−3.60	123.04	38.20	−0.88	−1.58	−1.66 (0.05)
12 Israel	1.62	3.04	11.57	8.28	−0.22	−0.26	−0.35 (0.08)
13 Italy	0.26	2.23	5.32	4.17	−0.44	−0.50	−0.66 (0.07)
14 Japan	2.12	2.31	8.14	4.17	−0.28	−0.39	−0.50 (0.07)
15 Luxembourg	0.68	2.01	19.10	6.17	−0.23	−0.40	−0.52 (0.10)
16 Netherlands	0.77	2.03	18.38	5.31	−0.30	−0.56	−0.72 (0.16)
17 New Zealand	1.58	2.07	12.16	8.02	−0.50	−0.62	−0.67 (0.06)
18 Norway	2.18	4.52	14.83	5.56	−0.41	−0.67	−0.73 (0.06)
19 Singapore	3.33	2.23	20.63	8.92	−0.20	−0.30	−0.27 (0.07)
20 Slovenia	1.78	4.10	10.44	6.09	−0.32	−0.42	−0.46 (0.09)
21 South Korea	4.33	7.68	24.35	13.19	−0.32	−0.43	−0.54 (0.05)
22 Spain	0.77	2.50	8.06	4.03	−0.21	−0.30	−0.49 (0.09)
23 Sweden	1.85	1.40	7.73	4.05	−0.42	−0.58	−0.50 (0.07)
24 Switzerland	2.87	−1.57	16.09	4.97	−0.91	−1.64	−1.49 (0.04)

25 Taiwan	5.[illegible]3	3.42	17.29	7.11	−0.22	−0.34	−0.33 (0.08)
26 UK	1.[illegible]3	1.70	8.84	7.37	−0.65	−0.71	−0.75 (0.05)
27 USA	2.[illegible]0	3.59	5.91	5.09	−0.50	−0.54	−0.58 (0.04)
Mean (*Developed*)	2.[illegible]3	2.55	17.17	7.65	−0.38	−0.54	−0.65 (0.01)
Developing countries							
28 Colombia	2.[illegible]0	4.50	7.53	4.41	−0.31	−0.41	−0.70 (0.09)
29 Czech Republic	2.[illegible]0	2.83	13.42	8.8	−0.36	−0.44	−0.49 (0.10)
30 Estonia	4.[illegible]7	5.29	34.72	17.42	−0.40	−0.56	−0.44 (0.09)
31 Greece	0.[illegible]9	2.51	36.26	7.57	−0.26	−0.57	−0.72 (0.15)
32 Hungary	1.[illegible]8	6.71	15.71	11.98	−0.32	−0.37	−0.45 (0.08)
33 India	3.[illegible]4	6.84	19.54	40.85	−0.18	−0.12	−0.17 (0.03)
34 Latvia	4.[illegible]3	5.15	83.93	36.19	−0.29	−0.44	−0.67 (0.13)
35 Lithuania	5.[illegible]7	3.44	55.40	22.60	−0.40	−0.63	−0.43 (0.12)
36 Malaysia	5.[illegible]6	1.99	17.68	2.73	−0.39	−0.99	−0.68 (0.28)
37 Mexico	1.[illegible]4	4.36	18.30	10.39	−0.46	−0.61	−0.67 (0.10)
38 Philippines	3.[illegible]4	4.08	2.56	4.76	−0.10	−0.07	−0.03 (0.08)
39 Poland	3.[illegible]5	4.57	33.15	23.96	−0.39	−0.46	−0.80 (0.05)
40 Portugal	1.[illegible]8	1.59	29.38	26.88	−0.55	−0.58	−0.80 (0.06)
41 Slovakia	3.[illegible]9	3.48	27.97	16.00	−0.43	−0.57	−0.50 (0.08)
42 South Africa	1.[illegible]5	9.38	17.05	13.71	−0.43	−0.48	−0.47 (0.05)
43 Sri Lanka	3.[illegible]2	9.13	100.98	48.79	−0.45	−0.65	−0.80 (0.07)
44 Thailand	3.[illegible]5	4.45	47.20	12.89	−0.16	−0.31	0.37 (0.13)
45 Turkey	2.[illegible]7	16.75	31.87	33.97	−0.22	−0.21	−0.28 (0.08)
Mean (*Developing*)	3.[illegible]9	5.39	32.93	19.11	−0.34	−0.47	−0.49 (0.03)
Mean (*All countries*)	2.[illegible]1	3.69	23.47	12.23	−0.37	−0.51	−0.59 (0.01)

Note: Columns (2) and (3) are to be div[illegible]ded by 100, and columns (4) and (5) are to be divided by 10,000.

The overall annual price growth in the 45 countries presented in column (3) of the table varies between −3.6 percent (Ireland) and 16.8 percent (Turkey) with an overall cross-country average of 3.7 percent per annum. It is also observable that the overall cross-country average price growth in developing countries is twice that of the growth in the developed countries. Columns (4) and (5) of the table present the quantity and price variances for each country averaged over the sample period for each country. As before, the last row of the table gives the mean variance for each country averaged over the whole sample period. A comparison of these two variances reveals that the Divisia quantity variances systematically exceed the corresponding Divisia price variances. To confirm this relationship, in Figure 3.1, we plot $\sqrt{\bar{K}^c}$ against $\sqrt{\bar{\Pi}^c}$ for $c=1, \ldots, 45$. As can be seen, most of the points lie above the 45o line, indicating that, on average, the quantity variance systematically exceeds the price variance. This pattern agrees well with the results of Chen (2001), Clements (1982), Clements et al. (2020), Meisner (1979), Rathnayaka et al. (2019), Selvanathan and Selvanathan (1993, 2003), and Theil and Suhm (1981).

Column (6) of Table 3.9 presents the mean Divisia price-quantity correlations for each country averaged over the whole sample period. As can be seen, all correlations presented in the table are negative with a cross-country average of −0.4. Figure 3.2 plots a frequency histogram of all the price-quantity correlations pooled over time and countries (ρ_{ct} for $t=1, \ldots, T$ and $c=1, 2, \ldots, 45$), given in Table 3.8. Again, the majority of the correlations are negative with a central value around −0.4. The negative correlation values reflect the tendency of the consumer to move away from commodities having above average price increases. Column (7) of Table 3.9 presents the

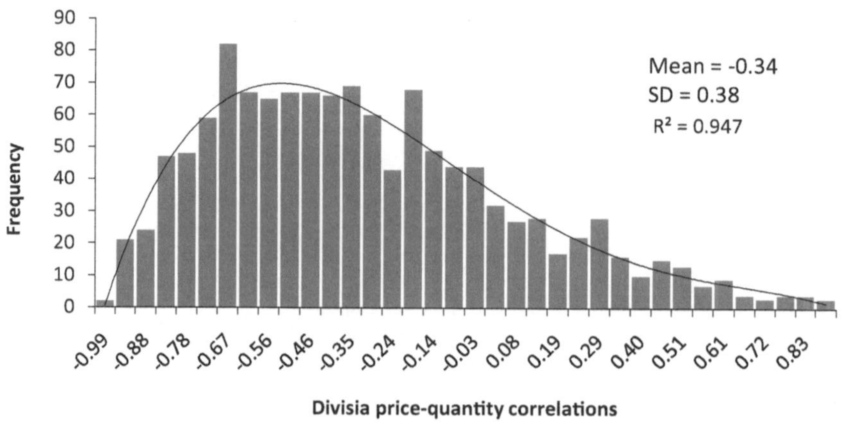

Figure 3.1 Quantity standard deviation vs price standard deviation, all countries (at sample means).

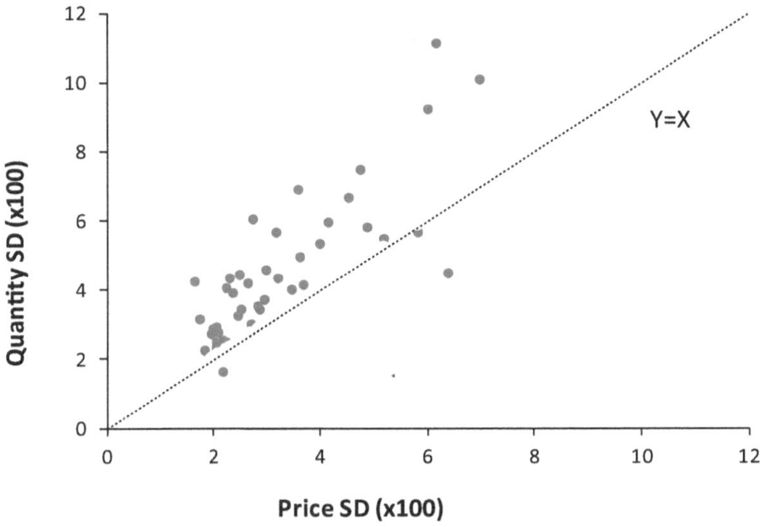

Figure 3.2 Frequency distribution of price-quantity correlations, all countries.

estimates of income flexibility ϕ calculated as in equation (3.15). As can be seen, all the estimates in that column are negative as they should be and are close to −0.5, which is well in agreement with previous studies (Clements et al. 2020, Rathnayaka et al. 2019, Selvanathan and Selvanathan 1993, 2003, and Theil and Suhm 1981). We shall discuss the last column of Table 3.9 in Section 3.4.

3.4 Relative Prices, Relative Consumption and Income Flexibility

Now we analyse the movements of relative consumption and relative prices in the form of frequency distributions and scatter plots. As a byproduct of this analysis, we derive estimates for income flexibility and construct its sampling distribution.

Table 3.10 presents a frequency distribution (in percentages) of joint signs of relative consumption and relative prices for the 45 countries for all goods. To obtain these percentage frequency distributions for a country for all goods, we first group all the pairs (relative consumption, relative prices) into four subgroups, namely, (a) (positive relative consumption, positive relative prices), (b) (positive relative consumption, negative relative prices), (c) (negative relative consumption, positive relative prices), and (d) (negative relative consumption, negative relative prices); next, we count the frequencies for each group and express each frequency as a proportion of the total number of paired observations. Columns (2) and (3) of the table give the summary in percentage of (a) (positive relative consumption, positive relative prices)

Table 3.10 Frequencies of joint signs of relative consumption and relative price changes for all goods combined (in percentages)

	Positive consumption		*Negative consumption*		*Opposite signs*
Country	*Positive price*	*Negative price*	*Positive price*	*Negative price*	*(3) + (4)*
(1)	*(2)*	*(3)*	*(4)*	*(5)*	*(6)*
Developed countries					
1 Australia	14	34	34	19	68
2 Austria	18	36	28	18	64
3 Belgium	20	31	29	20	60
4 Canada	15	30	35	20	65
5 Denmark	16	32	30	22	62
6 Finland	21	33	29	18	62
7 France	19	29	31	21	60
8 Germany	15	36	33	15	69
9 Hong Kong	18	24	34	24	58
10 Iceland	16	33	31	20	64
11 Ireland	6	44	45	5	89
12 Israel	23	32	25	20	57
13 Italy	18	35	27	19	62
14 Japan	23	30	28	19	58
15 Luxembourg	20	31	27	22	58
16 Netherlands	21	33	28	18	61
17 New Zealand	15	33	34	18	67
18 Norway	15	31	36	18	67
19 Singapore	17	31	30	21	61
20 Slovenia	16	33	28	23	61
21 South Korea	21	33	26	21	59
22 Spain	20	32	24	24	56
23 Sweden	19	33	33	15	66
24 Switzerland	5	44	46	5	90
25 Taiwan	19	34	27	20	61
26 UK	15	35	38	11	73
27 USA	13	38	37	12	75
Mean (*Developed*)	17	33	32	18	65
Developing countries					
28 Colombia	17	33	30	20	63
29 Czech Republic	18	37	28	18	65
30 Estonia	21	32	28	19	60
31 Greece	21	28	29	23	57
32 Hungary	13	35	32	20	67
33 India	16	28	29	27	57
34 Latvia	20	35	27	18	62
35 Lithuania	18	28	30	24	58
36 Malaysia	13	38	27	22	65
37 Mexico	11	35	33	22	68
38 Philippines	22	26	28	24	54
39 Poland	21	32	27	20	59
40 Portugal	18	31	39	13	70
41 Slovakia	21	37	28	14	65
42 South Africa	18	34	31	16	65
43 Sri Lanka	15	32	30	23	62
44 Thailand	17	26	27	30	53
45 Turkey	19	34	29	18	63
Mean (*Developing*)	18	32	30	21	62
Mean (*All countries*)	17	33	31	19	64

and (b) (positive relative consumption, negative relative prices), respectively. That is, the column (2) entry for a particular country gives the proportion of positive consumption that corresponds to positive price during the sample period. Similarly, column (3) gives the proportion of positive consumption that corresponds to negative prices, column (4) gives the proportion of negative consumption that corresponds to positive prices and column (5) gives the proportion of negative consumption that corresponds to negative prices. For example, in Australia, relative prices and relative consumption for all goods move in the opposite direction 34 + 34 = 68 percent of the time while they move in the same direction 14 + 19 = 33 percent of the time. Column (6) presents, for each country, the total percentage of opposite signs of relative consumption and relative prices. As can be seen, from the "all countries" row, overall, 33 + 31 = 64 percent of the pairs of relative prices and consumption across the 45 countries have opposite signs, while 17 + 19 = 36 percent have the same sign. Among the developed countries, 65 percent of the relative prices and relative consumption have the opposite signs, and among the developing countries, 62 percent of the relative prices and relative consumption have the opposite signs. These results clearly support the *law of demand*, that is, other things being equal, an increase in the relative price of a commodity causes its consumption to fall.

We now use scatter plots of relative consumption against relative prices and obtain estimates for income flexibility under certain assumptions. These estimates of income flexibility have only a preliminary status and we formally estimate the income flexibility in the next chapter. The estimate of income flexibility is exclusively used as an input for general equilibrium models, where the price elasticities are estimated based on the ϕ value. The study of income flexibility is important for a number of reasons. One of them is to test the well-known Frisch's (1959) conjecture, which states that the income elasticity of the marginal utility of income ($1/\phi$) decreases in absolute value as the consumer (or country) becomes more affluent. Frisch (1959, p.189) provides some numerical conjectures for the dependence of the elasticity on the level of real income. The value of the elasticity varies from −10 (for an extremely poor population), −2 (for the middle-income bracket) to −0.1 (for the rich part of the population). In the next section, we verify whether Frisch's conjecture is supported by our cross-country data.

In Chapter 2, we derived the finite-change version of the CBS/PI demand equation under preference independence for commodity i, which we reproduce here,

$$\bar{w}_{it}\left(Dq_{it} - DQ_t\right) = \beta_i\, DQ_t + \phi\left(\beta_i + \bar{w}_{it}\right)\left(Dp_{it} - DP_t'\right), \quad i = 1,\ldots,n, \; t = 1,\ldots,T \tag{3.16}$$

where $DP_t' = \sum_j \left(\beta_j + \bar{w}_{jt}\right) Dp_{jt}$. The income elasticity under equation (3.16) is given by $\eta_i = 1 + \dfrac{\beta_i}{\bar{w}_i}$.

Under the assumption of unitary income elasticity of commodity i, $\beta_i = 0$. Therefore, equation (3.16) under unitary income elasticity for commodity i becomes

$$(Dq_{it} - DQ_t) = \phi(Dp_{it} - DP_t), \quad i = 1,\ldots,n, \; t = 1,\ldots,T \tag{3.17}$$

where $DP_t = \sum_j \bar{w}_{jt} Dp_{jt}$ is the Divisia price index given by equation (3.9). For a given i, if we regress the growth in the consumption of i relative to the overall growth in consumption, $(Dq_{it} - DQ_t)$, against the growth in relative price $(Dp_{it} - DP_t)$ of i for t =1, …, T, the slope of the regression line can be interpreted as ϕ, the income flexibility. For each country, we obtain the estimates of ϕ for $i = 1$, …, n. Since we have the number of commodities $n = 12$ for most countries with 45 countries, we have 512 estimates of ϕ. Table 3.11 presents these estimates for the income flexibility ϕ for 12 commodities in 45 countries, and the frequency histograms of all these estimates are presented in Figure 3.3. As can be seen, the overall cross-country average is −0.50 with a standard error of 0.03 (with developed country average −0.53 and developing country average −0.40). These estimates of ϕ are well in agreement with previous empirical findings reported in the literature (for example, see Chen 2001, Clements et al. 2020, Rathnayaka et al. 2019, Selvanathan and Selvanathan 1993, 2003, and Theil and Suhm 1981).

In the above regression model (3.17), as ϕ is the same for all $i = 1$, …, 12, for each country, we can also perform a restricted pooled regression by considering $(Dq_{it} - DQ_t)$ against $(Dp_{it} - DP_t)$ for all $i = 1$, …, n and $t = 1$, …, T. That is, we plot $(Dq_{it} - DQ_t)$ against $(Dp_{it} - DP_t)$ for $t = 1$, …, T and $i = 1$, …, n for each country and obtain 45 such estimates for ϕ. The last column of Table 3.9 presents all such estimates for ϕ. As can be seen, all the estimates are negative (except for Thailand) with an average of −0.59.

Instead of pooling the data across commodities and time, alternatively, one could pool them over countries and time. In order to achieve this, in equation (3.17) for commodity i, we add a country superscript c (=1, …, 45):

$$\left(Dq_{it}^c - DQ_t^c\right) = \phi\left(Dp_{it}^c - DP_t^c\right), \quad i = 1,\ldots,n. \tag{3.18}$$

Summing both sides over $t = 1$, …, T and dividing by T for each country c (=1, …, 45) and commodity i, we get

$$\left(D\bar{q}_i^c - D\bar{Q}^c\right) = \phi\left(D\bar{p}_i^c - D\bar{P}^c\right), \quad i = 1,\ldots,n. \tag{3.19}$$

The values of $\left(D\bar{q}_i^c - D\bar{Q}^c\right)$ and $\left(D\bar{p}_i^c - D\bar{P}^c\right)$ are relative consumption and relative prices, respectively. Now, for each commodity i (=1, …, 12), if we plot $(D\bar{q}_i^c - D\bar{Q}^c)$ against $(D\bar{p}_i^c - D\bar{P}^c)$, c=1,…, 45, the resulting slope of the regression line (3.19) is also an estimate for ϕ. Figure 3.4 gives the plots for

Table 3.11 512 Estimates of income flexibility, 12 commodities and 45 countries

Country	Food	Alcohol	Clothing	Housing	Durables	Health	Transport	Communication	Recreation	Education	Restaurant	Miscellaneous	Mean
(1)	(2)	(3)	(4)	(5)	(6)	(7)	(8)	(9)	(10)	(11)	(12)	(13)	(14)
Developed countries													
1 Australia	−0.64	−0.39	−0.99	−0.23	−0.58	−0.66	0.14	−0.25	−0.28	−0.31	−0.24	−0.80	−0.43
2 Austria	−0.37	0.45	−1.04	−0.32	−0.81	−0.62	−0.18	−1.48	−1.16	−0.41	0.04	−0.04	−0.50
3 Belgium	0.55	−0.01	−0.90	0.18	−0.88	−0.05	−0.31	−0.31	−1.27	−0.67	−0.58	0.09	−0.35
4 Canada	−0.22	−0.29	−0.98	0.03	−0.44	−0.54	−0.20	−0.55	0.16	−0.28	−1.17	−0.08	−0.38
5 Denmark	−0.18	−0.87	−0.24	−1.08	−0.98	0.05	0.96	−1.09	−0.65	0.37	−1.63	−0.79	−0.51
6 Finland	−0.29	−0.40	−0.47	−0.16	0.06	−0.07	−0.43	−0.29	−0.57	−1.77	−0.63	−0.11	−0.43
7 France	−0.19	−0.35	−0.52	0.27	−0.86	−0.87	−0.88	−0.48	−0.50	−1.04	−0.71	−0.01	−0.51
8 Germany	−0.54	−1.08	−0.53	−0.34	−1.48	−0.48	−0.97	−1.52	−0.76	−0.61	−1.17	0.19	−0.77
9 Hong Kong	−0.01	–	0.58	−0.03	−0.09	−1.14	−0.27	–	−0.42	–	–	0.14	−0.15
10 Iceland	0.30	−0.42	−0.91	−0.89	−1.41	−0.61	−1.03	−1.99	−0.54	−0.37	−0.37	−0.45	−0.72
11 Ireland	−1.99	−1.66	−1.89	−1.05	−1.86	−1.53	−2.07	−1.63	−1.92	−2.04	−1.68	−1.68	−1.75
12 Israel	−0.08	−0.08	−0.47	0.05	0.02	0.60	−0.19	−0.55	−0.18	0.13	−0.53	−0.05	−0.11
13 Italy	−0.29	−0.61	−0.72	−0.47	−0.64	−0.48	−0.83	−0.22	−0.23	−0.37	−0.96	0.05	−0.48
14 Japan	0.24	–	−0.15	−0.45	−0.64	−0.68	−0.62	–	−0.50	–	–	−0.51	−0.41
15 Luxembourg	−0.48	−1.74	−0.01	−0.11	−0.09	−0.36	0.59	−0.41	−0.60	−0.70	0.46	−0.10	−0.30
16 Netherlands	0.00	−0.29	−0.19	0.15	−1.11	−3.67	−0.28	−0.83	−1.26	−0.59	−1.29	0.02	−0.78
17 New Zealand	0.58	−0.47	−0.64	−0.33	1.11	−0.27	−0.68	−1.25	−0.66	−0.67	−1.19	−0.36	−0.40
18 Norway	−0.76	−0.98	−0.96	−0.11	−0.85	−1.11	−0.87	−0.39	−0.74	−0.81	−0.63	−0.41	−0.72
19 Singapore	−0.30	–	0.44	−0.05	−0.69	−0.02	−0.42	–	−0.66	–	–	−0.34	−0.25
20 Slovenia	−0.20	−0.47	−0.81	0.13	−0.63	−0.98	−0.87	−0.02	−0.44	−0.24	−0.50	0.06	−0.41
21 South Korea	0.01	−0.38	−0.43	0.00	−0.38	−0.83	−0.56	−0.55	−0.01	0.00	−0.42	−0.64	−0.35
22 Spain	−0.19	−0.50	−0.80	0.24	0.00	−0.59	−0.62	0.18	−0.16	1.15	0.02	0.04	−0.10
23 Sweden	−0.11	−0.96	−0.91	0.13	−1.26	−0.51	−0.02	−0.15	−0.97	0.22	−0.51	0.19	−0.41
24 Switzerland	−1.67	−1.95	−1.45	−1.74	−1.71	−1.98	−1.86	−1.20	−1.63	−1.93	−1.88	−2.42	−1.78
25 Taiwan	−0.01	–	−0.41	−0.15	−0.03	−0.26	−0.66	–	−0.43	–	–	−0.55	−0.31
26 UK	−0.06	−0.25	−0.96	−0.50	−1.32	−0.35	−0.66	−1.09	−1.02	−0.27	−0.73	0.05	−0.59
27 USA	−0.39	−0.43	−0.59	−0.60	−1.31	−0.36	−0.42	−0.65	−0.67	−0.47	−0.18	−0.11	−0.52
Mean (*Developed*)	−0.27	−0.61	−0.63	−0.27	−0.70	−0.68	−0.53	−0.73	−0.67	−0.51	−0.72	−0.32	−0.53

(*Continued*)

Table 3.11 512 Estimates of income flexibility, 12 commodities and 45 countries (*Continued*)

Country (1)	Food (2)	Alcohol (3)	Clothing (4)	Housing (5)	Durables (6)	Health (7)	Transport (8)	Communication (9)	Recreation (10)	Education (11)	Restaurant (12)	Miscellaneous (13)	Mean (14)
Developing countries													
28 Colombia	−0.10	−0.51	0.18	−0.25	−0.15	−1.07	0.23	−0.99	−0.33	0.63	−0.48	−0.46	−0.27
29 Czech Republic	−0.31	−0.07	−0.34	−0.08	−0.57	−0.62	−0.20	−0.46	−0.50	0.06	−0.85	−1.60	−0.46
30 Estonia	0.23	−0.63	0.35	−0.19	−0.67	−0.36	−0.68	−0.44	−0.28	0.09	−0.39	−0.45	−0.29
31 Greece	−0.27	−0.71	1.44	0.38	−0.55	−1.84	−1.06	−0.46	−0.98	0.01	−0.18	−0.68	−0.41
32 Hungary	−0.28	−1.04	−0.53	0.36	−0.71	−0.97	−0.36	0.18	−0.54	−0.33	−0.78	−0.16	−0.43
33 India	−0.19	–	−0.21	−0.04	−0.19	−0.22	−0.05	–	−0.16	–	–	−0.22	−0.16
34 Latvia	0.07	0.27	−0.53	−0.77	−1.38	−0.35	−0.38	−0.89	−0.44	−0.40	−1.63	−0.54	−0.58
35 Lithuania	−0.04	−0.65	−0.52	−1.01	0.71	−0.34	0.37	−0.34	0.19	0.60	−1.08	−0.37	−0.21
36 Malaysia	−1.44	–	2.50	0.11	−0.63	−2.10	−0.22	–	−2.74	–	–	−2.71	−0.90
37 Mexico	−0.25	−0.98	−0.18	−0.35	−0.55	−0.15	−0.33	−0.91	−2.26	−1.52	−0.49	−0.57	−0.71
38 Philippines	0.09	–	−0.58	0.08	−0.59	−0.31	0.11	–	−0.29	–	–	−0.30	−0.23
39 Poland	−0.07	−0.22	−1.26	0.13	−0.55	−0.82	−0.88	−0.47	−0.87	0.96	0.90	0.76	−0.20
40 Portugal	−0.86	−0.60	−0.46	−1.24	−0.32	−0.77	−0.66	−0.98	0.43	−0.98	−0.61	−0.37	−0.62
41 Slovakia	−0.50	−0.18	−0.59	−0.47	−0.89	−0.64	−0.51	−0.41	−0.92	−0.57	−1.15	−0.32	−0.60
42 South Africa	−0.51	–	−0.92	−0.39	−0.57	−0.41	−0.77	–	−0.46	−0.44	0.06	−0.70	−0.51
43 Sri Lanka	−0.84	–	−0.89	−0.47	−0.47	−0.64	−0.53	–	−1.02	–	–	−1.04	−0.74
44 Thailand	0.18	–	0.11	0.01	−0.52	0.24	−0.36	–	1.00	–	–	2.22	0.36
45 Turkey	−0.52	–	0.35	0.16	0.59	−0.42	−0.99	–	−0.64	−0.33	−1.33	0.01	−0.31
Mean (*Developing*)	−0.31	−0.48	−0.12	−0.22	−0.44	−0.66	−0.40	−0.56	−0.60	−0.17	−0.62	−0.42	−0.40
Mean (*All Countries*)	−0.29	−0.57	−0.42	−0.25	−0.60	−0.67	−0.48	−0.67	−0.64	−0.39	−0.68	−0.36	−0.48

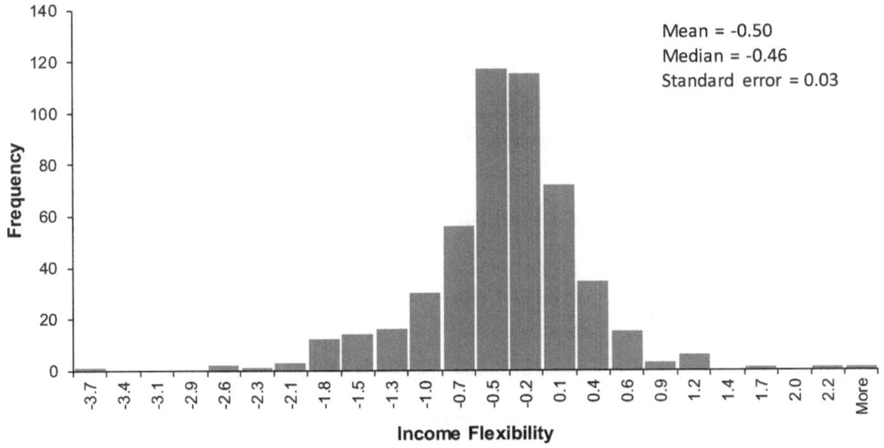

Figure 3.3 Frequency histogram of the 512 income flexibility estimates.

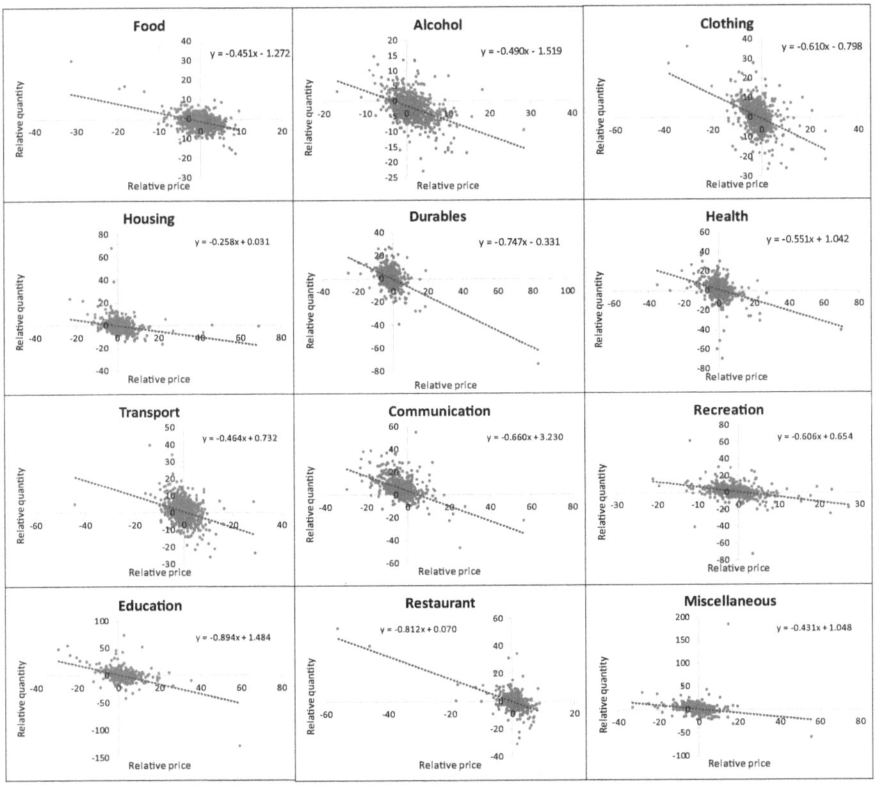

Figure 3.4 Relative quantity versus relative price for 12 commodities, all countries combined.

each of the 12 commodity groups. As can be seen, in all plots, all the points are scattered around a negatively sloping straight line. The slopes of the lines are in the range −0.2 to −0.8 and most of them are close to −0.6. In Table 3.12, we present the resulting estimate of ϕ for each commodity group. As can be seen, the overall average over the 12 commodities is $\phi = -0.58$.

3.5 Food Budget Share and Income

One of the most important empirical regularities in consumption economics is *Engel's law*. This law states that the budget share for food (w_{Ft}) falls with increasing income (M_t). Working (1943) and then Leser (1963) modelled the *Engel's law* into a linear regression framework, which is known as *Working's model*,

$$w_{Ft} = \alpha_F + \beta_F \log M_t. \tag{3.20}$$

Choosing $M_t = 1$ for some year t in equation (3.20), α_F can be interpreted as the budget share of food during that year t. The coefficient β_F gives 100 times the change in the budget share of food resulting from a 1 percent increase in income.

Table 3.13 presents the estimates for the Working's model parameters, α_F, β_F and the income elasticity for food derived as $[1+(\beta_F/w_F)]$, for each country. As can be seen from column (3), all the income coefficients are negative and are statistically significant. The cross-country average for the 45 countries is $\beta_F = -0.389$ (standard error = 0.07). All the income elasticity estimates in column (5) are less than 1, indicating that food is a necessity in all countries. This clearly shows that *Engel's law* is well supported by the data. Irrespective of the level of income, food is a necessity for all countries. However, the income elasticity for food is slightly higher in the developing countries than in the developed countries.

Table 3.12 Estimates of income flexibility, all countries combined

	Commodity (1)	*Slope* (2)	*Standard error* (3)
1	Food	−0.45	0.03
2	Alcohol	−0.49	0.04
3	Clothing	−0.61	0.04
4	Housing	−0.26	0.03
5	Durables	−0.75	0.04
6	Health	−0.55	0.04
7	Transport	−0.46	0.04
8	Communication	−0.66	0.04
9	Recreation	−0.61	0.04
10	Education	−0.89	0.06
11	Restaurants	−0.81	0.04
12	Miscellaneous	−0.43	0.05
	Mean	−0.58	0.01

Table 3.13 Estimates of Working's model for food

Country	Intercept $\alpha_F \times 100$	Income coefficient $\beta_F \times 100$	R^2	Income elasticities η_F
(1)	*(2)*	*(3)*	*(4)*	*(5)*
Developed countries				
1 Australia	27.49 (1.21)	−1.68 (0.12)	0.87	0.84
2 Austria	33.51 (2.47)	−2.39 (0.25)	0.82	0.76
3 Belgium	45.86 (5.46)	−3.41 (0.57)	0.66	0.74
4 Canada	43.93 (1.77)	−3.42 (0.18)	0.91	0.67
5 Denmark	51.54 (5.16)	−3.38 (0.43)	0.75	0.71
6 Finland	68.06 (2.48)	−5.72 (0.27)	0.91	0.64
7 France	43.61 (0.72)	−3.17 (0.08)	0.96	0.80
8 Germany	51.09 (3.53)	−4.18 (0.36)	0.87	0.61
9 Hong Kong	78.45 (2.85)	−5.51 (0.26)	0.91	0.70
10 Iceland	58.82 (11.34)	−3.08 (0.78)	0.46	0.78
11 Ireland	64.38 (3.45)	−5.61 (0.36)	0.93	0.46
12 Israel	18.11 (4.80)	−0.22 (0.44)	0.01	0.98
13 Italy	63.40 (2.43)	−5.04 (0.25)	0.95	0.66
14 Japan	86.33 (3.25)	−8.99 (0.43)	0.90	0.54
15 Luxembourg	16.31 (5.79)	−0.67 (0.57)	0.06	0.92
16 Netherlands	29.77 (6.56)	−1.94 (0.68)	0.31	0.82
17 New Zealand	6.58 (1.90)	0.77 (0.19)	0.37	1.05
18 Norway	160.45 (3.82)	−12.25 (0.32)	0.97	0.26
19 Singapore	78.99 (1.50)	−6.95 (0.16)	0.97	0.56
20 Slovenia	39.49 (2.26)	−2.66 (0.25)	0.85	0.83
21 South Korea	114.64 (3.30)	−6.28 (0.22)	0.94	0.72
22 Spain	67.09 (3.12)	−5.71 (0.33)	0.94	0.58
23 Sweden	39.50 (5.93)	−2.27 (0.50)	0.49	0.82
24 Switzerland	29.99 (6.06)	−1.95 (0.57)	0.40	0.79
25 Taiwan	92.29 (1.89)	−6.13 (0.16)	0.96	0.74
26 UK	21.24 (4.27)	−1.32 (0.45)	0.31	0.84
27 USA	41.65 (0.80)	−3.39 (0.08)	0.97	0.63
Mean (*Developed*)	54.54 (0.82)	−3.94 (0.07)	0.72	0.71
Developing countries				
28 Colombia	47.48 (5.33)	−1.83 (0.34)	0.68	0.90
29 Czech Republic	65.74 (7.54)	−4.16 (0.63)	0.69	0.74
30 Estonia	51.81 (6.09)	−3.71 (0.73)	0.57	0.82
31 Greece	23.75 (5.29)	−0.80 (0.57)	0.09	0.95
32 Hungary	67.47 (4.84)	−3.54 (0.350)	0.84	0.80
33 India	115.22 (2.65)	−7.60 (0.30)	0.93	0.85
34 Latvia	81.52 (5.67)	−7.13 (0.70)	0.85	0.70
35 Lithuania	97.97 (7.93)	−8.52 (0.96)	0.81	0.69
36 Malaysia	60.81 (7.31)	−3.92 (0.77)	0.63	0.83
37 Mexico	−16.91 (10.93)	3.51 (0.97)	0.56	1.15
38 Philippines	42.79 (7.69)	0.03 (0.70)	0.00	1.00
39 Poland	91.74 (2.42)	−7.28 (0.25)	0.97	0.66
40 Portugal	38.07 (5.49)	−2.32 (0.60)	0.43	0.86
41 Slovakia	85.91 (3.44)	−7.73 (0.40)	0.95	0.62
42 South Africa	44.28 (1.40)	−1.78 (0.15)	0.77	0.93
43 Sri Lanka	110.53 (3.04)	−5.61 (0.29)	0.90	0.89
44 Thailand	84.10 (4.54)	−5.09 (0.45)	0.72	0.84
45 Turkey	37.05 (2.04)	−1.16 (0.23)	0.62	0.95
Mean (*Developing*)	62.74 (1.35)	−3.81 (0.13)	0.67	0.85
Mean (*All countries*)	57.82 (0.73)	−3.89 (0.07)	0.70	0.79

Note: Standard errors are in parentheses.

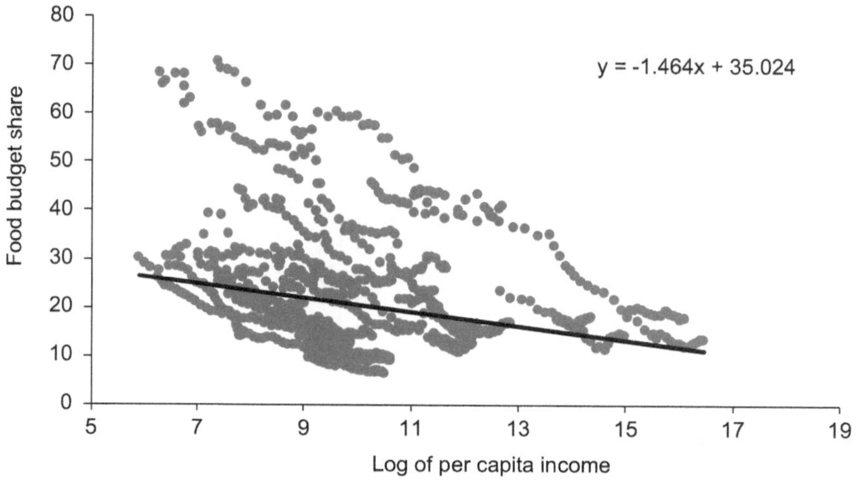

Figure 3.5 Food budget share versus log of per capita income, all countries combined.

In Figure 3.5, we pool the data across the 45 countries and plot the budget shares (w_{Ftc}) against the logarithm of income ($\log M_{tc}$) in one graph. As can be seen, the slope the line $\beta_F = -0.1464$ is negative as expected. Based on this slope value and the mean cross-country budget share of $w_F = 0.1069$ from Table 3.5, we can estimate the income elasticity of food for the 45 countries as $[1 + (\beta_F/w_F)] = [1 + (-0.1464/0.1069)] = 0.86$.

3.6 Double-log Demand System

Double-log demand equations, introduced earlier in Section 2.4, are one of the types of demand equations that are specified without reference to any utility function. In this section, we use the double-log demand equations to obtain preliminary estimates for the income and price elasticities. Double-log demand equations were very popular during the early days of estimating consumer demand due their simplicity in terms of estimation and interpretation. The coefficients of double-log demand equations have the easy interpretation that they are the income and price elasticities.

We consider here the double-log demand equation for commodity i in finite-change form as

$$Dq_{it} = \alpha_i + \eta_i \, DQ_t + \eta_{ii} \left[Dp_{it} - DP_t \right] + \varepsilon_{it}, \quad i = 1, \ldots, n, \tag{3.21}$$

where α_i is an autonomous trend term; η_i is the income elasticity of commodity i; η_{ii} is the Slutsky own-price elasticity; and ε_{it} is a disturbance term. It is worth noting that this double-log demand equation includes only the own-relative price and no other prices. We estimate equation (3.21) by least squares (LS) for each country separately. Tables 3.14 and 3.15 present the estimates for the income elasticity (η_i) and own-price elasticity (η_{ii}), respectively, for each commodity for the 45 countries. The last row of the tables presents the elasticities for each commodity averaged over the 45 countries. We also give the mean elasticities for developed and developing countries separately.

As can be seen from Table 3.14, all the income elasticities, except a few, are positive. However, none of the negative elasticities are statistically significant. All the elasticities in column (2) for food are less than one, indicating that food is a necessity in all countries. The average value of the food income elasticity for the 45 countries is 0.5. On average, the income elasticities for clothing, durables, transport, communication, recreation and restaurants are larger than 1, indicating that these commodities are luxuries in most countries, while the income elasticities for alcohol, housing, health and education are less than 1, indicating that they are necessities.

In Table 3.15, most of the own-price elasticities are negative as they should be. Most of the own-price elasticities are negative (some are positive but a majority of them are statistically insignificant) and less than one in absolute value, indicating that demand for all 12 commodities is price inelastic.

3.7 Frisch's Conjecture

Frish's (1959) conjecture states that the income elasticity of the marginal utility of income ($1/\phi$) decreases in absolute value as the consumer (or country) becomes more affluent. Alternatively, ϕ should increase in absolute value as the consumer (or country) becomes more affluent.

Below, we verify whether Frisch's conjecture is supported by data from all 45 countries as well as by the two groups, developed and developing countries. To do this, we estimate a linear relationship of the form,

$$\phi^c = \lambda + \mu y^c + \varepsilon^c, \tag{3.22}$$

where λ and μ are parameters to be estimated; the superscript c denotes country c; y^c is per capita real GDP (in international dollars) of country c; and ε^c is an independent disturbance term with zero mean. If the Frish's (1959) conjecture is true, then the data should reject the null hypothesis, Ho: $\mu = 0$.

We estimate equation (3.22) using the estimates of ϕ^c from column (7) of Table 3.9 together with the values of per capita real GDP (in international dollars) of country c, y^c, from Table 3.2. The t-test statistic value and the corresponding p-value for testing the null hypothesis Ho: $\mu = 0$ for the 45 countries are ($t = -2.49$, p-value $= 0.02$); for the 27 developed countries ($t = -2.36$, p-value $= 0.03$); and for the 18 developing countries ($t = -1.49$, p-value $= 0.16$). For all countries combined and the developed countries group, as the p-values are less than the level of significance $\alpha = 0.05$, we reject the null hypothesis, Ho: $\mu = 0$. This means that ϕ is dependent on real income and hence

Table 3.14a Income elasticities, 27 developed countries, 12 commodities

Country (1)		*Food* (2)	*Alcohol* (3)	*Clothing* (4)	*Housing* (5)	*Durables* (6)	*Health* (7)	*Transport* (8)	*Communication* (9)	*Recreation* (10)	*Education* (11)	*Restaurants* (12)	*Miscellaneous* (13)
1	Australia	0.46 (0.19)	0.91 (0.23)	1.15 (0.32)	0.33 (0.06)	1.06 (0.32)	0.18 (0.32)	2.06 (0.32)	1.14 (0.53)	1.57 (0.26)	0.46 (0.27)	1.66 (0.36)	0.86 (0.41)
2	Austria	0.31 (0.16)	0.42 (0.49)	0.09 (0.29)	0.90 (0.26)	0.83 (0.24)	0.52 (0.38)	1.88 (0.41)	3.02 (1.50)	1.44 (0.31)	0.83 (0.88)	0.44 (0.40)	0.96 (0.20)
3	Belgium	−0.35 (0.37)	0.85 (0.60)	−0.80 (0.62)	0.7 (0.23)	1.03 (0.41)	0.61 (0.23)	2.17 (0.47)	1.95 (1.27)	1.02 (0.56)	0.35 (0.69)	0.58 (0.43)	2.35 (0.47)
4	Canada	0.18 (0.07)	0.52 (0.21)	1.42 (0.14)	0.03 (0.08)	2.08 (0.14)	0.46 (0.24)	2.29 (0.19)	0.64 (0.24)	1.46 (0.17)	−0.03 (0.15)	1.42 (0.19)	0.88 (0.16)
5	Denmark	0.53 (0.12)	−0.32 (0.25)	0.61 (0.36)	0.15 (0.18)	1.49(0.24)	0.33 (0.26)	3.04 (0.43)	1.36 (0.68)	1.54 (0.25)	−0.04 (0.51)	1.34 (0.28)	0.96 (0.36)
6	Finland	0.32 (0.10)	0.74 (0.19)	1.71 (0.20)	−0.11 (0.08)	1.98(0.16)	0.90 (0.24)	2.35 (0.20)	1.53 (0.36)	1.51 (0.13)	0.17 (0.65)	1.43 (0.14)	1.14 (0.23)
7	France	0.45 (0.05)	0.48 (0.13)	1.12 (0.13)	0.97 (0.12)	1.39 (0.13)	0.36 (0.19)	1.94 (0.15)	1.14 (0.44)	1.40 (0.10)	0.22 (0.38)	0.59 (0.14)	1.17 (0.19)
8	Germany	0.81 (0.49)	−0.01 (0.65)	0.76 (0.57)	0.23 (0.39)	2.15 (0.89)	−0.65 (0.81)	1.63 (0.80)	1.77 (1.68)	1.51 (0.50)	1.08 (0.76)	1.41 (0.64)	1.07 (0.44)
9	Hong Kong	0.45 (0.10)	–	2.56 (0.19)	0.13 (0.10)	1.90 (0.26)	0.83 (0.26)	1.07 (0.17)	–	0.76 (0.14)	–	–	0.72 (0.14)
10	Iceland	0.40 (0.15)	0.82 (0.30)	0.91 (0.34)	0.27 (0.29)	1.20 (0.44)	0.20 (0.19)	2.95 (0.40)	1.79 (0.61)	1.18 (0.31)	−0.15 (0.15)	1.18 (0.22)	0.96 (0.36)
11	Ireland	0.81 (0.06)	0.82 (0.06)	0.88 (0.06)	1.21 (0.13)	1.04 (0.05)	0.46 (0.12)	0.73 (0.06)	0.70 (0.09)	0.91 (0.04)	0.59 (0.08)	0.91(0.04)	1.55 (0.16)
12	Israel	0.21 (0.13)	−0.06 (0.33)	0.98 (0.58)	0.29 (0.10)	1.95 (0.28)	1.28 (0.23)	2.43 (0.25)	1.99 (0.96)	1.41 (0.30)	0.60 (0.35)	1.70 (0.82)	0.74 (0.25)
13	Italy	0.59 (0.11)	0.80 (0.29)	1.52 (0.20)	0.22 (0.12)	1.60 (0.18)	1.04 (0.29)	1.64 (0.22)	2.19 (0.43)	1.58 (0.23)	0.67 (0.20)	1.01 (0.22)	0.48 (0.27)
14	Japan	0.85 (0.15)	–	1.55 (0.35)	0.65 (0.11)	1.72 (0.35)	0.34 (0.20)	1.64 (0.20)	–	1.27 (0.20)	–	–	1.47 (0.19)
15	Luxembourg	0.38 (0.35)	3.08 (0.87)	0.10 (0.44)	0.55 (0.25)	0.77 (0.32)	0.18 (1.30)	0.97 (0.31)	0.17 (0.35)	0.79 (0.35)	1.39 (0.82)	0.65 (0.28)	1.08 (0.64)
16	Netherlands	0.30 (0.08)	0.50 (0.26)	0.97 (0.26)	0.08 (0.17)	1.68 (0.26)	2.07 (1.93)	1.45 (0.19)	3.70 (0.54)	1.18 (0.18)	0.30 (0.59)	1.02 (0.23)	1.00 (0.16)
17	New Zealand	0.64 (0.13)	0.31 (0.27)	0.96 (0.32)	0.26 (0.10)	1.15 (0.27)	−0.12 (0.63)	2.31 (0.29)	0.36 (0.48)	1.26 (0.27)	0.49 (0.81)	2.12 (0.48)	0.83 (0.25)
18	Norway	0.49 (0.10)	0.59 (0.17)	1.25 (0.14)	0.19 (0.10)	1.24 (0.17)	−0.10 (0.21)	2.99 (0.22)	0.66 (0.54)	1.17 (0.16)	0.27 (0.56)	0.74 (0.22)	0.59 (0.16)
19	Singapore	0.47 (0.09)	–	1.37 (0.17)	0.32 (0.14)	0.85 (0.12)	0.67 (0.17)	1.39 (0.18)	–	1.41 (0.12)	–	–	1.38 (0.15)
20	Slovenia	0.74 (0.12)	0.41 (0.40)	1.63 (0.37)	0.34 (0.12)	1.86 (0.44)	0.77 (0.39)	0.88 (0.26)	1.21 (0.60)	1.62 (0.33)	0.77 (0.47)	0.90 (0.28)	1.14 (0.22)
21	South Korea	0.66 (0.10)	0.39 (0.16)	1.77 (0.18)	0.36 (0.10)	2.25 (0.21)	0.89 (0.30)	1.44 (0.13)	1.31 (0.39)	1.64 (0.17)	0.41 (0.14)	1.10 (0.13)	1.23 (0.17)
22	Spain	0.34 (0.13)	0.61 (0.27)	1.62 (0.19)	0.33 (0.13)	1.59 (0.12)	0.52 (0.12)	1.66 (0.24)	1.61 (0.30)	1.48 (0.15)	0.32 (0.22)	1.43 (0.17)	1.26 (0.19)
23	Sweden	0.41 (0.20)	−0.27 (0.49)	1.89 (0.29)	0.09 (0.13)	2.01 (0.33)	0.03 (0.56)	2.50 (0.49)	1.80 (0.83)	1.63 (0.26)	0.11 (0.27)	0.73 (0.32)	1.35 (0.29)
24	Switzerland	0.89 (0.24)	0.59 (0.19)	1.15 (0.25)	0.95 (0.15)	1.03 (0.15)	0.71 (0.12)	1.25 (0.22)	0.35 (0.44)	0.96 (0.20)	0.73 (0.17)	0.60 (0.15)	1.62 (0.34)
25	Taiwan	0.55 (0.06)	–	1.28 (0.10)	0.70 (0.12)	1.37 (0.16)	1.06 (0.45)	2.20 (0.26)	–	1.08 (0.14)	–	–	1.29 (0.23)
26	UK	0.64 (0.14)	0.65 (0.25)	0.69 (0.17)	0.35 (0.09)	1.83 (0.32)	0.49 (0.46)	1.19 (0.15)	1.56 (0.39)	1.64 (0.22)	0.37 (0.54)	1.14 (0.24)	1.56 (0.24)
27	USA	0.37 (0.10)	0.49 (0.15)	1.24 (0.12)	0.45 (0.08)	1.73 (0.14)	0.38 (0.12)	2.46 (0.19)	0.82 (0.17)	1.4 (0.11)	0.55 (0.12)	0.88 (0.13)	1.34 (0.16)
Mean (*Developed*)		0.48 (0.03)	0.58 (0.06)	1.12 (0.06)	0.40 (0.03)	1.51 (0.06)	0.53 (0.11)	1.87 (0.06)	1.42 (0.13)	1.33 (0.05)	0.46 (0.09)	1.09 (0.06)	1.15 (0.06)

Table 3.14b Income elasticities, 18 developing countries, 12 commodities (cont.)

Country (1)	*Food* (2)	*Alcohol* (3)	*Clothing* (4)	*Housing* (5)	*Durables* (6)	*Health* (7)	*Transport* (8)	*Communication* (9)	*Recreation* (10)	*Education* (11)	*Restaurants* (12)	*Miscellaneous* (13)
1 Colombia	0.58 (0.13)	0.16 (0.44)	2.04 (0.42	0.16 (0.10)	1.15 (0.21)	0.83 (0.34)	1.43 (0.34)	1.71 (0.94)	1.29 (0.42)	0.67 (0.19)	1.11 (0.26)	1.20 (0.17)
2 Czech Republic	0.45 (0.20)	0.17 (0.27)	1.18 (0.32	0.27 (0.17)	1.28 (0.28)	1.54 (0.90)	1.68 (0.34)	1.76 (0.77)	1.59 (0.22)	2.59 (0.92)	0.73 (0.37)	2.74 (0.52)
3 Estonia	0.50 (0.13)	0.57 (0.20)	1.26 (0.16	0.71 (0.20)	1.76 (0.18)	0.94 (0.18)	1.64 (0.17)	0.64 (0.31)	1.81 (0.16)	1.36 (0.38)	0.98 (0.19)	1.27 (0.15)
4 Greece	0.74 (0.23)	0.87 (0.34)	1.88 (0.24	0.27 (0.14)	1.93 (0.30)	2.00 (0.46)	1.36 (0.41)	1.75 (0.68)	1.30 (0.22)	1.19 (0.66)	0.70 (0.27)	0.90 (0.32)
5 Hungary	0.84 (0.14)	0.93 (0.22)	1.46 (0.42	0.66 (0.16)	1.71 (0.32)	1.13 (0.29)	2.09 (0.29)	0.89 (0.52)	1.23 (0.17)	0.43 (0.58)	0.57 (0.28)	0.53 (0.26)
6 India	0.92 (0.12)	–	1.32 (0.38	0.28 (0.07)	1.24 (0.27)	0.34 (0.34)	0.56 (0.17)	–	0.64 (0.29)	–	–	1.18 (0.29)
7 Latvia	0.74 (0.13)	0.79 (0.37)	1.52 (0.28	0.02 (0.21)	1.73 (0.28)	1.00 (0.32)	1.82 (0.22)	0.68 (0.50)	1.74 (0.43)	0.56 (1.27)	1.76 (0.57)	1.34 (0.39)
8 Lithuania	0.93 (0.10)	0.25 (0.15)	1.45 (0.31	0.39 (0.16)	1.31 (0.24)	1.19 (0.49)	1.46 (0.23)	−0.19 (0.59)	1.54 (0.34)	1.08 (0.68)	1.10 (0.33)	1.77 (0.39)
9 Malaysia	0.31 (0.18)	–	3.27 (0.63	0.42 (0.19)	1.46 (0.39)	0.66 (0.52)	1.27 (0.16)	–	1.52 (0.29)	–	–	1.43 (0.34)
10 Mexico	0.29 (0.11)	0.39 (0.46)	1.05 (0.37	0.76 (0.16)	0.93 (0.21)	0.38 (0.27)	2.34 (0.22)	0.50 (0.51)	1.92 (0.75)	0.08 (0.10)	1.05 (0.18)	0.50 (0.18)
11 Philippines	0.89 (0.11)	–	−0.19 (0.50	1.01 (0.37)	0.55 (0.62)	1.35 (0.38)	1.35 (0.37)	–	0.92 (0.23)	–	–	1.43 (0.36)
12 Poland	0.67 (0.17)	1.07 (0.39)	0.18 (0.43	0.84 (0.38)	1.11 (0.41)	1.42 (0.42)	2.63 (0.45)	1.04 (1.20)	1.69 (0.75)	1.37 (0.56)	0.30 (0.72)	1.20 (0.74)
13 Portugal	0.30 (0.22)	0.77 (0.33)	0.82 (0.30	−0.02 (0.09)	1.23 (0.12)	0.58 (0.27)	2.22 (0.26)	1.33 (0.47)	1.03 (0.15)	0.42 (0.33)	0.82 (0.15)	0.45 (0.32)
14 Slovakia	0.65 (0.20)	0.83 (0.19)	1.08 (0.40	0.57 (0.30)	1.71 (0.30)	1.95 (1.16)	0.97 (0.27)	1.04 (0.38)	1.39 (0.17)	0.90 (0.78)	1.16 (0.40)	1.62 (0.27)
15 South Africa	0.58 (0.11)	–	1.25 (0.15	0.34 (0.18)	1.23 (0.07)	0.57 (0.20)	1.65 (0.20)	–	1.09 (0.22)	0.66 (0.31)	1.84 (0.29)	1.43 (0.24)
16 Sri Lanka	0.92 (0.13)	–	1.06 (0.31	1.81 (0.44)	0.50 (0.49)	0.83 (0.46)	0.84 (0.29)	–	1.90 (0.59)	–	–	0.31 (0.58)
17 Thailand	0.51 (0.08)	–	0.68 (0.14	0.14 (0.12)	1.15 (0.18)	1.12 (0.26)	1.82 (0.18)	–	1.54 (0.25)	–	–	−0.84 (1.04)
18 Turkey	0.32 (0.14)	–	1.18 (0.44	0.26 (0.07)	1.87 (0.27)	0.42 (0.40)	2.04 (0.28)	–	1.72 (0.38)	0.80 (0.34)	1.25 (0.38)	1.58 (0.27)
Mean (*Developing*)	0.62 (0.04)	0.62 (0.06)	1.25 (0.09	0.49 (0.05)	1.32 (0.07)	1.01 (0.11)	1.62 (0.07)	1.01 (0.12)	1.44 (0.09)	0.93 (0.13)	1.03 (0.07)	1.11 (0.10)
Mean (*All countries*)	0.53 (0.03)	0.59 (0.05)	1.17 (0.05	0.44 (0.03)	1.44 (0.05)	0.72 (0.08)	1.77 (0.04)	1.29 (0.09)	1.37 (0.05	0.63 (0.07)	1.06 (0.05)	1.13 (0.05)

Table 3.15a Own-price elasticities, 27 developed countries, 12 commodities

	Country (1)	*Food* (2)	*Alcohol* (3)	*Clothing* (4)	*Housing* (5)	*Durables* (6)
1	Australia	−0.43 (0.17)	−0.39 (0.12)	−1.00 (0.27)	−0.28 (0.06)	−0.59 (0.37)
2	Austria	−0.47 (0.13)	0.22 (0.50)	−1.00 (0.28)	−0.31 (0.24)	−0.85 (0.24)
3	Belgium	0.27 (0.29)	−0.03 (0.29)	−1.06 (0.45)	0.22 (0.20)	−0.87 (0.31)
4	Canada	−0.06 (0.06)	−0.33 (0.07)	−0.94 (0.13)	−0.24 (0.18)	−0.45 (0.24)
5	Denmark	−0.23 (0.14)	−1.11 (0.25)	−0.18 (0.51)	−0.86 (0.63)	−0.91 (0.45)
6	Finland	−0.33 (0.09)	−0.42 (0.14)	−0.51 (0.32)	−0.43 (0.10)	−0.11 (0.28)
7	France	−0.26 (0.06)	−0.47 (0.08)	−0.49 (0.17)	0.28 (0.16)	−0.59 (0.18)
8	Germany	−0.54 (0.23)	−1.22 (0.31)	−0.52 (0.37)	0.16 (0.43)	−1.41 (0.79)
9	Hong Kong	0.01 (0.17)	–	−0.45 (0.20)	−0.36 (0.15)	0.10 (0.43)
10	Iceland	−0.07 (0.18)	−0.45 (0.26)	−0.94 (0.26)	−0.57 (0.19)	−1.33 (0.34)
11	Ireland	−1.79 (0.19)	−1.70 (0.18)	−1.94 (0.11)	−1.58 (0.39)	−1.82 (0.09)
12	Israel	−0.13 (0.12)	−0.24 (0.16)	−0.47 (0.45)	−0.01 (0.08)	−0.32 (0.32)
13	Italy	−0.67 (0.16)	−0.72 (0.27)	−0.85 (0.36)	−0.28 (0.24)	−0.40 (0.34)
14	Japan	0.11 (0.21)	–	−0.30 (0.24)	−0.32 (0.11)	−0.62 (0.22)
15	Luxembourg	−0.73 (0.43)	−0.77 (1.04)	−0.19 (0.56)	−0.33 (0.63)	−0.20 (0.48)
16	Netherlands	−0.23 (0.10)	−0.45 (0.23)	−0.18 (0.36)	−0.14 (0.34)	−1.02 (0.49)
17	New Zealand	−0.68 (0.13)	−0.67 (0.25)	−0.66 (0.44)	−0.13 (0.07)	1.09 (0.40)
18	Norway	−0.65 (0.16)	−1.04 (0.13)	−0.97 (0.10)	−0.18 (0.12)	−0.81 (0.34)
19	Singapore	−0.35 (0.16)	–	−0.50 (0.27)	−0.18 (0.13)	−0.69 (0.18)
20	Slovenia	−0.30 (0.14)	−0.62 (0.26)	−0.76 (0.52)	0.49 (0.15)	−0.40 (0.56)
21	South Korea	−0.17 (0.14)	−0.39 (0.10)	−0.39 (0.19)	0.12 (0.10)	−0.42 (0.21)
22	Spain	−0.51 (0.26)	−0.66 (0.21)	−1.25 (0.40)	0.32 (0.35)	0.44 (0.39)
23	Sweden	−0.15 (0.11)	−1.13 (0.29)	−1.14 (0.26)	−0.09 (0.14)	−1.20 (0.34)
24	Switzerland	−1.65 (0.29)	−1.76 (0.18)	−1.44 (0.13)	−1.70 (0.25)	−1.71 (0.10)
25	Taiwan	−0.20 (0.08)	–	−0.40 (0.11)	−0.10 (0.22)	−0.07 (0.10)
26	UK	−0.26 (0.12)	−0.37 (0.17)	−0.97 (0.12)	−0.25 (0.18)	−0.42 (0.52)
27	USA	−0.44 (0.08)	−0.48 (0.08)	−0.60 (0.13)	−0.40 (0.13)	−1.27 (0.18)
Mean (*Developed*)		−0.40 (0.03)	−0.66 (0.06)	−0.74 (0.06)	−0.26 (0.05)	−0.62 (0.07)

there is support for the Frisch's (1959) conjecture. On the other hand, for the developing countries, as the p-value = 0.16 is greater than $\alpha = 0.05$, we do not reject the null hypothesis and conclude that ϕ is independent of real income and there is no support for the Frisch's (1959) conjecture. The finding that for the developed countries data support Frisch's (1959) conjecture is in contrast to results from a number of previous studies (e.g., Clements and Theil 1996; Selvanathan 1993; Selvanathan and Selvanathan 2003; Theil 1980; Theil 1987).

Health (7)	*Transport* (8)	*Communication* (9)	*Recreation* (10)	*Education* (11)	*Restaurants* (12)	*Miscellaneous* (13)
−0.57 (0.17)	−0.07 (0.19)	−0.26 (0.23)	−0.01 (0.30)	−0.37 (0.21)	−0.49 (0.41)	−0.86 (0.38)
−0.55 (0.23)	−0.40 (0.19)	−1.19 (0.31)	−1.08 (0.27)	−0.42 (0.18)	−0.15 (0.62)	−0.04 (0.09)
−0.07 (0.07)	−0.46 (0.23)	−0.49 (0.41)	−1.26 (0.37)	−0.74 (0.52)	−0.77 (0.35)	0.01 (0.12)
−0.72 (0.43)	−0.36 (0.14)	−0.59 (0.14)	0.13 (0.31)	−0.50 (0.09)	−0.80 (0.34)	−0.03 (0.25)
0.00 (0.37)	−0.04 (0.50)	−1.17 (0.45)	−0.70 (0.30)	0.26 (0.85)	−1.76 (0.81)	−0.81 (0.39)
−0.07 (0.28)	−0.59 (0.19)	−0.28 (0.16)	−0.63 (0.21)	−1.38 (0.84)	−0.69 (0.20)	−0.14 (0.17)
−0.73 (0.22)	−0.51 (0.18)	−0.50 (0.16)	−0.61 (0.13)	−1.10 (0.35)	−0.54 (0.21)	−0.08 (0.12)
−0.48 (0.26)	−1.06 (0.34)	−1.39 (0.39)	−0.78 (0.27)	−0.61 (0.18)	−1.09 (0.51)	−0.18 (0.13)
−1.16 (0.34)	−0.27 (0.24)	–	−0.31 (0.20)	–	–	0.26 (0.21)
−0.29 (0.28)	0.15 (0.44)	−1.95 (0.56)	−0.43 (0.39)	0.21 (0.16)	−0.39 (0.52)	−0.45 (0.35)
−1.59 (0.16)	−2.43 (0.11)	−1.84 (0.11)	−1.98 (0.09)	−2.00 (0.04)	−1.58 (0.13)	−1.70 (0.19)
0.59 (0.32)	−0.32 (0.24)	−0.58 (0.36)	−0.25 (0.26)	0.14 (0.63)	−0.76 (0.91)	−0.16 (0.31)
−0.48 (0.31)	−0.81 (0.18)	−0.32 (0.28)	−0.26 (0.37)	−0.51 (0.32)	−0.97 (0.55)	0.23 (0.17)
−0.69 (0.13)	−0.70 (0.23)	–	−0.53 (0.18)	–	–	−0.41 (0.24)
−0.52 (0.59)	0.59 (0.22)	−0.52 (0.20)	−0.67 (0.35)	−0.72 (0.47)	0.28 (0.37)	−0.13 (0.38)
−3.80 (2.77)	−0.31 (0.28)	−0.69 (0.26)	−1.21 (0.33)	−0.44 (0.96)	−1.28 (0.35)	0.02 (0.08)
0.00 (0.56)	−0.53 (0.20)	−1.19 (0.19)	−0.58 (0.35)	−0.65 (0.20)	0.07 (0.98)	−0.40 (0.26)
−0.59 (0.25)	−0.97 (0.37)	−0.40 (0.24)	−0.73 (0.37)	−0.79 (0.65)	−0.67 (0.29)	−0.38 (0.14)
−0.14 (0.21)	−0.52 (0.23)	–	−0.58 (0.23)	–	–	−0.46 (0.20)
−0.99 (0.58)	−0.89 (0.23)	−0.05 (0.47)	−0.42 (0.70)	−0.25 (0.59)	−0.50 (0.24)	0.03 (0.13)
−0.83 (0.33)	−0.47 (0.15)	−0.52 (0.13)	−0.22 (0.23)	0.13 (0.12)	−0.45 (0.20)	−0.63 (0.19)
−0.65 (0.20)	−0.56 (0.31)	0.17 (0.32)	−0.28 (0.26)	0.57 (0.40)	−0.30 (0.43)	−0.02 (0.15)
−0.12 (0.36)	−0.33 (0.50)	−0.06 (0.32)	−0.92 (0.31)	0.34 (0.11)	−0.48 (0.47)	0.13 (0.16)
−1.97 (0.20)	−1.81 (0.26)	−1.28 (0.13)	−1.61 (0.24)	−1.89 (0.10)	−2.00 (0.10)	−2.36 (0.25)
−0.25 (0.39)	−0.40 (0.29)	–	−0.44 (0.12)	–	–	−0.62 (0.34)
−0.03 (0.63)	−0.69 (0.17)	−0.93 (0.27)	−0.98 (0.25)	−0.36 (0.35)	−0.83 (0.47)	−0.11 (0.17)
−0.32 (0.13)	−0.32 (0.10)	−0.63 (0.11)	−0.71 (0.19)	−0.51 (0.13)	−0.17 (0.29)	−0.28 (0.22)
−0.63 (0.12)	−0.56 (0.05)	−0.72 (0.05)	−0.67 (0.06)	−0.50 (0.08)	−0.71 (0.09)	−0.35 (0.04)

3.8 Is There Support for the Preference Independence Structure?

Preference independence assumption is an attractive option for the simplification of demand equations, especially when the number of commodities is large. There are two distinct justifications for this assumption (Clements 1987; Clements and Selvanathan 1994): (i) The economic justification in terms of preference independence plausible when the commodities in

Table 3.15b Own-price elasticities, 18 developing countries, 12 commodities (cont.)

Country (1)	*Food* (2)	*Alcohol* (3)	*Clothing* (4)	*Housing* (5)	*Durables* (6)
1 Colombia	−0.09 (0.10)	−0.42 (0.25)	0.13 (0.38)	0.48 (0.21)	−0.16 (0.23)
2 Czech Republic	−0.42 (0.16)	−0.25 (0.26)	−0.35 (0.23)	0.02 (0.15)	−0.60 (0.49)
3 Estonia	0.04 (0.31)	−0.90 (0.30)	−0.13 (0.43)	0.09 (0.41)	−0.06 (0.27)
4 Greece	−0.23 (0.43)	−0.72 (0.29)	0.56 (0.73)	0.91 (0.33)	−0.53 (0.52)
5 Hungary	−0.31 (0.12)	−1.04 (0.20)	−0.78 (0.55)	0.22 (0.20)	−0.63 (0.48)
6 India	−0.18 (0.13)	–	−0.20 (0.12)	0.00 (0.02)	−0.19 (0.12)
7 Latvia	−0.18 (0.31)	0.04 (0.49)	−0.40 (0.36)	−0.10 (0.17)	−0.54 (0.60)
8 Lithuania	−0.06 (0.15)	−0.96 (0.18)	−0.66 (0.31)	−0.47 (0.27)	0.82 (0.54)
9 Malaysia	−0.94 (0.47)	–	4.34 (2.44)	−0.26 (0.59)	−0.15 (1.28)
10 Mexico	−0.37 (0.23)	−1.22 (0.40)	−0.18 (0.15)	−0.20 (0.22)	−0.57 (0.29)
11 Philippines	0.09 (0.10)	–	−0.28 (0.28)	0.08 (0.16)	−0.47 (0.35)
12 Poland	−0.17 (0.15)	−0.23 (0.34)	−1.18 (0.22)	0.18 (0.38)	−0.54 (0.56)
13 Portugal	−1.06 (0.09)	−0.56 (0.45)	−0.27 (0.49)	−0.58 (0.09)	−0.46 (0.15)
14 Slovakia	−0.45 (0.24)	−0.27 (0.20)	−0.60 (0.55)	−0.22 (0.35)	−0.81 (0.29)
15 South Africa	−0.41 (0.13)	–	−0.88 (0.12)	−0.23 (0.15)	−0.56 (0.12)
16 Sri Lanka	−0.80 (0.16)	–	−0.89 (0.15)	−0.60 (0.25)	−1.00 (0.17)
17 Thailand	0.11 (0.10)	–	0.14 (0.14)	0.00 (0.06)	−0.51 (0.23)
18 Turkey	−0.24 (0.14)	–	0.30 (0.47)	0.10 (0.04)	−0.39 (0.33)
Mean (*Developing*)	−0.32 (0.05)	−0.59 (0.06)	−0.07 (0.16)	−0.03 (0.06)	−0.41 (0.11)
Mean (*All countries*)	−0.37 (0.03)	−0.64 (0.04)	−0.48 (0.07)	−0.17 (0.04)	−0.54 (0.06)

question are broad aggregates; and (ii) the statistical justification that the assumption reduces the number of unknown coefficients to be estimated from the order of $n2$ to n. However, whether it is truly legitimate to invoke the assumption of preference independence is largely an empirical question. In this section, we use the data from the 45 countries to investigate this issue at a preliminary level. We will revisit this issue formally in later chapters.

Under preference independence, the income and own-price elasticities are related in the following way:

$$\eta_{ii} = \phi\eta_i, \quad i = 1,2,\ldots,n, \tag{3.23}$$

with η_i being the income elasticity and η_{ii} being the own-price elasticity of i. The relationship given by equation (3.23) means that under preference independence, own-price elasticities are proportional to income elasticities with ϕ being the factor of proportionality. In other words, luxuries are more price elastic than necessities (Deaton 1974, Pigou 1910).

Health (7)	*Transport* (8)	*Communication* (9)	*Recreation* (10)	*Education* (11)	*Restaurants* (12)	*Miscellaneous* (13)
−1.08 (0.51)	0.22 (0.36)	−0.84 (0.39)	−0.23 (0.47)	0.59 (0.26)	−0.57 (0.43)	−0.30 (0.31)
−0.60 (0.53)	−0.19 (0.33)	−0.61 (0.31)	−0.62 (0.25)	0.04 (0.79)	−0.85 (0.45)	−1.41 (0.63)
−0.37 (0.35)	−0.84 (0.27)	−0.49 (0.36)	−0.70 (0.24)	0.12 (0.37)	−0.39 (0.55)	−0.47 (0.14)
−1.97 (1.11)	−0.72 (0.85)	−0.23 (0.73)	−0.89 (0.39)	−0.29 (1.53)	−0.15 (0.39)	−0.68 (0.38)
−1.00 (0.15)	−0.24 (0.27)	0.20 (0.31)	−0.61 (0.30)	−0.13 (0.46)	−0.47 (0.45)	−0.06 (0.22)
−0.24 (0.09)	−0.06 (0.06)	–	−0.14 (0.13)	–	–	−0.22 (0.12)
−0.36 (0.37)	0.02 (0.37)	−0.94 (0.29)	0.53 (0.83)	−0.83 (1.65)	−0.62 (1.53)	−0.41 (0.53)
−0.21 (0.66)	0.22 (0.31)	−0.09 (0.34)	0.32 (0.67)	0.63 (0.83)	−1.07 (0.38)	0.04 (0.53)
−2.66 (1.69)	−0.30 (0.21)	–	−2.26 (1.01)	–	–	−0.63 (0.94)
−0.27(0.35)	−0.34 (0.25)	−0.90 (0.43)	−1.81 (0.65)	−0.19 (0.31)	−0.51 (0.30)	−0.71 (0.20)
−0.26 (0.23	0.13 (0.13)	–	−0.30 (0.14)	–	–	−0.37 (0.21)
−0.81(0.30)	−0.48 (0.30)	−0.47 (0.34)	−0.97 (0.18)	0.93 (0.47)	−0.95 (0.09)	−0.78 (0.28)
−0.58 (0.34)	−0.97 (0.34)	−1.17 (0.49)	−0.44 (0.16)	−0.62 (0.43)	−0.49 (0.32)	−0.03 (0.27)
−0.38 (0.52)	−0.52 (0.24)	−0.41 (0.16)	−0.77 (0.31)	−0.57 (0.38)	−1.07 (0.40)	−0.31 (0.18)
−0.48 (0.17)	−0.64 (0.15)	–	−0.45 (0.11)	−0.46 (0.15)	−0.04 (0.20)	−0.63 (0.21)
−0.67 (0.17)	−0.55 (0.16)	–	−1.17 (0.40)	–	–	−1.18 (0.26)
0.21 (0.30)	−0.19 (0.16)	–	0.85 (0.33)	–	–	2.05 (0.79)
−0.50 (0.30)	−0.37 (0.29)	–	−0.50 (0.26)	−0.30 (0.20)	−1.47 (0.39)	0.04 (0.11)
−0.68 (0.14)	−0.32 (0.08)	−0.54 (0.07)	−0.56 (0.11)	−0.08 (0.15)	−0.66 (0.11)	−0.33 (0.10)
−0.65 (0.09)	−0.46 (0.04)	−0.66 (0.04)	−0.63 (0.06)	−0.35 (0.08)	−0.69 (0.07)	−0.35 (0.05)

To analyse the proportionality relationship (3.23), we use the income and own-price elasticity estimates presented in Tables 3.14 and 3.15. Figure 3.6 plots each pair of the own-price elasticity (η_{ii}) against the income elasticity (η_i), and the solid line is the LS line. The points are scattered around a negatively sloping line, and the location of the points gives evidence that luxuries tend to be more price elastic. The estimate of the factor of proportionality is −0.35 with standard error 0.03, which is not far from the estimates of ϕ presented in Tables 3.9, 3.11 and 3.12. The significance of the factor of proportionality gives indirect evidence to the preference independence hypothesis. Even though our findings are in contrast to Deaton's (1974) findings, however, acceptance of preference independence was supported by a number of other previous studies (e.g., Chen 2001; Clements et al. 1984; Rathnayaka et al. 2019; Selvanathan 1993; Selvanathan and Selvanathan 2003). We shall formally test the hypothesis of preference independence in Chapter 4.

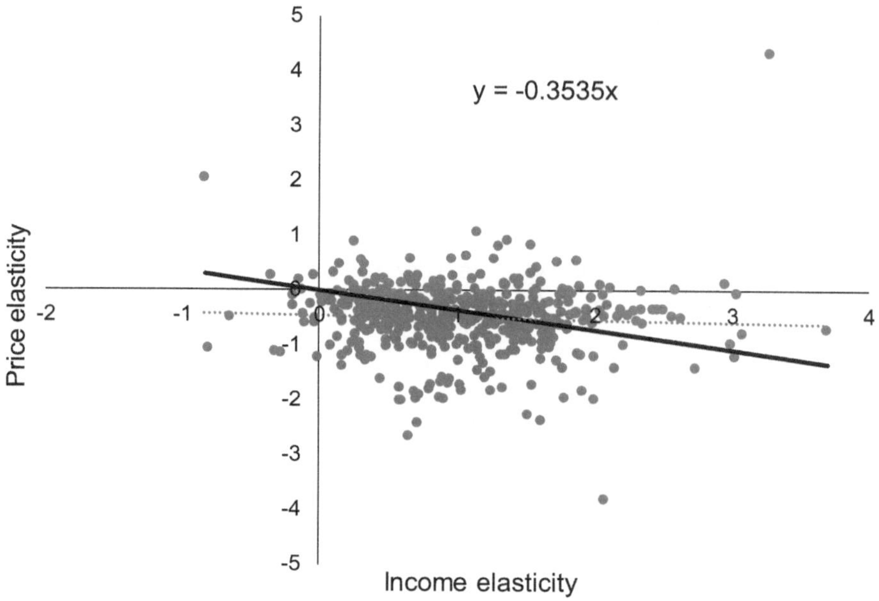

Figure 3.6 Price elasticity vs Income elasticity, all countries combined.

3.9 Concluding Comments

In this chapter, we present a preliminary data analysis of the consumption patterns of consumers in 45 countries, consisting of 27 developed countries and 18 developing countries. The results show some similarities as well as dissimilarities between the developed and developing countries in the consumption patterns of 12 broad commodity groups. The analysis further provides support for the law of demand, Engel's law, Frisch conjecture and preference independence. We also found that the income flexibility is an international constant with an estimated value of around −0.5.

In Chapter 4, we formally estimate a system of demand equations derived in Chapter 2; perform tests of a number of demand theory hypotheses and, using measures of goodness-of-fit, select the best model and also present the implied income and price elasticities.

References

Chen, D.L. 2001. *World consumption economics*. Singapore, London: World Scientific.

Clements, K.W. 1982. Divisia Moments of Australian consumption. *Economics Letters* 9: 43–48.

Clements, K.W. 1983. The demand for energy used in transport. *Australian Journal of Management* 8: 27–56.

Clements, K.W. 1987. Chapter 1: Alternative approaches to consumption theory, in H. Theil and K.W. Clements (eds.), *Applied Demand Analysis: Results from System-Wide Approaches.* Cambridge, MA: Ballinger Publishing Company.

Clements, K.W., S. Kappelle, and E.J. Roberts. 1984. Are luxuries more price elastic than necessities? McKethan-Matherly Discussion Paper MM6, Graduate School of Business, University of Florida, Gainesville.

Clements, K.W. and S. Selvanathan. 1994. Understanding consumption patterns. *Empirical Economics* 19: 69–110.

Clements, K.W., J. Si, E.A. Selvanathan, and S. Selvanathan. (2020). Demand elasticities for 9 goods in 37 countries. *Applied Economics* 52(24): 2636–2655.

Clements, K.W., and H. Theil. 1996. Chapter 7: A cross-country analysis of consumption patterns, in H. Theil (ed.), *Studies in Global Economics.* Advanced Studies in Theoretical and Applied Econometrics. Boston, MA: Kluwer Academic Publishers, pp. 95–108.

Deaton, A.S. 1974. The analysis of consumer demand in the United Kingdom, 1900–1970. *Econometrica* 42: 341–367.

Frisch, R. 1959. A complete scheme for computing all direct and cross demand elasticities in a model with many sectors. *Econometrica* 27: 177–196.

Leser, C.E.V. 1963. Forms of Engel functions. *Econometrica* 31: 694–703.

Meisner, J.F. 1979. Divisia Moments of U.S. industry, 1947–1978. *Economics Letters* 4: 239–242.

Pigou, A.C. 1910. A method of determining the numerical values of elasticities of demand. *Economic Journal* 20: 636–640.

Rathnayaka, S D., E.A. Selvanathan and S. Selvanathan. 2019. Consumption atterns in Sri Lanka: A decomposition analysis. *Applied Economics* 51 (37): 4056–4072.

Selvanathan, E.A., and K.W. Clements. 1995. *Recent Developments in applied demand analysis.* London: Springer.

Selvanathan, E.A., and S. Selvanathan. 1993. A cross-country analysis of consumption patterns. *Applied Economics* 25: 1245–1259.

Selvanathan, E.A., and S. Selvanathan. 2003. *International consumption comparisons: OECD versus LDC.* Singapore: World Scientific.

Selvanathan, S. 1993. *A system-wide analysis of international consumption patterns.* Advanced Studies in Theoretical and Applied Econometrics. Boston, MA: Kluwer Academic Publishers.

Theil, H. 1980. *The system-wide approach to microeconomics.* Chicago, NY: University of Chicago Press.

Theil, H. 1987. Chapter 3: The economics of demand systems, in H. Theil and K.W. Clements (eds.), *Applied Demand Analysis: Results from System-wide Approaches.* Cambridge, MA: Ballinger Publishing Company.

Theil, H., and K.W. Clements. 1987. *Applied demand analysis: Results from system-wide approaches.* Cambridge, MA: Ballinger Publishing Company.

Theil, H., and R. Finke. 1984. A time-series analysis of a demand system based on cross-country coefficient estimates. *Economics Letters* 15: 245–250.

Theil, H., J.L. Seale, Jr., and C. F. Chung. 1987. A regional analysis of food consumption in China. *Empirical Economics* 12: 129–135.

Theil, H., and F.E. Suhm. 1981. *International consumption comparisons: A system-wide approach.* Amsterdam: North-Holland Publishing Company.

Working, H. 1943. Statistical laws of family expenditure. *Journal of the American Statistical Association* 38: 43–56.

4 Demand System Estimation

E A Selvanathan, S Selvanathan and M Jayasinghe

4.1 Introduction

One of the primary objectives of applied demand analysis is to estimate demand systems to analyse the responses to changes in income and prices on demand for consumer goods. In Chapter 3, we presented a preliminary analysis of the consumption data for 12 commodities in 45 countries; investigated the empirical regularities in the consumption patterns and verified consumption laws, including Engel's Law and the Law of demand; and derived preliminary demand elasticities. In this chapter, we use three of the demand systems introduced in Chapter 2, the Rotterdam demand model, CBS model and Almost Ideal Demand System (AIDS), to formally model and estimate the demand for nine consumer goods[1] in the 45 countries. We also present results on testing various demand theory hypotheses such as demand homogeneity, Slutsky symmetry and preference independence, and present the implied income and price elasticities. The demand elasticities are useful inputs for policy analysts and researchers, because an understanding of price and income responses is a very important element in the formulation of fiscal policy or any other type of economic program.

4.2 Demand Systems for Estimation

In this section, we present three selected demand systems introduced in Chapter 2 for estimation.

4.2.1 Rotterdam Demand System

In Chapter 2, we derived the finite-change version of the Rotterdam demand system (2.112) in absolute prices in Section 2.11, which we reproduce here,

$$\bar{w}_{it} Dq_{it} = \theta_i DQ_t + \sum_{j=1}^{n} \pi_{ij} Dp_{jt}, \quad i = 1,\ldots,n. \tag{4.1}$$

DOI: 10.4324/9780429200120-4

where $Dq_{it} = \log q_{it} - \log q_{it-1}$ is the finite log-change in consumption of commodity i from period $t-1$ and to t, and $Dp_{it} = \log p_{it} - \log p_{it-1}$ is the finite log-change in price of i from period $t-1$ and to t; $\bar{w}_{it} = ½(w_{i,t} + w_{i,t-1})$ is the arithmetic average of the budget shares in period t and $t-1$; and $DQ_t = \sum_{i=1}^{n} \bar{w}_{it} Dq_{it}$ is the finite-change version of the Divisia volume index. The coefficient θ_i is the marginal share of i and π_{ij} is the (i, j)th Slutsky coefficient.

When the coefficients of equation (4.1), θ_i and π_{ij}, are treated as constants it is known as the ith demand equation of the absolute price version of the Rotterdam demand model.

Dividing both sides of equation (4.1) by $\bar{w}_{it}$, we find that the income and compensated price elasticities are

$$\eta_i = \frac{\theta_i}{\bar{w}_{it}}, \qquad \eta_{ij} = \frac{\pi_{ij}}{\bar{w}_{it}}, \qquad i = 1, 2, \ldots, n. \tag{4.2}$$

As before, we classify a commodity as a necessity (luxury) if its income elasticity is less (greater) than 1.

In view of the demand system (4.1), demand homogeneity and Slutsky symmetry can be tested as

$$\sum_{j=1}^{n} \pi_{ij} = 0, \quad i = 1, 2, \ldots, n, \tag{4.3}$$

and

$$\pi_{ij} = \pi_{ji}, \quad i, j = 1, 2, \ldots, n. \tag{4.4}$$

4.2.2 Working's-Rotterdam Demand System

We derived the Working's model re-parameterisation of the Rotterdam demand system in absolute prices (2.119) in Section 2.12 of Chapter 2, which we reproduce here:

$$\bar{w}_{it}\left(Dq_{it} - DQ_t\right) = \beta_i DQ_t + \sum_{j=1}^{n} \pi_{ij} Dp_{jt}, \quad i = 1, 2, \ldots, n. \tag{4.5}$$

Dividing both sides of equation (4.5) by $\bar{w}_{it}$, we obtain the income and price elasticity of commodity i as

$$\eta_i = 1 + \frac{\beta_i}{\bar{w}_{it}}, \qquad \eta_{ij} = \frac{\pi_{ij}}{\bar{w}_{it}}, \qquad i, j = 1, 2, \ldots, n. \tag{4.6}$$

As can be seen, the income elasticity is less (greater) than one depending on whether the income coefficient β_i in equation (4.5) is less (greater) than zero. That is, a commodity is classified as a necessity or luxury depending on whether β_i is less than 0 or greater than 0.

4.2.3 Almost Ideal Demand System (AIDS)

In Section 2.12 of Chapter 2, we introduced the linearised version of the AIDS given by equation (2.132), which we reproduce here:

$$w_i = \alpha_i + \beta_i \log\frac{M}{P} + \sum_{j=1}^{n} \gamma_{ij} \log p_j, \quad i = 1,2,\ldots,n, \tag{4.7}$$

where $\log P = \sum_k w_k \log p_k$ is the Stone's price index and α_i's, β_i's and γ_{ij}'s are all constants.

The income and uncompensated price elasticities implied by AIDS (4.7) are

$$\eta_i = 1 + \frac{\beta_i}{w_i}, \quad i = 1,2,\ldots,n, \tag{4.8}$$

and

$$\eta_{ij} = -\delta_{ij} + \frac{1}{w_i}\left[\gamma_{ij} - \beta_i w_j\right], \quad i,j = 1,2,\ldots,n. \tag{4.9}$$

As can be seen, the Working (1943) model is a special case of the AIDS and the income elasticity given by both models is the same.

4.2.4 Demand System under Preference Independence

In Sections 2.8 and 2.11, we discussed the preference independent utility function and the demand system under preference independence given by equation (2.113) of Chapter 2, which we reproduce here:

$$\bar{w}_{it} Dq_{it} = \theta_i DQ_t + \phi\theta_i\left(Dp_{it} - DP'_{it}\right), \quad i = 1,2,\ldots,n, \tag{4.10}$$

where the coefficients ϕ and θ_i are specified as constants.

Under the Working model parametrisation, we have $\theta_i = w_i + \beta_i$. $i = 1, 2, \ldots, n$, and the Rotterdam-Working (W-R) model under preference independence is given by equation (2.120), which we reproduce here,

$$\bar{w}_{it}\left(Dq_{it} - DQ_t\right) = \beta_i DQ_t + \phi\left(\beta_i + \bar{w}_{it}\right)\left(Dp_{it} - DP'_t\right), \tag{4.11}$$

where the coefficients ϕ and β_i are specified as constants and $DP'_t = \Sigma_j\left(\beta_j + \bar{w}_{jt}\right)Dp_{jt}$.

4.3 Estimating the Rotterdam Demand System

Estimating a system of demand equations such as equation (4.1) in an unrestricted fashion requires the estimation of an impossibly large number of coefficients. When we have n such demand equations, we have $(n - 1)$ marginal shares and $n(n-1)$ Slutsky coefficients as free parameters need to be estimated. For example, if $n = 10$, then we have 99 free parameters (9 marginal shares and 90 Slutsky coefficients) to be estimated. It is a common practice in demand analysis applications, *a priori* restrictions such as demand homogeneity (4.3) and/or Slutsky symmetry (4.4) or preference independence restrictions are imposed, thus reducing the number of unknown parameters. When $n = 10$, imposing homogeneity and symmetry reduces the number of Slutsky coefficients to be estimated from 90 to 45 or imposing preference independence from 90 to 1, which is a significant reduction in the unknown parameters to be estimated.

Various aspects of testing demand theory hypotheses have also been researched by many researchers (for example, see Barten 1977; Bera et al. 1981; Bewley 1983; Cribari-Neto and Zarkos 1997; Deschamps 2000; Karagiannis and Mergos 2002; Keuzenkamp 2000; Keuzenkamp and Barten 1995; Laitinen 1978; Pollak and Wales 1992; and Theil and Clements 1987). As the sample size for most of the 45 countries considered in our database is around 21, in this chapter, we use the finite-sample test developed by Laitinen (1978) for testing homogeneity.

4.3.1 The Rotterdam Demand Model

We write equation (4.1) for commodity i (=1, 2, …, n, the number of goods) and period t (=1, 2, …, T, the sample size after lagging), with an error term added as

$$\bar{w}_{it} Dq_{it} = \theta_i DQ_t + \sum_{j=1}^{n} \pi_{ij} Dp_{jt} + \varepsilon_{it}. \tag{4.12}$$

where θ_i is the ith marginal share satisfying $\Sigma_{i=1}^{n} \theta_i = 1$; π_{ij} is the (i, j)th Slutsky coefficient satisfying $\Sigma_{i=1}^{n} \pi_{ij} = 0$; and all other notations are as before. The error terms are assumed to be normally distributed with zero mean and are independent over time. If we sum both sides of equation (4.12) over $i = 1$, 2, …, n, we get $\Sigma_{i=1}^{n} \varepsilon_{it} = 0$ for $t = 1, 2, …, T$. Therefore, the ε_{it}'s are linearly dependent and one of the equations is redundant and can be deleted (Barten 1964). We delete the nth equation. It can be shown that the best linear unbiased estimators of the parameters for the system of equations (4.12) for $i = 1, 2, …, n$ are the same as those obtained by estimating each equation separately by least squares (LS). See Theil (1971) for details.

Let Σ be the $(n-1)\times(n-1)$ contemporaneous covariance matrix of the disturbance term ε_{it} of (4.12) for $i = 1, ..., n-1$. In general, Σ is unknown. For estimation and hypothesis testing, it is common practice to approximate this matrix by its unbiased estimator **S**, the matrix of mean squares and cross-products of the LS residuals.

Denoting $y_{it} = \bar{w}_{it} Dq_{it}$, $\mathbf{y}_i = [\theta_i \, \pi_{i1} \, \ldots \, \pi_{in}]'$ and $\mathbf{x}_t = [DQ_t \; Dp_{1t} \ldots Dp_{nt}]'$, and deleting the nth equation, (4.12) can be written for $t = 1, 2, \ldots, T$ in vector form as

$$y_i = \mathbf{X}\gamma_i + \varepsilon_i, \quad i = 1,2,\ldots,n, \tag{4.13}$$

where $y_i = [y_{it}]$ is a T-vector; $\mathbf{X}$ is a $T \times (n + 1)$ matrix whose tth row is $\mathbf{x}_t'$; and $\varepsilon_i = [\varepsilon_{it}]$ is a T-vector. We write equation (4.13) for $i = 1, \ldots, n - 1$ as

$$y = (\mathbf{I}_{n-1} \otimes \mathbf{X})\gamma + \varepsilon \tag{4.14}$$

where $\mathbf{I}_{n-1}$ is the identity matrix of order $(n - 1)$; $y = [y_i]$, $y = [y_i]$ and $\varepsilon = [\varepsilon_i]$ are vectors consisting of $(n - 1)$ subvectors; and $\otimes$ is the Kronecker product.

4.3.2 Testing Demand Homogeneity

Let $\boldsymbol{a} = [0 \; 1 \; \ldots \; 1]'$ be a $(n+1)$-vector. Then, demand homogeneity, (4.3), can be written in vector form as

$$\boldsymbol{a}'\gamma_i = 0, \quad i = 1,\ldots,n.$$

For $i = 1, \ldots, n - 1$, this can be expressed as

$$\mathbf{R}\gamma = 0, \tag{4.15}$$

where $\mathbf{R} = \mathbf{I}_{n-1} \otimes \boldsymbol{a}'$.

The test statistic for testing the homogeneity restriction (4.15) is

$$\frac{(\mathbf{R}\hat{\gamma})'\Sigma^{-1}(\mathbf{R}\hat{\gamma})/\mathbf{a}'(\mathbf{X}'\mathbf{X})^{-1}\mathbf{a}}{\operatorname{tr}\Sigma^{-1}\mathbf{S}}, \tag{4.16}$$

where $\hat{\gamma}$ is the LS estimator of γ; Σ is the error covariance matrix; and $\mathbf{S}$ is the LS residual moment matrix, an unbiased estimator of Σ (Theil, 1971). When Σ is known, under the null hypothesis, equation (4.16) is distributed as F with $(n-1)$ and $(n-1)(T-n-2)$ degrees of freedom. Usually, the error covariance matrix Σ is unknown and is replaced by its estimator $\mathbf{S}$. The test statistic for homogeneity then becomes

$$\Psi_H = \frac{(\mathbf{R}\hat{\gamma})'\mathbf{S}^{-1}(\mathbf{R}\hat{\gamma})}{\mathbf{a}'(\mathbf{X}'\mathbf{X})^{-1}\mathbf{a}} \tag{4.17}$$

Under the null hypothesis, it can be easily shown that Ψ_H has an asymptotic $\chi 2$ distribution with $(n - 1)$ degrees of freedom. It is worth noting that as equation (4.17) involves $\mathbf{S}^{-1}$, $\mathbf{S}$ must be non-singular. The necessary condition for $\mathbf{S}$ to be non-singular is that $T-2n \geq 1$ (Laitinen 1978).

Laitinen (1978) derived the exact finite-sample distribution of Ψ_H in equation (4.17) under the null hypothesis of demand homogeneity restriction.

Laitin).en showed that Ψ_H is distributed as a Hotelling's T^2, which itself is distributed as a constant multiple $(n-1)(T-n-1)/(T-2n+1)$ of $F(n-1,T-2n+1)$. This exact test is very useful in applications where the sample size is relatively small.

We present the test results for testing the homogeneity hypothesis for the Rotterdam model (4.1) in Table 4.1. Columns (1)–(3) present the country, the number of commodities (n) and the sample size after lagging (T). Column (4) gives the value of the test statistic (4.17) and next two columns give the two degrees of freedom $(n-1)$ and $(T-2n+1)$ for the F-test statistic and column (7) gives the value of the multiplier for the F-test. Column (8) gives the corresponding p-value for the F-test statistic value presented in column (4). Column (9) presents the conclusion of the test. As can be seen, for a majority of the 45 countries homogeneity is acceptable at the 5 percent level of significance and, for almost all countries, it is acceptable at the 1 percent level. Therefore, we use the model with the homogeneity restriction imposed.

The homogeneity-constrained version of model (4.1) is obtained by imposing the homogeneity restriction (4.3) on (4.1),

$$y_{it} = \theta_i DQ_t + \sum_{j=1}^{n-1} \pi_{ij}\left(Dp_{jt} - Dp_{nt}\right) + \varepsilon_{it}, \quad i = 1,\ldots,n; \; t = 1,2,\ldots,T. \tag{4.18}$$

Let $\gamma_i^H = [\theta_i \; \pi_{i1} \; \ldots \; \pi_{in-1}]'$ and $\mathbf{X}_t^H = [DQ_t \; (Dp_{1t} - Dp_{nt}) \; \ldots \; (Dp_{n-1,t} - Dp_{nt})]'$. Then, equation (4.18) can be written as

$$y_i = \mathbf{X}^H \gamma_i^H + \varepsilon_i, \quad i = 1,\ldots,n, \tag{4.19}$$

where $\mathbf{X}^H$ is a $T \times n$ matrix whose tth row is $\mathbf{X}_t^{H\prime}$; and y_i and ε_i are as previously defined. As done earlier, we delete the nth equation and write equation (4.19) in matrix form as

$$y = \left(\mathbf{I} \otimes \mathbf{X}^H\right)\gamma^H + \varepsilon, \tag{4.20}$$

where $\mathbf{I}$ is the identity matrix of order $(n-1)$; $Y^H = [y_i^H]$ is a vector consisting of $(n-1)$ subvectors; and y and ε are as defined before. Let $\hat{y}_i^H$ be the LS estimator of Y_i^H for $i = 1, \ldots, n$; and $\hat{Y}^H = \left[\hat{y}_i^H\right]$ be the vector consisting of $(n-1)$ subvectors.

4.3.3 Testing Slutsky Symmetry

In vector form, for $i, j = 1, \ldots, n-1$, the symmetry restrictions (4.4) can be written as

$$\mathbf{R}\gamma^H = 0, \tag{4.21}$$

where $\mathbf{R}$ is a $q \times n(n-1)$ matrix with $q = \frac{1}{2}(n-1)(n-2)$ and each row of $\mathbf{R}$ consists of zeros except for a 1 and a -1 corresponding to π_{ij} and π_{ji} for some $i \neq j$.

Table 4.1 Testing homogeneity and symmetry – Rotterdam demand system, 45 countries

				Testing homogeneity (F-test)						Testing symmetry (χ^2-test)		
	Country	n	T (after lagging)	Test statistic	df1	df2	Multiplier	p-value	Decision	Test statistic	p-value	Decision
	(1)	(2)	(3)	(4)	(5)	(6)	(7)	(8)	(9)	(10)	(11)	(12)
Developed countries												
1	Australia	9	29	13.2	8	12	12.7	0.457	Accept	41.8	0.045	Accept
2	Austria	9	20	31.3	8	3	26.7	0.497	Accept	93.1	0.000	Reject
3	Belgium	9	19	1203.6	8	2	36.0	0.029	*Accept	134.4	0.000	Reject
4	Canada	9	34	12.7	8	17	11.3	0.398	Accept	58.2	0.001	Reject
5	Denmark	9	20	1736.5	8	3	26.7	0.003	Reject	43.4	0.032	*Accept
6	Finland	9	40	10.2	8	23	10.4	0.477	Accept	49.5	0.007	Reject
7	France	9	56	12.3	8	39	9.4	0.270	Accept	31.9	0.278	Accept
8	Germany	9	19	6.9	8	2	36.0	0.964	Accept	32.1	0.270	Accept
9	Hong Kong	8	45	21.8	7	30	8.4	0.032	*Accept	25.3	0.236	Accept
10	Iceland	9	19	91.1	8	2	36.0	0.314	Accept	74.9	0.000	Reject
11	Ireland	8	18	103.9	7	3	21.0	0.108	Accept	46.1	0.001	Reject
12	Israel	9	19	37.7	8	2	36.0	0.576	Accept	86.2	0.000	Reject
13	Italy	9	19	95.5	8	2	36.0	0.302	Accept	68.4	0.000	Reject
14	Japan	9	19	28.8	8	2	36.0	0.663	Accept	59.1	0.001	Reject
15	Luxembourg	9	20	8.7	8	3	26.7	0.909	Accept	52.1	0.004	Reject
16	Netherlands	9	19	4.7	8	2	36.0	0.986	Accept	64.9	0.000	Reject
17	New Zealand	9	27	27.2	8	10	13.6	0.151	Accept	83.0	0.000	Reject
18	Norway	9	27	9.5	8	10	13.6	0.687	Accept	62.0	0.000	Reject
19	Singapore	8	27	16.0	7	12	10.5	0.249	Accept	41.3	0.005	Reject
20	Slovenia	9	19	40.3	8	2	36.0	0.553	Accept	117.2	0.000	Reject
21	South Korea	9	45	49.7	8	28	10.0	0.001	Reject	59.6	0.000	Reject
22	Spain	9	19	58.7	8	2	36.0	0.435	Accept	195.4	0.000	Reject
23	Sweden	9	22	18.5	8	5	19.2	0.542	Accept	36.1	0.141	Accept
24	Switzerland	8	18	559.0	7	3	21.0	0.011	*Accept	25.7	0.218	Accept
25	Taiwan	8	54	6.7	7	39	8.1	0.568	Accept	25.7	0.217	Accept
26	UK	9	20	125.6	8	3	26.7	0.115	Accept	88.4	0.000	Reject
27	USA	9	45	52.3	8	28	10.0	0.000	Reject	61.9	0.000	Reject

Developing countries												
28	Colombia	6	14	13.9	5	3	11.7	0.471	Accept	21.0	0.021	*Accept
29	Czech Republic	9	20	700.9	8	3	26.7	0.011	*Accept	34.4	0.189	Accept
30	Estonia	9	20	48.4	8	3	26.7	0.338	Accept	141.2	0.000	Reject
31	Greece	9	20	39.3	8	3	26.7	0.411	Accept	33.6	0.215	Accept
32	Hungary	9	20	12.3	8	3	26.7	0.830	Accept	102.7	0.000	Reject
33	India	8	45	42.9	7	30	8.4	0.001	Reject	38.1	0.013	*Accept
34	Latvia	9	19	26.6	8	2	36.0	0.688	Accept	46.3	0.016	*Accept
35	Lithuania	9	19	108.9	8	2	36.0	0.272	Accept	43.4	0.032	*Accept
36	Malaysia	7	16	19.8	6	3	16.0	0.466	Accept	40.7	0.000	Reject
37	Mexico	5	11	8.7	4	2	10.0	0.598	Accept	4.7	0.588	Accept
38	Philippines	8	18	63.8	7	3	21.0	0.195	Accept	28.3	0.132	Reject
39	Poland	9	20	44.2	8	3	26.7	0.369	Accept	91.9	0.000	Reject
40	Portugal	9	20	40.8	8	3	26.7	0.397	Accept	67.1	0.000	Reject
41	Slovakia	9	20	14.5	8	3	26.7	0.781	Accept	133.4	0.000	Reject
42	South Africa	9	39	15.9	8	22	10.5	0.210	Accept	36.2	0.137	Accept
43	Sri Lanka	8	41	17.7	7	26	8.6	0.085	Accept	28.0	0.141	Accept
44	Thailand	8	48	9.9	7	33	8.3	0.329	Accept	40.1	0.007	Reject
45	Turkey	7	16	24.4	6	3	16.0	0.392	Accept	67.1	0.000	Reject

Note: $df1 = n - 1$; $df2 = T - 2n + 1$; Multiplier = $df1*(T - n - 1)/df2$. *Accept means acceptable at the 1 percent level of significance. Among the 45 countries, the homogeneity hypothesis is rejected for 8 percent of the countries and the homogeneity and symmetry hypothesis is rejected for 60 percent of the countries.

The test statistic for symmetry is given by (see, e.g., Theil, 1971)

$$\frac{\left(\mathbf{R}\hat{\gamma}^{H}\right)'\left\{\mathbf{R}\left[\Sigma\otimes\left(\mathbf{X}^{H\prime}\mathbf{X}^{H}\right)^{-1}\right]\mathbf{R}'\right\}^{-1}\left(\mathbf{R}\hat{\gamma}^{H}\right)}{[q/(n-1)]\operatorname{tr}\Sigma^{-1}\mathbf{S}}, \tag{4.22}$$

where Σ is the error covariance matrix of model (4.18) for $i = 1, \ldots, n-1$. Under the null hypothesis of symmetry, equation (4.22) is distributed as F with q and $(n-1)(T\ n)$ degrees of freedom. As before, we replace Σ by its estimator **S** (when **S** is nonsingular) and the test statistic becomes

$$\Psi_S = \left(\mathbf{R}\hat{\gamma}^{H}\right)'\left\{\mathbf{R}\left[\mathbf{S}\otimes\left(\mathbf{X}^{H\prime}\mathbf{X}^{H}\right)^{-1}\right]\mathbf{R}'\right\}^{-1}\left(\mathbf{R}\hat{\gamma}^{H}\right), \tag{4.23}$$

which has an asymptotic $\chi 2$ distribution with q degrees of freedom.

Columns (10)–(12) of Table 4.1 present the test results for the Slutsky symmetry hypothesis. Columns (10) and (11) give the value of the test statistic for symmetry given by equation (4.23) and the corresponding p-value for the 45 countries, and column (12) presents the resulting symmetry test conclusion. As can be seen, the symmetry hypothesis is not supported by most of the countries at the 5 percent level of significance.

4.3.4 Testing Preference Independence

Now we test the preference independence hypothesis using a distribution-free test based on Barnard's (1963) Monte Carlo simulation procedure developed for preference independence in Selvanathan (1987). The basic idea behind the Monte Carlo simulation procedure is to simulate a large number of values of the test statistic under the null hypothesis to construct its empirical distribution. The observed value of the test statistic is then compared with this distribution. Below, we set out this Monte Carlo procedure and then present its application to preference independence.

Using the standard notation, consider the system of equations $\mathbf{y} = \mathbf{X}\boldsymbol{\beta} + \varepsilon$. Suppose we are interested in testing the null hypothesis $\mathbf{R}\boldsymbol{\beta} = \mathbf{b}$ using a test statistic τ. Obviously τ is a function of the estimate of the parameter vector $\boldsymbol{\beta}$. In general, the Monte Carlo procedure can be summarised as follows:

Step 1: Estimate the unrestricted model and obtain the data-based value $\tau 1$ of τ.

Step 2: Estimate the model under the null hypothesis $\mathbf{R}\beta = \mathbf{b}$ and obtain the estimate **S** of the covariance matrix Σ of the disturbances.

Step 3: Generate quasi-normal error terms with zero means and covariance matrix **S** and use these errors together with the observed value of **X** and the restricted estimates to generate a new data set for **y** under the null hypothesis. Use the generated data to estimate the unrestricted model.

Step 4: Repeat Step 3 a certain number of times, say N, and in each case calculate the simulated value of the test statistic τ.

Step 5: Let $\tau_2, \tau_3 \ldots \tau_M$ be the values of the test statistic τ obtained from the simulated data, where $M = N + 1$. For a one-tailed test, we reject the null hypothesis for the observed sample at the α percent significance level if τ_l is among the M' largest values of the τ_i's such that $(M'/M) \times 100 = \alpha$.

The number of replications (N) is usually chosen to be sufficiently large to reduce the 'blurring effect', which leads to loss of power (see Marriot 1979). However, after a certain number of replications, the return for increased computing time diminishes. According to Besag and Diggle (1977), the suggested number of replications to reduce the 'blurring effect' for a 5 percent significance test is 999. If we use $\alpha = 5$ percent significance level and $N = 999$ simulations, for a one-tailed test, we reject the null hypothesis if the rank of τl is 951, ..., 999 or 1,000. For $\alpha = 1$ percent and $N = 999$ simulations, for a one-tailed test, we reject the null hypothesis if the rank of τl is 991, ..., 999 or 1,000.

We now apply this simulation procedure to test the preference independence hypothesis for the 45 countries. Table 4.2 presents the test results. As can be seen, except for four countries (Canada, Ireland, USA, and Philippines), the preference independence hypothesis is widely supported by data from most countries.

4.3.5 Final Estimates under the Rotterdam Demand System

Since preference independence among the nine commodity groups is widely acceptable for the 45 countries data, we report only the estimation results from the Rotterdam demand model under preference independence, given by equation (4.10), for all countries in Table 4.3. Columns (2)–(10) present the estimated marginal shares (θ_i s), and the last column gives the estimate for the income flexibility ϕ. As can be seen, all the estimates for the marginal shares (except food and clothing for Belgium, housing for Germany and health care for Sweden) are positive and all estimates for income flexibility are negative and almost all of them are statistically significant.

Table 4.4 presents the implied income elasticities for the nine commodity groups under preference independence. As can be seen, all the income elasticity estimates for food are less than one (except for Belgium, Luxembourg, Switzerland and Portugal), indicating that food is a necessity. Housing and health are, generally, necessities while clothing, durables, transport and communication, education and restaurants are luxuries. The mean income elasticity across the 45 countries for food is 0.64, housing 0.45 and health care 0.89 which are less than one, indicating that overall, these three commodities are necessities. The mean income elasticity for clothing is 1.29, durables 1.50, transport 1.60, education 1.32 and restaurants 1.20, which are all greater than one, indicating that these five commodities are luxuries.

Table 4.2 Testing preference independence – Rotterdam demand system, 45 countries

	Country	Observed value of the test statistic	Rank	Decision at the 5 percent level	Decision at the 1 percent level
	(1)	(2)	(3)	(4)	(5)
Developed countries					
1	Australia	79.63	939	Accept	Accept
2	Austria	120.38	929	Accept	Accept
3	Belgium	116.41	753	Accept	Accept
4	Canada	102.32	999	Reject	Reject
5	Denmark	75.59	413	Accept	Accept
6	Finland	54.19	689	Accept	Accept
7	France	71.45	990	Reject	Accept
8	Germany	58.00	103	Accept	Accept
9	Hong Kong	46.64	882	Accept	Accept
10	Iceland	126.28	881	Accept	Accept
11	Ireland	128.61	995	Reject	Reject
12	Israel	98.46	538	Accept	Accept
13	Italy	140.06	892	Accept	Accept
14	Japan	132.80	887	Accept	Accept
15	Luxembourg	107.48	841	Accept	Accept
16	Netherlands	99.32	586	Accept	Accept
17	New Zealand	81.78	934	Accept	Accept
18	Norway	53.37	769	Accept	Accept
19	Singapore	34.82	620	Accept	Accept
20	Slovenia	154.10	986	Reject	Accept
21	South Korea	46.76	564	Accept	Accept
22	Spain	158.69	962	Reject	Accept
23	Sweden	87.68	815	Accept	Accept
24	Switzerland	36.20	76	Accept	Accept
25	Taiwan	43.56	894	Accept	Accept
26	UK	80.76	531	Accept	Accept
27	USA	83.44	998	Reject	Reject
Developing countries					
28	Colombia	54.78	904	Accept	Accept
29	Czech Republic	92.39	672	Accept	Accept
30	Estonia	107.59	844	Accept	Accept
31	Greece	53.01	74	Accept	Accept
32	Hungary	94.20	727	Accept	Accept
33	India	50.09	943	Accept	Accept
34	Latvia	105.74	692	Accept	Accept
35	Lithuania	102.11	614	Accept	Accept
36	Malaysia	55.37	692	Accept	Accept
37	Mexico	40.99	905	Accept	Accept
38	Philippines	124.91	992	Reject	Reject
39	Poland	138.73	976	Reject	Accept
40	Portugal	101.58	753	Accept	Accept
41	Slovakia	82.98	546	Accept	Accept
42	South Africa	61.66	876	Accept	Accept
43	Sri Lanka	55.05	972	Reject	Accept
44	Thailand	58.15	991	Reject	Accept
45	Turkey	60.78	779	Accept	Accept

Note: Among the 45 countries, the preference independence hypothesis is rejected at the 5 percent level of significance for 20 percent of the countries and at the 1 percent level for 9 percent of the countries.

Table 4.3 Marginal shares and income flexibility – Rotterdam demand system under preference independence, 45 countries

Country	Marginal shares									Income flexibility
Country	*Food*	*Clothing*	*Housing*	*Durables*	*Health*	*Transport*	*Education*	*Restaurants*	*Miscellaneous*	*Income flexibility*
(1)	*(2)*	*(3)*	*(4)*	*(5)*	*(6)*	*(7)*	*(8)*	*(9)*	*(10)*	*(11)*
Developed countries										
1 Australia	0.09 (0.21)	0.06 (0.01)	0.08 (0.01)	0.08 (0.02)	0.04 (0.01)	0.21 (0.04)	0.14 (0.02)	0.11 (0.02)	0.19 (0.04)	−0.46 (0.06)
2 Austria	0.04 (0.02)	0.02 (0.02)	0.19 (0.04)	0.07 (0.01)	0.02 (0.01)	0.33 (0.05)	0.20 (0.03)	0.07 (0.04)	0.08 (0.02)	−0.27 (0.06)
3 Belgium	−0.02 (0.04)	−0.03 (0.03)	0.17 (0.05)	0.08 (0.02)	0.03 (0.01)	0.26 (0.05)	0.14 (0.05)	0.05 (0.02)	0.31 (0.06)	−0.14 (0.04)
4 Canada	0.07 (0.01)	0.09 (0.01)	0.01 (0.02)	0.13 (0.01)	0.02 (0.01)	0.32 (0.03)	0.12 (0.01)	0.12 (0.01)	0.11 (0.02)	−0.34 (0.05)
5 Denmark	0.08 (0.01)	0.03 (0.01)	0.01 (0.04)	0.08 (0.01)	0.01 (0.01)	0.36 (0.04)	0.17 (0.02)	0.08 (0.01)	0.19 (0.03)	−0.50 (0.08)
6 Finland	0.10 (0.02)	0.09 (0.01)	0.01 (0.02)	0.09 (0.01)	0.02 (0.01)	0.31 (0.03)	0.17 (0.01)	0.11 (0.01)	0.11 (0.02)	−0.37 (0.05)
7 France	0.13 (0.01)	0.12 (0.01)	0.14 (0.02)	0.11 (0.01)	0.00 (0.01)	0.25 (0.02)	0.12 (0.01)	0.04 (0.01)	0.08 (0.02)	−0.44 (0.04)
8 Germany	0.14 (0.03)	0.05 (0.02)	−0.04 (0.08)	0.13 (0.05)	0.02 (0.02)	0.39 (0.08)	0.15 (0.03)	0.11 (0.02)	0.05 (0.02)	−0.44 (0.07)
9 Hong Kong	0.09 (0.02)	0.42 (0.03)	0.04 (0.01)	0.14 (0.02)	0.04 (0.01)	0.08 (0.01)	–	0.06 (0.01)	0.14 (0.03)	−0.25 (0.07)
10 Iceland	0.06 (0.02)	0.06 (0.01)	0.19 (0.04)	0.08 (0.01)	0.00 (0.01)	0.34 (0.03)	0.10 (0.02)	0.10 (0.02)	0.07 (0.01)	−0.68 (0.08)
11 Ireland	0.16 (0.01)	0.06 (0.00)	0.23 (0.02)	0.07 (0.00)	0.04 (0.00)	0.18 (0.01)	–	0.20 (0.01)	0.06 (0.01)	−1.60 (0.07)
12 Israel	0.06 (0.02)	0.03 (0.02)	0.09 (0.02)	0.12 (0.01)	0.04 (0.01)	0.38 (0.03)	0.11 (0.02)	0.07 (0.04)	0.10 (0.02)	−0.06 (0.07)
13 Italy	0.16 (0.01)	0.10 (0.01)	0.04 (0.02)	0.11 (0.01)	0.04 (0.01)	0.27 (0.03)	0.13 (0.02)	0.08 (0.02)	0.07 (0.02)	−0.33 (0.05)
14 Japan	0.16 (0.02)	0.11 (0.02)	0.09 (0.02)	0.10 (0.02)	0.03 (0.02)	0.17 (0.02)	–	0.14 (0.02)	0.20 (0.05)	−0.41 (0.05)
15 Luxembourg	0.23 (0.03)	0.05 (0.01)	0.21 (0.02)	0.06 (0.01)	0.01 (0.01)	0.15 (0.02)	0.08 (0.01)	0.07 (0.01)	0.16 (0.02)	−0.16 (0.08)
16 Netherlands	0.07 (0.01)	0.05 (0.01)	0.03 (0.03)	0.11 (0.02)	0.09 (0.07)	0.27 (0.03)	0.15 (0.02)	0.08 (0.02)	0.15 (0.02)	−0.11 (0.05)
17 New Zealand	0.17 (0.02)	0.04 (0.01)	0.15 (0.02)	0.06 (0.02)	0.01 (0.01)	0.28 (0.03)	0.12 (0.02)	0.08 (0.02)	0.09 (0.01)	−0.49 (0.07)
18 Norway	0.16 (0.02)	0.09 (0.01)	0.07 (0.02)	0.09 (0.01)	0.01 (0.00)	0.41 (0.02)	0.11 (0.01)	0.03 (0.01)	0.06 (0.01)	−0.79 (0.07)
19 Singapore	0.10 (0.02)	0.07 (0.01)	0.04 (0.01)	0.07 (0.01)	0.02 (0.01)	0.21 (0.03)	–	0.30 (0.03)	0.19 (0.02)	−0.42 (0.09)
20 Slovenia	0.17 (0.02)	0.09 (0.02)	0.11 (0.03)	0.07 (0.02)	0.03 (0.01)	0.20 (0.03)	0.15 (0.03)	0.09 (0.01)	0.09 (0.02)	−0.31 (0.06)
21 South Korea	0.17 (0.03)	0.13 (0.02)	0.05 (0.02)	0.10 (0.01)	0.03 (0.01)	0.19 (0.01)	0.11 (0.01)	0.09 (0.01)	0.13 (0.02)	−0.20 (0.04)
22 Spain	0.09 (0.02)	0.08 (0.01)	0.03 (0.02)	0.08 (0.01)	0.02 (0.01)	0.24 (0.02)	0.12 (0.01)	0.22 (0.02)	0.12 (0.02)	−0.30 (0.05)
23 Sweden	0.11 (0.03)	0.09 (0.01)	0.16 (0.03)	0.09 (0.01)	−0.03 (0.01)	0.31 (0.06)	0.24 (0.03)	0.01 (0.02)	0.01 (0.02)	−0.46 (0.07)
24 Switzerland	0.15 (0.01)	0.03 (0.00)	0.22 (0.01)	0.04 (0.00)	0.11 (0.01)	0.11 (0.01)	–	0.17 (0.01)	0.18 (0.01)	−1.92 (0.06)
25 Taiwan	0.17 (0.02)	0.08 (0.01)	0.14 (0.02)	0.05 (0.01)	0.04 (0.01)	0.25 (0.03)	–	0.10 (0.02)	0.17 (0.03)	−0.21 (0.04)
26 UK	0.07 (0.01)	0.06 (0.01)	0.10 (0.02)	0.10 (0.01)	0.03 (0.01)	0.16 (0.01)	0.22 (0.02)	0.14 (0.02)	0.11 (0.02)	−0.77 (0.05)
27 USA	0.06 (0.01)	0.07 (0.01)	0.10 (0.01)	0.11 (0.01)	0.05 (0.02)	0.26 (0.02)	0.12 (0.01)	0.07 (0.01)	0.16 (0.02)	−0.45 (0.04)
Mean (*Developed*)	0.11(0.01)	0.08 (0.00)	0.10 (0.01)	0.09 (0.00)	0.03 (0.00)	0.26 (0.01)	0.14 (0.00)	0.10 (0.00)	0.13 (0.00)	−0.48 (0.01)

(Continued)

Table 4.3 Marginal shares and income flexibility – Rotterdam demand system under preference independence, 45 countries (*Continued*)

Country	Marginal shares									Income flexibility
	Food	*Clothing*	*Housing*	*Durables*	*Health*	*Transport*	*Education*	*Restaurants*	*Miscellaneous*	
(1)	*(2)*	*(3)*	*(4)*	*(5)*	*(6)*	*(7)*	*(8)*	*(9)*	*(10)*	*(11)*
Developing countries										
28 Colombia	0.12 (0.03)	0.13 (0.02)	0.04 (0.02)	0.05 (0.01)	0.03 (0.01)	–	–	–	0.64 (0.03)	−0.21 (0.11)
29 Czech Republic	0.12 (0.03)	0.05 (0.01)	0.08 (0.03)	0.07 (0.01)	0.03 (0.01)	0.20 (0.03)	0.17 (0.02)	0.07 (0.02)	0.22 (0.04)	−0.41 (0.06)
30 Estonia	0.17 (0.03)	0.07 (0.01)	0.16 (0.03)	0.07 (0.01)	0.02 (0.00)	0.21 (0.02)	0.14 (0.01)	0.06 (0.01)	0.10 (0.01)	−0.51 (0.05)
31 Greece	0.15 (0.04)	0.09 (0.01)	0.06 (0.03)	0.09 (0.01)	0.08 (0.02)	0.25 (0.05)	0.09 (0.01)	0.10 (0.03)	0.08 (0.03)	−0.28 (0.12)
32 Hungary	0.18 (0.02)	0.06 (0.01)	0.09 (0.02)	0.10 (0.02)	0.08 (0.01)	0.29 (0.04)	0.12 (0.02)	0.06 (0.02)	0.02 (0.02)	−0.61 (0.06)
33 India	0.48 (0.07)	0.15 (0.03)	0.03 (0.01)	0.06 (0.01)	0.01 (0.01)	0.14 (0.03)	–	0.02 (0.01)	0.10 (0.02)	−0.10 (0.03)
34 Latvia	0.20 (0.03)	0.07 (0.01)	0.04 (0.04)	0.06 (0.01)	0.04 (0.01)	0.24 (0.02)	0.16 (0.02)	0.13 (0.02)	0.07 (0.02)	−0.55 (0.11)
35 Lithuania	0.27 (0.03)	0.01 (0.02)	0.07 (0.02)	0.06 (0.01)	0.07 (0.01)	0.21 (0.03)	0.09 (0.01)	0.04 (0.01)	0.11 (0.02)	−0.31 (0.08)
36 Malaysia	0.07 (0.04)	0.07 (0.02)	0.07 (0.02)	0.08 (0.02)	0.02 (0.01)	0.26 (0.03)	–	–	0.43 (0.05)	−0.36 (0.12)
37 Mexico	0.08 (0.02)	0.01 (0.00)	0.23 (0.03)	–	0.05 (0.01)	–	–	–	0.63 (0.04)	−0.97 (0.12)
38 Philippines	0.38 (0.05)	0.00 (0.01)	0.06 (0.04)	0.04 (0.03)	0.04 (0.01)	0.16 (0.04)	–	0.06 (0.01)	0.27 (0.05)	−0.16 (0.05)
39 Poland	0.15 (0.02)	0.07 (0.01)	0.11 (0.04)	0.08 (0.01)	0.09 (0.01)	0.21 (0.03)	0.16 (0.03)	0.06 (0.01)	0.07 (0.03)	−0.52 (0.05)
40 Portugal	0.24 (0.05)	0.06 (0.01)	−0.03 (0.02)	0.07 (0.01)	0.03 (0.01)	0.36 (0.03)	0.08 (0.01)	0.09 (0.02)	0.09 (0.03)	−0.23 (0.07)
41 Slovakia	0.20 (0.04)	0.05 (0.01)	0.15 (0.05)	0.09 (0.01)	0.04 (0.02)	0.11 (0.02)	0.12 (0.01)	0.11 (0.02)	0.13 (0.02)	−0.41 (0.05)
42 South Africa	0.19 (0.03)	0.09 (0.01)	0.04 (0.02)	0.12 (0.01)	0.05 (0.01)	0.24 (0.03)	0.09 (0.01)	0.05 (0.01)	0.14 (0.02)	−0.36 (0.04)
43 Sri Lanka	0.47 (0.05)	0.10 (0.02)	0.07 (0.02)	0.07 (0.01)	0.02 (0.00)	0.15 (0.03)	–	0.06 (0.02)	0.07 (0.01)	−0.63 (0.08)
44 Thailand	0.14 (0.03)	0.05 (0.01)	0.01 (0.01)	0.06 (0.01)	0.05 (0.01)	0.25 (0.02)	–	0.39 (0.07)	0.05 (0.04)	−0.04 (0.06)
45 Turkey	0.10 (0.03)	0.06 (0.03)	0.05 (0.01)	0.16 (0.02)	0.04 (0.01)	–	–	0.35 (0.03)	0.25 (0.04)	−0.24 (0.06)
Mean (*Developing*)	0.21(0.01)	0.07 (0.00)	0.07 (0.01)	0.08 (0.00)	0.04 (0.00)	0.22 (0.01)	0.12 (0.00)	0.11 (0.01)	0.19 (0.01)	−0.38 (0.02)
Mean (*All countries*)	0.15(0.01)	0.07 (0.00)	0.09 (0.00)	0.09 (0.00)	0.03 (0.00)	0.24 (0.00)	0.14 (0.00)	0.11 (0.00)	0.15 (0.00)	−0.44 (0.01)

Table 4.4 Income elasticities of nine commodities, Rotterdam demand system under preference independence, 45 countries

	Country (1)	*Food* (2)	*Clothing* (3)	*Housing* (4)	*Durables* (5)	*Health* (6)	*Transport* (7)	*Education* (8)	*Restaurants* (9)	*Miscellaneous* (10)
Developed countries										
1	Australia	0.617	1.472	0.374	1.346	0.776	1.473	1.011	1.585	1.327
2	Austria	0.288	0.328	0.915	0.988	0.411	2.146	1.742	0.594	0.712
3	Belgium	–0.091	–0.513	0.713	1.364	0.512	1.862	1.489	0.899	2.325
4	Canada	0.508	1.757	0.042	2.174	0.644	1.943	1.204	1.623	0.815
5	Denmark	0.472	0.702	0.026	1.523	0.241	2.510	1.418	1.457	1.508
6	Finland	0.438	1.785	0.045	1.721	0.721	2.054	1.492	1.525	1.204
7	France	0.64	1.561	0.698	1.609	0.111	1.643	1.317	0.716	0.735
8	Germany	0.996	0.984	–0.172	1.795	0.390	2.285	1.474	2.148	0.435
9	Hong Kong	0.502	2.567	0.215	1.728	0.961	0.960	–	0.714	0.717
10	Iceland	0.295	1.231	0.967	1.251	0.104	1.982	0.786	1.191	0.790
11	Ireland	0.953	1.243	1.139	1.122	1.207	1.182	–	0.875	0.556
12	Israel	0.353	0.916	0.401	1.755	1.144	2.104	1.118	1.224	0.813
13	Italy	0.820	1.397	0.216	1.515	1.143	1.745	1.561	0.938	0.701
14	Japan	0.816	1.971	0.443	1.864	0.308	1.558	1.176	–	1.354
15	Luxembourg	1.202	0.890	0.975	0.900	0.406	0.811	0.953	0.903	1.297
16	Netherlands	0.465	0.988	0.165	1.678	2.390	1.565	1.238	1.150	1.089
17	New Zealand	0.867	0.923	0.575	0.965	0.661	1.681	1.055	1.452	1.004
18	Norway	0.767	1.197	0.340	1.325	0.241	2.419	0.990	0.655	0.415
19	Singapore	0.646	1.176	0.345	0.874	0.502	1.460	–	1.278	1.193
20	Slovenia	0.826	1.605	0.588	1.286	0.824	1.084	1.372	1.288	0.940
21	South Korea	0.625	1.695	0.359	2.495	0.932	1.477	0.941	1.036	1.253
22	Spain	0.478	1.540	0.185	1.495	0.572	1.701	1.236	1.341	1.263
23	Sweden	0.684	1.813	0.563	2.012	–0.868	1.910	2.059	0.259	0.134
24	Switzerland	1.107	0.822	0.895	0.884	0.896	0.986	–	0.933	1.387
25	Taiwan	0.726	1.426	0.725	1.170	0.977	1.815	–	0.666	1.173
26	UK	0.554	1.123	0.393	2.034	1.773	1.065	1.866	1.503	0.860
27	USA	0.491	1.379	0.514	2.010	0.341	1.863	1.156	1.057	1.300
Mean (*Developed*)		0.631	1.258	0.468	1.514	0.679	1.677	1.302	1.116	1.011

(*Continued*)

Table 4.4 Income elasticities of nine commodities, Rotterdam demand system under preference independence, 45 countries (*Continued*)

Country (*1*)	*Food* (*2*)	*Clothing* (*3*)	*Housing* (*4*)	*Durables* (*5*)	*Health* (*6*)	*Transport* (*7*)	*Education* (*8*)	*Restaurants* (*9*)	*Miscellaneous* (*10*)
Developing countries									
28 Colombia	0.545	1.882	0.250	1.052	0.853	–	–	–	1.365
29 Czech Republic	0.496	1.263	0.317	1.197	1.248	1.593	1.551	0.847	2.670
30 Estonia	0.602	1.115	0.787	1.532	0.838	1.408	1.517	0.876	1.402
31 Greece	0.741	1.751	0.338	2.094	1.849	1.405	1.403	0.695	0.974
32 Hungary	0.711	1.809	0.485	1.809	1.906	1.631	1.301	0.866	0.227
33 India	0.956	1.465	0.297	1.429	0.486	1.08	–	0.583	1.881
34 Latvia	0.598	1.319	0.192	1.936	1.079	1.69	1.545	2.368	1.317
35 Lithuania	0.776	1.498	0.432	1.032	1.599	1.266	1.272	1.329	1.642
36 Malaysia	0.278	2.620	0.425	1.473	0.910	1.316	–	–	1.473
37 Mexico	0.251	1.174	0.864	–	1.098	–	–	–	1.468
38 Philippines	0.877	0.076	0.455	0.711	1.694	1.188	–	0.990	1.670
39 Poland	0.501	1.488	0.531	1.798	2.387	1.579	1.787	1.892	0.581
40 Portugal	1.199	0.972	–0.200	1.187	0.646	2.088	0.924	0.876	0.769
41 Slovakia	0.759	1.109	0.632	1.621	1.277	1.013	1.200	1.683	1.384
42 South Africa	0.658	1.402	0.321	1.291	0.788	1.564	1.119	1.688	1.268
43 Sri Lanka	0.873	1.317	0.931	1.445	0.871	0.895	–	1.699	1.605
44 Thailand	0.424	0.800	0.101	1.372	1.257	1.981	–	1.741	0.658
45 Turkey	0.383	0.869	0.282	2.049	1.015	–	–	1.914	1.287
Mean (*Developing*)	0.646	1.329	0.413	1.472	1.211	1.446	1.362	1.336	1.313
Mean (*All countries*)	0.637	1.287	0.446	1.498	0.892	1.595	1.321	1.197	1.132

Comparing the mean income elasticities between developed and developing countries presented in the table, it can be seen that the income elasticities are broadly similar for all commodities except health care. Health care is a necessity in most of the developed countries while it is a luxury in most of the developing countries.

Table 4.5 presents the own-price elasticities for the nine commodity groups. As can be seen, all own-price elasticities are negative and are mostly less than one in absolute value. The last row shows the mean own-price elasticities for the nine commodities across all countries: −0.26 (food), −0.50 (clothing), −0.20 (housing), −0.56 (durables), −0.36 (health), −0.50 (transport), −0.45 (education), −0.46 (restaurants) and −0.38 (miscellaneous), respectively, indicating that the demand for all goods is price inelastic. Comparing the mean own-price elasticities between developed and developing countries presented in the table, we can see that on average they are broadly similar between the two groups of countries with all elasticities being negative and less than one in absolute value.

4.4 Estimating the Workings-Rotterdam (W-R) Demand System

In this section, we test the validity of the demand theory hypotheses with respect to the W-R model (4.5) and present the estimation results and the implied demand elasticities. Table 4.6 presents the results for testing the homogeneity (4.3) and Slutsky symmetry (4.4) hypotheses. As can be seen from column (9), in a majority of the 45 countries, homogeneity is acceptable at the 5 percent level of significance and is acceptable for almost all countries at the 1 percent level. The last three columns of Table 4.6 present the test results for Slutsky symmetry. Column (10) gives the value of the test statistics, column (11) gives the corresponding p-values and column (12) presents the conclusion of the symmetry test. As can be seen, the symmetry hypothesis is not supported by the data for many countries.

We now apply the Monte Carlo simulation procedure described in Section 4.3 to test the preference independence hypothesis for the 45 countries. Table 4.7 presents the test results. As can be seen, except for two countries (Canada and Ireland), the preference independence hypothesis is supported by the data from most countries. Table 4.8 presents the estimation results of the W-R model under preference independence (4.11). Columns (2)–(10) present the income coefficients β_i s, and the last column gives the estimate for the income flexibility ϕ. As can be seen, almost all the estimates for the income coefficients for all commodities are negative and statistically significant at the 5 percent level of significance. All estimated income flexibility estimates are negative and almost all are statistically significant.

Table 4.9 presents the implied income elasticities for the nine commodity groups. As can be seen, all but four of the income elasticity estimates for food are less than one, indicating that food is a necessity. The results

Table 4.5 Own-price elasticities of nine commodities, Rotterdam demand system, 45 countries

Country (1)	*Food* (2)	*Clothing* (3)	*Housing* (4)	*Durables* (5)	*Health* (6)	*Transport* (7)	*Education* (8)	*Restaurants* (9)	*Miscellaneous* (10)
Developed countries									
1 Australia	−0.260	−0.638	−0.160	−0.576	−0.345	−0.540	−0.402	−0.652	−0.496
2 Austria	−0.075	−0.087	−0.201	−0.249	−0.109	−0.390	−0.379	−0.150	−0.178
3 Belgium	0.013	0.074	−0.083	−0.175	−0.070	−0.192	−0.179	−0.120	−0.226
4 Canada	−0.159	−0.539	−0.014	−0.638	−0.213	−0.446	−0.358	−0.484	−0.247
5 Denmark	−0.219	−0.341	−0.013	−0.703	−0.120	−0.806	−0.591	−0.673	−0.615
6 Finland	−0.147	−0.602	−0.017	−0.581	−0.261	−0.524	−0.461	−0.509	−0.400
7 France	−0.245	−0.610	−0.265	−0.635	−0.049	−0.543	−0.510	−0.303	−0.298
8 Germany	−0.372	−0.406	0.078	−0.683	−0.167	−0.609	−0.545	−0.835	−0.179
9 Hong Kong	−0.113	−0.370	−0.051	−0.368	−0.230	−0.220	–	−0.167	−0.153
10 Iceland	−0.189	−0.782	−0.530	−0.779	−0.070	−0.884	−0.480	−0.729	−0.501
11 Ireland	−1.279	−1.864	−1.411	−1.676	−1.854	−1.560	–	−1.119	−0.841
12 Israel	−0.019	−0.051	−0.021	−0.088	−0.063	−0.075	−0.057	−0.065	−0.042
13 Italy	−0.231	−0.421	−0.069	−0.451	−0.368	−0.423	−0.456	−0.288	−0.218
14 Japan	−0.278	−0.715	−0.163	−0.683	−0.121	−0.526	–	−0.412	−0.441
15 Luxembourg	−0.145	−0.132	−0.120	−0.132	−0.063	−0.108	−0.138	−0.132	−0.170
16 Netherlands	−0.050	−0.107	−0.018	−0.171	−0.247	−0.131	−0.120	−0.120	−0.106
17 New Zealand	−0.353	−0.434	−0.241	−0.446	−0.320	−0.592	−0.458	−0.653	−0.450
18 Norway	−0.504	−0.865	−0.248	−0.949	−0.188	−1.119	−0.693	−0.497	−0.314
19 Singapore	−0.245	−0.461	−0.139	−0.345	−0.207	−0.488	–	−0.380	−0.410
20 Slovenia	−0.210	−0.449	−0.161	−0.366	−0.246	−0.267	−0.359	−0.362	−0.264
21 South Korea	−0.102	−0.287	−0.066	−0.439	−0.176	−0.234	−0.163	−0.185	−0.212
22 Spain	−0.133	−0.429	−0.054	−0.419	−0.171	−0.393	−0.331	−0.318	−0.338
23 Sweden	−0.276	−0.755	−0.216	−0.830	0.406	−0.598	−0.718	−0.116	−0.060
24 Switzerland	−1.805	−1.528	−1.347	−1.630	−1.521	−1.673	–	−1.491	−2.193
25 Taiwan	−0.129	−0.280	−0.134	−0.238	−0.202	−0.292	–	−0.128	−0.209
26 UK	−0.394	−0.809	−0.271	−1.396	−1.322	−0.683	−1.116	−0.988	−0.584
27 USA	−0.206	−0.571	−0.207	−0.798	−0.144	−0.617	−0.454	−0.439	−0.486
Mean (*Developed*)	−0.301	−0.536	−0.227	−0.609	−0.313	−0.553	−0.427	−0.456	−0.394

Developing countries										
28	Colombia	−0.099	−0.340	−0.050	−0.207	−0.171	–	–	–	−0.103
29	Czech Republic	−0.181	−0.496	−0.121	−0.463	−0.504	−0.529	−0.535	−0.327	−0.860
30	Estonia	−0.252	−0.522	−0.336	−0.719	−0.414	−0.564	−0.663	−0.418	−0.636
31	Greece	−0.177	−0.450	−0.089	−0.535	−0.477	−0.298	−0.358	−0.177	−0.252
32	Hungary	−0.354	−1.031	−0.268	−0.991	−1.073	−0.708	−0.694	−0.498	−0.135
33	India	−0.049	−0.125	−0.029	−0.134	−0.048	−0.094	–	−0.057	−0.169
34	Latvia	−0.265	−0.679	−0.102	−1.004	−0.570	−0.705	−0.720	−1.135	−0.676
35	Lithuania	−0.174	−0.419	−0.124	−0.302	−0.462	−0.311	−0.359	−0.395	−0.454
36	Malaysia	−0.092	−0.866	−0.140	−0.483	−0.317	−0.347	–	–	−0.300
37	Mexico	−0.347	−0.132	−0.276	–	−0.459	–	–	–	−0.226
38	Philippines	−0.088	−0.012	−0.069	−0.110	−0.262	−0.160	–	−0.150	−0.196
39	Poland	−0.221	−0.712	−0.244	−0.854	−1.118	−0.642	−0.774	−0.923	−0.280
40	Portugal	−0.206	−0.207	0.047	−0.250	−0.142	−0.302	−0.193	−0.180	−0.160
41	Slovakia	−0.247	−0.426	−0.218	−0.599	−0.498	−0.364	−0.429	−0.607	−0.490
42	South Africa	−0.190	−0.455	−0.109	−0.404	−0.268	−0.421	−0.365	−0.573	−0.388
43	Sri Lanka	−0.292	−0.749	−0.541	−0.844	−0.538	−0.475	–	−1.002	−0.942
44	Thailand	−0.015	−0.031	−0.004	−0.053	−0.049	−0.061	–	−0.044	−0.026
45	Turkey	−0.083	−0.198	−0.065	−0.418	−0.237	–	–	−0.304	−0.235
Mean (*Developing*)		−0.185	−0.436	−0.152	−0.492	−0.423	−0.399	−0.509	−0.453	−0.363
Mean (*All countries*)		−0.255	−0.496	−0.197	−0.564	−0.357	−0.498	−0.453	−0.455	−0.381

Table 4.6 Testing homogeneity and symmetry – Workings-Rotterdam demand system, 45 countries

				Testing homogeneity (F-test)						Testing symmetry (Chi-squared test)		
	Country	n	T (after lagging)	Test statistic	df1	df2	Multiplier	p-value	Decision	Test statistic	p-value	Decision
	(1)	(2)	(3)	(4)	(5)	(6)	(7)	(8)	(9)	(10)	(11)	(12)
Developed countries												
1	Australia	9	29	13.5	8	12	12.7	0.443	Accept	42.7	0.037	*Accept
2	Austria	9	20	29.5	8	3	26.7	0.520	Accept	92.5	0.000	Reject
3	Belgium	9	19	704.6	8	2	36.0	0.050	Accept	124.4	0.000	Reject
4	Canada	9	34	12.9	8	17	11.3	0.384	Accept	57.6	0.001	Reject
5	Denmark	9	20	1,108.3	8	3	26.7	0.005	Reject	42.7	0.037	*Accept
6	Finland	9	40	11.0	8	23	10.4	0.429	Accept	57.1	0.001	Reject
7	France	9	56	11.5	8	39	9.4	0.312	Accept	42.2	0.042	*Accept
8	Germany	9	19	6.9	8	2	36.0	0.965	Accept	32.5	0.256	Accept
9	Hong Kong	8	45	23.1	7	30	8.4	0.025	*Accept	28.1	0.138	Accept
10	Iceland	9	19	101.8	8	2	36.0	0.287	Accept	73.1	0.000	Reject
11	Ireland	8	18	42.9	7	3	21.0	0.299	Accept	70.8	0.000	Reject
12	Israel	9	19	42.0	8	2	36.0	0.540	Accept	82.8	0.000	Reject
13	Italy	9	19	257.5	8	2	36.0	0.128	Accept	64.3	0.000	Reject
14	Japan	9	19	33.1	8	2	36.0	0.618	Accept	60.3	0.000	Reject
15	Luxembourg	9	20	8.2	8	3	26.7	0.918	Accept	64.2	0.000	Reject
16	Netherlands	9	19	5.3	8	2	36.0	0.981	Accept	63.7	0.000	Reject
17	New Zealand	9	27	25.8	8	10	13.6	0.169	Accept	81.1	0.000	Reject
18	Norway	9	27	16.6	8	10	13.6	0.375	Accept	61.6	0.000	Reject
19	Singapore	8	27	18.6	7	12	10.5	0.183	Accept	39.0	0.010	*Accept
20	Slovenia	9	19	40.5	8	2	36.0	0.552	Accept	119.8	0.000	Reject
21	South Korea	9	45	15.7	8	28	10.0	0.177	Accept	64.3	0.000	Reject
22	Spain	9	19	60.0	8	2	36.0	0.428	Accept	195.4	0.000	Reject
23	Sweden	9	22	18.3	8	5	19.2	0.548	Accept	36.1	0.141	Accept
24	Switzerland	8	18	303.1	7	3	21.0	0.025	*Accept	25.7	0.218	Accept
25	Taiwan	8	54	16.7	7	39	8.1	0.070	Accept	25.7	0.217	Accept
26	UK	9	20	125.4	8	3	26.7	0.115	Accept	88.4	0.000	Reject
27	USA	9	45	46.6	8	28	10.0	0.001	Reject	61.9	0.000	Reject

Developing countries												
28	Colombia	6	14	16.1	5	3	11.7	0.421	Accept	21.4	0.019	*Accept
29	Czech Republic	9	20	847.8	8	3	26.7	0.008	Reject	29.5	0.389	Accept
30	Estonia	9	20	39.1	8	3	26.7	0.413	Accept	125.9	0.000	Reject
31	Greece	9	20	39.2	8	3	26.7	0.412	Accept	33.5	0.217	Accept
32	Hungary	9	20	12.8	8	3	26.7	0.818	Accept	101.6	0.000	Reject
33	India	8	45	44.6	7	30	8.4	0.000	Reject	36.3	0.020	*Accept
34	Latvia	9	19	23.6	8	2	36.0	0.725	Accept	56.4	0.001	Reject
35	Lithuania	9	19	231.1	8	2	36.0	0.142	Accept	41.4	0.049	*Accept
36	Malaysia	7	16	21.2	6	3	16.0	0.442	Accept	48.1	0.000	Reject
37	Mexico	5	11	8.1	4	2	10.0	0.619	Accept	4.5	0.605	Accept
38	Philippines	8	18	32.3	7	3	21.0	0.392	Accept	33.5	0.041	*Accept
39	Poland	9	20	1,171.9	8	3	26.7	0.005	Reject	97.8	0.000	Reject
40	Portugal	9	20	42.4	8	3	26.7	0.383	Accept	59.5	0.000	Reject
41	Slovakia	9	20	27.2	8	3	26.7	0.552	Accept	132.2	0.000	Reject
42	South Africa	9	39	15.7	8	22	10.5	0.217	Accept	39.6	0.072	*Accept
43	Sri Lanka	8	41	17.1	7	26	8.6	0.096	Accept	34.2	0.034	*Accept
44	Thailand	8	48	9.1	7	33	8.3	0.386	Accept	32.7	0.049	*Accept
45	Turkey	7	16	18.0	6	3	16.0	0.501	Accept	57.2	0.000	Reject

Note: $df1 = n - 1$; $df2 = T - 2n + 1$; Multiplier = $df1*(T - n - 1)/df2$. *Accept means acceptable at the 1 percent level of significance. Among the 45 countries, the percentage rejection of the homogeneity hypothesis is 6 percent of the countries and the percentage rejection of the symmetry hypothesis is 58 percent of the countries.

Table 4.7 Testing preference independence, Workings-Rotterdam demand system

	Country (1)	*Observed value* (2)	*Rank* (3)	*Decision at the 5 percent level* (4)	*Decision at the 1 percent level* (5)
Developed countries					
1	Australia	75.0	906	Accept	Accept
2	Austria	123.2	938	Accept	Accept
3	Belgium	112.0	711	Accept	Accept
4	Canada	97.7	998	Reject	Reject
5	Denmark	76.9	437	Accept	Accept
6	Finland	55.8	769	Accept	Accept
7	France	70.3	988	Reject	Accept
8	Germany	58.1	110	Accept	Accept
9	Hong Kong	47.0	897	Accept	Accept
10	Iceland	128.5	904	Accept	Accept
11	Ireland	151.2	999	Reject	Reject
12	Israel	101.0	572	Accept	Accept
13	Italy	140.1	892	Accept	Accept
14	Japan	129.3	877	Accept	Accept
15	Luxembourg	106.7	844	Accept	Accept
16	Netherlands	95.8	533	Accept	Accept
17	New Zealand	85.4	956	Reject	Accept
18	Norway	48.3	833	Accept	Accept
19	Singapore	27.4	373	Accept	Accept
20	Slovenia	151.2	988	Reject	Accept
21	South Korea	56.1	856	Accept	Accept
22	Spain	142.8	932	Accept	Accept
23	Sweden	85.9	793	Accept	Accept
24	Switzerland	42.6	235	Accept	Accept
25	Taiwan	36.5	742	Accept	Accept
26	UK	78.4	486	Accept	Accept
27	USA	71.4	983	Reject	Accept
Developing countries					
28	Colombia	49.8	852	Accept	Accept
29	Czech Republic	89.1	634	Accept	Accept
30	Estonia	112.0	872	Accept	Accept
31	Greece	51.3	61	Accept	Accept
32	Hungary	83.5	592	Accept	Accept
33	India	41.0	807	Accept	Accept
34	Latvia	112.2	758	Accept	Accept
35	Lithuania	99.3	582	Accept	Accept
36	Malaysia	53.5	653	Accept	Accept
37	Mexico	40.0	892	Accept	Accept
38	Philippines	116.0	985	Reject	Accept
39	Poland	127.3	958	Reject	Accept
40	Portugal	105.9	797	Accept	Accept
41	Slovakia	97.1	751	Accept	Accept
42	South Africa	61.7	903	Accept	Accept
43	Sri Lanka	48.6	936	Accept	Accept
44	Thailand	56.7	983	Reject	Accept
45	Turkey	62.4	796	Accept	Accept

Note: Among the 45 countries, the preference independence hypothesis is rejected at the 5 percent level of significance for 20 percent of the countries and at the 1 percent level for only 4 percent of the countries.

Table 4.8 Income coefficients and income flexibility, Workings-Rotterdam demand system

		Income coefficients									
	Country	*Food*	*Clothing*	*Housing*	*Durables*	*Health*	*Transport*	*Education*	*Restaurant*	*Miscellaneous*	*Income flexibility*
	(1)	*(2)*	*(3)*	*(4)*	*(5)*	*(6)*	*(7)*	*(8)*	*(9)*	*(10)*	*(11)*
Developed countries											
1	Australia	−0.06 (0.02)	0.02 (0.01)	−0.13 (0.01)	0.02 (0.02)	0.00 (0.01)	0.05 (0.04)	−0.01 (0.02)	0.04 (0.02)	0.06 (0.04)	−0.51(0.06)
2	Austria	−0.10 (0.02)	−0.05 (0.02)	−0.01 (0.04)	0.00 (0.02)	−0.02 (0.01)	0.17 (0.05)	0.09 (0.03)	−0.05 (0.04)	−0.03 (0.02)	−0.24(0.06)
3	Belgium	−0.19 (0.04)	−0.08 (0.03)	−0.07 (0.05)	0.02 (0.02)	−0.03 (0.01)	0.12 (0.05)	0.05 (0.05)	−0.01 (0.02)	0.17 (0.06)	−0.14(0.04)
4	Canada	−0.08 (0.02)	0.04 (0.01)	−0.22 (0.02)	0.07 (0.01)	−0.01 (0.01)	0.16 (0.03)	0.02 (0.01)	0.04 (0.01)	−0.02 (0.02)	−0.38(0.05)
5	Denmark	−0.08 (0.01)	−0.01 (0.01)	−0.26 (0.04)	0.03 (0.01)	−0.02 (0.01)	0.21 (0.04)	0.05 (0.02)	0.03 (0.01)	0.06 (0.03)	−0.49(0.08)
6	Finland	−0.13 (0.02)	0.04 (0.01)	−0.20 (0.02)	0.04 (0.01)	−0.01 (0.01)	0.16 (0.03)	0.06 (0.01)	0.03 (0.01)	0.01 (0.02)	−0.38(0.05)
7	France	−0.12 (0.01)	0.01 (0.01)	−0.04 (0.02)	0.03 (0.01)	−0.02 (0.01)	0.13 (0.02)	0.03 (0.01)	−0.01 (0.01)	0.00 (0.02)	−0.38(0.04)
8	Germany	0.00 (0.03)	0.00 (0.02)	−0.29 (0.08)	0.06 (0.05)	−0.02 (0.02)	0.21 (0.08)	0.06 (0.03)	0.06 (0.02)	−0.07 (0.02)	−0.44(0.07)
9	Hong Kong	−0.12 (0.02)	0.25 (0.03)	−0.14 (0.02)	0.06 (0.02)	0.00 (0.01)	0.00 (0.01)	–	−0.02 (0.01)	−0.04 (0.03)	−0.24(0.07)
10	Iceland	−0.11 (0.02)	0.02 (0.01)	−0.01 (0.04)	0.01 (0.01)	−0.03 (0.01)	0.14 (0.03)	−0.05 (0.02)	0.02 (0.02)	0.01 (0.01)	−0.65(0.07)
11	Ireland	−0.01 (0.01)	0.00 (0.00)	0.08 (0.02)	0.00 (0.00)	−0.01 (0.00)	0.02 (0.01)	–	−0.04 (0.01)	−0.05 (0.01)	−1.60(0.07)
12	Israel	−0.11 (0.02)	0.00 (0.02)	−0.13 (0.02)	0.05 (0.01)	0.00 (0.01)	0.19 (0.03)	0.01 (0.02)	0.01 (0.04)	−0.02 (0.02)	−0.01(0.07)
13	Italy	−0.04 (0.01)	0.03 (0.01)	−0.17 (0.02)	0.04 (0.01)	0.00 (0.01)	0.12 (0.03)	0.04 (0.02)	−0.01 (0.02)	−0.03 (0.02)	−0.33(0.05)
14	Japan	−0.10 (0.02)	0.03 (0.02)	−0.07 (0.02)	0.03 (0.02)	−0.05 (0.02)	0.08 (0.02)	–	0.04 (0.02)	0.05 (0.02)	−0.42(0.05)
15	Luxembourg	0.04 (0.03)	−0.01 (0.01)	−0.01 (0.02)	−0.01 (0.01)	−0.01 (0.01)	−0.04 (0.02)	0.00 (0.01)	−0.01 (0.01)	0.04 (0.02)	−0.24(0.09)
16	Netherlands	−0.08 (0.01)	0.00 (0.01)	−0.16 (0.03)	0.04 (0.02)	0.05 (0.07)	0.11 (0.03)	0.03 (0.02)	0.01 (0.02)	0.01 (0.02)	−0.12(0.05)
17	New Zealand	−0.03 (0.02)	0.00 (0.01)	−0.10 (0.02)	−0.01 (0.02)	−0.01 (0.01)	0.11 (0.03)	0.00 (0.02)	0.03 (0.02)	0.00 (0.01)	−0.50(0.07)
18	Norway	−0.07 (0.02)	0.01 (0.01)	−0.14 (0.02)	0.02 (0.01)	−0.01 (0.00)	0.24 (0.02)	0.01 (0.01)	−0.01 (0.01)	−0.04 (0.01)	−0.88(0.07)
19	Singapore	−0.07 (0.01)	0.01 (0.01)	−0.09 (0.01)	−0.01 (0.01)	−0.02 (0.01)	0.07 (0.03)	–	0.08 (0.03)	0.04 (0.02)	−0.39(0.07)
20	Slovenia	−0.03 (0.02)	0.04 (0.02)	−0.08 (0.03)	0.02 (0.02)	−0.01 (0.01)	0.02 (0.03)	0.04 (0.03)	0.02 (0.01)	−0.01 (0.02)	−0.31(0.06)
21	South Korea	−0.08 (0.02)	0.06 (0.02)	−0.11 (0.02)	0.05 (0.01)	0.00 (0.01)	0.06 (0.01)	−0.01 (0.01)	0.01 (0.01)	0.02 (0.02)	−0.17(0.04)
22	Spain	−0.09 (0.02)	0.03 (0.01)	−0.15 (0.02)	0.03 (0.01)	−0.02 (0.00)	0.10 (0.02)	0.02 (0.01)	0.06 (0.03)	0.03 (0.02)	−0.30(0.05)
23	Sweden	−0.05 (0.03)	0.04 (0.01)	−0.13 (0.03)	0.05 (0.01)	−0.06 (0.01)	0.15 (0.06)	0.12 (0.03)	−0.04 (0.02)	−0.08 (0.02)	−0.43(0.07)
24	Switzerland	0.02 (0.01)	−0.01 (0.00)	−0.04 (0.02)	0.00 (0.00)	−0.01 (0.01)	0.00 (0.01)	–	−0.01 (0.01)	0.04 (0.02)	−1.84(0.06)
25	Taiwan	−0.11 (0.01)	0.02 (0.01)	−0.05 (0.02)	0.01 (0.01)	0.00 (0.01)	0.11 (0.03)	–	−0.01 (0.02)	0.03 (0.03)	−0.24(0.04)
26	UK	−0.05 (0.01)	0.01 (0.01)	−0.15 (0.02)	0.05 (0.01)	0.01 (0.01)	0.00 (0.01)	0.10 (0.02)	0.05 (0.02)	−0.03 (0.02)	−0.76(0.05)
27	USA	−0.07 (0.01)	0.02 (0.01)	−0.10 (0.01)	0.05 (0.01)	−0.09 (0.02)	0.12 (0.02)	0.02 (0.01)	0.00 (0.01)	0.05 (0.02)	−0.46(0.04)
Mean (*Developed*)		−0.07(0.00)	0.02 (0.00)	−0.11 (0.01)	0.03 (0.00)	−0.01 (0.00)	0.10 (0.01)	0.03 (0.00)	0.01 (0.00)	0.01 (0.00	−0.48 (0.01)

(*Continued*)

Table 4.8 Income coefficients and income flexibility, Workings-Rotterdam demand system (*Continued*)

	Country	Income coefficients									Income flexibility
		Food	*Clothing*	*Housing*	*Durables*	*Health*	*Transport*	*Education*	*Restaurant*	*Miscellaneous*	
	(1)	*(2)*	*(3)*	*(4)*	*(5)*	*(6)*	*(7)*	*(8)*	*(9)*	*(10)*	*(11)*
Developing countries											
28	Colombia	−0.10 (0.03)	0.06 (0.02)	−0.12 (0.02)	0.00 (0.01)	−0.01 (0.01)	–	–	–	0.16 (0.04)	−0.09 (0.11)
29	Czech Republic	−0.13 (0.03)	0.01 (0.01)	−0.16 (0.03)	0.01 (0.01)	0.00 (0.01)	0.08 (0.03)	0.06 (0.02)	−0.01 (0.02)	0.15 (0.04)	−0.41 (0.07)
30	Estonia	−0.12 (0.03)	0.01 (0.01)	−0.04 (0.03)	0.02 (0.01)	0.00 (0.00)	0.06 (0.02)	0.05 (0.01)	−0.01 (0.01)	0.03 (0.01)	−0.51 (0.05)
31	Greece	−0.05 (0.04)	0.04 (0.01)	−0.14 (0.03)	0.05 (0.01)	0.04 (0.02)	0.07 (0.05)	0.03 (0.01)	−0.04 (0.03)	0.00 (0.03)	−0.26 (0.11)
32	Hungary	−0.08 (0.02)	0.03 (0.01)	−0.10 (0.02)	0.05 (0.02)	0.04 (0.01)	0.11 (0.04)	0.03 (0.02)	−0.01 (0.02)	−0.06 (0.02)	−0.61 (0.06)
33	India	0.03 (0.05)	0.04 (0.03)	−0.07 (0.01)	0.02 (0.01)	−0.01 (0.01)	−0.01 (0.02)	–	−0.02 (0.01)	0.03 (0.02)	−0.13 (0.03)
34	Latvia	−0.11 (0.03)	0.02 (0.01)	−0.16 (0.04)	0.02 (0.01)	0.00 (0.01)	0.09 (0.02)	0.05 (0.02)	0.07 (0.02)	0.01 (0.02)	−0.61 (0.10)
35	Lithuania	−0.06 (0.03)	0.03 (0.02)	−0.08 (0.03)	0.00 (0.01)	0.02 (0.01)	0.03 (0.03)	0.02 (0.01)	0.01 (0.01)	0.03 (0.02)	−0.33 (0.08)
36	Malaysia	−0.17 (0.05)	0.05 (0.02)	−0.09 (0.03)	0.03 (0.02)	0.00 (0.01)	0.06 (0.03)	–	–	0.13 (0.06)	−0.33 (0.12)
37	Mexico	−0.16 (0.02)	−0.02 (0.00)	−0.02 (0.03)	–	−0.01 (0.01)	–	–	–	0.21 (0.03)	−0.99 (0.10)
38	Philippines	−0.06 (0.05)	−0.01 (0.01)	−0.07 (0.04)	0.00 (0.03)	0.01 (0.01)	0.02 (0.04)	–	0.00 (0.01)	0.11 (0.05)	−0.15 (0.05)
39	Poland	−0.16 (0.02)	0.03 (0.02)	−0.13 (0.04)	0.03 (0.01)	0.07 (0.01)	0.11 (0.03)	0.06 (0.03)	0.03 (0.01)	−0.03 (0.03)	−0.52 (0.06)
40	Portugal	0.04 (0.05)	0.00 (0.02)	−0.18 (0.02)	0.01 (0.01)	−0.02 (0.01)	0.19 (0.03)	−0.01 (0.01)	−0.01 (0.02)	−0.02 (0.03)	−0.23 (0.06)
41	Slovakia	−0.09 (0.04)	0.00 (0.02)	−0.07 (0.05)	0.04 (0.01)	0.01 (0.02)	0.00 (0.02)	0.03 (0.01)	0.04 (0.02)	0.05 (0.02)	−0.41 (0.05)
42	South Africa	−0.09 (0.03)	0.02 (0.01)	−0.08 (0.02)	0.03 (0.01)	−0.02 (0.01)	0.08 (0.02)	0.00 (0.01)	0.02 (0.01)	0.04 (0.02)	−0.42 (0.05)
43	Sri Lanka	−0.05 (0.05)	0.02 (0.02)	−0.02 (0.02)	0.01 (0.01)	0.00 (0.00)	−0.01 (0.03)	–	0.02 (0.02)	0.02 (0.01)	−0.68 (0.09)
44	Thailand	−0.17 (0.03)	−0.02 (0.01)	−0.09 (0.01)	0.01 (0.01)	0.01 (0.01)	0.12 (0.02)	–	0.18 (0.07)	−0.04 (0.04)	−0.06 (0.06)
45	Turkey	−0.19 (0.04)	−0.01 (0.03)	−0.12 (0.02)	0.08 (0.02)	0.00 (0.01)	0.18 (0.04)	–	–	0.06 (0.04)	−0.14 (0.07)
Mean (*Developing*)		−0.10(0.01)	0.02 (0.00)	−0.10 (0.01)	0.02 (0.00)	0.01 (0.00)	0.07 (0.01)	0.03 (0.00)	0.02 (0.01)	0.05 (0.01)	−0.38 (0.02)
Mean (*All countries*)		−0.08(0.00)	0.02 (0.00)	−0.10 (0.00)	0.03 (0.00)	−0.01 (0.00)	0.09 (0.00)	0.03 (0.00)	0.01 (0.00)	0.02 (0.00)	−0.44 (0.01)

Note: p-values are in parentheses.

Table 4.9 Income elasticities, Workings–Rotterdam demand system

	Country (1)	*Food* (2)	*Clothing* (3)	*Housing* (4)	*Durables* (5)	*Health* (6)	*Transport* (7)	*Education* (8)	*Restaurants* (9)	*Miscellaneous* (10)
Developed countries										
1	Australia	0.602	1.561	0.396	1.411	0.950	1.355	0.957	1.560	1.376
2	Austria	0.281	0.272	0.943	0.992	0.406	2.081	1.764	0.610	0.753
3	Belgium	−0.102	−0.567	0.721	1.343	0.539	1.876	1.483	0.916	2.325
4	Canada	0.489	1.701	0.061	2.127	0.762	1.945	1.174	1.579	0.860
5	Denmark	0.491	0.710	0.028	1.522	0.245	2.472	1.406	1.490	1.518
6	Finland	0.416	1.777	0.122	1.695	0.711	2.033	1.49	1.506	1.142
7	France	0.406	1.065	0.813	1.416	0.389	1.868	1.335	0.782	0.961
8	Germany	0.996	1.012	−0.204	1.799	0.439	2.218	1.531	2.239	0.472
9	Hong Kong	0.326	2.543	0.252	1.780	1.008	1.029	–	0.753	0.793
10	Iceland	0.416	1.402	0.964	1.172	0.029	1.806	0.632	1.213	1.079
11	Ireland	0.956	0.967	1.379	1.053	0.741	1.158	–	0.842	0.534
12	Israel	0.378	0.392	0.432	1.712	1.133	2.081	1.083	1.229	0.810
13	Italy	0.816	1.403	0.197	1.523	1.121	1.772	1.549	0.936	0.713
14	Japan	0.507	1.542	0.663	1.539	0.519	1.692	–	1.315	1.355
15	Luxembourg	1.194	0.387	0.964	0.919	0.404	0.809	0.962	0.905	1.314
16	Netherlands	0.437	0.969	0.187	1.644	2.363	1.620	1.244	1.141	1.047
17	New Zealand	0.868	0.908	0.591	0.918	0.658	1.674	1.037	1.453	1.033
18	Norway	0.696	1.[illegible]66	0.352	1.259	0.428	2.398	1.068	0.745	0.478
19	Singapore	0.555	1.[illegible]02	0.311	0.839	0.587	1.452	–	1.342	1.249
20	Slovenia	0.846	1.52	0.583	1.278	0.798	1.094	1.347	1.297	0.911
21	South Korea	0.700	1.734	0.226	2.359	0.986	1.459	0.946	1.083	1.227
22	Spain	0.480	1.532	0.158	1.500	0.565	1.689	1.242	1.354	1.305
23	Sweden	0.678	1.375	0.546	2.099	−0.870	1.905	2.010	0.239	0.197
24	Switzerland	1.167	0.346	0.847	0.908	0.910	1.017	–	0.961	1.319
25	Taiwan	0.534	1.300	0.718	1.273	1.034	1.801	–	0.962	1.209
26	UK	0.584	1.223	0.407	2.026	1.739	1.023	1.871	1.557	0.779
27	USA	0.407	1.318	0.486	1.933	0.397	1.883	1.191	1.018	1.382
Mean (*Developed*)		0.597	1.213	0.487	1.483	0.703	1.674	1.301	1.149	1.042

(*Continued*)

Table 4.9 Income elasticities, Workings-Rotterdam demand system (*Continued*)

	Country (1)	*Food* (2)	*Clothing* (3)	*Housing* (4)	*Durables* (5)	*Health* (6)	*Transport* (7)	*Education* (8)	*Restaurants* (9)	*Miscellaneous* (10)
Developing countries										
28	Colombia	0.535	1.952	0.268	1.084	0.838	–	–	–	1.351
29	Czech Republic	0.468	1.135	0.351	1.15	1.218	1.612	1.513	0.885	2.742
30	Estonia	0.599	1.115	0.796	1.438	0.848	1.430	1.503	0.928	1.373
31	Greece	0.743	1.829	0.270	2.061	1.905	1.422	1.371	0.743	0.972
32	Hungary	0.705	1.76	0.473	1.813	1.937	1.612	1.300	0.892	0.294
33	India	1.055	1.358	0.302	1.394	0.493	0.897	–	0.551	1.621
34	Latvia	0.680	1.294	0.219	1.779	1.057	1.644	1.465	2.227	1.254
35	Lithuania	0.837	1.451	0.495	1.010	1.522	1.193	1.213	1.375	1.493
36	Malaysia	0.288	2.65	0.444	1.504	0.954	1.289	–	–	1.460
37	Mexico	0.351	0.251	0.920	–	0.854		–	–	1.474
38	Philippines	0.852	0.438	0.473	1.022	1.578	1.116	–	0.963	1.679
39	Poland	0.445	1.648	0.366	1.720	2.698	1.789	1.628	2.001	0.730
40	Portugal	1.174	0.938	−0.227	1.180	0.664	2.114	0.930	0.871	0.824
41	Slovakia	0.654	1.039	0.693	1.721	1.311	0.977	1.259	1.587	1.540
42	South Africa	0.692	1.377	0.369	1.294	0.747	1.485	1.046	1.601	1.343
43	Sri Lanka	0.903	1.299	0.778	1.294	0.866	0.974	–	1.599	1.482
44	Thailand	0.508	0.699	0.016	1.248	1.158	1.934	–	1.812	0.473
45	Turkey	0.304	0.914	0.32	1.975	0.897	2.018	–	–	1.299
Mean (*Developing*)		0.655	1.286	0.407	1.452	1.197	1.469	1.323	1.288	1.300
Mean (*All countries*)		0.620	1.242	0.455	1.471	0.901	1.598	1.308	1.197	1.145

show that, overall, food, housing and health care are necessities while clothing, durables, transport, education and restaurants are luxuries. This can also be confirmed from the last row of the table, where the mean income elasticity across the 45 countries for food is 0.62, housing 0.46 and health care 0.90, indicating that these three are necessities and the mean income elasticity for clothing is 1.24, durables 1.47, transport 1.60, education 1.31 and restaurants 1.20, indicating that these five commodities are luxuries. However, comparing the mean income elasticities under the W-R demand system for developed and developing countries in the table, there is similarity regarding the elasticities for all but one commodity, health, among the two groups of countries. Food and housing are necessities, and clothing, durables, transport, education and restaurants are luxuries in both groups of countries. These findings are generally in line with previous studies (see, for example, Clements et al. 2006; Clements et al. 2020). Considering the mean income elasticity for health care, we find that it is a necessity for developed countries (0.70) while it is a luxury for developing countries (1.20). Similar results were found in Farag et al. (2012).

Table 4.10 presents the implied own-price elasticities for the nine commodity groups. As can also be seen, all own-price elasticities are negative and are mostly less than one in absolute value. The mean own-price elasticities for the nine commodities across the 45 countries are −0.25 (food), −0.49 (clothing), −0.21 (housing), −0.55 (durables), −0.36 (health), −0.50 (transport), −0.45 (education), −0.47 (restaurants) and −0.40 (miscellaneous), indicating that demand for all goods is price inelastic. Comparing the mean own-price elasticities for developed and developing countries presented in the table, there is similarity in the elasticities for all commodities between the two groups of countries.

4.5 Estimating the Almost Ideal Demand System (AIDS)

In this section, we use the AIDS model given by equation (4.7) to test demand theory hypothesis and also obtain model estimates and implied elasticities. Table 4.11 presents the hypotheses tests results for demand homogeneity and Slutsky symmetry. As can be seen, under AIDS, homogeneity is acceptable for 76 percent of the countries while symmetry is acceptable for 64 percent of the countries. Tables 4.12 and 4.13 present the estimated income coefficients and the own-price coefficients by estimating the AIDS model under homogeneity and symmetry imposed. Tables 4.14 and 4.15 present the implied income and own-price elasticities calculated from equations (4.8) and (4.9) and the AIDS parameter estimates from Tables 4.12 and 4.13. As can be seen from Table 4.14, income elasticity estimates for food and housing are generally less than 1, indicating that food and housing are necessities in most countries. Clothing is a necessity in developed countries, while it is a luxury in developing countries. Income elasticity estimates for all other commodities are greater than 1 indicating that they are luxuries.

Table 4.10 Own-price elasticities, Workings-Rotterdam demand system

	Country (1)	*Food* (2)	*Clothing* (3)	*Housing* (4)	*Durables* (5)	*Health* (6)	*Transport* (7)	*Education* (8)	*Restaurant* (9)	*Miscellaneous* (10)
Developed countries										
1	Australia	−0.278	−0.737	−0.184	−0.657	−0.457	−0.554	−0.419	−0.703	−0.557
2	Austria	−0.066	−0.065	−0.185	−0.225	−0.097	−0.345	−0.345	−0.138	−0.169
3	Belgium	0.014	0.080	−0.082	−0.170	−0.072	−0.190	−0.175	−0.119	−0.222
4	Canada	−0.172	−0.584	−0.023	−0.699	−0.280	−0.498	−0.391	−0.528	−0.289
5	Denmark	−0.220	−0.334	−0.013	−0.678	−0.118	−0.773	−0.567	−0.664	−0.597
6	Finland	−0.144	−0.615	−0.045	−0.587	−0.264	−0.534	−0.472	−0.515	−0.391
7	France	−0.143	−0.377	−0.261	−0.493	−0.148	−0.513	−0.449	−0.286	−0.329
8	Germany	−0.374	−0.419	0.094	−0.688	−0.188	−0.606	−0.565	−0.870	−0.195
9	Hong Kong	−0.075	−0.364	−0.059	−0.371	−0.237	−0.231	–	−0.172	−0.164
10	Iceland	−0.248	−0.842	−0.505	−0.700	−0.019	−0.804	−0.376	−0.707	−0.636
11	Ireland	−1.282	−1.471	−1.602	−1.578	−1.157	−1.534	–	−1.086	−0.808
12	Israel	−0.003	−0.007	−0.003	−0.012	−0.009	−0.010	−0.008	−0.009	−0.006
13	Italy	−0.226	−0.415	−0.062	−0.445	−0.354	−0.419	−0.445	−0.281	−0.217
14	Japan	−0.191	−0.592	−0.239	−0.593	−0.205	−0.578	–	−0.466	−0.456
15	Luxembourg	−0.221	−0.202	−0.182	−0.206	−0.096	−0.164	−0.212	−0.202	−0.262
16	Netherlands	−0.048	−0.107	−0.021	−0.171	−0.249	−0.137	−0.123	−0.122	−0.104
17	New Zealand	−0.357	−0.432	−0.249	−0.430	−0.322	−0.596	−0.456	−0.660	−0.466
18	Norway	−0.519	−0.941	−0.285	−1.010	−0.371	−1.244	−0.826	−0.627	−0.402
19	Singapore	−0.197	−0.401	−0.117	−0.307	−0.223	−0.449	–	−0.361	−0.392
20	Slovenia	−0.217	−0.459	−0.162	−0.369	−0.242	−0.272	−0.359	−0.369	−0.260
21	South Korea	−0.097	−0.257	−0.038	−0.366	−0.163	−0.203	−0.144	−0.169	−0.183
22	Spain	−0.133	−0.425	−0.046	−0.418	−0.168	−0.389	−0.330	−0.319	−0.346
23	Sweden	−0.258	−0.733	−0.198	−0.812	0.383	−0.562	−0.665	−0.101	−0.083
24	Switzerland	−1.811	−1.510	−1.242	−1.607	−1.482	−1.652	–	−1.467	−2.024
25	Taiwan	−0.110	−0.285	−0.147	−0.285	−0.236	−0.321	–	−0.195	−0.237
26	UK	−0.412	−0.874	−0.279	−1.388	−1.294	−0.659	−1.115	−1.015	−0.534
27	USA	−0.177	−0.559	−0.201	−0.787	−0.170	−0.635	−0.476	−0.433	−0.521
Mean (*Developed*)		−0.295	−0.516	−0.235	−0.595	−0.305	−0.551	−0.425	−0.466	−0.402

Developing countries										
28	Colombia	−0.043	−0.154	−0.023	−0.093	−0.074	–	–	–	−0.045
29	Czech Republic	−0.171	−0.446	−0.132	−0.443	−0.490	−0.530	−0.521	−0.339	−0.871
30	Estonia	−0.252	−0.525	−0.341	−0.682	−0.421	−0.574	−0.662	−0.443	−0.628
31	Greece	−0.162	−0.428	−0.066	−0.483	−0.449	−0.275	−0.321	−0.172	−0.230
32	Hungary	−0.352	−1.006	−0.262	−0.994	−1.090	−0.703	−0.694	−0.512	−0.175
33	India	−0.065	−0.154	−0.038	−0.172	−0.064	−0.105	–	−0.071	−0.194
34	Latvia	−0.321	−0.733	−0.127	−1.019	−0.614	−0.761	−0.758	−1.184	−0.710
35	Lithuania	−0.196	−0.437	−0.151	−0.317	−0.473	−0.319	−0.369	−0.438	−0.447
36	Malaysia	−0.090	−0.819	−0.137	−0.460	−0.311	−0.321	–	–	−0.281
37	Mexico	−0.317	−0.246	−0.710	–	−0.803	–	–	–	−0.523
38	Philippines	−0.083	−0.067	−0.068	−0.149	−0.233	−0.145	–	−0.139	−0.188
39	Poland	−0.202	−0.788	−0.176	−0.827	−1.258	−0.708	−0.723	−0.981	−0.349
40	Portugal	−0.205	−0.202	0.054	−0.250	−0.147	−0.305	−0.196	−0.181	−0.172
41	Slovakia	−0.222	−0.403	−0.237	−0.637	−0.515	−0.356	−0.451	−0.580	−0.540
42	South Africa	−0.235	−0.533	−0.149	−0.482	−0.303	−0.483	−0.408	−0.648	−0.485
43	Sri Lanka	−0.316	−0.797	−0.494	−0.821	−0.577	−0.548	–	−1.020	−0.942
44	Thailand	−0.026	−0.041	−0.001	−0.073	−0.069	−0.090	–	−0.067	−0.028
45	Turkey	−0.039	−0.118	−0.042	−0.231	−0.120	–	–	−0.177	−0.135
Mean (*Developing*)		−0.183	−0.439	−0.172	−0.478	−0.445	−0.415	−0.510	−0.463	−0.386
Mean (*All countries*)		−0.250	−0.485	−0.210	−0.550	−0.361	−0.502	−0.452	−0.465	−0.395

Table 4.11 Homogeneity and symmetry hypothesis testing, AIDS, 45 countries

			Homogeneity			Symmetry		
Country	n	T	Test statistic	$F_{critical}$	Decision	Test statistic	$F_{critical}$	Decision
(1)	(2)	(3)	(4)	(5)	(6)	(7)	(8)	(9)
Developed countries								
1 Australia	9	29	2.186	0.033	Accept	1.974	0.003	Reject
2 Austria	9	21	1.172	0.328	Accept	1.060	0.408	Accept
3 Belgium	9	19	1.101	0.377	Accept	1.175	0.289	Accept
4 Canada	9	34	2.343	0.021	Accept	3.426	0.000	Reject
5 Denmark	9	20	0.851	0.562	Accept	1.094	0.370	Accept
6 Finland	9	40	2.740	0.007	Reject	2.993	0.000	Reject
7 France	9	56	3.711	0.000	Reject	4.606	0.000	Reject
8 Germany	9	19	0.882	0.537	Accept	1.074	0.398	Accept
9 Hong Kong	8	45	3.876	0.001	Reject	4.141	0.000	Reject
10 Iceland	9	19	0.930	0.499	Accept	1.449	0.105	Accept
11 Ireland	8	18	1.097	0.380	Accept	1.655	0.061	Accept
12 Israel	9	19	1.039	0.419	Accept	1.246	0.226	Accept
13 Italy	9	19	0.951	0.483	Accept	1.193	0.272	Accept
14 Japan	9	19	0.547	0.816	Accept	0.826	0.727	Accept
15 Luxembourg	9	20	1.016	0.433	Accept	1.221	0.240	Accept
16 Netherlands	9	19	0.248	0.979	Accept	1.066	0.408	Accept
17 New Zealand	9	27	1.899	0.067	Accept	1.985	0.003	Reject
18 Norway	9	27	3.260	0.002	Reject	3.610	0.000	Reject
19 Singapore	8	27	2.659	0.014	Accept	3.637	0.000	Reject
20 Slovenia	9	19	1.094	0.381	Accept	1.432	0.112	Accept
21 South Korea	9	45	3.419	0.001	Reject	3.482	0.000	Reject
22 Spain	9	19	3.178	0.005	Reject	2.688	0.000	Reject
23 Sweden	9	22	1.325	0.244	Accept	1.254	0.202	Accept
24 Switzerland	8	18	1.205	0.318	Accept	2.020	0.016	Accept
25 Taiwan	8	54	2.924	0.006	Reject	3.651	0.000	Reject
26 UK	9	20	1.225	0.299	Accept	1.232	0.231	Accept
27 USA	9	45	3.607	0.001	Reject	4.065	0.000	Reject
Developing countries								
28 Colombia	6	14	1.181	0.348	Accept	1.457	0.199	Accept
29 Czech Republic	9	20	1.195	0.316	Accept	1.195	0.264	Accept
30 Estonia	9	20	0.999	0.446	Accept	1.758	0.025	Accept
31 Greece	9	20	1.103	0.373	Accept	1.107	0.355	Accept
32 Hungary	9	20	0.891	0.529	Accept	1.393	0.124	Accept
33 India	8	45	3.240	0.003	Reject	4.393	0.000	Reject
34 Latvia	9	19	0.878	0.541	Accept	1.204	0.262	Accept
35 Lithuania	9	19	1.067	0.399	Accept	1.229	0.240	Accept
36 Malaysia	7	16	1.026	0.425	Accept	1.255	0.270	Accept
37 Mexico	5	11	1.084	0.407	Accept	0.865	0.585	Accept
38 Philippines	8	18	0.877	0.532	Accept	1.205	0.279	Accept
39 Poland	9	20	1.065	0.399	Accept	1.306	0.175	Accept
40 Portugal	9	20	1.145	0.347	Accept	1.194	0.265	Accept
41 Slovakia	9	20	1.143	0.348	Accept	1.065	0.405	Accept
42 South Africa	9	39	3.178	0.002	Reject	2.688	0.000	Reject
43 Sri Lanka	8	41	2.711	0.011	Accept	3.339	0.000	Reject
44 Thailand	8	48	3.483	0.001	Reject	4.285	0.000	Reject
45 Turkey	7	16	0.853	0.538	Accept	1.053	0.435	Accept
Percentage Rejection				24 percent			36 percent	

Note: k = Number of parameters in each equation. Degrees of freedom for homogeneity F-test, $df1 = q = n - 1$, $df2 = (n - 2)(T - k)$. For example, with constant, $n = 9$, $T = 21$, $k = 11$, $df1 = 8$, $df2 = 70$. Degrees of freedom for homogeneity and symmetry, F-test, $df1 = q = n(n - 1)/2$, $df2 = (n - 2)(T - k)$. For example, with constant, $n = 9$, $T = 21$, $k = 11$, $df1 = 36$, $df2 = 70$.

Table 4.12 Income coefficients, AIDS under homogeneity and symmetry, 45 countries

Country (1)	*Food* (2)	*Clothing* (3)	*Housing* (4)	*Durables* (5)	*Health* (6)	*Transport* (7)	*Education* (8)	*Restaurant* (9)	*Miscellaneous* (10)
Developed countries									
1 Australia	−0.10 (0.01)	−0.02 (0.01)	0.00 (0.00)	−0.02 (0.01)	0.01 (0.01)	0.08 (0.01)	0.12 (0.02)	−0.03 (0.01)	−0.03 (0.04)
2 Austria	−0.06 (0.02)	−0.06 (0.01)	−0.08 (0.02)	−0.01 (0.01)	0.00 (0.00)	0.22 (0.02)	0.00 (0.00)	−0.07 (0.03)	0.05 (0.05)
3 Belgium	−0.12 (0.03)	−0.16 (0.02)	−0.03 (0.01)	−0.01 (0.01)	0.02 (0.01)	0.17 (0.02)	0.00 (0.00)	0.00 (0.00)	0.13 (0.05)
4 Canada	−0.09 (0.01)	−0.04 (0.01)	−0.13 (0.02)	0.00 (0.00)	0.02 (0.00)	0.06 (0.01)	0.10 (0.01)	0.02 (0.01)	0.05 (0.03)
5 Denmark	−0.11 (0.01)	−0.01 (0.02)	−0.30 (0.03)	0.02 (0.01)	−0.02 (0.01)	0.22 (0.04)	0.09 (0.02)	0.05 (0.01)	0.06 (0.06)
6 Finland	−0.17 (0.01)	0.00 (0.00)	0.07 (0.02)	−0.04 (0.01)	0.00 (0.00)	0.03 (0.01)	0.03 (0.01)	0.02 (0.01)	0.06 (0.03)
7 France	−0.10 (0.00)	−0.05 (0.00)	0.10 (0.01)	−0.02 (0.00)	0.00 (0.00)	0.05 (0.00)	0.03 (0.00)	−0.03 (0.01)	0.03 (0.01)
8 Germany	−0.12 (0.03)	−0.09 (0.02)	−0.17 (0.04)	0.07 (0.03)	0.08 (0.02)	0.09 (0.05)	0.05 (0.03)	0.01 (0.02)	0.08 (0.08)
9 Hong Kong	−0.21 (0.01)	0.05 (0.02)	0.04 (0.01)	0.09 (0.01)	0.04 (0.00)	0.01 (0.01)	–	−0.03 (0.01)	0.02 (0.03)
10 Iceland	0.01 (0.02)	0.01 (0.01)	0.06 (0.03)	−0.05 (0.02)	0.01 (0.01)	−0.09 (0.03)	−0.05 (0.02)	0.03 (0.02)	0.08 (0.05)
11 Ireland	−0.04 (0.00)	−0.03 (0.01)	0.05 (0.01)	−0.01 (0.00)	0.01 (0.00)	−0.01 (0.00)	–	−0.02 (0.01)	0.04 (0.01)
12 Israel	−0.12 (0.02)	−0.05 (0.02)	−0.07 (0.03)	0.06 (0.01)	0.02 (0.01)	0.22 (0.03)	−0.01 (0.01)	0.01 (0.07)	−0.06 (0.08)
13 Italy	−0.10 (0.02)	0.07 (0.01)	−0.15 (0.01)	0.03 (0.01)	0.02 (0.01)	0.10 (0.02)	0.09 (0.01)	−0.03 (0.02)	−0.03 (0.05)
14 Japan	−0.23 (0.15)	0.08 (0.08)	−0.15 (0.11)	−0.07 (0.06)	−0.14 (0.05)	0.04 (0.07)	−0.07 (0.07)	0.09 (0.04)	0.44 (0.24)
15 Luxembourg	0.01 (0.01)	0.01 (0.00)	0.03 (0.01)	−0.04 (0.01)	−0.02 (0.00)	−0.02 (0.01)	−0.02 (0.01)	−0.01 (0.00)	0.06 (0.03)
16 Netherlands	−0.12 (0.01)	0.00 (0.00)	−0.15 (0.02)	0.02 (0.01)	0.11 (0.03)	0.17 (0.02)	−0.02 (0.01)	−0.02 (0.01)	0.01 (0.03)
17 New Zealand	−0.01 (0.02)	0.00 (0.00)	−0.11 (0.02)	0.05 (0.01)	0.01 (0.02)	0.05 (0.02)	0.03 (0.03)	0.00 (0.00)	−0.02 (0.06)
18 Norway	−0.13 (0.01)	−0.06 (0.01)	−0.04 (0.01)	0.04 (0.01)	0.03 (0.00)	0.05 (0.02)	0.13 (0.01)	0.02 (0.01)	−0.02 (0.03)
19 Singapore	−0.12 (0.01)	−0.02 (0.00)	−0.01 (0.01)	−0.03 (0.00)	0.01 (0.00)	0.04 (0.01)	–	0.09 (0.02)	0.03 (0.02)
20 Slovenia	−0.13 (0.01)	0.00 (0.00)	−0.03 (0.02)	−0.02 (0.01)	0.00 (0.00)	0.06 (0.01)	0.05 (0.02)	0.02 (0.01)	0.04 (0.03)
21 South Korea	−0.20 (0.01)	−0.01 (0.01)	0.00 (0.00)	−0.01 (0.01)	0.01 (0.01)	0.05 (0.01)	0.08 (0.01)	0.02 (0.01)	0.06 (0.02)
22 Spain	−0.05 (0.03)	−0.09 (0.01)	0.18 (0.02)	−0.03 (0.01)	−0.04 (0.01)	−0.05 (0.02)	−0.03 (0.01)	0.03 (0.01)	0.07 (0.05)
23 Sweden	−0.11 (0.02)	0.04 (0.02)	−0.30 (0.02)	0.09 (0.01)	−0.03 (0.01)	0.20 (0.04)	0.09 (0.01)	0.01 (0.03)	0.01 (0.06)
24 Switzerland	0.05 (0.01)	−0.01 (0.01)	0.09 (0.02)	0.01 (0.00)	−0.08 (0.01)	−0.01 (0.01)	–	0.00 (0.00)	−0.05 (0.03)
25 Taiwan	−0.15 (0.01)	0.00 (0.00)	0.00 (0.00)	0.03 (0.00)	0.00 (0.00)	0.07 (0.01)	–	0.05 (0.00)	0.00 (0.00)
26 UK	−0.04 (0.01)	0.01 (0.01)	−0.15 (0.02)	0.04 (0.01)	0.06 (0.01)	0.02 (0.02)	0.04 (0.02)	−0.05 (0.01)	0.07 (0.04)
27 USA	−0.10 (0.01)	−0.04 (0.01)	−0.03 (0.02)	−0.01 (0.02)	0.01 (0.04)	0.06 (0.02)	0.05 (0.02)	0.02 (0.01)	0.04 (0.05)
Mean (*Developed*)	−0.10 (0.01)	−0.02 (0.00)	−0.05 (0.01)	0.01 (0.00)	0.01 (0.00)	0.07 (0.00)	0.04 (0.00)	0.01 (0.00)	0.05 (0.01)

(*Continued*)

Table 4.12 Income coefficients, AIDS under homogeneity and symmetry, 45 countries (*Continued*)

Country (*1*)	*Food* (*2*)	*Clothing* (*3*)	*Housing* (*4*)	*Durables* (*5*)	*Health* (*6*)	*Transport* (*7*)	*Education* (*8*)	*Restaurant* (*9*)	*Miscellaneous* (*10*)
Developing countries									
28 Colombia	−0.12 (0.01)	0.03 (0.01)	−0.06 (0.01)	−0.01 (0.00)	−0.01 (0.00)	–	–	–	0.18 (0.02)
29 Czech Republic	−0.17 (0.04)	0.00 (0.00)	−0.16 (0.04)	0.02 (0.01)	0.03 (0.01)	0.06 (0.02)	0.06 (0.02)	0.00 (0.00)	0.15 (0.07)
30 Estonia	0.00 (0.00)	0.02 (0.01)	−0.15 (0.03)	0.04 (0.00)	0.01 (0.00)	0.04 (0.01)	0.01 (0.01)	0.00 (0.00)	0.04 (0.05)
31 Greece	−0.03 (0.02)	0.04 (0.01)	−0.21 (0.02)	0.04 (0.01)	0.06 (0.01)	0.11 (0.03)	0.03 (0.01)	−0.04 (0.02)	0.00 (0.00)
32 Hungary	−0.10 (0.02)	−0.02 (0.01)	0.01 (0.03)	0.09 (0.01)	−0.03 (0.02)	0.13 (0.02)	0.05 (0.02)	−0.15 (0.02)	0.01 (0.03)
33 India	−0.24 (0.01)	0.05 (0.00)	−0.04 (0.00)	0.04 (0.00)	−0.01 (0.00)	0.11 (0.01)	–	0.01 (0.00)	0.08 (0.02)
34 Latvia	−0.31 (0.04)	0.04 (0.01)	−0.02 (0.04)	0.03 (0.01)	0.05 (0.01)	0.06 (0.02)	0.13 (0.03)	0.02 (0.03)	0.00 (0.00)
35 Lithuania	−0.12 (0.01)	0.04 (0.01)	−0.09 (0.01)	0.03 (0.01)	0.00 (0.00)	0.06 (0.02)	0.03 (0.01)	0.01 (0.00)	0.03 (0.02)
36 Malaysia	−0.14 (0.05)	0.05 (0.02)	−0.14 (0.03)	0.04 (0.01)	0.00 (0.00)	0.07 (0.01)	–	–	0.12 (0.06)
37 Mexico	−0.08 (0.02)	−0.01 (0.01)	−0.09 (0.02)	–	0.00 (0.00)	–	–	–	0.17 (0.03)
38 Philippines	−0.04 (0.01)	−0.02 (0.00)	−0.02 (0.01)	−0.01 (0.00)	0.02 (0.00)	0.05 (0.01)	–	−0.01 (0.00)	0.04 (0.01)
39 Poland	−0.09 (0.03)	−0.06 (0.01)	0.00 (0.00)	0.01 (0.01)	0.03 (0.01)	0.08 (0.02)	−0.05 (0.02)	−0.03 (0.01)	0.12 (0.07)
40 Portugal	−0.08 (0.03)	0.08 (0.02)	−0.15 (0.02)	0.00 (0.00)	−0.05 (0.01)	0.33 (0.04)	−0.03 (0.02)	0.03 (0.02)	−0.13 (0.06)
41 Slovakia	−0.07 (0.03)	0.06 (0.02)	0.10 (0.06)	0.05 (0.01)	0.06 (0.03)	−0.13 (0.02)	−0.01 (0.01)	0.02 (0.02)	−0.07 (0.08)
42 South Africa	−0.05 (0.03)	−0.09 (0.01)	0.18 (0.02)	−0.03 (0.01)	−0.04 (0.01)	−0.05 (0.02)	−0.03 (0.01)	0.03 (0.01)	0.07 (0.05)
43 Sri Lanka	−0.18 (0.02)	−0.02 (0.00)	0.07 (0.01)	0.01 (0.00)	0.00 (0.00)	0.13 (0.01)	–	0.01 (0.01)	−0.01 (0.02)
44 Thailand	−0.12 (0.01)	0.00 (0.00)	−0.01 (0.00)	0.01 (0.00)	0.01 (0.00)	0.06 (0.00)	–	0.00 (0.00)	0.04 (0.01)
45 Turkey	−0.12 (0.01)	−0.12 (0.02)	−0.02 (0.02)	0.08 (0.01)	0.05 (0.01)	–	–	0.09 (0.01)	0.03 (0.03)
Mean (*Developing*)	−0.11 (0.01)	0.00 (0.00)	−0.04 (0.01)	0.03 (0.00)	0.01 (0.00)	0.07 (0.00)	0.02 (0.00)	0.00 (0.00)	0.05 (0.01)
Mean (*All countries*)	−0.10 (0.00)	−0.01 (0.00)	−0.05 (0.00)	0.01 (0.00)	0.01 (0.00)	0.07 (0.00)	0.03 (0.00)	0.00 (0.00)	0.05 (0.01)

Note: Standard errors are in parenthesis.

Table 4.13 Own-price coefficients, AIDS under homogeneity and symmetry, 45 countries

	Country	*Food*	*Clothing*	*Housing*	*Durables*	*Health*	*Transport*	*Education*	*Restaurant*	*Miscellaneous*
	(1)	*(2)*	*(3)*	*(4)*	*(5)*	*(6)*	*(7)*	*(8)*	*(9)*	*(10)*
Developed countries										
1	Australia	0.08 (0.02)	−0.01 (0.01)	0.13 (0.01)	0.00 (0.00)	0.00 (0.00)	0.08 (0.02)	0.03 (0.03)	0.06 (0.02)	−0.13 (0.05)
2	Austria	0.11 (0.02)	−0.04 (0.01)	0.21 (0.02)	0.04 (0.02)	0.01 (0.00)	0.09 (0.02)	−0.01 (0.02)	0.21 (0.03)	0.08 (0.06)
3	Belgium	0.09 (0.02)	0.01 (0.01)	0.30 (0.02)	0.19 (0.01)	0.05 (0.00)	0.08 (0.02)	0.08 (0.02)	0.00 (0.00)	0.12 (0.05)
4	Canada	0.11 (0.02)	0.02 (0.01)	0.31 (0.03)	0.03 (0.01)	0.01 (0.01)	0.14 (0.02)	0.11 (0.03)	−0.04 (0.01)	0.21 (0.06)
5	Denmark	0.07 (0.01)	0.03 (0.02)	0.29 (0.03)	−0.01 (0.01)	0.02 (0.00)	−0.06 (0.04)	0.06 (0.01)	−0.02 (0.03)	0.02 (0.05)
6	Finland	0.14 (0.01)	0.02 (0.01)	0.12 (0.03)	0.01 (0.01)	0.02 (0.00)	0.08 (0.02)	−0.01 (0.02)	0.02 (0.01)	0.06 (0.04)
7	France	0.08 (0.01)	0.05 (0.01)	0.16 (0.01)	0.00 (0.00)	−0.02 (0.00)	0.10 (0.01)	0.02 (0.00)	0.07 (0.01)	0.08 (0.02)
8	Germany	0.04 (0.02)	0.02 (0.01)	0.29 (0.05)	0.10 (0.04)	0.02 (0.01)	0.07 (0.03)	0.04 (0.01)	0.02 (0.01)	0.07 (0.08)
9	Hong Kong	0.27 (0.01)	0.17 (0.03)	0.16 (0.02)	0.06 (0.01)	−0.01 (0.00)	0.00 (0.00)	–	0.05 (0.01)	0.15 (0.04)
10	Iceland	−0.07 (0.02)	0.06 (0.01)	0.03 (0.02)	0.02 (0.01)	0.04 (0.00)	−0.10 (0.03)	0.08 (0.02)	−0.10 (0.03)	0.01 (0.05)
11	Ireland	−0.09 (0.01)	−0.06 (0.01)	−0.02 (0.01)	−0.05 (0.00)	0.00 (0.00)	−0.14 (0.01)	–	−0.01 (0.04)	0.06 (0.03)
12	Israel	0.12 (0.02)	0.02 (0.01)	0.19 (0.01)	0.04 (0.00)	0.06 (0.00)	0.16 (0.02)	−0.01 (0.02)	0.00 (0.00)	0.05 (0.07)
13	Italy	0.05 (0.04)	0.03 (0.02)	0.13 (0.01)	0.06 (0.01)	0.02 (0.01)	0.01 (0.02)	−0.05 (0.01)	−0.01 (0.05)	0.08 (0.07)
14	Japan	0.27 (0.10)	−0.20 (0.05)	0.33 (0.06)	0.02 (0.01)	−0.12 (0.01)	0.10 (0.03)	0.02 (0.01)	−0.12 (0.02)	−0.07 (0.13)
15	Luxembourg	−0.06 (0.03)	−0.05 (0.01)	−0.25 (0.04)	−0.05 (0.02)	−0.02 (0.01)	0.21 (0.03)	0.00 (0.00)	−0.02 (0.02)	0.08 (0.07)
16	Netherlands	0.10 (0.01)	0.03 (0.01)	0.29 (0.02)	0.01 (0.01)	−0.22 (0.05)	0.06 (0.04)	−0.07 (0.01)	0.05 (0.01)	0.09 (0.06)
17	New Zealand	0.09 (0.02)	0.00 (0.00)	0.16 (0.01)	−0.03 (0.02)	0.02 (0.01)	0.12 (0.02)	0.14 (0.02)	0.06 (0.04)	0.00 (0.00)
18	Norway	0.03 (0.02)	−0.02 (0.01)	−0.07 (0.03)	0.02 (0.02)	0.00 (0.00)	−0.14 (0.05)	−0.09 (0.01)	0.01 (0.03)	0.09 (0.07)
19	Singapore	0.07 (0.01)	0.03 (0.02)	0.12 (0.01)	0.02 (0.01)	0.04 (0.00)	0.07 (0.02)	–	0.12 (0.03)	0.00 (0.00)
20	Slovenia	0.09 (0.01)	0.00 (0.00)	0.05 (0.03)	0.04 (0.01)	0.05 (0.01)	−0.04 (0.02)	0.19 (0.04)	0.02 (0.01)	0.07 (0.06)
21	South Korea	0.18 (0.01)	0.08 (0.02)	0.14 (0.02)	0.03 (0.01)	−0.03 (0.02)	0.05 (0.01)	0.06 (0.01)	0.08 (0.01)	0.03 (0.04)
22	Spain	0.16 (0.03)	−0.01 (0.00)	0.02 (0.01)	0.05 (0.01)	0.09 (0.01)	0.06 (0.02)	0.04 (0.01)	0.00 (0.00)	0.02 (0.06)
23	Sweden	0.14 (0.02)	0.00 (0.00)	0.20 (0.02)	−0.03 (0.01)	0.04 (0.01)	0.22 (0.06)	−0.04 (0.01)	0.04 (0.03)	0.12 (0.07)
24	Switzerland	−0.11 (0.01)	−0.01 (0.01)	0.00 (0.00)	−0.03 (0.00)	−0.18 (0.01)	−0.12 (0.02)	–	−0.07 (0.01)	−0.14 (0.06)
25	Taiwan	0.21 (0.01)	0.04 (0.00)	0.13 (0.02)	0.02 (0.00)	0.06 (0.01)	0.18 (0.05)	–	0.05 (0.01)	−0.02 (0.07)
26	UK	0.06 (0.01)	−0.01 (0.01)	0.20 (0.03)	−0.05 (0.01)	−0.07 (0.01)	0.02 (0.03)	−0.01 (0.02)	0.18 (0.01)	0.11 (0.05)
27	USA	0.13 (0.01)	0.02 (0.00)	0.08 (0.01)	0.02 (0.01)	0.10 (0.01)	0.09 (0.01)	−0.01 (0.02)	0.08 (0.01)	0.01 (0.02)
Mean (*Developed*)		0.09 (0.00)	0.01 (0.00)	0.14 (0.00)	0.02 (0.00)	0.00 (0.00)	0.05 (0.01)	0.03 (0.00)	0.03 (0.00)	0.05 (0.01)

(*Continued*)

Table 4.13 Own-price coefficients, AIDS under homogeneity and symmetry, 45 countries (*Continued*)

Country	*Food*	*Clothing*	*Housing*	*Durables*	*Health*	*Transport*	*Education*	*Restaurant*	*Miscellaneous*
(1)	*(2)*	*(3)*	*(4)*	*(5)*	*(6)*	*(7)*	*(8)*	*(9)*	*(10)*
Developing countries									
28 Colombia	0.06 (0.04)	0.05 (0.03)	0.10 (0.02)	0.00 (0.00)	−0.01 (0.01)	–	–	–	−0.12 (0.05)
29 Czech Republic	0.05 (0.02)	−0.01 (0.01)	0.20 (0.02)	0.02 (0.01)	0.03 (0.01)	0.07 (0.02)	0.07 (0.01)	0.10 (0.02)	−0.10 (0.05)
30 Estonia	0.28 (0.03)	−0.01 (0.03)	0.22 (0.06)	0.05 (0.00)	0.05 (0.00)	0.07 (0.02)	0.16 (0.02)	0.06 (0.02)	0.03 (0.09)
31 Greece	0.10 (0.05)	0.20 (0.02)	0.42 (0.04)	0.06 (0.01)	−0.04 (0.02)	0.12 (0.06)	0.09 (0.02)	0.13 (0.04)	0.05 (0.11)
32 Hungary	0.16 (0.01)	0.01 (0.01)	0.19 (0.02)	0.08 (0.01)	0.02 (0.01)	0.13 (0.02)	0.05 (0.02)	0.21 (0.02)	0.13 (0.05)
33 India	0.23 (0.03)	0.09 (0.01)	0.08 (0.00)	0.02 (0.00)	0.02 (0.00)	0.15 (0.02)	–	0.04 (0.00)	0.03 (0.03)
34 Latvia	0.07 (0.06)	−0.01 (0.01)	0.05 (0.04)	−0.01 (0.00)	0.00 (0.00)	0.02 (0.02)	−0.04 (0.05)	0.10 (0.06)	0.02 (0.10)
35 Lithuania	0.16 (0.02)	0.02 (0.01)	0.09 (0.01)	0.04 (0.04)	0.03 (0.01)	0.15 (0.03)	−0.08 (0.01)	−0.02 (0.01)	−0.01 (0.07)
36 Malaysia	0.12 (0.14)	0.01 (0.02)	0.36 (0.10)	0.11 (0.07)	−0.04 (0.05)	0.10 (0.02)	–	–	0.34 (0.19)
37 Mexico	0.17 (0.02)	0.02 (0.01)	0.22 (0.03)	–	0.03 (0.01)	–	–	–	0.11 (0.03)
38 Philippines	0.27 (0.01)	0.03 (0.00)	0.11 (0.01)	0.05 (0.00)	0.01 (0.01)	0.19 (0.01)	–	0.05 (0.01)	0.08 (0.02)
39 Poland	0.27 (0.03)	−0.02 (0.01)	0.17 (0.06)	−0.01 (0.02)	−0.02 (0.01)	0.04 (0.02)	0.09 (0.03)	0.01 (0.00)	0.07 (0.08)
40 Portugal	−0.01 (0.03)	−0.02 (0.01)	0.10 (0.01)	0.03 (0.00)	0.01 (0.00)	0.19 (0.04)	0.04 (0.01)	0.05 (0.03)	0.14 (0.05)
41 Slovakia	0.12 (0.03)	0.16 (0.01)	−0.02 (0.05)	0.05 (0.00)	0.00 (0.00)	0.11 (0.02)	0.02 (0.01)	−0.03 (0.02)	0.05 (0.08)
42 South Africa	0.16 (0.03)	−0.01 (0.00)	0.02 (0.01)	0.05 (0.01)	0.09 (0.01)	0.06 (0.02)	0.04 (0.01)	0.00 (0.00)	0.02 (0.06)
43 Sri Lanka	0.03 (0.03)	−0.02 (0.01)	0.02 (0.01)	0.02 (0.01)	0.01 (0.00)	0.06 (0.02)	–	0.02 (0.01)	0.01 (0.06)
44 Thailand	0.19 (0.02)	0.05 (0.01)	0.01 (0.01)	0.01 (0.01)	0.01 (0.01)	0.08 (0.02)	–	0.19 (0.03)	−0.01 (0.01)
45 Turkey	0.07 (0.01)	0.09 (0.02)	0.14 (0.01)	0.07 (0.02)	0.03 (0.00)	–	–	0.07 (0.02)	0.09 (0.04)
Mean (*Developing*)	0.14 (0.01)	0.04 (0.00)	0.14 (0.01)	0.04 (0.00)	0.01 (0.00)	0.10 (0.01)	0.04 (0.00)	0.07 (0.01)	0.05 (0.02)
Mean (*All countries*)	0.11 (0.01)	0.02 (0.00)	0.14 (0.00)	0.03 (0.00)	0.00 (0.00)	0.07 (0.00)	0.03 (0.00)	0.04 (0.00)	0.05 (0.01)

Note: Standard errors are in parenthesis.

Table 4.14 Income elasticities, AIDS under homogeneity and symmetry, 45 countries

	Country (1)	*Food* (2)	*Clothing* (3)	*Housing* (4)	*Durables* (5)	*Health* (6)	*Transport* (7)	*Education* (8)	*Restaurant* (9)	*Miscellaneous* (10)
Developed countries										
1	Australia	0.330	0.435	0.980	0.607	1.199	1.565	1.857	0.506	0.812
2	Austria	0.584	0.026	0.621	0.850	1.009	2.469	1.007	0.438	1.470
3	Belgium	0.330	−2.068	0.862	0.859	1.271	2.173	1.032	0.998	1.885
4	Canada	0.358	0.266	0.467	1.073	1.732	1.332	2.022	1.294	1.392
5	Denmark	0.299	0.841	−0.117	1.412	0.217	2.525	1.770	1.848	1.519
6	Finland	0.241	0.910	1.333	0.217	0.943	1.181	1.282	1.295	1.709
7	France	0.497	0.308	1.475	0.666	1.031	1.316	1.288	0.566	1.270
8	Germany	0.136	−0.627	0.302	2.005	2.902	1.503	1.480	1.154	1.686
9	Hong Kong	−0.157	1.296	1.217	2.112	2.074	1.111	–	0.605	1.096
10	Iceland	1.071	1.257	1.281	0.310	1.233	0.457	0.580	1.307	1.941
11	Ireland	0.795	0.435	1.268	0.892	1.299	0.904	–	0.917	1.405
12	Israel	0.366	−0.357	0.709	1.798	1.556	2.219	0.881	1.117	0.524
13	Italy	0.503	1.961	0.287	1.361	1.581	1.630	2.078	0.687	0.731
14	Japan	−0.302	2.749	0.362	−0.596	−2.624	1.298	0.462	2.351	4.277
15	Luxembourg	1.069	1.195	1.124	0.460	−0.193	0.877	0.769	0.842	1.491
16	Netherlands	0.141	0.926	0.258	1.301	3.885	1.978	0.874	0.728	1.101
17	New Zealand	0.930	0.932	0.586	1.883	1.253	1.320	1.253	0.948	0.813
18	Norway	0.380	0.096	0.789	1.559	2.113	1.267	2.170	1.445	0.757
19	Singapore	0.269	0.626	0.896	0.660	1.307	1.311	–	1.373	1.223
20	Slovenia	0.381	0.962	0.821	0.684	1.148	1.347	1.483	1.302	1.469
21	South Korea	0.269	0.928	0.990	0.814	1.330	1.356	1.682	1.210	1.544
22	Spain	0.834	−0.354	2.360	0.700	0.363	0.707	0.598	2.128	1.603
23	Sweden	0.345	1.749	−0.057	3.012	−0.093	2.200	1.828	1.134	1.107
24	Switzerland	1.345	0.784	1.371	1.161	0.381	0.934	–	1.027	0.577
25	Taiwan	0.397	1.057	1.011	1.579	0.919	1.500	–	1.330	0.992
26	UK	0.717	1.278	0.415	1.801	4.940	1.105	1.307	0.452	1.528
27	USA	0.140	0.317	0.867	0.871	1.035	1.445	1.466	1.264	1.291
Mean (*Developed*)		0.454	0.664	0.833	1.113	1.252	1.446	1.326	1.121	1.378

(*Continued*)

Table 4.14 Income elasticities, AIDS under homogeneity and symmetry, 45 countries (*Continued*)

	Country (1)	*Food* (2)	*Clothing* (3)	*Housing* (4)	*Durables* (5)	*Health* (6)	*Transport* (7)	*Education* (8)	*Restaurant* (9)	*Miscellaneous* (10)
Developed countries										
28	Colombia	0.452	1.382	0.651	0.820	0.597	–	–	–	1.378
29	Czech Republic	0.313	1.030	0.349	1.296	2.562	1.520	1.527	1.022	2.829
30	Estonia	0.990	1.276	0.252	1.919	1.216	1.247	1.124	0.958	1.501
31	Greece	0.861	1.698	−0.080	1.925	2.294	1.636	1.464	0.679	1.012
32	Hungary	0.626	0.553	1.039	2.600	0.361	1.731	1.519	−1.328	1.161
33	India	0.518	1.537	0.573	1.904	0.723	1.870	–	1.311	2.492
34	Latvia	0.047	1.745	0.892	2.075	2.356	1.401	2.330	1.417	0.998
35	Lithuania	0.667	1.637	0.475	1.476	1.104	1.366	1.385	1.491	1.537
36	Malaysia	0.432	2.664	0.172	1.710	1.004	1.338	–	–	1.429
37	Mexico	0.681	0.692	0.625	–	1.042	–	–	–	1.398
38	Philippines	0.910	−0.135	0.846	0.729	1.847	1.328	–	0.823	1.217
39	Poland	0.695	−0.189	0.986	1.234	1.651	1.559	0.446	0.153	2.028
40	Portugal	0.624	2.235	−0.015	0.934	−0.057	2.888	0.674	1.258	−0.148
41	Slovakia	0.717	2.223	1.422	2.002	2.970	−0.168	0.871	1.286	0.204
42	South Africa	0.834	−0.354	2.360	0.700	0.363	0.707	0.598	2.128	1.603
43	Sri Lanka	0.658	0.671	1.814	1.247	0.924	1.773	–	1.253	0.727
44	Thailand	0.658	0.994	0.904	1.203	1.323	1.482	–	0.999	1.532
45	Turkey	0.565	−0.704	0.875	2.089	2.516	–	–	1.523	1.158
Mean (*Developing*)		0.625	1.053	0.786	1.521	1.378	1.445	1.194	0.998	1.336
Mean (*All countries*)		0.523	0.820	0.814	1.271	1.302	1.445	1.285	1.077	1.362

The own-price elasticity estimates presented in Table 4.15 for food, clothing, housing, durables, transport, education and restaurants are generally less than one in absolute value, indicating that the demand for these goods is price inelastic. The demand for health in developed countries is generally price elastic, while it is price inelastic in developing countries.

Next, we compare the mean income elasticities and own-price elasticities for developed and developing countries in Tables 4.14 and 4.15. As can be seen, the mean income elasticity for clothing in developed countries is 0.66 and developing countries is 1.05, meaning that clothing is a necessity in developed countries while it is a luxury in developing countries. All other commodities, on average, have similar income and own-price elasticities in the two groups of countries. Overall, our results are in line with those of many previous studies (see, for example, Bustamante and Shimoga 2018; Clements et al. 2006; Clements et al. 2020).

4.6 A Comparison of the Three Demand Models Estimation Results

To choose the preferred model among the three, we first compare the test results to determine whether the models satisfy the demand theory hypotheses and preference independent utility structure. Then, we consider the implied demand elasticities. The test results show that demand homogeneity is generally acceptable by all three models, for 92 percent of the countries using the Rotterdam model, 94 percent using the W-R model and 76 percent using the AIDS model. The hypothesis of symmetry is supported by the AIDS model for 64 percent of the countries, by the Rotterdam model for only 40 percent of the countries and by the W-R model for 42 percent of the countries. However, the preference independence utility structure is accepted for 91 percent of the countries by the Rotterdam model and for 96 percent of the countries by the W-R model. Therefore, Rotterdam and W-R models[2] would be preferable under homogeneity or preference independence, and the AIDS model would be preferable where homogeneity and symmetry restrictions are imposed.

Table 4.16 presents a summary of the mean implied income and own-price elasticities obtained using the parameter estimates of the three demand models for developed countries, developing countries and all 45 countries. As can be seen, the implied income and own-price elasticities are similar regardless of the model used and also across developed or developing countries, except in the case of clothing and health, which has a different status for the two groups of countries.

4.7 Concluding Comments

In this chapter, we estimated three demand models for consumer goods grouped into nine broad categories, namely food, clothing, housing, durables, health, transport, education, restaurants and miscellaneous for the 45 countries. We tested the validity of the demand theory hypotheses, demand

Table 4.15 Own-price elasticities, AIDS under homogeneity and symmetry, 45 countries

	Country (1)	Food (2)	Clothing (3)	Housing (4)	Durables (5)	Health (6)	Transport (7)	Education (8)	Restaurant (9)	Miscellaneous (10)
Developed countries										
1	Australia	−0.371	−1.253	−0.367	−0.988	−1.046	−0.544	−0.876	−0.159	−1.883
2	Austria	−0.143	−1.576	0.097	−0.470	−0.735	−0.640	−1.049	0.896	−0.334
3	Belgium	−0.377	−0.555	0.286	2.055	−0.090	−0.596	−0.149	−1.032	−0.244
4	Canada	−0.169	−0.671	0.421	−0.442	−0.840	−0.236	−0.051	−1.504	0.583
5	Denmark	−0.434	−0.423	0.351	−1.215	−0.310	−1.624	−0.622	−1.332	−0.888
6	Finland	−0.179	−0.582	−0.544	−0.760	−0.274	−0.511	−1.086	−0.732	−0.371
7	France	−0.501	−0.317	−0.333	−1.004	−1.629	−0.419	−0.768	0.153	−0.324
8	Germany	−0.592	−0.597	0.385	0.317	−0.704	−0.690	−0.666	−0.566	−0.520
9	Hong Kong	0.691	0.007	−0.126	−0.312	−1.383	−1.059	–	−0.347	−0.239
10	Iceland	−1.383	0.067	−0.920	−0.596	0.309	−1.460	−0.279	−2.216	−0.918
11	Ireland	−1.469	−2.085	−1.172	−1.758	−0.956	−1.920	–	−1.011	−0.418
12	Israel	−0.245	−0.501	−0.106	−0.520	0.981	−0.312	−1.077	−1.043	−0.526
13	Italy	−0.666	−0.654	−0.217	−0.215	−0.383	−1.032	−1.675	−1.097	−0.219
14	Japan	0.753	−5.581	0.549	−0.369	−4.090	−0.313	−0.794	−2.867	−1.953
15	Luxembourg	−1.329	−1.985	−2.188	−1.779	−1.755	0.147	−0.929	−1.324	−0.421
16	Netherlands	−0.197	−0.536	0.594	−0.851	−6.580	−0.834	−1.603	−0.283	−0.338
17	New Zealand	−0.532	−1.027	−0.280	−1.503	−0.247	−0.330	0.292	0.066	−0.984
18	Norway	−0.736	−1.173	−1.305	−0.765	−1.116	−1.852	−1.974	−0.910	0.045
19	Singapore	−0.429	−0.515	−0.021	−0.748	−0.026	−0.583	–	−0.582	−1.041
20	Slovenia	−0.437	−0.942	−0.691	−0.361	−2.344	−0.052	−0.829	0.025	−1.044
21	South Korea	−0.154	−0.010	−0.005	−0.254	−1.735	−0.671	−0.525	−0.104	−0.779
22	Spain	−0.404	−1.025	−1.038	−0.434	0.567	−0.573	−0.473	−0.895	−0.930
23	Sweden	−0.044	−1.137	−0.008	−1.824	0.413	0.151	−1.404	−0.316	0.214
24	Switzerland	−1.878	−1.169	−1.101	−1.723	−2.363	−2.036	–	−1.426	−2.044
25	Taiwan	0.010	−0.312	−0.308	−0.668	0.772	0.228	–	−0.700	−1.123
26	UK	−0.499	−1.176	−0.054	−2.043	−5.689	−0.918	−1.143	0.999	−0.228
27	USA	0.182	−0.579	−0.574	−0.680	−0.351	−0.411	−1.108	0.270	−0.925
Mean (*Developed*)		−0.427	−0.974	−0.321	−0.737	−1.171	−0.707	−0.854	−0.668	−0.661

Developing countries										
28	Colombia	−0.629	−0.350	−0.331	−0.363	−1.353	–	–	–	−1.436
29	Czech Republic	−0.608	−1.140	−0.026	−0.618	0.259	−0.470	−0.372	0.200	−2.296
30	Estonia	−0.026	−1.098	0.273	−0.055	0.808	−0.545	0.821	−0.020	−0.694
31	Greece	−0.490	2.913	1.438	0.378	−2.005	−0.420	0.351	−0.017	−0.401
32	Hungary	−0.277	−0.785	−0.014	0.293	−0.514	−0.362	−0.499	2.332	0.530
33	India	−0.296	−0.208	−0.152	−0.497	−0.285	0.080	–	0.078	−0.467
34	Latvia	−0.489	−1.255	−0.723	−1.459	−1.040	−0.887	−1.485	0.711	−0.564
35	Lithuania	−0.425	−0.691	−0.370	−0.313	−0.362	−0.145	−2.256	−1.700	−1.174
36	Malaysia	−0.368	−0.665	1.261	0.896	−2.815	−0.567	–	–	0.052
37	Mexico	−0.226	−0.258	0.008	–	−0.552	–	–	–	−0.910
38	Philippines	−0.329	0.624	−0.118	0.095	−0.496	0.303	–	−0.147	−0.514
39	Poland	0.007	−1.260	−0.191	−1.178	−1.438	−0.751	0.061	−0.547	−0.511
40	Portugal	−0.950	−1.414	−0.157	−0.516	−0.647	−0.252	−0.521	−0.584	0.435
41	Slovakia	−0.483	2.233	−1.195	−0.072	−0.913	0.085	−0.739	−1.480	−0.418
42	South Africa	−0.404	−1.025	−1.038	−0.434	0.567	−0.573	−0.473	−0.895	−0.930
43	Sri Lanka	−0.752	−1.295	−0.826	−0.627	−0.164	−0.773	–	−0.426	−0.792
44	Thailand	−0.328	−0.151	−0.883	−0.723	−0.768	−0.425	–	−0.138	−1.898
45	Turkey	−0.607	0.334	−0.158	−0.238	−0.158	–	–	−0.697	−0.542
Mean (*Developing*)		−0.427	−0.305	−0.178	−0.319	−0.660	−0.380	−0.511	−0.222	−0.696
Mean (*All countries*)		−0.427	−0.707	−0.264	−0.576	−0.966	−0.590	−0.747	−0.509	−0.675

Table 4.16 Summary mean income and own-price elasticities, three models, nine commodities, developed, developing and all countries

Model (1)	*Food* (2)	*Clothing* (3)	*Housing* (4)	*Durables* (5)	*Health* (6)	*Transport* (7)	*Education* (8)	*Restaurant* (9)	*Miscellaneous* (10)
Income elasticity									
Rotterdam demand system									
Developed	0.631	1.258	0.468	1.514	0.679	1.677	1.302	1.116	1.011
Developing	0.646	1.329	0.413	1.472	1.211	1.446	1.362	1.336	1.313
All countries	0.637	1.287	0.446	1.498	0.892	1.595	1.321	1.197	1.132
Workings–Rotterdam demand system									
Developed	0.597	1.213	0.487	1.483	0.703	1.674	1.301	1.149	1.042
Developing	0.655	1.286	0.407	1.452	1.197	1.469	1.323	1.288	1.300
All countries	0.620	1.242	0.455	1.471	0.901	1.598	1.308	1.197	1.145
AIDS									
Developed	0.454	0.664	0.833	1.113	1.252	1.446	1.326	1.121	1.378
Developing	0.625	1.053	0.786	1.521	1.378	1.445	1.194	0.998	1.336
All countries	0.523	0.820	0.814	1.271	1.302	1.445	1.285	1.077	1.362
Own–price elasticity									
Rotterdam demand system									
Developed	−0.301	−0.536	−0.227	−0.609	−0.313	−0.553	−0.427	−0.456	−0.394
Developing	−0.185	−0.436	−0.152	−0.492	−0.423	−0.399	−0.509	−0.453	−0.363
All countries	−0.255	−0.496	−0.197	−0.564	−0.357	−0.498	−0.453	−0.455	−0.381
Workings–Rotterdam demand system									
Developed	−0.295	−0.516	−0.235	−0.595	−0.305	−0.551	−0.425	−0.466	−0.402
Developing	−0.183	−0.439	−0.172	−0.478	−0.445	−0.415	−0.510	−0.463	−0.386
All countries	−0.250	−0.485	−0.210	−0.550	−0.361	−0.502	−0.452	−0.465	−0.395
AIDS									
Developed	−0.427	−0.974	−0.321	−0.737	−1.171	−0.707	−0.854	−0.668	−0.661
Developing	−0.427	−0.305	−0.178	−0.319	−0.660	−0.380	−0.511	−0.222	−0.696
All countries	−0.427	−0.707	−0.264	−0.576	−0.966	−0.590	−0.747	−0.509	−0.675

homogeneity and Slutsky symmetry. We also tested the preference independence utility structure of the nine broad commodity groups and found that it is supported by almost all countries.

Based on the implied income and own-price elasticities obtained using the parameter estimates of the models, we found that across all three models, food and housing are necessities and the other commodities are generally luxuries in most developed and developing countries. The only dissimilarity found is that health is mostly a necessity in developed countries, whereas it is a luxury in developing countries. The demand for all commodities is generally price inelastic in both groups of countries. The mean income flexibility is −0.48 for developed countries and −0.38 for developing countries, which is in line with past studies where income flexibility values close to −0.5 have been the norm mainly for developed countries. Overall, using recent data, our results further confirm the findings of previous studies (see, for example, Clements et al. 2006; Clements et al, 2020; Farag et al. 2012; Selvanathan and Selvanathan 2003, Selvanathan et al. 2021) with respect to developed and developing countries.

In the next chapter, we will analyse the consumption patterns of consumers in developed and developing countries in South Asia using cross-sectional survey data.

Notes

1 In Chapter 3, we used 12 commodity groups for most of the countries for the preliminary data analysis. In this chapter for model estimation, we use nine commodity groups so that the conditions for model estimation are met as well as for comparative purposes across countries. Some of the 12 commodity groups are combined to make the nine commodity groups.

2 In a review article on the performance of the Rotterdam demand model and other popular demand models, Clements and Gao (2015) cite the works of Barnett and Kanyama (2013) and Barnett and Seck (2008), which uses Monte Carlo techniques to show that under most circumstances the Rotterdam model performs better than the AIDS model.

References

Barnard, G.A. 1963. Comment. *Journal of the Royal Statistical Society: Series B (Statistical Methodology)* 25: 294.

Barnett, W.A., and I. Kanyama. 2013. Time-varying parameters in the almost ideal demand system and the Rotterdam model: Will the best specification please stand up? *Applied Economics* 45: 4169–4183.

Barnett, W.A., and O. Seck. 2008. Rotterdam versus almost ideal model: Will the best specification please stand up? *Journal of Applied Economics* 23: 798–824.

Barten, A.P. 1964. Consumer demand functions under conditions of almost additive preferences. *Econometrica* 32: 1–38.

Barten, A.P. 1977. The systems of consumer demand Functions approach: A review. *Econometrica,* 45: 23–51.

Bera, A.K., R.P. Byron, and C.M. Jarque. 1981. Further evidence on asymptotic tests for homogeneity and symmetry in large demand systems. *Economics Letters* 8(2): 101–105.

Besag, J., and D.J. Diggle. 1977. Simple Monte Carlo tests of spatial pattern. *Applied Statistics* 26: 327–333.

Bewley, R.A. 1983. Tests of restrictions in large demand systems. *European Economic Review* 20(1–3): 257–269.

Bustamante, A.V., and S. Shimoga. 2018. Comparing the income elasticity of health spending in middle-income and high-income countries: The role of financial protection. *International Journal of Health Policy and Management* 7(3): 255–263.

Clements, K.W., and G. Gao. 2015. The Rotterdam demand model half a century on. *Economic Modelling* 49: 91–103.

Clements, K.W., J. Si, E.A. Selvanathan, and S. Selvanathan. 2020. Demand elasticities for 9 goods in 37 countries. *Applied Economics* 52(24): 2636–2655.

Clements, K.W., Y. Wu, and J. Zhang. 2006. Comparing international consumption patterns. *Empirical Economics* 31, 1–30.

Cribari-Neto, F., and S.G. Zarkos. 1997. Finite-sample adjustments for homogeneity and symmetry tests in systems of demand equations: A Monte Carlo evaluation. *Computational Economics* 10(4): 337–351.

Deschamps, P. J. 2000. Exact small-sample inference in stationary, fully regular, dynamic demand models. *Journal of Econometrics* 97(1): 51–91.

Farag, M., A.K. Nandakumar, S. Wallack, D. Hodgkin, G. Gaumer, and C. Erbil. 2012. The income elasticity of health care spending in developing and developed countries. *International Journal of Health Care Finance and Economics* 12(2):145–162.

Karagiannis, G., and G.J. Mergos. 2002. Estimating theoretically consistent demand systems using cointegration techniques with application to Greek food data. *Economics Letters* 74(2): 137–143.

Keuzenkamp, H.A. 2000. *Probability, econometrics and truth: The methodology of econometrics*. Cambridge: Cambridge University Press.

Keuzenkamp, H.A., and A.P. Barten 1995. Rejection without falsification on the history of testing the homogeneity condition in the theory of consumer demand. *Journal of Econometrics* 67(1): 103–127.

Laitinen, K. 1978. Why is demand homogeneity so often rejected? *Economic Letters* 1: 187–191.

Marriott, F.H. 1979. Barnard's Monte Carlo tests: How many simulations? *Journal of the Royal Statistical Society: Series C (Applied Statistics)* 28(1): 75–77.

Pollak, A.A., and T.J. Wales. 1992. *Demand system specification and estimation*. New York and Oxford: Oxford University Press.

Selvanathan, S. 1987. A Monte Carlo test of preference independence. *Economic Letters* 25: 259–261.

Selvanathan, E.A., and S. Selvanathan. 2003. *International consumption comparisons*. Singapore: World Scientific Publications.

Selvanathan, E.A., S. Selvanathan, L. Wong, L., and M. Jayasinghe. 2021. Modelling regional consumption patterns in Australia. *Economic Record* 97(317): 141–156.

Theil, H. 1971. An economic theory of the second moments of disturbances of behavioral equations. *The American Economic Review* 61(1): 190–194.

Theil, H., and K. W. Clements. 1987. *Applied demand analysis: Results from system-wide approaches*. Cambridge, MA: Ballinger Publishing Company.

Working, H. 1943. Statistical law of family expenditure. *Journal of the American Statistical Association* 38: 43–56.

5 Household Demand in the Asia Pacific Countries

M Jayasinghe, E A Selvanathan, S Selvanathan and R K Mondal

5.1 Introduction

Since the pioneering work of Engel (1857), Engel curves have become an integral part in many areas of consumption economics. Early studies on the analysis of household expenditures, however, mainly used linear Engel curves (see, for example, Allen and Bowley 1935; Nicholson 1949). The poor performance of these linear forms of Engel curves led researchers to investigate other functional forms to estimate Engel curves. One of the leading-edge works in this regard was carried out by Prais and Houthakker (1955), who estimated five different forms of Engel functions, namely linear, semi-log, hyperbolic, double-log and log-inverse. Despite the apparent need to use the appropriate functional form to analyse household budgets, it is a challenging task to find the appropriate functional form. Nevertheless, the work of Box and Cox (1964), Poirier (1978) and Zarembka (1974), on transformation of variables, facilitates the specification of a functional form which is determined by the data. Demand elasticities derived from estimation of these functional forms give varying results, depending on the data used in empirical estimations. Houthakker (1957) and Houthakker (1965) found that although, in some instances, income elasticity of various commodity groups tends to vary from country to country, there are also some similarities. For example, in many studies, food has been consistently identified as a necessity (with income elasticity less than 1) (see, for example, Clements and Gao 2012; Clements and Si 2017 Clements et al. 2020; Haque 2005; Jayasinghe et al. 2019; Selvanathan 1993; Selvanathan and Selvanathan 2003a; Selvanathan et al. 2021).

A majority of the recent work on Engel function estimations has made allowances for household size and compositional differences by introducing an additional variable on household size into the Engel curve specification together with household expenditure (M) (see, for example, Beneito 2003, and Rajapakse 2011). Other studies use per capita expenditure (PCE) as an independent variable in the Engel model specification (see, for example, Mori et al. 2006 and Nie and Sousa-Poza 2016). Another method widely used

DOI: 10.4324/9780429200120-5

in the literature in controlling for the effects of household size and compositional differences is to use expenditure per equivalent adult (EPEA). The EPEA is obtained using household equivalence scales. The intuition here is that due to the existence of consumption economies of scale, household equivalence scales do not increase as rapidly as household size. The Organisation for Economic Co-operation and Development (OECD)-modified scales that assign a value of 1 to the first household member, 0.5 to each additional adult and 0.3 to each child are widely used by policy makers and statisticians (Eurostat 2014). Based on the OECD-modified equivalence scales, for example, the effective household size for a two-adult and one-child household will be 1.8 (=1 + 0.5 + 0.3) instead of 3. EPEA is obtained by dividing the household expenditure by 1.8 (in this example) to obtain EPEA instead of dividing by 3 which results in PCE. It is widely accepted that such EPEA takes the economics of scale in consumption and the differences in the needs of individuals, such as children and adults in the household, into consideration (see, for example, Lanjouw and Ravallion 1995, Deaton and Paxson 1998, Jayasinghe 2022).

In Chapter 4, we considered nine broadly defined commodity groups and estimated income and price elasticities based on time-series consumption data. In this chapter, we estimate income[1] elasticities for the same nine commodity groups: (1) food (food and beverages, including dining at restaurants), (2) alcohol (alcohol and tobacco), (3) clothing (clothing and footwear), (4) housing (housing and durables), (5) health (health and personal care), (6) transport (transport and communication), (7) recreation, (8) education and (9) miscellaneous, using household-level expenditure data for Australia, Bangladesh, India and Sri Lanka. The difference between Chapter 4 and this chapter is that Chapter 4 uses time-series data whereas this chapter uses cross-sectional household level survey data for a particular year. The income elasticities are calculated using the Box-Cox Engel functions estimated under three different specifications: total expenditure (M), PCE and EPEA. We then compare the income elasticities of a developed country (Australia) with a group of developing countries from South Asia (Bangladesh, India and Sri Lanka).[2]

The remainder of this chapter is organised as follows. Section 5.2 discusses the Box-Cox transformation to the Engel curve estimation, and Section 5.3 discusses the best model selection measure known as the information inaccuracy. Sections 5.4 and 5.5 describe the cross-sectional household survey data and their summary statistics for the four countries and Section 5.6 presents the estimation procedure and discusses the empirical results. Section 5.7 presents the concluding comments.

5.2 Box-Cox Transformation and Income Elasticities

The focus of this section is to discuss the role of the Box-Cox transformation in relation to Engel curve estimation.

5.2.1 Engel Curves

Various econometric methods have been utilised to estimate the Engel curves (see, for example, Blundell et al. 1998; Byrne et al. 1996; Haque 2005; Hausman et al. 1995; Houthakker 1957, McDowell et al. 1997; Working 1943; You 2003). The conventional approach of estimating the income elasticities is to select an appropriate functional form, such as linear, log-linear or log-log for each commodity to estimate Engel curves and then to use the estimated parameters to obtain the income elasticity estimates at any level of household income.

The traditional demand functions we introduced in Chapter 2 are derived by maximising the consumer's utility function subject to his/her budget constraint. These demand functions express the quantity demanded of a good as a function of its own price, prices of other goods and the income of the individual consumer. These demand equations should satisfy adding-up restrictions and a number of additional theoretical restrictions such as homogeneity, symmetry and negativity (Deaton and Muellbauer 1980). However, the use of cross-sectional data to estimate demand equations and thereby demand elasticities partly simplifies the estimation. This is because in cross-sectional data, information on prices is not usually available and hence the demand for a certain good is expected to depend only on the income level of the individual. Accordingly, the only condition that needs to be satisfied is the adding-up restriction. Although some of the early studies such as Allen and Bowley (1935) and Prais and Houthakker (1955) analyse the demand for consumer goods without any reference to a utility function and using single equation estimation, a majority of the recent studies focus on estimating utility-based demand equations as a system of equations that satisfies the adding-up restriction. These models include the Addilog model (Houthakker 1960), the Rotterdam Demand System (Barten 1964; Theil 1965) and the Almost Ideal Demand System (AIDS) (Deaton and Muellbauer 1980). Most of these demand systems have been discussed in Chapter 2.

A simple form of Engel curve for a given commodity i (i = 1, 2, ..., n) in share-linear form can be written as

$$w_i = \alpha_i + \beta_i M, \quad i = 1, 2, \ldots, n, \tag{5.1}$$

where w_i is the budget share on commodity i, and M is household expenditure (or income for short). The coefficients α_i and β_i are the parameters to be estimated. Under this specification, the income elasticity, η_i, is given by

$$\eta_i = 1 + \frac{\beta_i}{w_i} M, \quad i = 1, 2, \ldots, n. \tag{5.2}$$

Equations (5.1) and (5.2) are special cases when λ = 1 of the Box-Cox Engel function given in equations (2.22) and (2.29) in Section 2.4 of Chapter 2.

Studies have shown that there are some inconsistencies with theoretical propositions and empirical findings in relation to the linear form of Engel curves such as equation (5.1) (Haque 2005).

In addition to the share-linear specification, the most commonly used functional form is the semi-log form, the well-known Working's (1943) model which we introduced in Section 2.4, which we reproduce here:

$$w_i = \alpha_i + \beta_i \log(M), \quad i = 1,2,\ldots,n. \tag{5.3}$$

Income elasticity of specification (5.3) is

$$\eta_i = 1 + \frac{\beta_i}{w_i}, \quad i = 1,2,\ldots,n. \tag{5.4}$$

Under the Working's model specification, a commodity will be classified as a necessity with income elasticity less than one (luxury with income elasticity greater than one) if β_i is negative (positive).

An important issue associated with linear Engel curve estimation is the use of linear functional forms when the relationship may not be linear. Many applied studies on the Engel curve analysis identified a non-linear relationship between expenditure shares of individual items and household expenditure (see, for example, Bhalotra and Attfield 1998; Grigg 1994, Jayasinghe 2022; and Lewbel 2008). To resolve this issue, the Box-Cox Engel function, which is based on Box and Cox (1964) transformation, is currently being used, which we introduced in Section 2.4 of Chapter 2 and will reproduce below. The main advantage of this method is that this flexible functional form specification allows the data to determine the best suitable functional form to estimate the demand equation.

5.2.2 Estimation of Box-Cox Engel Function

Taking the Engel curve specified in equation (5.1) as the starting point, the Box-Cox Engel function for commodity *i* can be written as

$$w_i = \alpha_i + \beta_i M^{(\lambda)} + u_i, \quad i = 1,2,\ldots,n, \tag{5.5}$$

where w_i is the budget share on commodity i ($i = 1, 2, \ldots, n$) consumed, $M^{(\lambda)}$ is the Box-Cox transformed household expenditure and u_i is a stochastic disturbance term that satisfies the usual regression model assumptions. Under Box-Cox transformation, we write

$$M^{(\lambda)} = \begin{cases} \dfrac{M^{\lambda} - 1}{\lambda} & \text{if} \quad \lambda \neq 0 \\ \log M & \text{if} \quad \lambda = 0, \end{cases} \tag{5.6}$$

Where l is the Box-Cox transformation parameter.

Equation (5.5) provides a non-linear specification for the system of Engel curves. For the adding-up restriction to be satisfied, the parameters of model (5.5) are expected to satisfy the following conditions:

$$\sum_{i=1}^{n} \alpha_i = 1 \text{ and } \sum_{i=1}^{n} \beta_i = 0. \tag{5.7}$$

Estimation of the non-linear system of equations (5.5) for $i = 1, 2, \ldots, n$, subject to (5.7), will provide an estimate for Box-Cox transformation parameter λ. The Box-Cox method assigns an initial value for λ and continues searching for an optimal value for λ using equation (5.6).

Equation (5.5) represents the basic Engel curve specification, which displays the relationship between the budget share of a given commodity against expenditure. Studies have also shown that household socio-demographic factors significantly affect household consumption patterns (Bosch-Domènech 1991; Jayasinghe 2022). To incorporate the possible effect of these factors, in addition to household expenditure, variables relating to socio-demographic aspects have also been included in the model. These include household size, the square of household size, gender of the head of the household, residential area classification, and ethnicity/religion. Accordingly, the augmented version of equation (5.5) takes the form

$$w_i = \alpha_i + \beta_i M^{(\lambda)} + \gamma_i Z + \kappa_i (Z)^2 + \sum_{j=1}^{K} \delta_{ij} d_j + u_i, \quad i = 1,2,\ldots,n, \tag{5.8}$$

where Z is the household size, $(Z)^2$ is the square of the household size and d_j, $j = 1,2,\ldots,K$, are dummy variables representing the K household characteristics other than the household size.

5.2.3 Income Elasticities

We derived the income elasticity of commodity i in equation (2.29) in Section 2.4 of Chapter 2 as

$$\eta_i = \begin{cases} 1 + \dfrac{\beta_i}{w_i} M^{\lambda} & \text{when } \lambda \neq 0 \\ 1 + \dfrac{\beta_i}{w_i} & \text{when } \lambda = 0, \end{cases} \qquad i = 1,2,\ldots,n. \tag{5.9}$$

5.2.4 Adjustments for the Differences in Household Size and Composition

For the purpose of incorporating household size (Z) and compositional effects into our regression model specification, instead of including Z and $(Z)^2$ as additional explanatory variables in the model as in equation (5.8), in one model, we replace M with PCE and in another model, we replace M with EPEA.

The new regression models corresponding to equation (5.8) with PCE and EPEA can be presented as

$$w_i = \alpha_i + \beta_i \ \mathrm{PCE}^{(\lambda)} + \sum_{j=1}^{K} \delta_{ij} d_j + u_i, \quad i = 1,2,\ldots,n, \tag{5.10}$$

$$w_i = \alpha_i + \beta_i \ \mathrm{EPEA}^{(\lambda)} + \sum_{j=1}^{K} \delta_{ij} d_j + u_i, \quad i = 1,2,\ldots,n. \tag{5.11}$$

Since the household size aspect has already been incorporated in PCE and EPEA, household size related variables (Z and Z^2) have been omitted when we re-specified equation (5.8) as equations (5.10) and (5.11) with PCE and EPEA, respectively.

The PCE and EPEA income elasticities based on the models given in equations (5.10) and (5.11), respectively, can be derived as[3]

$$\eta_i = 1 + \frac{\beta_i}{w_i} \cdot \mathrm{PCE}^{(\lambda)}, \quad i = 1,2,\ldots,n, \tag{5.12}$$

$$\eta_i = 1 + \frac{\beta_i}{w_i} \cdot \mathrm{EPEA}^{(\lambda)}, \quad i = 1,2,\ldots,n. \tag{5.13}$$

Estimation results of the three models (5.8), (5.10) and (5.11) that make allocations for household size and compositional differences in three different ways would enable us to compare the differences in income elasticities estimated using equations (5.9), (5.12) and (5.13).

Using cross-sectional household survey data for Australia, Bangladesh, India and Sri Lanka, we estimate the regression models (5.8), (5.10) and (5.11), which we reproduce here with household (h) subscripts included:

$$w_{ih} = \alpha_i + \beta_i M_h^{(\lambda)} + \gamma_i Z_h + \kappa_i (Z_h)^2 + \sum_{j=1}^{K} \delta_{ij} d_j + u_{ih}, \quad i = 1,2,\ldots,n; \ h = 1,2,\ldots,H, \tag{5.14}$$

where n is the number of commodities and H is the number of households.

$$w_{ih} = \alpha_i + \beta_i \ \mathrm{PCE}_h^{(\lambda)} + \sum_{j=1}^{K} \delta_{ij} d_j + u_{ih}, \quad i = 1,2,\ldots,n; \ h = 1,2,\ldots,H, \tag{5.15}$$

$$w_{ih} = \alpha_i + \beta_i \ \mathrm{EPEA}_h^{(\lambda)} + \sum_{j=1}^{K} \delta_{ij} d_j + u_{ih}, \quad i = 1,2,\ldots,n; \ h = 1,2,\ldots,H, \tag{5.16}$$

where w_{ih} is the expenditure share on ith commodity by household h.

In equation (5.14), $M_h^{(\lambda)}$ is the Box-Cox transformed household expenditure; in equation (5.15), $\mathrm{PCE}_h^{(\lambda)}$ is the Box-Cox transformed PCE; and in equation (5.16), $\mathrm{EPEA}_h^{(\lambda)}$ is the Box-Cox transformed EPEA for the household h, Z_h is the household size of household h, $(Z_h)^2$ is the square of household size and d_h is a dummy variable for the gender of the head of the household h. The number of dummy variables used for each country varies based on the nature of the data available for each country. Where necessary, we provide an explanation in the results section. The coefficients, α_i, β_i, γ_i, κ_i and δ_{ij} (j = 1, 2, ..., K) are the corresponding parameters for the ith commodity group, and u_{ih} is the stochastic disturbance term of the ith equation.

Equations (5.14)–(5.16) for i = 1, 2, ..., n and h = 1, 2, ..., H are estimated as a system of equations using the Seemingly Unrelated Regression Estimation (SURE) method as discussed in Zellner (1962). There are n equations in the system, one for each commodity. As the system of n demand equations satisfies the adding-up restriction, the variance-covariance matrix of the system to be estimated becomes singular; hence, for estimation we drop one of the equations from the system. Barten (1964) has shown that the estimation results would be the same irrespective of which equation is dropped. Thus, during the estimation of system of equations, we drop the equation for the miscellaneous group. We then obtain the estimates corresponding to the miscellaneous group using the adding-up restrictions. The maximum likelihood parameter estimates of this system of equation models (5.14)–(5.16) are then used to calculate the income elasticities given by equations (5.9), (5.12) and (5.13), respectively.

5.3 Model Selection and Information Inaccuracies

To compare and select the best model, we investigate the performance of the three M, PCE and EPEA models (5.14)–(5.16) in two levels. First, we use the goodness-of-fit measure, the information inaccuracy, calculated based on the observed and predicted budget shares of the three models (see Theil 1975, pp. 215–220). Second, we use the commodity-level information inaccuracies to compare each expenditure sub-category, separately.

For the n commodities, if we denote $w_{1h}, w_{2h}, \ldots, w_{nh}$, as the observed budget shares for household h and $\hat{w}_{1h}, \hat{w}_{2h}, \ldots, \hat{w}_{nh}$ as the predicted budget shares from the estimated model, then the information inaccuracy of these predictions for household h is written as

$$I_h = \sum_{i=1}^{n} w_{ih} \cdot \log\left(\frac{w_{ih}}{\hat{w}_{ih}}\right), \quad h = 1, 2, \ldots, H, \tag{5.17}$$

where $\hat{w}_{ih} = w_{ih} - \hat{u}_{ih}$ and log is the natural logarithm. If the model predictions are perfect, then $\hat{w}_{ih} = w_{ih}$ and $I_h = 0$; otherwise, $I_h > 0$.

Similarly, we can also write the information inaccuracy for good i and its complements for household h as

$$I_{ih} = w_{ih} \log\left(\frac{w_{ih}}{\hat{w}_{ih}}\right) + (1 - w_{ih}) \log\left(\frac{1 - w_{ih}}{1 - \hat{w}_{ih}}\right), \quad i = 1, 2, \ldots, n; \; h = 1, 2, \ldots, H. \tag{5.18}$$

We average the information inaccuracies over the households to obtain the information inaccuracies for the overall model as

$$I = \frac{1}{H} \sum_{h=1}^{H} I_h \tag{5.19}$$

and for a particular commodity i as

$$I_i = \frac{1}{H} \sum_{h=1}^{H} I_{ih}, \quad i = 1, 2, \ldots, n. \tag{5.20}$$

5.4 Household Expenditure Surveys Data

In this section, we present a detailed description of the cross-sectional household survey data for the four countries used for the analysis in this chapter and in Section 5.5 present some summary statistics about the characteristics of households in the four countries.

Due to access, availability and consistency issues with household survey data for various countries, we have selected three developing countries from South Asia with various characteristics, Bangladesh, India and Sri Lanka, and one developed country, Australia, for the cross-sectional analysis in this chapter. Figure 5.1 presents a part-map of the Asia Pacific region, which includes the four countries. We use the latest available cross-sectional Household Expenditure Survey (HES) data of Australia (2015–2016), Bangladesh (2016), India (2011–2012) and Sri Lanka (2016). The three countries from

South Asia have some commonality by being in the same geographical area, while differences also exist in various ways. For example, by population size, India is the largest (about 1.4 billion), Bangladesh is in the middle (about 164 million) and Sri Lanka the smallest (about 22 million). By religion, Bangladesh has mostly Muslims, India has mostly Hindus and Sri Lanka has mostly Buddhists. These three countries are considered as developing or lower-middle income countries (World Bank 2020). The per capita GDP of Bangladesh, India and Sri Lanka are US$1876, US$2014 and US$3854, respectively (World Bank 2020). On the other hand, Australia is an island nation of western culture with about 25.5 million people and a majority of them follow the Christian religion. It is a developed country belonging to the OECD, with a per capita GDP of US$54,907 (World Bank, 2020).

The household income and expenditure survey data for all four countries used in this chapter have been collected through direct interviews using a survey questionnaire by the respective country statistical agencies. The

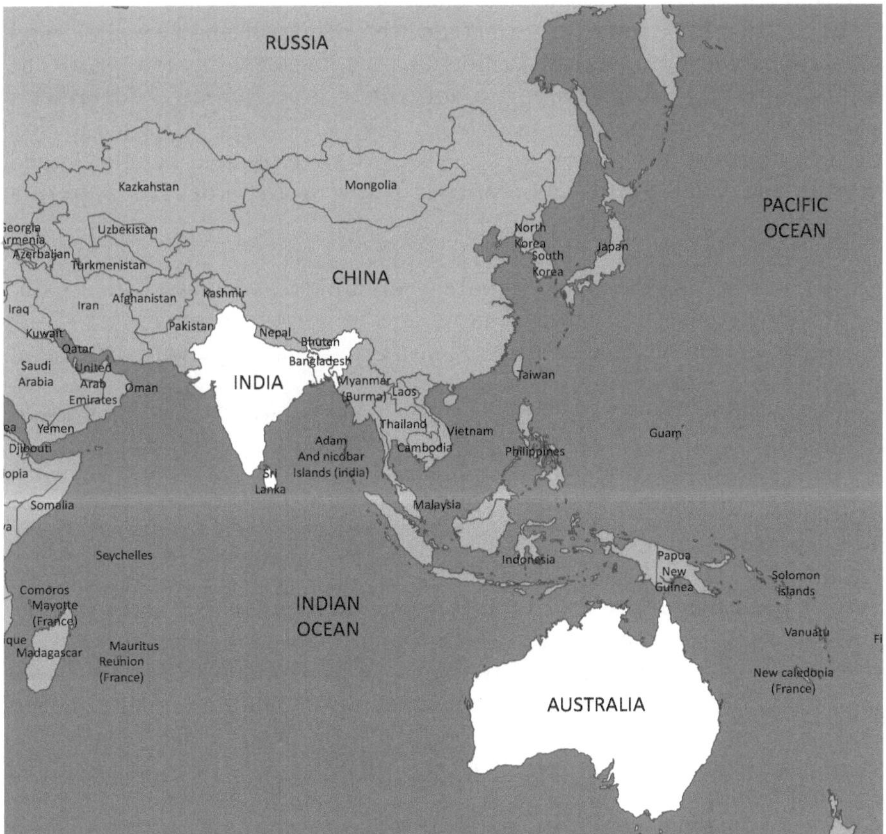

Figure 5.1 Map showing Australia, Bangladesh, India and Sri Lanka.

questionnaire covers three main areas: data on demographic characteristics of all household members, household expenditure (on food, non-food and alcohol and tobacco), and income received by each household member in the form of monetary and non-monetary income.

The household is the unit of analysis in all cross-sectional data analysis discussions in this book. The United Nations' definition of a household is, 'a household is a small group of persons who share the same living accommodation, who pool some, or all, of their income and wealth and who consume certain types of goods and services collectively, mainly housing and food.' A one-person household is a unit where a person lives by himself/herself and makes separate provision for his/her food, whereas a multi-person household is a group of two or more persons who live together and have common meal arrangements. In all four household expenditure survey data sets used in this book, consumption expenditure data are collected and recorded at the household level.

In the context of Bangladesh, India and Sri Lanka, the head of the household is usually expected to make household decisions. The head of the household is defined as a person who resides in the household and who is accepted by the other members of the household as the head. The Australian HES does not identify a household head. Instead, it identifies a household reference person. As noted in ABS (2017), the reference person for each household is chosen by applying, to all household members aged 15 years and older, the selection criteria below, in the order listed, until a single appropriate reference person is identified:

- the person with the highest tenure when ranked as follows: owner without a mortgage, owner with a mortgage, renter, other tenure
- one of the partners in a registered or de facto marriage, with dependent children
- one of the partners in a registered or de facto marriage, without dependent children
- a lone parent with dependent children
- the person with the highest income
- the eldest person

Overall, the expenditure data of all four countries are mostly comparable. However, there are some features in the four cross-sectional surveys that are worth noting. In the Bangladesh, Indian and Sri Lankan household surveys, the home production of food for own consumption and the freely received food have also been valued and recorded, separately, in the form of imputed values. Furthermore, imputed rent values for owner occupied houses were not available for India. In the Australian data, all expenditures are given on a weekly basis. In the original Bangladesh and Sri Lankan data, food expenditure is recorded on a weekly basis and non-food expenditure is recorded on a monthly, bi-annual or annual basis. In Indian data, food expenditure and some non-food expenditures are recorded on a monthly basis, while the remaining non-food expenditures are given on an annual basis. For the purpose of analysis in this chapter, all expenditures are converted to a monthly equivalent.

Table 5.1 provides a detailed description of the commodity groups covered in all four household expenditure surveys. Columns (1) and (2) of Table 5.1 present the expenditure categories (commodities) that are covered in the surveys of all four countries, in general, and their detailed descriptions. Column (3) provides the reclassified commodity group names for the purpose of the analysis in this chapter and in line with the commodity group classification in the other chapters. Below, we discuss the household (income and) expenditure surveys for the four countries in detail.

5.4.1 Australia

For Australia, we use the latest national household survey, *Household Expenditure Survey (HES) 2015/16*, conducted by the ABS. The HES is conducted every six years. The sample of 2015/16 HES was selected through a stratified, multistage cluster design from the private dwelling framework of the ABS Population Survey Master Sample (ABS 2017). The data were collected over a period of 12 months to ensure that survey results are representative of income and expenditure patterns across the year. At the most detailed level, the HES covers over 600 household consumption items, including food, non-food items, alcohol and tobacco. At the broadest level, it consists of 20 expenditure groups that are in line with the expenditure sub-categories given in Table 5.1.

5.4.2 Bangladesh

The data for Bangladesh are based on the micro-level national household survey, *Household Income and Expenditure Survey (HIES) 2016*, conducted by the Bangladesh Bureau of Statistics (BBS). The Bangladesh HIES is the standalone data source for estimating household income, expenditure and consumption, among other things, in Bangladesh. The first round of the Bangladesh HES was conducted in 1973–1974 following the independence of Bangladesh in 1971. The survey was renamed as the HIES in 2000. The 2016 HIES is the 16th in the series. The HIES 2016 followed a stratified two-stage cluster sampling design. The main stratum comprises the eight administrative divisions that were stratified by three basic localities: rural, urban and city corporation. The second stratum comprises 64 districts in Bangladesh. According to BBS (2017), an urban area is a densely populated area with at least 5,000 population, where the majority of the population are engaged in non-agriculture occupations and there exists an identified central place with amenities, such as paved roads, improved communication services, electricity, gas, water supply, sewerage and sanitation. The BBS defines an urban

Table 5.1 Description of household expenditure sub-categories, nine commodity groups

Commodity groups (1)	*Description* (2)	*Reclassified commodity groups* (3)
Food and beverages	Expenditure on all food and beverages, including the expenditure on food away from home.	*Food*
Alcohol and tobacco	Expenditure on alcohol, tobacco and other intoxicants.	*Alcohol*[a]
Clothing, textiles and footwear	Expenditures on purchase of clothing, clothing materials, tailoring charges, shoes, bags, umbrellas and repair charges.	*Clothing*
Housing	Refers to the average payment of rent, mortgages, water bills and taxes per month. For owner-occupied houses, an estimated rent has been included.	*Housing*
Fuel and light	Average monthly expenditure towards electricity, gas, other fuel and related items such as bulbs.	
Non-durable household goods	Expenditure on washing soap and powder, insecticides of household use.	
Household services	Expenditures on wages to servants, laundry charges and grinding charges.	
Durable household goods	Expenses on household appliances and utensils, furniture, purchase of motor vehicles, bicycles, etc. in the past 6 months and 12 months.	
Health care	Expenses on practitioner's fee, medicines, pharmaceutical products, hospital charges and payments to medical laboratories for tests analysis.	*Health care*
Personal care	Expenses on toiletries, cosmetics and beauty services in the past month.	
Transport	Expenditure on public and private transport and maintenance of private vehicles, including annual revenue license and insurance.	*Transport*
Communication	Expenses towards telephone, internet and postal charges.	
Recreation and entertainment	Expenditure towards cinema, books, newspapers, gambling, pilgrimages, sports, pets, toys and maintenance of televisions and other audio-visual equipment.	*Recreation*
Education	Education fees for schooling and higher education, school textbooks and stationery.	*Education*
Miscellaneous	Expenditure on provident funds, trade union contributions, insurance, payment of debts, income tax, other savings, weddings and funerals, donations, and other social activities.	*Miscellaneous*

[a] The Bangladesh data set does not provide data on alcohol consumption and reports expenditure on tobacco consumption only. Expenditure on both alcohol and tobacco is included in this category for the other three countries.

centre with a population of 100,000 or more as a 'city'. Major cities (of about 200,000 population) are governed by City Corporations. In this book, the urban areas consist of both urban centres and City Corporations.

Food expenditure data in the Bangladesh HIES cover about 150 varieties of food and non-alcoholic beverages classified under 16 sub-categories: food grains, pulses, fish, eggs, meat, vegetables, milk and milk products, sweetmeat, fats and oils, fruits, sugar and molasses, spices, dining out, betel leaf and chew goods, miscellaneous food and non-alcoholic beverages. In order to circumvent seasonal variation in food expenditure, food consumption by households is monitored over a 14-day period in 12 consecutive months. In the Bangladesh HIES, household non-food expenditures have been collected for 19 sub-categories. These expenditure groups are mostly in line with expenditure sub-categories given in Table 5.1.

5.4.3 India

For India, we use the data from the second round of *Indian Human Development Survey (IHDS-II) 2011/12*, conducted by University of Maryland and the National Council of Applied Economic Research. This data set (IHDS II, 2018) has been widely used to analyse human development outcomes in the context of India (Desai and Vanneman 2018). It is a nationally representative multi-topic survey of 42,152 urban and rural households, covering 33 states and union territories, 384 districts, 1,503 villages and 971 urban blocks, located in 276 towns and cities across India. The IHDS-II comprises mostly re-interviews of households interviewed for the first wave of the survey IHDS-I in 2004–2005, with an additional replacement sample of 6,911 households. The primary sampling unit (PSU) consists of villages and urban blocks.

The survey covered several socio-economic and demographic topics related to human development, such as economic status, consumption and standard of living, health care, education, marriage, gender relations and social capital. This book utilises the household-level demographic and consumption data of IHDS-II. The consumption data in this survey cover both food and non-food expenditures reported at a sub-category level, not at the commodity level. Expenditure on food (and beverages) consists of monthly expenditure on rice, wheat/flour, sugar and sweets, cereal products, pulses and pulses products, spices, vegetables, meat, eggs, processed food, fruits and nuts, restaurant food and tea and coffee. Expenditure on non-food consists of monthly or annual spending on housing, clothing (and footwear), education, health care, transport (and communication), recreation and other miscellaneous expenses and these sub-categories are mostly comparable with the sub-categories of other cross-sectional survey data used in this book.

5.4.4 Sri Lanka

For Sri Lanka, the data are based on the micro-level national household survey, the latest *Household Income and Expenditure Survey (HIES) 2016*, conducted by the Department of Census and Statistics (DCS) in Sri Lanka. The HIES is usually conducted every five years, with the first HIES conducted in 1990/1991. The HIES 2016 is the ninth in the HIES series. The data were collected from an island-wide representative sample during 12 consecutive monthly rounds, in order to capture seasonal variations in income, expenditure and consumption of households.

The survey uses a two-stage stratified sample design and the district is the main domain used for the stratification. The urban, rural and estate sectors in each district of the country are the second selection domains. There are 25 administrative districts in Sri Lanka. Based on the common traditional practice adapted for sub-national classification of households for policy analysis, the households in Sri Lanka are categorised into three regions, generally known as sectors: urban, rural and estate. The DCS defines the areas governed by either municipal council or urban council as the urban sector. The plantation areas, mainly tea but include rubber plantations as well, which are more than 20 acres in extent and which have not fewer than 10 residential labourers, are known as the estate sector. The residential areas that do not belong to either the urban sector or the estate sector are classified as the rural sector (DCS 2011).

Food expenditure in the Sri Lankan survey includes the expenditure on food and non-alcoholic beverages consumed by the households. It covers a total of 249 food and non-alcoholic beverages, classified under 18 sub-categories: cereal, prepared food, pulses, vegetables, yams, meat, fish, dried fish, eggs, coconuts, condiments, other foods, milk and milk products, fats and oils, sugar, fruits, confectionery and non-alcoholic beverages. In order to circumvent seasonal variation in food expenditure, food consumption by households is monitored over a seven-day period in 12 consecutive months. The consumption expenditure in the data set is the average of this weekly consumption across these 12 months (DCS 2011). The expenditure on non-food items covers 14 subgroups that are consistent with those categories listed in Table 5.1.

5.5 Summary Statistics

Tables 5.2 and 5.3 present a number of summary statistics relating to the household survey data for the four countries.

5.5.1 Australia

Part A of Table 5.2 presents the summary statistics for Australia based on the survey data. The average household size in Australia is 2.4. About 56 percent of household reference persons in this survey are male. A majority of the households in the survey sample were drawn from major cities (72.4 percent), followed by 17 percent from inner regional areas, 9.1 percent from outer regional areas and 1.5 percent from remote areas. The sample represents each of the six states and two territories and consists of 22.4 percent of New South Wales households, 23.9 percent of Victorian households, 14.8 percent of Queensland households, 13.1 percent of South Australian households, 11.9 percent of Western Australian households and 7.7 percent

Table 5.2 Demographic characteristics, four countries

A: Australia (2015/16): *Sample size 7,903*	
Household size	2.4
Gender of the reference person (in percent)	
Male	56.1
Female	43.9
Remoteness area (in percent)	
Major cities	72.4
Inner regional	17.0
Outer regional	9.1
Remote	1.5
State or territory of residence (in percent)	
New South Wales (NSW)	22.4
Victoria (VIC)	23.9
Queensland (QLD)	14.8
South Australia (SA)	13.1
Western Australia (WA)	11.9
Tasmania (TAS)	7.7
Northern Territory (NT)	3.3
Australian Capital Territory (ACT)	2.9

B: Bangladesh (2016): *Sample size 42,307*	
Household size	4.1
Household headship (in percent)	
Male	87.5
Female	12.5
Religion (in percent)	
Muslim	87.0
Hindu	10.0
Christian	0.5
Buddhist	2.4
Other	0.1
Residential sector (in percent)	
Urban	68.6
Rural	31.4

C: India (2011/12): *Sample size 41,572*	
Household size	4.8
Household headship (in percent)	
Male	85.7
Female	14.3
Religion (in percent)	
Hindu	81.6
Muslim	11.7
Christian	2.9
Sikh	2.3
Buddhist	0.6
Other	0.9
Residential sector (in percent)	
Urban	34.5
Rural	65.5

D: Sri Lanka (2016): *Sample size 21,733*	
Household size	4.1
Household headship (in percent)	
Male	74.1
Female	25.9
Ethnicity (in percent)	
Sinhala	72.5
Tamil	27.1
Other	0.4
Religion (in percent)	
Buddhist	70.2
Hindu	12.6
Muslim	9.7
Christian	7.5
Residential sector (in percent)	
Urban	15.5
Rural	80.5
Estate	4.0

Source: Based on ABS (2016), BBS (2017), DCS (2017) and IHDS II (2018).

of Tasmanian households. Around 6 percent of the sample is drawn from the Northern Territory (3.3 percent) and the Australian Capital Territory (2.9 percent).

As can be seen from Table 5.3, in terms of consumption, on average, Australian households allocate about 18.7 percent of their total expenditure on food, 3.5 percent on alcohol and the remaining 77.8 percent on non-food

Table 5.3 Budget shares by commodity group, four countries

Commodity	*Australia*	*Bangladesh*	*India*	*Sri Lanka*
Food	18.7	47.9	47.3	44.8
Alcohol/Tobacco	3.5	3.1[a]	1.9	2.4
Non-food items	77.8	49.0	50.8	52.8
Clothing	2.7	6.9	4.5	3.3
Housing	32.4	19.7	11.2	19.9
Health care	8.0	8.5	13.3	4.6
Transport	17.0	5.9	10.1	8.6
Recreation	10.6	0.3	0.5	1.2
Education	1.7	4.2	4.7	3.2
Miscellaneous	5.5	3.6	6.5	12.0

Source: Based on ABS (2016), BBS (2017), DCS (2017) and IHDS II (2018).
[a] For Bangladesh, data for alcohol are not available and this entry is for tobacco only.

items. Among the non-food items, the highest expenditure share is allocated on housing and household effects, such as household durable goods, fuel and power, and household services and operations (32.4 percent), followed by transport and communication (17 percent) and recreation (10.6 percent). On average, a household allocates about 8 percent of total expenditure on health care. Clothing and miscellaneous sub-categories represent about 2.7 percent and 5.5 percent of total household expenditure, respectively. The lowest budget share is allocated to education (1.7 percent).

5.5.2 Bangladesh

As can be seen from Part B of Table 5.2, the average household size in Bangladesh in 2016 is 4.1. The majority (87.5 percent) of the households in the sample is headed by a male. While about 87 percent of the households follow the Islamic faith, the remaining 13 percent consists of Hindus (10 percent), Buddhists (2.4 percent), Christians (0.5 percent) and others (0.1 percent). About 69 percent of the households live in the urban areas of Bangladesh. When considering the household expenditure (see Table 5.3), on average, households spend about 47.9 percent on food and beverages, 3.1 percent on tobacco and 49 percent on non-food items. Bangladesh HIES does not provide expenditure data on alcohol consumption. Among the non-food expenditure, expenditure on housing (which consists of fuel and lighting, household textile, housing, cooking, furniture and household durable goods) dominates the household non-food expenditure, accounting for about 19.7 percent of total household expenditure. Health care expenses stood at 8.5 percent followed by clothing (6.9 percent). Transport accounts for about 6 percent of total household expenditure, while education represents about 4.2 percent. Miscellaneous expenditure (that consists of taxes, remittances, purchase of gold and insurance payment) accounts for about 3.6 percent of total household expenditure. Bangladeshi households spend the lowest budget share on recreation (0.3 percent).

5.5.3 India

As shown in Part C of Table 5.2, India's average household size is about 4.8. Data suggest that about 86 percent of households are headed by male. The majority of the household heads (82 percent) are Hindus, followed by Muslims (12 percent). India has a large proportion (about 65 percent) of households living in the rural localities. As can be seen from Table 5.3, 47 percent of total household budget was spent on food and beverages. The household expenditure on alcohol, tobacco and other intoxicants represents about 2 percent of total household expenditure. Among the non-food expenditure sub-categories, Indian households, on average, allocated the most of their household budget on health care (13.3 percent), followed by expenditure on housing (11.2 percent) and transport and communication (10.1 percent). Expenditure on recreation recorded the lowest percentage of budget allocation (0.5 percent).

5.5.4 Sri Lanka

Part D of Table 5.2 presents the summary statistics for demographic characteristics and household expenditure data for Sri Lanka. The average household size in Sri Lanka is 4.1. One quarter of households in the sample in Sri Lanka have a female head. In terms of the distribution of the ethnic groups in the country, the Sinhala-speaking population dominates at 72.5 percent and the Tamil-speaking population accounts for around 27 percent. As can be seen from Table 5.3, in Sri Lanka, overall, households allocate a major share of their budget on non-food items (52.9 percent) compared with food items (44.8 percent), excluding expenditure on alcohol. Among the non-food expenditure sub-categories, the budget share on housing is the highest (around 20 percent), followed by miscellaneous (including taxes, debt and insurance payments) (12 percent). While transport and communication expenditure accounts for about 8.6 percent of total household expenditure, health care and personal expenditure share is about 4.6 percent. The lowest budget shares are seen in clothing and footwear (3.3 percent), education (3.2 percent) and recreation (1.2 percent).

In summary, Table 5.3 reveals that households in developed countries such as Australia allocate only less than one-fifth of their budget share on food while developing countries such as Bangladesh (48 percent), India (47 percent) and Sri Lanka (45 percent) allocate almost half of their budget on food, intuitively supporting the Working's (1943) model that food budget share falls with increasing income. On the other hand, households in developed countries like Australia allocate a significantly higher proportion of their income (32.4 percent) on housing compared with households in developing countries, such as Bangladesh (19.7 percent), India (11.2 percent) and Sri Lanka (19.9 percent). The same disproportions are seen with transport and communication expenditure share, where Australian households allocate 17 percent of their income compared to the allocation of households in Bangladesh 5.9 percent, India 10.1 percent and Sri Lanka 8.6 percent.

Table 5.4 Estimation results, models (5.14), (5.15) and (5.16), Australia

Commodity group	Constant			Expenditure			HH size	HH size square	Gender		
	M	*PCE*	*EPEA*	*M*	*PCE*	*EPEA*	*M*	*M*	*M*	*PCE*	*EPEA*
(1)	*(2)*	*(3)*	*(4)*	*(5)*	*(6)*	*(7)*	*(8)*	*(9)*	*(10)*	*(11)*	*(12)*
1 Food	0.390[a]	0.627[a]	0.760[a]	−0.015[a]	−0.059[a]	−0.075[a]	0.045[a]	−0.004[a]	−0.003[b]	−0.002	−0.005[a]
	(0.000)	(0.000)	(0.000)	(0.000)	(0.000)	(0.000)	(0.000)	(0.000)	(0.071)	(0.347)	(0.005)
2 Alcohol	0.049[a]	−0.008	0.026[a]	0.000	0.006[a]	0.002	−0.006[a]	0.000	−0.009[a]	−0.007[a]	−0.007[a]
	(0.000)	(0.504)	(0.000)	(0.724)	(0.009)	(0.386)	(0.002)	(0.355)	(0.000)	(0.000)	(0.000)
3 Clothing	−0.025[a]	0.005	−0.043[a]	0.002[a]	0.003[a]	0.009[a]	0.002	0.000	0.006[a]	0.005[a]	0.005[a]
	(0.000)	(0.543)	(0.000)	(0.000)	(0.000)	(0.000)	(0.141)	(0.573)	(0.000)	(0.000)	(0.000)
4 Housing	0.635[a]	0.605[a]	0.769[a]	−0.018[a]	−0.042[a]	−0.063[a]	−0.007	0.003[a]	0.011[a]	0.020[a]	0.017[a]
	(0.000)	(0.000)	(0.000)	(0.000)	(0.000)	(0.000)	(0.155)	(0.000)	(0.001)	(0.000)	(0.000)
5 Health	0.091[a]	0.046[a]	0.102[a]	−0.001[b]	0.004[a]	−0.004[b]	0.005[a]	−0.002[a]	0.003[a]	0.005[a]	0.005[a]
	(0.000)	(0.001)	(0.000)	(0.073)	(0.043)	(0.077)	(0.022)	(0.000)	(0.040)	(0.004)	(0.004)
6 Transport	0.074[a]	0.096[a]	0.030	0.006[a]	0.013[a]	0.021[a]	−0.001	0.000	−0.015[a]	−0.018[a]	−0.017[a]
	(0.000)	(0.000)	(0.244)	(0.000)	(0.000)	(0.000)	(0.815)	(0.913)	(0.000)	(0.000)	(0.000)
7 Recreation	−0.077[a]	−0.241[a]	−0.338[a]	0.013[a]	0.048[a]	0.060[a]	−0.026[a]	0.002[a]	0.003	0.001	0.004
	(0.000)	(0.000)	(0.000)	(0.000)	(0.000)	(0.000)	(0.000)	(0.000)	(0.166)	(0.657)	(0.104)
8 Education	−0.060[a]	0.030[a]	−0.058[a]	0.003[a]	−0.002[b]	0.010[a]	0.005[a]	0.000	0.002[a]	−0.001	−0.001
	(0.000)	(0.001)	(0.000)	(0.000)	(0.064)	(0.000)	(0.001)	(0.302)	(0.035)	(0.316)	(0.415)
9 Miscellaneous	−0.078[a]	−0.161[a]	−0.248[a]	0.009[a]	0.030[a]	0.041[a]	−0.019[a]	0.002[a]	0.000	−0.002[a]	0.000[a]
	(0.000)	(0.000)	(0.000)	(0.000)	(0.000)	(0.000)	(0.000)	(0.000)	(0.111)	(0.000)	(0.000)

The Box-Cox transformation value for M is $\lambda = 0.1691$, PCE is $\lambda = -0.0099$ and EPEA is $\lambda = -0.0175$. *p*-values are in parentheses.

[a] significant at 5 percent level.

[b] significant at 10 percent level.

Developing country households spend more than 3 percent (Bangladesh 4.2 percent, India 4.7 percent and Sri Lanka 3.2 percent) of their income on education, while developed country households spend less than 2 percent (Australia 1.7 percent) on education.

5.6 Estimation Results and Discussion

5.6.1 Australia

Table 5.4 presents the coefficient estimates of total expenditure (M), per capita expenditure (PCE) and expenditure per equivalent adult (EPEA) models given by equations (5.14)–(5.16), respectively, for Australia. These results are obtained by estimating the system of the Box-Cox Engel curves.

As can be seen from columns (5) to (7) of Table 5.4, all estimated expenditure coefficients are statistically significant at the 5 percent level or 10 percent level, except for the alcohol coefficient in the M and EPEA models. We also observe that in most of the cases, the estimated income coefficients are of the same sign across the three model specifications (except for health care and education), although with different magnitudes. As household income increases, the budget share on food, housing and health care declines, while that of alcohol, clothing and footwear, health and personal care, transport and communication, education, recreation, and miscellaneous goods increases in Australia.

The coefficient estimates of household size and the square of household size variables are presented in columns (8) and (9) of Table 5.4 for model (5.14). As can be seen, the positive and statistically significant household size coefficient coupled with the negative household size squared coefficient for food and health expenditure implies an 'inverted U' relationship, indicating that when household size increases, the budget share on food and health increases at a decreasing rate up to a certain point and then starts to decline. The estimated household size squared coefficient is positive and statistically significant for housing and recreation, indicating a 'U shaped' relationship, meaning that with increasing household size the budget share for these goods decreases up to a certain point and then starts to increase. The household size and household size squared terms have been omitted in the PCE (5.15) and EPEA (5.16) models, as the household size has already been incorporated when calculating PCE and EPEA.

The signs of the gender (where male = 0 and female = 1) coefficient estimates for food, alcohol, transport and communications are negative, while those for clothing, housing and health are positive and statistically significant across the three model specifications, M, PCE and EPEA. This means that, in Australia, if the response person is a female, then that household allocates a lower budget share on food, alcohol and transport and communication and a higher budget share on clothing, housing and health than a household whose response person is a male. The estimated coefficients for recreation and education are not statistically significant, indicating that there is no difference in budget share allocation on recreation and education between a male or female response person.

Table 5.5 presents the income elasticities for Australia under M, PCE and EPEA models at the national level. As can be seen, food and housing are necessities ($\eta < 1$), while alcohol, clothing, transport, recreation and education are luxuries ($\eta > 1$) for Australian households.

Health is borderline with income elasticity close to one and therefore, close to being a luxury in Australia. The results are consistent across the three models, except for health and education in the PCE model.

Table 5.6 presents the elasticity estimates by income groups: low-income (bottom 25 percent), lower-middle income (25–50 percent), upper-middle income (50–75 percent), and high-income (top 25 percent) groups, under the three models (M, PCE and EPEA). As can be seen, although the magnitude of income elasticities is different across the three models, in most cases, the broader elasticity classification of commodity groups, a necessity or a luxury, is consistent across the three models and income groups. More specifically, in all three models and in all four income groups, food is a necessity ($\eta < 1$), while alcohol, clothing and health care, recreation, education and miscellaneous commodity groups are luxuries ($\eta > 1$). While housing is a necessity for all income groups, it is a luxury good for low-income households under PCE and EPEA models. Transport is a necessity for middle-income Australians, while it is a luxury for upper middle- and high-income households. However, it gives mixed results for low-income households based on the model specification, M, PCE or EPEA.

Table 5.7 presents the income elasticities for the nine commodity groups by states and territory level in Australia. As can be seen, the broader elasticity classification, whether a necessity or a luxury, remains the same in the majority of commodity groups. For all states and territories, food and housing income elasticity estimates are less than 1, indicating that these goods are a necessity for households in all states and territories. On the

Table 5.5 Income elasticities of nine commodities, Australia

Commodity group (1)	*M* (2)	*PCE* (3)	*EPEA* (4)
1 Food	0.673 (0.000)	0.707 (0.001)	0.647 (0.000)
2 Alcohol	1.017 (0.000)	1.167 (0.000)	1.040 (0.000)
3 Clothing	1.361 (0.000)	1.097 (0.000)	1.289 (0.000)
4 Housing	0.772 (0.000)	0.879 (0.000)	0.831 (0.000)
5 Health	0.955 (0.000)	1.041 (0.000)	0.958 (0.000)
6 Transport	1.148 (0.000)	1.307 (0.000)	1.109 (0.000)
7 Recreation	1.505 (0.000)	1.422 (0.000)	1.494 (0.000)
8 Education	1.731 (0.000)	0.885 (0.000)	1.492 (0.000)
9 Miscellaneous	1.668 (0.000)	1.498 (0.000)	1.844 (0.000)

Note: Standard errors of estimated income elasticities are given in parentheses.

Table 5.6 Income elasticities of nine commodities by level of income, Australia

Commodity group	Low-income			Lower-middle income			Upper-middle income			High-income		
	M	*PCE*	*EPEA*	*M*	*PCE*	*EPEA*	*M*	*PCE*	*EPEA*	*M*	*PCE*	*EPEA*
(1)	*(2)*	*(3)*	*(4)*	*(5)*	*(6)*	*(7)*	*(8)*	*(9)*	*(10)*	*(11)*	*(12)*	*(13)*
1 Food	0.564	0.691	0.465	0.795	0.764	0.597	0.772	0.740	0.654	0.553	0.710	0.507
	(0.000)	(0.000)	(0.001)	(0.000)	(0.000)	(0.001)	(0.000)	(0.000)	(0.000)	(0.000)	(0.000)	(0.000)
2 Alcohol	1.290	1.077	1.532	1.007	1.077	1.599	1.132	1.203	1.244	1.020	1.109	1.051
	(0.000)	(0.000)	(0.000)	(0.000)	(0.000)	(0.000)	(0.000)	(0.000)	(0.000)	(0.000)	(0.000)	(0.000)
3 Clothing	1.610	1.219	1.195	1.745	1.219	1.101	1.487	1.342	1.269	1.129	1.002	1.010
	(0.000)	(0.000)	(0.000)	(0.000)	(0.000)	(0.000)	(0.000)	(0.000)	(0.000)	(0.000)	(0.000)	(0.000)
4 Housing	0.828	1.005	1.035	0.712	0.930	0.942	0.801	0.934	0.948	0.805	0.960	0.921
	(0.000)	(0.001)	(0.001)	(0.000)	(0.001)	(0.001)	(0.000)	(0.001)	(0.002)	(0.000)	(0.001)	(0.002)
5 Health care	1.085	1.011	0.929	1.200	1.129	1.142	1.165	1.192	1.271	0.994	1.059	1.001
	(0.000)	(0.000)	(0.000)	(0.000)	(0.000)	(0.000)	(0.000)	(0.000)	(0.000)	(0.000)	(0.000)	(0.000)
6 Transport	1.048	0.939	0.885	0.832	0.994	0.931	1.370	1.076	1.097	1.025	1.010	0.998
	(0.000)	(0.000)	(0.000)	(0.000)	(0.000)	(0.000)	(0.000)	(0.000)	(0.001)	(0.000)	(0.000)	(0.001)
7 Recreation	1.938	1.476	1.803	1.655	1.447	1.883	1.039	1.246	1.351	1.253	1.374	1.526
	(0.000)	(0.000)	(0.000)	(0.000)	(0.000)	(0.000)	(0.000)	(0.000)	(0.000)	(0.000)	(0.000)	(0.000)
8 Education	1.157	1.321	1.211	2.583	1.345	1.185	0.979	1.001	1.010	1.231	1.120	1.118
	(0.000)	(0.000)	(0.000)	(0.000)	(0.000)	(0.000)	(0.000)	(0.000)	(0.000)	(0.000)	(0.000)	(0.000)
9 Miscellaneous	1.663	1.555	1.859	1.929	1.284	1.541	1.158	1.458	1.689	2.044	1.407	1.665
	(0.000)	(0.000)	(0.000)	(0.000)	(0.000)	(0.000)	(0.000)	(0.000)	(0.000)	(0.000)	(0.000)	(0.000)

Note: Standard errors of estimated income elasticities are given in parentheses.

Table 5.7 Income elasticities of nine commodities by state, Australia

Commodity group	NSW			Victoria			Queensland		
	M	*PCE*	*EPEA*	*M*	*PCE*	*EPEA*	*M*	*PCE*	*EPEA*
(1)	*(2)*	*(3)*	*(4)*	*(5)*	*(6)*	*(7)*	*(8)*	*(9)*	*(10)*
1 Food	0.681	0.712	0.657	0.679	0.702	0.647	0.699	0.743	0.679
	(0.000)	(0.001)	(0.001)	(0.000)	(0.001)	(0.001)	(0.000)	(0.001)	(0.001)
2 Alcohol	1.002	1.197	1.046	1.147	1.154	1.126	0.881	1.132	0.936
	(0.000)	(0.000)	(0.000)	(0.000)	(0.000)	(0.000)	(0.000)	(0.000)	(0.000)
3 Clothing	1.316	1.044	1.260	1.414	1.137	1.363	1.361	1.101	1.288
	(0.000)	(0.000)	(0.000)	(0.000)	(0.000)	(0.000)	(0.000)	(0.000)	(0.000)
4 Housing	0.806	0.904	0.864	0.785	0.905	0.849	0.730	0.832	0.787
	(0.000)	(0.003)	(0.004)	(0.000)	(0.002)	(0.003)	(0.000)	(0.003)	(0.005)
5 Health care	0.926	1.031	0.942	0.873	0.980	0.869	1.022	1.062	1.010
	(0.000)	(0.000)	(0.000)	(0.000)	(0.000)	(0.000)	(0.000)	(0.000)	(0.001)
6 Transport	1.138	1.053	1.096	1.157	1.078	1.118	1.100	1.056	1.066
	(0.000)	(0.001)	(0.001)	(0.000)	(0.001)	(0.001)	(0.000)	(0.001)	(0.002)
7 Recreation	1.522	1.448	1.513	1.445	1.382	1.441	1.591	1.482	1.571
	(0.000)	(0.001)	(0.001)	(0.000)	(0.001)	(0.001)	(0.000)	(0.001)	(0.001)
8 Education	1.651	0.692	1.319	1.770	1.034	1.618	1.585	0.811	1.328
	(0.000)	(0.000)	(0.000)	(0.000)	(0.000)	(0.000)	(0.000)	(0.000)	(0.000)
9 Miscellaneous	1.597	1.422	1.554	1.576	1.438	1.556	1.835	1.577	1.791
	(0.000)	(0.001)	(0.001)	(0.000)	(0.001)	(0.001)	(0.000)	(0.001)	(0.001)

Note: Standard errors of estimated income elasticities are given in parentheses.

Table 5.7 Income elasticities of nine commodities by state, Australia (Cont.)

Commodity group	*SA*			*WA*			*Tasmania*			*NT*			*ACT*		
	M	*PCE*	*EPEA*	*M*	*PCE*	*EPEA*	*M*	*PCE*	*EPEA*	*M*	*PCE*	*EPEA*	*M*	*PCE*	*EPEA*
(1)	*(2)*	*(3)*	*(4)*	*(5)*	*(6)*	*(7)*	*(8)*	*(9)*	*(10)*	*(11)*	*(12)*	*(13)*	*(14)*	*(15)*	*(16)*
1 Food	0.671	0.700	0.653	0.604	0.669	0.592	0.667	0.722	0.644	0.678	0.694	0.651	0.726	0.735	0.702
	(0.000)	(0.001)	(0.002)	(0.000)	(0.001)	(0.001)	(0.000)	(0.001)	(0.002)	(0.000)	(0.002)	(0.003)	(0.000)	(0.002)	(0.003)
2 Alcohol	1.116	1.247	1.116	0.811	1.033	0.894	1.080	1.099	1.036	0.403	1.203	0.788	1.479	1.239	1.337
	(0.000)	(0.000)	(0.000)	(0.000)	(0.000)	(0.000)	(0.000)	(0.000)	(0.000)	(0.000)	(0.000)	(0.001)	(0.000)	(0.000)	(0.000)
3 Clothing	1.389	1.204	1.361	1.389	1.135	1.295	1.038	0.777	0.910	1.692	1.258	1.563	1.563	1.272	1.502
	(0.000)	(0.000)	(0.000)	(0.000)	(0.000)	(0.000)	(0.000)	(0.000)	(0.000)	(0.000)	(0.000)	(0.000)	(0.000)	(0.000)	(0.000)
4 Housing	0.698	0.817	0.751	0.829	0.904	0.874	0.732	0.878	0.797	0.876	0.899	87	0.752	0.876	0.804
	(0.000)	(0.003)	(0.004)	(0.000)	(0.004)	(0.005)	(0.000)	(0.004)	(0.005)	(0.001)	(0.008)	(0.012)	(0.000)	(0.007)	(0.010)
5 Health care	0.955	1.022	0.933	1.050	1.147	1.070	0.957	1.055	0.969	0.933	1.01	0.989	1.121	1.133	1.124
	(0.000)	(0.000)	(0.001)	(0.000)	(0.000)	(0.001)	(0.000)	(0.001)	(0.001)	(0.000)	(0.000)	(0.001)	(0.000)	(0.001)	(0.001)
6 Transport	1.232	1.118	1.186	1.115	1.057	1.081	1.220	1.092	1.181	1.109	1.150	1.116	0.942	0.909	0.923
	(0.000)	(0.001)	(0.002)	(0.000)	(0.001)	(0.002)	(0.000)	(0.002)	(0.003)	(0.000)	(0.002)	(0.003)	(0.000)	(0.002)	(0.003)
7 Recreation	1.592	1.489	1.583	1.476	1.362	1.445	1.461	1.370	1.441	1.299	1.278	1.326	1.507	1.457	1.496
	(0.000)	(0.001)	(0.001)	(0.000)	(0.001)	(0.001)	(0.000)	(0.001)	(0.001)	(0.000)	(0.002)	(0.002)	(0.000)	(0.002)	(0.003)
8 Education	1.693	1.021	1.572	1.924	1.008	1.623	1.874	0.609	1.627	1.680	0.472	1.039	1.601	0.955	1.505
	(0.000)	(0.000)	(0.000)	(0.000)	(0.000)	(0.000)	(0.000)	(0.000)	(0.000)	(0.000)	(0.000)	(0.000)	(0.000)	(0.000)	(0.000)
9 Miscellaneous	1.724	1.591	1.723	1.609	1.487	1.597	1.667	1.593	1.712	1.986	1.511	1.788	1.660	1.486	1.628
	(0.000)	(0.001)	(0.001)	(0.000)	(0.001)	(0.001)	(0.000)	(0.001)	(0.001)	(0.000)	(0.001)	(0.001)	(0.000)	(0.001)	(0.001)

Note: Standard errors of estimated income elasticities are given in parentheses.

other hand, in general, alcohol (except in NT, Queensland and WA), clothing (except Tasmania), transport (except in ACT), recreation and education have income elasticity mostly greater than 1, indicating that these goods are luxuries for household in all states and territories. While health care is generally a necessity in SA, Tasmania, NT, NSW and Victoria, it is a luxury in Queensland, WA and ACT.

To identify the best model, we calculate the information inaccuracies discussed in Section 5.3. Table 5.8 presents the calculated information inaccuracies for the three models given by equation (5.19) and for the individual commodities given by equation (5.20) for Australia. The overall model information inaccuracies (I) reveal that the lowest information inaccuracy can be seen for the M model, indicating that it is the best model. The second lowest information inaccuracy is seen in the EPEA model, while the highest information inaccuracy is produced in the PCE model for Australia. Therefore, for aggregate household-level data, household expenditure with household size and the square of household size variables, model (5.14), appears to be the best model. When considering the individual commodity-level information inaccuracies (I_i), in a majority of the cases model M has the lowest information inaccuracies in six out of nine commodity groups. The PCE model has the lowest information inaccuracy for food, clothing and miscellaneous while EPEA performs well for food only.

Table 5.9 presents the coefficient estimates corresponding to the three model specifications with respect to total expenditure M model (5.14), per capita expenditure PCE model (5.15) and expenditure per adult equivalent EPEA model (5.16), for Bangladesh.

As can be seen, most of the estimated coefficients are statistically significant at the 5 percent or 10 percent levels. We observe that the estimated expenditure coefficients are of the same sign across all three model specifications with differing magnitudes. Estimation results indicate that as household income increases, the budget share on food, tobacco and clothing decline, while that of housing, health, transport, recreation, education and miscellaneous goods increase. The coefficient estimates of household size

Table 5.8 Information inaccuracies of the three models, Australia

Commodity (1)	*M* (2)	*PCE* (3)	*EPEA* (4)
1 Food	20,600	20,548	20,548
2 Alcohol	22,399	22,866	22,753
3 Clothing	16,808	16,615	16,632
4 Housing	52,389	53,988	53,609
5 Health care	28,333	29,056	29,004
6 Transport	38,751	39,050	38,967
7 Recreation	42,069	42,081	42,480
8 Education	17,735	20,180	19,846
9 Miscellaneous	33,026	32,915	33,129
All commodities	272,107	277,299	276,967

Note: Information inaccuracies are all multiplied by 10^6.

Table 5.9 Estimation results, models (5.14), (5.15) and (5.16), Bangladesh

Commodity group	Constant			Expenditure			HH size	HH size²	Gender		
	M	*PCE*	*EPEA*	*M*	*PCE*	*EPEA*	*M*	*M*	*M*	*PCE*	*EPEA*
(1)	*(2)*	*(3)*	*(4)*	*(5)*	*(6)*	*(7)*	*(8)*	*(9)*	*(10)*	*(11)*	*(12)*
1 Food	1.693[a]	3.900[a]	3.937[a]	−0.265[a]	−1.076[a]	−0.975[a]	0.037[a]	−0.002[a]	−0.019[a]	0.000	−0.016[a]
	(0.000)	(0.000)	(0.000)	(0.000)	(0.000)	(0.000)	(0.000)	(0.000)	(0.000)	(0.936)	(0.000)
2 Tobacco	0.147[a]	0.282[a]	0.338[a]	−0.014[a]	−0.079[a]	−0.075[a]	−0.002[a]	0.000[a]	−0.011[a]	−0.007[a]	−0.009[a]
	(0.000)	(0.000)	(0.000)	(0.000)	(0.000)	(0.000)	(0.000)	(0.000)	(0.000)	(0.000)	(0.000)
3 Clothing	0.088[a]	0.249[a]	0.187[a]	−0.015[a]	−0.047[a]	−0.038[a]	0.007[a]	0.000[a]	−0.002[a]	−0.005[a]	−0.006[a]
	(0.000)	(0.000)	(0.000)	(0.000)	(0.000)	(0.000)	(0.000)	(0.000)	(0.000)	(0.000)	(0.000)
4 Housing	−0.079[a]	−0.930[a]	−0.746[a]	0.037[a]	0.332[a]	0.271[a]	−0.031[a]	0.002[a]	0.017[a]	0.026[a]	0.031[a]
	(0.000)	(0.000)	(0.000)	(0.000)	(0.000)	(0.000)	(0.000)	(0.000)	(0.000)	(0.000)	(0.000)
5 Health care	0.011[a]	−0.233[a]	−0.165[a]	0.011[b]	0.098[a]	0.071[a]	−0.010[a]	0.001[a]	−0.002[a]	0.001	0.002[a]
	(0.000)	(0.000)	(0.000)	(0.078)	(0.000)	(0.000)	(0.000)	(0.000)	(0.000)	(0.501)	(0.024)
6 Transport	−0.154[a]	−0.545[a]	−0.551[a]	0.039[a]	0.178[a]	0.182[a]	−0.006[a]	0.000[a]	−0.009[a]	−0.012[a]	−0.009[a]
	(0.000)	(0.000)	(0.000)	(0.000)	(0.000)	(0.000)	(0.000)	(0.000)	(0.000)	(0.000)	(0.000)
7 Recreation	−0.016[a]	−0.052[a]	−0.053[a]	0.002[a]	0.015[a]	0.014[a]	−0.001[a]	0.000[a]	0.000[a]	−0.001[a]	0.000[a]
	(0.000)	(0.000)	(0.000)	(0.000)	(0.000)	(0.000)	(0.000)	(0.014)	(0.000)	(0.000)	(0.000)
8 Education	−0.233[a]	−0.381[a]	−0.613[a]	0.031[a]	0.124[a]	0.176[a]	0.020[a]	−0.002[a]	0.018[a]	−0.001	0.001
	(0.000)	(0.000)	(0.000)	(0.000)	(0.000)	(0.000)	(0.000)	(0.000)	(0.000)	(0.124)	(0.425)
9 Miscellaneous	−0.457[a]	−1.290[a]	−1.333[a]	0.174[a]	0.455[a]	0.374[a]	−0.015[a]	0.001[a]	0.009[a]	0.001[a]	0.007[a]
	(0.000)	(0.000)	(0.000)	(0.000)	(0.000)	(0.000)	(0.000)	(0.000)	(0.000)	(0.000)	(0.000)

Note: The Box-Cox transformation value for M is $\lambda = -0.0350$, PCE is $\lambda = -0.2790$ and EPEA is $\lambda = -0.2451$. *p*-values are in parentheses.
[a] and [b] refer to significance at the 5 percent and 10 percent levels, respectively.

and the square of household size variables are statistically significant at the 5 percent level. This indicates that household size plays a significant role in determining the household spending patterns in Bangladesh. As can be seen from columns (8) and (9) of Table 5.9, the food and education commodity groups have a positive sign for household size coefficient followed by a negative sign for the square of household size, indicating an inverse 'U' relationship. This indicates that as household size increases, the budget share on these commodities increases at a decreasing rate. Since these items can be considered as household private goods, it is expected that the budget shares of these goods would increase with increasing household size. However, due to the presence of some consumption economies of scale, we still see that budget shares do not increase as rapidly as household size but increases at a decreasing rate. On the other hand, budget shares on tobacco, clothing, housing, health care, transport, recreation and miscellaneous goods decrease at an increasing rate with household size, as indicated by the negative household size coefficient and a positive square of household size variable. This declining budget share with increasing household size is expected in the presence of consumption economies of scale in large households.

The gender coefficient estimates (where male = 0 and female = 1) are presented in columns (10)–(12) of Table 5.9. For all commodities in the M model and EPEA model (except education), the gender coefficient is statistically significant at the 5 percent level. This indicates that overall, gender (of the household head) plays a significant role in budget allocations of Bangladeshi households. We observe that female headship is associated with a lower budget share on food, tobacco, clothing and transport, and a greater budget share on housing, education and miscellaneous goods. The budget share on recreation shows mixed results with a positive coefficient in the M and EPEA models and a negative coefficient in the PCE model. Although these gender coefficients in the recreation equation are significant, the magnitude is negligible.

Table 5.10 presents the income elasticities at the national level, estimated at sample means. Overall, food, tobacco and clothing are necessities, while housing, health care, transport, recreation, education and miscellaneous are luxuries.

Table 5.10 Income elasticities of nine commodities, Bangladesh

Commodity group (1)	*M* (2)	*PCE* (3)	*EPEA* (4)
1 Food	0.622 (0.000)	0.783 (0.001)	0.772 (0.000)
2 Tobacco	0.783 (0.000)	0.826 (0.000)	0.809 (0.000)
3 Clothing	0.842 (0.000)	0.930 (0.000)	0.934 (0.000)
4 Housing	1.146 (0.000)	1.185 (0.000)	1.176 (0.000)
5 Health care	1.094 (0.000)	1.119 (0.000)	1.100 (0.000)
6 Transport	1.486 (0.000)	1.313 (0.000)	1.372 (0.000)
7 Recreation	1.301 (0.000)	1.320 (0.000)	1.346 (0.000)
8 Education	1.314 (0.000)	1.178 (0.000)	1.292 (0.000)
9 Miscellaneous	3.826 (0.000)	2.045 (0.000)	1.997 (0.000)

Note: Standard errors of estimated income elasticities are given in parentheses.

The elasticity classification is consistent across the three types of expenditure (M, PCE and EPEA). Table 5.11 presents the elasticity estimates by income for various groups under the M, PCE and EPEA models. Tables 5.12 and 5.13 present income elasticity estimates by residential sector (urban and rural) and religion (Islam and other), respectively. As can be seen, the broader elasticity classification of commodities is consistent across the three models and the elasticity classification remains unchanged irrespective of their expenditure (or income) levels, sector of residence and religion, except that clothing is a necessity for households with Islam religion and a luxury for others. Overall, in Bangladesh, food, tobacco and clothing are necessities (income elasticities are less than one), while housing, health care, transportation, recreation, education and miscellaneous are luxuries (income elasticities are greater than 1).

These income elasticities are in line with previous studies about developing countries (see Rajapakse 2011, Selvanathan 1993, and Selvanathan and Selvanathan 2003b). However, we observe that the magnitudes of the elasticity estimates are slightly different.

Table 5.14 presents the information inaccuracies for the three models given by equation (5.19) and for the individual commodities given by equation (5.20). Our results indicate that the model (5.14) with M has the lowest information inaccuracies in total as well as in all other instances, except for 'recreation'. These results indicate that the M model outperforms the other two models. Therefore, we suggest that if an analysis of income elasticities is needed using data at the household level, household expenditure M with household size and the square of household size variables, model (5.14) appears to be the best model.

5.6.2 India

Table 5.15 presents the coefficient estimates corresponding to the three expenditure specifications given by models (5.14)–(5.16) for India estimated using the system of Box-Cox Engel curves.

As can be seen from columns (5) to (7) of Table 5.15, all estimated expenditure coefficients are statistically significant at the 5 percent level. In most of the cases, the estimated coefficients are of the same sign across the three model specifications (except for housing), although the magnitude is different. With Indian data, we observe that the budget share on food, alcohol and clothing declines with increasing expenditure levels, while that of health care, transport, education, recreation and miscellaneous goods increases with expenditure across all three expenditure specifications: M, PCE and EPEA. However, the results indicate that the housing budget share has a positive and significant relationship with total expenditure (M), while the relationship is a negative and significant relationship with PCE and EPEA.

The coefficient estimates of household size and the square of household size variables are presented in columns (8) and (9) of Table 5.15. As can be seen, most of the estimated coefficients are statistically significant at the

Table 5.11 Income elasticities of nine commodities by level of income, Bangladesh

Commodity group	Low-income			Lower-middle income			Upper-middle income			High-income		
	M	*PCE*	*EPEA*	*M*	*PCE*	*EPEA*	*M*	*PCE*	*EPEA*	*M*	*PCE*	*EPEA*
(1)	*(2)*	*(3)*	*(4)*	*(5)*	*(6)*	*(7)*	*(8)*	*(9)*	*(10)*	*(11)*	*(12)*	*(13)*
1 Food	0.917	0.921	0.919	0.784	0.775	0.767	0.742	0.755	0.734	0.585	0.576	0.568
	(0.001)	(0.044)	(0.041)	(0.001)	(0.045)	(0.034)	(0.001)	(0.034)	(0.012)	(0.001)	(0.049)	(0.038)
2 Tobacco	0.915	0.925	0.920	0.879	0.776	0.721	0.717	0.658	0.562	0.603	0.678	0.622
	(0.000)	(0.002)	(0.001)	(0.000)	(0.001)	(0.001)	(0.000)	(0.001)	(0.001)	(0.000)	(0.001)	(0.001)
3 Clothing	0.876	0.890	0.881	0.946	0.900	0.932	0.976	0.933	0.935	1.011	0.998	0.979
	(0.000)	(0.001)	(0.001)	(0.000)	(0.001)	(0.001)	(0.000)	(0.003)	(0.002)	(0.000)	(0.002)	(0.002)
4 Housing	0.995	0.997	0.992	1.197	1.234	1.202	1.313	1.146	1.134	1.263	1.245	1.221
	(0.000)	(0.007)	(0.005)	(0.000)	(0.010)	(0.012)	(0.000)	(0.015)	(0.014)	(0.000)	(0.012)	(0.010)
5 Health care	1.085	1.165	1.135	1.204	1.156	1.127	1.149	1.110	1.079	0.932	1.001	1.011
	(0.000)	(0.002)	(0.002)	(0.000)	(0.001)	(0.001)	(0.000)	(0.005)	(0.004)	(0.000)	(0.003)	(0.003)
6 Transport	1.327	1.376	1.357	1.341	1.471	1.485	1.172	1.255	1.268	1.435	1.462	1.479
	(0.000)	(0.001)	(0.001)	(0.000)	(0.001)	(0.002)	(0.000)	(0.003)	(0.004)	(0.000)	(0.002)	(0.002)
7 Recreation	1.306	1.343	1.332	1.671	2.844	2.921	1.327	1.333	1.351	1.459	1.581	1.672
	(0.000)	(0.000)	(0.000)	(0.000)	(0.000)	(0.000)	(0.000)	(0.000)	(0.000)	(0.000)	(0.000)	(0.000)
8 Education	1.352	1.378	1.365	1.493	1.291	1.467	1.302	1.240	1.125	1.200	1.291	1.321
	(0.000)	(0.001)	(0.001)	(0.000)	(0.001)	(0.003)	(0.000)	(0.001)	(0.003)	(0.000)	(0.003)	(0.002)
9 Miscellaneous	1.473	1.578	1.432	1.732	2.561	1.897	2.086	1.751	1.816	2.196	2.321	2.164
	(0.000)	(0.000)	(0.000)	(0.000)	(0.000)	(0.000)	(0.000)	(0.002)	(0.000)	(0.000)	(0.000)	(0.000)

Note: Standard errors of estimated income elasticities are given in parentheses.

Table 5.12 Income elasticities of nine commodities by residential sector, Bangladesh

Commodity group	*Urban*			*Rural*		
	M	*PCE*	*EPEA*	*M*	*PCE*	*EPEA*
(1)	*(2)*	*(3)*	*(4)*	*(5)*	*(6)*	*(7)*
1 Food	0.723	0.750	0.734	0.783	0.800	0.792
	(0.002)	(0.088)	(0.066)	(0.001)	(0.063)	(0.049)
2 Tobacco	0.535	0.592	0.541	0.735	0.805	0.729
	(0.000)	(0.002)	(0.001)	(0.000)	(0.001)	(0.001)
3 Clothing	0.938	0.917	0.934	0.944	0.914	0.945
	(0.000)	(0.004)	(0.003)	(0.000)	(0.003)	(0.002)
4 Housing	1.210	1.224	1.207	1.163	1.178	1.147
	(0.000)	(0.035)	(0.027)	(0.000)	(0.016)	(0.012)
5 Health care	1.059	1.065	1.056	1.122	1.143	1.114
	0.000)	(0.008)	(0.006)	(0.000)	(0.005)	(0.004)
6 Transport	1.394	1.365	1.375	1.346	1.315	1.334
	(0.000)	(0.006)	(0.004)	(0.000)	(0.003)	(0.002)
7 Recreation	1.975	1.902	1.959	1.685	1.653	1.688
	(0.000)	(0.000)	(0.000)	(0.000)	(0.000)	(0.000)
8 Education	1.548	1.371	1.539	1.469	1.303	1.515
	(0.000)	(0.006)	(0.004)	(0.000)	0.002)	(0.002)
9 Miscellaneous	2.289	2.127	2.219	2.475	2.316	2.403
	(0.000)	(0.000)	(0.000)	(0.000)	(0.001)	(0.001)

Note: Standard errors of estimated income elasticities are given in parentheses.

Table 5.13 Income elasticities of nine commodities by religion, Bangladesh

Commodity group	*Islam*			*Other*		
	M	*PCE*	*EPEA*	*M*	*PCE*	*EPEA*
(1)	*(2)*	*(3)*	*(4)*	*(5)*	*(6)*	*(7)*
1 Food	0.772	0.792	0.783	0.704	0.730	0.709
	(0.001)	(0.056)	(0.043)	(0.003)	(0.136)	(0.106)
2 Tobacco	0.668	0.736	0.666	0.734	0.798	0.745
	(0.000)	(0.001)	(0.001)	(0.000)	(0.003)	(0.002)
3 Clothing	0.930	0.903	0.929	1.046	1.001	1.043
	(0.000)	(0.003)	(0.002)	(0.000)	(0.006)	(0.005)
4 Housing	1.187	1.198	1.173	1.153	1.187	1.152
	(0.000)	(0.016)	(0.012)	(0.001)	(0.039)	(0.031)
5 Health care	1.076	1.097	1.071	1.292	1.278	1.290
	(0.000)	(0.005)	(0.004)	(0.000)	(0.012)	(0.009)
6 Transport	1.352	1.320	1.334	1.475	1.435	1.468
	(0.000)	(0.003)	(0.002)	(0.000)	(0.008)	(0.006)
7 Recreation	1.833	1.771	1.817	1.911	1.853	1.905
	(0.000)	(0.000)	(0.000)	(0.000)	(0.000)	(0.000)
8 Education	1.494	1.326	1.523	1.588	1.377	1.574
	(0.000)	(0.002)	(0.002)	(0.000)	(0.008)	(0.006)
9 Miscellaneous	2.367	1.000	1.011	2.770	2.584	2.703
	(0.000)	(0.003)	(0.003)	(0.000)	(0.003)	(0.002)

Note: Standard errors of estimated income elasticities are given in parentheses.

Table 5.14 Information inaccuracies of the three models, Bangladesh

Commodity group (1)	*M* (2)	*PCE* (3)	*EPEA* (4)
1 Food	30,000	30,887	30,708
2 Tobacco	9,959	10,292	10,086
3 Clothing	9,977	10,057	10,102
4 Housing	28,892	29,335	29,674
5 Health care	20,885	20,909	20,979
6 Transport	19,989	20,034	20,120
7 Recreation	2,714	2,710	2,701
8 Education	21,110	22,387	22,235
9 Miscellaneous	25,424	25,936	25,621
All commodities	168,949	172,546	172,226

Note: Information inaccuracies are given in ($\times 10^6$).

5 percent level of significance, indicating that household size plays a significant role in household budget allocations in India. Budget shares on food, clothing and education have a positive sign for household size coefficient, followed by a negative sign for the square of household size variable. This indicates that as household size increases, the budget shares on these commodities increase at a decreasing rate. In contrast, the negative household size coefficient followed by the positive square of household size variable of alcohol, housing, health care, transport, recreation and miscellaneous goods implies that budget shares on these commodity groups decrease at an increasing rate with increasing household size in India. However, in several commodity types, the magnitude of the coefficients is quite small.

As shown in Table 5.15, the signs of the gender (where male = 0 and female = 1) coefficient estimates are mostly consistent across the three models, except for some inconsistencies observed for the food and education budget shares. The results suggest that female headship is associated with increased budget share on housing, health care, recreation and miscellaneous, while showing a decreased budget share on alcohol, clothing and transport in India.

Table 5.16 presents the income elasticities based on the three models for India. As can be seen, at the national level, food, alcohol, clothing and housing are necessities, while health care, transport, recreation, education and miscellaneous are luxuries in India. The elasticity classification is consistent across the three types of expenditure (M, PCE and EPEA). The elasticity estimates by expenditure group (low, lower middle, upper middle and high) under the M, PCE and EPEA models are reported in Table 5.17. As can be seen, although the magnitudes of income elasticities are different across the three models, the broader elasticity classification of commodity groups; a necessity or a luxury is consistent across the three models and income groups. More specifically, in all three models and in all three expenditure quartiles, food, alcohol, clothing and housing are necessities, while

Table 5.15 Estimation results, models (5.14), (5.15) and (5.16), India

Commodity group	Constant			Expenditure			HH size	HH size^2	Gender		
	M	*PCE*	*EPEA*	*M*	*PCE*	*EPEA*	*M*	*M*	*M*	*PCE*	*EPEA*
(1)	*(2)*	*(3)*	*(4)*	*(5)*	*(6)*	*(7)*	*(8)*	*(9)*	*(10)*	*(11)*	*(12)*
1 Food	1.526[a]	2.369[a]	2.657[a]	−0.126[a]	−0.460[a]	−0.477[a]	0.030[a]	−0.001[a]	−0.008[a]	0.015[a]	0.000
	(0.000)	(0.000)	(0.000)	(0.000)	(0.000)	(0.000)	(0.000)	(0.000)	(0.000)	(0.000)	(0.841)
2 Alcohol	0.096[a]	0.131[a]	0.163[a]	−0.008[a]	−0.027[a]	−0.031[a]	0.000[a]	0.000[a]	−0.010[a]	−0.008[a]	−0.009[a]
	(0.000)	(0.000)	(0.000)	(0.000)	(0.000)	(0.000)	(0.602)	(0.026)	(0.000)	(0.000)	(0.000)
3 Clothing	0.095[a]	0.183[a]	0.182[a]	−0.007[a]	−0.033[a]	−0.030[a]	0.005[a]	−0.001[a]	−0.001[a]	−0.002[a]	−0.002[a]
	(0.000)	(0.000)	(0.000)	(0.000)	(0.000)	(0.000)	(0.000)	(0.000)	(0.011)	(0.000)	(0.000)
4 Housing	0.283[a]	0.272[a]	0.357[a]	0.013[a]	−0.032[a]	−0.047[a]	−0.005[a]	0.000[a]	0.000	0.009[a]	0.007[a]
	(0.000)	(0.000)	(0.000)	(0.000)	(0.000)	(0.000)	(0.000)	(0.000)	(0.676)	(0.000)	(0.000)
5 Health care	−0.038[a]	−0.270[a]	−0.282[a]	0.020[a]	0.091[a]	0.085[a]	−0.013[a]	0.001[a]	0.010[a]	0.010[a]	0.013[a]
	(0.000)	(0.000)	(0.000)	(0.000)	(0.000)	(0.000)	(0.000)	(0.000)	(0.000)	(0.000)	(0.000)
6 Transport	−0.370[a]	−0.720[a]	−0.844[a]	0.055[a]	0.198[a]	0.206[a]	−0.012[a]	0.001[a]	−0.003[a]	−0.015[a]	−0.008[a]
	(0.000)	(0.000)	(0.000)	(0.000)	(0.000)	(0.000)	(0.011)	(0.001)	(0.010)	(0.000)	(0.000)
7 Recreation	−0.028[a]	−0.055[a]	−0.065[a]	0.004[a]	0.015[a]	0.016[a]	−0.001[a]	0.000[a]	0.000	−0.001[a]	0.000
	(0.000)	(0.000)	(0.000)	(0.000)	(0.000)	(0.000)	(0.000)	(0.029)	(0.612)	(0.002)	(0.434)
8 Education	−0.202[a]	−0.225[a]	−0.379[a]	0.025[a]	0.069[a]	0.095[a]	0.009[a]	−0.001[a]	0.007[a]	−0.006[a]	−0.003[a]
	(0.000)	(0.000)	(0.000)	(0.000)	(0.000)	(0.000)	(0.000)	(0.000)	(0.000)	(0.000)	(0.006)
9 Miscellaneous	−0.363[a]	−0.684[a]	−0.788[a]	0.050[a]	0.179[a]	0.184[a]	−0.013[a]	0.001[a]	0.001[a]	−0.003[a]	0.002[a]
	(0.000)	(0.000)	(0.000)	(0.000)	(0.000)	(0.000)	(0.000)	(0.000)	(0.000)	(0.000)	(0.000)

Note: The Box-Cox transformation value for M is $\lambda = 0.0109$, PCE is $\lambda = -0.1743$ and EPEA is $\lambda = -0.1533$. *p*-values are in parentheses.
[a] Significant at the 5 percent level.

Table 5.16 Income elasticities of nine commodities, India

Commodity group (1)	*M* (2)	*PCE* (3)	*EPEA* (4)
1 Food	0.706 (0.000)	0744 (0.001)	0.713 (0.000)
2 Alcohol	0.527 (0.000)	0.634 (0.000)	0.543 (0.000)
3 Clothing	0.815 (0.000)	0.801 (0.000)	0.807 (0.000)
4 Housing	0.869 (0.000)	0.924 (0.000)	0.880 (0.000)
5 Health care	1.169 (0.000)	1.180 (0.000)	1.181 (0.000)
6 Transport	1.607 (0.000)	1.518 (0.000)	1.581 (0.000)
7 Recreation	1.899 (0.000)	1.770 (0.000)	1.860 (0.000)
8 Education	1.592 (0.000)	1.387 (0.000)	1.578 (0.000)
9 Miscellaneous	1.844 (0.000)	1.720 (0.000)	1.801 (0.000)

Note: Standard errors of estimated income elasticities are given in parentheses.

transportation, education, recreation and miscellaneous commodity groups are luxuries. While health care is a luxury for low, middle and upper-middle income households, it is a necessity for the high-income households.

Table 5.18 presents the income elasticities for the nine commodity groups by religion. In the interest of brevity, we have combined Christian, Sikh, Buddhist and other religions into one group here. As can be seen, the broader elasticity classification, whether a necessity or a luxury, remains the same for all commodity groups. For all three religions, income elasticity for food, alcohol, clothing and housing is less than 1, indicating that these goods are necessities for Indian households, irrespective of their religion. On the other hand, health care, transport, education, recreation and miscellaneous goods have income elasticity greater than 1, indicating that these goods are luxuries for all households, irrespective of their religion.

The income elasticities by the residential area – urban and rural – are presented in Table 5.19. Income elasticities are mostly consistent across the three models for both rural and urban households. In general, food, alcohol, clothing and housing are a necessity, while health care is a luxury.

Table 5.20 presents the calculated overall and individual commodity information inaccuracies for the three models for India. The overall model information inaccuracies (I) reveal that the M model is the best with lowest information inaccuracy, followed by the EPEA model and the PCE model for India. When considering the individual commodity-level information inaccuracies (I_i), in six commodity groups out of nine (except for

Table 5.17 Income elasticities of nine commodities by level of income, India

Commodity group	Low-income			Lower-middle income			Upper-middle income			High-income		
	M	*PCE*	*EPEA*	*M*	*PCE*	*EPEA*	*M*	*PCE*	*EPEA*	*M*	*PCE*	*EPEA*
(1)	*(2)*	*(3)*	*(4)*	*(5)*	*(6)*	*(7)*	*(8)*	*(9)*	*(10)*	*(11)*	*(12)*	*(13)*
1 Food	0.926	0.932	0.942	0.920	0.922	0.907	0.635	0.672	0.645	0.535	0.574	0.565
	(0.000)	(0.007)	(0.043)	(0.000)	(0.006)	(0.038)	(0.000)	(0.005)	(0.031)	(0.001)	(0.049)	(0.038)
2 Alcohol	0.675	0.723	0.754	0.593	0.651	0.575	0.408	0.432	0.459	0.528	0.578	0.551
	(0.000)	(0.000)	(0.002)	(0.000)	(0.000)	(0.001)	(0.000)	(0.000)	(0.000)	(0.000)	(0.001)	(0.001)
3 Clothing	0.913	0.932	0.915	0.899	0.832	0.877	0.773	0.793	0.760	0.701	0.698	0.779
	(0.000)	(0.000)	(0.001)	(0.000)	(0.000)	(0.001)	(0.000)	(0.000)	(0.001)	(0.000)	(0.002)	(0.002)
4 Housing	0.806	0.874	0.862	0.784	0.792	0.756	0.984	0.942	0.937	0.969	0.978	0.971
	(0.000)	(0.000)	(0.005)	(0.000)	(0.001)	(0.008)	(0.000)	(0.001)	(0.012)	(0.000)	(0.012)	(0.010)
5 Health care	1.192	1.159	1.190	1.185	1.145	1.273	1.068	1.040	1.121	0.983	0.998	0.987
	(0.000)	(0.001)	(0.002)	(0.000)	(0.001)	(0.004)	(0.000)	(0.002)	(0.007)	(0.000)	(0.003)	(0.003)
6 Transport	1.516	1.396	1.537	1.383	1.279	1.399	1.821	1.543	1.621	1.314	1.452	1.469
	(0.000)	(0.000)	(0.002)	(0.000)	(0.001)	(0.004)	(0.000)	(0.001)	(0.008)	(0.000)	(0.002)	(0.002)
7 Recreation	1.690	1.363	1.647	1.416	1.387	1.374	1.439	1.167	1.290	1.664	1.481	1.674
	(0.000)	(0.000)	(0.000)	(0.000)	(0.000)	(0.000)	(0.000)	(0.000)	(0.001)	(0.000)	(0.000)	(0.000)
8 Education	1.288	1.218	1.756	1.154	1.123	1.334	1.726	1.174	1.375	1.273	1.391	1.321
	(0.000)	(0.000)	(0.001)	(0.000)	(0.000)	(0.002)	(0.000)	(0.001)	(0.004)	(0.000)	(0.003)	(0.002)
9 Miscellaneous	1.449	1.315	1.150	1.350	1.247	1.445	1.724	1.498	1.667	1.970	1.321	1.564
	(0.000)	(0.000)	(0.001)	(0.000)	(0.000)	(0.000)	(0.000)	(0.000)	(0.001)	(0.000)	(0.000)	(0.000)

Note: Standard errors of estimated income elasticities are given in parentheses.

Table 5.18 Income elasticities of nine commodities by religion, India

Commodity group	*Hindu*			*Muslim*			*Christian, Sikh, Buddhist and other*		
	M	*PCE*	*EPEA*	*M*	*PCE*	*EPEA*	*M*	*PCE*	*EPEA*
(1)	*(2)*	*(3)*	*(4)*	*(5)*	*(6)*	*(7)*	*(8)*	*(9)*	*(10)*
1 Food	0.706	0.745	0.714	0.704	0.736	0.704	0.705	0.746	0.721
	(0.000)	(0.007)	(0.006)	(0.001)	(0.020)	(0.019)	(0.001)	(0.021)	(0.018)
2 Alcohol	0.532	0.641	0.549	0.565	0.662	0.570	0.441	0.537	0.467
	(0.000)	(0.000)	(0.000)	(0.000)	(0.000)	(0.000)	(0.000)	(0.000)	(0.000)
3 Clothing	0.813	0.800	0.805	0.800	0.792	0.796	0.844	0.824	0.835
	(0.000)	(0.000)	(0.000)	(0.000)	(0.000)	(0.000)	(0.000)	(0.001)	(0.001)
4 Housing	0.856	0.912	0.866	0.941	0.983	0.952	0.924	0.980	0.943
	(0.000)	(0.001)	(0.001)	(0.000)	(0.003)	(0.003)	(0.000)	(0.004)	(0.004)
5 Health care	1.163	1.175	1.175	1.232	1.239	1.245	1.134	1.138	1.137
	(0.000)	(0.002)	(0.002)	(0.000)	(0.006)	(0.005)	(0.000)	(0.005)	(0.005)
6 Transport	1.608	1.519	1.582	1.708	1.614	1.689	1.494	1.422	1.466
	(0.000)	(0.001)	(0.001)	(0.000)	(0.002)	(0.002)	(0.000)	(0.005)	(0.005)
7 Recreation	1.893	1.763	1.850	2.107	1.987	2.075	1.537	1.432	1.509
	(0.000)	(0.000)	(0.000)	(0.000)	(0.000)	(0.000)	(0.000)	(0.000)	(0.000)
8 Education	1.582	1.377	1.569	1.590	1.402	1.609	1.614	1.429	1.571
	(0.000)	(0.000)	(0.000)	(0.000)	(0.001)	(0.001)	(0.000)	(0.003)	(0.002)
9 Miscellaneous	1.843	1.717	(0.003)	1.945	1.818	1.916	1.665	1.579	1.610
	(0.001)	(0.003)		(0.000)	(0.002)	(0.002)	(0.001)	(0.002)	(0.002)

Note: Standard errors of estimated income elasticities are given in parentheses.

Table 5.19 Income elasticities of nine commodities by residential sector, India

Commodity group	*Urban*			*Rural*		
	M	*PCE*	*EPEA*	*M*	*PCE*	*EPEA*
(1)	*(2)*	*(3)*	*(4)*	*(5)*	*(6)*	*(7)*
1 Food	0.659	0.704	0.667	0.727	0.760	0.732
	(0.001)	(0.009)	(0.008)	(0.000)	(0.008)	(0.007)
2 Alcohol	0.708	0.767	0.719	0.719	0.785	0.727
	(0.000)	(0.000)	(0.000)	(0.000)	(0.000)	(0.000)
3 Clothing	0.832	0.824	0.824	0.810	0.793	0.803
	(0.000)	(0.000)	(0.000)	(0.000)	(0.000)	(0.000)
4 Housing	0.968	1.019	0.995	0.793	0.855	0.796
	(0.001)	(0.003)	(0.002)	(0.000)	(0.001)	(0.001)
5 Health care	1.094	1.097	1.094	1.206	1.218	1.221
	(0.001)	(0.003)	(0.002)	(0.000)	(0.002)	(0.002)
6 Transport	1.501	1.433	1.477	1.639	1.546	1.617
	(0.001)	(0.002)	(0.002)	(0.000)	(0.001)	(0.001)
7 Recreation	1.341	1.305	1.336	1.185	1.155	1.176
	(0.000)	(0.000)	(0.000)	(0.000)	(0.000)	(0.000)
8 Education	1.373	1.247	1.363	1.387	1.250	1.381
	(0.001)	(0.002)	(0.002)	(0.000)	(0.001)	(0.000)
9 Miscellaneous	1.735	1.632	1.691	1.858	1.733	1.820
	(0.000)	(0.001)	(0.001)	(0.002)	(0.010)	(0.009)

Note: Standard errors of estimated income elasticities are given in parentheses.

Table 5.20 Information inaccuracies of the three models, India

Commodity group	*M*	*PCE*	*EPEA*
(1)	*(2)*	*(3)*	*(4)*
1 Food	24,499	29,961	26,092
2 Alcohol	8,450	8,430	8,478
3 Clothing	4,834	4,884	4,812
4 Housing	27,454	2,9417	2,8187
5 Health care	22,903	23,640	23,440
6 Transport	51,746	51,676	51,781
7 Recreation	27,303	28,340	27,945
8 Education	32,095	32,731	32,551
9 Miscellaneous	9,600	10,043	9,841
All commodities	222,021	227,621	22,5081

Note: Information inaccuracies are given in ($\times 10^6$).

alcohol, clothing and transport), the M model has the lowest information inaccuracies. Therefore, for household-level data, household expenditure M with household size and the square of household size variables appear to be the best model. Therefore, we suggest that if an analysis of income elasticities is needed at the household level, the precision of results appears to be higher if M is used instead of PCE or EPEA for India.

5.6.3 Sri Lanka

Table 5.21 presents the coefficient estimates corresponding to the three expenditure specifications given by models (5.14)–(5.16), estimated as a system of Box-Cox Engel curves using the 2016 HIES data for Sri Lanka. As can be seen from columns (5)–(7), all estimated expenditure coefficients are statistically significant at the 5 percent level. The estimated coefficients are of the same sign across the three model specifications, although with different magnitudes. While the budget share on food, alcohol and clothing declines with increasing income, the budget shares on housing, health care, education, recreation and miscellaneous goods increase with increasing income in Sri Lanka. The coefficient estimates of household size and the square of household size variables in Table 5.21 are statistically significant at the 5 percent level of significance, indicating that household size plays a significant role in determining the household expenditure allocations of Sri Lankan households. In particular, as can be seen in columns (8) and (9), the positive sign of the household size coefficient followed by the negative sign of the square of household size variables for food, clothing, transport and education indicates that as household size increases, budget share on these commodity groups increase at a decreasing rate. Due to a lower level of economies of scale in consumption in these types of private goods, initially budget share increases with household size. However, in very large households, there is a possibility of harvesting economies of scale in consumption by various means, such as bulk purchase of food and passing on clothing to younger siblings (Jayasinghe 2022), hence increasing budget share at a decreasing rate. On the other hand, the negative household size coefficient followed by the positive square of household size variable for alcohol, housing, health care, recreation and miscellaneous indicates budget shares decreasing at an increasing rate as household size increases in Sri Lanka.

The gender coefficients (where male = 0 and female = 1) presented in Table 5.21 are mostly of the same sign across the three models and are mostly statistically significant at the 5 percent level. The estimated coefficient for food is generally negative. The smaller family size and different household compositions – more children than adults – of female-headed households may lead them to have a lower budget share on food compared with male-headed households. The negative coefficient for EPEA could be supported by the fact that female-headed households consist of more children and appear to reap greater food consumption economies of scale (Jayasinghe 2022). However, under PCE, the gender coefficient for food is positive, reflecting that female-headed households spend a greater share of their expenditure on food compared with male-headed households. This is probably because PCE ignores the possibilities of household size and compositional differences. The estimated coefficients for alcohol and transport are negative, indicating that female-headed households allocate less of their household budget on these goods. The positive and significant signs of the

Table 5.21 Estimation results, models (5.14), (5.15) and (5.16), Sri Lanka

Commodity group	Constant			Expenditure			HH size	HH size^2	Gender		
	M	PCE	EPEA	M	PCE	EPEA	M	M	M	PCE	EPEA
(1)	(2)	(3)	(4)	(5)	(6)	(7)	(8)	(9)	(10)	(11)	(12)
1 Food	3.916[a]	10.111	12.331	−0.539[a]	−3.153[a]	−3.760[a]	0.046[a]	−0.002[a]	−0.016[a]	0.008[a]	−0.007[a]
	(0.000)	(0.000)	(0.000)	(0.000)	(0.000)	(0.000)	(0.000)	(0.000)	(0.000)	(0.000)	(0.000)
2 Alcohol	0.141[a]	0.214	0.380	−0.016[a]	−0.062[a]	−0.113[a]	−0.005[a]	0.001[a]	−0.017[a]	−0.014[a]	−0.015[a]
	(0.000)	(0.000)	(0.000)	(0.000)	(0.000)	(0.000)	(0.000)	(0.000)	(0.000)	(0.000)	(0.000)
3 Clothing	0.043[a]	0.178	0.079	−0.005[a]	−0.049[a]	−0.017[a]	0.007[a]	−0.001[a]	0.002[a]	0.001[aab]	0.001[aab]
	(0.000)	(0.000)	(0.000)	(0.000)	(0.000)	(0.013)	(0.000)	(0.000)	(0.000)	(0.094)	(0.081)
4 Housing	0.140[a]	−0.754	−0.349	0.037[a]	0.333[a]	0.196[a]	−0.031[a]	0.002[a]	0.016[a]	0.023[a]	0.023[a]
	(0.000)	(0.000)	(0.000)	(0.000)	(0.000)	(0.000)	(0.000)	(0.000)	(0.000)	(0.000)	(0.000)
5 Health care	−0.006	−0.217	−0.132	0.011[a]	0.086[a]	0.057[a]	−0.009[a]	0.001[a]	0.001	0.003[a]	0.003[a]
	(0.576)	(0.000)	(0.000)	(0.000)	(0.000)	(0.000)	(0.000)	(0.000)	(0.148)	(0.002)	(0.001)
6 Transport	−0.493[a]	−1.339	−1.832	0.086[a]	0.466[a]	0.607[a]	0.003[a]	−0.001[a]	−0.009[a]	−0.016[a]	−0.013[a]
	(0.000)	(0.000)	(0.000)	(0.000)	(0.000)	(0.000)	(0.011)	(0.001)	(0.000)	(0.000)	(0.000)
7 Recreation	−0.151[a]	−0.466	−0.540	0.026[a]	0.156[a]	0.174[a]	−0.005[a]	0.001[a]	0.001[a]	0.001	0.001[a]
	(0.000)	(0.000)	(0.000)	(0.000)	(0.000)	(0.000)	(0.000)	(0.000)	(0.046)	(0.349)	(0.031)
8 Education	−0.168[a]	−0.144	−0.673	0.023[a]	0.060[a]	0.224[a]	0.021[a]	−0.002[a]	0.006[a]	−0.001	−0.000
	(0.000)	(0.000)	(0.000)	(0.000)	(0.000)	(0.000)	(0.000)	(0.000)	(0.000)	(0.138)	(0.983)
9 Miscellaneous	−2.799[a]	−6.582	−8.265	0.377[a]	2.163[a]	2.632[a]	−0.027[a]	0.001[a]	0.016[a]	−0.005[a]	0.007[a]
	(0.000)	(0.000)	(0.000)	(0.000)	(0.000)	(0.000)	(0.000)	(0.000)	(0.000)	(0.000)	(0.000)

Note: The Box-Cox transformation value fo M is −0.0936, PCE is $\lambda = -0.3065$ and EPEA is $\lambda = -0.2991$. *p*-values are in parentheses.
[a] and [b] denote significance at the 5 percent and 10 percent levels, respectively.

coefficient estimate of gender for clothing, housing, health care, education and recreation indicate that female-headed households would allocate more of their expenditure on these goods.

Table 5.22 presents the income elasticities for the three models. As can be seen, overall, food, alcohol and clothing are necessities while the remaining household goods are luxuries for Sri Lankan households. These income elasticities are in line with previous studies about Sri Lanka as well as those about the least developed countries (see Rajapakse 2011, Selvanathan 1993, and Selvanathan and Selvanathan 2003a). When considering the elasticity estimates in Table 5.22, it can be seen that the elasticity classification of any commodity group, that is, whether a necessity or a luxury, remains unchanged irrespective of whether we use M, PCE or EPEA. Nevertheless, the magnitude of the elasticity estimates is different based on the model. These differences are based on the way in which we incorporate household size and compositional differences into account in the three models.

The elasticity estimates by income groups under M, PCE and EPEA models are reported in Table 5.23. As can be seen, there are notable differences in income elasticities of goods by income groups. Food is a necessity for households in all income groups, under all three model specifications. While alcohol is a necessity for households in lower-middle, upper-middle and high-income groups, it is a luxury for households in the low-income group. Clothing is a luxury for households in low- and lower-middle-income

Table 5.22 Income elasticities of nine commodities, Sri Lanka

Commodity group (1)	*M* (2)	*PCE* (3)	*EPEA* (4)
1 Food	0.564 (0.000)	0.528 (0.001)	0.488 (0.000)
2 Alcohol	0.708 (0.000)	0.823 (0.000)	0.707 (0.000)
3 Clothing	0.935 (0.000)	0.900 (0.000)	0.969 (0.000)
4 Housing	1.080 (0.000)	1.112 (0.000)	1.060 (0.000)
5 Health care	1.104 (0.000)	1.127 (0.000)	1.076 (0.000)
6 Transport	1.427 (0.000)	1.361 (0.000)	1.427 (0.000)
7 Recreation	1.963 (0.000)	1.902 (0.000)	1.915 (0.000)
8 Education	1.309 (0.000)	1.126 (0.000)	1.427 (0.000)
9 Miscellaneous	2.356 (0.000)	2.215 (0.000)	2.344 (0.000)

Note: Standard errors of estimated income elasticities are given in parentheses.

Table 5.23 Income elasticities of nine commodities by level of income, Sri Lanka

Commodity group	Low-income			Lower-middle income			Upper-middle income			High-income		
	M	*PCE*	*EPEA*	*M*	*PCE*	*EPEA*	*M*	*PCE*	*EPEA*	*M*	*PCE*	*EPEA*
(1)	*(2)*	*(3)*	*(4)*	*(5)*	*(6)*	*(7)*	*(8)*	*(9)*	*(10)*	*(11)*	*(12)*	*(13)*
1 Food	0.750	0.786	0.788	0.570	0.642	0.475	0.470	0.478	0.349	0.391	0.390	0.372
	(0.004)	(0.108)	(0.124)	(0.004)	(0.108)	(0.124)	(0.004)	(0.122)	(0.139)	(0.004)	(0.122)	(0.158)
2 Alcohol	1.481	1.174	1.298	0.360	0.870	0794	0.575	0.302	0.520	0.232	0.437	0.318
	(0.000)	(0.002)	(0.003)	(0.000)	(0.002)	(0.003)	(0.000)	(0.003)	(0.003)	(0.000)	(0.003)	(0.003)
3 Clothing	1.179	1.250	1.325	1.014	0.706	1.203	0.786	0.982	0.852	0.511	0.649	0.581
	(0.000)	(0.004)	(0.005)	(0.000)	(0.004)	(0.005)	(0.000)	(0.005)	(0.006)	(0.000)	(0.005)	(0.007)
4 Housing	1.171	1.061	1.005	1.287	1.179	1.158	1.188	1.257	1.312	1.112	1.116	1.189
	(0.001)	(0.079)	(0.098)	(0.001)	(0.079)	(0.098)	(0.002)	(0.089)	(0.109)	(0.002)	(0.089)	(0.124)
5 Health care	1.461	1.183	1.238	1.233	1.149	1.041	1.212	1.179	1.191	1.123	1.096	1.088
	(0.000)	(0.008)	(0.010)	(0.000)	(0.008)	(0.010)	(0.000)	(0.009)	(0.011)	(0.000)	(0.009)	(0.013)
6 Transport	1.572	1.576	1.525	1.746	1.393	1.454	1.559	1.345	1.403	1.070	1.081	1.064
	(0.000)	(0.025)	(0.030)	(0.000)	(0.025)	(0.030)	(0.000)	(0.028)	(0.034)	(0.000)	(0.028)	(0.038)
7 Recreation	1.946	1.909	1.674	2.472	2.511	1.866	1.720	1.830	1.922	1.688	1.637	1.578
	(0.000)	(0.002)	(0.002)	(0.000)	(0.002)	(0.002)	(0.000)	(0.002)	(0.003)	(0.000)	(0.002)	(0.003)
8 Education	1.601	1.957	2.523	1.588	1.333	1.337	1.429	1.285	1.524	0.994	0.939	1.971
	(0.000)	(0.012)	(0.015)	(0.000)	(0.012)	(0.015)	(0.000)	(0.014)	(0.017)	(0.000)	(0.014)	(0.019)
9 Miscellaneous	5.784	5.298	5.740	3.280	2.849	2.205	2.295	1.961	2.074	1.632	1.384	1.436
	(0.000)	(0.001)	(0.012)	(0.000)	(0.001)	(0.012)	(0.000)	(0.001)	(0.013)	(0.001)	(0.001)	(0.028)

Note: Standard errors of estimated income elasticities are given in parentheses.

groups, while it is a necessity for upper-middle and high-income households. Housing, health care, transport, recreation, education and miscellaneous goods are luxuries for all households for all three models.

Table 5.24 presents the income elasticities for the nine goods by different ethnic groups. As can be seen, the elasticity classification (necessity and luxury) remains the same for most of the commodity groups, except for clothing and health care, across the three ethnic groups. The income elasticity for food and alcohol is less than 1 for households in all ethnic groups under all three models. For all three ethnic groups income elasticity for housing, transport, education, recreation and miscellaneous exceeds 1, indicating that these goods are luxuries. While clothing is a necessity for Sinhalese and other ethnic groups, it is a luxury for Tamils. Income elasticity of alcohol reported is less than but closer to 1 making it a near luxury, particularly for Tamils.

Table 5.25 presents the income elasticity for the nine goods by residential sectors: urban, rural and estate. Income elasticities for food are less than 1 for households in all three sectors, reflecting the necessity nature of food. Alcohol is a near luxury for the households in the estate sector. Housing and health appear to be a luxury, or near luxury for households in all three sectors. While clothing is a necessity for households living in urban and rural sectors, it is a luxury for estate sector households. Income elasticities for transport, education, and recreation are all greater than 1 indicating that these are luxuries for households in all three sectors. Table 5.26 presents the calculated overall and individual commodity information inaccuracies given by equations (5.19) and (5.20) for the three models. The overall model information inaccuracies (I) and the individual commodity level information inaccuracies (I_i) reveal that the M model outperforms the other two models.

In summary, the M model outperforms the other two models in terms of information inaccuracy measures in all countries under consideration: Australia, Bangladesh, India and Sri Lanka. In Table 5.27, we provide a summary of income elasticity estimates for the full sample using the M model specification for all four countries. The elasticity estimates have been derived at the mean total expenditure and budget shares of the respective countries. As can be seen, in all four countries in general, food is a necessity and transport, recreation and education are luxuries, irrespective of the level of economic development of a country. Alcohol is a luxury in Australia while it is a necessity in India and Sri Lanka. Tobacco is surprisingly a necessity in Bangladesh. While clothing is a luxury in Australia, it is a necessity in Bangladesh, India and Sri Lanka. Housing is mixed, a necessity in Australia and India and it is a luxury in Bangladesh and Sri Lanka. Health care is a necessity in Australia but a luxury in the other three countries. Similar results have also been reported in Jayasinghe et al. (2019) with respect to Sri Lanka during 2006 and 2016.

Table 5.24 Income elasticities of nine commodities by ethnicity, Sri Lanka

Commodity group	*Sinhalese*			*Tamils*			*Other*		
(1)	*M* *(2)*	*PCE* *(3)*	*EPEA* *(4)*	*M* *(5)*	*PCE* *(6)*	*EPEA* *(7)*	*M* *(8)*	*PCE* *(9)*	*EPEA* *(10)*
1 Food	0.543	0.600	0.561	0.609	0.563	0.626	0.578	0.654	0.608
	(0.004)	(0.201)	(0.222)	(0.010)	(0.429)	(0.516)	(0.060)	(3.123)	(3.657)
2 Alcohol	0.788	0.858	0.798	0.911	0.999	0.913	0.903	0.875	0.888
	(0.000)	(0.007)	(0.009)	(0.000)	(0.014)	(0.017)	(0.003)	(0.158)	(0.196)
3 Clothing	0.892	0.862	0.926	1.060	1.033	1.099	0.781	0.701	0.785
	(0.000)	(0.003)	(0.004)	(0.000)	(0.008)	(0.010)	(0.000)	(0.054)	(0.068)
4 Housing	1.063	1.088	1.044	1.115	1.150	1.094	1.274	1.279	1.257
	(0.002)	(0.087)	(0.104)	(0.003)	(0.097)	(0.123)	(0.037)	(1.775)	(1.260)
5 Health care	1.099	1.119	1.058	1.280	1.294	1.239	0.943	0.911	0.851
	(0.000)	(0.007)	(0.009)	(0.000)	(0.008)	(0.011)	(0.003)	(0.133)	(0.165)
6 Transport	1.396	1.321	1.394	1.647	1.531	1.610	1.579	1.470	1.513
	(0.001)	(0.024)	(0.028)	(0.001)	(0.025)	(0.032)	(0.005)	(0.225)	(0.279)
7 Recreation	2.289	2.152	2.167	1.661	1.531	1.636	1.540	1.524	1.594
	(0.000)	(0.001)	(0.002)	(0.000)	(0.001)	(0.002)	(0.006)	(0.014)	(0.017)
8 Education	1.175	1.080	1.255	1.263	1.062	1.329	1.726	1.542	1.763
	(0.000)	(0.010)	(0.012)	(0.000)	(0.012)	(0.015)	(0.003)	(0.272)	(0.328)
9 Miscellaneous	2.736	2.494	2.658	3.333	2.937	3.230	2.135	1.853	2.036
	(0.042)	(0.085)	(0.008)	(0.003)	(0.018)	(0.019)	(0.002)	(0.012)	(0.013)

Note: Standard errors of estimated income elasticities are given in parentheses.

Table 5.25 Income elasticities of nine commodities by residential sector, Sri Lanka

Commodity group	*Urban*			*Rural*			*Estate*		
(1)	*M* *(2)*	*PCE* *(3)*	*EPEA* *(4)*	*M* *(5)*	*PCE* *(6)*	*EPEA* *(7)*	*M* *(8)*	*PCE* *(9)*	*EPEA* *(10)*
1 Food	0.542	0.599	0.562	0.563	0.616	0.579	0.645	0.720	0.665
	(0.009)	(0.450)	(0.529)	(0.004)	(0.205)	(0.229)	(0.029)	(1.033)	(1.270)
2 Alcohol	0.877	0.910	0.886	0.801	0.880	0.804	0.972	1.105	0.988
	(0.000)	(0.018)	(0.022)	(0.000)	(0.007)	(0.008)	(0.002)	(0.062)	(0.080)
3 Clothing	0.939	0.918	0.969	0.924	0.898	0.960	1.234	1.112	1.261
	(0.000)	(0.008)	(0.009)	(0.000)	(0.004)	(0.004)	(0.001)	(0.020)	(0.026)
4 Housing	1.082	1.120	1.076	1.074	1.099	1.053	0.898	1.002	0.896
	(0.006)	(0.317)	(0.392)	(0.002)	(0.069)	(0.083)	(0.004)	(0.152)	(0.196)
5 Health care	1.190	1.232	1.157	1.131	1.151	1.090	0.943	0.938	0.911
	(0.000)	(0.016)	(0.020)	(0.000)	(0.006)	(0.008)	(0.000)	(0.014)	(0.018)
6 Transport	1.602	1.493	1.571	1.411	1.340	1.413	1.459	1.259	1.356
	(0.001)	(0.055)	(0.067)	(0.000)	(0.020)	(0.024)	(0.001)	(0.048)	(0.062)
7 Recreation	2.297	1.121	2.224	2.098	1.991	2.005	1.593	1.479	1.595
	(0.000)	(0.004)	(0.005)	(0.000)	(0.001)	(0.001)	(0.000)	(0.002)	(0.003)
8 Education	1.251	1.110	1.278	1.180	1.072	1.267	1.468	1.029	1.537
	(0.001)	(0.035)	(0.042)	(0.000)	(0.008)	(0.010)	(0.000)	(0.015)	(0.020)
9 Miscellaneous	2.910	2.570	2.810	2.850	2.593	2.769	2.690	2.308	2.608
	(0.002)	(0.012)	(0.022)	(0.000)	(0.111)	(0.022)	(0.003)	(0.060)	(0.065)

Note: Standard errors of estimated income elasticities are given in parentheses.

Table 5.26 Information inaccuracies of the three models, Sri Lanka

Commodity group (1)	*M* (2)	*PCE* (3)	*EPEA* (4)
1 Food	24,499	29,961	26,092
2 Alcohol	21,451	22,244	21,831
3 Clothing	9,899	9,923	10,009
4 Housing	35,112	35,852	36,148
5 Health care	21,172	21,305	21,370
6 Transport	27,097	27,922	27,512
7 Recreation	11,848	11,755	11,852
8 Education	18,222	19,984	19,719
9 Miscellaneous	59,230	63,565	74,437
All commodities	228,529	242,511	248,214

Note: Information inaccuracies are given in ($\times 10^6$).

Table 5.27 Summary of income elasticities for the four countries based on the preferred 'M' model

Commodity group (1)	*Australia* (2)	*Bangladesh* (3)	*India* (4)	*Sri Lanka* (5)
1 Food	0.673	0.622	0.706	0.564
	(0.000)	(0.000)	(0.000)	(0.000)
2 Alcohol	1.017	-	0.527	0.708
	(0.000)		(0.000)	(0.000)
Tobacco	-	0.783	-	-
		(0.000)		
3 Clothing	1.361	0.842	0.815	0.935
	(0.000)	(0.000)	(0.000)	(0.000)
4 Housing	0.772	1.146	0.869	1.080
	(0.000)	(0.000)	(0.000)	(0.000)
5 Health care	0.955	1.094	1.169	1.104
	(0.000)	(0.000)	(0.000)	(0.000)
6 Transport	1.148	1.486	1.607	1.427
	(0.000)	(0.000)	(0.000)	(0.000)
7 Recreation	1.505	1.301	1.899	1.963
	(0.000)	(0.000)	(0.000)	(0.000)
8 Education	1.731	1.314	1.592	1.309
	(0.000)	(0.000)	(0.000)	(0.000)
9 Miscellaneous	1.668	3.826	1.844	2.356
	(0.000)	(0.000)	(0.000)	(0.000)

Note: Standard errors of estimated income elasticities are given in parentheses. The Bangladesh dataset does not provide data on alcohol consumption and reports expenditure on tobacco consumption only.

5.7 Concluding Comments and Policy Implications

In this chapter, we used the Box-Cox Engel functions to estimate income elasticities for Australia, Bangladesh, India and Sri Lanka. We estimated three models of a complete system of non-linear Engel curves to incorporate household size and compositional differences into the model and compared the differences in elasticity estimates across the three models. In these three models, budget shares as dependent variables were modelled taking the M, PCE and EPEA, separately, as independent variables together with a set of other socio-economic variables. We used information inaccuracies to select the preferred model.

The estimation results reveal some important similarities and differences between income elasticities in developing and developed countries. In general, household consumption economies of scale were observed in almost all commodity groups and household size played an important role in determining household budget allocations, except for Australia. This was what we anticipated as the average household size in a developed country like Australia is lower than that of developing countries, such as Bangladesh, India and Sri Lanka. We also observed that the impact of the state/region/residential sector is somewhat minimum on the household budget allocations in Australia, compared with that of Bangladesh, India and Sri Lanka. We also observed some ethnic/religious differences in household spending patterns in Bangladesh, India and Sri Lanka.

However, the socio-demographic factors, such as household size, ethnicity, religion and residential area, appeared to have a minimum impact on the broader elasticity classification of commodity groups in all four countries. Nevertheless, our results revealed that the level of economic development of a country (classified as developed vs developing countries) does have implications on the broader elasticity classification of commodities. For example, we found that food is a necessity and transport education, recreation and miscellaneous goods are luxuries in all four countries. We also observed that while health care is a necessity for households in Australia, it is a luxury for households in developing countries, such as Bangladesh, India and Sri Lanka. On the other hand, alcohol and clothing are necessities for those households in developing countries, whereas these goods are luxury items for Australian households. No consistent results were found with respect to housing. Housing is a luxury in Bangladesh and Sri Lanka, while it is a necessity in Australia and India.

While, in general, the model specifications, M, PCE, and EPEA did not have significant implications on the relationship between the budget shares of various commodity groups and income, the information inaccuracy analysis indicated that the M model is the best performing model in all countries. While the EPEA specification was identified as the second-best model in Australia, Bangladesh and India, the PCE model appeared as the second-best model in Sri Lanka.

The elasticity estimates presented in this study provide some useful insights with respect to investment decisions of manufacturing firms and government policy decisions. Household income levels have been increasing considerably over the past decade in all the countries under consideration in this chapter. This can be expected to grow even further in the years to come, particularly in the developing countries. As a result, we could expect the household demand for commodities that have been recognised as luxury goods, such as health care, transport, education and recreation, to increase. This means that luxury services such as travel, dining out, obtaining private health services and having private education for children will, undoubtedly, become a greater part of consumers' total expenditure as income rises. While the luxury nature of health, automobiles, consumer durables and recreational services provides an important guide for investment decisions for industries engaged in these businesses, it also provides some important signals for governments, particularly when designing tax policies. For example, if a tax such as a Value Added Tax is imposed, the cost of production of goods and services is expected to increase, resulting in a decline of quantity supplied. However, as the demand for luxury goods, such as health care and telecommunication, is expected to grow with rising household income, equating to a rise in quantity demanded, there may be a sharp increase in price due to lower quantity supplied. Therefore, these goods will increasingly become luxury goods for lower-income households. While such a tax policy will support government revenue objectives, this may have an adverse impact on low-income households in developing countries. For example, with a considerably high proportion of aging people, needing private health care service, in all these countries, the price rise in health services may discourage and exclude low-income households from accessing improved health care. The impact of tax revisions for food, however, is comparatively lower as food is a necessity whose demand is less responsive to the changes in income. Overall, our results prove useful and relevant for demand and pricing policies in both developed and developing countries.

Notes

1 Most consumer demand studies refer to total expenditure as income, which is followed in this book as well. Hence, expenditure shares and budget shares are used interchangeably, and expenditure elasticities are referred to as income elasticities throughout the book.
2 The selection of the countries is based on access to comparable household-level survey data.
3 The derivation of equations (5.12) and (5.13) is similar to that of equation (5.9), but with PCE and EPEA, instead of *M*.

References

Allen, R.G.D., and A.L. Bowley 1935. *Family expenditure*. London: Staple Press.

ABS 2016. Household expenditure survey 2015–2016: Expanded Confidential Unit Record Files (CURF). DataLab, Findings based on use of ABS Microdata.

ABS 2017. Household expenditure survey and survey of income and housing, User guide, Australia, 2015–16, ABS cat no. 6503.0. Australian Bureau of Statistics, Canberra, Ausralia.

BBS 2017. Preliminary report on household income and expenditure survey 2016. Bangladesh Bureau of Statistics, Dhaka, Bangladesh.

Barten, A.P. 1964. Family composition, prices and expenditure patterns, in P. Hart and G. Mills (eds.), *Economic analysis for national economic planning.* London: Butterworth.

Beneito, P. 2003. A complete system of Engel curves in the Spanish economy. *Applied Economics* 35(7): 803–816.

Bhalotra, S., and C. Attfield 1998. Intrahousehold resource allocation in rural Pakistan: A semiparametric analysis. *Journal of Applied Econometrics* 13(5): 463–480.

Blundell, R., D. Alan, and K. Pendakur. 1998. Semiparametric estimation and consumer demand. *Journal of Applied Econometrics* 13(5): 435–461.

Bosch-Domènech, A. 1991. Economies of scale, location, age, and sex discrimination in household demand. *European Economic Review* 35(8): 1589–1595.

Box, G.E.P., and D.R. Cox. 1964. An analysis of transformations. *Journal of the Royal Statistical Society* 26: 211–252.

Byrne, P.J., O. Capps, and A. Saha. 1996. Analysis of food-away-from-home expenditure patterns for U.S. housheolds, 1982–89. *American Journal of Agricultural Economics* 78(3): 614–627.

Clements, K.W., and G. Gao. 2012. Quality, quantity, spending and prices. *European Economic Review* 56(7): 1376–1391.

Clements, K.W., and J. Si. 2017. Simplifying the big mac index. *Journal of International Financial Management and Accounting* 28(1): 86–99.

Clements, K.W., J. Si, E.A. Selvanathan, and S. Selvanathan. 2020. Demand elasticities for 9 goods in 37 countries. *Applied Economics* 52(24): 2636–2655.

DCS 2011. Household income and expenditure survey -2009/10. Department of Census and Statistics, Colombo, Sri Lanka.

DCS 2017. Household income and expenditure survey -2016. Department of Census and Statistics, Colombo, Sri Lanka.

Deaton, A., and J. Muellbauer. 1980. *Economics and consumer behavior.* Cambridge: Cambridge University Press.

Deaton, A., and C. Paxson.1998. Economies of scale, household size, and the demand for food. *The Journal of Political Economy* 106(5): 897–930.

Desai, S., and R. Vanneman. 2018. India human development survey-II (IHDS-II), 2011–12.

Engel, E. 1857. Die lebenskosten belgischer arbeiter-familien fruher und jetzt. *International Statistical Institute Bulletin* 9: 1–74.

Eurostat. 2014. Glossary: Equivalised disposable income. Retrieved from http://ec.europa.eu/eurostat/statistics-explained/index.php/Glossary:Equivalised_disposable_income

Grigg, D. 1994. Food expenditure and economic development. *GeoJournal* 33(4), 377–382. doi:10.1007/BF00806419.

Haque, M.O. 2005. Income elasticity and economic development: Methods and applications (Vol. 42). Dordrecht: Springer.

Hausman, J.A., W.K. Newey, and J.L. Powell. 1995. Nonlinear errors in variables estimation of some Engel curves. *Journal of Econometrics* 65(1): 205–233.

Houthakker, H.S. 1957. An international comparison of household expenditure patterns, commemorating the centenary of Engel's law. *Econometrica* 25(4): 532–551.

Houthakker, H.S. 1960. Additive preferences. *Econometrica* 28: 244–257.

Houthakker, H.S. 1965. New evidence on demand elasticities. *Econometrica* 33(2): 277–288.

IHDS II 2018. *India Human Development Survey-II, 2011–12.* IHDS Series, Version V6, Data sharing for demographic research. doi:10.3886/ICPSR36151.v6.

Jayasinghe, M. 2022. *Poverty, Food Consumption, and Economic Development*. Singapore: Springer. doi:10.1007/978-981-16-8743-3.

Jayasinghe, M., E.A. Selvanathan, and S. Selvanathan. 2019. An intertemporal analysis of expenditure elasticities under three expenditure specifications for sri Lanka. *Applied Economics* 51(59): 6376–6392.

Lanjouw, P., and M. Ravallion. 1995. Poverty and household size. *The Economic Journal* 105(433): 1415–1434.

Lewbel, A. 2008. Engel curves, in S.N. Durlauf and L.E. Blume (eds.), *The New palgrave dictionary of economics* (2nd ed.). Basingstoke: Palgrave Macmillan.

McDowell, D.R., J.E. Allen-Smith, and P.E. McLean-Meyinsse. 1997. Food expenditures and socioeconomic characteristics: Focus on income class. *American Journal of Agricultural Economics* 79(5): 1444–1451.

Mori, H., K. Ishibashi, D. Clason, and J. Dyck. 2006. *Age-free income elasticities of demand for foods: New evidence from Japan*. Accessed on 10th January 2022. Retreived from https://citeseerx.ist.psu.edu/viewdoc/download?doi=10.1.1.574.422&rep=rep1&type=pdf.

Nicholson, J.L. 1949. Variations in working class family expenditure. *Journal of the Royal Statistical Society. series A (general)* 112(4): 359–418.

Nie, P., and A. Sousa-Poza. 2016. A fresh look at calorie income elasticities in China. *China Agricultural Economic Review* 8(1): 55–80.

Poirier, D.J. 1978. The use of the Box-Cox transformation in limited dependent variable models. *Journal of the American Statistical Association 73*(362): 284–287.

Prais, S., and H. Houthakker. 1955. *The analysis of family budgets* (2nd ed.). Cambridge: Cambridge University Press.

Rajapakse, S. 2011. Estimation of a complete system of nonlinear Engel curves: Further evidence from Box-Cox Engel curves for Sri Lanka. *Applied Economics* 43(3): 371–385.

Selvanathan, S. 1993. *A system-wide analysis of international consumption patterns*. The Netherlands: Kluwer Academic Publishers.

Selvanathan, E.A., and S. Selvanathan. 2003a. *International consumption comparisons: OECD versus LDC*. River Edge, NJ, Singapore: World Scientific.

Selvanathan, E.A., and S. Selvanathan. 2003b. Similarities in the consumption patterns of the five Asian tigers. *Asian Economic Journal* 17: 297–323.

Selvanathan, E.A., S. Selvanathan, L. Wong, and M. Jayasinghe. 2021. Modelling regional consumption patterns in Australia. *Economic Record* 97(317): 141–156.

Theil, H. 1965. The information approach to demand analysis. *Econometrica* 33: 67–87.

Theil, H. 1975. *Theory and measurement of consumer demand*. Volume 1, Amsterdam: North Holland.

Working, H. 1943. Statistical laws of family expenditure. *Journal of the American Statistical Association* 38: 43–56.

World Bank 2020. *World development indicators*. https://datacatalog.worldbank.org/dataset/ world-development-indicators.

You, J. 2003. Robust estimation of models of Engel curves. *Empirical Economics* 28(1): 61–73.

Zarembka, P. 1974. *Frontiers in econometrics*. New York: Academic Press.

Zellner, A. 1962. An efficient method of estimating seemingly unrelated regressions and tests for aggregation bias. *Journal of the American Statistical Association* 57(298): 348–368.

6 Demand for Food, Alcohol, Tobacco, Restaurants and Soft Drinks

S Selvanathan, M Jayasinghe and E A Selvanathan

6.1 Introduction

In the previous chapters, we considered food and alcohol as one group, namely 'food', and analysed the demand for the food group together with another eight or nine broad commodity groups such as clothing, housing, health and restaurant meals unconditionally. In Chapter 4, we used time-series data from 45 countries and in Chapter 5 we used cross-sectional data for a selected number of countries in the Asia Pacific region. In this chapter, we analyse the consumption of the food group disaggregated into food, alcohol, tobacco, soft drinks and restaurant meals conditionally within the food group for the countries considered in Chapters 4 and 5 using time-series data as well cross-sectional data. In Sections 2.9–2.11 of Chapter 2, we introduced the conditional demand equations under block independence. In this chapter, we use them to analyse the consumption of food, alcohol, tobacco, soft drinks and restaurant meals conditionally within the food group.

6.2 Demand for Food – A Review

Consumer demand for food is an important consideration for policy makers and agribusiness market participants to plan and implement social, welfare and food security-related policies and business policies. Of further importance is the impact of food prices on demand for food (Andreyeva et al. 2010). Factors such as increasing population, food price volatility and adverse climatic changes pose significant challenges for global food and nutritional security (Abbott and de Battisti 2011). Achieving food security and improving the nutritional food intake of people are recognised as important development challenges globally. Thus, these aspects have received high priority in the United Nations' *2015 Sustainable Development Goals.*[1]

Kearney (2010) highlights that volatility of food prices has implications on individual household incomes and their food consumption patterns. Several studies have indicated that rising household income over time has resulted in increased consumption of food away from home (restaurant meals) both in developed and developing countries (Jensen and Yen 1996; Liu et al. 2015). On the other hand, food availability is closely linked to food prices and income variability (Kearney 2010). For example, research suggests that households

DOI: 10.4324/9780429200120-6

in developing countries allocate a major share of their household income on food compared with non-food items (Jayasinghe et al. 2019). Research also highlights that household dietary patterns change with increasing income levels where individuals tend to consume more calories, especially animal-based calories (Bodirsky et al. 2015). These findings suggest that in the event of high food prices and a decrease in income or lack of enough income, low-income people may not be able to acquire adequate food to fulfil their daily calorie intake (D'Souza and Jolliffe 2012), resulting in a significant impact on household food consumption levels. It is often hard to quantify to what extent households are affected by these external factors. However, the magnitude of change in food demand in response to a change in price and income can be predicted and quantified through income and price elasticities.

Alcohol consumption patterns are also of great interest to many stakeholders. Worldwide, the harmful use of alcohol results in 3 million deaths annually, representing about 5.3 percent of the global deaths (WHO 2018). A large body of consumer demand literature has noted that reducing the affordability of alcohol (i.e., by increasing its price) has shown significant effectiveness in controlling alcohol consumption. In particular, the change in consumption of alcohol in response to a change in price – commonly known as the price elasticity of alcohol demand – indicates how much prices must increase in order to achieve the intended reduction in consumption.

To this end, accurate estimates of price elasticities serve as an important policy tool in designing food and welfare policies and alcohol taxation and pricing policies. Furthermore, the analysis of food and alcohol demand conveys signals to the farmers, producers and sellers on their investment, production and sales decisions and thereby enables them to dovetail with the household demand effectively. In what follows, we present a concise review of recent literature on elasticity estimates of food, alcohol and restaurants.

Lluch and Powell (1975), using the linear expenditure system of Stone (1954), analysed the personal consumption expenditures on eight commodity groups of 19 countries. The study found that own-price and expenditure elasticity estimates of food decline as real per capita Gross National Product increases. Selvanathan and Selvanathan (1993) compared consumption by commodity group across 18 OECD countries using a static AIDS model over the period 1960–1981. The study found that food is a necessity (income elasticity < 1). Similar results were found in Selvanathan and Selvanathan (2003a) with respect to the consumption patterns of the five strongest Asian economies (Hong Kong, Japan, South Korea, Singapore and Taiwan) and Clements et al. (2020) with respect to all 37 OECD countries. Seale et al. (2003) estimated income and price elasticities of demand for nine broad commodity categories, including food, and eight food sub-categories: bread and cereals, meat, fish, dairy products, oils and fats, fruits and vegetables, beverages and tobacco, and other food products across 114 countries, using *1996 International Comparison Program data*. The study employed the two-stage, cross-country demand system based on the Florida Model. The analysis revealed that low-, middle-, and high-income countries all respond differently to changes in income and food prices. Furthermore, low-income countries are more responsive to price and income changes than high-income countries. In particular, staple food like cereals has smaller demand responses to income changes than higher-valued food items such as meat, fish and dairy.

Using household consumption data from Peru, Gil and Molina (2005) found that tobacco is a necessity. Using time-series data for 43 countries consisting of 24 developed countries and 19 developing countries, Selvanathan and Selvanathan (2006) analysed the consumption patterns of four commodities: food, tobacco, alcohol and soft drinks. The estimated results based on the Rotterdam Demand System revealed that tobacco and alcohol are necessities in most of the developed countries and luxuries in a majority of developing countries. While food is a necessity, soft drinks are a luxury in most countries. The own-price elasticity estimates revealed that demand for all four commodities is price inelastic in all countries. In a systematic review of research on the price elasticity of demand for food in the USA between 1938 and 2007, Andreyeva et al. (2010) found that food-away-from-home was most responsive to changes in prices (−0.81) and more elastic than demand for food at home (−0.59). Wong et al. (2017) analysed private consumption patterns of Australia utilising a system-wide approach and three demand models: the AIDS, Rotterdam and CBS demand systems. The study revealed that Australian consumers, on average, allocate about two-thirds of their income on food, housing, transport and recreation. In particular, the estimated income elasticities using time-series data for Australia reveal that food, alcohol and tobacco are necessities and that demand for these goods is price inelastic. Jayasinghe et al. (2019), using Sri Lankan Household Survey data, revealed that food and alcohol are necessities for Sri Lankan households, although the magnitude of expenditure elasticities vary by different expenditure groups, ethnicity of household head, and the residential sector.

6.3 Consumption of Food, Soft Drinks, Tobacco and Alcohol – A Cross-Country Analysis

6.3.1 Food Consumption

A number of recent cross-country consumption studies have found that there is a significant difference in the budget allocation of consumers' income on food (see, for example, Clements et al. 2020; Selvanathan 1993; Selvanathan and Selvanathan 2003b). According to these studies, while consumers in most of the developed countries allocate less than one sixth of their income to the food group, consumers in developing countries allocate at least one-fourth of their income to the food group. For example, budget share allocated to the food group varies from as low as 9 percent by the consumers in the USA to nearly 50 percent by consumers in India. Therefore, a complete scientific analysis of demand for food as a group as well as the conditional demand for goods such as food, alcohol, tobacco, restaurant meals and non-alcoholic beverages (soft drinks) within the food group at a cross-country level is very important.

Figure 6.1 presents the budget share for food in the 45 developed and developing countries considered in Chapters 3 and 4. As can be seen, consumers in the rich (developed) countries tend to allocate a smaller proportion of their income on food while consumers in the poor (developing) countries allocate a larger proportion of their income on food. This is further demonstrated in Figure 6.2, where we plot the average food budget share for each country against the natural logarithm of income for that country. As can be seen, there is a negative relationship between food budget share and consumer income, supporting the well-known Engel's (1857) Law.

6.3.2 Soft Drinks Consumption

While soft drinks (carbonated) continue to be a favourite refreshment, especially among the younger age group, its consumption is also considered as

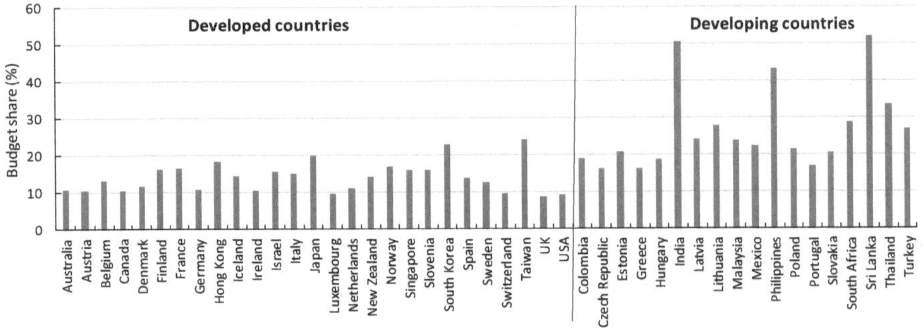

Figure 6.1 Food budget share, 45 selected developed and developing countries.

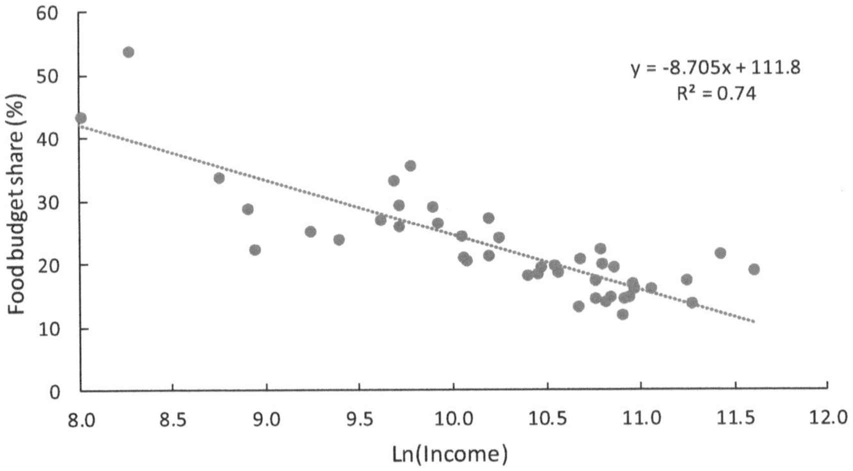

Figure 6.2 Food budget share vs log(income), 45 developed and developing countries.

one of the main causes of obesity, Type 2 diabetes and tooth decay among young children and hence a health and economic burden to the whole of society. There are calls from various health organisations to impose a tax on Sugar-Sweetened Beverages (SSB), with the objective of reducing soft drinks consumption to improve public health. For example, The World Health Organization's (WHO) *Global Action Plan for the Prevention and Control of Non-communicable Diseases 2013–2020*[2] recommended member states consider taxing sugary drinks to address Type 2 diabetes, obesity and tooth decay. Over 30 countries around the globe have introduced taxes on SSBs, in line with the WHO Action Plan recommendations. A number of countries such as Hungary have gone further and introduced taxes on confectionery, salty snacks and other products as well. While the health experts have given strong support for the SSBs tax in many countries, there are a lot of views on who should bear the burden of this tax, consumers or the soft drinks industry. Many economists argue that such a tax will have adverse consequences for the soft drinks industry and its employees. Therefore, analysing soft drinks as part of food consumption has community significance.

Figure 6.3 shows the per capita consumption of soft drinks in 2018 (in litres) of the top ten countries globally. As can be seen, the highest per capita consumption of soft drinks is in Mexico (634 litres) followed closely by the USA (618 litres) and then Brazil (280 litres) and Germany (121 litres). The remainder of the top ten countries only consumed less than 62 litres per capita in 2018.

In 2020, during the COVID-19 pandemic, the USA soft drinks market was estimated to be worth $269.6 billion. The global soft drinks market value is still on the increase and is predicted to reach $1.4 trillion in 2027. The world's second largest economy, China, is forecasted to reach a projected soft drinks market size of US$284.6 billion by 2027 (GlobeNewswire, 2020). Due to

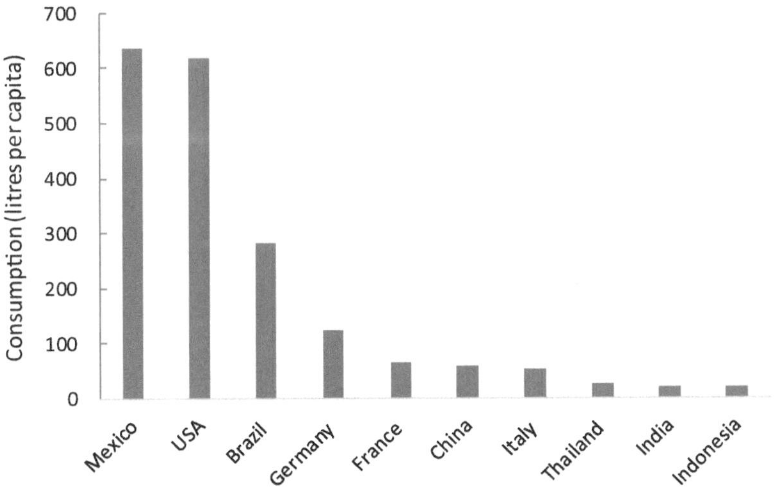

Figure 6.3 Soft drinks consumption, top ten countries, 2018.

continued health warnings, a significant number of people have begun substituting their soft drinks consumption habit with bottled water consumption.

Figure 6.4 presents the per capita bottled water consumption in the top 20 countries (based on 2018 ranking) in 2013 and 2018. As can be seen, in 2018, Mexico and Thailand consumed the most (72 gallons per capita) bottled water followed by Italy (50 gallons) and the USA (42 gallons). Between 2013 and 2018, the consumption of bottled water increased in almost all countries, with the largest increases seen in Thailand, Indonesia, the USA, South Korea, Mexico and the UAE.

6.3.3 Tobacco Consumption

In most developing countries, it is well understood by most consumers that smoking can do serious harm not only to them but also to others in proximity through passive smoking. However, there is still a significant proportion of the population in many countries who smoke for pleasure. In many countries, smoking is totally banned at workplaces and public spaces, and advertising of tobacco products in the media is also banned. However, in a number of less developed countries, health messages about the harmful effects of tobacco use are not well understood by the general public and tobacco companies can easily infiltrate into these countries and still manage to sell their tobacco products.

Columns (2)–(8) of Table 6.1 show the global cigar consumption (in billions) by regions, Africa, America, China, East Mediterranean, Europe,

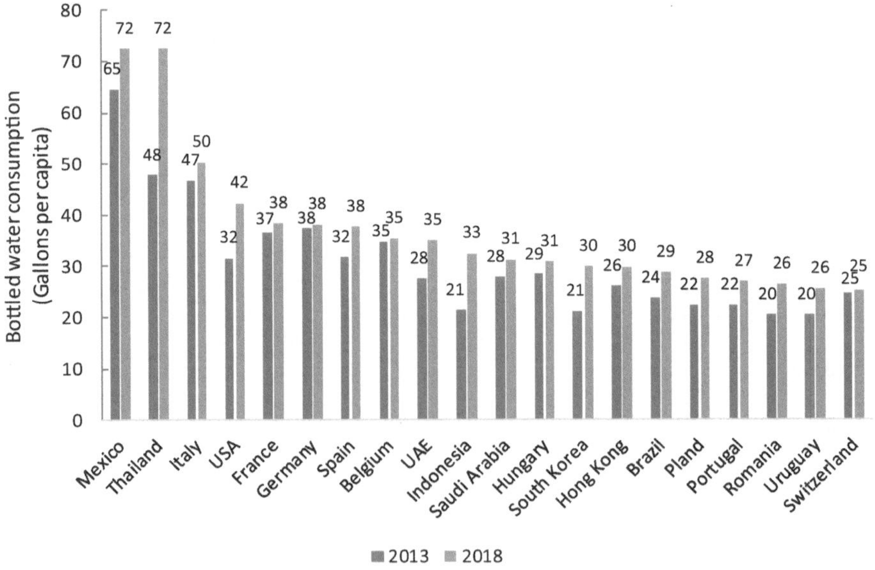

Figure 6.4 Bottled water consumption, top 20 countries, 2013 and 2018.

Table 6.1 Global cigar consumption and its growth rate by regions, 1999–2016

	Consumption (billions)							*Consumption growth rate (percent)*						
Year	*Africa*	*America*	*China*	*East Mediterranean*	*Europe*	*Southeast Asia*	*Western Pacific (excl China)*	*Africa*	*America*	*China*	*East Mediterranean*	*Europe*	*Southeast Asia*	*Western Pacific (excl China)*
(1)	*(2)*	*(3)*	*(4)*	*(5)*	*(6)*	*(7)*	*(8)*	*(9)*	*(10)*	*(11)*	*(12)*	*(13)*	*(14)*	*(15)*
1999	124	774	1638	282	1443	346	622							
2000	123	755	1667	294	1470	354	626	−0.8	−2.5	1.8	4.3	1.9	2.3	0.5
2001	122	749	1702	304	1514	388	617	−0.3	−0.8	2.1	3.1	3.0	9.6	−1.4
2002	126	719	1720	306	1539	422	612	3.0	−3.9	1.0	0.7	1.7	8.8	−0.7
2003	127	734	1760	319	1565	428	611	0.4	2.0	2.3	4.3	1.6	1.4	−0.2
2004	127	720	1817	342	1551	436	620	0.4	−1.9	3.3	7.2	−0.9	1.9	1.5
2005	129	713	1885	353	1567	443	594	1.3	−0.8	3.7	3.1	1.0	1.4	−4.2
2006	130	705	1949	372	1568	465	588	1.0	−1.2	3.4	5.5	0.1	5.1	−1.0
2007	132	683	2058	378	1568	466	592	1.2	−3.1	5.6	1.6	0.0	0.1	0.7
2008	133	658	2143	392	1582	491	581	1.1	−3.6	4.1	3.7	0.9	5.3	−1.9
2009	136	614	2229	393	1548	509	568	2.0	−6.6	4.0	0.4	−2.1	3.6	−2.2
2010	139	599	2317	369	1482	521	557	2.2	−2.5	3.9	−6.3	−4.3	2.5	−1.9
2011	143	582	2406	363	1442	542	534	2.9	−2.8	3.9	−1.7	−2.7	3.9	−4.2
2012	150	563	2462	368	1407	569	540	4.9	−3.4	2.3	1.5	−2.4	5.0	1.2
2013	151	535	2491	376	1325	578	520	1.1	−4.9	1.2	2.3	−5.8	1.6	−3.8
2014	153	518	2550	363	1269	582	488	0.8	−3.3	2.4	−3.4	−4.2	0.7	−6.0
2015	154	505	2490	358	1234	583	462	0.9	−2.5	−2.4	−1.3	−2.8	0.1	−5.3
2016	155	480	2351	371	1209	578	461	0.8	−5.0	−5.6	3.5	−2.0	−0.9	−0.2
Mean	136	645	2091	350	1460	483	566	1.3	−2.8	2.2	1.7	−1.0	3.1	−1.7

Source: The Tobacco Atlas (2016).

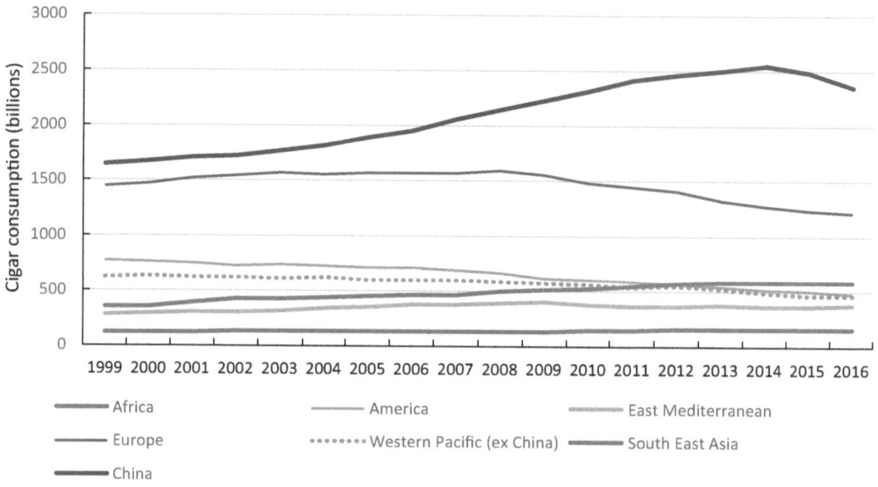

Figure 6.5 Global cigar consumption by regions, 1999–2016.
Source: The Tobacco Atlas (2016).

Southeast Asia and Western Pacific (excluding China), over the years 1999–2016. Figure 6.5 presents a graphical representation of the regional cigar consumption patterns during 1999–2016. Columns (9)–(15) of Table 6.1 give the corresponding growth rates in cigar consumption. The last row presents the sample mean of each column. As can be seen, cigar consumption in numbers has increased in Africa, China, East Mediterranean and Southeast Asia and has fallen in America, Europe and Western Pacific countries. The mean values presented in the last row of the last six columns indicate that, on average, cigar consumption has grown, at a rate of 1.3 percent per annum in Africa, 2.2 percent in China, 1.7 percent in East Mediterranean and 3.1 percent in Southeast Asia, while it has, on average, fallen at a rate of 2.8 percent per annum in America, 1 percent in Europe and 1.7 percent in the Western Pacific regions.

Figure 6.6 shows the rate of smoking in 2015 in the top 25 countries globally by all, male and female persons. As can be seen, the top three countries by all smokers are Kiribati (52.4 percent), Nauru (47.5 percent) and Greece (42.7 percent). By male smokers, the top three countries are Indonesia (76.2 percent), Jordan (70.2 percent) and Kiribati (63.9 percent). The top three countries by female smokers are Nauru (52 percent), Kiribati (40.9 percent) and Serbia (39.7 percent). As can be seen, the smoking rate of males is much higher than that of females in most countries. For example, in Russia, the rate of smoking of males is 59 percent while that of females is only 22.8 percent. Considering Indonesia, males have the highest rate of smoking of 76.2 percent in the world, while female rate of smoking in Indonesia is not even in the top 20 countries. Therefore, countries need to develop policies to reduce the prevalence of smoking among the male population.

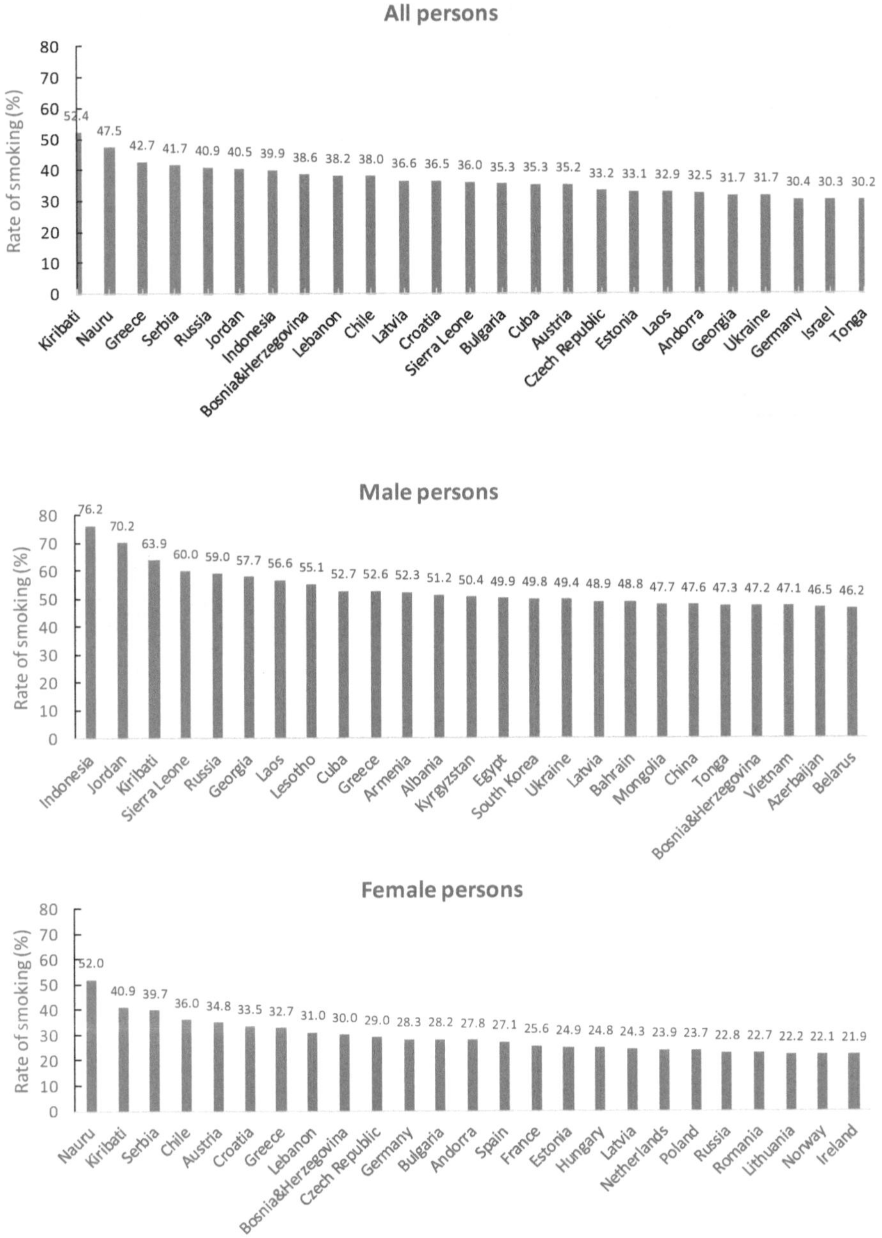

Figure 6.6 Rate of smoking in the top 25 countries, 2015.

Table 6.2 and Figures 6.7 and 6.8 present the rate of smoking in 2015 among males and females in the 45 developed and developing countries. As can be seen, the rate of smoking among males in developing countries

Table 6.2 Rate of smoking by gender, 45 developed and developing countries, 2015

	Country (1)	*All persons* (2)	*Male* (3)	*Female* (4)
Developed countries				
1	Australia	14.9	16.7	13.1
2	Austria	35.2	35.5	34.8
3	Belgium	23.3	26.5	20.0
4	Canada	15.0	17.7	12.2
5	Denmark	17.0	17.6	16.4
6	Finland	20.9	23.2	18.5
7	France	27.7	29.8	25.6
8	Germany	30.4	32.4	28.3
9	Hong Kong	–	–	–
10	Iceland	16.1	17.0	15.1
11	Ireland	22.2	22.4	21.9
12	Israel	30.3	41.2	19.3
13	Italy	24.0	28.3	19.7
14	Japan	22.2	33.7	10.6
15	Luxembourg	23.6	25.8	21.4
16	Netherlands	25.1	26.2	23.9
17	New Zealand	–	–	–
18	Norway	22.3	22.4	22.1
19	Singapore	16.5	28.0	5.0
20	Slovenia	20.2	22.3	18.1
21	South Korea	27.0	49.8	4.2
22	Spain	29.2	31.3	27.1
23	Sweden	20.6	20.4	20.8
24	Switzerland	23.3	26.9	19.7
25	Taiwan	–	–	–
26	UK	19.2	19.9	18.4
27	USA	17.3	19.5	15.0
Mean (*Developed*)		22.6	26.4	18.8
Developing countries				
28	Colombia	11.1	16.0	6.2
29	Czech Republic	33.2	37.4	29.0
30	Estonia	33.1	41.2	24.9
31	Greece	42.7	52.6	32.7
32	Hungary	28.4	32.0	24.8
33	India	11.2	20.4	1.9
34	Latvia	36.6	48.9	24.3
35	Lithuania	30.2	38.1	22.2
36	Malaysia	22.2	43.0	1.4
37	Mexico	13.7	20.8	6.6
38	Philippines	25.8	43.0	8.5
39	Poland	28.1	32.4	23.7
40	Portugal	22.6	31.5	13.7
41	Slovakia	28.7	39.7	17.6
42	South Africa	19.0	31.4	6.5
43	Sri Lanka	14.4	28.4	0.4
44	Thailand	21.9	41.4	2.3
45	Turkey	26.0	39.5	12.4
Mean (*Developing*)		24.9	35.4	14.4
Mean (*All countries*)		23.6	30.3	16.9

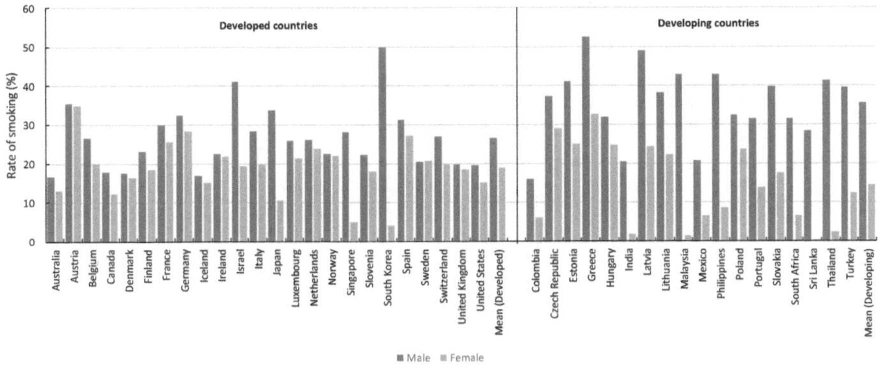

Figure 6.7 Rate of smoking by gender, 45 developed and developing countries, 2015.

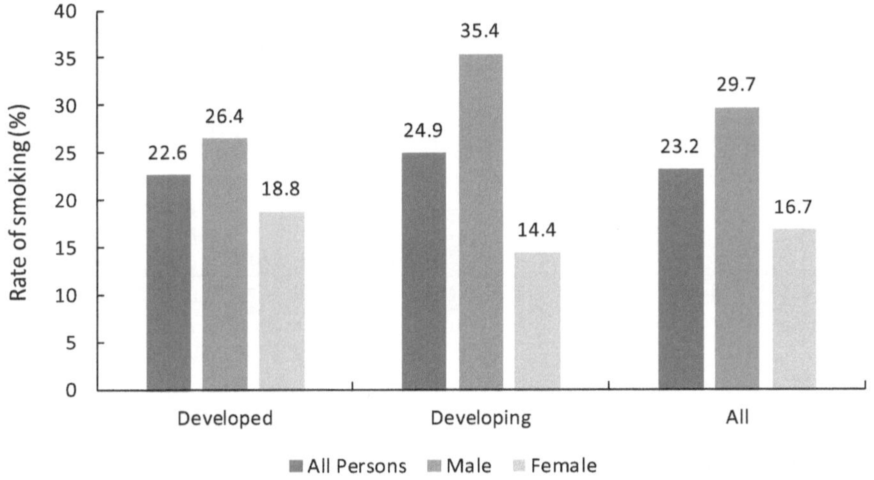

Figure 6.8 Rate of smoking by gender, developed vs developing countries, 2015.

is consistently greater than that in the developed countries. However, the difference in the rate of smoking between males and females in developing countries is much greater than that in developed countries. That is, smoking is a major issue among males in the developing countries.

Figures 6.9 and 6.10 present the number of cigarettes smoked as well as the rate of smoking between males and females in the OECD (developed) countries in 2019. OECD countries are mostly developed countries. Greece followed by Turkey and Israel have the highest cigarette consumption among the OECD countries. A further comparison of the gender-based rate of smoking in all OECD countries shows, as before, the rate of smoking is higher among males than females, except in Iceland. Greece and Turkey have the highest proportion of male smokers (greater than 40 percent) followed by Latvia, Lithuania and Hungary. Greece also has the highest

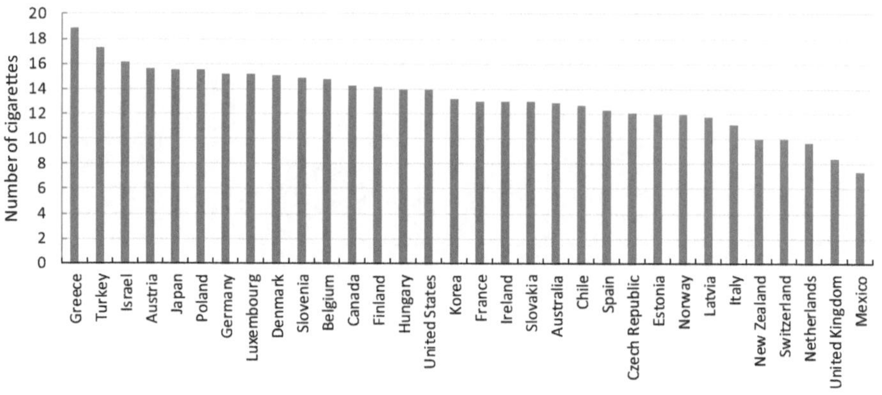

Figure 6.9 Number of cigarettes per smoker per day, aged 15+, OECD countries, 2019.

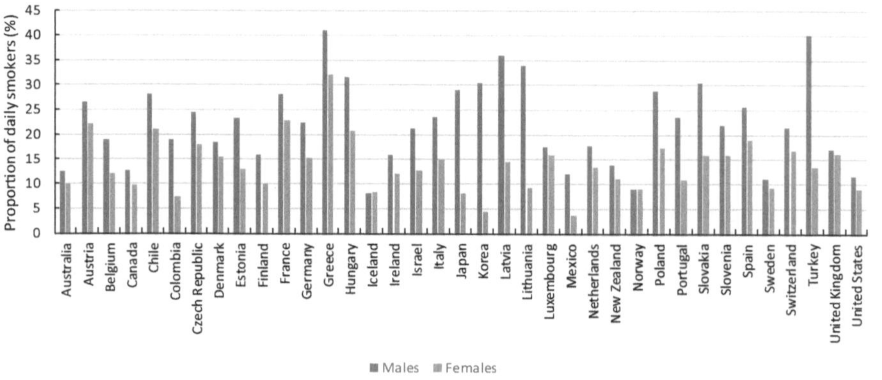

Figure 6.10 Proportion of population (15+) who are daily smokers by gender, OECD countries, 2019.

proportion of female smokers (greater than 30 percent) followed by France, Austria, Chile and Hungary (greater than 20 percent).

Table 6.3 presents time-series data for the percentage prevalence of smoking among males for selected years between 2007 and 2018 for the 45 developed and developing countries. As can be seen from the trend over time, the rate of tobacco consumption among males has declined over the 12-year period in all but four countries (France, Singapore, Portugal and Slovakia), with major decline in countries such as Austria, Canada, Denmark, Sweden, the UK and India.

6.3.4 *Alcohol Consumption*

Alcohol is the most widely used legal drug around the world for celebration, relaxation and pleasure. Alcohol consumption plays an important role in generating 'pleasantries' for many people, thousands of jobs and tax

Table 6.3 Prevalence of tobacco use (percent of adults), developed and developing countries, 2007–2018

	Country (1)	*2007* (2)	*2010* (3)	*2012* (4)	*2014* (5)	*2016* (6)	*2018* (7)
Developed countries							
1	Australia	22.4	20.4	19.3	18.2	17.1	16.2
2	Austria	39.4	36.1	34.2	32.5	30.7	29.1
3	Belgium	27.8	27.0	26.5	25.9	25.5	25.0
4	Canada	28.1	24.7	22.6	20.7	19.1	17.5
5	Denmark	28.5	25.3	23.4	21.6	20.0	18.6
6	Finland	25.0	23.4	22.3	21.3	20.4	19.7
7	France	34.5	34.5	34.5	34.6	34.6	34.6
8	Germany	31.2	30.3	29.7	29.1	28.6	28.0
9	Hong Kong	–	–	–	–	–	–
10	Iceland	22.1	19.4	17.8	16.4	15.0	13.8
11	Ireland	30.2	28.2	26.9	25.9	24.6	23.6
12	Israel	28.7	27.8	27.2	26.6	26.0	25.5
13	Italy	25.1	24.7	24.3	24.0	23.6	23.4
14	Japan	28.3	26.4	25.1	23.9	22.8	21.9
15	Luxembourg	26.2	24.9	24.0	23.3	22.5	21.7
16	Netherlands	28.4	27.0	26.1	25.1	24.3	23.4
17	New Zealand	22.5	20.1	18.6	17.3	16.0	14.8
18	Norway	20.7	18.2	16.7	15.4	14.1	13.0
19	Singapore	16.5	16.5	16.5	16.5	16.6	16.5
20	Slovenia	24.3	23.8	23.5	23.3	23.0	22.7
21	South Korea	29.1	26.9	25.7	24.4	23.3	22.0
22	Spain	33.3	31.6	30.6	29.6	28.8	27.9
23	Sweden	41.7	37.6	35.1	32.9	30.8	28.8
24	Switzerland	27.1	26.6	26.2	25.9	25.4	25.1
25	Taiwan	–	–	–	–	–	–
26	UK	30.3	25.4	23.7	22.0	20.6	19.2
27	USA	29.1	27.9	27.2	26.4	25.7	25.1
Mean (*Developed*)		28.0	26.2	25.1	24.1	23.2	22.3
Developing countries							
28	Colombia	12.4	11.0	10.1	9.3	8.6	7.9
29	Czech Republic	33.4	32.9	32.5	32.2	31.9	31.5
30	Estonia	36.4	34.7	33.6	32.4	31.5	30.5
31	Greece	45.3	43.4	42.1	41.2	40.2	39.1
32	Hungary	35.9	34.2	33.5	32.4	31.4	30.6
33	India	38.5	34.8	32.6	30.6	28.8	27.0
34	Latvia	39.0	38.4	37.9	37.5	37.1	36.7
35	Lithuania	32.4	30.8	29.8	29.0	28.0	27.1
36	Malaysia	25.7	24.5	23.8	23.1	22.5	21.8
37	Mexico	19.4	17.7	16.7	15.7	14.8	13.9
38	Philippines	30.5	28.6	27.4	26.2	25.1	24.3
39	Poland	34.1	31.6	30.1	28.6	27.4	26.0
40	Portugal	26.1	26.4	26.8	27.1	27.5	27.9
41	Slovakia	31.9	31.9	32.0	32.1	32.1	32.3
42	South Africa	35.0	33.9	33.1	32.5	32.0	31.4
43	Sri Lanka	25.5	24.6	24.1	23.6	23.3	22.9
44	Thailand	28.1	26.5	25.4	24.5	23.6	22.8
45	Turkey	32.6	31.7	31.0	30.4	29.8	29.3
Mean (*Developing*)		31.2	29.9	29.0	28.2	27.5	26.8
Mean (*All countries*)		28.8	27.2	26.2	25.3	24.5	23.7

revenue for governments, but binge drinking by a small but significant section of the population impacts heavily on not just the individual drinker but society as a whole. Alcohol misuse results in serious negative issues such as personal health problems, costs to the health system, loss of productivity due to work absenteeism, domestic violence, road accidents/deaths, and costs to the criminal justice system due to various alcohol-related offences. Around the world, drinking alcohol is now considered as one of the major risk factors, most harmful after tobacco. To set up alcohol control policies to reduce alcohol consumption, such as some form of a tax on alcohol, the key input would be the demand elasticities of alcohol. Therefore, analysing the demand for alcohol is an important aspect and the first step in deciding on suitable alcohol control policies.

Figure 6.11 plots the litres per capita of pure alcohol consumption in the OECD countries for the year 2018. As can be seen, countries such as Austria, the Czech Republic, France and Latvia have the highest level of alcohol consumption of about 12 litres per capita of pure alcohol while Israel and Turkey are the lowest alcohol consuming countries with below 3 litres per capita of pure alcohol consumption among the OECD countries. Figure 6.12 plots the alcohol consumption ranking of the top 25 countries by gender, for the year 2018. As can be seen, considering the litres per capita of pure alcohol consumption for all persons, the top three countries are Seychelles (20.5 litres), Uganda (15.1 litres) and the Czech Republic (14.5 litres). Among males, considering the litres per capita of pure alcohol consumption, the top three countries are again Seychelles (32 litres), Uganda (24.6 litres) and the Czech Republic (22.3 litres); among females, the top three countries are Seychelles (9.5 litres), Czech Republic (7 litres) and Lithuania (6.6 litres).

Table 6.4 presents the time-series data of total alcohol consumption per capita (litres of pure alcohol, 15+ years of age) by all persons as well as by gender for the 27 developed and 18 developing countries, respectively, as

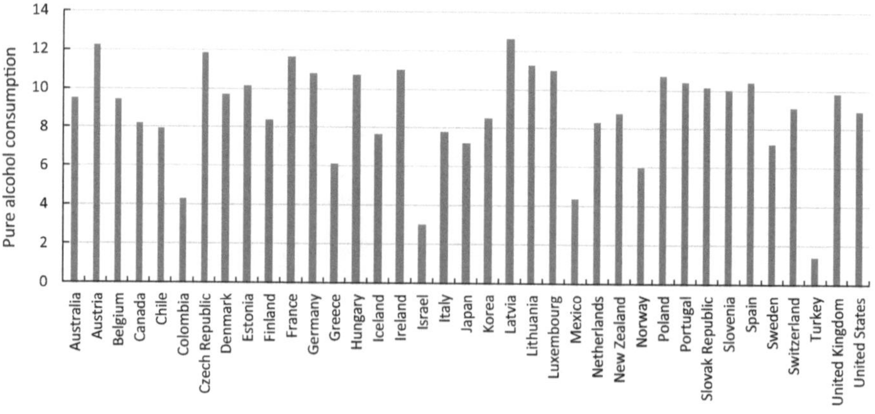

Figure 6.11 Per capita pure alcohol consumption, total population aged 15+, OECD countries, 2018.

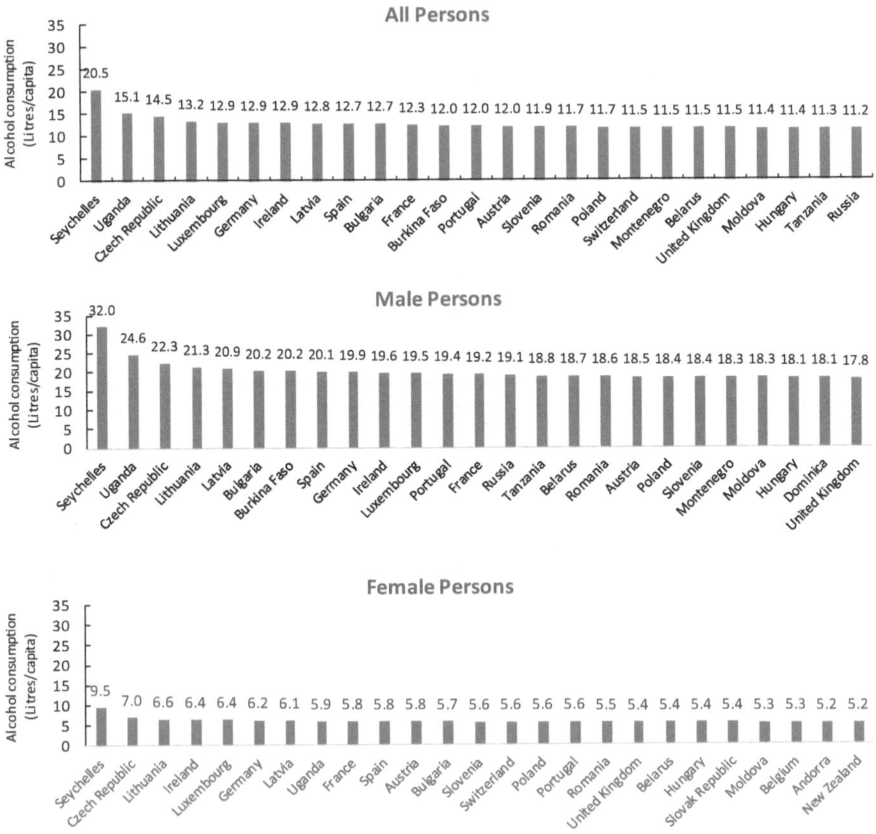

Figure 6.12 Per capita pure alcohol consumption in top 25 countries, 2018.

considered in Chapters 3 and 4 for selected years during 2000–2018. As can be seen, on average, there is a clear slow but steadily decreasing trend among the developed countries among all persons (10.9 litres to 10 litres) as well as across males (16.8 litres to 15.4 litres) and females (5.3 litres to 4.8 litres) between 2000 and 2018. But there is no clear trend among the developing countries in regard to their alcohol consumption. In 2018, the average per capita pure alcohol consumption among the developed countries was 10 litres for all persons, 15.4 litres for males and 4.8 litres for females. The corresponding average consumption for developing countries was 8.6 litres for all persons, 13.7 litres for males and 3.8 litres for females. Overall, in contrast to tobacco consumption discussed in the previous section, alcohol consumption among the three categories (all persons, males and females) appears to be lower in the developing countries compared with the developed countries. In both groups of countries, the average alcohol consumption among females is much lower than among males.

Table 6.4 Total alcohol consumption per capita (litres of pure alcohol, 15+ years of age)

	Country	*All persons*					*Male*					*Female*				
		2000	2005	2010	2015	2018	2000	2005	2010	2015	2018	2000	2005	2010	2015	2018
	(1)	*(2)*	*(3)*	*(4)*	*(5)*	*(6)*	*(7)*	*(8)*	*(9)*	*(10)*	*(11)*	*(12)*	*(13)*	*(14)*	*(15)*	*(16)*
Developed countries																
1	Australia	11.7	12.1	12.4	10.8	10.5	17.9	18.3	18.7	16.4	16.0	5.7	6.0	6.1	5.3	5.2
2	Austria	13.1	12.8	12.2	12.1	12.0	20.4	19.9	19.0	18.7	18.5	6.4	6.2	5.9	5.8	5.8
3	Belgium	12.5	13.1	11.4	11.8	11.1	19.4	20.3	17.7	18.3	17.2	6.0	6.3	5.4	5.6	5.3
4	Canada	–	–	10.1	8.9	8.9	–	–	15.8	13.9	14.0	–	–	4.6	4.0	4.1
5	Denmark	12.7	12.3	11.0	10.4	10.3	19.5	18.9	16.9	16.0	15.8	6.1	5.9	5.2	4.9	4.9
6	Finland	11.7	13.1	12.6	11.2	10.8	18.3	20.4	19.5	17.4	16.8	5.5	6.3	6.0	5.3	5.1
7	France	14.1	13.1	12.4	12.6	12.3	21.8	20.3	19.3	19.7	19.2	6.8	6.3	5.9	6.0	5.8
8	Germany	14.2	13.3	12.6	13.1	12.9	22.0	20.6	19.6	20.1	19.9	6.8	6.4	6.0	6.3	6.2
9	Hong Kong	–	–	–	–	–	–	–	–	–	–	–	–	–	–	–
10	Iceland	7.0	7.7	7.5	8.7	9.1	10.8	11.8	11.4	13.3	13.9	3.3	3.7	3.5	4.2	4.3
11	Ireland	15.1	14.2	12.1	12.5	12.9	22.7	21.3	18.3	19.0	19.6	7.7	7.2	6.0	6.1	6.4
12	Israel	3.1	2.7	3.1	3.9	4.2	4.9	4.3	4.9	6.1	6.6	1.4	1.2	1.4	1.8	1.9
13	Italy	10.4	9.4	7.3	7.6	7.8	16.3	14.9	11.7	12.1	12.5	4.9	4.4	3.3	3.4	3.5
14	Japan	8.2	8.0	7.2	7.9	8.0	12.6	12.3	11.1	12.2	12.3	4.0	3.9	3.5	3.8	3.9
15	Luxembourg	14.3	13.6	13.0	13.2	12.9	21.8	20.7	19.7	19.8	19.5	7.2	6.8	6.4	6.5	6.4
16	Netherlands	11.1	10.7	10.2	9.6	9.6	17.1	16.5	15.7	14.8	14.8	5.3	5.1	4.8	4.5	4.5
17	New Zealand	10.4	10.9	11.3	10.4	10.6	16.2	16.9	17.5	16.1	16.4	5.0	5.3	5.5	5.1	5.2
18	Norway	8.0	8.9	8.9	7.5	7.4	12.2	13.6	13.6	11.4	11.2	3.9	4.3	4.4	3.6	3.6
19	Singapore	2.5	1.8	2.2	2.1	2.0	3.7	2.7	3.3	3.1	3.1	1.3	0.9	1.1	1.1	1.0
20	Slovenia	12.6	12.3	11.5	12.7	11.9	19.6	19.1	17.8	19.7	18.4	6.0	5.9	5.5	6.0	5.6
21	South Korea	12.3	10.6	10.0	10.0	9.7	18.6	16.0	15.1	15.2	14.7	6.2	5.2	4.9	5.0	4.8
22	Spain	12.4	12.8	10.0	11.3	12.7	19.3	19.9	15.7	17.9	20.1	5.9	6.1	4.6	5.1	5.8
23	Sweden	8.5	8.6	9.5	9.1	8.9	13.3	13.4	14.7	14.0	13.7	3.9	4.0	4.4	4.3	4.2
24	Switzerland	12.5	11.6	11.4	11.6	11.5	19.3	18.0	17.6	17.7	17.7	6.1	5.7	5.6	5.6	5.6
25	Taiwan	–	–	–	–	–	–	–	–	–	–	–	–	–	–	–
26	UK	13.7	13.9	12.1	11.2	11.5	21.4	21.5	18.7	17.4	17.8	6.6	6.8	5.7	5.3	5.4
27	USA	9.2	9.5	9.4	9.8	9.9	14.3	14.7	14.5	15.2	15.3	4.3	4.5	4.4	4.6	4.6
Mean (*Developed*)		10.9	10.7	10.1	10.0	10.0	16.8	16.5	15.5	15.4	15.4	5.3	5.2	4.8	4.8	4.8

Developing countries																
28	Colombia	5.6	5.4	5.0	5.8	5.7	9.0	8.8	8.2	9.4	9.3	2.3	2.2	2.1	2.4	2.4
29	Czech Republic	15.0	14.8	14.1	14.3	14.5	23.2	22.8	21.6	22.0	22.3	7.4	7.3	6.9	6.9	7.0
30	Estonia	9.6	15.7	12.4	12.4	9.2	15.8	25.3	20.1	20.1	15.0	4.4	7.6	5.9	5.9	4.4
31	Greece	10.2	10.7	9.7	10.5	10.2	15.9	16.7	15.2	16.6	16.2	4.6	4.9	4.4	4.6	4.5
32	Hungary	14.3	14.6	12.1	11.6	11.4	22.5	23.0	19.3	18.5	18.1	7.0	7.2	5.8	5.5	5.4
33	India	2.3	2.3	4.4	5.5	5.5	3.7	3.8	7.1	9.0	9.0	0.8	0.8	1.5	1.9	1.9
34	Latvia	8.8	12.0	11.6	12.6	12.8	14.7	19.7	19.2	20.7	20.9	4.0	5.7	5.5	6.0	6.1
35	Lithuania	13.4	16.1	15.3	15.4	13.2	21.7	25.8	24.6	24.7	21.3	6.4	8.0	7.6	7.7	6.6
36	Malaysia	1.5	1.3	1.3	0.9	0.9	2.5	2.1	2.1	1.4	1.4	0.6	0.5	0.5	0.3	0.3
37	Mexico	6.4	6.5	5.2	4.9	5.0	10.2	10.3	8.3	7.8	8.0	2.8	2.8	2.2	2.1	2.1
38	Philippines	6.1	5.7	7.0	6.7	6.9	9.7	9.1	11.1	10.7	11.0	2.5	2.3	2.8	2.7	2.8
39	Poland	9.2	10.6	11.2	11.6	11.7	14.6	16.7	17.6	18.3	18.4	4.2	5.0	5.3	5.5	5.6
40	Portugal	14.1	13.4	12.5	11.9	12.0	22.1	21.0	19.9	19.2	19.4	6.8	6.4	5.9	5.5	5.6
41	Slovakia	12.5	12.1	12.0	11.5	11.1	19.6	18.9	18.7	18.0	17.4	5.9	5.8	5.8	5.6	5.4
42	South Africa	10.0	9.6	10.0	9.6	9.5	16.7	15.9	16.7	16.1	15.9	3.8	3.6	3.7	3.5	3.5
43	Sri Lanka	2.2	2.6	3.9	4.1	4.1	3.6	4.2	6.4	6.8	6.8	0.9	1.0	1.6	1.7	1.7
44	Thailand	6.5	6.8	7.7	8.4	8.3	10.5	11.0	12.5	13.5	13.4	2.7	2.9	3.2	3.5	3.5
45	Turkey	2.4	2.1	2.3	2.1	2.1	4.3	3.7	4.1	3.8	3.6	0.7	0.6	0.6	0.6	0.6
Mean (*Developing*)		8.3	9.0	8.8	8.9	8.6	13.3	14.4	14.0	14.2	13.7	3.7	4.1	4.0	4.0	3.8
Mean (*All countries*)		9.8	10.0	9.5	9.5	9.4	15.4	15.6	14.9	14.9	14.7	4.6	4.7	4.5	4.5	4.4

6.4 Preliminary Data Analysis of the Disaggregated Food Group – Time-Series Data

In Chapter 3, we used disaggregated data where a consumer basket consists of 12 commodities, including food, alcohol and restaurants. In Chapter 4, alcohol was combined with food. In this section, as discussed earlier, we disaggregate the food group into three commodities, namely food, alcohol and restaurants. We further use the price and consumption data for food, alcohol and restaurants, used in Chapter 3, to present some preliminary conditional data analysis in the form of budget shares, Divisia indices and scatter plots.

Table 6.5 presents the unconditional and conditional budget shares for food, alcohol and restaurants and the budget share of the food group consisting of these three items for the 45 countries. The unconditional budget shares ($\overline{w}_{it}$) in columns (2)–(4) are reproduced from Table 3.5 (columns (2), (3) and (12)) of Chapter 3, and the group budget share ($\overline{W}_{gt}$) in column (5) is a simple addition of the three unconditional budget shares in columns (2)–(4). The conditional budget shares ($\overline{w}'_{it}$) presented in columns (6)–(8) for each item are the proportion of expenditures on food, alcohol and restaurants expressed as proportion of the total expenditure on the food group. Alternatively, the conditional budget shares ($\overline{w}'_{it}$) can also be calculated as the unconditional budget share of each item in columns (2)–(4) divided by the group budget share in column (5). As can be seen from the last row of the table, the mean unconditional budget shares for all countries combined for food, alcohol and restaurants are 15.4 percent, 5 percent and 7.5 percent, respectively. The mean food group unconditional budget share for all countries is 28.8 percent. This means that a typical consumer allocates about one-third of their income on the food group. The mean conditional budget for all countries for food, alcohol and restaurants within the food group are 54.6 percent, 18.0 percent and 27.3 percent, respectively. This means that, if a consumer allocates \$100 on food group expenditure, out of that \$100, \$54.60 will be spent on food, \$18 on alcohol and \$27.30 on restaurants.

In Chapter 3, we summarised the consumption data of all consumer goods in the form of Divisia index numbers. Now, we summarise the consumption data for food, alcohol and restaurants in the form of conditional Divisia index for a group.

To measure the growth in consumption of the food group, we use the conditional Divisia volume index for a group S_g, DQ_{gt}, for period t, which is the weighted sum of individual quantity log-changes of items within the group S_g with weights being the corresponding conditional budget shares $\overline{w}'_{it}$ defined as

$$DQ_{gt} = \sum_{i \in S_g} \overline{w}'_{it} Dq_{it}, \quad t = 1,\ldots,T, \tag{6.1}$$

Table 6.5 Unconditional and conditional budget shares at sample means, food group, 45 countries

		Unconditional				*Conditional*		
	Country (1)	*Food* (2)	*Alcohol* (3)	*Restaurants* (4)	*Food group* (5)	*Food* (6)	*Alcohol* (7)	*Restaurants* (8)
Developed countries								
1	Australia	10.8	3.8	7.0	21.6	49.8	17.8	32.4
2	Austria	10.3	3.5	11.7	25.4	40.4	13.6	46.0
3	Belgium	13.2	3.9	5.6	22.8	58.2	17.2	24.6
4	Canada	10.6	4.1	7.3	22.0	48.0	18.6	33.5
5	Denmark	11.7	4.3	5.5	21.5	54.5	19.8	25.7
6	Finland	16.1	5.9	6.6	28.6	55.5	20.9	23.7
7	France	16.5	4.2	6.1	26.7	61.2	15.5	23.3
8	Germany	10.8	3.5	5.0	19.4	55.8	18.2	26.0
9	Hong Kong[a]	–	–	–	18.4	–	–	–
10	Iceland	14.4	4.9	8.2	27.5	52.1	18.0	29.9
11	Ireland	10.5	6.7	13.9	31.1	43.3	27.6	29.1
12	Israel	15.7	2.4	6.1	24.2	64.9	10.0	25.1
13	Italy	15.1	4.2	8.9	28.2	53.5	15.0	31.5
14	Japan[a]	–	–	–	19.8	–	–	–
15	Luxembourg	9.5	9.2	7.3	26.0	36.6	35.2	28.2
16	Netherlands	11.1	3.2	7.2	21.5	51.7	14.8	33.5
17	New Zealand	14.2	5.4	5.8	25.3	56.0	21.1	22.9
18	Norway	16.7	4.8	5.1	26.6	62.1	18.0	19.8
19	Singapore[a]	–	–	–	16.0	–	–	–
20	Slovenia	15.8	5.3	6.7	27.9	56.8	19.1	24.1
21	South Korea	22.8	4.1	8.4	35.4	62.4	11.3	26.3
22	Spain	13.8	4.3	16.4	34.4	40.1	12.3	47.6
23	Sweden	12.6	4.0	5.2	21.8	58.22	18.81	22.98
24	Switzerland	9.4	4.1	7.5	21.0	44.8	19.4	35.9
25	Taiwan[a]	–	–	–	24.1	–	–	–
26	UK	8.6	4.3	9.5	22.4	38.5	19.3	42.3
27	USA	9.2	2.5	6.6	18.3	49.6	13.7	36.7
Mean (*Developed*)		13.0	4.5	7.7	24.4	51.9	18.1	30.0
Developing countries								
28	Colombia	18.9	3.4	11.2	33.4	56.4	10.2	33.4
29	Czech Republic	16.1	8.2	8.0	32.3	49.7	25.3	25.0
30	Estonia	20.9	8.0	6.6	35.4	58.8	22.6	18.6
31	Greece	16.3	4.5	13.7	34.5	47.2	13.0	39.8
32	Hungary	18.5	7.2	6.4	32.1	57.6	22.4	20.1
33	India[a]	–	–	–	50.6	–	–	–
34	Latvia	24.1	8.9	5.5	38.5	62.1	23.1	14.8
35	Lithuania	27.8	7.6	2.9	38.4	72.2	20.1	7.7
36	Malaysia[a]	–	–	–	23.8	–	–	–
37	Mexico	22.3	2.7	4.5	29.4	75.7	9.1	15.2
38	Philippines[a]	–	–	–	43.2	–	–	–
39	Poland	21.4	7.8	3.0	32.2	66.4	24.3	9.3
40	Portugal	16.9	3.4	10.7	31.0	54.4	11.0	34.6
41	Slovakia	20.5	5.7	6.6	32.8	62.3	17.3	20.4
42	South Africa[a]	–	–	–	31.4	–	–	–
43	Sri Lanka[a]	–	–	–	53.6	–	–	–
44	Thailand[a]	–	–	–	33.6	–	–	–
45	Turkey[a]	–	–	–	33.1	–	–	–
Mean (*Developing*)		20.3	6.1	7.2	35.5	60.3	18.0	21.7
Mean (*All countries*)		15.4	5.0	7.5	28.8	54.6	18.0	27.3

[a] Disaggregated data are not available.

where $\bar{w}'_{it} = (1/2)(w'_{it} + w'_{it-1})$ is the arithmetic average of the conditional budget shares of commodity i in periods t and $t-1$. The Divisia volume index for the group S_g averaged over the whole sample period for each country is calculated as

$$D\bar{Q}_g = \frac{1}{T}\sum_{t=1}^{T} DQ_{gt}. \tag{6.2}$$

Growth in the price of the food group can be measured by the Divisia price index for group S_g, DP_{gt}, for period t, which is the weighted sum of individual price log-changes with the corresponding conditional budget shares being the weights, and is given by

$$DP_{gt} = \sum_{i \in S_g} \bar{w}'_{it} Dp_{it}, \quad t = 1, \ldots, T. \tag{6.3}$$

The Divisia price index for the group S_g averaged over the whole sample period for each country is calculated as,

$$D\bar{P}_g = \frac{1}{T}\sum_{t=1}^{T} DP_{gt} \tag{6.4}$$

The Divisia quantity index (DQ_{gt}) and the Divisia price index (DP_{gt}) are first-order moments for the group. The second-order moments for the group, the Divisia quantity and price variances that correspond to the Divisia volume and price indices for the group S_g are

$$K_{gt} = \sum_{i \in Sg} \bar{w}'_{it}\left[Dq_{it} - DQ_{gt}\right]^2, \quad t = 1, \ldots, T, \tag{6.5}$$

and

$$\Pi_{gt} = \sum_{i \in Sg} \bar{w}'_{it}\left[Dp_{it} - DP_{gt}\right]^2, \quad t = 1, \ldots, T. \tag{6.6}$$

These two variances measure the degree to which the quantities and prices of the individual commodities change disproportionately within the group. When all quantities and prices change proportionately, these two variances will vanish.

To measure the co-movement of prices and quantities within the group, we define the Divisia price-quantity correlation for group S_g as

$$\rho_{gt} = \frac{\Gamma_{gt}}{\sqrt{K_{gt}\Pi_{gt}}}, \quad t = 1, \ldots, T, \tag{6.7}$$

where $\Gamma_{gt} = \sum_{i \in S_g} \overline{w}'_{it}\left(Dp_{it} - DP_{gt}\right)\left(Dq_{it} - DQ_{gt}\right)$ is the Divisia price-quantity covariance between price and quantities of the group S_g. Since relative prices and relative consumptions are expected to move in the opposite direction, we would expect the Divisia price-quantity correlation for the group S_g to be negative. The corresponding variances and correlation sample period averages for each country are calculated as

$$\bar{K}_g = \frac{1}{T}\sum_{t=1}^{T} K_{gt},\ \bar{\Pi}_g = \frac{1}{T}\sum_{t=1}^{T} \Pi_{gt},\ \text{and}\ \bar{\rho}_g = \frac{1}{T}\sum_{t=1}^{T} \rho_{gt}. \tag{6.8}$$

Furthermore, if we regress relative consumption $(Dq_{it} - DQ_{gt})$ against relative price, $(Dp_{it} - DP_{gt})$, then under the assumption of unitary income elasticity, we can show that the Weighted Least Squares (WLS) estimate of the slope of this regression line is Γ_{gt}/Π_{gt}, which is income flexibility ϕ_t, introduced in Chapter 3 (for example, see Selvanathan and Selvanathan 2003b) which is calculated as

$$\phi_{gt} = \frac{\Gamma_{gt}}{\Pi_{gt}} = \rho_{gt}\sqrt{\frac{K_{gt}}{\Pi_{gt}}}. \tag{6.9}$$

The income flexibility for the group S_g averaged over the whole sample period for each country is calculated as,

$$\bar{\phi}_g = \frac{1}{T}\sum_{t=1}^{T} \phi_{gt} \tag{6.10}$$

Table 6.6 presents the price-consumption data for the group in the form of Divisia summary measures. Column (2) of the table gives the average growth in consumption of the food group given by equation (6.2) for each country, column (3) gives the average growth in prices of the food group given by equation (6.4), column (4) gives the quantity variance, column (5) gives the price variance, and column (6) gives the price-quantity correlations given by equation (6.8). As can be seen from the overall 45 country average given in the last row of the table, consumption of the food group has increased on average at a rate of 1.11 percent per annum and price of the food group has increased at a rate of 3.41 percent per annum. A comparison of columns (4) and (5) for each country reveals that, for a majority of the countries, quantity variance systematically exceeds the price variance. This can be further observed in Figure 6.13 where we plot the quantity variance against the price variance together with a 45° line. As can be seen, most of the data points are scattered above the 45° line, indicating that the quantity variance systematically exceeds the price variance. Considering the Divisia

Table 6.6 Mean Divisia price and quantity indices, variances and correlation, and income flexibility, food group, 45 countries

	Country *(1)*	*Divisia quantity index (DQ)* *(2)*	*Divisia price index (DP)* *(3)*	*Divisia quantity variance* *(4)*	*Divisia price variance* *(5)*	*Divisia price-quantity correlation* *(6)*	*Income flexibility* *(7)*
Developed countries							
1	Australia	0.48	3.83	3.87	3.22	−0.48	−0.53
2	Austria	0.48	2.23	1.77	0.49	−0.26	−0.49
3	Belgium	−0.06	2.44	2.40	1.01	−0.06	−0.09
4	Canada	0.00	3.21	3.04	4.84	−0.34	−0.27
5	Denmark	−0.03	1.96	3.97	1.10	−0.25	−0.47
6	Finland	0.72	3.97	4.41	4.91	−0.24	−0.23
7	France	1.02	4.35	1.45	2.09	−0.43	−0.36
8	Germany	−0.32	1.74	3.97	1.53	−0.54	−0.87
9	Hong Kong[a]	–	–	–	–	–	–
10	Iceland	3.04	4.42	9.69	4.67	−0.15	−0.22
11	Ireland	4.01	−1.83	34.37	10.90	−0.87	−1.54
12	Israel	0.66	4.28	10.67	4.48	−0.21	−0.32
13	Italy	0.13	2.18	2.14	1.12	−0.45	−0.62
14	Japan[a]	–	–	–	–	–	–
15	Luxembourg	−1.00	2.97	19.98	1.21	−0.21	−0.85
16	Netherlands	0.30	2.45	2.84	1.66	−0.17	−0.22
17	New Zealand	0.69	2.84	7.47	2.26	−0.46	−0.84
18	Norway	1.01	4.93	5.01	2.35	−0.35	−0.51
19	Singapore[a]	–	–	–	–	–	–
20	Slovenia	0.57	4.77	4.43	4.39	−0.41	−0.41
21	South Korea	2.20	7.95	5.76	6.52	−0.14	−0.13
22	Spain	−0.74	2.96	3.48	2.18	0.07	0.09
23	Sweden	−0.96	3.88	28.84	35.61	−0.54	−0.49
24	Switzerland	0.82	−0.32	9.67	3.01	−0.85	−1.52
25	Taiwan[a]	–	–	–	–	–	–
26	UK	0.09	2.87	1.86	2.89	−0.28	−0.22
27	USA	0.52	3.98	2.11	2.39	−0.12	−0.11
Mean (*Developed*)		0.59	3.13	7.53	4.56	−0.34	−0.49

Developing countries							
28	Colombia	1.52	5.44	2.95	2.26	−0.29	−0.33
29	Czech Republic	1.49	3.00	4.45	3.69	−0.23	−0.25
30	Estonia	3.89	5.23	15.57	6.80	−0.31	−0.47
31	Greece	0.61	2.91	18.19	8.73	−0.45	−0.65
32	Hungary	0.84	7.53	6.77	7.95	−0.52	−0.48
33	India[a]	–	–	–	–	–	–
34	Latvia	3.21	4.80	44.89	5.61	0.11	0.31
35	Lithuania	3.77	3.08	13.97	8.57	−0.37	−0.47
36	Malaysia[a]	–	–	–	–	–	–
37	Mexico	0.88	5.25	4.64	2.79	−0.20	−0.26
38	Philippines[a]	–	–	–	–	–	–
39	Poland	1.66	4.19	22.05	20.75	−0.33	−0.34
40	Portugal	4.20	−0.74	32.80	34.58	−0.64	−0.62
41	Slovakia	2.04	3.03	10.27	5.22	−0.07	−0.10
42	South Africa[a]	–	–	–	–	–	–
43	Sri Lanka[a]	–	–	–	–	–	–
44	Thailand[a]	–	–	–	–	–	–
45	Turkey[a]	–	–	–	–	–	–
Mean (*Developing*)		2.19	3.97	16.05	9.72	−0.30	−0.33
Mean (*All countries*)		1.11	3.41	10.29	6.23	−0.32	−0.44

Note: All entries in columns (2) and (3) are to be divided by 100, and entries in column (4) and (5) are to be divided by 10,000.
[a] Disaggregated data are not available.

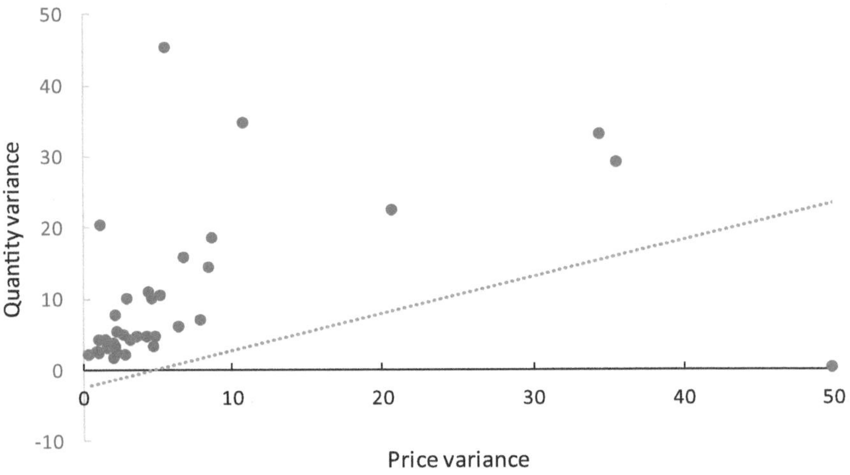

Figure 6.13 Quantity variance against price variance, 45 countries.

price-quantity correlations presented in column (6), it can be seen that most of the correlations are negative as they should be with an average of −0.32. The last column of the table gives the estimates for income flexibility calculated using equation (6.10). As can be seen, most of the estimates are negative with a cross-country average of −0.44. The above observations are well in agreement with the unconditional analysis presented in Chapter 3 as well as with many previous studies (e.g., see Chen 2001; Clements et al. 2020; Rathnayaka et al. 2019; Selvanathan et al. 2021).

Table 6.7 tabulates the percentage signs of relative prices (RP) and relative consumption (RC) in the form of four combinations (positive RP, positive RC), (positive RP, negative RC), (negative RP, positive RC) and (negative RP, negative RC). As can be seen, more than two-thirds of the pair (RP, RC) observations fall in the (positive RP, negative RC) and (negative RP, positive RC) categories, for each group of countries as well as for all 45 countries, giving support for the law of demand, meaning that the demand for a commodity falls when relative price increases.

In Figure 6.14, for ten selected countries, we plot relative consumption against relative price for the food group. Table 6.8 presents, for each country, the slope of the fitted regression line for each individual and pooled data across the three commodities. The slope can be interpreted as an estimate for income flexibility, ϕ. As can be seen, a majority of the ϕ estimates are in the range −0.4 to −0.6, with an overall average very close to −0.6. We have observed such values of income flexibility with unconditional data as well, as seen in the last column of Table 6.8 and these values are well in agreement with the value −0.5 reported in many previous studies (e.g., Clements et al. 2020; Rathnayaka et al. 2019; Theil and Suhm 1981).

Table 6.7 Frequency of same and opposite signs of relative prices and relative consumption of the food group, 45 countries

Country	*Positive consumption*		*Negative consumption*		*Opposite signs*
	Positive price	*Negative price*	*Positive price*	*Negative price*	*(3) + (4)*
(1)	*(2)*	*(3)*	*(4)*	*(5)*	*(6)*
Developed countries					
1 Australia	16	30	34	20	64
2 Austria	17	37	33	13	70
3 Belgium	26	23	30	21	53
4 Canada	23	26	30	21	56
5 Denmark	18	27	28	27	55
6 Finland	28	24	29	19	53
7 France	18	31	35	17	66
8 Germany	16	39	30	16	69
9 Hong Kong[a]	–	–	–	–	–
10 Iceland	25	25	26	25	51
11 Ireland	4	44	48	4	92
12 Israel	25	21	26	28	47
13 Italy	12	37	39	12	76
14 Japan[a]	–	–	–	–	–
15 Luxembourg	22	28	25	25	53
16 Netherlands	19	21	35	25	56
17 New Zealand	14	30	35	22	65
18 Norway	12	31	41	16	72
19 Singapore[a]	–	–	–	–	–
20 Slovenia	15	28	38	18	66
21 South Korea	19	29	27	24	56
22 Spain	30	30	21	19	51
23 Sweden	17	43	33	7	76
24 Switzerland	4	41	48	7	89
25 Taiwan[a]	–	–	–	–	–
26 UK	25	35	27	13	62
27 USA	19	30	32	19	62
Mean (*Developed*)	18	31	33	18	64
Developing countries					
28 Colombia	17	29	31	24	60
29 Czech Republic	22	25	28	25	53
30 Estonia	20	33	32	15	65
31 Greece	15	37	35	13	72
32 Hungary	13	35	43	8	78
33 India[a]	–	–	–	–	–
34 Latvia	30	21	25	25	46
35 Lithuania	12	35	39	14	74
36 Malaysia	–	–	–	–	–
37 Mexico	15	30	36	18	66
38 Philippines[a]	–	–	–	–	–
39 Poland	15	28	38	18	66
40 Portugal	10	28	55	7	83
41 Slovakia	22	32	25	22	57
42 South Africa[a]	–	–	–	–	–
43 Sri Lanka[a]	–	–	–	–	–
44 Thailand[a]	–	–	–	–	–
45 Turkey[a]	–	–	–	–	–
Mean (*Developing*)	17	30	35	17	65
Mean (*All countries*)	18	31	33	18	64

[a] Disaggregated data are not available.

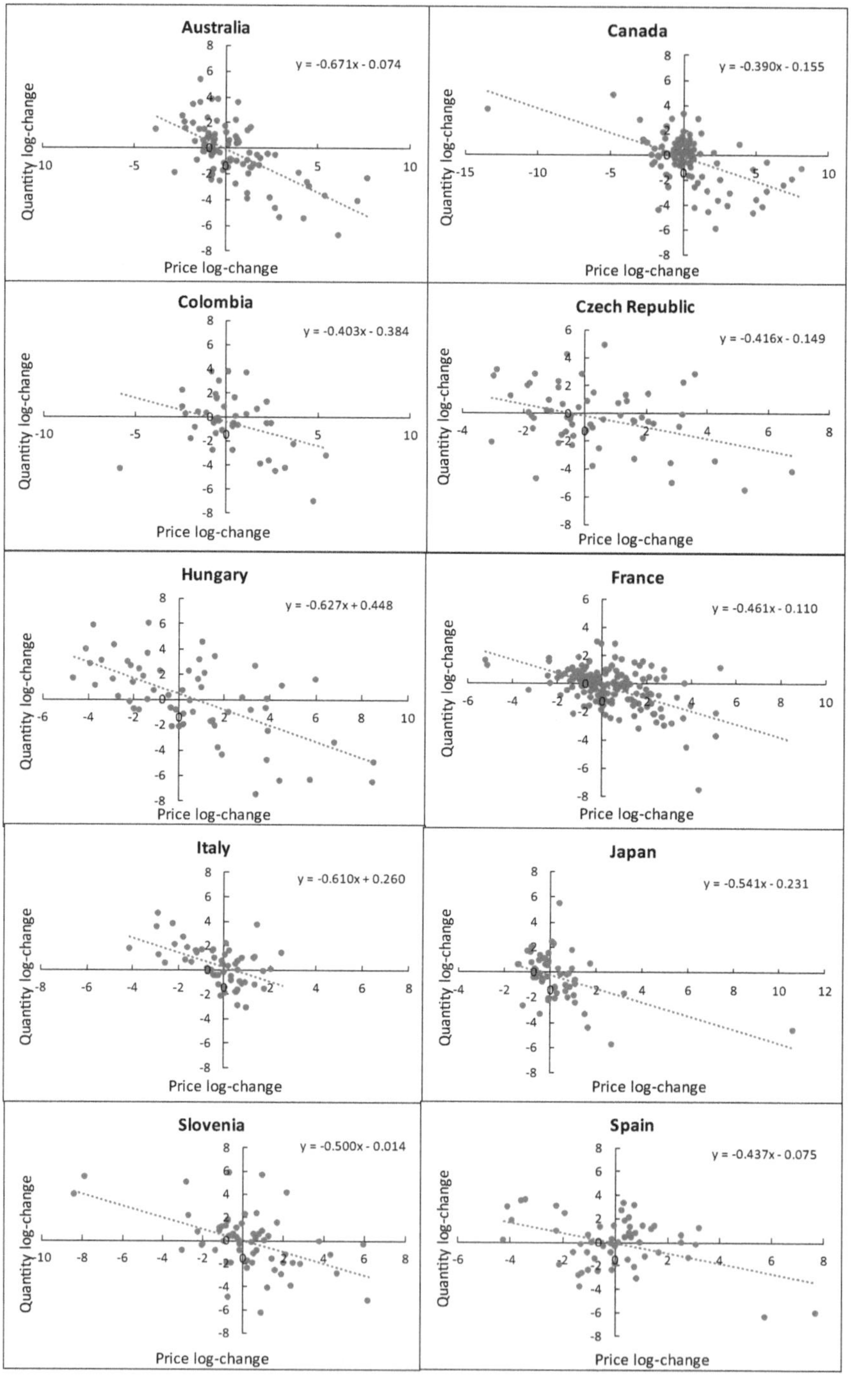

Figure 6.14 Relative quantity vs relative price, food group, ten selected countries.

Table 6.8 Estimates of income flexibility for the food group and disaggregated food group, 45 countries

	Country (1)	*Food* (2)	*Alcohol* (3)	*Restaurants* (4)	*Food group*[b] (5)
Developed countries					
1	Australia	−0.42	−0.51	−0.58	−0.67
2	Austria	−0.96	0.25	−1.04	−0.23
3	Belgium	−0.43	−0.17	−0.69	−0.24
4	Canada	−0.52	−0.28	−0.45	−0.39
5	Denmark	−0.50	−0.91	−0.76	−0.75
6	Finland	−0.40	−0.46	−0.10	−0.38
7	France	−0.48	−0.44	−0.56	−0.46
8	Germany	−0.89	−1.04	−1.04	−1.07
9	Hong Kong[a]	–	–	–	–
10	Iceland	0.14	−0.59	0.16	−0.33
11	Ireland	−1.82	−1.79	−2.03	−1.65
12	Israel	−0.40	−0.19	−0.05	−0.21
13	Italy	−0.82	−0.69	−0.44	−0.61
14	Japan[a]	–	–	–	–
15	Luxembourg	−0.36	−1.46	−1.45	−0.88
16	Netherlands	−0.46	−0.67	−0.47	−0.68
17	New Zealand	−0.96	−0.70	0.21	−0.84
18	Norway	−0.99	−1.08	−0.48	−0.80
19	Singapore[a]	–	–	–	–
20	Slovenia	−0.71	−0.39	−0.52	−0.50
21	South Korea	−0.33	−0.43	−0.19	−0.36
22	Spain	−0.31	−0.52	0.78	−0.44
23	Sweden	−0.51	−0.92	−0.87	−0.86
24	Switzerland	−1.70	−1.80	−1.89	−1.73
25	Taiwan[a]	–	–	–	–
26	UK	−0.16	−0.31	0.09	−0.23
27	USA	−0.54	−0.47	−0.40	−0.45
Mean (*Developed*)		−0.63	−0.68	−0.56	−0.64
Developing countries					
28	Colombia	−0.06	−0.22	1.46	−0.40
29	Czech Republic	−0.12	0.10	−0.55	−0.42
30	Estonia	−0.50	−0.31	−0.50	−0.35
31	Greece	−0.59	−0.83	−0.36	−0.72
32	Hungary	−0.62	−0.96	−0.27	−0.63
33	India[a]	–	–	–	–
34	Latvia	−0.50	0.18	1.02	0.28
35	Lithuania	−0.53	−0.55	−1.03	−0.81
36	Malaysia[a]	–	–	–	–
37	Mexico	−0.58	−0.91	−0.18	−0.67
38	Philippines	–	–	–	–
39	Poland	−0.84	−0.53	−0.93	−0.94
40	Portugal	−0.90	−0.78	−0.92	−0.91
41	Slovakia	−0.86	−0.32	−0.97	−0.70
42	South Africa[a]	–	–	–	–
43	Sri Lanka[a]	–	–	–	–
44	Thailand[a]	–	–	–	–
45	Turkey[a]	–	–	–	–
Mean (*Developing*)		−0.56	−0.47	−0.29	−0.57
Mean (*All countries*)		−0.61	−0.61	−0.47	−0.62

[a] Disaggregated data are not available.

[b] The income flexibility presented in Table 6.6 for the food group may not be the same as that in column (5) due to differences in the methods used.

Table 6.9 Estimated income and own-price elasticities, double-log demand equation, food group, 45 countries

Country		*Income elasticity*			*Price elasticity*		
	Country (1)	*Food* (2)	*Alcohol* (3)	*Restaurants* (4)	*Food* (5)	*Alcohol* (6)	*Restaurants* (7)
Developed countries							
1	Australia	0.61 (0.12)	0.58 (0.22)	1.84 (0.19)	−0.39 (0.16)	−0.56 (0.14)	−0.66 (0.24)
2	Austria	0.69 (0.28)	1.49 (0.48)	1.18 (0.32)	−0.83 (0.33)	0.26 (0.45)	−0.91 (0.53)
3	Belgium	1.06 (0.23)	1.47 (0.50)	0.63 (0.44)	−0.42 (0.38)	−0.17 (0.36)	−0.61 (0.47)
4	Canada	0.32 (0.08)	0.98 (0.22)	1.90 (0.16)	−0.14 (0.08)	−0.28 (0.08)	−0.41 (0.22)
5	Denmark	0.75 (0.13)	0.42 (0.38)	2.10 (0.18)	−0.62 (0.33)	−0.92 (0.38)	−1.19 (0.26)
6	Finland	0.64 (0.09)	1.17 (0.18)	1.68 (0.18)	−0.41 (0.12)	−0.45 (0.11)	−0.28 (0.22)
7	France	0.83 (0.06)	1.04 (0.20)	1.48 (0.18)	−0.43 (0.10)	−0.44 (0.09)	−0.74 (0.15)
8	Germany	1.01 (0.20)	0.23 (0.47)	1.56 (0.30)	−0.89 (0.28)	−0.89 (0.30)	−1.11 (0.37)
9	Hong Kong[a]	–	–	–	–	–	–
10	Iceland	0.74 (0.08)	1.00 (0.21)	1.50 (0.18)	−0.02 (0.23)	−0.64 (0.29)	−0.27 (0.42)
11	Ireland	0.97 (0.05)	0.96 (0.05)	1.05 (0.05)	−1.77 (0.21)	−1.78 (0.13)	−1.95 (0.14)
12	Israel	0.38 (0.14)	−0.17 (0.33)	2.97 (0.41)	−0.46 (0.30)	−0.19 (0.15)	−0.20 (0.48)
13	Italy	0.73 (0.07)	1.18 (0.21)	1.73 (0.16)	−1.14 (0.22)	−0.64 (0.23)	−1.80 (0.37)
14	Japan	–	–	–	–	–	–
15	Luxembourg	0.87 (0.13)	1.31 (0.16)	0.78 (0.08)	−0.37 (0.86)	−0.12 (1.01)	−0.75 (0.92)
16	Netherlands	0.51 (0.07)	0.76 (0.23)	1.83 (0.15)	−0.26 (0.19)	−0.73 (0.24)	−0.50 (0.31)
17	New Zealand	0.89 (0.08)	0.67 (0.16)	1.54 (0.26)	−0.95 (0.26)	−0.74 (0.22)	−0.15 (0.91)
18	Norway	0.94 (0.07)	1.01 (0.16)	1.12 (0.19)	−0.92 (0.21)	−1.08 (0.16)	−0.44 (0.31)
19	Singapore[a]	–	–	–	–	–	–
20	Slovenia	0.89 (0.08)	1.18 (0.30)	1.18 (0.19)	−0.65 (0.16)	−0.34 (0.24)	−0.52 (0.20)
21	South Korea	0.90 (0.06)	0.72 (0.15)	1.30 (0.13)	−0.41 (0.15)	−0.42 (0.09)	−0.27 (0.15)
22	Spain	0.48 (0.11)	0.75 (0.21)	1.42 (0.12)	−0.40 (0.35)	−0.61 (0.17)	−0.05 (0.39)
23	Sweden	1.02 (0.02)	0.78 (0.09)	1.35 (0.05)	−0.43 (0.13)	−0.68 (0.10)	−0.43 (0.07)
24	Switzerland	1.06 (0.08)	0.74 (0.12)	0.94 (0.08)	−1.77 (0.22)	−1.58 (0.18)	−1.97 (0.13)
25	Taiwan[a]	–	–	–	–	–	–
26	UK	0.72 (0.10)	0.76 (0.21)	1.36 (0.17)	−0.32 (0.14)	−0.39 (0.19)	−0.32 (0.27)
27	USA	0.83 (0.08)	0.60 (0.18)	1.44 (0.13)	−0.58 (0.10)	−0.49 (0.08)	−0.67 (0.18)
Mean (*Developed*)		0.77 (0.03)	0.85 (0.06)	1.47 (0.04)	−0.63 (0.06)	−0.60 (0.06)	−0.70 (0.08)

Developing countries							
28	Colombia	0.82 (0.13)	0.83 (0.55)	1.54 (0.30)	−0.14 (0.17)	−0.23 (0.25)	−0.60 (0.29)
29	Czech	0.83 (0.19)	0.78 (0.20)	1.61 (0.29)	−0.24 (0.30)	0.17 (0.26)	−0.71 (0.24)
30	Estonia	0.82 (0.11)	1.23 (0.23)	1.29 (0.26)	−0.27 (0.43)	−0.15 (0.32)	−0.69 (0.48)
31	Greece	1.08 (0.18)	1.19 (0.31)	0.84 (0.28)	−0.59 (0.35)	−0.82 (0.24)	−0.33 (0.45)
32	Hungary	0.99 (0.08)	1.12 (0.19)	0.83 (0.22)	−0.62 (0.11)	−0.97 (0.14)	−0.21 (0.25)
33	India	–	–	–	–	–	–
34	Latvia	0.69 (0.13)	0.76 (0.19)	2.17 (0.39)	0.39 (0.68)	−0.17 (0.38)	−0.34 (1.31)
35	Lithuania	1.08 (0.05)	0.52 (0.18)	1.45 (0.29)	−0.58 (0.19)	−0.65 (0.21)	−1.03 (0.29)
36	Malaysia[a]	–	–	–	–	–	–
37	Mexico	0.72 (0.10)	1.85 (0.73)	1.85 (0.35)	−0.63 (0.28)	−0.82 (0.36)	−0.47 (0.32)
38	Philippines[a]	–	–	–	–	–	–
39	Poland	0.73 (0.11)	1.15 (0.26)	1.48 (0.56)	−0.51 (0.21)	−0.61 (0.27)	−0.86 (0.11)
40	Portugal	0.85 (0.16)	1.05 (0.30)	1.12 (0.24)	−1.12 (0.24)	−0.83 (0.33)	−1.06 (0.28)
41	Slovakia	0.92 (0.11)	0.84 (0.13)	1.42 (0.31)	−0.81 (0.24)	−0.36 (0.16)	−0.82 (0.34)
42	South Africa[a]	–	–	–	–	–	–
43	Sri Lanka[a]	–	–	–	–	–	–
44	Thailand[a]	–	–	–	–	–	–
45	Turkey[a]	–	–	–	–	–	–
Mean (*Developing*)		0.87 (0.04)	1.03 (0.10)	1.42 (0.10)	−0.46 (0.10)	−0.49 (0.08)	−0.65 (0.15)
Mean (*All countries*)		0.80 (0.02)	0.91 (0.05)	1.46 (0.04)	−0.58 (0.05)	−0.57 (0.05)	−0.69 (0.07)

Note: Standard errors are in parentheses.
[a] Disaggregated data are not available.

Table 6.9 presents the conditional income and price elasticities based on the double-log demand system introduced in Section 2.4. As can be seen, almost all conditional income elasticities for food are less than 1, with an average of 0.8, indicating that food is a necessity. The conditional income elasticity estimates for alcohol are mixed, that is, alcohol is a luxury in some countries and a necessity in others. The income elasticity for restaurant meals is generally above unity with an average of 1.46, indicating that in most countries, meals consumed at restaurants is a luxury. The own-price elasticities for food, alcohol and restaurants are negative and less than one in absolute value, indicating that the demand for these goods is price inelastic.

6.5 Modelling the Demand for Food, Alcohol and Restaurant Meals

The elasticities presented in the previous section have only a preliminary status as they are based on the basic demand system, the double-log demand system. In this section, we present the conditional demand equations for estimation, test the demand theory hypotheses, and present the model estimates as well as the implied income and price elasticities.

From Section 2.11 of Chapter 2, we have the finitechange version of the absolute price version of the conditional demand equation (2.116) for $i \in S_g$, which we reproduce here:

$$\bar{w}_{it} Dq_{it} = \theta_i' W_{gt} DQ_{gt} + \sum_{j \in S_g} \pi_{ij}^g Dp_{jt}, \quad i \in S_g, \tag{6.11}$$

where the conditional coefficients, conditional marginal shares θ_i' and conditional Slutsky coefficient, π_{ij}^g, are specified as constants. The conditional Slutsky coefficients satisfy the demand homogeneity,

$$\sum_{j \in S_g} \pi_{ij}^g = 0, \quad i \in S_g, \tag{6.12}$$

and Slutsky symmetry,

$$\pi_{ij}^g = \pi_{ji}^g, \quad i, j \in S_g. \tag{6.13}$$

Table 6.10 presents the results for the hypothesis testing of demand homogeneity and Slutsky symmetry. We have $n = 3$ commodities, and the sample size T varies country to country. As can be seen from column (9), for most of the countries the demand homogeneity property is acceptable. Similarly, results presented in column (12) of the table reveal that the symmetry hypothesis is also acceptable by most countries.

Table 6.10 Testing homogeneity and symmetry, food group, 45 countries

				Testing homogeneity (F-test)						Testing symmetry (χ^2-test)		
	Country (1)	n (2)	T (after lagging) (3)	Test statistic (4)	df1 (5)	df2 (6)	Multiplier (7)	p-value (8)	Decision (5% level) (9)	Test statistic (10)	p-value (11)	Decision (5% level) (12)
Developed countries												
1	Australia	3	29	1.88	2	23	2.09	0.18	Accept	0.12	0.73	Accept
2	Austria	3	20	1.57	2	14	2.14	0.24	Accept	1.97	0.16	Accept
3	Belgium	3	19	8.03	2	13	2.15	0.01	Accept[b]	4.22	0.04	Accept[b]
4	Canada	3	34	0.53	2	28	2.07	0.60	Accept	0.00	1.00	Accept
5	Denmark	3	20	2.24	2	14	2.14	0.14	Accept	4.17	0.04	Accept[b]
6	Finland	3	40	0.51	2	34	2.06	0.61	Accept	1.47	0.23	Accept
7	France	3	56	0.67	2	50	2.04	0.52	Accept	0.80	0.37	Accept
8	Germany	3	19	0.67	2	13	2.15	0.53	Accept	5.77	0.02	Accept[b]
9	Hong Kong[a]	–	–	–	–	–	–	–	–	–	–	–
10	Iceland	3	19	2.23	2	13	2.15	0.15	Accept	0.22	0.64	Accept
11	Ireland	3	18	0.75	2	12	2.17	0.50	Accept	0.05	0.82	Accept
12	Israel	3	19	0.97	2	13	2.15	0.40	Accept	3.13	0.08	Accept
13	Italy	3	19	0.04	2	13	2.15	0.96	Accept	1.91	0.17	Accept
14	Japan[a]	3	19	0.68	2	13	2.15	0.52	Accept	0.17	0.68	Accept
15	Luxembourg	3	20	0.62	2	14	2.14	0.55	Accept	0.20	0.65	Accept
16	Netherlands	3	19	0.74	2	13	2.15	0.50	Accept	0.83	0.36	Accept
17	New Zealand	3	27	1.00	2	21	2.10	0.39	Accept	0.97	0.32	Accept
18	Norway	3	44	0.32	2	38	2.05	0.73	Accept	3.10	0.08	Accept
19	Singapore[a]	–	–	–	–	–	–	–	–	–	–	–
20	Slovenia	3	20	2.33	2	14	2.14	0.13	Accept	0.68	0.41	Accept
21	South Korea	3	45	10.89	2	39	2.05	0.00	Reject	2.94	0.09	Accept
22	Spain	3	19	0.08	2	13	2.15	0.92	Accept	0.74	0.39	Accept
23	Sweden	3	18	2.12	2	12	2.17	0.16	Accept	0.45	0.05	Accept
24	Switzerland	3	18	4.46	2	12	2.17	0.04	Accept[b]	1.90	0.17	Accept
25	Taiwan[a]	–	–	–	–	–	–	–	–	–	–	–
26	UK	3	20	1.50	2	14	2.14	0.26	Accept	0.00	1.00	Accept
27	USA	3	45	0.14	2	39	2.05	0.87	Accept	1.41	0.24	Accept

(*Continued*)

Table 6.10 Testing homogeneity and symmetry, food group, 45 countries (*Continued*)

	Country (1)	n (2)	T (after lagging) (3)	Testing homogeneity (F-test): Test statistic (4)	df1 (5)	df2 (6)	Multiplier (7)	p-value (8)	Decision (5% level) (9)	Testing symmetry (χ^2-test): Test statistic (10)	p-value (11)	Decision (5% level) (12)
Developing countries												
28	Colombia	3	14	0.77	2	8	2.25	0.49	Accept	0.23	0.63	Accept
29	Czech Republic	3	20	3.77	2	14	2.14	0.05	Accept	0.00	1.00	Accept
30	Estonia	3	20	1.39	2	14	2.14	0.28	Accept	0.08	0.78	Accept
31	Greece	3	20	0.26	2	14	2.14	0.77	Accept	0.01	0.92	Accept
32	Hungary	3	20	2.11	2	14	2.14	0.16	Accept	0.01	0.92	Accept
33	India[a]	–	–	–	–	–	–	–	–	–	–	–
34	Latviaa	3	19	0.70	2	13	2.15	0.51	Accept	2.67	0.10	Accept
35	Lithuania	3	19	7.38	2	13	2.15	0.01	Accept[b]	0.86	0.35	Accept
36	Malaysia	–	–	–	–	–	–	–	–	–	–	–
37	Mexico	3	11	2.50	2	5	2.40	0.18	Accept	0.46	0.50	Accept
38	Philippines	–	–	–	–	–	–	–	–	–	–	–
39	Poland	3	20	0.03	2	14	2.14	0.97	Accept	0.61	0.43	Accept
40	Portugal	3	20	0.32	2	14	2.14	0.73	Accept	0.52	0.47	Accept
41	Slovakia	3	20	0.45	2	14	2.14	0.65	Accept	1.82	0.18	Accept
42	South Africa[a]	–	–	–	–	–	–	–	–	–	–	–
43	Sri Lanka[a]	–	–	–	–	–	–	–	–	–	–	–
44	Thailand[a]	–	–	–	–	–	–	–	–	–	–	–
45	Turkey[a]	–	–	–	–	–	–	–	–	–	–	–

Note: $df1 = n - 1$; $df2 = T - 2n$; Multiplier = $[df1\ ′\ (T - n - 2)/df2]$.

[a] Disaggregated data are not available.

[b] Acceptable at the 1 percent level of significance.

Table 6.11 Implied income and price elasticities, food group, 45 countries

	Country	Income elasticity			Own-price elasticity			Cross-price elasticity					
		Food	*Alcohol*	*Restaurant*	*Food*	*Alcohol*	*Restaurant*	*Food-Alcohol*	*Food-Restaurant*	*Alcohol-Food*	*Alcohol-Restaurant*	*Restaurant-Food*	*Restaurant-Alcohol*
	(1)	*(2)*	*(3)*	*(4)*	*(5)*	*(6)*	*(7)*	*(8)*	*(9)*	*(10)*	*(11)*	*(12)*	*(13)*
Developed countries													
1	Australia	0.60	0.54	1.86	−0.21	−0.52	−0.47	0.05	0.17	0.13	0.40	0.26	0.22
2	Austria	0.68	1.42	1.16	−0.49	0.23	−0.34	0.01	0.47	0.04	−0.27	0.42	−0.08
3	Belgium	1.01	1.46	0.65	−0.19	−0.11	−0.58	−0.01	0.20	−0.04	0.15	0.48	0.10
4	Canada	0.31	1.06	1.95	−0.07	−0.25	−0.15	0.03	0.04	0.07	0.18	0.05	0.10
5	Denmark	0.72	0.36	2.09	−0.38	−0.66	−0.89	0.10	0.28	0.28	0.39	0.59	0.30
6	Finland	0.63	1.22	1.66	−0.18	−0.34	−0.18	0.12	0.06	0.31	0.03	0.15	0.03
7	France	0.81	0.95	1.54	−0.20	−0.41	−0.57	0.04	0.16	0.16	0.25	0.41	0.17
8	Germany	1.02	0.19	1.53	−0.43	−0.77	−0.97	0.12	0.31	0.36	0.42	0.67	0.29
9	Hong Kong[a]	–	–	–	–	–	–	–	–	–	–	–	–
10	Iceland	0.65	1.03	1.59	0.02	−0.49	−0.27	0.00	−0.02	0.00	0.50	−0.03	0.30
11	Ireland	0.98	0.99	1.04	−0.99	−1.29	−1.38	0.44	0.55	0.69	0.60	0.81	0.57
12	Israel	0.39	−0.16	3.05	−0.04	−0.31	−0.10	0.03	0.02	0.16	0.14	0.04	0.06
13	Italy	0.57	1.08	1.70	−0.68	−0.58	−1.28	0.05	0.64	0.16	0.42	1.08	0.20
14	Japan[a]	–	–	–	–	–	–	–	–	–	–	–	–
15	Luxembourg	0.85	1.35	0.75	−0.09	0.10	−0.63	−0.25	0.33	−0.26	0.16	0.43	0.20
16	Netherlands	0.51	0.77	1.85	−0.14	−0.63	−0.39	0.04	0.11	0.12	0.51	0.16	0.22
17	New Zealand	0.90	0.72	1.52	−0.40	−0.43	−0.15	0.25	0.15	0.67	−0.24	0.37	−0.22
18	Norway	1.02	0.97	0.96	−0.31	−0.83	−0.44	0.21	0.11	0.71	0.12	0.33	0.11
19	Singapore[a]	–	–	–	–	–	–	–	–	–	–	–	–
20	Slovenia	0.89	1.06	1.22	−0.23	−0.44	−0.45	0.28	0.32	0.09	0.13	0.14	0.16
21	South Korea	0.91	0.75	1.33	−0.19	−0.35	−0.28	0.07	0.12	0.37	−0.02	0.28	−0.01
22	Spain	0.52	0.76	1.46	−0.15	−0.53	−0.09	0.10	0.05	0.32	0.21	0.04	0.05
23	Sweden	0.99	0.83	1.16	−0.16	−0.54	−0.30	0.11	0.05	0.34	0.21	0.14	0.17
24	Switzerland	1.04	0.88	1.02	−1.06	−1.40	−1.24	0.79	0.90	0.34	0.33	0.73	0.62
25	Taiwan[a]	–	–	–	–	–	–	–	–	–	–	–	–
26	UK	0.76	0.76	1.33	−0.18	−0.31	−0.16	0.08	0.10	0.15	0.16	0.09	0.07
27	USA	0.84	0.63	1.36	−0.32	−0.40	−0.33	0.09	0.22	0.33	0.07	0.30	0.03
Mean (*Developed*)		0.76	0.85	1.47	−0.31	−0.49	−0.51	0.12	0.23	0.24	0.21	0.34	0.16

(Continued)

Table 6.11 Implied income and price elasticities, food group, 45 countries (*Continued*)

		Income elasticity			Own-price elasticity			Cross-price elasticity					
	Country (1)	Food (2)	Alcohol (3)	Restaurant (4)	Food (5)	Alcohol (6)	Restaurant (7)	Food-Alcohol (8)	Food-Restaurant (9)	Alcohol-Food (10)	Alcohol-Restaurant (11)	Restaurant-Food (12)	Restaurant-Alcohol (13)
Developing countries													
28	Colombia	0.73	0.42	1.64	−0.09	−0.36	−0.46	−0.06	0.15	−0.32	0.68	0.25	0.21
29	Czech	0.84	0.65	1.67	−0.06	0.16	−0.52	−0.14	0.20	−0.28	0.12	0.40	0.12
30	Estonia	0.79	1.24	1.36	−0.16	−0.12	−0.59	0.01	0.15	0.02	0.10	0.47	0.12
31	Greece	1.08	1.22	0.83	−0.31	−0.78	−0.19	0.18	0.13	0.65	0.13	0.15	0.04
32	Hungary	0.98	1.10	0.95	−0.24	−0.88	−0.58	0.19	0.05	0.48	0.39	0.14	0.44
33	India[a]	–	–	–	–	–	–	–	–	–	–	–	–
34	Latvia	0.74	0.76	2.47	−0.03	−0.09	0.22	0.06	−0.03	0.16	−0.07	−0.11	−0.11
35	Lithuania	1.08	0.51	1.52	−0.16	−0.59	−1.00	0.11	0.05	0.40	0.20	0.49	0.51
36	Malaysia	–	–	–	–	–	–	–	–	–	–	–	–
37	Mexico	0.73	1.83	1.84	−0.14	−0.73	−0.43	0.07	0.07	0.59	0.14	0.35	0.09
38	Philippines[a]	–	–	–	–	–	–	–	–	–	–	–	–
39	Poland	0.76	1.48	1.49	−0.14	−0.38	−0.64	0.10	0.04	0.26	0.13	0.31	0.33
40	Portugal	0.84	1.38	1.13	−0.53	−0.40	−0.51	0.14	0.39	0.70	−0.30	0.61	−0.10
41	Slovakia	0.93	0.81	1.39	−0.26	−0.12	−0.44	0.07	0.19	0.27	−0.15	0.57	−0.12
42	South Africa[a]	–	–	–	–	–	–	–	–	–	–	–	–
43	Sri Lanka[a]	–	–	–	–	–	–	–	–	–	–	–	–
44	Thailand[a]	–	–	–	–	–	–	–	–	–	–	–	–
45	Turkey[a]	–	–	–	–	–	–	–	–	–	–	–	–
Mean (*Developing*)		0.86	1.04	1.48	−0.19	−0.39	−0.47	0.07	0.13	0.27	0.12	0.33	0.14
Mean (*All countries*)		0.80	0.91	1.47	−0.27	−0.46	−0.49	0.10	0.20	0.25	0.18	0.34	0.15

[a] Disaggregated data are not available.

Table 6.11 presents the implied income, own-price and cross-price elasticities based on the homogeneity and symmetry constrained estimates. As can be seen from columns (2)–(4) of the table, in almost all countries, food is a necessity (income elasticity < 1) and restaurant is a luxury (income elasticity > 1). Alcohol is mixed, and in a majority of the countries it is a necessity or near luxury. On average, all own-price elasticities presented in columns (5)–(7) are negative and less than one in absolute value, indicating that the demand for food, alcohol and restaurant is price inelastic. A majority of the cross-price elasticities presented in columns (8)–(13) are positive, indicating that food, alcohol and restaurants are pairwise substitutes. However, in a small number of countries, the cross-price elasticities are negative, revealing some level of complementarity between food, alcohol and restaurants in some countries. This strong substitutability points in the direction of preference independence of food, alcohol and restaurant in the consumer's utility structure.

We now test for the preference independence of the utility structure based on the Monte Carlo simulation test described in Chapter 4, and the results are presented in Table 6.12. As most of the ranks of the observed test statistics value are below 950, we conclude that at the 5 percent level of significance, the preference independence hypothesis is supported by the data from most countries.

Under preference independence, the Rotterdam conditional demand equation (2.115) given in Chapter 2 for commodity i takes the form

$$\bar{w}_{it} Dq_{it} = \theta_i' W_{gt} DQ_{gt} + \phi\theta_g\theta_i' \left(Dp_{it} - DP_{gt}' \right), \quad i \in S_g, \tag{6.14}$$

where the coefficients ϕ and θ_i are specified as constants. Tables 6.13 and 6.14 present the model estimation results for the system of demand equations (6.14) and the implied income and price elasticities, respectively, for the three commodities in the 45 countries. The marginal shares presented in columns (2)–(4) of Table 6.13 can be interpreted as follows. For example, if there is a dollar increase in the food group expenditure in Australia, out of that one-dollar increase, on average, consumers allocate 27 cents on food, 13 cents on alcohol and the remaining 60 cents on restaurant meals. In the majority of the developed countries, a higher share of the extra dollar in expenditure in the food group is allocated to restaurants. The estimates of income flexibility presented in the last column reveal that most of the estimates are negative as they should be and with an average of −0.65.

The income elasticities presented in columns (2)–(4) of Table 6.14 reveal that in most countries, food is a necessity, but restaurant meals is a luxury. While alcohol is a necessity in some countries, and a luxury for others, it is on the borderline in some countries. The own-price elasticities presented in columns (5)–(7) reveal that the demand for food, alcohol and restaurant

Table 6.12 Monte Carlo test results of preference independence, food group, 45 countries

	Country (1)	*Observed value* (2)	*Rank* (3)	*Decision at the 5 % level* (4)
Developed countries				
1	Australia	1.94	552	Accept
2	Austria	4.74	863	Accept
3	Belgium	2.50	617	Accept
4	Canada	0.26	103	Accept
5	Denmark	0.92	332	Accept
6	Finland	2.84	748	Accept
7	France	1.12	417	Accept
8	Germany	2.15	599	Accept
9	Hong Kong[a]	–	–	–
10	Iceland	2.73	628	Accept
11	Ireland	0.53	184	Accept
12	Israel	5.58	913	Accept
13	Italy	5.58	909	Accept
14	Japan[a]	–	–	–
15	Luxembourg	0.72	228	Accept
16	Netherlands	1.75	490	Accept
17	New Zealand	2.31	607	Accept
18	Norway	0.96	323	Accept
19	Singapore[a]	–	–	–
20	Slovenia	3.17	728	Accept
21	South Korea	2.38	654	Accept
22	Spain	1.48	465	Accept
23	Sweden	19.71	1000	Reject
24	Switzerland	2.88	654	Accept
25	Taiwan[a]	–	–	–
26	UK	0.60	208	Accept
27	USA	2.39	666	Accept
Developing countries				
28	Colombia	5.79	855	Accept
29	Czech Republic	6.52	913	Accept
30	Estonia	1.37	387	Accept
31	Greece	0.80	293	Accept
32	Hungary	6.26	906	Accept
33	India[a]	–	–	–
34	Latvia	0.31	111	Accept
35	Lithuania	3.37	712	Accept
36	Malaysia[a]	–	–	–
37	Mexico	0.42	114	Accept
38	Philippines[a]	–	–	–
39	Poland	0.54	193	Accept
40	Portugal	3.49	756	Accept
41	Slovakia	3.34	740	Accept
42	South Africa[a]	–	–	–
43	Sri Lanka[a]	–	–	–
44	Thailand[a]	–	–	–
45	Turkey[a]	–	–	–
Percentage of rejection			2.9 percent	

[a] Disaggregated data are not available.

Table 6.13 Estimation results of model under preference independence, food group, 45 countries

Country (1)		Marginal shares: Food (2)	Marginal shares: Alcohol (3)	Marginal shares: Restaurants (4)	Income flexibility (5)
Developed countries					
1	Australia	0.27 (0.05)	0.13 (0.03)	0.60 (0.06)	−0.68 (0.16)
2	Austria	0.25 (0.11)	0.18 (0.06)	0.57 (0.12)	−0.40 (0.28)
3	Belgium	0.60 (0.12)	0.25 (0.08)	0.16 (0.10)	−0.23 (0.24)
4	Canada	0.15 (0.04)	0.20 (0.04)	0.65 (0.05)	−0.29 (0.09)
5	Denmark	0.35 (0.05)	0.12 (0.04)	0.54 (0.05)	−0.97 (0.20)
6	Finland	0.36 (0.04)	0.25 (0.03)	0.39 (0.04)	−0.40 (0.09)
7	France	0.50 (0.04)	0.15 (0.02)	0.35 (0.04)	−0.51 (0.09)
8	Germany	0.45 (0.07)	0.13 (0.04)	0.42 (0.07)	−1.10 (0.22)
9	Hong Kong[a]	–	–	–	–
10	Iceland	0.32 (0.05)	0.23 (0.05)	0.45 (0.07)	−0.22 (0.18)
11	Ireland	0.42 (0.02)	0.27 (0.01)	0.31 (0.01)	−1.82 (0.11)
12	Israel	0.25 (0.09)	0.03 (0.02)	0.72 (0.10)	−0.55 (0.34)
13	Italy	0.35 (0.03)	0.10 (0.02)	0.55 (0.04)	−1.54 (0.23)
14	Japan[a]	–	–	–	–
15	Luxembourg	0.33 (0.04)	0.46 (0.05)	0.21 (0.02)	−0.69 (0.72)
16	Netherlands	0.26 (0.04)	0.13 (0.03)	0.61 (0.04)	−0.57 (0.19)
17	New Zealand	0.50 (0.04)	0.15 (0.03)	0.35 (0.06)	−1.04 (0.24)
18	Norway	0.65 (0.04)	0.19 (0.02)	0.17 (0.03)	−0.95 (0.18)
19	Singapore[a]	–	–	–	–
20	Slovenia	0.51 (0.04)	0.20 (0.04)	0.29 (0.04)	−0.53 (0.12)
21	South Korea	0.57 (0.04)	0.09 (0.02)	0.35 (0.04)	−0.45 (0.10)
22	Spain	0.18 (0.04)	0.10 (0.02)	0.73 (0.04)	−0.67 (0.27)
23	Sweden	0.63 (0.01)	0.09 (0.02)	0.29 (0.01)	−0.38 (0.06)
24	Switzerland	0.47 (0.03)	0.17 (0.02)	0.36 (0.02)	−1.92 (0.13)
25	Taiwan[a]	–	–	–	–
26	UK	0.27 (0.04)	0.15 (0.03)	0.58 (0.06)	−0.40 (0.15)
27	USA	0.40 (0.04)	0.09 (0.02)	0.51 (0.04)	−0.71 (0.11)
Mean (*Developed*)		0.39 (0.01)	0.17 (0.01)	0.44 (0.01)	−0.74 (0.05)
Developing countries					
28	Colombia	0.43 (0.06)	0.09 (0.04)	0.48 (0.08)	−0.24 (0.15)
29	Czech Republic	0.40 (0.07)	0.10 (0.05)	0.41 (0.07)	0.36 (0.16)
30	Estonia	0.49 (0.06)	0.26 (0.04)	0.25 (0.04)	−0.33 (0.22)
31	Greece	0.54 (0.07)	0.17 (0.03)	0.29 (0.09)	−0.72 (0.16)
32	Hungary	0.55 (0.04)	0.29 (0.04)	0.16 (0.04)	−0.66 (0.09)
33	India[a]	–	–	–	–
34	Latvia	0.44 (0.06)	0.18 (0.04)	0.38 (0.06)	−0.11 (0.42)
35	Lithuania	0.77 (0.03)	0.12 (0.03)	0.11 (0.02)	−0.73 (0.17)
36	Malaysia[a]	–	–	–	–
37	Mexico	0.54 (0.06)	0.18 (0.05)	0.28 (0.05)	−0.40 (0.14)
38	Philippines[a]	–	–	–	–
39	Poland	0.52 (0.07)	0.33 (0.06)	0.15 (0.04)	−0.46 (0.14)
40	Portugal	0.53 (0.07)	0.11 (0.03)	0.36 (0.07)	−0.96 (0.17)
41	Slovakia	0.57 (0.06)	0.14 (0.02)	0.28 (0.05)	−0.47 (0.16)
42	South Africa[a]	–	–	–	–
43	Sri Lanka[a]	–	–	–	–
44	Thailand[a]	–	–	–	–
45	Turkey[a]	–	–	–	–
Mean (*Developing*)		0.53 (0.02)	0.19 (0.01)	0.29 (0.02)	−0.49 (0.06)
Mean (*All countries*)		0.44 (0.01)	0.17 (0.01)	0.39 (0.01)	−0.65 (0.04)

Note: Standard errors are in parentheses.
[a] Disaggregated data are not available.

Table 6.14 Implied income and own-price elasticities, food group, 45 countries

Country (1)		Income elasticity Food (2)	Income elasticity Alcohol (3)	Income elasticity Restaurants (4)	Price elasticity Food (5)	Price elasticity Alcohol (6)	Price elasticity Restaurants (7)
Developed countries							
1	Australia	0.604	0.543	1.858	−0.212	−0.522	−0.474
2	Austria	0.684	1.416	1.155	−0.485	0.234	−0.336
3	Belgium	1.014	1.457	0.648	−0.190	−0.110	−0.581
4	Canada	0.314	1.055	1.950	−0.065	−0.249	−0.150
5	Denmark	0.722	0.355	2.091	−0.376	−0.66	−0.885
6	Finland	0.632	1.224	1.661	−0.179	−0.335	−0.175
7	France	0.808	0.948	1.539	−0.197	−0.413	−0.573
8	Germany	1.015	0.194	1.534	−0.429	−0.773	−0.965
9	Hong Kong[a]	–	–	–	–	–	–
10	Iceland	0.653	1.029	1.586	0.019	−0.494	−0.270
11	Ireland	0.977	0.992	1.041	−0.989	−1.287	−1.375
12	Israel	0.386	−0.157	3.049	−0.040	−0.306	−0.097
13	Italy	0.567	1.078	1.696	−0.681	−0.584	−1.278
14	Japan[a]	–	–	–	–	–	–
15	Luxembourg	0.853	1.352	0.748	−0.087	0.098	−0.632
16	Netherlands	0.512	0.766	1.854	−0.141	−0.633	−0.387
17	New Zealand	0.895	0.715	1.522	−0.402	−0.432	−0.152
18	Norway	1.020	0.972	0.961	−0.313	−0.832	−0.440
19	Singapore[a]	–	–	–	–	–	–
20	Slovenia	0.888	1.057	1.220	−0.232	−0.444	−0.453
21	South Korea	0.905	0.754	1.332	−0.186	−0.350	−0.277
22	Spain	0.522	0.763	1.461	−0.145	−0.525	−0.092
23	Sweden	0.991	0.829	1.161	−0.162	−0.54	−0.303
24	Switzerland	1.038	0.883	1.015	−1.064	−1.403	−1.235
25	Taiwan[a]	–	–	–	–	–	–
26	UK	0.756	0.755	1.333	−0.178	−0.308	−0.164
27	USA	0.836	0.627	1.361	−0.316	−0.399	−0.328
Mean (*Developed*)		0.765	0.852	1.469	−0.307	−0.490	−0.505
Developing countries							
28	Colombia	0.727	0.420	1.639	−0.091	−0.360	−0.458
29	Czech Republic	0.842	0.651	1.667	−0.059	0.162	−0.522
30	Estonia	0.793	1.241	1.357	−0.159	−0.122	−0.592
31	Greece	1.084	1.219	0.829	−0.307	−0.776	−0.194
32	Hungary	0.982	1.097	0.945	−0.237	−0.878	−0.580
33	Indiaa	–	–	–	–	–	–
34	Latvia	0.736	0.761	2.474	−0.034	−0.093	0.219
35	Lithuania	1.080	0.514	1.518	−0.163	−0.591	−0.997
36	Malaysia[a]	–	–	–	–	–	–
37	Mexico	0.731	1.834	1.839	−0.141	−0.733	−0.433
38	Philippines[a]	–	–	–	–	–	–
39	Poland	0.757	1.475	1.489	−0.138	−0.384	−0.641
40	Portugal	0.841	1.381	1.128	−0.528	−0.399	−0.512
41	Slovakia	0.926	0.810	1.387	−0.259	−0.120	−0.442
42	South Africa[a]	–	–	–	–	–	–
43	Sri Lanka[a]	–	–	–	–	–	–
44	Thailand[a]	–	–	–	–	–	–
45	Turkey[a]	–	–	–	–	–	–
Mean (*Developing*)		0.864	1.037	1.479	−0.192	−0.390	−0.468
Mean (*All countries*)		0.797	0.912	1.472	−0.270	−0.458	−0.493

[a] Disaggregated data are not available.

meals is price inelastic as almost all of them are less than one in absolute value.

6.6 Conditional Demand Analysis of the Disaggregated Food Group with Cross-Sectional Data

In Chapter 5, we analysed the household demand for consumers in Australia, Bangladesh,[3] India and Sri Lanka using single-country Household Expenditure Survey (HES) data sets. The analysis presented in that chapter is for broad aggregate commodities. We obtain income elasticities[4] for those broad commodity groups in relation to various household characteristics such as income level, age and location. In this section, we extend that analysis for goods within the food group based on the same HES data for the commodity disaggregation within the food group, food, alcohol and restaurants.

In Section 2.12 of Chapter 2, we introduced the conditional generalised Working's model (CGWM) given by equation (2.136) and the corresponding income elasticities given by equation (2.138), which we reproduce below.

The conditional version of the Generalised Working's (1943) model is,

$$w_i' = a_i' + b_i' M_g^{\lambda}, \tag{6.15}$$

where $\sum_{i \in S_g} a_i' = 1$ and $\sum_{i \in S_g} b_i' = 0$.

The implied conditional income elasticity of CGWM is given by

$$\eta_i' = (1+\lambda) - \lambda \frac{a_i'}{w_i'}. \tag{6.16}$$

We disaggregate the food group into food, alcohol, tobacco, restaurants and soft drinks. Below, we present the cross-sectional analysis of the demand for these disaggregated food groups using household survey data for three countries, Australia, India and Sri Lanka.

6.6.1 Australia

Table 6.15 presents the average budget share of the food group and conditional budget shares within the food group for food, alcohol, tobacco, restaurants and soft drinks, for Australia. As can be seen at the national level, the food group budget allocation is only 22.3 percent. Considering the goods within the food group, the low-income group allocates 25.6 percent, the lower-middle-income group allocates 23.6 percent, the upper-middle-income group allocates 22.4 percent, while the high-income group allocates only 19.1 percent of their total expenditure on food.

Within the food group, at the national level, Australian consumers allocate more than half (51.7 percent) of their food group expenditure on

Table 6.15 Average budget share of food group and conditional budget shares within the food group, Australia

Household location/income level	*Average food group budget share (as a % of the total household expenditure)*	*Average conditional budget shares (as a % of the total food expenditure)*[a]				
		Food	*Alcohol*	*Tobacco*	*Restaurants*	*Soft drinks*
(1)	*(2)*	*(3)*	*(4)*	*(5)*	*(6)*	*(7)*
National	22.3	51.7	11.3	5.2	30.1	1.6
Income level						
Low-income (lower 25 percent)	25.6	54.1	10.8	8.8	24.6	1.7
Lower-middle-income (25–50 percent)	23.6	52.3	10.9	5.7	29.3	1.8
Upper-middle-income (50–75 percent)	22.4	52.8	10.8	4.5	30.2	1.6
High-income (upper 25 percent)	19.1	48.8	12.4	3.2	34.3	1.3
Age group						
18–34	20.3	47.0	11.3	4.1	36.0	1.6
35–49	21.4	52.5	10.7	5.3	29.8	1.6
50–64	23.4	51.8	11.9	6.0	28.6	1.6
65 and above	24.3	55.5	11.5	5.1	26.5	1.4

Notes: The sample size is 6,768.
[a] Total conditional budget share may not add to 100 due to rounding off.

Table 6.16 Income elasticities of food group and individual commodities within the food group by income level and age group, Australia

Commodity	*National*	*Income level*				*Age group*			
		Low-income	*Lower-middle-income*	*Upper-middle-income*	*High-income*	*18–34*	*35–49*	*50–64*	*65 and above*
(1)	*(2)*	*(3)*	*(4)*	*(5)*	*(6)*	*(7)*	*(8)*	*(9)*	*(10)*
Food group	0.67 (0.01)	0.76 (0.04)	0.59 (0.01)	0.63 (0.03)	0.55 (0.03)	0.82 (0.03)	0.69 (0.00)	0.68 (0.00)	0.61 (0.02)
Food	0.80 (0.01)	0.86 (0.02)	0.75 (0.02)	0.76 (0.02)	0.72 (0.02)	0.71 (0.02)	0.82 (0.01)	0.76 (0.01)	0.81 (0.01)
Alcohol	1.63 (0.03)	1.52 (0.07)	1.81 (0.06)	1.76 (0.06)	1.85 (0.05)	1.68 (0.06)	1.56 (0.05)	1.64 (0.05)	1.67 (0.05)
Tobacco	1.28 (0.06)	1.83 (0.10)	2.30 (0.11)	1.58 (0.13)	1.37 (0.16)	1.01 (0.13)	1.04 (0.10)	1.28 (0.10)	1.66 (0.12)
Restaurants	1.07 (0.13)	0.82 (0.04)	0.90 (0.03)	1.08 (0.30)	1.08 (0.03)	1.19 (0.03)	1.13 (0.02)	1.14 (0.03)	1.00 (0.03)
Soft drinks	0.60 (0.45)	0.49 (0.99)	0.79 (0.89)	0.71 (5.66)	0.54 (1.17)	0.33 (0.99)	0.71 (0.80)	0.63 (0.81)	0.58 (0.99)

Note: Standard errors are in parentheses.

food, followed by 30.1 percent on restaurant meals, 11.3 percent on alcohol, 5.2 percent on tobacco, and the remaining 1.6 percent on soft drinks. In terms of the age groups, at the national level, the younger age group allocates 20.3 percent and the older age group allocates 24.3 percent of their total budget on the food group. While allocation on the food group differs among Australian consumers across differing income levels and age groups, the conditional allocation on food alone also differs slightly across income levels (low-income 54.1 percent, high-income 48.8 percent) as well as age groups (47 percent for the younger age group to 55.5 percent for the older age group). While there is not much difference in the alcohol and soft drinks share of expenditure, there are differences in the allocation on tobacco as well as on restaurants. For example, while the low-income group allocates about 8.8 percent of their food group expenditure on tobacco, the high-income group allocates only about 3.2 percent of their food group expenditure on tobacco. While the low-income group allocates about 24.6 percent of their food group expenditure on restaurant meals, the high-income group allocates about 34 percent. There is not much difference in the expenditure percentages on alcohol, tobacco or soft drinks among differing age groups, but there is a significant difference of expenditure allocated to restaurant meals (36 percent by the younger age group compared with 26.5 percent by the older age group).

Table 6.16 presents the implied income elasticities by income level and age group. As can be seen from the table, the income elasticity for the food group as well as food is less than one at the national level and across income levels and age groups, indicating that food as a group or food as a single commodity within the food group is a necessity. The income elasticities for alcohol, tobacco and restaurants are all greater than 1 and for soft drinks is below 1 at the national level, across all income levels and all age groups, meaning that alcohol, tobacco and restaurants are luxuries and soft drinks is a necessity.

6.6.2 India

Table 6.17 presents the summary information on the food group budget share as well as for the commodities forming the food group based on Indian Human Development Survey data. As can be seen at the national level, the food group budget allocation is 48.3 percent, while the low-income group allocates a much higher 59.3 percent, the lower-middle group allocates 53.5 percent, the upper-middle group allocates 46.9 percent, and the high-income group allocates only 33.3 percent of their total expenditure on food. Comparing this with Table 6.15 for Australia, a developed country, where the budget share allocation on the food group was less than 26 percent at all income levels, shows a similarity with the high-income group in India, a developing country. For all other income groups in India, the food group budget share is more than 47 percent.

Table 6.17 Average budget share of food group and conditional budget shares within the food group, India

Household location/income level	*Average food group budget share (as a % of the total household expenditure)*	*Average conditional budget shares (as a % of the total food group expenditure)*[a]		
		Food	*Alcohol and Tobacco*	*Restaurants*
(1)	*(2)*	*(3)*	*(4)*	*(5)*
National	48.3	82.4	11.1	6.4
Income level				
Low-income (lower 25 percent)	59.3	82.5	13.7	3.7
Lower-middle-income (25–50 percent)	53.5	83.4	11.8	4.7
Upper-middle-income (50–75 percent)	46.9	82.8	10.3	6.7
High-income (upper 25 percent)	33.3	80.9	8.2	10.7
Age group				
18–34	52.1	82.6	11.8	5.6
35–49	48.1	82.4	11.0	6.5
50–64	47.2	82.4	10.6	7.0
65 and above	47.7	82.3	11.4	6.4

Note: The sample size is 7,470.
[a] Total conditional budget share may not sum to 100 due to rounding off.

Table 6.18 Income elasticities of food group and individual commodities within the food group by income level and age group, India

Commodity	*National*	*Income level*				*Age group*			
		Low-income	*Lower-middle-income*	*Upper-middle-income*	*High-income*	*18–34*	*35–49*	*50–64*	*65 and above*
(1)	*(2)*	*(3)*	*(4)*	*(5)*	*(6)*	*(7)*	*(8)*	*(9)*	*(10)*
Food group	0.70 (0.01)	0.91 (0.01)	0.81 (0.02)	0.74 (0.02)	0.59 (0.02)	0.75 (0.07)	0.70 (0.01)	0.67 (0.01)	0.70 (0.01)
Food	0.96 (0.00)	0.99 (0.01)	0.95 (0.01)	0.94 (0.01)	0.91 (0.01)	0.97 (0.01)	0.96 (0.004)	0.96 (0.004)	0.98 (0.01)
Alcohol and tobacco	0.82 (0.02)	0.88 (0.04)	1.28 (0.05)	1.29 (0.06)	1.14 (0.06)	0.81 (0.04)	0.85 (0.03)	0.85 (0.03)	0.70 (0.04)
Restaurants	1.79 (0.04)	1.624 (0.18)	1.27 (0.16)	1.30 (0.12)	1.61 (0.07)	1.89 (0.13)	1.76 (0.07)	1.77 (0.07)	1.82 (0.09)

$\lambda = -0.1720; \lambda_g = 0.0329$

Note: Standard errors are in parentheses.

Within the food group, at the national level, Indian consumers allocate 82.4 percent of their food group expenditure on food, 11.1 percent on alcohol and tobacco combined and the remaining 6.4 percent on restaurants. In terms of the age groups, at the national level, the younger age group allocates 4.4 percent more than the older age group who spend 47.7 percent of their total expenditure on the food group. While allocation on the food group differs among Indian consumers across differing income levels and age groups, the allocation of food group expenditure on food alone exceeds 81 percent and is very comparable across income levels as well as age groups. However, there is a significant difference in the allocation on alcohol and tobacco as well as on restaurants. For example, while the low-income group allocates about 14 percent of their food group expenditure on alcohol and tobacco, the high-income group allocates only about 8 percent of their food group expenditure in this way. While the low-income group allocates only about 4 percent of their food group expenditure on restaurant meals, the high-income group allocates about 11 percent. There is not much difference in expenditure proportions on alcohol and tobacco or on restaurants among differing age groups.

Table 6.18 presents the income elasticities for the food group as a whole and the conditional income elasticities of food, alcohol, tobacco and restaurants for India. The income elasticity for the food group as well as food individually is less than one at the national level and across all income levels and age groups, indicating that food as a group or food as a single item is a necessity. The income elasticity for alcohol and tobacco is less than unity at the national level and the low-income level meaning it is a necessity, while for all other income groups, it is a luxury. For all age groups, alcohol and tobacco is a necessity. Across all levels, national, income and age, restaurant meals is a luxury.

6.6.3 Sri Lanka

Table 6.19 presents the average budget share of the food group and the conditional budget shares within the food group for food, alcohol, tobacco, restaurants and soft drinks, for Sri Lanka. At the national level, Sri Lankan consumers allocate about 47 percent of their total expenditure on the food group. There is a significant difference in allocation on the food group across differing income levels but not by age groups. While the low-income group allocates 61 percent of their income on the food group, the high-income group allocates only half of that proportion at 30 percent. Allocation on food alone is similar across income levels as well as age groups. However, there is a significant difference in the allocation on alcohol, tobacco, restaurants as well as soft drinks. For example, while the low-income group allocates about 1.4 percent of their food group expenditure on alcohol, 2.8 percent on tobacco, 13.5 percent on restaurants and 0.1 percent on soft drinks, the high-income group allocates 2.3 percent, 1.9 percent, 11.1

Table 6.19 Average budget share of food group and conditional budget shares within the food group, Sri Lanka

Household location/income level	*Average food group share (as a % of the total household expenditure)*	*Average conditional shares (as a % of the total food expenditure)*[a]				
		Food	*Alcohol*	*Tobacco*	*Restaurants*	*Soft drinks*
(1)	*(2)*	*(3)*	*(4)*	*(5)*	*(6)*	*(7)*
National	47.0	84.3	2.0	2.4	11.1	0.3
Income level						
Low-income (lower 25 percent)	61.1	82.0	1.4	2.8	13.5	0.1
Lower-middle-income (25–50 percent)	52.7	85.7	1.9	2.5	9.7	0.2
Upper-middle-income (50–75 percent)	44.1	85.3	2.2	2.2	10.0	0.3
High-income (upper 25 percent)	29.9	84.1	2.3	1.9	11.1	0.5
Age group						
18–34	47.6	82.9	1.6	2.0	13.2	0.4
35–49	45.7	85.1	2.2	2.2	10.3	0.3
50–64	47.2	84.9	2.3	2.7	9.9	0.2
65 and above	48.1	82.8	1.4	2.4	13.2	0.2

Note: The sample size is 21,474.
[a] Total conditional budget share may not sum to 100 due to rounding off.

Table 6.20 Income elasticities of food group and individual commodities within the food group by income level and age group, Sri Lanka

Commodity	*National*	*Income level*				*Age group (years)*			
		Low-income	*Lower-middle-income*	*Upper-middle-income*	*High-income*	*18–34*	*35–49*	*50–64*	*65 and above*
(1)	*(2)*	*(3)*	*(4)*	*(5)*	*(6)*	*(7)*	*(8)*	*(9)*	*(10)*
Food group	0.55 (0.00)	0.80 (0.01)	0.68 (0.01)	0.59 (0.00)	0.37 (0.01)	0.51 (0.01)	0.52 (0.01)	0.54 (0.01)	0.56 (0.01)
Food	0.86 (0.00)	0.76 (0.01)	0.80 (0.01)	0.82 (0.01)	0.81 (0.01)	0.81 (0.01)	0.85 (0.01)	0.86 (0.01)	0.91 (0.01)
Alcohol	3.05 (0.06)	3.62 (0.16)	3.88 (0.15)	3.67 (0.14)	3.47 (0.12)	2.75 (0.22)	3.02 (0.10)	3.12 (0.09)	2.85 (0.15)
Tobacco	1.25 (0.04)	1.47 (0.07)	1.63 (0.08)	1.88 (0.09)	1.79 (0.09)	1.59 (0.14)	1.36 (0.07)	1.29 (0.05)	0.93 (0.07)
Restaurants	1.58 (0.03)	2.05 (0.06)	2.00 (0.07)	1.73 (0.06)	1.75 (0.04)	1.84 (0.08)	1.72 (0.04)	1.57 (0.04)	1.36 (0.05)
Soft drinks	2.82 (1.63)	2.58 (12.88)	2.11 (5.77)	2.43 (3.30)	2.48 (1.49)	2.96 (3.82)	2.79 (2.35)	3.24 (3.41)	2.90 (5.29)

$\lambda = -0.3109$; $\lambda_g = -0.0148$

Note: Standard errors are in parentheses.

percent and 0.5 percent, respectively. There is not much difference on any sub-category within the food group across differing age groups.

Table 6.20 presents the income elasticities for the food group as a whole and the food group divided into food, alcohol, tobacco, restaurants and soft drinks for Sri Lanka. The income elasticity for the food group as well as food alone is less than one at the national level and across income levels and age groups, indicating that food as a group, or food as a single item within the food group, is a necessity. The income elasticities for alcohol, tobacco, restaurants and soft drinks are all greater than one at the national level, and at all income levels and age group. Therefore, across all levels, food is a necessity and all other commodities are luxuries. As food dominates the food group individual items in terms of budget share (more than 80 percent), even though the other four commodities in the food group are luxuries, the food group as a whole is a necessity at all levels as it is influenced by the individual food category, which is a necessity at all levels.

6.7 Concluding Comments

In this chapter, we analysed the demand for food as a group and demand for food, alcohol, tobacco, restaurants and soft drinks conditionally within the aggregated food group formed by these commodities. We presented a preliminary analysis of consumption patterns of these commodities using time-series data for food, alcohol and restaurants for 27 developed and 18 developing countries by presenting the budget shares and Divisia measures of consumption and prices for the food as a group and its individual items.

While, on average, consumers in the developing countries allocate more than one-third of their income on the food group, in the developed countries, consumers allocate less than one-fourth of their income on the food group. All consumers allocate about the same percentage of their income on restaurant meals, about 8 percent, while there is a significant difference in the expenditure on individual items, food and alcohol, between consumers in developed (food 13.0 percent, alcohol 4.5 percent) and developing (food 20.3 percent, alcohol 6.1 percent) countries. Among the 45 countries, on average, food prices grew at a rate of 3.4 percent per annum and consumption at a rate of 1.1 percent per annum.

Using the conditional demand equations, we then tested the demand theory hypotheses and estimated the model to obtain final estimates of income and price elasticities of food, alcohol and restaurants for the 45 countries. The results show that demand homogeneity and Slutsky symmetry hypotheses are supported by the data for most countries. The estimation results using time-series data indicate that, within the food group, food is a necessity but restaurant meals is a luxury. The results for alcohol are mixed and borderline to being a necessity or a luxury. On average, alcohol is a necessity in developed countries and is a luxury or near-luxury in developing countries.

The own- and cross-price elasticities indicate that the demand for food, alcohol and restaurants are price inelastic and while, in general, all three are pairwise substitutes, in some countries, there exist some complementarity between the three commodities.

We also estimated the demand for the disaggregated goods, food, alcohol, tobacco, restaurants and soft drinks, using cross-sectional data from HESs for Australia, India and Sri Lanka. For household-level data, the results show that food is a necessity across countries, across varying levels of income and age groups. Alcohol, tobacco and restaurant meals are generally a luxury, while soft drinks is a necessity in Australia (a developed country) and a luxury in Sri Lanka (a developing country). The estimated demand elasticities are useful inputs for policy formulation by governments, related industries and researchers working in the consumer demand area.

Notes

1 https://sdgs.un.org/goals.
2 https://www.who.int/publications/i/item/9789241506236.
3 Since disaggregated data for the food group are unavailable for Bangladesh, we have not included Bangladesh in this section.
4 As household-level data do not provide information on prices, we calculated only the income elasticities.

References

Abbott, P., and A. de Battisti. 2011. Recent global food price shocks: causes, consequences and lessons for African governments and donors. *Journal of African Economies* 20(1): i12–i62.

Andreyeva, T., M.W. Long, and K.D. Brownell. 2010. The Impact of food prices on consumption: A systematic review of research on the price elasticity of demand for food. *American Journal of Public Health* 100(2): 216–222.

Bodirsky, B.L., S. Rolinski, A. Biewald, I. Weindl, A. Popp, and H. Lotze-Campen. 2015. Global food demand scenarios for the 21st century. *PLoS One*, 10(11): e0139201. doi:10.1371/journal.pone.0139201.

Chen, D.L. 2001. *World consumption economics*. Singapore, London: World Scientific.

Clements, K.W., J. Si, E.A. Selvanathan, and S. Selvanathan. 2020. Demand elasticities for 9 goods in 37 countries. *Applied Economics* 52(24): 2636–2655.

D'Souza, A., and D. Jolliffe. 2012. Rising food prices and coping strategies: Household-level evidence from Afghanistan. *The Journal of Development Studies*, 48(2): 282–299.

Engel, E. 1857. Die lebenskosten belgischer arbeiter-familien fruher und jetzt. *International Statistical Institute Bulletin* 9: 1–74.

Gil, A.I., and J.A. Molina. 2005. The Demand Behaviour of Consumers in Peru: A demographic analysis using the QUAIDS. *The Journal of Developing Areas* 39: 191–206.

GlobeNewswire 2020. *Global soft drinks industry*. Accessed on 10th February 2022. Retrieved from https://www.globenewswire.com/news-release/2020/07/08/2059404/0/en/Global-Soft-Drinks-Industry.html.

Jayasinghe, M., E.A. Selvanathan, and S. Selvanathan. 2019. An intertemporal analysis of expenditure elasticities under three expenditure specifications for Sri Lanka. *Applied Economics* 51(59): 6376–6392.

Jensen, H., and S.T. Yen. 1996. Food expenditure away from home by type of meal. *Canadian Journal of Agricultural Economics* 44: 67–80.

Kearney J. 2010. Food consumption trends and drivers. *Philosophical transactions of the Royal Society of London. Series B, Biological sciences* 365(1554), 2793–2807.

Liu, H., T.I. Wahl, J.L. Seale, and J. Bai. 2015. Household composition, income, and food-away-from-home expenditure in urban China. *Food Policy* 51: 97–100.

Lluch, C., and A. Powell. 1975. International comparisons of expenditure patterns. *European Economic Review* 6(3): 275–303.

Rathnayaka, S.D., E.A. Selvanathan, and S. Selvanathan. 2019. Consumption patterns in Sri Lanka: A decomposition analysis. *Applied Economics* 51(37): 4056–4072.

Seale, J.L., A. Regmi, and J. Bernstein. 2003. *International evidence on food consumption patterns.* Economic Research Service, US Department of Agriculture, Washington D.C.

Selvanathan, S. 1993. *A system-wide analysis of international consumption patterns.* Advanced Studies in Theoretical and Applied Econometrics. Boston, MA: Kluwer Academic Publishers.

Selvanathan, S., and E.A. Selvanathan. 1993. A cross-country analysis of consumption patterns. *Applied Economics 25*: 1245–1259.

Selvanathan, E.A., and S. Selvanathan. 2003a. Similarities in the consumption patterns of the five Asian tigers. *Asian Economic Journal* 17:297–323.

Selvanathan, E.A., and S. Selvanathan. 2003b. *International consumption comparisons: OECD versus LDC.* Singapore: World Scientific.

Selvanathan, S., and E.A. Selvanathan. 2006. Consumption patterns of food, tobacco and beverages: A cross-country analysis. *Applied Economics* 38(13): 1567–1584.

Selvanathan, E.A., S. Selvanathan, L. Wong, L., and M. Jayasinghe. 2021. Modelling regional consumption patterns in Australia. *Economic Record* 97(317): 141–156.

Stone, R. 1954. Linear expenditure systems and demand analysis: An application to the pattern of British demand. *The Economic Journal* 64(255): 511–527.

Theil, H., and F.E. Suhm. 1981. *International Consumption Comparisons: A System-wide Approach.* Amsterdam: North-Holland Publishing Company.

The Tobacco Atlas 2016. Accessed on 10th February 2022. Global Cigarette Consumption. Retrieved from https://tobaccoatlas.org/topic/consumption/.

WHO 2018. *Alcohol-Key facts.* Accessed on 10th February 2022. Retrieved from https://www.who.int/news-room/fact-sheets/detail/alcohol.

Wong, L., E.A. Selvanathan, and S. Selvanathan. 2017. 'Empirical analysis of Australian consumption patterns. *Empirical Economics* 52(2): 799–823.

Working, H. 1943. Statistical laws of family expenditure. *Journal of the American Statistical Association* 38: 43–56.

7 Demand for Transport, Communication and Housing

E A Selvanathan, S Selvanathan and M Jayasinghe

7.1 Introduction

In Chapter 6, we presented an analysis of the demand for the food group consisting of food, restaurants, soft drinks, alcohol and tobacco in the 45 countries and estimated conditional demand equations for the three items within food, namely food, alcohol and restaurants. In this chapter, we analyse the demand for another important commodity group consisting of transport, communication and housing (TCH group), conditionally for the 45 countries. In some ways, the three commodities TCH are interlinked. In some situations, communication acts as a substitute for transport (for example, depending on circumstances, instead of travelling to meet someone, it may be sufficient to discuss via the telephone) and in other situations communication could act as a complement for transport (for example a telephone communication could lead to travel). Similarly, the location of a person's house would determine the amount he/she has to spend on transport and the cost of travel could also determine how much a person can afford to spend on housing. A number of studies have appeared in the literature in the past ten years that analyse the link between TCH (for example, see Dewita et al. 2018, 2020; Hassan et al. 2018; and Mattingly and Morrissey 2014). As in Chapter 6, (1) we use the conditional demand equations under block independence derived in Chapter 2 for estimation and to obtain the implied income and price elasticities of the three goods within the TCH group for the same 45 countries, and (2) we follow a similar analysis using the household expenditure survey (HES) data for three countries, Australia, India and Sri Lanka.

As can be seen from Table 3.5 of Chapter 3, at sample means, consumers in developing countries allocate 21.2 percent of their income on housing, 12.9 percent on transport and 2.4 percent on communication, giving a total of about 37 percent of their income on the TCH group. In developing countries, consumers allocate 16.9 percent on housing, 13.7 percent on transport and 3.1 percent on communication, with a total of about 34 percent of their income on the TCH group. These figures clearly show that, in most countries, the TCH group occupies a significant part of the household expenditure and a study of the demand for TCH has some significance.

DOI: 10.4324/9780429200120-7

Analysis of demand for TCH has also become an important area of policy interest. The transport and communication sectors have seen an exponential growth followed by astonishing growth in travel, communication technologies and economic activities across the globe. The travel behaviour of people has changed, particularly as a result of rising income and the widespread use of cars. Similarly, with the advancement of the internet and other online communication platforms, the communication behaviour of people has changed. On the other hand, shelter is considered as one of the basic needs (together with food and clothing). The demand elasticities, both price and income, of transport, communication and housing are important tools to assess the impact of pricing policies. For example, price elasticity of transport demand is one of the most important parameters to understand how pricing policies will affect transport demand. An understanding of demand for TCH in developed and developing countries will be valuable for anticipating future use of these goods and even energy demand (both household and transport related) and addressing environmental concerns, such as carbon dioxide emissions. For example, if price elasticities for transport demand are low and falling, then high taxes on (or prices of) carbon are likely to have little effect on overall transport use (Fouquet 2012).

Section 7.2 presents a literature review of the demand for the TCH group and its three individual commodities. Section 7.3 presents a preliminary analysis based on the time-series data for the 45 countries and in Section 7.4 we present the model estimation results and discuss the implications of the model coefficient estimates and their implied demand elasticities. Section 7.5 presents the analysis based on cross-sectional data and also analyses the effect of the various characteristics on the estimates and elasticities. Finally, Section 7.6 presents the concluding comments.

7.2 Demand for Transport, Communication and Housing (TCH): A Review

Choo et al. (2007) analysed the aggregate consumer expenditure on transportation and communication in the USA between 1984 and 2002, applying the linear approximate Almost Ideal Demand System (AIDS) method. The results indicated that transportation and communications expenditure groups have both substitution and complementarity relationships. Clements et al. (2020) estimated income and price elasticities for nine commodities, including housing for all 37 OECD countries, using the differential demand system approach. The study used time-series data for the period 1995–2015. The results revealed that housing is a necessity item for OECD consumers. Furthermore, own-price elasticity estimates revealed that the demand for housing is price inelastic. Fouquet (2012) examined the trends in income and price elasticities in the UK between 1850 and 2010. The results indicate that income and price elasticities were very high in the mid-19th century and declined continuously since then. Land transport demand became price inelastic (i.e., less than one) in the early 1920s and income inelastic at the end of the 1930s and in the early 1940s. In 2010, long-run income and price elasticity of aggregate land transport demand were estimated to be 0.8 and −0.6, respectively. Jayasinghe et al. (2019), using Household Income and Expenditure Survey data for Sri Lanka, analysed consumer demand for nine commodity groups, including TCH. The study estimated a system of demand curves adopting the Box-Cox Engel curves approach. The implied elasticity estimated revealed that TCH are luxury goods with expenditure elasticities greater than one. Selvanathan and Selvanathan (1994) investigated the substitution/complementarity relationship between consumer demand for private transport, public transport and communication in the UK and Australia for the period 1960–1986 using the Rotterdam Demand System approach. The results revealed significant similarities and some important differences in consumption of these goods in the two countries. The results also indicated that in both countries: (a) private transport is a luxury and public transport is a necessity; (b) the demand for all three goods is price inelastic; and (c) public transport, private transport and communications are pairwise substitutes.

When considering the literature on the consumer demand for housing, Ahmad (2015) analysed demand for housing and its attributes in urban Bangladesh using a survey of 4,400 households. The study found that housing demand is inelastic with respect to income and price and that price elasticity is less than income elasticity in absolute terms. Clements et al. (2021) using *2015/16 Australian Household Expenditure Survey* data found that the income elasticity of housing for the one-consumer case is 0.954. With quintiles, this elasticity was found to be above unity for both the lowest and highest income groups, while the middle-income groups have lower elasticities (between 0.688 and 0.922). Gallin (2003) estimated the long-run income elasticity of housing demand in the USA using time-series data for the period 1975–2002 and found the income elasticity to be between 1.45 and 1.71. Jayasinghe et al. (2019) found that housing is a luxury good in Sri Lanka. While Lopez et al. (1998) obtained a value of 1.20, Martinez and Maza (2003) found income elasticities of housing closer to 2.80 for Spain. By using a cross-sectional analysis, a number of studies have found that income elasticity of housing ranges between 0.69 and 1.00 in the USA and between 0.80 and 1.00 in Spain (see, for example, Fernández-Kranz and Hon 2006; Goodman and Kawai 1982, 1986; Manrique and Ojah 2003; Polinsky 1977). Using time-series data between 1966 and 1994, a study by Tse and Raftery (1999) revealed that the short-run income elasticity of housing in Hong Kong is generally less than unity and the adjustment parameter is about 0.81. Overall, studies have found mixed results with respect to income elasticity of housing, ranging from being a necessity to a luxury, both in developing and developed countries. The results appear to be particularly sensitive for the type of data used – cross-sectional or time-series.

There is a growing body of literature examining the demand for housing and housing affordability together with demand for transport. This is particularly important because housing location has significant implications on transport costs. For example, Dewita et al. (2018) noted that households are compelled to make trade-offs between transport and housing by either spending more on housing in the inner city with lower transport costs or choosing more affordable housing in suburban areas, with a higher commuting cost. Dewita et al. (2018) found that the overall housing affordability is affected by housing type, choice of transport modes and distance to work and school. Dewita et al. (2020) further confirm that housing affordability is affected not only by housing type but also by the choice of transport modes. Using the Location Housing Affordability Index, which combines the housing affordability with transport expenditure, Hassan et al. (2018) found that household location significantly influences household affordability. In particular, this study found that houses in the urban area were seriously unaffordable for the low- and middle-income groups generating serious implications on their transport budgets. Mattingly and Morrissey (2014) argue that traditional measures of housing affordability are expressed solely as a function of housing cost and income. This unidimensional view of affordability ignores transportation costs, which represent a significant proportion of household budgets. The study examined the combined housing and transport affordability in intra-metropolitan areas in Auckland, New Zealand. The results reveal that once commuting costs are incorporated into measures, a very different pattern of affordability emerges. In summary, these results highlight the need to analyse housing expenditure in combination with transport and communication expenditures.

7.3 Preliminary Data Analysis – Time-Series Data

As in Chapter 6 (Section 6.4), in this section, we present a preliminary data analysis of the price and consumption data of the TCH group in the form of budget shares, Divisia indices and scatter plots.

Table 7.1 presents the unconditional and conditional budget shares for TCH and the budget share for the group consisting of these three items. The unconditional budget shares in columns (2)–(4) are reproduced from Table 3.5, and the group budget share in column (5) is a simple addition of the three unconditional budget shares in columns (2)–(4). The conditional budget shares presented in columns (6)–(8) for each commodity are the proportion of expenditures on the TCH group expressed as a proportion of the total expenditure on the group. As can be seen, the mean unconditional budget shares of TCH for the 45 countries are 13.3 percent, 2.8 percent and 19.1 percent, respectively, giving a total of 35.1 percent for the group. This means that a typical consumer allocates about one-third of their income on the TCH group. The mean conditional budget shares for TCH are 35.2 percent, 7.2 percent and 57.6 percent, respectively. Now we summarise the consumption data in the form of Divisia measures given by equations (6.1)–(6.10) for the TCH group. As in Chapter 6, for a group S_g for period t, we use the Divisia volume index (DQ_{gt}) and the Divisia price index (DP_{gt}) to measure the growth in consumption and prices, the corresponding Divisia quantity variance (K_{gt}) and Divisia price variance (Π_{gt}) to measure the variation in consumption and prices, and the Divisia price-quantity correlation (ρ_{gt}) to measure the strength

Table 7.1 Unconditional and conditional budget shares at sample means, TCH group, 45 countries

Country		*Unconditional budget share (percent)*				*Conditional budget share (percent)*		
	Country (1)	*Transport* (2)	*Communication* (3)	*Housing* (4)	*Group* (5)	*Transport* (6)	*Communication* (7)	*Housing* (8)
Developed countries								
1	Australia	12.0	2.2	20.7	34.9	34.5	6.2	59.3
2	Austria	12.9	2.3	20.6	35.8	36.1	6.5	57.5
3	Belgium	11.7	2.4	23.7	37.8	31.0	6.3	62.8
4	Canada	14.5	2.1	23.6	40.2	36.0	5.3	58.8
5	Denmark	12.4	2.0	27.2	41.6	29.7	4.8	65.4
6	Finland	13.3	2.0	22.4	37.7	35.6	5.1	59.3
7	France	13.4	1.9	20.3	35.6	38.2	5.1	56.8
8	Germany	14.3	2.6	24.1	41.0	34.9	6.4	58.7
9	Hong Kong[a]	–	–	–	–	–	–	–
10	Iceland	15.0	2.2	19.8	37.0	40.8	5.8	53.4
11	Ireland	12.2	2.7	19.9	34.8	35.2	7.7	57.1
12	Israel	14.0	3.9	23.0	40.9	34.2	9.4	56.4
13	Italy	13.0	2.7	20.6	36.3	35.9	7.4	56.7
14	Japan	10.9	2.5	23.5	36.9	29.6	6.7	63.7
15	Luxembourg	16.7	1.7	21.5	39.9	41.8	4.2	54.1
16	Netherlands	13.4	3.5	20.2	37.1	36.1	9.4	54.4
17	New Zealand	14.0	2.8	25.4	42.2	33.3	6.7	60.1
18	Norway	14.8	2.2	21.2	38.2	38.8	5.6	55.6
19	Singapore[a]	–	–	–	–	–	–	–
20	Slovenia	15.7	2.8	18.8	37.3	42.0	7.6	50.5
21	South Korea	10.3	2.4	14.5	27.2	39.2	7.7	53.1
22	Spain	11.6	2.5	18.3	32.4	36.2	7.6	56.2
23	Sweden	13.3	3.1	28.0	44.4	26.2	6.3	67.5
24	Switzerland	9.3	2.3	24.0	35.6	26.2	6.3	67.5
25	Taiwan[a]	13.7	–	18.9	32.6	–	–	–
26	UK	13.4	2.0	25.5	40.9	32.8	4.8	62.5
27	USA	11.7	2.1	18.8	32.6	35.9	6.5	57.6
Mean (*Developed*)		12.9	2.4	21.3	36.6	35.1	6.4	58.5

Developing countries							
28 Colombia	10.6	4.2	16.7	31.6	33.6	13.3	53.1
29 Czech	9.7	2.8	24.3	36.7	26.7	7.4	65.9
30 Estonia	11.6	3.0	19.5	34.2	34.1	8.8	57.1
31 Greece	14.2	3.4	19.0	36.6	39.1	9.2	51.8
32 Hungary	13.9	3.7	19.2	36.7	37.8	9.9	52.4
33 India	12.5	–	10.5	23.0	–	–	–
34 Latvia	11.6	2.8	20.1	34.4	33.8	7.9	58.3
35 Lithuania	13.7	2.4	16.5	32.5	42.0	7.2	50.9
36 Malaysia	19.7	–	17.0	36.7	–	–	–
37 Mexico	18.1	3.5	21.6	43.2	41.9	8.2	49.9
38 Philippines	13.7	–	12.3	26.0	–	–	–
39 Poland	10.7	2.7	20.7	34.1	31.3	8.0	60.7
40 Portugal	14.6	2.8	14.9	32.3	45.3	8.7	46.0
41 Slovakia	7.9	3.3	23.5	34.7	23.1	9.4	67.5
42 South Africa[a]	15.6	–	13.0	28.6	–	–	–
43 Sri Lanka[a]	17.2	–	8.0	25.2	–	–	–
44 Thailand[a]	12.8	–	9.3	22.0	–	–	–
45 Turkey[a]	18.0	–	17.4	35.4	–	–	–
Mean (*Developing*)	13.7	3.1	16.9	33.7	35.3	8.9	55.8
Mean (*All countries*)	13.3	2.8	19.1	35.1	35.2	7.2	57.6

[a] Disaggregated data are not available.

and direction of the relationship between consumption and prices, and their sample means for each country. Furthermore, as in Chapter 6, we obtain the income flexibility ϕ_t as Γ_{gt}/Π_{gt} and its sample mean for each country.

Table 7.2 presents these summary measures. Columns (2) and (3) of the table give the mean Divisia quantity and price indices, respectively; columns (4) and (5) present the mean Divisia quantity variance and price variance, respectively, while column (6) gives the mean price-quantity correlation for each country. As can be seen from the last row of the table, which gives the average across all countries, the price of the TCH group has increased at a rate of 3.30 percent per annum and consumption of the group has increased at a rate of 2.40 percent per annum. The price increase of the group in developing countries (4.96 percent) is almost twice that of developed countries (2.55 percent). A comparison of column (4) with column (5) for each country reveals that, for a majority of the countries, quantity variance systematically exceeds the price variance. This can be further observed in Figure 7.1 where we plot the quantity variance against the price variance together with a 45° line. As can be seen, most of the data points are scattered above the 45° line, indicating that quantity variance systematically exceeds the price variance. As can be seen from column (6) of Table 7.2, a majority of the correlations are negative with an average of –0.45. The last column of the table gives the sample mean income flexibility for each country. As can be seen, most of the estimates are negative with a cross-country average of –0.66. The above observations are well in agreement with the unconditional analysis presented in Chapter 3 as well as with many previous cross-country demand studies.

Table 7.3 tabulates the percentage signs of relative prices (RP) and relative consumption (RC) in the form of four combinations: (positive RP, positive RC), (positive RP, negative RC), (negative RP, positive RC) and (negative

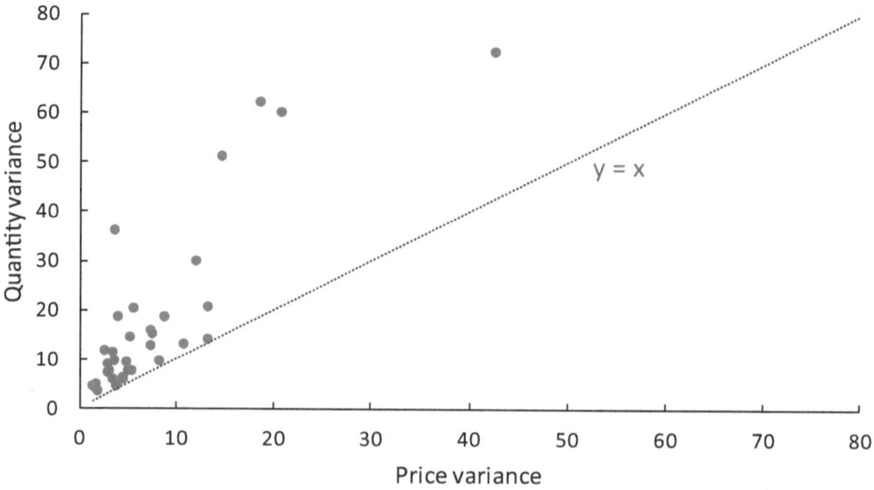

Figure 7.1 Divisia quantity variance against price variance, TCH group, 45 countries.

Table 7.2 Mean Divisia price and quantity indices, variances and correlation, and income flexibility, TCH group, 45 countries

Country (1)	Divisia quantity index (DQ) (2)	Divisia price index (DP) (3)	Divisia quantity variance (4)	Divisia price variance (5)	Divisia price-quantity correlation (6)	Income flexibility (7)
Developed countries						
1 Australia	1.99	3.19	4.41	4.02	−0.36	−0.38
2 Austria	0.93	2.18	7.53	5.63	−0.44	−0.51
3 Belgium	0.86	2.11	4.79	1.93	−0.45	−0.71
4 Canada	1.78	2.68	4.30	1.63	−0.21	−0.34
5 Denmark	0.51	2.28	11.70	2.79	−0.49	−1.00
6 Finland	2.07	4.26	14.30	5.45	−0.41	−0.66
7 France	2.89	4.57	6.00	3.65	−0.54	−0.69
8 Germany	0.82	1.62	7.23	3.09	−0.75	−1.15
9 Hong Kong[a]	–	–	–	–	–	–
10 Iceland	3.21	5.50	62.00	18.81	−0.48	−0.87
11 Ireland	9.75	−4.07	60.08	20.83	−0.89	−1.51
12 Israel	2.16	3.43	12.59	7.47	−0.18	−0.23
13 Italy	0.50	2.81	7.45	5.22	−0.68	−0.81
14 Japan	1.41	−0.14	4.49	1.54	−0.41	−0.70
15 Luxembourg	0.55	2.12	5.77	4.73	−0.38	−0.42
16 Netherlands	1.00	2.61	11.49	3.65	−0.21	−0.37
17 New Zealand	1.66	2.25	13.22	10.91	−0.69	−0.76
18 Norway	2.21	4.82	18.72	4.12	−0.20	−0.43
19 Singapore[a]	–	–	–	–	–	–
20 Slovenia	1.63	4.36	7.71	3.20	−0.45	−0.70
21 South Korea	5.23	8.47	20.48	13.44	−0.60	−0.74
22 Spain	2.15	2.89	8.86	3.14	−0.52	−0.87
23 Sweden	3.20	−1.53	9.16	5.01	−0.81	−1.10
24 Switzerland	3.20	−1.53	9.16	5.01	−0.81	−1.10
25 Taiwan[a]	–	–	–	–	–	–
26 UK	1.03	2.47	3.46	2.13	−0.61	−0.78
27 USA	1.69	3.80	6.29	4.67	−0.71	−0.82
Mean (*Developed*)	2.18	2.55	13.38	5.92	−0.51	−0.74

(*Continued*)

Table 7.2 Mean Divisia price and quantity indices, variances and correlation, and income flexibility, TCH group, 45 countries (*Continued*)

Country *(1)*	*Divisia quantity index (DQ)* *(2)*	*Divisia price index (DP)* *(3)*	*Divisia quantity variance* *(4)*	*Divisia price variance* *(5)*	*Divisia price-quantity correlation* *(6)*	*Income flexibility* *(7)*
Developing countries						
28 Colombia	3.24	4.55	9.71	3.82	0.20	0.32
29 Czech Republic	1.85	3.98	9.58	8.52	−0.48	−0.51
30 Estonia	4.33	6.30	29.95	12.20	−0.47	−0.74
31 Greece	1.57	2.27	35.94	3.78	−0.31	−0.96
32 Hungary	2.34	6.80	15.11	7.65	−0.16	−0.22
33 Indiaa	–	–	–	–	–	–
34 Latvia	4.31	6.94	72.37	42.71	−0.43	−0.56
35 Lithuania	4.45	5.38	51.15	14.91	−0.38	−0.70
36 Malaysia[a]	–	–	–	–	–	–
37 Mexico	1.77	4.05	15.81	7.62	−0.20	−0.29
38 Philippines[a]	–	–	–	–	–	–
39 Poland	4.09	5.39	18.51	9.03	−0.40	−0.57
40 Portugal	0.29	3.99	20.16	5.66	−0.43	−0.81
41 Slovakia	3.37	4.87	14.06	13.48	−0.56	−0.57
42 South Africa[a]	–	–	–	–	–	–
43 Sri Lanka[a]	–	–	–	–	–	–
44 Thailand[a]	–	–	–	–	–	–
45 Turkey[a]	–	–	–	–	–	–
Mean (*Developing*)	2.87	4.96	26.58	11.76	−0.33	−0.51
Mean (*All countries*)	2.40	3.30	17.53	7.76	−0.45	−0.66

Note: All entries in columns (2) and (3) are to be divided by 100 and those in columns (4) and (5) are to be divided by 10,000.
a Disaggregated TCH data are unavailable.

Table 7.3 Frequency of same and opposite signs of relative prices and relative consumption of transport, communication and housing group, 45 countries

Country	*Positive consumption*		*Negative consumption*		*Opposite signs*
	Positive price	*Negative price*	*Positive price*	*Negative price*	*(3) + (4)*
(1)	*(2)*	*(3)*	*(4)*	*(5)*	*(6)*
Developed countries					
1 Australia	15	34	29	22	63
2 Austria	13	45	30	12	75
3 Belgium	19	28	21	32	49
4 Canada	20	26	28	25	54
5 Denmark	13	42	27	18	69
6 Finland	16	38	28	18	66
7 France	17	39	27	17	66
8 Germany	14	47	32	7	79
9 Hong Kong[a]	–	–	–	–	–
10 Iceland	11	39	32	19	71
11 Ireland	9	44	39	7	83
12 Israel	19	35	28	18	63
13 Italy	11	49	35	5	84
14 Japan	30	19	12	39	31
15 Luxembourg	23	32	17	28	49
16 Netherlands	19	32	28	21	60
17 New Zealand	12	51	25	12	76
18 Norway	23	25	23	30	48
19 Singapore[a]	–	–	–	–	–
20 Slovenia	18	32	23	27	55
21 South Korea	16	40	28	16	68
22 Spain	19	37	28	16	65
23 Sweden	9	46	37	7	83
24 Switzerland	9	46	37	7	
25 Taiwan[a]					
26 UK	15	43	30	12	73
27 USA	11	41	33	14	74
Mean (*Developed*)	16	38	28	18	65

(*Continued*)

Table 7.3 Frequency of same and opposite signs of relative prices and relative consumption of transport, communication and housing group, 45 countries (*Continued*)

	Positive consumption		*Negative consumption*		*Opposite signs*
Country (1)	*Positive price* (2)	*Negative price* (3)	*Positive price* (4)	*Negative price* (5)	*(3) + (4)* (6)
Developing countries					
28 Colombia	33	26	19	21	45
29 Czech Republic	17	35	28	20	63
30 Estonia	15	37	30	18	67
31 Greece	23	27	27	23	54
32 Hungary	20	30	27	23	57
33 India[a]	–	–	–	–	–
34 Latvia	14	42	33	11	75
35 Lithuania	11	30	37	23	67
36 Malaysia[a]	–	–	–	–	–
37 Mexico	18	30	21	30	51
38 Philippines[a]	–	–	–	–	–
39 Poland	15	37	23	25	60
40 Portugal	15	48	22	15	70
41 Slovakia	15	42	30	13	72
42 South Africa[a]	–	–	–	–	–
43 Sri Lanka[a]	–	–	–	–	–
44 Thailand[a]	–	–	–	–	–
45 Turkey[a]	–	–	–	–	–
Mean (*Developing*)	18	35	27	20	62
Mean (*All countries*)	16	37	28	19	64

a Disaggregated data are not available.

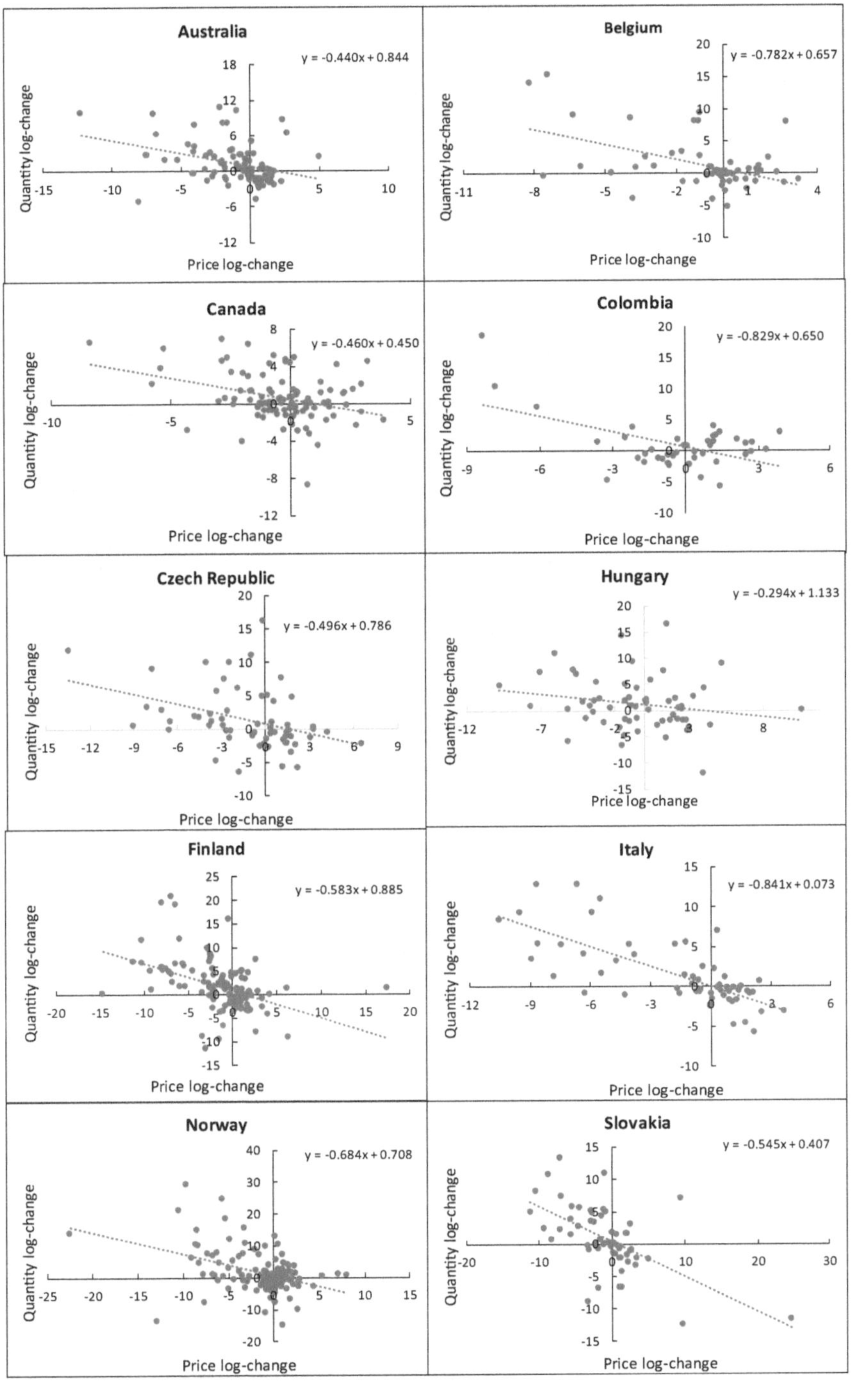

Figure 7.2 Relative quantity vs relative prices, TCH group, ten selected countries.

Table 7.4 Estimates of income flexibility for TCH, 45 countries

Country *(1)*	*Transport* *(2)*	*Communication* *(3)*	*Housing* *(4)*	*Group (Figure 7.2)* *(5)*
Developed countries				
1 Australia	0.02	−0.08	0.09	−0.44
2 Austria	−0.31	−1.36	−0.50	−1.07
3 Belgium	−0.22	−0.38	−0.08	−0.78
4 Canada	−0.08	−0.45	−0.09	−0.46
5 Denmark	1.02	−1.10	1.06	−1.02
6 Finland	−0.30	−0.32	−0.47	−0.58
7 France	−0.47	−0.59	−0.20	−0.85
8 Germany	−0.99	−1.45	−1.01	−1.34
9 Hong Kong[a]	–	–	–	–
10 Iceland	−1.27	−1.50	−1.23	−1.42
11 Ireland	−1.42	−1.58	−1.48	−1.52
12 Israel	−0.09	−0.54	−0.04	−0.55
13 Italy	−0.73	−0.43	−0.80	−0.84
14 Japan	0.22	−0.77	0.06	−0.90
15 Luxembourg	0.61	−0.17	0.59	−0.58
16 Netherlands	−0.06	−0.84	−0.50	−1.01
17 New Zealand	−0.61	−1.15	−0.61	−1.03
18 Norway	−0.19	−0.44	−0.24	−0.68
19 Singapore[a]	–	–	–	–
20 Slovenia	−0.37	−0.31	−0.28	−0.70
21 South Korea	−0.53	−0.61	−0.38	−0.72
22 Spain	−0.37	−0.13	−0.47	−0.79
23 Sweden	−1.80	−1.20	−1.66	−1.22
24 Switzerland	−1.80	−1.20	−1.66	−1.22
25 Taiwan[a]	–	–	–	–
26 UK	−0.54	−1.15	−0.56	−1.03
27 USA	−0.45	−0.70	−0.58	−0.73
Mean (*Developed*)	−0.45	−0.77	−0.46	−0.89
Developing countries				
28 Colombia	0.23	−0.99	−0.46	−0.83
29 Czech Republic	0.04	−0.51	0.09	−0.50
30 Estonia	−0.84	−0.43	−0.84	−0.84
31 Greece	−0.43	−0.35	−0.35	−0.92
32 Hungary	−0.21	−0.10	0.02	−0.29
33 India[a]	–	–	–	–
34 Latvia	−1.00	−0.75	−0.88	−0.87
35 Lithuania	0.00	−0.24	−0.13	−0.47
36 Malaysia[a]	–	–	–	–
37 Mexico	−0.60	−0.74	−0.38	−0.82
38 Philippines[a]	–	–	–	–
39 Poland	−0.60	−0.55	−0.25	−0.62
40 Portugal	−1.13	−1.97	−1.18	−0.98
41 Slovakia	−0.78	−0.51	−0.41	−0.55
42 South Africa[a]	–	–	–	–
43 Sri Lanka[a]	–	–	–	–
44 Thailand[a]	–	–	–	–
45 Turkey[a]	–	–	–	–
Mean (*Developing*)	−0.48	−0.65	−0.44	−0.70
Mean (*All countries*)	−0.46	−0.73	−0.45	−0.83

[a] Disaggregated data are not available.

Table 7.5 Estimated conditional income and own-price elasticities, double-log demand equation, 45 countries

	Income elasticity			*Price elasticity*		
Country (1)	*Transport* (2)	*Communication* (3)	*Housing* (4)	*Transport* (5)	*Communication* (6)	*Housing* (7)
Developed countries						
1 Australia	2.16 (0.16)	1.29 (0.46)	0.29 (0.07)	−0.20 (0.13)	−0.11 (0.22)	−0.16 (0.11)
2 Austria	1.14 (0.15)	1.06 (0.80)	0.71 (0.11)	−0.37 (0.16)	−1.35 (0.29)	−0.49 (0.21)
3 Belgium	1.51 (0.30)	1.70 (0.82)	0.71 (0.13)	−0.15 (0.38)	−0.39 (0.38)	0.00 (0.34)
4 Canada	2.46 (0.16)	0.61 (0.27)	0.13 (0.08)	−0.15 (0.16)	−0.50 (0.16)	−0.06 (0.15)
5 Denmark	2.95 (0.30)	0.49 (0.64)	0.16 (0.14)	−0.65 (0.57)	−0.98 (0.50)	−0.65 (0.57)
6 Finland	2.47 (0.15)	1.42 (0.37)	0.03 (0.09)	−0.33 (0.16)	−0.32 (0.16)	−0.50 (0.14)
7 France	1.46 (0.10)	0.89 (0.30)	0.76 (0.07)	−0.02 (0.20)	−0.56 (0.17)	0.01 (0.20)
8 Germany	1.49 (0.39)	1.57 (0.67)	0.55 (0.20)	−0.81 (0.37)	−1.42 (0.22)	−0.51 (0.40)
9 Hong Kong[a]	–	–	–	–	–	–
10 Iceland	1.74 (0.33)	1.05 (0.57)	0.40 (0.21)	−0.93 (0.32)	−1.50 (0.47)	−0.87 (0.27)
11 Ireland	0.74 (0.10)	0.72 (0.10)	1.21 (0.11)	−2.21 (0.26)	−1.75 (0.12)	−2.17 (0.41)
12 Israel	1.54 (0.17)	1.76 (0.51)	0.48 (0.07)	−0.12 (0.25)	−0.51 (0.27)	0.05 (0.13)
13 Italy	1.85 (0.17)	2.45 (0.41)	0.33 (0.11)	−0.35 (0.19)	−0.79 (0.26)	−0.35 (0.21)
14 Japan	1.22 (0.32)	1.80 (0.61)	0.77 (0.10)	−0.07 (0.37)	−1.16 (0.43)	0.01 (0.27)
15 Luxembourg	0.92 (0.08)	1.11 (0.13)	1.05 (0.06)	0.60 (0.27)	−0.11 (0.21)	0.56 (0.28)
16 Netherlands	1.37 (0.20)	3.75 (0.45)	0.30 (0.15)	−0.18 (0.35)	−0.80 (0.24)	−0.67 (0.38)
17 New Zealand	2.13 (0.18)	0.33 (0.32)	0.51 (0.10)	−0.13 (0.15)	−1.14 (0.17)	−0.34 (0.13)
18 Norway	2.06 (0.10)	0.37 (0.33)	0.30 (0.07)	−0.17 (0.25)	−0.40 (0.23)	−0.38 (0.23)
19 Singapore[a]	–	–	–	–	–	–
20 Slovenia	1.43 (0.23)	1.14 (0.52)	0.54 (0.14)	−0.05 (0.34)	−0.32 (0.48)	0.21 (0.27)
21 South Korea	1.40 (0.14)	1.73 (0.32)	0.60 (0.08)	−0.35 (0.18)	−0.55 (0.11)	−0.12 (0.13)
22 Spain	1.11 (0.25)	1.83 (0.28)	0.64 (0.15)	−0.44 (0.51)	−0.61 (0.19)	0.62 (0.53)
23 Sweden	1.24 (0.13)	0.61 (0.36)	0.96 (0.05)	−1.78 (0.18)	−1.23 (0.13)	−1.64 (0.14)
24 Switzerland	1.24 (0.13)	0.61 (0.36)	0.96 (0.05)	−1.78 (0.18)	−1.23 (0.13)	−1.64 (0.14)
25 Taiwan[a]	–	–	–	–	–	–
26 UK	1.68 (0.22)	2.14 (0.52)	0.54 (0.10)	−0.52 (0.20)	−0.97 (0.23)	−0.47 (0.17)
27 USA	2.08 (0.10)	0.66 (0.14)	0.37 (0.06)	−0.21 (0.09)	−0.62 (0.10)	−0.26 (0.10)
Mean (*Developed*)	1.64 (0.04)	1.29 (0.10)	0.55 (0.02)	−0.47 (0.06)	−0.80 (0.06)	−0.41 (0.06)

(*Continued*)

Table 7.5 Estimated conditional income and own-price elasticities, double-log demand equation, 45 countries (*Continued*)

	Income elasticity			Price elasticity		
Country (1)	*Transport (2)*	*Communication (3)*	*Housing (4)*	*Transport (5)*	*Communication (6)*	*Housing (7)*
Developing countries						
28 Colombia	1.36 (0.13)	1.76 (0.44)	0.44 (0.07)	−0.03 (0.29)	−0.60 (0.42)	−0.11 (0.26)
29 Czech	1.90 (0.29)	2.08 (0.46)	0.50 (0.12)	0.04 (0.20)	−0.70 (0.26)	−0.08 (0.17)
30 Estonia	1.31 (0.16)	0.55 (0.26)	0.87 (0.09)	−0.67 (0.34)	−0.69 (0.41)	−0.69 (0.29)
31 Greece	2.00 (0.22)	1.48 (0.65)	0.19 (0.15)	0.85 (0.62)	−0.25 (0.71)	1.14 (0.56)
32 Hungary	1.74 (0.18)	1.01 (0.41)	0.51 (0.12)	−0.09 (0.28)	−0.10 (0.33)	−0.12 (0.24)
33 India	–	–	–	–	–	–
34 Latvia	1.80 (0.38)	0.45 (0.71)	0.50 (0.19)	−0.51 (0.36)	−0.88 (0.32)	−0.49 (0.23)
35 Lithuania	1.71 (0.22)	0.24 (0.58)	0.53 (0.15)	0.45 (0.54)	−0.19 (0.33)	−0.03 (0.33)
36 Malaysia[a]	–	–	–	–	–	–
37 Mexico	1.72 (0.17)	0.31 (0.40)	0.56 (0.10)	−0.23 (0.33)	−0.79 (0.44)	−0.13 (0.23)
38 Philippines[a]	–	–	–	–	–	–
39 Poland	1.35 (0.34)	0.83 (0.64)	0.76 (0.18)	−0.37 (0.50)	−0.57 (0.32)	−0.01 (0.37)
40 Portugal	2.16 (0.14)	0.80 (0.39)	0.07 (0.13)	−0.62 (0.28)	−1.88 (0.70)	−0.75 (0.33)
41 Slovakia	0.49 (0.33)	1.11 (0.36)	1.13 (0.16)	−0.85 (0.28)	−0.52 (0.15)	−0.44 (0.31)
42 South Africa[a]	–	–		–	–	–
43 Sri Lanka[a]	–	–		–	–	–
44 Thailand[a]	–	–		–	–	–
45 Turkey[a]	–	–		–	–	–
Mean (*Developing*)	1.59 (0.07)	0.97 (0.15)	0.54 (0.04)	−0.19 (0.12)	−0.65 (0.13)	−0.16 (0.10)
Mean (*All countries*)	1.63 (0.04)	1.19 (0.08)	0.55 (0.02)	−0.38 (0.05)	−0.76 (0.06)	−0.33 (0.05)

Note: Standard errors are in parenthesis.
[a] Disaggregated data are unavailable.

RP, negative RC). As can be seen, more than two-thirds of the pair (RP, RC) observations are falling in the (positive RP, negative RC) and (negative RP, positive RC) categories, giving support for the law of demand, meaning that the demand for a good falls when relative price increases.

In Figure 7.2, for selected countries, we plot RC against RP of the TCH. Table 7.4 presents, for each country, the slope of the fitted regression line for each individual and pooled data across the three commodities. The slope can be interpreted as an estimate for income flexibility. As can be seen, the average values are –0.46 (transport), –0.73 (communication) and –0.45 (housing). We have observed such values of income flexibility with unconditional data and these results are also similar to the values reported in many previous cross-country studies (Chen 2001; Clements et al. 2020; Meisner 1979; Rathnayaka et al. 2019; Selvanathan 1993; Selvanathan and Selvanathan 1993, 2003a, 2003b; Selvanathan et al. 2021; Theil and Suhm, 1981).

Table 7.5 presents the conditional income and price elasticities based on the double-log demand system. As can be seen, on average, the conditional income elasticity estimates for transport (1.63) and communication (1.19) are greater than one, implying that transport and communication are luxuries and the conditional income elasticity for housing (0.55) is less than one, implying that it is a necessity. The own-price elasticity of transport (–0.38), communication (–0.76) and housing (–0.33) are all less than one in absolute value, indicating that the demand for these three commodities is price inelastic.

7.4 Modelling the Demand for Transport, Communication and Housing

In this section, we present the conditional demand equations for estimation, test the demand theory hypotheses, estimate the model and present the implied income and price elasticities. From Section 2.11 of Chapter 2, we have the finite-change version of the absolute price version of the conditional demand equation (2.116) for $i \in S_g$, which we reproduce here:

$$\bar{w}_{it} Dq_{it} = \theta_i' W_{gt} DQ_{gt} + \sum_{j \in S_g} \pi_{ij}^g Dp_{jt}, \tag{7.1}$$

where the conditional marginal share, θ_i', and Slutsky coefficient, π_{ij}^g, are specified as constants.

The conditional Slutsky coefficients satisfy demand homogeneity,

$$\sum_{j \in S_g} \pi_{ij}^g = 0, \quad i \in S_g, \tag{7.2}$$

and Slutsky symmetry,

$$\pi_{ij}^g = \pi_{ji}^g, \quad i, j \in S_g. \tag{7.3}$$

Table 7.6 presents the results for the testing of demand homogeneity and Slutsky symmetry hypotheses. We have n = 3 commodities, and the sample

Table 7.6 Testing homogeneity and symmetry, TCH group, 45 countries

	Country (1)	n (2)	T (after lagging) (3)	Testing homogeneity (F-test): Test statistic (4)	df1 (5)	df2 (6)	Multiplier (7)	p-value (8)	Decision (5 % level) (9)	Testing symmetry (χ^2-test): Test statistic (10)	p-value (11)	Decision (5 % level) (12)
	Developed countries											
1	Australia	3	29	5.78	2	23	2.09	0.01	Accept[b]	1.54	0.21	Accept
2	Austria	3	20	0.81	2	14	2.14	0.46	Accept	0.94	0.33	Accept
3	Belgium	3	19	1.82	2	13	2.15	0.20	Accept	0.00	1.00	Accept
4	Canada	3	34	1.86	2	28	2.07	0.17	Accept	4.21	0.04	Accept[b]
5	Denmark	3	20	0.77	2	14	2.14	0.48	Accept	3.92	0.05	Accept
6	Finland	3	40	5.45	2	34	2.06	0.01	Accept[b]	2.87	0.09	Accept
7	France	3	56	1.84	2	50	2.04	0.17	Accept	7.75	0.01	Accept[b]
8	Germany	3	19	0.80	2	13	2.15	0.47	Accept	0.50	0.48	Accept
9	Hong Kong[a]	–	–	–	–	–	–	–	–	–	–	–
10	Iceland	3	19	0.74	2	13	2.15	0.49	Accept	0.22	0.64	Accept
11	Ireland	3	18	8.16	2	12	2.17	0.01	Accept[b]	0.25	0.62	Accept
12	Israel	3	19	0.65	2	13	2.15	0.54	Accept	0.63	0.43	Accept
13	Italy	3	19	5.35	2	13	2.15	0.02	Accept[b]	0.04	0.84	Accept
14	Japan	3	19	0.35	2	13	2.15	0.71	Accept	13.31	0.00	Reject
15	Luxembourg	3	20	1.90	2	14	2.14	0.19	Accept	0.00	1.00	Accept
16	Netherlands	3	19	0.55	2	13	2.15	0.59	Accept	1.20	0.27	Accept
17	New Zealand	3	27	0.05	2	21	2.10	0.95	Accept	1.18	0.28	Accept
18	Norway	3	44	3.82	2	38	2.05	0.03	Accept[b]	1.11	0.29	Accept
19	Singapore[a]	–	–	–	–	–	–	–	–	–	–	–
20	Slovenia	3	20	7.22	2	14	2.14	0.01	Accept[b]	0.23	0.63	Accept
21	South Korea	3	45	4.80	2	39	2.05	0.01	Accept[b]	0.50	0.48	Accept
22	Spain	3	19	1.31	2	13	2.15	0.30	Accept	0.23	0.63	Accept
23	Sweden	3	18	0.01	2	12	2.17	0.99	Accept	0.48	0.49	Accept
24	Switzerland	3	18	1.51	2	12	2.17	0.26	Accept	1.65	0.20	Accept
25	Taiwan[a]	–	–	–	–	–	–	–	–	–	–	–
26	UK	3	20	7.84	2	14	2.14	0.01	Accept[b]	0.29	0.59	Accept
27	USA	3	45	3.09	2	39	2.05	0.06	Accept	1.87	0.17	Accept

Developing countries												
28	Colombia	3	14	3.60	2	8	2.25	0.08	Accept	0.92	0.34	Accept
29	Czech	3	20	0.94	2	14	2.14	0.41	Accept	0.10	0.75	Accept
30	Estonia	3	20	2.47	2	14	2.14	0.12	Accept	3.45	0.06	Accept
31	Greece	3	20	0.45	2	14	2.14	0.65	Accept	1.18	0.28	Accept
32	Hungary	3	20	3.30	2	14	2.14	0.07	Accept	0.39	0.53	Accept
33	India[a]	–	–	–	–	–	–	–	–	–	–	–
34	Latvia	3	19	2.00	2	13	2.15	0.18	Accept	0.14	0.71	Accept
35	Lithuania	3	19	5.56	2	13	2.15	0.02	Accept[b]	0.23	0.63	Accept
36	Malaysia[a]	–	–	–	–	–	–	–	–	–	–	–
37	Mexico	3	11	0.18	2	5	2.40	0.84	Accept	0.00	1.00	Accept
38	Philippines[a]	–	–	–	–	–	–	–	–	–	–	–
39	Poland	3	20	1.39	2	14	2.14	0.28	Accept	0.01	0.92	Accept
40	Portugal	3	20	12.86	2	14	2.14	0.00	Reject	1.41	0.24	Accept
41	Slovakia	3	20	3.38	2	14	2.14	0.06	Accept	6.26	0.01	Accept[b]
42	South Africa[a]	–	–	–	–	–	–	–	–	–	–	–
43	Sri Lanka[a]	–	–	–	–	–	–	–	–	–	–	–
44	Thailand[a]	–	–	–	–	–	–	–	–	–	–	–
45	Turkey[a]	–	–	–	–	–	–	–	–	–	–	–
Percentage of rejection									17.6			2.9

Note: $df1 = n - 1$; $df2 = T - 2n$; Multiplier = $[df1\ '\ (T - n - 2)/df2]$.
a Disaggregated data are unavailable.
b Acceptable at the 1 percent level of significance.

size T varies from country to country. As can be seen from column (9), for most of the countries, the demand homogeneity property is acceptable. Similarly, results presented in column (12) of the table reveal that the symmetry hypothesis is also acceptable for most countries at the 5 percent level of significance.

Under preference independence, the Rotterdam conditional demand equation (2.115) given in Chapter 2 for commodity i takes the form

$$\bar{w}_{it} Dq_{it} = \theta_i' W_{gt} DQ_{gt} + \phi\theta_g\theta_i' \left(Dp_{it} - DP_{gt}' \right), \quad i \in S_g, \tag{7.4}$$

where the coefficients ϕ and θ_i' are specified as constants. We test for the preference independence of the three goods, transport, communication and housing, using the Monte Carlo simulation test described in Chapter 4 and the results are presented in Table 7.7. As most of the ranks of the observed value of the test statistic are below 950, we conclude that, at the 5 percent level of significance, the preference independence hypothesis is generally acceptable for most countries' data.

Table 7.8 presents the estimation results for model (7.4), and Tables 7.9, 7.10 presents the implied income, own-price and cross-price elasticities. The marginal shares presented in columns (2)–(4) of Table 7.8 have the following interpretation. If there is, for example, a dollar increase in the TCH group expenditure in Australia, out of that one dollar, on average, consumers will allocate 76 cents on transport, 8 cents on communication and the remaining 17 cents on housing. The estimates of income flexibility presented in the last column reveal that most of the estimates are negative as they should be with an average value for all countries of −0.59.

The implied income elasticities based on time-series data presented in columns (2)–(4) of Tables 7.9, 7.10 reveal that, in most countries, transport (1.73) and communication (1.10) are luxuries and housing (0.52) is a necessity. Similar results were found in Clements et al. (2020), Fernández-Kranz and Hon (2006), Goodman and Kawai (1982, 1986), Manrique and Ojah (2003), Polinsky (1977), and Tse and Raftery (1999), where time-series data were used. The income elasticity classification of housing as a necessity, however, is substantially different from those estimates based on cross-sectional data in Clements et al. (2021) and Jayasinghe et al. (2019). The own-price elasticities presented in columns (5)–(7) reveal that the demand for TCH is price inelastic, as they are all less than one in absolute value. Similar results were found in Clements et al. (2020), Fouquet (2012) and Selvanathan and Selvanathan (1994). The sample averages of cross-price elasticities are all positive, indicating that transport, communication and housing are pairwise substitutes. However, at the individual country level, in some countries, there is complimentarity between transport, communication and housing. The substitutability between transport and communication was also found in Choo et al. (2007) and Selvanathan and Selvanathan (1994).

Table 7.7 Monte Carlo test results of preference independence, TCH group, 45 countries

	Country *(1)*	*Observed value* *(2)*	*Rank* *(3)*	*Decision at 5 % level* *(4)*
1	Australia	0.16	75	Accept
2	Austria	90.21	641	Accept
3	Belgium	0.47	193	Accept
4	Canada	0.06	28	Accept
5	Denmark	0.26	84	Accept
6	Finland	9.64	980	Accept
7	France	17.17	1,000	Reject
8	Germany	0.13	48	Accept
9	Hong Kong[a]	–	–	–
10	Iceland	3.57	751	Accept
11	Ireland	3.33	694	Accept
12	Israel	2.75	692	Accept
13	Italy	3.64	762	Accept
14	Japan	1.78	522	Accept
15	Luxembourg	8.81	976	Accept
16	Netherlands	7.35	940	Accept
17	New Zealand	17.19	1,000	Reject
18	Norway	4.33	867	Accept
19	Singapore[a]	–	–	–
20	Slovenia	4.69	848	Accept
21	South Korea	3.18	771	Accept
22	Spain	0.67	222	Accept
23	Sweden	1.03	328	Accept
24	Switzerland	0.76	273	Accept
25	Taiwan[a]	–	–	–
26	UK	0.05	25	Accept
27	USA	8.52	981	Accept
28	Colombia	1.39	404	Accept
29	Czech	3.42	737	Accept
30	Estonia	2.08	547	Accept
31	Greece	6.23	918	Accept
32	Hungary	0.28	114	Accept
33	India[a]	–	–	–
34	Latvia	0.75	265	Accept
35	Lithuania	1.54	474	Accept
36	Malaysia[a]	–	–	–
37	Mexico	5.91	836	Accept
38	Philippines[a]	–	–	–
39	Poland	3.58	750	Accept
40	Portugal	7.00	941	Accept
41	Slovakia	3.22	715	Accept
42	South Africa[a]	–	–	–
43	Sri Lanka[a]	–	–	–
44	Thailand[a]	–	–	–
45	Turkey[a]	–	–	–
Percentage of rejection				5.7 percent

[a] Disaggregated data are unavailable.

Table 7.8 Estimation results of model under preference independence, TCH group, 45 countries

Country (1)		Marginal shares: Transport (2)	Communication (3)	Housing (4)	Income flexibility (5)
1	Australia	0.76 (0.05)	0.08 (0.03)	0.17 (0.04)	−0.22 (0.12)
2	Austria	0.29 (0.09)	0.02 (0.29)	0.69 (0.20)	−1.07 (0.10)
3	Belgium	0.46 (0.09)	0.09 (0.05)	0.45 (0.08)	−0.20 (0.19)
4	Canada	0.90 (0.05)	0.03 (0.01)	0.07 (0.04)	−0.44 (0.26)
5	Denmark	0.88 (0.07)	0.02 (0.02)	0.09 (0.06)	−1.74 (1.41)
6	Finland	0.88 (0.05)	0.03 (0.02)	0.09 (0.04)	−0.71 (0.39)
7	France	0.56 (0.04)	0.04 (0.01)	0.40 (0.04)	−0.61 (0.14)
8	Germany	0.52 (0.10)	0.12 (0.03)	0.36 (0.10)	−0.73 (0.19)
9	Hong Kong[a]	–	–	–	–
10	Iceland	0.62 (0.09)	0.07 (0.02)	0.32 (0.09)	−1.26 (0.24)
11	Ireland	0.26 (0.05)	0.05 (0.01)	0.70 (0.06)	−2.77 (0.64)
12	Israel	0.60 (0.06)	0.19 (0.06)	0.21 (0.04)	−0.12 (0.13)
13	Italy	0.63 (0.06)	0.18 (0.03)	0.18 (0.05)	−0.36 (0.09)
14	Japan	0.72 (0.06)	0.03 (0.04)	0.25 (0.04)	−0.02 (0.14)
15	Luxembourg	0.38 (0.03)	0.05 (0.00)	0.58 (0.03)	−0.05 (0.15)
16	Netherlands	0.46 (0.07)	0.31 (0.04)	0.22 (0.08)	−0.28 (0.09)
17	New Zealand	0.63 (0.06)	0.07 (0.02)	0.31 (0.06)	−0.53 (0.11)
18	Norway	0.82 (0.04)	0.02 (0.02)	0.16 (0.03)	−0.55 (0.34)
19	Singapore[a]	–	–	–	–
20	Slovenia	0.64 (0.09)	0.08 (0.04)	0.28 (0.06)	0.20 (0.24)
21	South Korea	0.58 (0.05)	0.10 (0.03)	0.32 (0.04)	−0.22 (0.10)
22	Spain	0.66 (0.07)	0.12 (0.03)	0.21 (0.07)	−0.17 (0.18)
23	Sweden	0.31 (0.03)	0.05 (0.01)	0.64 (0.03)	−1.58 (0.14)
24	Switzerland	0.31 (0.03)	0.05 (0.01)	0.64 (0.03)	−1.58 (0.14)
25	Taiwan[a]	–	–	–	–
26	UK	0.56 (0.06)	0.10 (0.02)	0.34 (0.06)	−0.49 (0.12)
27	USA	0.77 (0.03)	0.05 (0.01)	0.18 (0.03)	−0.47 (0.08)
Mean (*Developed*)		0.59 (0.01)	0.08 (0.01)	0.33 (0.01)	−0.66 (0.07)
28	Colombia	0.55 (0.07)	0.34 (0.08)	0.11 (0.05)	−0.26 (0.21)
29	Czech	0.51 (0.09)	0.16 (0.04)	0.34 (0.08)	−0.26 (0.12)
30	Estonia	0.45 (0.05)	0.05 (0.02)	0.49 (0.05)	−0.75 (0.25)
31	Greece	0.69 (0.08)	0.13 (0.05)	0.18 (0.07)	0.05 (0.40)
32	Hungary	0.64 (0.06)	0.10 (0.03)	0.26 (0.05)	−0.12 (0.17)
33	India[a]	–	–	–	–
34	Latvia	0.58 (0.09)	0.10 (0.02)	0.32 (0.10)	−0.66 (0.16)
35	Lithuania	0.75 (0.07)	−0.01 (0.02)	0.26 (0.07)	0.24 (0.46)
36	Malaysia[a]	–	–	–	–
37	Mexico	0.67 (0.06)	0.04 (0.03)	0.29 (0.04)	−0.19 (0.21)
38	Philippines[a]	–	–	–	–
39	Poland	0.44 (0.09)	0.08 (0.04)	0.49 (0.10)	−0.34 (0.26)
40	Portugal	0.89 (0.06)	0.05 (0.03)	0.06 (0.04)	−1.67 (0.77)
41	Slovakia	0.21 (0.07)	0.11 (0.03)	0.68 (0.10)	−0.68 (0.21)
42	South Africa[a]	–	–	–	–
43	Sri Lanka[a]	–	–	–	–
44	Thailand[a]	–	–	–	–
45	Turkey[a]	–	–	–	–
Mean (*Developing*)		0.58 (0.02)	0.10 (0.01)	0.32 (0.02)	−0.42 (0.02)
Mean (*All countries*)		0.59 (0.01)	0.09 (0.01)	0.32 (0.01)	−0.59 (0.06)

Standard errors are in parentheses.
[a] Disaggregated data are unavailable.

Table 7.9 Implied income and price elasticities for TCH group, 45 countries

Country	Income elasticity			Own-price elasticity			Cross-price elasticity					
	Transport	*Communication*	*Housing*	*Transport*	*Communication*	*Housing*	*Transport–Communication*	*Transport – Housing*	*Communication–Transport*	*Communication–Housing*	*Housing – Transport*	*Housing–Communication*
(1)	*(2)*	*(3)*	*(4)*	*(5)*	*(6)*	*(7)*	*(8)*	*(9)*	*(10)*	*(11)*	*(12)*	*(13)*
Developed countries												
1 Australia	2.19	1.23	0.28	−0.14	−0.22	−0.05	0.05	0.09	0.26	−0.03	0.05	0.00
2 Austria	1.25	1.01	0.84	−0.23	−1.34	−0.19	0.08	0.15	0.45	0.89	0.09	0.10
3 Belgium	1.51	1.34	0.71	−0.08	−0.36	−0.02	0.06	0.02	0.30	0.06	0.01	0.01
4 Canada	2.50	0.63	0.12	−0.11	−0.25	−0.04	0.04	0.07	0.29	−0.04	0.04	0.00
5 Denmark	2.92	0.46	0.17	−0.49	−0.94	−0.21	0.09	0.40	0.55	0.39	0.18	0.03
6 Finland	2.59	1.28	0.02	−0.19	−0.33	−0.18	−0.03	0.22	−0.24	0.56	0.14	0.05
7 France	1.49	0.31	0.73	−0.10	−0.71	−0.02	0.08	0.02	0.60	0.11	0.01	0.01
8 Germany	1.55	1.67	0.60	−0.48	−1.17	−0.29	0.11	0.37	0.59	0.58	0.22	0.06
9 Hong Kong[a]	–	–	–	–	–	–	–	–	–	–	–	–
10 Iceland	1.86	0.54	0.39	−0.47	−1.18	−0.43	0.04	0.43	0.30	0.88	0.33	0.10
11 Ireland	0.84	0.93	1.11	−1.39	−1.47	−0.79	0.21	1.17	0.96	0.51	0.72	0.07
12 Israel	1.77	1.91	0.38	−0.17	−0.52	0.01	0.17	0.00	0.59	−0.07	0.00	−0.01
13 Italy	1.87	2.33	0.27	−0.19	−0.83	−0.18	0.04	0.15	0.20	0.63	0.09	0.08
14 Japan	2.45	0.36	0.40	0.05	−0.51	−0.03	0.01	−0.05	0.03	0.49	−0.03	0.05
15 Luxembourg	0.91	1.04	1.07	0.34	−0.32	0.19	−0.03	−0.31	−0.34	0.66	−0.24	0.05
16 Netherlands	1.37	3.41	0.33	−0.12	−0.76	−0.30	−0.07	0.18	−0.26	1.02	0.12	0.18
17 New Zealand	2.13	0.16	0.47	−0.14	−0.74	−0.13	0.02	0.11	0.11	0.64	0.06	0.07
18 Norway	2.12	0.32	0.29	−0.10	−0.43	−0.18	−0.04	0.15	−0.29	0.72	0.10	0.07
19 Singaporea	–	–	–	–	–	–	–	–	–	–	–	–
20 Slovenia	1.43	1.66	0.55	−0.08	−0.07	0.14	0.13	−0.05	0.73	−0.66	−0.04	−0.10
21 South Korea	1.46	1.39	0.60	−0.23	−0.30	−0.08	0.09	0.14	0.46	−0.16	0.10	−0.02
22 Spain	1.87	1.60	0.36	0.04	−0.33	0.03	0.04	−0.08	0.19	0.13	−0.05	0.02
23 Sweden	1.24	0.47	0.96	−1.27	−1.09	−0.54	0.07	1.20	0.29	0.80	0.47	0.07
24 Switzerland	1.24	0.47	0.96	−1.27	−1.09	−0.54	0.07	1.20	0.29	0.80	0.47	0.07
25 Taiwana	–	–	–	–	–	–	–	–	–	–	–	–
26 The UK	1.70	2.13	0.55	−0.38	−0.89	−0.19	0.08	0.30	0.55	0.34	0.16	0.03
27 USA	2.13	0.62	0.34	−0.17	−0.64	−0.13	0.03	0.13	0.19	0.45	0.08	0.05
Mean (*Developed*)	1.77	1.14	0.52	−0.31	−0.69	−0.17	−0.06	0.25	0.28	0.40	0.13	0.04

a Disaggregated data are unavailable.

Table 7.10 Implied income and price elasticities for TCH group, 45 countries (Cont.)

Country	*Income elasticity*			*Own-price elasticity*			*Cross-price elasticity*					
	Transport	*Communication*	*Housing*	*Transport*	*Communication*	*Housing*	*Transport – Communication*	*Transport – Housing*	*Communication – Transport*	*Communication – Housing*	*Housing – Transport*	*Housing – Communication*
(1)	*(2)*	*(3)*	*(4)*	*(5)*	*(6)*	*(7)*	*(8)*	*(9)*	*(10)*	*(11)*	*(12)*	*(13)*
Developing countries												
28 Colombia	1.72	2.16	0.25	−0.11	−0.64	0.02	0.20	−0.09	0.50	0.14	−0.06	0.04
29 Czech	1.94	2.01	0.51	0.03	−0.66	0.02	0.10	−0.13	0.35	0.32	−0.05	0.04
30 Estonia	1.38	0.39	0.87	−0.49	−0.95	−0.29	0.13	0.36	0.50	0.45	0.22	0.07
31 Greece	1.98	1.51	0.17	0.56	−0.46	0.61	0.18	−0.74	0.75	−0.29	−0.56	−0.05
32 Hungary	1.71	1.03	0.48	−0.03	−0.16	−0.05	0.00	0.03	0.00	0.16	0.02	0.03
33 India[a]	–	–	–	–	–	–	–	–	–	–	–	–
34 Latvia	1.87	0.96	0.50	−0.30	−0.66	−0.21	0.04	0.25	0.19	0.47	0.15	0.06
35 Lithuania	1.77	0.05	0.49	0.18	−0.15	0.08	−0.03	−0.15	−0.17	0.31	−0.12	0.05
36 Malaysia[a]	–	–	–	–	–	–	–	–	–	–	–	–
37 Mexico	1.65	0.31	0.57	−0.17	−0.75	−0.06	0.13	0.04	0.64	0.12	0.04	0.02
38 Philippines[a]	–	–	–	–	–	–	–	–	–	–	–	–
39 Poland	1.45	1.06	0.76	−0.41	−0.52	−0.05	0.23	0.19	0.89	−0.38	0.10	−0.05
40 Portugal	2.01	0.71	0.06	−0.32	−2.26	−0.58	0.09	0.23	0.44	1.82	0.23	0.35
41 Slovakia	0.66	1.14	1.10	−0.54	−0.61	−0.14	0.20	0.35	0.48	0.14	0.12	0.02
42 South Africa[a]	–	–	–	–	–	–	–	–	–	–	–	–
43 Sri Lanka[a]	–	–	–	–	–	–	–	–	–	–	–	–
44 Thailand[a]	–	–	–	–	–	–	–	–	–	–	–	–
45 Turkey[a]	–	–	–	–	–	–	–	–	–	–	–	–
Mean (*Developing*)	1.65	1.03	0.52	−0.15	−0.71	−0.06	0.12	0.03	0.42	0.30	0.01	0.05
Mean (*All countries*)	1.73	1.10	0.52	−0.26	−0.69	−0.14	0.07	0.18	0.32	0.37	0.09	0.05

[a] Disaggregated data are unavailable.

7.5 Conditional Demand Analysis of the Disaggregated TCH Group with Cross-Sectional Data

As in Chapter 6, in this section, we extend the conditional demand analysis for the TCH group based on cross-sectional HES data for a developed country, Australia, and two developing countries, India and Sri Lanka considered in Section 6.6 for the food group. We use the conditional version of the generalised Working's model given by equation (6.15) and the implied conditional income elasticity given by equation (6.16) in Chapter 6 for the three commodities as individual goods within that group.

7.5.1 Australia

Table 7.11 presents the summary information on the TCH group budget share as well as for the commodities forming the group for Australian Household Expenditure Survey data. As can be seen, at the national level, the group budget allocation for the TCH group is 47.6 percent, which is not too far from the group budget share presented in Table 7.1. By income level, the Australian low-income group allocates 51.4 percent, lower-middle-income group allocates 48.4 percent, upper-middle-income group allocates 46.8 percent and the high-income group allocates 45.1 percent of their total expenditure on the group as a whole. This allocation of nearly 50 percent of the budget on the TCH group shows the importance of this group in the

Table 7.11 Average budget share of TCH group and conditional budget shares within the TCH group, Australia

Household income level/location	*Average group share (as a percent of the total household expenditure)*	*Average conditional shares (as a percent of the total group expenditure)*[a]		
		Transport	*Communication*	*Housing*
(1)	*(2)*	*(3)*	*(4)*	*(5)*
National (Australia)	47.6	28.3	8.5	63.1
Income level				
Low-income (lower 25 percent)	51.4	21.3	10.3	68.3
Lower-middle-income (25–50 percent)	48.4	25.0	9.2	65.7
Upper-middle-income (50–75 percent)	46.8	29.4	8.4	62.2
High-income (upper 25 percent)	45.1	35.7	6.8	58.5
Remoteness level (location)				
Major cities	47.3	27.6	8.3	64.0
Inner regional	48.9	30.1	8.4	61.4
Outer regional	47.1	30.3	9.5	60.1
Remote Australia	43.7	28.9	9.2	61.9

Note: The sample size is 6,768.
[a] Due to rounding-off of values to one decimal, the total may not add to 100.

consumer basket. Within the group, at the national level, Australian consumers allocate 28.3 percent of their TCH group expenditure on transport, 8.5 percent on communication and the remaining 63 percent on housing. That is, expenditure on housing, or in other words cost of housing, is much higher than the expenditure on transport and communication in Australia.

While budget allocation for the TCH group differs among Australian consumers across differing income levels, the budget allocation on transport, communication and housing individually also varies very much across income levels. The budget share allocation by location shows not much difference at the group level or at the individual commodity level.

Table 7.12 presents the implied income elasticities by income level and location. As can be seen from the table, the income elasticity for the TCH group is about 0.91 at the national level, indicating that the TCH group as a whole is a necessity. However, the income elasticity for the TCH group is slightly above one for all income levels except for the low-income households. This means that the TCH group is a necessity for the low-income households and a luxury for all others. Considering the location, the group income elasticity is less than one for households in the outer regional and remote Australia, meaning that the TCH group is a luxury for consumers in the outer regional and remote Australia. Considering the income elasticity for transport, transport is a luxury for Australians at the national level as well as all locations and all income levels except the low-income and lower-middle-income groups, for whom it is a near luxury. Communication is a necessity at the national level, across all income levels and for all locations in Australia. Housing is a necessity or near luxury at the national level, as well as for households in all locations and for the high-income group. Housing is a luxury for the low-income, lower-middle-income and upper-middle-income groups.

Table 7.12 Income elasticities of TCH group and individual commodities within the TCH group by income level and location, Australia

Commodity (1)	National (2)	*Income level* Low-income (3)	Lower-middle-income (4)	Upper-middle-income (5)	High-income (6)	*Location* Major cities (7)	Inner regional (8)	Outer regional (9)	Remote Australia (10)
TCH group	0.91	0.96	1.04	1.04	1.02	0.90	0.89	1.01	1.05
	(0.01)	(0.02)	(0.02)	(0.03)	(0.02)	(0.01)	(0.02)	(0.03)	(0.06)
Transport	1.24	0.93	0.98	1.10	1.15	1.19	1.41	1.36	1.32
	(0.02)	(0.04)	(0.04)	(0.03)	(0.03)	(0.02)	(0.03)	(0.05)	(0.10)
Communication	0.46	0.55	0.48	0.39	0.32	0.44	0.55	0.47	0.59
	(0.07)	(0.13)	(0.14)	(0.17)	(0.21)	(0.06)	(0.12)	(0.21)	(0.44)
Housing	0.97	1.09	1.09	1.04	0.99	0.99	0.86	0.90	0.91
	(0.01)	(0.01)	(0.01)	(0.02)	(0.02)	(0.001)	(0.00)	(0.01)	(0.04)
$\lambda = -0.0681$; $\lambda_g = -0.0059$									

Note: Standard errors are in parentheses.

7.5.2 India

Table 7.13 presents the budget shares allocated to the TCH group by Indian households with various income levels as well as those residing in rural or urban areas using Indian Human Development Survey (IHDS) data. As can be seen, at the national level, the budget allocation for the TCH group is 22.3 percent, while low-income and lower-middle-income groups both allocate about 18 percent, upper-middle-income groups allocate 23 percent and high-income groups allocate 29 percent on the TCH group consumption. Within the group, at the national level, Indian households allocate about 35 percent of their TCH group expenditure on transport, 13 percent on communication and the remaining 53 percent on housing. While allocation on the TCH group differs among Indian households across differing income levels and location, the allocation on transport, communication and housing individually also varies substantially across income levels as well as location. For example, within the TCH group, transport budget share is lower for households living in rural areas than those living in the urban areas, whereas budget share allocated to communication is higher for rural households than urban households.

Table 7.14 presents the income elasticities for the TCH group and for the disaggregated goods within the group overall and by various income levels and by the location where the household lives. The income elasticity for the TCH group is 1.27 at the national level, indicating that the TCH group is a luxury. Considering transport individually by income level, it can be seen

Table 7.13 Average budget share of TCH group and conditional budget shares within the TCH group, India

Household income level/ location	*Average group share (as a percent of the total household expenditure)*	*Average conditional shares (as a percent of the total group expenditure)*[a]		
		Transport	*Communication*	*Housing*
(1)	*(2)*	*(3)*	*(4)*	*(5)*
National (India)	22.3	34.7	12.5	52.7
Income level				
Low-income (lower 25 percent)	18.3	26.0	9.2	64.8
Lower-middle-income (25–50 percent)	18.9	28.4	13.3	58.1
Upper-middle-income (50–75 percent)	23.1	36.9	14.5	48.6
High-income (upper 25 percent)	28.8	47.5	13.0	39.4
Remoteness level (location)				
Rural	26.7	24.8	14.4	50.8
Urban	19.7	34.7	11.5	53.9

Note: The sample size is 7,470.
[a] Due to rounding-off of values to one decimal, the total may not add to100.

Table 7.14 Income elasticities of TCH group and individual commodities within the TCH group by income level and location, India

Commodity (1)	National (2)	Income level: Low-income (3)	Lower-middle-income (4)	Upper-middle-income (5)	High-income (6)	Location: Rural (7)	Urban (8)
TCH group	1.27	1.12	1.15	1.29	1.23	1.21	1.21
	(0.01)	(0.03)	(0.04)	(0.04)	(0.03)	(0.02)	(0.02)
Transport	1.26	1.11	1.22	1.25	1.20	1.29	1.33
	(0.01)	(0.03)	(0.03)	(0.02)	(0.01)	(0.01)	(0.01)
Communication	1.03	1.31	1.09	0.75	0.74	0.86	1.07
	(0.03)	(0.12)	(0.08)	(0.07)	(0.07)	(0.04)	(0.04)
Housing	0.82	0.91	0.87	0.89	0.85	0.84	0.77
	(0.01)	(0.01)	(0.01)	(0.02)	(0.02)	(0.01)	(0.01)
$\lambda = -0.1720; \lambda_g = -0.0625$							

Note: Standard errors are in parentheses.

that the income elasticity (1.11–1.25) is greater than one, indicating that it is a luxury. In contrast, the income elasticity for housing (0.85–0.91) is less than one, implying that it is a necessity for Indian households. Communication is a near luxury at the national level and a luxury for low-income to lower-middle-income households. For upper-middle-income and high-income households, communication is a necessity. This shows that, considering transport, communication and housing individually, there are differences in the behaviour of consumers at different income levels in India. In terms of the location of the households, transport is a luxury and housing is a necessity for both rural and urban households. However, communication is a necessity for rural households but is a luxury for urban households. This could be attributed to the fact that communication plays a major role in expanding and strengthening social networks; increases people's ability to deal with emergencies; reduces travel costs; maximises the outcomes of necessary journeys; increases temporal accessibility; and amplifies efficiency of activities in rural areas (Sife et al. 2010).

7.5.3 Sri Lanka

Table 7.15 presents the TCH group budget share as well as the budget share for the three disaggregated commodities within the group using the Sri Lankan Household Income and Expenditure Survey data. As can be seen at the national level, in Sri Lanka, the budget allocation on the TCH group is 29.2 percent. The low-income households allocate 25.5 percent, the lower-middle-income households allocate about 28 percent, the upper-middle-income households allocate 30 percent and the high-income households allocate about 33 percent of their income on the consumption

Table 7.15 Average budget share of TCH group and conditional budget shares within the TCH group, Sri Lanka

Household location/income level (1)	*Average group share (as a percent of the total household expenditure)* (2)	*Average conditional shares (as a percent of group expenditure)*[a] *Transport* (3)	*Communication* (4)	*Housing* (5)
National	29.2	22.6	7.4	70.0
Income level				
Low-income (lower 25 percent)	25.5	15.2	6.6	78.2
Lower-middle-income (25–50 percent)	27.9	21.3	7.8	70.9
Upper-middle-income (50–75 percent)	30.2	25.2	7.7	67.1
High-income (upper 25 percent)	33.2	28.7	7.5	63.8
Residential sector (location)				
Rural	28.2	23.7	7.4	68.9
Urban	36.2	17.5	6.8	75.6
Estate	20.5	21.6	8.8	69.6

Note: The sample size is 21,474.
[a] Due to rounding-off of values to one decimal, the total may not add to 100.

of the TCH group. That is, the higher the income level, the greater the share of budget allocation on the TCH group. Within the TCH group, at the national level, Sri Lankan consumers allocate 23 percent of their group budget on transport, 7 percent on communication and the remaining 70 percent on housing. That is, in Sri Lanka, housing occupies the largest share among the TCH group. Considering the budget allocation on the TCH group by location, urban households allocate the highest, 36 percent, share of their income on the group while rural households allocate 28 percent and estate households allocate only 21 percent. While the budget allocation on the TCH group differs among Sri Lankan consumers across income levels and location, the allocation on transport, communication and housing individually also varies substantially across income levels as well as location.

Table 7.16 presents the income elasticities for the TCH group as well as TCH individually by income levels and location. The income elasticity for the TCH group ranges between 1.06 and 1.38, across income levels and location, indicating that TCH as a group is a luxury for all households, which is very similar to the results for Indian households discussed above. The income elasticity for transport is greater than one (1.04–1.40), indicating that it is a luxury. Communication is a necessity or near luxury at the national level as well as across various income levels and location of the households. Housing is a near luxury at all income levels (income elasticity 0.98–1.01) but more of a necessity for estate households than urban and rural households in Sri Lanka. Similar results have been found in Jayasinghe et al. (2019).

Table 7.16 Income elasticities of TCH group and individual commodities within the TCH group by income level and location, Sri Lanka

Commodity	National level	Income level				Location		
		Low-income	Lower-middle-income	Upper-middle-income	High-income	Rural	Urban	Estate
(1)	(2)	(3)	(4)	(5)	(6)	(7)	(8)	(9)
TCH group	1.20	1.22	1.38	1.29	1.07	1.15	1.20	1.06
	(0.01)	(0.02)	(0.02)	(0.02)	(0.02)	(0.01)	(0.01)	(0.04)
Transport	1.20	1.13	1.11	1.04	1.04	1.23	1.31	1.40
	(0.02)	(0.02)	(0.02)	(0.02)	(0.01)	(0.01)	(0.02)	(0.04)
Communication	0.93	0.92	0.83	0.78	0.77	0.93	0.99	0.99
	(0.24)	(0.08)	(0.08)	(0.08)	(0.08)	(0.03)	(0.07)	(0.15)
Housing	0.94	0.98	0.99	1.01	1.01	0.93	0.93	0.88
	(0.00)	(0.01)	(0.01)	(0.01)	(0.01)	(0.003)	(0.01)	(0.01)

$\lambda = -0.3109$; $\lambda_g = -0.0613$

Note: Standard errors are in parentheses.

7.6 Concluding Comments

In this chapter, we carried out an in-depth analysis of the conditional demand for another important commodity group consisting of transport, communication and housing (the TCH group). We first analysed using time-series data for this commodity group for the 45 countries and then using household cross-sectional data for three countries, Australia, India and Sri Lanka. Following a preliminary analysis of the data, using the conditional demand equations, we estimated income, own-price and cross-price elasticities for the TCH group. We also tested demand theory hypotheses comprising demand homogeneity and Slutsky symmetry and the preference independence of the utility structure.

Overall, we observed that on average, consumers allocate about one-third of their income on the TCH group. Within the group, the highest budget share is allocated for housing (57.6 percent), followed by transport (35.2 percent) and communication (7.2 percent). Although some individual country-level heterogeneities were observed, in general, a similar pattern was found in both developed and developing countries. In particular, on average, out of a 36.6 percent budget allocated on this group by households in developed countries, 35.1 percent was spent on transport, 6.4 percent was spent on communication and 58.5 percent was spent on housing. Households in developing countries allocated 35.3 percent on transport, 8.9 percent on communication and 55.8 percent on housing, out of a 33.7 percent allocation of total budget on this group of commodities.

The estimated income elasticities revealed that overall, transport and communication are luxuries and housing is a necessity, both in the developed and developing countries under consideration. The own-price elasticities suggested that, in both developed and developing countries, demand for transport, communication and housing are price inelastic. The sample averages of cross-price elasticities indicated that transport, communication and housing are pairwise substitutes, except the negative cross-price elasticity is at the individual country level, suggesting that these are complementary goods.

The cross-sectional analysis based on the HES data for Australia, India and Sri Lanka revealed that Australian households allocated almost twice the budget share for the TCH group compared with Indian and Sri Lankan households, nationally as well as at all income levels and locations. Within the group, households in all three countries spent the highest conditional budget share on housing, followed by transport and communication.

The estimated income elasticities at the national level indicated that TCH as a whole is a necessity for an average Australian household and a luxury for an average Indian and Sri Lankan household. Nevertheless, notable differences were observed by income level and regional level (remoteness level/urban and rural), especially for Australian households. For example, for an average household in the low-income group in Australia, TCH is a necessity, while it is a luxury for lower-middle, upper-middle and high-income households. While TCH is a necessity for Australian households who are living in major cities and inner regional locations, it is a luxury for outer regional and remote Australians. Income-based differences were observed in 'communication' in India and 'housing' in Sri Lanka (a luxury for lower- and middle-income households and a necessity for upper-middle and high-income households).

A growing body of literature identifies that household budget allocation on housing is inextricably linked with household transport budget allocations. Therefore, the conditional income, own-price and cross-price elasticities derived within the TCH group in this chapter, both in developed and developing countries, provide important policy insights.

References

Ahmad S. 2015. Housing demand and housing policy in urban Bangladesh. *Urban Studies* 52(4):738–755.

Chen, D.L. 2001. *World consumption economics.* Singapore, London: World Scientific.

Choo, S., T. Lee, and P.L. Mokhtarian. 2007. Relationships between US consumer expenditures on communications and transportation using Almost Ideal Demand System Modeling: 1984–2002. *Transportation Planning and Technology* 30(5): 431–453.

Clements, K.W., J. Si, E.A. Selvanathan, and S. Selvanathan. 2020. Demand elasticities for 9 goods in 37 countries. *Applied Economics* 52(24): 2636–2655.

Clements, K.W., M.J.M. Mariano, and G. Verikios. 2021. Expenditure patterns, heterogeneity and long-term structural change. Economics Discussion/Working Papers 21-10, The University of Western Australia, Department of Economics.

Dewita, Y., M. Burke, and B.T. Yen. 2020. The relationship between transport, housing and urban form: Affordability of transport and housing in Indonesia. *Case Studies on Transport Policy* 8(1): 252–262.

Dewita, Y., B.T. Yen, and M. Burke. 2018. The effect of transport cost on housing affordability: Experiences from the Bandung metropolitan area, Indonesia. *Land use policy* 79: 507–519.

Fernández-Kranz, D., and M.T.A. Hon. 2006. Cross-section analysis of the income elasticity of housing demand in Spain: Is there a real estate bubble? *The Journal of Real Estate Finance and Economics* 32: 449–470.

Fouquet, R. 2012. Trends in income and price elasticities of transport demand (1850–2010). *Energy Policy* 50: 50–61.

Gallin, J. 2003. The long-run relationship between house prices and income: Evidence from local housing markets. doi:10.2139/ssrn.410808.

Goodman, A., and M. Kawai. 1982. Permanent income, hedonic prices, and demand for housing: New evidence. *Journal of Urban Economics* 12:214–237.

Goodman, A., and M. Kawai. 1986. 'Functional form, sample selection, and housing demand. *Journal of Urban Economics* 20:155–167.

Hassan, M.A., H. Hamdan, J. Abdullah, and Y.A. Abdullah. 2018. Housing and transport expenditure: An assessment of location Housing affordability. *Planning Malaysia* 16(6): 99–108.

Jayasinghe, M., E.A. Selvanathan, and S. Selvanathan. 2019. An intertemporal analysis of expenditure elasticities under three expenditure specifications for Sri Lanka. *Applied Economics* 51(59): 6376–6392.

Lopez, C., E. Aguayo, and P. Exposito. 1998. El comportamiento de los precios de la vivienda en las regiones españolas: principales determinantes. *Economic Development* 34, University of Santiago de Compostela. Faculty of Economics and Business. Econometrics.

Manrique, J., and K. Ojah. 2003. The demand for housing in Spain: An endogenous switching regression analysis. *Applied Economics* 35: 323–336.

Martiınez J., and L.A. Maza. 2003. Analysis of house prices in Spain. Bank of Spain, Working Paper no. 0307.

Mattingly, K., and J. Morrissey. 2014. Housing and transport expenditure: Socio-spatial indicators of affordability in Auckland. *Cities* 38: 69–83.

Meisner, J.F. 1979. Divisia Moments of U.S. Industry, 1947–1978. *Economics Letters* 4: 239–242.

Polinsky, A. 1977. The demand for housing: A study in specification and grouping. *Econometrica* 45: 447–461.

Rathnayaka, S.D., E.A. Selvanathan, and S. Selvanathan. 2019. Consumption patterns in Sri Lanka: A decomposition analysis. *Applied Economics* 51 (37): 4056–4072.

Selvanathan, S. (1993). *A System-wide analysis of international consumption patterns.* Advanced Studies in Theoretical and Applied Econometrics. Boston: Kluwer Academic Publishers.

Selvanathan, S., and E.A. Selvanathan. 1993. A Cross-country analysis of consumption patterns. *Applied Economics* 25: 1245–1259.

Selvanathan, E.A., and S. Selvanathan. 1994. The demand for transport and communications in the United Kingdom and Australia. *Transportation Research B* 28 (1): 1–9.

Selvanathan, E.A., and S. Selvanathan. 2003a. Similarities in the consumption patterns of the five Asian tigers. *Asian Economic Journal* 17: 297–323.

Selvanathan, E.A., and S. Selvanathan. 2003b. *International consumption comparisons: OECD versus LDC.* World Scientific, Singapore.

Selvanathan, E.A., S. Selvanathan, L. Wong, L., and M. Jayasinghe. (2021). Modelling regional consumption patterns in Australia. *Economic Record* 97(317): 141–156.

Sife, A.S., E. Kiondo, and J.G. Lyimo-Macha. 2010. Contribution of mobile phones to rural livelihoods and poverty reduction in Morogoro region, Tanzania', *The Electronic Journal of Information Systems in Developing Countries* 42: 1–15.

Theil, H., and F.E. Suhm. 1981. *International consumption comparisons: A system-wide approach.* Amsterdam: North-Holland Publishing Company.

Tse, R.Y., and J. Raftery. 1999. Income elasticity of housing consumption in Hong Kong: A cointegration approach. *Journal of Property Research* 16: 123–138.

8 Demand for Health, Recreation and Education

M Jayasinghe, E A Selvanathan and S Selvanathan

8.1 Introduction

In Chapter 6, we considered the demand for the food group consisting of food, alcohol and restaurant meals. In Chapter 7, we analysed the demand for transport, communication and housing (TCH) in the same 45 countries using time-series data as well as in a selected number of countries using cross-sectional Household Expenditure Survey (HES) data by estimating conditional demand equations. In this chapter, we extend the same methodology to analyse the demand for another group of commodities consisting of health, recreation and education (HRE). As in Chapters 6 and 7, in this chapter also we use the conditional demand equations under block independence derived in Section 2.12 of Chapter 2.

Rising household income levels, changing demographic composition in countries with noticeable population aging and an increasing level of international and local travel facilitated by rapidly growing transport, health, education and recreation sectors have become important considerations in household budget allocations. For example, several studies have observed a connection between rising national income and higher spending on health care, leisure and education (see, for example, Boppart and Ngai 2021; Boustan et al. 2013; Martín et al. 2010). However, people with different income levels within a country may demand these commodities differently and they may also respond differently to their income changes. In this chapter, we analyse the demand for the HRE group for the 45 countries considered in the previous chapters. These 45 countries consist of both developed and developing countries and thereby provide insights on the differences in the way in which consumers in developed and developing countries respond to price and income changes with respect to these goods. Such analysis will provide important policy insights for optimal allocation of resources in the economy and the efficient proportion of public and private expenditure, especially in health care and education, to ensure the well-being of people. For example, Costa-Font et al. (2009) suggested that if health care is a necessity, it highlights the need for greater redistribution of health care resources and greater public involvement in health care.

DOI: 10.4324/9780429200120-8

8.2 Demand for Health, Recreation and Education (HRE): A Review

Several empirical findings on the necessity or luxury status of healthcare to consumers show mixed results. While some studies suggest that healthcare is a luxury, other studies show that it is a necessity. The findings appear sensitive to the type of health care examined – whether private or public or aggregate data or household data, period covered, econometric techniques used and whether the data are cross-sectional or time-series. For example, Getzen (2000) suggested that health care is a necessity for individuals but a luxury at the national level. Particularly, when health insurance data are taken into consideration, income elasticities of individuals are typically near zero, while national health expenditure elasticities are commonly greater than 1. Several studies that investigate the income elasticity of health care in developed countries found that health care was a luxury good (see, for example, Gerdtham et al. 1992; Gerdtham and Jonsson 2000). On the other hand, Farag et al. (2012) found that health care is a necessity in low-, middle- and high-income countries. However, Xu and Saksena (2011) analysed the health care expenditure patterns of 143 countries over the period 1995–2008 and found that health care in low-income countries is a luxury and in middle- and high-income countries it is a necessity. Freeman (2003), using health care expenditures and disposable personal income data for the individual States in the USA for the period 1966–1998, estimated the income elasticity of health care. The results, based on the dynamic ordinary least squares regressions, revealed that the income elasticity of health care lies between 0.817 and 0.844, confirming that health care, even at the aggregate level, is a necessity for consumers in the USA. Khan and Mahumud (2015) examined the consumer demand for health care in the South-East Asian countries during 1995–2010. The results revealed that health care is a necessity when provided through the public sector and a luxury when delivered by the private sector. Lépine (2015) examined the relationship between permanent and current income and health care expenditure in rural Senegal and found that health care is a necessity. Using cross-country data for 84 countries from 2010 to 2011 on gross domestic product and national expenditure on vaccines, Alfonso et al. (2016) estimated and compared the income elasticity of vaccine expenditure and general health care expenditure. The study found that income elasticities for health care expenditure and vaccine expenditure are 0.844 and 0.336. Based on pseudo panel modelling during 2006–2016, Jayasinghe et al. (2019) found that health and personal care is a necessity for Sri Lankan households. Overall, the income elasticity estimates of health care ranges from a necessity to luxury, depending on the level of economic development in a given country and the type of data used.

Jenkins et al. (2019) examined the determinants of educational expenditure by households in Nigeria, using data from the *Nigerian General Household Survey* 2012/2013. The results showed that household income, the age, education, gender of the household heads and urban versus rural residence have a significant impact on the decision to spend on education. The study also revealed that expenditure on education is income elastic but it varies greatly in magnitude for low-income families compared with higher-income families. Similar results were found in Jayasinghe et al. (2019) in Sri Lanka and in Acerenza and Gandelman (2019) in Latin America and the Caribbean.

Recreation and leisure expenditure patterns have been studied extensively in the context of travel and tourism using both time-series and cross-sectional data (see, for example, Boman et al. 2013; Fredman and Wilström 2018; Knapman and Stoeckl 1995; Njegovan 2006), and most of these studies have found that travel and tourism-related recreation activities are luxury goods. Using 1988–1989 German Consumer Expenditure Survey data on active, passive and social entertainment, Pawlowski and Breuer (2012) estimated expenditure elasticities in the range of 0.40–0.72, indicating that goods consumed in the course of those activities were necessities. Using Consumer Expenditure Survey data, Zheng and Zhang (2013) examined the different impacts of household socio-economic characteristics on leisure travel expenditure patterns between 1996 and 2006. Results indicated that sightseeing and entertainment activities are luxury goods. Jayasinghe et al. (2019) found that recreation was a luxury for Sri Lankan households during 2006–2016.

Several studies have highlighted the potential link between health, recreation and education expenditures. For example, Mueller et al. (2019) have shown that increasing government spending on recreation improves public health, thus reducing health expenditure. Sato et al. (2019), using data for the USA, found that access to parks and recreational facilities was negatively associated with older adults' health care costs. Ross and Wu (1995) revealed that the well-educated report a greater sense of control over their lives and their health, are less likely to smoke, are more likely to exercise and to drink moderately, all of which are associated with good health. Kino et al. (2018) found that greater expenditure on education had a negative association with co-occurrence of health-risk behaviours in a representative sample from 27 European countries. Raghupathi and Raghupathi (2020) using empirical data from the OECD and the World Bank for 26 OECD countries for the years 1995–2015 found that adults with higher educational attainment have better health and lifespans compared with their less-educated peers.

8.3 Preliminary Data Analysis – Time-Series Data

As in earlier chapters, in this section we also present some preliminary data analysis of the price and consumption data of health, education and recreation by presenting budget shares, consumption and price growth rates using Divisa indices and the relationship between consumption and prices using a number of scatter plots.

Table 8.1 presents the unconditional and conditional budget shares for health, recreation and education and the budget share of the group consisting of these three items. The unconditional budget shares in columns (2)–(4) are reproduced from Table 3.5, and the group budget share in column (5) is a simple addition of the three unconditional budget shares in columns (2)–(4). The conditional budget shares presented in columns (6)–(8) for each item are the proportion of expenditures on health, recreation and education expressed as a proportion of the total expenditure on the HRE group. As can be seen, across the countries, the mean unconditional budget shares of health, recreation and education are 3.9 percent, 9.1 percent and 1.4 percent, respectively, giving a total budget share of 14.2 percent for the group. This means that a typical consumer allocates about 14 percent of their income on the HRE group. The corresponding mean conditional budget share for health, recreation and education are 29.4 percent, 59.8 percent and 10.7 percent, respectively. That is, within the HRE group, on average, recreation occupies a major proportion (about 60 percent) of the HRE budget.

Now, we summarise the consumption and price data for the HRE group in the form of Divisia indices given by equations (6.1)–(6.10) of Chapter 6 as presented in Table 8.2 for the 45 countries. The Divisia price and quantity indices in columns (2) and (3) of the table measure the growth in price and consumption of the HRE group. The Divisia price and quantity variances given in columns (4) and (5) measure the variation in price and consumption, respectively, of the HRE group. The Divisia price-quantity correlation in column (6) gives the measure of the strength and the direction of the relationship between price and consumption of the HRE group. The final column (7) gives the income flexibility. As can be seen from the last row of Table 8.2, which gives the average across all 45 countries, on average, prices of the HRE group have increased at a rate of 2.9 percent per annum and consumption of the group has quantity correlations in column (6) of the table; a majority of the correlations are negative with an average of −0.4, confirming that there is a negative linear relationship between relative prices and consumption. As can be seen from the last column of the table, as expected from the literature, most of the income flexibility estimates are negative with a cross-country average of −0.55 (Figure 8.1).

Table 8.3 presents the percentage of the signs of relative prices (RP) and relative consumption (RC) in the form of four combinations (positive RP, positive RC), (positive RP, negative RC), (negative RP, positive RC) and (negative RP, negative RC) for the HRE group. As can be seen from the last row, overall, nearly three-fourths of the pairs (RP, RC) of observations fall in the (positive RP, negative RC) or (negative RP, positive RC) categories, giving support for the law of demand, meaning that demand for the HRE group falls when the group's relative price increases. This result is in line with that of the other groups of commodities considered in Chapters 6 and 7.

Table 8.1 Unconditional and conditional budget shares at sample means, HRE group, 45 countries

		Unconditional				*Conditional*		
	Country (1)	*Health* (2)	*Recreation* (3)	*Education* (4)	*Group* (5)	*Health* (6)	*Recreation* (7)	*Education* (8)
Developed countries								
1	Australia	5.1	10.8	3.2	19.1	26.7	56.8	16.5
2	Austria	3.7	10.5	0.7	14.9	24.7	70.4	5.0
3	Belgium	5.6	9.2	0.4	15.2	36.7	60.6	2.7
4	Canada	3.4	9.0	1.1	13.4	24.8	67.1	8.1
5	Denmark	2.7	11.2	0.8	14.7	18.4	76.4	5.2
6	Finland	3.4	10.9	0.4	14.6	22.8	74.8	2.4
7	France	3.0	8.7	0.7	12.4	24.0	70.7	5.3
8	Germany	4.4	9.6	0.7	14.6	29.7	65.6	4.7
9	Hong Kong[a]	3.8	8.2	–	12.0	–	–	–
10	Iceland	3.0	11.4	1.2	15.6	19.2	72.8	8.0
11	Ireland	3.5	7.0	2.3	12.8	26.7	55.4	17.8
12	Israel	3.2	7.0	2.7	12.9	24.5	54.4	21.1
13	Italy	3.3	7.1	1.0	11.3	28.9	62.4	8.7
14	Japan	3.8	10.4	2.2	22.9	23.0	63.5	13.5
15	Luxembourg	2.0	7.2	0.7	9.8	19.9	73.3	6.8
16	Netherlands	4.0	11.4	0.7	16.0	24.5	71.1	4.4
17	New Zealand	2.2	10.0	0.9	13.1	16.9	76.5	6.6
18	Norway	2.3	10.5	0.5	13.3	62.1	18.0	19.8
19	Singapore	4.3	23.2	–	27.5	–	–	–
20	Slovenia	3.4	9.8	1.1	14.2	23.7	68.8	7.6
21	South Korea	3.7	6.3	5.3	15.4	24.8	40.3	34.9
22	Spain	3.4	8.1	1.6	13.1	26.1	62.0	11.9
23	Sweden	3.0	11.2	0.3	14.5	22.0	76.2	1.9
24	Switzerland	12.7	9.7	0.5	22.9	55.3	42.5	2.2
25	Taiwan	3.6	15.1	–	18.8	–	–	–
26	UK	1.5	10.4	1.3	13.3	11.5	78.7	9.8
27	USA	15.4	8.6	1.8	25.8	59.1	34.1	6.8
Mean (*Developed*)		4.2	10.1	1.3	15.5	28.2	62.2	9.7
Developing countries								
28	Colombia	3.3	4.9	5.0	13.1	24.8	37.5	37.8
29	Czech	2.0	10.2	0.6	12.8	16.0	79.7	4.4
30	Estonia	2.8	8.0	0.9	11.7	24.0	68.4	7.6
31	Greece	4.5	4.6	2.1	11.1	40.3	41.2	18.4
32	Hungary	3.9	7.9	1.5	13.4	29.3	59.1	11.5
33	India[a]	2.8	3.5	–	6.3	–	–	–
34	Latvia	3.9	8.2	1.7	13.9	28.8	59.2	12.0
35	Lithuania	4.1	6.3	0.6	11.0	37.5	57.1	5.4
36	Malaysia[a]	2.3	15.6	–	17.9	–	–	–
37	Mexico	4.4	4.2	1.6	10.2	43.3	41.4	15.3
38	Philippines[a]	2.4	5.7	–	8.1	–	–	–
39	Poland	3.9	7.9	1.1	12.9	30.1	61.1	8.8
40	Portugal	4.7	7.4	1.2	13.2	35.6	55.7	8.8
41	Slovakia	3.0	8.7	1.2	12.9	22.9	68.5	8.7
42	South Africa	5.8	5.5	2.1	13.4	42.3	42.7	15.0
43	Sri Lanka[a]	1.7	3.6	–	5.3	–	–	–
44	Thailand[a]	3.6	22.3	–	25.9	–	–	–
45	Turkey	3.5	4.5	1.1	9.0	38.5	49.5	12.0
Mean (*Developing*)		3.5	7.7	1.6	12.3	31.8	55.5	12.7
Mean (*All countries*)		3.9	9.1	1.4	14.2	29.4	59.8	10.7

[a] Disaggregated data are not available.

Table 8.2 Mean Divisia price and quantity indices, variances, and correlations, and income flexibility, HRE group, 45 countries

Country (1)	Divisia price index (DP) (2)	Divisia quantity index (DQ) (3)	Divisia price variance (4)	Divisia quantity variance (5)	Divisia price-quantity correlation (6)	Income flexibility (7)
Developed countries						
1 Australia	2.86	2.98	5.37	4.40	−0.49	−0.44
2 Austria	0.95	1.94	3.20	3.51	−0.57	−0.60
3 Belgium	1.23	1.55	2.81	2.91	−0.31	−0.32
4 Canada	2.19	2.68	1.90	2.12	−0.01	−0.01
5 Denmark	0.69	2.21	1.08	3.60	−0.26	−0.47
6 Finland	3.56	2.88	1.34	5.68	−0.19	−0.39
7 France	2.98	3.83	1.15	4.01	−0.45	−0.84
8 Germany	0.32	2.70	2.51	3.52	−0.26	−0.31
9 Hong Kong[a]	–	–	–	–	–	–
10 Iceland	3.66	3.18	4.06	9.68	−0.34	−0.52
11 Ireland	−2.93	7.14	85.65	244.30	−0.86	−1.45
12 Israel	2.01	1.88	2.65	2.44	0.00	0.00
13 Italy	1.42	0.89	1.61	2.34	−0.57	−0.69
14 Japan	−2.70	2.90	16.22	20.86	−0.72	−0.82
15 Luxembourg	1.46	0.36	3.73	19.67	−0.03	−0.07
16 Netherlands	1.41	1.08	0.91	60.93	−0.08	−0.65
17 New Zealand	1.16	2.56	6.28	12.87	−0.33	−0.47
18 Norway	4.93	1.01	2.35	5.01	−0.35	−0.51
19 Singapore[a]	–	–	–	–	–	–
20 Slovenia	3.63	2.85	0.80	6.85	−0.09	−0.26
21 South Korea	7.78	5.98	12.13	23.70	−0.43	−0.60
22 Spain	1.66	1.61	1.24	3.98	−0.20	−0.36
23 Sweden	−0.39	2.95	1.77	1.46	−0.04	−0.04
24 Switzerland	−2.64	4.47	1.29	6.87	−0.91	−2.10
25 Taiwan[a]	–	–	–	–	–	–
26 UK	−0.16	3.99	8.62	9.23	−0.76	−0.79
27 USA	3.87	3.07	4.31	3.88	−0.64	−0.61
Mean (*Developed*)	1.62	2.78	7.21	19.33	−0.37	−0.56
Developing countries						
28 Colombia	3.96	2.66	3.68	8.67	−0.69	−1.06
29 Czech Republic	1.96	2.39	4.15	10.23	−0.29	−0.46
30 Estonia	5.49	5.63	6.83	15.95	−0.04	−0.06
31 Greece	2.93	0.49	3.22	31.34	−0.04	−0.12
32 Hungary	6.55	2.04	11.94	15.81	−0.38	−0.44
33 India[a]	–	–	–	–	–	–
34 Latvia	4.62	8.55	5.66	74.50	−0.09	−0.33
35 Lithuania	2.40	10.82	9.54	56.95	−0.24	−0.59
36 Malaysia[a]	–	–	–	–	–	–
37 Mexico	4.46	1.03	5.14	43.66	−0.58	−1.69
38 Philippines[a]	–	–	–	–	–	–
39 Poland	6.48	2.59	16.51	27.88	−0.15	−0.19
40 Portugal	1.95	0.98	3.36	6.76	−0.40	−0.57
41 Slovakia	2.58	6.11	17.13	38.66	−0.48	−0.72
42 South Africa	9.91	1.84	18.58	14.02	−0.36	−0.31
43 Sri Lanka[a]	–	–	–	–	–	–
44 Thailand[a]	–	–	–	–	–	–
45 Turkey	14.58	3.66	29.70	38.78	−0.53	−0.61
Mean (*Developing*)	5.22	3.75	10.42	29.48	−0.33	−0.55
Mean (*All countries*)	2.89	3.12	8.34	22.89	−0.36	−0.55

Note: All entries in columns (2) and (3) are to be divided by 100, and those in columns (4) and (5) are to be divided by 10,000.

[a] Disaggregated data are unavailable.

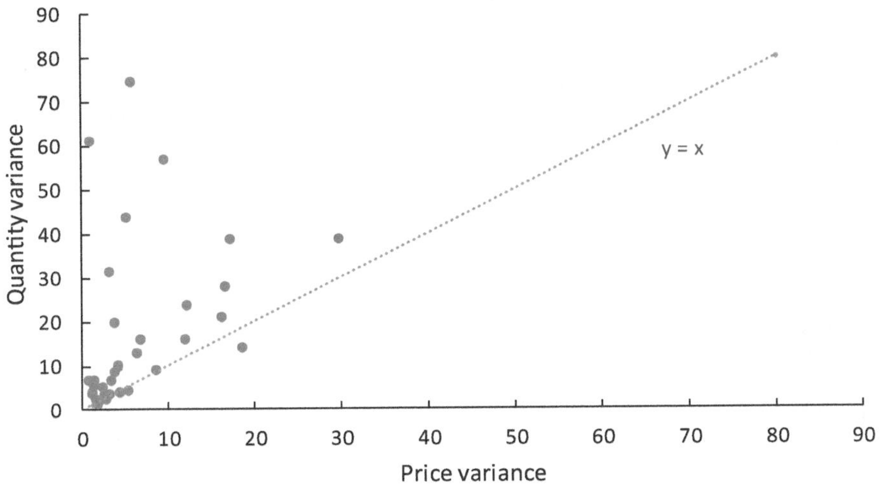

Figure 8.1 Divisia quantity variance against price variance, HRE group, 45 countries (excluding Ireland).

In Figure 8.2, for selected countries, we plot the RC against the RP for the combined HRE group. Table 8.4 presents the slope of the fitted regression line for each individual and pooled data across the three commodities. The slope can be interpreted as an estimate for income flexibility. As can be seen, a majority of the estimates are closer to −0.5 with a cross-country overall average of −0.66. We observed a similar range of values of income flexibility with unconditional data in the last column of Table 8.2.

In Table 8.5, we present the income and own-price elasticities obtained from the double-log demand equations introduced in Section 2.4 of Chapter 2. Columns (2)–(4) give the income elasticities and columns (5)–(7) give the own-price elasticities for health, recreation and education, respectively. As can be seen, the mean income elasticities for health and education are 0.8 and 0.6 (less than one), respectively, indicating that health and education are necessities in most of the countries. The mean income elasticity for recreation is 1.19 (greater than one), indicating that it is a luxury. The own-price elasticities of health, recreation and education are −0.69, −0.72 and −0.46, respectively, all less than one in absolute value, thus indicating that the demand for all three commodities is price inelastic.

8.4 Modelling the Demand for Health, Recreation and Education

In this section, we model the demand for the three commodities in the HRE group using conditional demand equations. We also present the estimation results, test the demand theory hypotheses, and present the implied income and price elasticities for the three commodities, health, recreation

Table 8.3 Frequency of same and opposite signs of relative prices and relative consumption of HRE group, 45 countries

		Positive consumption		*Negative consumption*		*Opposite signs*
	Country (1)	*Positive price* (2)	*Negative price* (3)	*Positive price* (4)	*Negative price* (5)	*(3) + (4)* (6)
Developed countries						
1	Australia	10	32	48	9	80
2	Austria	15	30	48	7	78
3	Belgium	18	26	37	19	63
4	Canada	10	30	52	8	82
5	Denmark	20	25	42	13	67
6	Finland	14	26	43	17	69
7	France	14	27	45	13	72
8	Germany	7	32	51	11	83
9	Hong Kong[a]	–	–	–	–	–
10	Iceland	11	28	44	18	72
11	Ireland	2	56	41	2	97
12	Israel	30	21	33	16	54
13	Italy	14	26	49	11	75
14	Japan	7	33	56	4	89
15	Luxembourg	15	33	37	15	70
16	Netherlands	37	25	23	16	48
17	New Zealand	19	33	40	9	73
18	Norway	12	31	41	16	72
19	Singapore[a]	–	–	–	–	–
20	Slovenia	27	25	25	23	–
21	South Korea	14	41	29	16	70
22	Spain	18	25	47	11	72
23	Sweden	17	33	47	3	80
24	Switzerland	6	43	44	7	87
25	Taiwan[a]	–	–	–	–	–
26	UK	8	32	55	5	–
27	USA	5	33	60	2	93
Mean (*Developed*)		15	31	43	11	75
Developing countries						
28	Colombia	26	26	31	17	57
29	Czech Republic	22	28	40	10	68
30	Estonia	30	20	20	30	40
31	Greece	22	25	30	23	55
32	Hungary	5	40	42	13	82
33	India[a]	–	–	–	–	–
34	Latvia	25	30	30	16	60
35	Lithuania	21	23	35	21	58
36	Malaysia	–	–	–	–	–
37	Mexico	12	33	45	9	78
38	Philippines[a]	–	–	–	–	–
39	Poland	15	28	48	8	76
40	Portugal	18	32	40	10	72
41	Slovakia	22	20	38	20	58
42	South Africa	18	28	36	18	64
43	Sri Lanka[a]	–	–	–	–	–
44	Thailand[a]	–	–	–	–	–
45	Turkey	19	25	35	21	60
Mean (*Developing*)		20	28	36	17	64
Mean (*All countries*)		16	30	41	13	72

[a] Disaggregated data are not available.

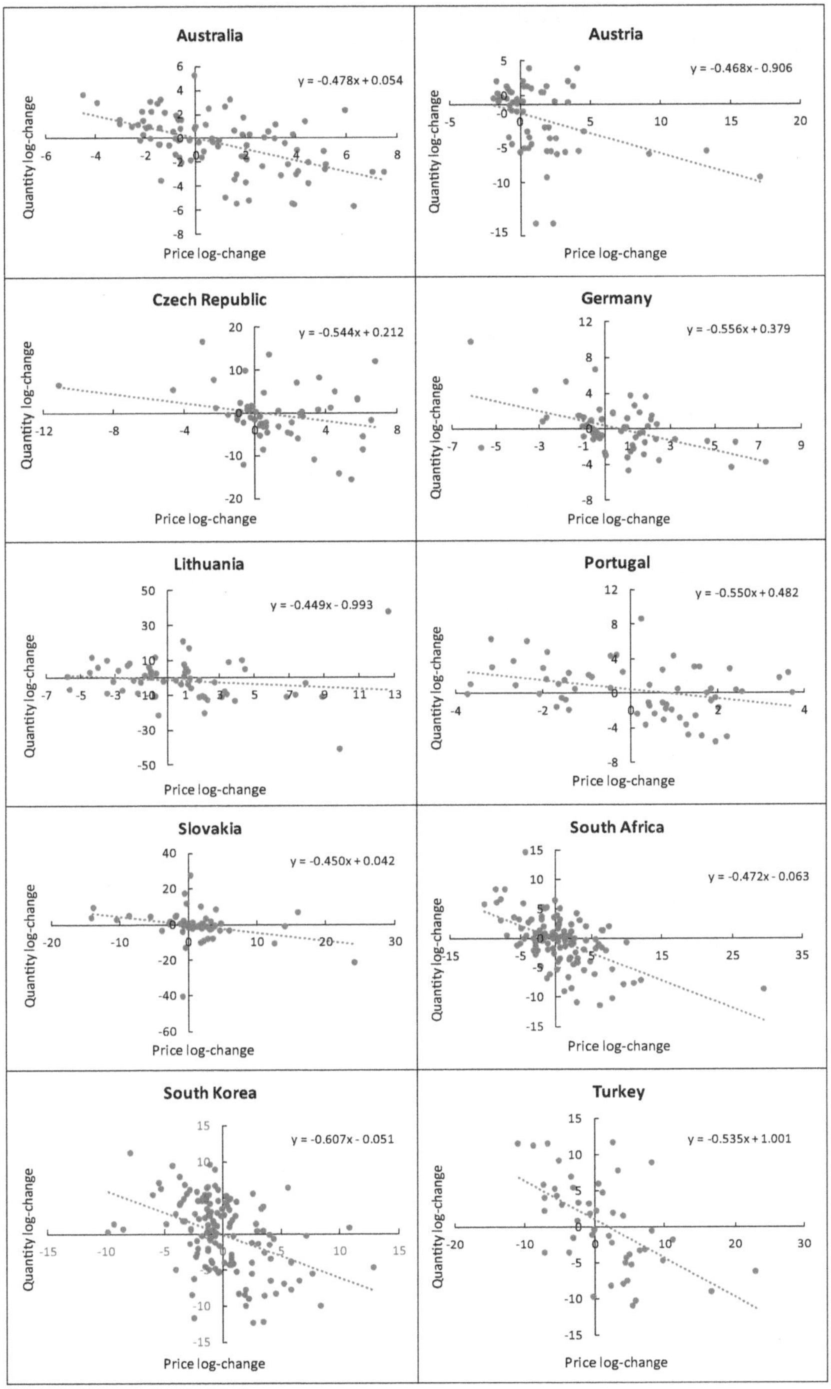

Figure 8.2 Relative quantity vs relative prices, HRE group, ten selected countries.

Table 8.4 Estimates of income flexibility for HRE group, 45 countries

	Country (1)	*Health (2)*	*Recreation (3)*	*Education (4)*	*HRE Group (5)*
Developed countries					
1	Australia	−0.72	−0.60	−0.36	−0.48
2	Austria	−1.04	−0.77	−0.38	−0.47
3	Belgium	−0.32	−0.34	−0.34	−0.45
4	Canada	0.01	0.10	−0.26	−0.29
5	Denmark	−0.61	−0.69	−0.10	−0.64
6	Finland	−0.02	−0.05	−1.93	−1.01
7	France	−0.92	−0.78	−1.04	−0.96
8	Germany	−0.68	−0.83	−0.63	−0.56
9	Hong Kong[a]	-	-	-	-
10	Iceland	−0.77	−1.09	−0.73	−0.73
11	Ireland	−1.67	−1.94	−2.00	−1.59
12	Israel	−0.25	−0.09	0.33	−0.03
13	Italy	−0.47	−0.41	−0.47	−0.61
14	Japan	−1.00	−1.11	−1.11	−1.02
15	Luxembourg	−0.51	−0.58	−0.74	−0.41
16	Netherlands	−7.69	−6.24	−0.19	−2.14
17	New Zealand	−0.68	−1.14	−0.75	−0.53
18	Norway	−0.99	−1.08	−0.48	−0.80
19	Singapore[a]	–	–	–	–
20	Slovenia	−0.50	−0.21	−0.23	−0.24
21	South Korea	−0.66	−0.35	−0.17	−0.61
22	Spain	−0.20	0.51	0.61	−0.27
23	Sweden	−0.88	−0.73	0.07	−0.20
24	Switzerland	−1.66	−1.67	−1.93	−2.04
25	Taiwan[a]	–	–	–	–
26	UK	−1.67	−0.33	−0.17	−0.75
27	USA	−0.62	−0.76	−0.54	−0.79
Mean (*Developed*)		−1.02	−0.88	−0.56	−0.73
Developing countries					
28	Colombia	0.14	0.02	0.43	−1.04
29	Czech	−0.63	−0.31	−0.47	−0.54
30	Estonia	−0.64	0.42	−0.05	−0.05
31	Greece	−0.84	−0.60	−0.62	−0.70
32	Hungary	−1.04	−1.36	−0.39	−0.70
33	Indiaa	–	–	–	–
34	Latviaa	–	−0.25	−0.22	0.10
35	Lithuania	0.07	0.37	−0.56	−0.45
36	Malaysia[a]	–	–	–	–
37	Mexico[a]	–	–	–	–
38	Philippines[a]	–	–	–	–
39	Poland	−1.00	−0.92	−0.73	−0.73
40	Portugal	−0.60	−0.55	−0.61	−0.55
41	Slovakia	−0.39	−0.34	−0.64	−0.45
42	South Africa	−0.62	−0.62	−0.37	−0.47
43	Sri Lanka[a]	–	–	–	–
44	Thailand[a]	–	–	–	–
45	Turkey	−0.43	−0.68	−0.57	−0.53
Mean (*Developing*)		−0.48	−0.40	−0.40	−0.51
Mean (*All countries*)		−0.84	−0.72	−0.51	−0.66

[a] Disaggregated data not available.

Table 8.5 Estimated conditional income and own-price elasticities, double-log demand equation, HRE group, 45 countries

	Country (1)	Income elasticity: Health (2)	Income elasticity: Recreation (3)	Income elasticity: Education (4)	Price elasticity: Health (5)	Price elasticity: Recreation (6)	Price elasticity: Education (7)
Developed countries							
1	Australia	0.44 (0.27)	1.47 (0.14)	0.58 (0.22)	−0.64 (0.20)	−0.48 (0.26)	−0.35 (0.21)
2	Austria	0.48 (0.18)	1.22 (0.08)	0.65 (0.53)	−0.94 (0.24)	−0.74 (0.23)	−0.40 (0.21)
3	Belgium	0.19 (0.11)	1.52 (0.07)	0.18 (0.33)	−0.21 (0.11)	−0.21 (0.12)	−1.15 (0.80)
4	Canada	0.61 (0.16)	1.24 (0.06)	0.04 (0.12)	0.04 (0.43)	−0.18 (0.38)	−0.47 (0.10)
5	Denmark	0.27 (0.15)	1.24 (0.04)	−0.09 (0.33)	−0.33 (0.27)	−0.40 (0.27)	0.06 (0.67)
6	Finland	0.71 (0.15)	1.14 (0.04)	0.12 (0.41)	−0.10 (0.35)	−0.20 (0.35)	−1.49 (0.67)
7	France	0.48 (0.15)	1.25 (0.05)	0.36 (0.32)	−0.79 (0.23)	−0.65 (0.21)	−1.05 (0.33)
8	Germany	0.69 (0.38)	1.18 (0.15)	0.33 (0.47)	−0.68 (0.31)	−0.79 (0.29)	−0.54 (0.22)
9	Hong Kong[a]	–	–	–	–	–	–
10	Iceland	0.48 (0.18)	1.21 (0.07)	0.19 (0.18)	−0.04 (0.38)	−0.20 (0.39)	0.06 (0.24)
11	Ireland	0.82 (0.08)	1.11 (0.06)	0.95 (0.06)	−1.60 (0.16)	−2.06 (0.18)	−2.01 (0.05)
12	Israel	0.88 (0.15)	1.15 (0.06)	0.75 (0.16)	−0.19 (0.34)	−0.03 (0.21)	0.37 (0.43)
13	Italy	0.82 (0.14)	1.16 (0.06)	0.47 (0.10)	−0.48 (0.34)	−0.50 (0.32)	−0.80 (0.26)
14	Japan	0.28 (0.22)	1.59 (0.11)	−0.18 (0.20)	−0.30 (0.25)	−0.15 (0.19)	0.08 (0.26)
15	Luxembourg	0.77 (0.29)	1.04 (0.07)	1.41 (0.24)	−0.58 (0.53)	−0.67 (0.53)	−0.65 (0.47)
16	Netherlands	2.98 (0.35)	0.32 (0.12)	0.26 (0.26)	−5.16 (1.24)	−3.94 (1.05)	−0.07 (0.52)
17	New Zealand	0.31 (0.39)	1.12 (0.09)	1.28 (0.43)	−0.53 (0.61)	−1.06 (0.40)	−0.77 (0.18)
18	Norway	0.94 (0.07)	1.01 (0.16)	1.12 (0.19)	−0.92 (0.21)	−1.08 (0.16)	−0.44 (0.31)
19	Singapore[a]	–	–	–	–	–	–
20	Slovenia	0.70 (0.20)	1.17 (0.08)	0.58 (0.28)	−0.81 (0.72)	−0.73 (0.88)	−0.06 (0.63)
21	South Korea	1.20 (0.18)	1.33 (0.09)	0.42 (0.10)	−0.57 (0.25)	−0.37 (0.23)	0.02 (0.15)
22	Spain	0.56 (0.12)	1.39 (0.07)	0.02 (0.20)	−0.48 (0.46)	−0.35 (0.40)	−0.61 (0.53)
23	Sweden	0.46 (0.33)	1.16 (0.10)	0.87 (0.28)	−0.59 (0.51)	−0.44 (0.52)	0.11 (0.18)
24	Switzerland	0.96 (0.06)	1.06 (0.09)	0.91 (0.10)	−1.68 (0.19)	−1.68 (0.21)	−1.94 (0.08)
25	Taiwan[a]	–	–	–	–	–	–
26	UK	0.53 (0.33)	1.14 (0.05)	0.53 (0.28)	−0.89 (0.74)	−0.23 (0.43)	−0.16 (0.34)
27	USA	0.76 (0.10)	1.54 (0.17)	0.62 (0.14)	−0.65 (0.28)	−1.00 (0.30)	−0.57 (0.14)
Mean (*Developed*)		0.72 (0.05)	1.20 (0.02)	0.51 (0.06)	−0.80 (0.09)	−0.76 (0.08)	−0.53 (0.08)

(*Continued*)

		Income elasticity			*Price elasticity*		
	Country *(1)*	*Health* *(2)*	*Recreation* *(3)*	*Education* *(4)*	*Health* *(5)*	*Recreation* *(6)*	*Education* *(7)*
Developing countries							
28	Colombia	0.72 (0.19)	1.55 (0.20)	0.30 (0.17)	−0.29 (0.42)	−0.65 (0.30)	0.07 (0.35)
29	Czech Republic	1.48 (0.37)	0.89 (0.07)	1.71 (0.42)	−0.65 (0.40)	−0.32 (0.33)	−0.61 (0.58)
30	Estonia	0.70 (0.08)	1.11 (0.04)	0.94 (0.21)	0.08 (0.30)	0.09 (0.36)	−0.06 (0.30)
31	Greece	1.42 (0.15)	0.66 (0.14)	0.91 (0.29)	−0.94 (0.67)	−1.08 (0.55)	−0.37 (1.27)
32	Hungary	1.01 (0.19)	0.98 (0.09)	1.02 (0.42)	−1.04 (0.15)	−1.36 (0.18)	−0.40 (0.42)
33	India[a]	–	–	–	–	–	–
34	Latvia	0.72 (0.15)	1.31 (0.10)	1.02 (0.51)	−0.60 (0.68)	−2.10 (0.87)	−0.18 (2.14)
35	Lithuania	0.91 (0.13)	1.11 (0.08)	0.55 (0.29)	−0.13 (0.53)	0.01 (0.54)	−0.14 (0.86)
36	Malaysia[a]	–	–	–	–	–	–
37	Mexico	0.29 (0.16)	2.07 (0.21)	0.03 (0.09)	−0.39 (0.50)	−0.62 (0.49)	−0.16 (0.21)
38	Philippines[a]	–	–	–	–	–	–
39	Poland	0.51 (0.16)	1.35 (0.10)	0.01 (0.32)	−0.77 (0.13)	−0.54 (0.18)	−0.21 (0.29)
40	Portugal	1.01 (0.21)	1.04 (0.14)	0.78 (0.30)	−0.60 (0.25)	−0.55 (0.25)	−0.51 (0.54)
41	Slovakia	1.99 (0.29)	0.73 (0.10)	0.96 (0.36)	0.10 (0.34)	−0.10 (0.31)	−0.63 (0.38)
42	South Africa	0.79 (0.10)	1.13 (0.10)	0.96 (0.19)	−0.59 (0.11)	−0.60 (0.11)	−0.37 (0.14)
43	Sri Lanka[a]	–	–	–	–	–	–
44	Thailand[a]	–	–	–	–	–	–
45	Turkey	0.63 (0.21)	1.25 (0.17)	0.83 (0.15)	−0.43 (0.26)	−0.61 (0.24)	−0.51 (0.13)
Mean (*Developing*)		0.94 (0.05)	1.17 (0.04)	0.77 (0.09)	−0.48 (0.11)	−0.65 (0.11)	−0.31 (0.22)
Mean (*All countries*)		0.80 (0.04)	1.19 (0.02)	0.60 (0.05)	−0.69 (0.07)	−0.72 (0.07)	−0.46 (0.09)

Note: Standard errors are in parentheses.
[a] Disaggregated data are not available.

and education. We also consider the cross-commodity effect between the three commodities.

From Section 2.11 of Chapter 2, we provided the finitechange version of the absolute price version of the conditional demand equation, which we reproduce here:

$$\bar{w}_{it} Dq_{it} = \theta_i' W_{gt} DQ_{gt} + \sum_{j \in S_g} \pi_{ij}^g Dp_{jt}, \quad i \in S_g. \tag{8.1}$$

where the conditional coefficients θ_i' and π_{ij}^g are specified as constants. The conditional Slutsky coefficients also satisfy demand homogeneity,

$$\sum_{j \in S_g} \pi_{ij}^g = 0, \quad i \in S_g, \tag{8.2}$$

and Slutsky symmetry,

$$\pi_{ij}^g = \pi_{ji}^g, \quad i, j \in S_g. \tag{8.3}$$

Table 8.6 presents the results for testing the demand theory hypotheses demand homogeneity in columns (4)–(9) and Slutsky symmetry in columns (10)–(12) based on the testing procedures described in Chapter 4. As can be seen from columns (9) and (12), regardless of whether developed or developing country, homogeneity and symmetry are generally acceptable for every country.

Table 8.7 presents the implied income, own-price and cross-price elasticities based on the homogeneity and symmetry constrained estimates. As can be seen from columns (2)–(4) of the table, in almost all countries, health and education are necessities (income elasticity < 1) and recreation is a luxury (income elasticity > 1). On average, all own-price elasticities presented in columns (5)–(7) are negative and less than one in absolute value, indicating that the demand for health, recreation and education are price inelastic. A majority of the cross-price elasticities presented in columns (8)–(13) are positive, indicating that health, recreation and education are pairwise substitutes in a number of countries. However, in a small number of countries, the cross-price elasticities are negative, revealing some level of complementarity between the three commodities. This strong substitutability points in the direction of preference independence of health, recreation and education in the consumers' utility structure.

Now, we consider the model under preference independence. The Rotterdam conditional demand equation for commodity i under preference independence takes the form

$$\bar{w}_{it} Dq_{it} = \theta_i' W_{gt} DQ_{gt} + \phi \theta_g \theta_i' \left(Dp_{it} - DP_{gt}' \right), \quad i \in S_g, \tag{8.4}$$

Table 8.6 Testing homogeneity and symmetry, HRE group, 45 countries

	Country (1)	n (2)	T (after lagging) (3)	Testing homogeneity (F-test): Test statistic (4)	df1 (5)	df2 (6)	Multiplier (7)	p-value (8)	Decision (9)	Testing symmetry (χ2-test): Test statistic (10)	p-value (11)	Decision (1 percent) (12)
Developed countries												
1	Australia	3	29	0.00	2	23	2.09	1.00	Accept	0.01	0.92	Accept
2	Austria	3	20	1.67	2	14	2.14	0.22	Accept	0.02	0.89	Accept
3	Belgium	3	19	3.54	2	13	2.15	0.06	Accept	0.08	0.78	Accept
4	Canada	3	34	4.97	2	28	2.07	0.01	Accept[b]	0.15	0.70	Accept
5	Denmark	3	20	0.00	2	14	2.14	1.00	Accept	0.78	0.38	Accept
6	Finland	3	40	0.58	2	34	2.06	0.57	Accept	0.31	0.58	Accept
7	France	3	56	0.53	2	50	2.04	0.59	Accept	1.42	0.23	Accept
8	Germany	3	19	0.75	2	13	2.15	0.49	Accept	1.72	0.19	Accept
9	Hong Kong[a]	–	–	–	–	–	–	–	–	–	–	–
10	Iceland	3	19	2.49	2	13	2.15	0.12	Accept	0.87	0.35	Accept
11	Ireland	3	18	1.83	2	12	2.17	0.20	Accept	3.78	0.05	Accept
12	Israel	3	19	1.81	2	13	2.15	0.20	Accept	0.03	0.86	Accept
13	Italy	3	19	0.33	2	13	2.15	0.72	Accept	0.05	0.82	Accept
14	Japan	3	19	3.05	2	13	2.15	0.08	Accept	1.19	0.28	Accept
15	Luxembourg	3	20	0.14	2	14	2.14	0.87	Accept	1.58	0.21	Accept
16	Netherlands	3	19	0.41	2	13	2.15	0.67	Accept	0.86	0.35	Accept
17	New Zealand	3	27	0.16	2	21	2.10	0.85	Accept	0.64	0.42	Accept
18	Norway	3	44	0.15	2	38	2.05	0.86	Accept	3.34	0.07	Accept
19	Singapore[a]	–	–	–	–	–	–	–	–	–	–	–
20	Sloveni[a]	3	20	11.52	2	14	2.14	0.00	Reject	1.02	0.31	Accept
21	South Korea	3	45	3.56	2	39	2.05	0.04	Accept[b]	0.01	0.92	Accept
22	Spain	3	19	5.05	2	13	2.15	0.02	Accept[b]	0.37	0.54	Accept
23	Sweden	3	12	3.33	2	6	2.33	0.11	Accept	0.43	0.05	Accept
24	Switzerland	3	18	10.79	2	12	2.17	0.00	Reject	0.43	0.51	Accept
25	Taiwana	–	–	–	–	–	–	–	–	–	–	–
26	UK	3	20	0.20	2	14	2.14	0.82	Accept	0.26	0.61	Accept
27	USA	3	45	5.87	2	39	2.05	0.01	Accept[b]	1.27	0.26	Accept

Developing countries												
28	Colombia	3	14	3.13	2	8	2.25	0.10	Accept	0.89	0.35	Accept
29	Czech	3	20	0.51	2	14	2.14	0.61	Accept	0.26	0.61	Accept
30	Estonia	3	20	1.38	2	14	2.14	0.28	Accept	0.07	0.79	Accept
31	Greece	3	20	0.37	2	14	2.14	0.70	Accept	0.26	0.61	Accept
32	Hungary	3	20	1.00	2	14	2.14	0.39	Accept	7.15	0.01	Accept[b]
33	India[a]	–	–	–	–	–	–	–	–	–	–	–
34	Latvia	3	19	0.07	2	13	2.15	0.93	Accept	5.31	0.02	Accept[b]
35	Lithuania	3	19	0.38	2	13	2.15	0.69	Accept	0.07	0.79	Accept
36	Malaysia[a]	–	–	–	–	–	–	–	–	–	–	–
37	Mexico	3	11	1.51	2	5	2.40	0.31	Accept	0.24	0.62	Accept
38	Philippines[a]	–	–	–	–	–	–	–	–	–	–	–
39	Poland	3	20	3.32	2	14	2.14	0.07	Accept	0.86	0.35	Accept
40	Portugal	3	20	1.80	2	14	2.14	0.20	Accept	0.01	0.92	Accept
41	Slovakia	3	20	0.33	2	14	2.14	0.73	Accept	0.19	0.66	Accept
42	South Africa	3	39	2.99	2	33	2.06	0.06	Accept	0.81	0.37	Accept
43	Sri Lanka[a]	–	–	–	–	–	–	–	–	–	–	–
44	Thailand[a]	–	–	–	–	–	–	–	–	–	–	–
45	Turkey[a]	–	–	–	–	–	–	–	–	–	–	–

Note: $df1 = n - 1$; $df2 = T - 2n$; Multiplier = $[df1 ´ (T - n - 2)/df2]$.

[a] Disaggregated data are not available.

[b] Acceptable at the 1 percent level of significance.

Table 8.7 Implied income and price elasticities for HRE group, 45 countries

	Country (1)	*Income elasticity*			*Own-price elasticity*			*Cross-price elasticity*					
		Health (2)	Recreation (3)	Education (4)	Health (5)	Recreation (6)	Education (7)	Health-Recreation (8)	Health-Education (9)	Recreation-Health (10)	Recreation-Education (11)	Education-Health (12)	Education-Recreation (13)
Developed countries													
1	Australia	0.35	1.47	0.43	−0.45	−0.19	−0.23	0.36	0.10	0.17	0.02	0.16	0.07
2	Austria	0.48	1.21	0.64	−0.73	−0.24	−0.40	0.67	0.06	0.23	0.01	0.30	0.10
3	Belgium	0.17	1.53	0.29	−0.13	−0.13	−1.86	0.11	0.03	0.06	0.07	0.36	1.50
4	Canada	0.56	1.28	0.00	0.05	−0.03	−0.38	−0.05	−0.01	−0.02	0.05	−0.01	0.40
5	Denmark	0.25	1.24	0.09	0.14	−0.09	1.80	0.37	−0.51	0.09	0.00	−1.80	0.00
6	Finland	0.67	1.13	0.02	−0.11	−0.05	−1.35	0.06	0.05	0.02	0.03	0.51	0.84
7	France	0.35	1.27	0.29	−0.55	−0.10	−1.38	0.27	0.28	0.09	0.01	1.26	0.12
8	Germany	0.65	1.20	0.39	−0.47	−0.25	−0.64	0.46	0.01	0.21	0.04	0.08	0.56
9	Hong Kong[a]	–	–	–	–	–	–	–	–	–	–	–	–
10	Iceland	0.19	1.35	−0.19	−0.08	0.03	0.08	0.00	0.07	0.00	−0.03	0.17	−0.26
11	Ireland	0.85	1.18	0.67	−1.33	−0.91	−1.72	1.05	0.28	0.51	0.41	0.43	1.30
12	Israel	0.86	1.16	0.76	0.06	−0.01	0.51	0.20	−0.26	0.09	−0.08	−0.30	−0.21
13	Italy	0.83	1.15	0.48	−0.35	−0.20	−0.75	0.28	0.07	0.13	0.07	0.23	0.52
14	Japan	0.09	1.55	−0.04	−0.50	−0.03	−0.93	0.01	0.48	0.01	0.02	0.83	0.11
15	Luxembourg	0.84	1.00	1.48	−0.38	−0.12	−1.44	0.16	0.22	0.04	0.08	0.63	0.81
16	Netherlands	2.92	0.39	0.29	−4.30	−1.39	0.36	4.20	0.10	1.44	−0.06	0.55	−0.91
17	New Zealand	0.47	1.09	1.31	−0.51	−0.32	−0.58	0.87	−0.36	0.19	0.13	−0.90	1.48
18	Norway	1.02	0.97	0.96	−0.31	−0.83	−0.44	0.21	0.11	0.71	0.12	0.33	0.11
19	Singapore[a]	–	–	–	–	–	–	–	–	–	–	–	–
20	Slovenia	0.59	1.19	0.58	−0.64	−0.23	−0.24	0.61	0.03	0.21	0.02	0.08	0.16
21	South Korea	1.20	1.38	0.43	−0.72	−0.53	0.00	0.79	−0.07	0.49	0.04	−0.05	0.05
22	Spain	0.53	1.38	0.02	−0.46	−0.18	−0.54	0.32	0.13	0.13	0.05	0.30	0.25
23	Sweden	0.41	1.17	0.91	−0.54	−0.13	−0.18	0.49	0.05	0.14	−0.01	0.60	−0.42
24	Switzerland	0.98	1.03	0.90	−0.73	−0.93	−1.79	0.69	0.04	0.89	0.04	1.10	0.70
25	Taiwan[a]	–	–	–	–	–	–	–	–	–	–	–	–
26	UK	0.50	1.13	0.53	−0.89	−0.09	−0.21	0.66	0.24	0.10	−0.01	0.28	−0.07
27	USA	0.66	1.67	0.63	−0.30	−0.53	−0.52	0.27	0.03	0.48	0.05	0.25	0.27
Mean (*Developed*)		0.68	1.21	0.49	−0.59	−0.31	−0.53	0.54	0.05	0.27	0.04	0.22	0.31

Developing countries													
28	Colombia	1.06	1.49	0.48	0.18	0.13	0.42	0.13	−0.31	0.09	−0.22	−0.20	−0.21
29	Czech	1.38	0.89	1.70	−0.45	−0.10	−0.64	0.38	0.06	0.08	0.02	0.23	0.41
30	Estonia	0.71	1.11	0.97	0.11	0.06	−0.19	−0.17	0.06	−0.06	0.00	0.18	0.01
31	Greece	1.42	0.69	0.77	−0.14	−0.60	0.46	0.48	−0.34	0.47	0.13	−0.74	0.28
32	Hungary	1.02	0.99	1.00	−0.70	−0.63	−0.69	0.86	−0.15	0.42	0.21	−0.39	1.08
33	India[a]	–	–	–	–	–	–	–	–	–	–	–	–
34	Latvia	0.67	1.26	0.51	−0.78	−0.53	−1.76	0.57	0.21	0.27	0.26	0.50	1.26
35	Lithuania	1.05	1.02	0.50	0.02	0.10	−0.04	−0.09	0.07	−0.06	−0.04	0.47	−0.43
36	Malaysia[a]	–	–	–	–	–	–	–	–	–	–	–	–
37	Mexico	0.38	2.00	0.04	−0.20	−0.31	0.05	0.26	−0.06	0.27	0.04	−0.16	0.10
38	Philippines[a]	–	–	–	–	–	–	–	–	–	–	–	–
39	Poland	0.53	1.37	0.05	−0.43	−0.23	−0.12	0.43	0.01	0.21	0.02	0.02	0.10
40	Portugal	1.02	1.01	0.86	−0.37	−0.26	−0.49	0.33	0.04	0.21	0.05	0.16	0.33
41	Slovakia	1.91	0.72	0.83	0.03	0.01	−0.59	−0.15	0.12	−0.05	0.04	0.31	0.28
42	South Africa	0.82	1.24	0.83	−0.37	−0.29	−0.30	0.28	0.09	0.28	0.01	0.26	0.04
43	Sri Lanka[a]	–	–	–	–	–	–	–	–	–	–	–	–
44	Thailand[a]	–	–	–	–	–	–	–	–	–	–	–	–
45	Turkey	0.68	1.33	0.70	−0.25	−0.28	−0.34	0.25	0.00	0.20	0.08	0.00	0.34
Mean (*Developing*)		0.97	1.16	0.71	−0.26	−0.22	−0.32	0.27	−0.02	0.18	0.05	0.05	0.28
Mean (*All countries*)		0.78	1.20	0.57	−0.48	−0.28	−0.46	0.45	0.03	0.24	0.04	0.16	0.30

[a] Disaggregated data are not available.

where the coefficients ϕ and θ_i are specified as constants. We now test preference independence of the utility structure based on the Monte Carlo simulation test described in Chapter 4. Table 8.8 presents the test results. As can be seen from column 4, for all but three countries, preference independence of the three commodities is acceptable at the 5 percent level of significance and, for all countries, it is acceptable at the 1 percent level.

Table 8.9 presents the estimation results under preference independence. Columns (2)–(4) present the conditional marginal shares of health, recreation and education, respectively. The cross-country average marginal shares for health, recreation and education are 0.22, 0.69 and 0.06, respectively, meaning that when there is a dollar increase in expenditure on the HRE group, out of that dollar increase, 22 cents will be allocated on health, 69 cents on recreation and 6 cents on education. The estimated income flexibility for each country is presented in the last column of Table 8.9. As can be seen, almost all estimates are negative as they should be with a cross-country average of -0.8, which is slightly higher than the expected income flexibility of $\phi = -0.5$.

8.5 Conditional Demand Analysis of the HRE Group with Cross-Sectional Data

In Sections 8.2 and 8.3, we presented a conditional demand analysis of the HRE group using time-series data for 45 countries. As in Section 7.4 of Chapter 7, we now extend the conditional demand analysis for goods within the HRE group based on cross-sectional HES data for a developed country, Australia, and three developing countries, Bangladesh, India and Sri Lanka. We use the conditional version of the generalised Working's model given by equation (6.15) and the implied conditional income elasticity given by equation (6.16) in Chapter 6 for the three commodities as individual goods within that group.

8.5.1 Australia

Table 8.10 presents the budget shares for the HRE group as well as for the commodities forming the group at the national level, by income level as well as by location of the household using Australian Household Expenditure Survey data. As can be seen at the national level, the budget allocation for the HRE group is 21.3 percent, while low-income households allocate about 17 percent, lower-middle-income households allocate about 20 percent, upper-middle-income households allocate 22 percent and high-income households allocate 25 percent of their total expenditure on the group as a whole. Within the group, at the national level, Australian consumers allocate 40 percent of their group expenditure on health, 8 percent on education and the remaining 52 percent on recreation. The budget share allocation on HRE individually also varies across income levels as well as location. The

Table 8.8 Monte Carlo test results of preference independence, 45 countries

Country *(1)*	*Observed value* *(2)*	*Rank* *(3)*	*Decision at the 5% level* *(4)*
Developed countries			
1 Australia	3.18	748	Accept
2 Austria	1.48	466	Accept
3 Belgium	3.72	784	Accept
4 Canada	6.78	952	Accept[b]
5 Denmark	4.95	878	Accept
6 Finland	3.60	808	Accept
7 France	13.37	990	Accept
8 Germany	0.30	103	Accept
9 Hong Kong[a]	–	–	–
10 Iceland	2.67	702	Accept
11 Ireland	2.73	647	Accept
12 Israel	1.90	503	Accept
13 Italy	4.12	777	Accept
14 Japan	7.22	885	Accept
15 Luxembourg	3.43	762	Accept
16 Netherlands	2.49	643	Accept
17 New Zealand	12.16	989	Accept
18 Norway	0.99	386	Accept
19 Singapore[a]	–	–	–
20 Slovenia	0.29	121	Accept
21 South Korea	8.31	978	Accept[b]
22 Spain	0.76	254	Accept
23 Sweden	4.58	830	Accept
24 Switzerland	1.54	458	Accept
25 Taiwan[a]	–	–	–
26 UK	2.31	625	Accept
27 USA	0.18	81	Accept
Developing countries			
28 Colombia	2.16	524	Accept
29 Czech Republic	0.06	21	Accept
30 Estonia	1.47	416	Accept
31 Greece	2.46	636	Accept
32 Hungary	8.41	971	Accept[b]
33 India[a]	–	–	–
34 Latvia	0.41	162	Accept
35 Lithuania	0.51	175	Accept
36 Malaysia[a]	–	–	–
37 Mexico	3.50	696	Accept
38 Philippines[a]	–	–	–
39 Poland	0.10	34	Accept
40 Portugal	0.03	14	Accept
41 Slovakia	4.20	816	Accept
42 South Africa	4.19	837	Accept
43 Sri Lanka[a]	–	–	–
44 Thailand[a]	–	–	–
45 Turkey	0.81	252	Accept
Percentage of rejection			0

[a] Disaggregated data are not available.
[b] Acceptable at the 1 percent level only.

Table 8.9 Estimation results of model under preference independence, 45 countries

	Country (1)	Marginal shares: Health (2)	Marginal shares: Recreation (3)	Marginal shares: Education (4)	Income flexibility (5)
Developed countries					
1	Australia	0.15 (0.06)	0.79 (0.07)	0.06 (0.03)	−0.91 (0.34)
2	Austria	0.12 (0.04)	0.87 (0.05)	0.01 (0.01)	−1.60 (0.57)
3	Belgium	0.05 (0.03)	0.94 (0.04)	0.01 (0.01)	−1.01 (0.69)
4	Canada	0.07 (0.03)	0.95 (0.03)	−0.02 (0.01)	1.66 (0.62)
5	Denmark	−0.14 (0.03)	0.19 (0.03)	−0.05 (0.02)	−1.00 (0.77)
6	Finland	0.16 (0.03)	0.85 (0.03)	−0.01 (0.01)	−0.07 (0.41)
7	France	0.08 (0.03)	0.89 (0.04)	0.03 (0.01)	−1.52 (0.56)
8	Germany	0.16 (0.07)	0.82 (0.08)	0.03 (0.01)	−1.14 (0.45)
9	Hong Kong[a]	–	–	–	–
10	Iceland	0.04 (0.03)	0.97 (0.03)	−0.01 (0.01)	−0.72 (0.44)
11	Ireland	0.21 (0.02)	0.65 (0.03)	0.14 (0.01)	−2.34 (0.23)
12	Israel	0.21 (0.03)	0.63 (0.03)	0.16 (0.03)	−0.03 (0.19)
13	Italy	0.22 (0.04)	0.73 (0.03)	0.05 (0.01)	−0.86 (0.27)
14	Japan	0.04 (0.05)	1.00 (0.05)	−0.04 (0.02)	−0.45 (0.23)
15	Luxembourg	0.15 (0.04)	0.75 (0.04)	0.10 (0.01)	−0.91 (0.27)
16	Netherlands	0.74 (0.08)	0.26 (0.08)	0.00 (0.01)	−5.09 (1.57)
17	New Zealand	0.05 (0.06)	0.88 (0.06)	0.08 (0.03)	−0.56 (0.21)
18	Norway	0.65 (0.04)	0.19 (0.02)	0.17 (0.03)	−0.95 (0.18)
19	Singapore[a]	–	–	–	–
20	Slovenia	0.15 (0.04)	0.81 (0.05)	0.04 (0.02)	−0.86 (0.74)
21	South Korea	0.33 (0.04)	0.54 (0.04)	0.14 (0.03)	−0.49 (0.19)
22	Spain	0.13 (0.03)	0.86 (0.04)	0.02 (0.02)	−0.95 (0.77)
23	Sweden	0.05 (0.06)	0.93 (0.06)	0.02 (0.00)	0.11 (0.16)
24	Switzerland	0.57 (0.03)	0.40 (0.03)	0.02 (0.00)	−1.76 (0.12)
25	Taiwan[a]	–	–	–	–
26	UK	0.03 (0.03)	0.91 (0.03)	0.06 (0.02)	−0.40 (0.49)
27	USA	0.39 (0.05)	0.57 (0.05)	0.04 (0.01)	−0.79 (0.19)
Mean (*Developed*)		0.19 (0.01)	0.72 (0.01)	0.04 (0.00)	−0.94 (0.11)
Developing countries					
28	Colombia	0.25 (0.05)	0.55 (0.06)	0.20 (0.06)	0.26 (0.28)
29	Czech Republic	0.22 (0.05)	0.70 (0.06)	0.08 (0.02)	−0.42 (0.18)
30	Estonia	0.16 (0.02)	0.76 (0.02)	0.07 (0.01)	−0.07 (0.22)
31	Greece	0.54 (0.05)	0.30 (0.05)	0.16 (0.04)	−0.74 (0.51)
32	Hungary	0.29 (0.04)	0.64 (0.05)	0.07 (0.03)	-1.11 (0.16)
33	India[a]	–	–	–	–
34	Latvia	0.18 (0.04)	0.74 (0.05)	0.08 (0.03)	−1.63 (0.93)
35	Lithuania	0.39 (0.06)	0.59 (0.07)	0.02 (0.02)	−0.02 (0.50)
36	Malaysia[a]	–	–	–	–
37	Mexico	0.13 (0.07)	0.87 (0.07)	0.00 (0.01)	−0.28 (0.65)
38	Philippines[a]	–	–	–	–
39	Poland	0.16 (0.05)	0.83 (0.05)	0.01 (0.02)	−0.96 (0.19)
40	Portugal	0.36 (0.07)	0.57 (0.07)	0.08 (0.03)	−0.58 (0.21)
41	Slovakia	0.43 (0.06)	0.52 (0.06)	0.06 (0.03)	−0.11 (0.20)
42	South Africa	0.36 (0.04)	0.52 (0.05)	0.11 (0.02)	−0.54 (0.10)
43	Sri Lanka[a]	–	–	–	–
44	Thailand[a]	–	–	–	–
45	Turkey	0.23 (0.06)	0.69 (0.07)	0.09 (0.02)	−0.61 (0.12)
Mean (*Developing*)		0.28 (0.01)	0.64 (0.02)	0.08 (0.01)	−0.52 (0.11)
Mean (*All countries*)		0.22 (0.01)	0.69 (0.01)	0.06 (0.00)	−0.80 (0.08)

Note: Standard errors are in parentheses.
[a] Disaggregated data are not available.

Table 8.10 Average budget share of HRE group and conditional budget shares within the HRE group, Australia

Household income level/location (1)	*Average HRE group budget share (as a percent of the total household expenditure)* (2)	*Average conditional budget shares (as a percent of the total group expenditure)*		
		Health (3)	*Recreation* (4)	*Education* (5)
National (Australia)	21.3	40.0	52.1	7.8
Income level				
Low-income (lower 25 percent)	17.1	48.8	48.1	3.0
Lower-middle-income (25–50 percent)	20.0	40.9	52.2	6.9
Upper-middle-income (50–75 percent)	21.6	39.3	52.7	7.9
High-income (upper 25 percent)	24.8	34.3	54.0	11.6
Remoteness level (location)				
Major cities	21.8	39.7	51.8	8.6
Inner regional	20.1	41.5	52.3	6.2
Outer regional	20.2	40.6	53.9	5.6
Remote Australia	22.8	35.3	57.8	6.9

Note: The sample size is 21,474.

within-group budget share allocation on health varies between 34 percent (high-income) and 49 percent (low-income), recreation varies between 48 percent (low-income) and 54 percent (high-income) and education varies between 3 percent (low-income) and 12 percent (high-income). By location, the within-group allocation on health varies between 35 percent (remote) and 42 percent (inner regional), recreation varies between 52 percent (major cities) and 58 percent (remote) and education ranges between 5.6 percent (outer regional) and 8.6 percent (major cities).

The income elasticity for the HRE group and goods within the group is presented in Table 8.11. As can be seen, the income elasticity for the group varies between 1.18 and 1.49 at the national level, across income levels and locations, indicating that HRE as a group is a luxury. The income elasticity for health is less than one and education is greater than one at the national

Table 8.11 Income elasticities of HRE group and individual commodities within the HRE group by income level and location, Australia

Commodity (1)	National (2)	*Income level* Low-income (3)	Lower-middle-income (4)	Upper-middle-income (5)	High-income (6)	*Location* Major cities (7)	Inner regional (8)	Outer regional (9)	Remote Australia (10)
HRE group	1.35	1.31	1.24	1.18	1.30	1.34	1.39	1.30	1.49
	(0.01)	(0.06)	(0.05)	(0.04)	(0.02)	(0.02)	(0.04)	(0.05)	(0.10)
Health	0.85	0.95	0.89	0.85	0.79	0.84	0.85	0.92	0.88
	(0.10)	(0.02)	(0.02)	(0.02)	(0.01)	(0.01)	(0.02)	(0.03)	(0.06)
Recreation	1.23	0.45	0.96	1.16	1.27	1.28	1.18	0.64	0.53
	(0.13)	(0.13)	(0.08)	(0.07)	(0.03)	(0.03)	(0.08)	(0.12)	(0.21)
Education	1.08	1.09	1.09	1.09	1.08	1.07	1.10	1.10	1.13
	(0.02)	(0.08)	(0.02)	(0.02)	(0.01)	(0.01)	(0.02)	(0.03)	(0.05)

Note: Standard errors are in parentheses.

level, across income levels and location, which indicates that health is a necessity and education is a luxury. Recreation is a luxury at the national level, across income levels and location except for low-income, lower-middle-income and outer regional and remote Australian households for whom it is a necessity.

8.5.2 Bangladesh

Table 8.12 presents the budget shares for the HRE group as well as for the commodities forming the group at the national level, by income level as well as by location of the household using Bangladesh Household Income and Expenditure Survey data. As can be seen at the Bangladesh national level, the budget allocation for the HRE group is 13 percent, while, on average, low-income households allocate about 10 percent, lower-middle-income households allocate about 12 percent, upper-middle-income households allocate 13 percent and high-income households allocate 16 percent of their total expenditure on the HRE group as a whole. Within the group, at the national level, Bangladeshi households allocate 74 percent of their group expenditure on health, 24 percent on education and the remaining 2 percent on recreation. The allocation on health, education and recreation individually also varies across income as well as location. The within-group allocation on health varies between 64 percent (high-income households) and 85 percent (low-income), education varies between 14 percent (low-income) and 33 percent (high-income) and recreation varies between 1 percent (low-income) and 3 percent (high-income). By location, the within-group budget share allocated for health by urban households is 71 percent while

Table 8.12 Average budget share of HRE group and conditional budget shares within the HRE group, Bangladesh

Household income level/location (1)	*Average HRE group budget share (as a percent of the total household expenditure)* (2)	*Average conditional budget shares (as a percent of the total group expenditure)*		
		Health (3)	*Recreation* (4)	*Education* (5)
National (Bangladesh)	12.7	73.6	1.9	24.4
Income level				
Low-income (lower 25 percent)	10.1	85.0	1.2	13.9
Lower-middle-income (25–50 percent)	12.0	75.3	1.6	23.2
Upper-middle-income (50–75 percent)	13.2	70.5	2.0	27.5
High-income (upper 25 percent)	15.5	63.9	2.8	33.2
Remoteness level (location)				
Rural	12.3	75.0	1.6	23.4
Urban	13.5	70.6	2.6	26.8

Note: The sample size is 45,558.

for rural households it is 75 percent, education allocation is 23 percent for rural and 27 percent for urban households; and recreation allocation is very low with 1.6 percent for rural households and 2.6 percent for urban households in Bangladesh.

The income elasticity for the HRE group and goods within the group is presented in Table 8.13. As can be seen, the income elasticity for the group is above unity at the national level, across income levels and location except for the high-income group (0.88), indicating that HRE as a group is a luxury for all types except the high-income group for which it is a necessity. The income elasticity for health is less than one, and education and recreation are above one at the national level, across all income levels and locations, indicating that health is a necessity and education and recreation are luxury goods in Bangladesh.

8.5.3 India

Next, we present the budget shares for the HRE group as well as for the commodities forming the group at the national level, by income level as well as by locations of the households in Table 8.14 using Indian Human

Table 8.13 Income elasticities of HRE group and individual commodities within the HRE group by income level and location, Bangladesh

Commodity (1)	National (2)	*Income level* Low-income (3)	Lower-middle-income (4)	Upper-middle-income (5)	High-income (6)	*Location* Rural (7)	Urban (8)
HRE group	1.24 (0.02)	1.23 (0.04)	1.12 (0.05)	1.01 (0.06)	0.88 (0.08)	1.25 (0.03)	1.20 (0.04)
Health	0.83 (0.00)	0.88 (0.00)	0.81 (0.00)	0.77 (0.01)	0.79 (0.01)	0.84 (0.00)	0.79 (0.00)
Recreation	1.27 (0.09)	1.25 (0.32)	1.17 (0.30)	0.97 (0.23)	1.09 (0.16)	1.18 (0.13)	1.30 (0.12)
Education	1.50 (0.01)	1.70 (0.02)	1.62 (0.01)	1.58 (0.01)	1.39 (0.01)	1.49 (0.01)	1.52 (0.01)
$\lambda = -0.2836; \lambda_g = -0.0120$							

Note: Standard errors are in parentheses.

Table 8.14 Average budget share of HRE group and conditional budget shares within the HRE group, India

Household income level/location (1)	*Average group budget share (as a percent of the total household expenditure)* (2)	*Average conditional budget shares (as a percent of the total group expenditure)* Health (3)	Recreation (4)	Education (5)
National (India)	18.0	76.4	5.2	18.2
Income level				
Low-income (lower 25 percent)	13.8	88.5	2.6	8.9
Lower-middle-income (25–50 percent)	17.7	82.2	3.1	14.7
Upper-middle-income (50–75 percent)	18.6	74.0	5.6	20.3
High-income (upper 25 percent)	22.1	60.1	9.8	29.2
Remoteness level (location)				
Rural	17.9	67.2	8.6	24.2
Urban	18.1	81.7	3.4	14.9

Note: The sample size is 7,470.

Development Survey data. As can be seen at the national level, the group budget allocation for the HRE group is 18 percent, while low-income households allocate about 14 percent, lower-middle-income households allocate about 18 percent, upper-middle-income households allocate 19 percent and high-income households allocate 22 percent of their total expenditure on the HRE group as a whole. Considering the three commodities within the group, at the national level, Indian consumers allocate 76 percent of their group expenditure on health, 18 percent on education and the remaining 5 percent on recreation. The budget share allocation on HRE individually also varies across income levels as well as location. The within-group budget share allocation on health varies between 60 percent (high-income households) and 89 percent (low-income), education varies between 9 percent (low-income) and 29 percent (high-income) and recreation varies between 3 percent (low-income) and 10 percent (high-income). By location, the within-HRE group budget share allocated for health by urban households is 82 percent while for rural households it is 67 percent; education allocation is 24 percent for rural households and 15 percent for urban households; and recreation allocation is 9 percent for rural households and 3 percent for urban households in India.

The income elasticities for the HRE group and goods within the group by income level and location are presented in Table 8.15. As can be seen, the income elasticity for the HRE group varies between 1.05 and 1.42 at the national level, across income levels and location, indicating that HRE as a group is a luxury. The income elasticity for health is less than 1 and education is greater than 1 at the national level, across income levels and regardless of the location of the household, indicating that health is a necessity and education is a luxury. Recreation is a luxury at the national level as well for the rural and urban households, and for high-income households it is a near luxury.

8.5.4 Sri Lanka

Table 8.16 presents the summary information on the HRE group budget share as well as for the commodities forming the group using the Sri Lankan Household Income and Expenditure Survey data. As can be seen at

Table 8.15 Income elasticities of HRE group and individual commodities within the HRE group by income level and location, India

		Income level				*Location*	
Commodity	*National*	*Low-income*	*Lower-middle-income*	*Upper-middle-income*	*High-income*	*Rural*	*Urban*
(1)	*(2)*	*(3)*	*(4)*	*(5)*	*(6)*	*(7)*	*(8)*
HRE group	1.26 (0.01)	1.24 (0.05)	1.42 (0.05)	1.18 (0.05)	1.05 (0.04)	1.24 (0.02)	1.34 (0.02)
Health	0.91 (0.004)	1.00 (0.01)	0.99 (0.01)	0.96 (0.01)	0.89 (0.01)	0.85 (0.01)	0.95 (0.004)
Recreation	1.24 (0.07)	0.76 (0.27)	0.81 (0.30)	0.86 (0.18)	1.01 (0.10)	1.20 (0.08)	1.08 (0.13)
Education	1.32 (0.01)	1.10 (0.05)	1.09 (0.04)	1.17 (0.03)	1.24 (0.02)	1.34 (0.02)	1.25 (0.02)
$\lambda = -0.1720$; $\lambda_g = -0.0350$							

Note: Standard errors are in parentheses.

Table 8.16 Average budget share of HRE group and conditional budget shares within the HRE group, Sri Lanka

Household income level/location	*Average group budget share (as a percent of the total household expenditure)*	*Average conditional budget shares (as a percent of the total group expenditure)*		
		Health	*Recreation*	*Education*
(1)	*(2)*	*(3)*	*(4)*	*(5)*
National (Sri Lanka)	8.9	61.7	11.8	26.4
Income level				
Low-income (lower 25 percent)	6.5	78.0	8.4	13.6
Lower-middle-income (25–50 percent)	8.5	63.6	10.1	26.3
Upper-middle-income (50–75 percent)	9.7	56.2	12.4	31.4
High-income (upper 25 percent)	11.0	49.4	16.2	34.3
Remoteness level (location)				
Urban	9.6	58.8	12.3	28.9
Rural	8.9	62.2	11.6	26.2
Estate	6.5	64.2	13.7	22.2

Note: The sample size is 21,474.

the national level, the budget share allocation for the HRE group is only 9 percent, while low-income households allocate about 7 percent, lower-middle-income households allocate about 9 percent, upper-middle-income households allocate 10 percent and high-income households allocate 11 percent of their total expenditure on the HRE group as a whole. Within the HRE group, at the national level, Sri Lankan consumers allocate 62 percent of their group expenditure on health, 26 percent on education and the remaining 12 percent on recreation. Considering the within-group budget share allocation on the three goods, the within-group allocation on health varies between 49 percent (high-income households) and 78 percent (low-income); education varies between 14 percent (low-income) and 34 percent (high-income); and recreation varies between 8 percent (low-income) and 16 percent (high-income). By location, the within-HRE group budget allocation for health is 59 percent for urban households, 62 percent for rural households and 64 percent for estate households. Conditional budget share of education is 22 percent for estate households, 26 percent for rural households and 29 percent for urban households, and for recreation it is about 12 percent for rural and urban households, while it is 14 percent for estate households.

Table 8.17 Income elasticities of HRE group and individual commodities within the HRE group by income level and location, Sri Lanka

		Income level				*Location*		
Commodity	*National*	*Low-income*	*Lower-middle-income*	*Upper-middle-income*	*High-income*	*Urban*	*Rural*	*Estate*
(1)	*(2)*	*(3)*	*(4)*	*(5)*	*(6)*	*(7)*	*(8)*	*(9)*
Group	0.54	0.80	0.68	0.59	0.37	0.51	0.52	0.54
	(0.00)	(0.01)	(0.01)	(0.00)	(0.01)	(0.01)	(0.01)	(0.01)
Health	0.86	0.76	0.80	0.82	0.81	0.81	0.85	0.86
	(0.00)	(0.01)	(0.01)	(0.01)	(0.01)	(0.01)	(0.01)	(0.01)
Education	3.05	3.62	3.88	3.67	3.47	2.75	3.02	3.12
	(0.06)	(0.16)	(0.15)	(0.14)	(0.12)	(0.22)	(0.10)	(0.09)
Recreation	1.25	1.47	1.63	1.88	1.79	1.59	1.36	1.29
	(0.04)	(0.07)	(0.08)	(0.09)	(0.09)	(0.14)	(0.07)	(0.05)
$\lambda = -0.3109$; $\lambda_g = -0.0148$								

Note: Standard errors are in parentheses.

Table 8.17 presents the implied income elasticities for the HRE group and goods within the group by income level and location. As can be seen from the income elasticities for the HRE group at the national level, the HRE group is a necessity. And considering the three disaggregated goods, health is a necessity, and recreation and education are luxuries. The same results were found for households in Australia, Bangladesh and India nationally for disaggregated goods. The same results can also be seen regardless of the income level and location of the households in Sri Lanka.

8.6 Concluding Comments

A number of studies have concluded that involvement in recreational activities and a higher level of education leads to better health outcomes for consumers. In this chapter, we analysed the demand for health, recreation and education within the HRE group formed by these three commodities for a group of 45 developed and developing countries. We presented a preliminary analysis of the data and then estimated conditional demand equations to obtain final estimates of conditional income and price elasticities of health, recreation and education. We also tested the demand theory hypotheses demand homogeneity and Slutsky symmetry as well as the preference independence of the utility structure and found those hypotheses are generally acceptable by the data for the three commodities. Results also revealed that while HRE as a group is a luxury in Australia, India and Bangladesh, it is a necessity in Sri Lanka; health as a single commodity is a necessity, while education and recreation are luxuries. The estimated own- and cross-price elasticities indicate that the demand for health, recreation and education are price inelastic and while, in general, all three are pairwise substitutes, in some countries there exists some complementarity between the three commodities.

While, on average, consumers in the developed countries allocate 15.5 percent of their income on the HRE group, in the developing countries, consumers allocate slightly less, 12.3 percent of their income on the HRE group. While, on average, consumers in developing countries allocate 3.5 percent of their income on health, 7.7 percent on recreation and 1.6 percent on education, consumers in developed countries allocate 4.2 percent on health, 10.1 percent on recreation and 1.3 percent on education.

The estimation results using time-series data indicate that, within the HRE group, in both developed and developing countries, health and education are necessities while recreation is a luxury. The demand for the individual goods, health, recreation and education, are price inelastic.

We also estimated the demand for the disaggregated goods, health, recreation and education, using the HES data for Australia, Bangladesh, India and Sri Lanka. The results show that HRE as a group is a luxury in Australia, Bangladesh and India while it is a necessity in Sri Lanka. Health as a single commodity is a necessity and recreation and education are luxuries in all four countries. There is a difference in the results for education between time-series (a necessity) and cross-sectional data (a luxury). For both data sets, time-series and cross-sectional, health is a necessity and recreation is a luxury.

References

Acerenza, S., and N. Gandelman. 2019. Household education spending in Latin America and the Caribbean: Evidence from income and expenditure surveys. *Education Finance and Policy* 14(1): 61–87.

Alfonso, Y.N., G. Ding, and D. Bishai. 2016. Income elasticity of vaccines spending versus general healthcare spending. *Health Economics* 25: 860–872.

Boman, M., P. Fredman, L. Lundmark, and G. Ericsson. 2013. Outdoor recreation – A necessity or a luxury? Estimation of Engel curves for Sweden. *Journal of Outdoor Recreation and Tourism* 3–4: 49–56.

Boppart, T., and L.R. Ngai. 2021. Rising inequality and trends in leisure. *Journal Economic Growth* 26: 153–185.

Boustan, L.P., F.V. Ferreira, H.J. Winkler, and E.M. Zolt. 2013. The effect of rising income inequality on taxation and public expenditures: Evidence from U.S. municipalities and school districts, 1970–2000. *The Review of Economics and Statistics* 95(4): 1291–1302.

Costa-Font, J., M. Gemmill, and G. Rubert. 2009. Re-visiting the health care luxury good hypothesis: Aggregation, precision, and publication biases? Working paper, Health, Econometrics and Data Group (HEDG), York, UK.

Freeman, D.G. 2003. Is health care a necessity or a luxury? Pooled estimates of income elasticity from US state-level data. *Applied Economics* 35(5): 495–502.

Farag, M., A.K. Nandakumar, S. Wallack, D. Hodgkin, G. Gaumer, and C. Erbil. 2012. The income elasticity of health care spending in developing and developed countries. *International Journal of Health Care Finance and Economics* 12(2): 145–162.

Fredman, P., and D. Wikström. 2018. Income elasticity of demand for tourism at Fulufjället national park. *Tourism Economics* 24(1): 51–63.

Gerdtham, U., and B. Jonsson. 2000. International comparisons of health expenditure: Theory, data, and econometric analysis, in A.J. Culyer and J.P. Newhouse (eds.), *Handbook of health economics,* Volume 1A, North Holland Publishing. Amsterdam: Elsevier Science.

Gerdtham, U., J. Sogaard, F. Andersson, and B. Jonsson. 1992. An econometric analysis of health care expenditure: A cross-section study of the OECD countries. *Journal of Health Economics* 11: 63–84.

Jenkins, G.P., H.A. Anayabolu, and P. Bahramian. 2019. Family decision-making for educational expenditure: New evidence from survey data for Nigeria. *Applied Economics* 51(52): 5663–5673.

Getzen, T.E. 2000. Health care is an individual necessity and a national luxury: Applying multilevel decision models to the analysis of health care expenditures. *Journal of Health Economics* 19, 259–270.

Jayasinghe, M., E.A. Selvanathan, and S. Selvanathan. 2019. An intertemporal analysis of expenditure elasticities under three expenditure specifications for Sri Lanka. *Applied Economics* 51(59): 6376–6392.

Khan, J.A., and R.A. Mahumud. 2015. Is healthcare a 'necessity' or 'luxury'? An empirical evidence from public and private sector analyses of South-East Asian countries. *Health Economics Review* 5(1): 1–9.

Kino, S., E. Bernabé, and W. Sabbah. 2018. The role of healthcare and education systems in co-occurrence of health risk behaviours in 27 European countries. *European Journal of Public Health* 28(1): 186–192.

Knapman, B., and N. Stoeckl. 1995. Recreation user fees: An Australian empirical investigation. *Tourism Economics* 1(1): 5–15. doi:10.1177/135481669500100102.

Lépine, A. 2015. Is health a necessity in Sub-Saharan Africa? An investigation of income-elasticity of health expenditures in rural Senegal. *Journal of International Development* 27: 1153–1177. doi:10.1002/jid.3036.

Martín, J., P.M. López, and M. Dolores Cano García. 2010. Review of the literature on the determinants of healthcare expenditure. *Applied Economics* 43: 19–46.

Mueller, J. T., S.Y. Park, and A.J. Mowen. 2019. The relationship between parks and recreation per capita spending and mortality from 1980 to 2010: A fixed effects model. *Preventive Medicine Reports* 14: 100827.

Njegovan, N. 2006. Elasticities of demand for leisure air travel: A system modelling approach. *Journal of Air Transport Management* 12(1): 33–39.

Pawlowski, T., and C. Breuer. 2012. Expenditure elasticities of the demand for leisure services. *Applied Economics* 44(26): 3461–3477.

Ross, C.E., and C.L. Wu. 1995. The links between education and health. *American Sociological Review* 719–745.

Raghupathi, V., and W. Raghupathi. 2020. The influence of education on health: An empirical assessment of OECD countries for the period 1995–2015. *Archives of Public Health* 78(1): 1–18.

Sato, M., Y. Inoue, J. Du, and D.C. Funk. 2019. Access to parks and recreational facilities, physical activity, and health care costs for older adults: evidence from U.S. counties. *Journal of Leisure Research* 50(3): 220–238.
Xu, K., and P. Saksena. 2011. *The determinants of health expenditure: A country level panel data analysis*. Geneva: World Health Organisation (WHO).
Zheng, B., and Y. Zhang. 2013. Household expenditures for leisure tourism in the USA, 1996 and 2006. *International Journal of Tourism Research* 15(2): 197–208.

9 Demand for Consumer Goods

A Summary

M Jayasinghe, E A Selvanathan and S Selvanathan

9.1 Introduction

There are evidenced differences and similarities in household demand for consumer goods in countries around the globe. The comprehensive cross-country analysis presented in this book provides convincing evidence regarding the consumption patterns of consumer goods. We have presented an extensive three-dimensional analysis on the consumption patterns of 12 consumer goods across 45 countries and over time. The countries considered in the study consist of developed as well as developing countries with similar lifestyle characteristics within each group. The time periods considered are the most recent wherever possible. The 12 broad commodities included in the analysis are (1) food, (2) alcohol, (3) clothing, (4) housing, (5) durables, (6) health, (7) transport, (8) communication, (9) recreation, (10) education, (11) restaurants and (12) miscellaneous. The book also presented conditional analysis of related commodities as three groups to analyse the consumer behaviour and cross effects within the groups.

This chapter presents an overall summary of the conclusions about the consumption patterns of individual consumer goods as well as groups of goods presented in Chapters 1–8.

9.2 Demand for Food

An overview of the basic data for food shows that, at sample means, while consumers in the developing countries allocate about one-fourth of their income on food (ranging from 16 percent for the Czech Republic to 54 percent for Sri Lanka), consumers from developed countries allocate less than one-seventh of their income on food (ranging from 8.6 percent for the UK to 24 percent for Taiwan). Globally, on average, consumers allocate about one-fifth of their income on food. Aggregate food prices, on average, in the developing countries (5.10 percent) have increased at about double the rate of increase in the developed countries (2.74 percent). However, food consumption, on average, in the developing countries (2.21 percent) has increased at about triple the rate of increase in the developed countries (0.85 percent).

DOI: 10.4324/9780429200120-9

Analysis of the relationship between food budget share and income for select countries identified an approximate inverse linear relationship between the two variables, supporting the well-known Engel's Law, which states that the budget share for food falls with increasing income. A plot of the relative consumption of food against the relative price of food for select countries shows an approximate negative linear relationship supporting the basic law in economics, the law of demand. The slope of this plot is −0.45, which can be interpreted as an estimate of the consumption parameter, the income flexibility (which is considered as an international constant and equal to a value between −0.4 and −0.7). The analysis further provided support for the law of demand, Frisch conjecture and preference independence. The estimated marginal share of food for an average world consumer is 0.15, indicating that when income increases by one dollar, 15 cents of that increase will be allocated to food. The estimated average income elasticity across countries for food is in the range 0.5–0.8, depending on the demand model used for estimation, implying that food is a necessity for consumers in any country. When the countries are grouped into developed and developing countries, food is still identified as a necessity for both groups of countries. However, food is more of a necessity in developing countries than in developed countries. The estimated average own-price elasticity across countries for food is in the range −0.2 to −0.4 and indicates that internationally the demand for food is price inelastic.

9.3 Demand for Alcohol

On average, world consumers allocate about 5 percent of their income on alcohol consumption. Across the world, on average, alcohol consumption has increased at a rate of only 0.1 percent per annum and alcohol prices have increased at a rate of 4.5 percent per annum. While alcohol consumption has fallen at a rate of -0.4 percent per annum across the developed countries, it has increased at a rate of 0.9 percent per annum in the developing countries. A plot of relative consumption of alcohol against relative price of alcohol shows an approximate negative linear relationship, supporting the basic economic law, the law of demand. The slope of this plot is −0.49, which can be interpreted as an estimate of the consumption parameter, the income flexibility. The estimated average income elasticity across countries for alcohol is around 0.6 (less than one) which indicates that it is internationally a necessity. When the countries are grouped into developed and developing countries, the average income elasticity for alcohol is 0.58 (for developed countries) and 0.62 (for developing countries), indicating that alcohol is a necessity in most developed and developing countries. The estimated average own-price elasticity across countries for alcohol is −0.6, which indicates that, globally, the demand for alcohol is price inelastic.

The analysis in this book highlighted an interesting observation where the estimated income elasticities of alcohol vary based on the type of data used: cross-sectional or time-series. The income elasticity for alcohol based on time-series data for Australia is 0.91 (a necessity); however, the income elasticity calculated based on Household Expenditure Survey (HES) data is just above unity. Across various income groups (low-middle-high) or across Australian states, the estimated income elasticities are just above unity. For India, the estimated income elasticity, at the national level as well as across various income groups, religious groups and urban/rural locations, varies in the range 0.4–0.7, representing a necessity. Based on HES data, while the income elasticity for alcohol for Sri Lanka at the national level is about 0.7 (a necessity), it is a luxury to the low-income group and a necessity to all other income groups. For various ethnic groups and urban/rural/estate locations, alcohol is a near luxury with income elasticity in the range 0.8–1.0.

When alcohol is considered conditionally within the food group (food, alcohol and restaurant), about 18 percent of the food group expenditure is allocated to alcohol. Conditional mean income and price elasticities for alcohol across all 45 countries are 0.91 and −0.57, respectively.

9.4 Demand for Clothing

In developing countries, the proportion of income allocated to expenditure on clothing (about 6 percent) by consumers is about the same as that of consumers in developed countries. On average, world consumers allocate about 5.7 percent of their income on clothing. The prices of clothing increased at a faster rate in the developing countries (at a rate of about 3.6 percent per annum) than in the developed countries (at a rate of about 1.1 percent per annum). However, the consumption of clothing grew at a rate of 2–4 percent in both country groups. A plot of relative consumption of clothing against relative price of clothing shows an approximate negative linear relationship supporting the basic economic law, the law of demand. The slope of this plot is −0.61, which can be interpreted as an estimate of the consumption parameter, the income flexibility. The average estimated marginal share of clothing for a world consumer is 0.07, which indicates that when income increases by one dollar, 7 cents of that increase will be allocated to clothing. The estimated average income elasticity across countries for clothing is 1.3 (greater than one) which indicates that it is internationally a luxury, with estimates about the same for developed and developing countries. The estimated average own-price elasticity across countries for clothing is −0.5 which indicates that internationally the demand for clothing is price inelastic.

9.5 Demand for Housing

On average, world consumers allocate about 19.5 percent of their income on housing. There is a significant difference in the share of allocation of income on housing between developed countries (21.2 percent) and developing countries (16.9 percent). Across the world, on average, housing consumption has increased at a rate of 2.1 percent per annum and housing prices have increased at a rate of 4.8 percent per annum. A plot of relative consumption of housing against relative price of housing shows an approximate negative linear relationship supporting the basic economic law, the law of demand. The slope of this plot is −0.26, which can be interpreted as an estimate of the consumption parameter, the income flexibility. The average estimated marginal share of housing for a world consumer is 0.09, which indicates that when income increases by one dollar, 9 cents of that increase will be allocated to housing. The estimated average income elasticity across countries for housing is 0.4 (less than one), indicating that it is internationally a necessity, and the income elasticity is about the same for developed and developing countries. The estimated average own-price elasticity across countries for housing is −0.2, which indicates that internationally the demand for housing is price inelastic.

When the cross-sectional HES data are used, housing is found to be a necessity in Australia and India while it is a luxury in Bangladesh and Sri Lanka, again highlighting the fact that the classification of housing as a necessity or luxury is not the same across countries.

9.6 Demand for Durables

In both developed and developing countries, the proportion of consumer income allocated to expenditure on durables is about 6 percent. The consumption and prices of durables increased at a faster rate in the developing countries (at a rate of about 4 percent per annum) than in the developed countries (at a rate of about 2 percent per annum). A plot of relative consumption of durables against relative price of durables shows an approximate negative linear relationship supporting the basic economic law, the law of demand. The slope of this plot is −0.75, which can be interpreted as an estimate of the consumption parameter, the income flexibility. The average estimated marginal share of durables for a world consumer is 0.09, which indicates that when income increases by one dollar, 9 cents of that increase will be allocated to durables. The estimated average income elasticity across countries for durables is 1.5 (greater than one) which indicates that it is internationally a luxury, with about the same income elasticity for developed and developing countries. The estimated average own-price elasticity across countries for durables is in the range −0.5 to −0.6, which indicates that internationally the demand for durables is price inelastic.

9.7 Demand for Health Care

In both developed and developing countries, the proportion of consumers' income allocated to expenditure on health care is about 3.5–4.5 percent. The consumption of health care increased at a faster rate in the developing countries (at a rate of about 3.9 percent per annum) than in the developed countries (at a rate of about 2.9 percent per annum). The cost of health care in developing countries has increased at a rate of 5.7 percent per annum, which is double the rate of developed countries. A plot of relative consumption of healthcare against relative price of health care shows an approximate negative linear relationship supporting the basic economic law, the law of demand. The slope of this plot is -0.55, which can be interpreted as an estimate of the consumption parameter, the income flexibility. The average estimated marginal share of health care for a world consumer is 0.03, which indicates that when income increases by one dollar, 3 cents of that increase will be allocated to health care. The estimated average income elasticity across countries shows that health care is a necessity in developed countries and is a luxury in developing countries. The estimated average own-price elasticity across countries for health care is in the range −0.4 (for developing countries) to −0.3 (for developed countries), which indicates that globally the demand for health care is price inelastic.

There is not much difference in the estimated income elasticity for Australia based on time-series data (0.8–1.2, depending on the demand system used) and based on cross-sectional HES data (0.96–1.04). For India and Sri Lanka, there is a significant difference in the income elasticities based on the type of data used. For India, on average, the income elasticity based on time-series data is 0.6 and based on cross-sectional *Indian Human Development Survey II* data, the value is 1.2, while for Sri Lanka, based on time-series data the value is 0.9 and based on cross-sectional HES data average income elasticity is 1.1.

9.8 Demand for Transport

In developing countries, the proportion of income allocated to expenditure on transport (about 13.7 percent) by consumers is about the same as that of consumers in developed countries (about 12.9 percent). The prices of transport increased at a faster rate in the developing countries (at a rate of about 5.5 percent per annum) than in the developed countries (at a rate of about 2.7 percent per annum). The consumption of transport also grew at a faster rate in developing countries (at a rate of about 4.2 percent per annum) than in the developed countries (at a rate of about 2.3 percent per annum). A plot of relative consumption of transport against relative price of transport shows an approximate negative linear relationship supporting the basic economic law, the law of demand. The slope of this plot is −0.46, which can be interpreted as an estimate of the consumption parameter, the income flexibility. The average estimated marginal share of transport for a world consumer is 0.24, which indicates that when income increases by one dollar, 24 cents of that increase will be allocated to transport. The estimated average income elasticity across all 45 countries for transport is 1.6 (greater than one), which indicates that it is globally a luxury, with income elasticity about the same for developed and developing countries. The estimated average own-price elasticity across countries for transport is in the range of −0.5 to −0.6, which indicates that globally the demand for transport is price inelastic.

Based on HES data, the income elasticities of transport in Australia, Bangladesh, India and Sri Lanka are all greater than one and are very similar to the time-series data estimates, confirming that transport is a luxury in all countries.

9.9 Demand for Communication

In both groups of countries, the proportion of income allocated to expenditure on communication is about 3 percent. With the rapid advancement of communication tools and technology, consumption of communication has grown at a rate of 7–8 percent per annum in both developed and developing countries. On the other hand, the price of communication, on average, has fallen in the developed countries at a rate of about 1.3 percent per annum but has increased in the developing countries at a rate of 1.8 percent per annum. A plot of relative consumption of communication against relative price of communication shows an approximate negative linear relationship supporting the basic economic law, the law of demand. The slope of this plot is −0.66, which can be interpreted as an estimate of the consumption parameter, the income flexibility. The estimated average income elasticity across countries for communication is 1.3, indicating that it is globally a luxury. It is more of a luxury for developed countries (income elasticity 1.4) than developing countries (income elasticity 1.01). The estimated average own-price elasticity across countries for communication is −0.66 which indicates that internationally the demand for communication is price inelastic.

9.10 Demand for Recreation

The proportion of income allocated to expenditure on recreation, on average, in the developing countries is about 7.7 percent and in developed countries it is about 10.1 percent. The prices of recreation increased at a faster rate in the developing countries (4.6 percent per annum) than in the developed countries (1.5 percent per annum). However, the consumption of recreation, on average, grew at a more similar rate comparing the developed countries (3.2 percent per annum) with the developing countries (4.4 percent). A plot of relative consumption of communication against its relative price shows an approximate negative linear relationship supporting the basic economic law, the law of demand. The slope of this plot is −0.61, which can be interpreted as an estimate of the consumption parameter, the income flexibility. The estimated average income elasticity across countries for communication is 1.3 (greater than one), which indicates that it is internationally a luxury, with income elasticity about the same for developed and developing countries. The estimated average own-price elasticity across countries for recreation is −0.6, which indicates that internationally the demand for recreation is price inelastic.

Based on HES data, the income elasticities of recreation in Australia, Bangladesh, India and Sri Lanka are all larger than unity, indicating that recreation is a luxury even when cross-sectional survey data are used.

9.11 Demand for Education

On average, the proportion of income allocated to expenditure on education is in the range of 1.3 percent (developed countries) to 1.6 percent (developing countries) across the 45 countries. The price of education increased at a faster rate in the developing countries (at a rate of about 7 percent per annum) than in the developed countries (at a rate of about 3.8 percent per annum). However, consumption of education grew at a similar rate in the range of 2–3 percent per annum in both groups of countries. A plot of relative consumption of education against its relative price shows an approximate negative linear relationship supporting the law of demand. The slope of this plot is −0.89, which can be interpreted as an estimate of the consumption parameter, the income flexibility. The average estimated marginal share of education for a world consumer is 0.14, which indicates that when income increases by one dollar, 14 cents of that increase will be allocated to education. The estimated average income elasticity across countries for education is about 1.3, which indicates that it is internationally a luxury, with about the same income elasticity for developed and developing countries. The estimated average own-price elasticity across countries for education is in the range −0.5 to −0.8 (depending on the demand system used), which indicates that internationally the demand for education is price inelastic.

Based on HES data, the income elasticities of education in Australia, Bangladesh, India and Sri Lanka are all greater than one, indicating that education is a luxury, which is the same finding based on time-series data.

9.12 Demand for Restaurant Meals

On average, world consumers allocate about 7.4 percent of their income on restaurants. Across the world, on average, restaurant meals consumption has increased at a rate of 1.8 percent per annum and its prices have increased at a rate of 4.2 percent per annum. A plot of relative consumption of restaurant meals against its relative price shows an approximate negative linear relationship with a slope −0.81, which can be interpreted as an estimate of the consumption parameter, the income flexibility. The estimated average income elasticity across countries for restaurant meals is 1.1 (greater than unity), which indicates that it is internationally a luxury, and the income elasticity is about the same for developed and developing countries. The estimated average own-price elasticity across countries for restaurant meals is in the range −0.5 to −0.7, which indicates that internationally the demand for restaurant meals is price inelastic.

9.13 Conditional Demand Analysis of Groups of Goods

9.13.1 Food, Alcohol, Tobacco, Restaurants and Soft Drinks (Food) Group

Conditional analysis within the food group consisting of three individual items, food, alcohol and restaurants based on time-series data[1] reveals that, on average, consumers allocate about 29 percent of their income on the overall food group and within the food group, they allocate 54.6 percent on food, 18 percent on alcohol and 27.3 percent on restaurants. Estimation results indicate that for every additional dollar spent on the food group, 44 cents is spent on food, 17 cents on alcohol and 39 cents on restaurant meals. The demand theory hypotheses, demand homogeneity, Slutsky symmetry and preference independence hypotheses are also supported by the conditional demand systems.

The conditional income elasticity for food is 0.80 (a necessity), alcohol is 0.9 (a necessity) and restaurants is 1.5 (a luxury). The own-price conditional elasticities are −0.3 (food), −0.5 (alcohol) and −0.5 (restaurants), indicating that the demand for all three items is price inelastic. We also found substitutability among food, alcohol and restaurants in some countries while complementarity was found in other countries.

The results from the HES data reveal that food as a group (consisting of food, alcohol, tobacco, restaurants and soft drinks) is a necessity in Australia, India and Sri Lanka. Within the food group, in Australia food and soft drinks are necessities, while alcohol, tobacco and restaurants are luxuries. In India, food, alcohol and tobacco are necessities, while restaurant meals are a luxury. In Sri Lanka, food is a necessity, while alcohol, tobacco, restaurants and soft drinks are luxuries.

9.13.2 Transport, Communication and Housing (TCH) Group

Conditional analysis within the TCH group consisting of three individual items, transport, communication and housing based on time-series data reveals that, on average, consumers allocate about 35 percent of their income on the overall TCH group. Then within the TCH group, consumers allocate 35.2 percent on transport, 7.2 percent on communication and 57.6 percent on housing. Estimation results indicate that for every additional dollar spent on the TCH group, 59 cents is spent on transport, 9 cents on communication and 32 cents on housing. The demand theory hypotheses, demand homogeneity, Slutsky symmetry and preference independence hypotheses are supported by the conditional demand systems.

The conditional income elasticity for transport is 1.73 (a luxury), communication is 1.1 (a luxury) and housing is 0.5 (a necessity). The own-price conditional elasticities are −0.3 (transport), −0.7 (communication) and −0.14 (housing), indicating that the demand for all three items is price inelastic.

We also found substitutability among TCH in some countries while complementarity was found among others.

The analysis from the HES data for Australia, India and Sri Lanka reveals that TCH as a group is a near luxury in Australia, and a luxury in India and Sri Lanka. Within the THC group, the conditional analysis results reveal that, in Australia, transport and communication are luxuries, and housing is a near luxury. In India, transport and communication are luxuries and housing is a necessity. In Sri Lanka, transport is a luxury, and communication and housing are near luxuries. These findings further highlight differences in the elasticity estimates in developed and developing countries as well as the sensitivity of elasticity estimates for cross-sectional and time-series data.

9.13.3 Health, Recreation and Education (HRE) Group

Conditional analysis within the HRE group consisting of three individual items, health, recreation and education based on time-series data reveals that, on average, consumers allocate about 14.2 percent of their income on the HRE group. Within the HER group expenditure, on average, consumers allocate 29.4 percent on health, 59.8 percent on recreation and the remaining 10.7 percent on education. Conditional demand model estimation results indicate that for every additional dollar spent on the HRE group, 22 cents is spent on health, 69 cents on recreation and 6 cents on education. The demand theory hypotheses, demand homogeneity, Slutsky symmetry and preference independence hypotheses are also supported by the conditional demand systems.

The conditional income elasticity for health is 0.8 (a necessity), recreation is 1.2 (a luxury) and education is 0.6 (a necessity). The own-price conditional elasticities are −0.5 (health), −0.3 (recreation) and −0.6 (education), indicating that the demand for all three items is price inelastic. We also found substitutability among health, recreation and education in some countries while complementarity was found among other countries.

The results from the cross-sectional HES data reveal that HRE as a group is a luxury in Australia, Bangladesh and India and a necessity in Sri Lanka. Within the HRE group, in all four countries, health is a necessity, and recreation and education are luxuries.

9.14 Empirical Regularities in Consumption Patterns

The book also identified a number of empirical regularities in the consumption patterns of the 12 commodities. These empirical regularities include:

- The Engel's Law (an inverse relationship between budget share and income).
- The Law of Demand (all other things being equal, an increase in the relative price of a commodity causes its consumption to fall).

- Demand homogeneity (demand functions are homogeneous of degree zero or an equi-proportionate change in income and prices results in unchanged consumption of each good or, in other words, the consumer does not suffer from money illusion).
- Substitution effects are symmetrical (when real income is held constant, the effect of an increase in the price of commodity *j* on the demand for commodity *i* is equal to the effect of a price increase of commodity *i* on the demand for commodity *j*, also known as Slutsky symmetry).
- Consumers' tastes are preference independent (marginal utility of good *i* is independent of the consumption of good *j*, or consumers' tastes can be described by means of a utility function, which is the sum of *n* sub-utility functions, one for each good).
- Frisch's conjecture: income elasticity of the marginal utility of income ($1/\phi$) decreases in absolute value as the consumer (or country) becomes more affluent. Support was found for the Frisch's conjecture in the context of developed countries but not in developing countries.

Note

1 For time-series data, food includes food and soft drinks; and alcohol includes alcohol and tobacco.

Subject Index

Author Index